Turret versus Broadside

An Anatomy of British Naval Prestige, Revolution and Disaster, 1860-1870

Howard J. Fuller

 Helion & Company Limited

Helion & Company Limited
Unit 8 Amherst Business Centre
Budbrooke Road
Warwick
CV34 5WE
England
Tel. 01926 499 619
Email: info@helion.co.uk
Website: www.helion.co.uk
Twitter: @helionbooks
Visit our blog at blog.helion.co.uk

Published by Helion & Company 2020
Designed and typeset by Mary Woolley (www.battlefield-design.co.uk)
Cover designed by Paul Hewitt, Battlefield Design (www.battlefield-design.co.uk)

Text © Howard J. Fuller 2020
Images © as individually credited

Every reasonable effort has been made to trace copyright holders and to obtain their permission for the use of copyright material. The author and publisher apologise for any errors or omissions in this work and would be grateful if notified of any corrections that should be incorporated in future reprints or editions of this book.

ISBN 978-1-913336-22-6

British Library Cataloguing-in-Publication Data.
A catalogue record for this book is available from the British Library.

All rights reserved. No part of this publication may be reproduced, stored in a retrieval system, or transmitted, in any form, or by any means, electronic, mechanical, photocopying, recording or otherwise, without the express written consent of Helion & Company Limited.

For details of other military history titles published by Helion & Company Limited contact the above address, or visit our website: http://www.helion.co.uk.

We always welcome receiving book proposals from prospective authors.

To Annie,

the Beauty on the bow of the Ship

Contents

List of Illustrations — vii
The Wolverhampton Military Studies Series: Series Editor's Preface — xv
Acknowledgments — xvi
Prologue — xix
Introduction: *In deference to public opinion* — xxv

1 *'If we were the defendants of Cronstadt I should laugh at any attacking force'* — 36
   The strategic dilemma of the Crimean War—Siege of Sevastopol—Napier in the Baltic—a British coastal assault flotilla—iron-armoured floating batteries—Russian defences—iron-armoured pontoon-rafts—minefields—the Austrian ultimatum—Dundas and Wood's doubts of success—Clarendon and Orlov in Paris—Treaty of 1856—Anglo-American tensions over Central America

2 *'We are only copying the French'* — 53
   Decline of the Concert of Europe—technology and national defence—*Gloire* and *Warrior*—criticisms—winning a numbers game in 1861—improved *Warrior*s and wooden conversions—the American Civil War and blockade—the *Trent* Affair—concerns over British naval operations—the U.S. Ironclad Board—the *Monitor*

3 *'Such a proceeding on our part is simply impossible'* — 73
   The Battle of Hampton Roads—more monitors for the Union—British reactions—the *Royal Sovereign*—the mediation proposal of Autumn 1862—American resources for war—loss of the *Monitor*—the ironclad assault on Charleston, April 1863—capture of the CSS *Atlanta*—the Polish Insurrection crisis

4 *'We should be laughed at if we stood by'* — 92
   Coles, Reed and the *'Naughty Child'*—'guns vs. armour' considerations—U.S. assessments of monitors—the Danish intervention question of 1864—the *Rolf Krake* in action—Somerset warns Palmerston—the Laird Rams—new heavy guns for the British fleet—the *Royal Sovereign* decommissioned—the controversy over HMS *Pallas*

5   'We must go back very much to the recognized forms, the recognized proportions, and the recognised shapes'   112
Threatening Austria—the quarrel over British foreign policy—Palmerston retreats—commanding the Great Lakes—fortifications of the U.S.—new heavy ordnance delayed—Britain's neutrality and 'humiliation'—debate over seagoing ironclads—Reed and the *Hercules*—the Civil War question of forts vs. ships—British monitors for the St. Lawrence—general proliferation of ironclads by 1865

6   'Were we at war with America or France, the right thing would be done instantly'   133
Scrutinising American practices—the 15-inch gun vs. British armour plates—Parliament sounds the alarm—geopolitics in North America—target tests at Shoeburyness—Ericsson claims the 'turret system'—Commons critique of Royal Navy broadside-ironclads—Robinson counterattacks Coles—Somerset seeks 'un-prejudicial' review committee—seagoing turret-ship mandated

7   'Wherever these Monitors manage to get, we should have vessels of equal fighting powers'   154
Reaction against the turret system—the sail-and-turret *Monarch*—end of the American Civil War—the Anglo-French naval fête—death of Palmerston—Coles attacks Reed in the press—Board terminates relationship with Coles, January 1866—Coles 'put in his place' and reinstated—British public pressure against broadside-ironclads—Bourne advocates a British *Dictator*—Ericsson's philosophy of naval power

8   'If the American shipbuilders are right ours must be wrong'   175
Coles condemns the *Monarch*—Grey relents to Coles; genesis of HMS *Captain*—test-firing against the *Royal Sovereign*—Austro-Prussian war and Reform agitation in summer 1866—'The wolf in the fold': the USS *Miantonomoh* in Britain—Robinson outlines new ironclads

9   'We must not relax our efforts ... however great the expense'   195
Reports on the Channel Squadron at sea—more central-battery ships—the breastwork-monitor idea—Reed denounces plans for HMS *Captain*—responsibility for the *Captain*'s design—Bourne argues for low-freeboard monitors again—Coles suggests more sail-and-turret ironclads—'turret vs. broadside'-debate at RUSI, May 1867—A 15-inch Rodman and the '*Hercules* Target'

10   'Making our experiments with scrupulous care, and wasting nothing on methods which cannot succeed'   216
The American challenge recedes—the Controller's Department judges private ironclad designs—Robinson's plans for 1868—Parliamentary scrutiny of navy, dockyard efficiency—Reed threatens to resign—the Board questions Robinson's power—Reed's essay on 'Seagoing Turret-ships and Lowness of Freeboard'—1869 proposal for mastless HMS *Devastation*-class—*Our Iron-Clad Ships*

11 *'It is very desirable that we should shew our strength well'*   236
Initial sea trials of HMS *Captain*—Robinson reports negatively—outbreak of the Franco-Prussian War, July 1870—British fears for Belgium—more Royal Navy monitors ordered—Reed mocks *Captain*'s efficiency—Press questions Reed's resignation—news of *Captain* foundering—the Admiralty trail of responsibility—Pakington denies 'lack of trust' in Robinson and Reed's opinions

12 *'The Captain is gone, and we who opposed and resisted her have gone too'*   256
Verdict of the court martial—the Childers *Minute* accuses Robinson and Reed—replies by Reed in *The Times* backfire—the uselessness of France's seagoing ironclads against Prussia—objections to the 1871 Committee on Ship Designs—Robinson forced out of office—Committee notes similar lack of ironclads for littoral operations

Conclusion *'There was a time when this country was the arbitress of the world'*   273

Appendices:
I   British Ironclads (1860-1870)   282
II   British Ironclads (1860-1870) – Armour and Armament   288
III   'Penetrating Power of Projectiles Fired from the Service Heavy Muzzle Loading Guns' (Captain C. Orde Browne, 'Firing at Armour-Clads Reduced to a System', *Journal of the Royal United Service Institution*, Vol. 16, 1873, 684-700)   296
IV   Captain James Goodenough Reports on the Union Navy (May 1864)   297
V   The British consider a turret vs. broadside confrontation between the U.S. and Spain at Valparaiso (March 1866)   302
VI   Admiral Robinson reports on France's ironclad fleet and French naval ordnance (June 1867)   305
VII   Laminated armour and the 'Law of Resistance'   308
VIII   'English and American Iron-Clads Compared' (John Ericsson's critique of Edward Reed's *Our Iron-Clad Ships*, in *Army and Navy Journal*, Vol. 7, No. 26, 12 February 1870, 397-8)   311

Bibliography   313
Index   354

List of Illustrations

Photographic Section 1

Henry John Temple, 3rd Viscount Palmerston (1784-1865). (CDV courtesy of the National Portrait Gallery)   I

Sir Charles Wood, 1st Viscount Halifax (1800-1885). (CDV courtesy of the National Portrait Gallery)   I

John Russell, 1st Earl Russell (1792-1878). (CDV courtesy of the National Portrait Gallery)   I

William Ewart Gladstone (1809-1898). (CDV courtesy of the National Portrait Gallery)   I

The combined Anglo-French fleet engages Russian harbour defences at Sevastopol during the Crimean War (17 October 1854) The Illustrated London News-*supplement, 14 April 1855*. (Author's collection)   II

The heavily fortified Russian naval arsenal of Cronstadt: home of the Russian Navy in the Gulf of Finland, and guardian of the seaward approaches to the Imperial Russian capital of St. Petersburg (shown in the distance). Cronstadt defied two successive British naval campaigns in the Baltic between 1854 and 1855, and was preparing to check a third in the summer of 1856, had the war continued. (Author's collection)   III

French floating ironclad-battery *Foudroyant* (*Dévastation*-class), laid down in August 1854 and launched the following June. Armed with sixteen shell-firing smoothbores protected by 4.3-inch iron armour-plating, the mastless, screw-propelled vessel drew only nine-feet of water and posed a serious threat to coastal fortifications wherever she could be safely deployed. (Author's collection)   IV

The emergency Russian response to armoured floating batteries versus Cronstadt's defences was a flotilla of heavily armed pontoon rafts capable of floating in three-feet of water and partially-armoured with solid 4-inch-thick iron plates. (Author's collection)   IV

Model of HMS *Warrior*, laid down in 1859 as a response to the French iron-armoured screw-frigate *Gloire* (begun a year before). She was the Royal Navy's first seagoing ironclad, and the world's first iron-hulled armoured capital ship. Despite her impressive speed and firepower, *Warrior*'s extreme size and cost were controversial, along with her partial armour-configuration which left her stern and rudderhead exposed to a potential enemy. (Image courtesy of the National Maritime Museum, Greenwich) V

The Admiralty's decision to invest in the largest, fastest, most-powerfully-armed ironclads possible in the emerging naval arms race with Imperial France came at a heavy price—and only private firms could do the work. Thames Iron Works and Shipbuilding required financial relief to avoid bankruptcy in constructing the novel *Warrior* over two and half years (and still retain a '12½-percent' profit margin). 'Per ton' of iron, the subsequent *Defence* and *Resistance*—though much smaller—were even more expensive. All of Britain's early seagoing broadside-ironclads went over-budget and took substantially longer to complete than contracted for. VI

The Mid-Victorian public was fascinated (and disquieted) by the remarkable changes in naval architecture underway in the early 1860s. VII

The baroque armoured bow of HMS *Minotaur*, a 10,500-ton super broadside-ironclad, shown here drawing 27-feet. Although laid down in September 1861, she was not fully completed with a revised armament until 1867—by which time her 5-inch-thick iron-plating was long considered inadequate against the latest ordnance. (Image NH 71224 courtesy of Naval History and Heritage Command, Washington, D.C.) VII

Rare likeness of Edward Adolphus Seymour, 12th Duke of Somerset (1804-1885). (William Hurrell Mallock and Helen Guendolen Seymour Ramsden (eds.), *Letters, Remains, and Memoirs of Edward Adolphus Seymour Twelfth Duke of Somerset* (1893)) VIII

Edward James Reed (1830-1906). (CDV courtesy of the National Portrait Gallery) VIII

John Ericsson (1803-1889). (Image NH 305 courtesy of Naval History and Heritage Command, Washington, D.C.) VIII

Cowper Phipps Coles (1818-1870). (CDV courtesy of the National Portrait Gallery) VIII

Britain's popular response to the *Trent* Affair of November-December 1861 was brutally simple: either President Abraham Lincoln's administration would bend to Lord Palmerston's ultimatum to release two captured Confederate emissaries or face a hostile dose of British naval power. As the Prime Minister assured Queen Victoria, 'Great Britain is in a better state than at any former time to inflict a severe blow upon and read a lesson to the United States which will not soon be forgotten.' At the time the Royal Navy was still dominated by wooden steam-powered, screw-propelled ships-of-the-line. Both the Union Army and Navy was still mobilising for war. IX

Scarcely four months after the *Trent* Affair, news reached Britain of the Confederate Navy's spectacular attack against the Union blockade anchored at Hampton Roads, Virginia. The 'Naval Revolution' as depicted here was the obvious invulnerability of armoured warships to point-blank broadsides from powerfully-armed wooden men-of-war. The next day, the U.S. Navy responded to the CSS *Virginia*'s attack with a small turreted vessel, the *Monitor*, which John Ericsson named to 'startle and admonish' 'Downing Street' and 'the Lords of the Admiralty' as well as 'the leaders of the Southern Rebellion.' The implications for British naval power were brutally simple. X

Monitor vs. Virginia, by Lukasz Kasperczyk – The Battle of Hampton Roads (8-9 March 1862) was not just the first battle between armoured warships, but a turret vs. broadside duel. Here the effectiveness of the deep-draft casemated ironclad in coastal waters was limited by the ebbing tide—and the Confederate giant ran aground at a critical moment during the battle. (Image courtesy of Lukasz Kasperczyk) XI

Although the ironclad action at Hampton Roads was technically a draw (neither vessel was sunk), the Union blockade was preserved. The Northern States also made the most of the geopolitical implications of Ericsson's monitor-form of ironclad, which promised to reverse the humiliating resolution of the *Trent* Affair three months earlier. Britain's wooden navy was now clearly vulnerable against ironclads, and the Royal Navy's new seagoing broadside-ironclads were likewise at risk against mastless, low-freeboard, turreted 'machines'. This sort of love-hate rivalry dominated Anglo-American relations throughout the nineteenth-century. (Author's collection) XII

(Above Right) *Punch*, 31 January 1863; as a result of the Battle of Hampton Roads and the success of the USS *Monitor*, both Ericsson and Coles were idolized as inventors of state-of-the-art turret-ships which magnified the technological scope—and strategic limitations—of the ironclad revolution. XIII

Armstrong 8-inch caliber, 150-pounder, rifled muzzle-loader—captured at Fort Fisher in January 1865, and now a prize of the U.S. Military Academy at West Point, New York. Contrast the above with the Dahlgren 15-inch, 450-pounder smoothbore below, now at Filipstad, Sweden—one of a pair given by John Ericsson to his native country in 1865, to arm her first *Passaic*-class monitor. These are believed to be the sole remaining 15-inch Dahlgrens in the world. (Author's collection) XIV

The 'guns vs. armour'-contest in the 1860s was front-page news and intertwined with both the 'turret vs. broadside'-debate and the larger, long-term question of 'ships vs. forts'. Many elements of British public and professional society had a vested interest in the outcome of increasingly elaborate and expensive trials of experimental guns and armour configurations for ships and coastal forts. Here a '*Gloire* Target' resisted both the 68-pounder smoothbore and 110-pounder Armstrong rifled breech-loader at 200 yards but succumbed to the new '300-pounder', 12-ton 'shunt' gun muzzle-loader. XV

Model of HMS *Wivern*, originally contracted by Confederate agents to be built by John Lairds & Sons (Birkenhead, Merseyside) in April 1862. The Battle of Hampton Roads also suggested that ironclads with a turret main armament would be cheaper and quicker to build than larger broadside-ironclads, as well as being capable of carrying heavier (though fewer) guns. The ship displaced only 2,750-tons and drew 17-feet for coastal operations. Other innovations included in the design were a ram-bow, and tripod masts to minimize rigging which might otherwise interfere with the training of the guns when the hinged bulwarks were lowered for action. The two 'Laird Rams' were considered a deadly threat to the Union blockade, which consisted mostly of wooden warships. Under intense pressure from the U.S. minister to Great Britain, the vessels were seized by Palmerston's government before they could escape from Liverpool and were then incorporated into the Royal Navy. The Admiralty was not enthusiastic, however. The pioneering ironclads were underpowered compared with larger broadside-armed versions, and the whole concept of combining masts and sails with open deck turrets seemed inefficient and contradictory. Their cruising abilities were likewise impaired by the combination of rolling at sea with a relatively low freeboard. Coles and his supporters (both in and out of the navy) instead emphasised their tactical advantages as well as economy and argued that larger versions would be both faster and more seaworthy. (Image courtesy of the National Maritime Museum, Greenwich) XVI

Photographic Section 2
John Somerset Pakington, 1st Baron Hampton (1799-1880). (CDV courtesy of the National Portrait Gallery) XVII
Hugh Culling Eardley Childers, (1827-1896). (CDV courtesy of the National Portrait Gallery) XVII
Henry Thomas Lowry-Corry, (1803-1873). (CDV courtesy of the National Portrait Gallery) XVII
Sir Alexander Milne, 1st Baronet (1806-1896). (Author's collection) XVII
As a major source of national prestige, Britain's ironclad fleet was subject to intense scrutiny by respectable, tax-paying Victorians, worried that the Royal Navy would prove of an inferior status to those of rival powers. (Image courtesy of the National Maritime Museum, Greenwich) XVIII
[Sir Frederick Grey, First Naval Lord, minute]: '*The letter of Cap. Coles appears to me to have been written rather with the view of its appearance in a Blue Book, as a complaint against the Admiralty, than with any idea of assisting by his advice in the construction of a sea going Turret ship. Should he not be allowed to prepare his own design of a sea going Ship of not less than two turrets, and send it in for consideration of the Board[?]*' - 21 April 1866. (The National Archives, Kew, ADM 1/5794) XVIII
U.S. 'Target No. 61 Sept 20 [1864]': a rolled 5-inch-thick iron plate from John Brown & Company (Sheffield) backed by 20-inches of oak, penetrated by a solid 438-pound cast-iron shot fired by a 15-inch muzzle-loaded smoothbore with a 60lb charge. (U.S. National Archives, RG 74 (Bureau of Ordnance, Entry 98)) XIX

The American turret-ship experience during the Civil War offered mixed lessons, easily misinterpreted. Monitors, with their small numbers of very heavy guns, proved deadly against Confederate ironclads like the *Atlanta, Tennessee* and *Virginia II*, but were of correspondingly limited value in subduing fortifications. If battened down properly they were exceptionally seaworthy, but their lack of sails and small coal bunkers prohibited their use as long-range cruisers (never mind their long-term habitability). (John Ericsson, 'The Monitors', *The Century Magazine,* November 1885 to April 1886, Vol. XXXI, New Series Vol. IX) XX

Like Coles in Britain, Ericsson took pains to promote his invention to the American public. But the argument over who made the first turret-armed man-of-war in history overlooked a vital distinction in how the ships themselves were conceptualised. Whereas Coles always had a seagoing cruiser in mind, only armed with turrets rather than broadside-mounted guns, Ericsson envisaged a more radical 'machine'—a modern weapons system—where the ship was merely a platform for carrying a supreme, ship-killing gun. (Image courtesy of Navy Art Collection, Naval History and Heritage Command, Washington, D.C.) XXI

Extent of Armour on the Sides of Iron Cased Ships, 30 April 1866, and signed by Robert Spencer Robinson (Admiralty Controller) Contrast the partial armour protection scheme of *Warrior* and *Defence* to that of *Valiant*, then *Achilles* and the *Minotaur* class. Only the *Caledonia* and other *Royal Oak* class conversions featured full protection for their size. After that the tendency was clearly towards more concentrated, thicker armour schemes protecting fewer though heavier guns until the 'central battery' profiles themselves resembled American monitors and rams, though with full masts, sails, and extensive surrounding superstructures. (Image courtesy of the National Maritime Museum (Greenwich) XXII

The 'Turret vs. Broadside'-debate in Britain reached its peak in 1866, when Coles was sacked, rehired, and finally offered a chance to build his own 'perfect' sail-and-turret ship (HMS *Captain*); but also when the Controller's Department carried out a brutal test of turret armaments under fire, with Reed's central-battery ironclad HMS *Bellerophon* blasting away at HMS *Royal Sovereign,* a wooden line-of-battle ship cut down in 1862 and armed with Coles turrets. Meanwhile, the U.S. Navy despatched its newest monitor, the double-turreted USS *Miantonomoh* (shown here at St. John's, Newfoundland), on a goodwill tour of Europe and Russia. (Image NH 105802 courtesy of Naval History and Heritage Command , Washington, D.C.) XXIV

The *Miantonomoh's* to Britain in the summer of 1866 caused a wave of public indignation with Admiralty shipbuilding policy. Almost all of the Royal Navy's ironclads featured high-freeboard broadsides which could be penetrated by the American monitor, while none of their guns could retaliate. Although the Board had already taken steps to rectify this embarrassing situation, with new ships under construction mounting heavier guns behind thicker armour-plating, Coles and his supporters were now convinced that a low freeboard sail-and-turret ironclad was practicable.   XXV

HMS *Northumberland* plagued her original builders (Mare & Company) who transferred their contract to Millwall Ironworks in 1863. Millwall also went bankrupt in 1866 trying to complete the vessel. Her armour was added while she was still on the stocks, and upon launch she stuck halfway down the ways, straining her hull integrity. Repeated attempts to pull the *Northumberland* loose failed. The Admiralty was then called in to help, at an additional cost to the public of £20,000. The April 1866 crisis cast further doubt upon broadside-ironclads, when just launching such behemoths was considered a triumph. (The Illustrated London News, 14 April 1866)   XXVI

While the Admiralty seemed recalcitrant in adopting smaller, handier, less expensive and more powerfully-armed and armoured turret-ships, private British firms carried on developing a variety of shallow-draught, sail-and-turret and low-freeboard monitor-type ironclads for foreign powers.   XXVII

Reed's response to the American *Miantonomoh* as an apex ironclad capable of sinking any ironclad she could encounter—range permitting—was the 'coastal defence', mastless 'breastwork-monitor', starting with HMVS *Cerberus* (1868) for the British imperial colony of Victoria, Australia. Today her wreck—sunk as a breakwater in 1926—can still be seen in Half Moon Bay, near Melbourne. (Image courtesy of Lukasz Kasperczyk)   XXVIII

USS *Miantonomoh* - laid down 1862, launched 1863. (Author's collection)   XXIX

HMS *Sultan* (central-battery ironclad) - laid down 1868, launched 1870. (Image courtesy of the National Maritime Museum, Greenwich)   XXIX

HMS *Devastation* - laid down 1869, launched 1871. (Image courtesy of the National Maritime Museum, Greenwich)   XXX

HMS *Captain* - laid down 1867, launched 1869. (Image courtesy of the National Maritime Museum, Greenwich)   XXX

The Age of the Ironclad began when traditional 'Blue Water' naval power, in the form of oceangoing battlefleets of capital ships, proved unable to effect much against Russia during the Crimean War (1853-1856), obliging the French and British to fashion shallow-draft, iron-armoured floating-batteries which could engage coastal forts with a reasonable prospect of success. The American Civil War (1861-1865) subsequently gave rise to low-freeboard turreted ironclads which could sink broadside-batteries either defending Southern ports or threatening Northern ones. In a coastal *assault* role they required close coordination with land forces—combined operations—to achieve victory against strongholds such as Charleston or Fort Fisher. While the Mid-Victorian public was clearly fascinated by these developments, both the British and French navies persisted in developing ironclad fleets which could 'command the sea'. The Franco-Prussian War

(1870-1871) subsequently demonstrated again the limits of deep-draft seagoing ironclads against a continental power; a disaster for France, and a warning to Britain. 10 April 1869, 'The Volunteer Review at Dover: View of Dover from the Sea—The Naval Squadron Attacking the Forts'. *Illustrated London News* (Author's collection) XXXI

Captain Hugh Talbot Burgoyne, (1833 - 1870). (Author's collection) XXXII

'The only Survivors of H.M. late Ship "CAPTAIN" in the same Clothing they wore on landing at Finisterre.' No other ship has shared her name since then. (MLN/161/4, Milne Papers, National Maritime Museum, Greenwich) XXXII

The Wolverhampton Military Studies Series
Series Editor's Preface

As series editor, it is my great pleasure to introduce the *Wolverhampton Military Studies* Series to you. Our intention is that in this series of books you will find military history that is new and innovative, and academically rigorous with a strong basis in fact and in analytical research, but also is the kind of military history that is for all readers, whatever their particular interests, or their level of interest in the subject. To paraphrase an old aphorism: a military history book is not less important just because it is popular, and it is not more scholarly just because it is dull. With every one of our publications we want to bring you the kind of military history that you will want to read simply because it is a good and well-written book, as well as bringing new light, new perspectives, and new factual evidence to its subject.

In devising the *Wolverhampton Military Studies Series*, we gave much thought to the series title: this is a *military* series. We take the view that history is everything except the things that have not happened yet, and even then a good book about the military aspects of the future would find its way into this series. We are not bound to any particular time period or cut-off date. Writing military history often divides quite sharply into eras, from the modern through the early modern to the mediaeval and ancient; and into regions or continents, with a division between western military history and the military history of other countries and cultures being particularly marked. Inevitably, we have had to start somewhere, and the first books of the series deal with British military topics and events of the twentieth century and later nineteenth century. But this series is open to any book that challenges received and accepted ideas about any aspect of military history, and does so in a way that encourages its readers to enjoy the discovery.

In the same way, this series is not limited to being about wars, or about grand strategy, or wider defence matters, or the sociology of armed forces as institutions, or civilian society and culture at war. None of these are specifically excluded, and in some cases they play an important part in the books that comprise our series. But there are already many books in existence, some of them of the highest scholarly standards, which cater to these particular approaches. The main theme of the *Wolverhampton Military Studies Series* is the military aspects of wars, the preparation for wars or their prevention, and their aftermath. This includes some books whose main theme is the technical details of how armed forces have worked, some books on wars and battles, and some books that re-examine the evidence about the existing stories, to show in a different light what everyone thought they already knew and understood. As series editor, together with my fellow editorial board members, and our publisher Duncan Rogers of Helion, I have found that we have known immediately and almost by instinct the kind of books that fit within this series. They are very much the kind of well-written and challenging books that my students at the University of Wolverhampton would want to read. They are books which enhance knowledge, and offer new perspectives. Also, they are books for anyone with an interest in military history and events, from expert scholars to occasional readers. One of the great benefits of the study of military history is that it includes a large and often committed section of the wider population, who want to read the best military history that they can find; our aim for this series is to provide it.

Stephen Badsey
University of Wolverhampton

Acknowledgments

This is a fairly sombre history; events leading up to a tragedy at sea. But as this volume alludes, the general frustration of the Victorians with their naval power in the pivotal years of the mid-nineteenth century may have served other peoples—and peace—well enough. In the same sense I must hope that the sacrifices made by those who have supported me over recent years in researching and writing up this analytical-narrative will ultimately prove worthwhile. Most recently, I was greatly helped by Scarlet Faro, Gareth Bellis, Penny Allen, Lizelle de Jager, and Robert Blyth at the National Maritime Museum (Royal Museums Greenwich); for use of the Museum's fabulous collection of ship models, photographs, and documents from personal paper collections (notably Sir Alexander Milne's) as part of the Caird Archive and Library. Before that I was privileged with a Caird Short-Term Research Fellowship, allowing me to rake through their Library's collections where I found, for example, several large, leather-bound volumes of newspaper clippings on early ironclads which had been compiled by Cowper Phipps Coles and his wife (later widowed). The Institute of Historical Research (Senate House, London) also favoured me in 2017 with a Scouloudi Research Grant, while on the other side of the Atlantic I received additional support from the U.S. Navy's Naval History and Heritage Command (Washington, D.C.) in the form of a Vice-Admiral Edwin B. Hooper Research Grant. This builds on the research I was able to conduct in their Navy Department Library, the U.S. National Archives (Washington, D.C.), Library of Congress, American-Swedish Historical Foundation (Philadelphia), New York Public Library and the New York Historical Society (New York City) thanks to a Rear-Admiral John D. Hayes Fellowship in U.S. Naval History. I am also very grateful for the help with Russian-based archival sources provided by St. Petersburg-based researcher Yury Basilov.

Along the way I have received unreserved support—travel grants and sabbaticals—from the Centre for Historical Research at the University of Wolverhampton (UK), where I have also been teaching war studies-related courses since 2005. Both my colleagues and students here have patiently suffered my passion for this subject-area in particular, and I have indeed benefited from their input. In the meantime, I was also able to make good use of conference panel and seminar papers delivered in recent years, generously hosted by the Society for Military History (its 2019 Annual Meeting in Columbus, Ohio), the National Maritime Museum (Greenwich), the

Baltic Defence College (Tartu, Estonia), the National Museum of the Royal Navy (Portsmouth), George Mason University (and the Virginia Sesquicentennial of the American Civil War Commission), and the National Army Museum (London). These venues allowed me to sound out various theories and receive advance feedback and advice from peers. My special thanks as well to the eminent historians who were willing to read through advanced drafts of the manuscript and offer their comments. I have also been wonderfully accommodated by my editor Duncan Rogers and his team at Helion & Company. It has been a real pleasure working with this publisher.

Finally, of course, I must acknowledge that the most important support which I received in making this book possible was the most personal support possible— namely that of Annie and her parents, Wanda and Pete, and our two lovely lads, Carson and Henry. They daily reminded me that for all the death and sorrow of history, life goes on.

*Resignedly beneath the sky
The melancholy waters lie.
So blend the turrets and shadows there
That all seem pendulous in the air,
While from a proud tower in the town
Death looks gigantically down.*

—Edgar Allen Poe, *The City in the Sea*

Prologue

One hundred and fifty years ago.

The sea was menacing, as the sun went down on the evening of 6 September 1870; to the east, the distant coast of Portugal had faded into the gloom. The breeze had been fresh all day, from the southwest, but now the barometer was falling and a cold, blustery gale had swept in turning the waves into foam-crested mountains. Ocean swells were getting longer and higher, plunging the ship's black iron prow deeper into dark blue-green waters. Each time the vessel slowly rose, heaving off vast amounts of angry white foam, it inexorably pitched down again with a roaring force that trembled through the entire vessel. Strong winds meanwhile buffeted against her portside beam, so that the vessel heeled further starboard into the rushing wall of water with every long oscillating roll back and forth. Yet this was HMS Captain, *the Royal Navy's newest, proudest ironclad, being more heavily armed and armoured than any seagoing man-of-war afloat—and her captain and crew were stubbornly determined to press their course northward, back to England as ordered. Her steam was up, driving her twin screws, and her hoisted canvas had been reduced to double reefed topsails and the fore staysail only. Earlier that day, the controversial warship had been inspected by Admiral Sir Alexander Milne, in command of the combined Channel and Mediterranean squadrons. This was the greatest force of ironclads the navy had ever assembled, on manoeuvres before the Bay of Biscay in a political show of force while France and Prussia waged war (ostensibly over whose influence would reign over the Spanish throne). Hosting the well-respected Admiral was the commanding officer, Captain Hugh Talbot Burgoyne, and the ship's 'designer', Captain Cowper Phipps Coles, Britain's pioneer advocate of turret-armed vessels. For the real power—the menace—of the* Captain *lay in her guns: four wrought-iron, 12-inch calibre, 25-ton rifled muzzle-loaders. These could sink any ironclad afloat at effective combat ranges.*[1] *As Coles had argued with the Board of Admiralty four years before, only his experimental sail-and-turret-ship could wield such guns anywhere in the world, and fight behind the thickest possible armour scheme. This in turn was due in large part to the*

---

1 With an 85-lb. 'battering' charge the 12-inch 25-ton gun reached achieved an initial muzzle velocity of 1,300-feet per second (or 13 percent faster than the speed of sound)—imparting an impact-energy of 7,000 foot-tons. At 10° elevation, range was up to 4,800 yards (2.7 miles).

Captain's unusually low-freeboard, which submerged more of the hull below water, allowing for greater thickness of iron armour plating of the area exposed above the waterline.

But it was this very quality which made Milne nervous. A thin flying bridge ran across the narrow 'hurricane deck' which ran from the top of the forecastle back to the poop, over both of the massive gun turrets below. From here the Admiral and the other officers tightly gripped the rails, watching the *Captain's* prominent bow plough through even moderate swells, violently driving the frothing water across the entire length of the main deck and crashing up against the sides of the turrets before rushing back off into the sea. Anyone on the deck below them would in fact be swept overboard. At 7,700-tons, the *Captain* was swimming heavily as much through the water as floating upon it. Yet as everyone knew, this was because errors in her construction and fitting made her two feet deeper than the already foolhardy freeboard of just eight-feet above the waterline. This, when most sailors in the navy—including Captain Burgoyne—did not know how to swim.[2] Coles was not worried; it would make the ship even 'steadier' in a seaway as well as offer more protection against enemy fire by lowering her target profile. All Milne could see was a first-class warship practically inviting the waves to wash over her, seeking out any opening, any imperfection to mercilessly exploit. How could Coles and Burgoyne and his officers not see the danger? By 5:30pm the weather was rapidly turning for the worse, and Milne's oared cutter only just managed to get back to his flagship, the broadside-ironclad *Lord Warden;* a high-walled fortress against the sea by comparison. As he looked back to catch sight of the Coles turret-ship bobbing up and down defiantly through grey Atlantic combers, a black wisp of coal smoke from her single funnel, sails taught with increasingly gusty winds, he decided that while he perhaps had to respect her raw military power he did really not approve of her as a lady fit to be called home by sailors. Something about her did not bode well…something ill-favoured. And it was the last time he ever saw her.

By midnight the *Captain* was indeed faring badly. The gale was blowing fiercely, with squalls reducing visibility even further, as the vessel became increasingly unmanageable.[3]

2   'It seems strange that Men who are employed on the water, and who are always liable from one Cause or another to tumble into it, should not be instructed in the very Simple act of taking advantage of the lightness of the Human Body as compared with an equal Bulk of Saltwater', wrote Lord Palmerston to the First Lord of the Admiralty in February 1865. The First Lord agreed, adding it was 'not always easy to teach sailors to swim. In cold climates they dislike the water. In warm climates the sharks render swimming dangerous', 12 February 1865, Palmerston to Edward Adolphus Seymour, 12th Duke of Somerset, Somerset Papers Collection, Aylesbury, Buckinghamshire Record Office, D/RA/A/2A/41; 14 February 1865, Somerset to Palmerston, Palmerston Papers, University of Southampton ('Broadlands'), GC/50.

3   As George Ballard observed, the unusual hurricane-force winds around midnight 'either spilt or blew clean away no fewer than twenty-three of [the fleet's] sails in all, including fourteen reefed topsails. Not a single ship escaped loss of gear except the *Captain*, where unhappily the hemp and canvas was too stout for the cranky hull beneath', George A. Ballard (edited by G. A. Osborn and N. A. M. Rodger), *The Black Battlefleet: A Study of the Capital Ship in Transition* (London: Nautical Publishing Co., Lymington & the

Giant swells and strong winds (Force 11)[4] now had her heeling to starboard well past an accepted twelve-degree margin of safety, as one drenched and exhausted deck crew changed watch with another. Burgoyne had also come up from his cabin, barely dressed—and clearly alarmed. He had felt the vessel lurch sharply several times through deep rolls. Something wasn't right. The mood of the crew had also turned. When the captain shouted out over the shrieking storm for another reading from the ship's pendulum the terrified reply he got back— for a low-freeboard ship caught in a gale on the open ocean—was a death-sentence: eighteen-degrees and climbing.[5] Too late Burgoyne called for all available hands to lower the topsails in an effort to quickly reduce the added pressure aloft which helped prevent the Captain *from righting herself. Now her rolls brought the devouring seas well over her starboard gunwale and up to her turrets. Not enough water was being cast off before another wave struck. The ship was in real peril, inclining further over, even as Burgoyne cried out for the sails to be simply cut loose from their halliards. But by now the stability of the vessel had reached its vanishing point, tipping steadily onto her side with a groan, and then, capsizing fully over.*

Only the men on the open deck managed to leap off the Captain *in time, including Burgoyne, and one gunner who scrambled through the aft turret's sighting hatch. One steam-pinnace and an oared-launch had luckily washed off the hurricane deck as the waves rushed over it, otherwise no one would have likely survived that night. All those who could not find or reach these two small boats in the raging, freezing saltwater, through stinging sheets of rain, in the dark of night—where even the moon was obscured behind impenetrable clouds— were doomed.[6] As it was, the majority of the* Captain's *crew were asleep below deck when her rolling became so critical that men in their hammocks were swung at right angles to the deck, and then all toppled over. Beneath them, the 25-ton guns and their monstrous iron carriages broke from their mounts and crashed against the turret roofs while the gigantic armoured towers themselves ripped loose from the lower hull and wrenched off the hurricane deck from below; everything plummeting into the dark abyss while the ocean poured through the gaping wounds of the hull. Above them was far worse, as the overturned stokeholds poured down white-hot hell; from a long line of furnaces scattering out fire, and the huge, careening boilers exploded open to scald every single panic-stricken stoker they did not crush.*

    Society for Nautical Research, Greenwich, 1980), 111. The *Hampshire Telegraph and Naval Chronicle* of 24 September 1870 also noted the 'stern ports of the captain's cabin of [HMS] *Warrior* were smashed in, and a portion of her figure-head carried away by the sea.'

4   Winds noted by other ships in the ironclad squadron ranged from Force 9 to 11 on the Beaufort scale; with Force 11 winds moving over 60 knots/70mph and waves exceeding fifty feet—one factor short of a full hurricane.

5   As noted in J. J. Welch, *A Text Book of Naval Architecture for the Use of Officers of the Royal Navy* (London: Darling & Son, Ltd., 1891), with a freeboard of 6½-feet the position of maximum stability for HMS *Captain* was 21-degrees. By contrast, the maximum stability for the sail-and-turret ironclad HMS *Monarch*, with a freeboard of 14-feet, was 40-degrees, 41-3.

6   Most accounts credit 472 officers and men as lost; there were only 18 survivors.

Outside in the storm, those struggling into the launch and trying to stay on top of the overturned pinnace, like Burgoyne, could hear the muffled screams of hundreds of their shipmates coming up from the funnel and hatchways before they finally slipped below the waves. The captain himself would not be saved. It was unbearable. The end of the world. Burgoyne had insisted that the last man clinging to the slippery hull of the boat go save himself by swimming over to the launch, which had strained over the heaving swells to come nearby and was barely visible in this dark, howling night of unimaginable tragedy. Burgoyne was wounded from the ship—his ship—overturning. He was in shock. But hearing the moans of the men calling out from the sinking wreck of HMS Captain, *or those shouting out from the darkness around him, and fading fast as everything and everyone was quickly swept away, he knew more profoundly than any other thought or sensation that he would not survive because he* could *not survive. At any rate, no sooner was the last survivor flung into the launch then Burgoyne was already disappeared out of sight to the others—his stout heart already sunk to oblivion.*

* * *

News of the foundering of the *Captain* struck the people of Britain like nothing they'd ever heard before. 'A more unfortunate disaster…has rarely been the lot of an English journalist to record', proclaimed the *Daily Telegraph* on 10 September 1870. 'The pen is almost paralysed in seeking to record the terrible event which is reported from Vigo Bay', echoed the Liverpool *Daily Post*. 'The *Captain*, it will be remembered, was built by Messrs. Laird, of Birkenhead.' Indeed, a Birkenhead newspaper declared the ship's sinking was 'felt here as if it were a personal calamity…the *Captain* was not only the pride of the nation but the special pride of the port; and her loss is felt as keenly as if she had been manned from Birkenhead and Liverpool, instead of Plymouth and Devonport.'[7] In this respect the London *Times* thought it was 'no exaggeration to say that the loss of Her Majesty's ship *Captain* is regarded as a domestic calamity throughout the southern and western divisions of this country. She was, by commission, a west country ship, and the majority of her company, officers included, were closely connected, either by birth or marriage, with that part of England.' Both Burgoyne and Coles were from Portsmouth, while at least 'one-third of the crew of the *Captain* were obtained from Plymouth, and therefore the reception of the startling intelligence fell like a thunderbolt upon the entire community.' The *Daily News*, while referring to the loss of the *Captain* as 'one of the most starling and stupendous calamites which the British Navy has ever experienced', also stressed how it was 'difficult to conceive the wide-spread ruin such a calamity as the loss of five-hundred men involves. It is not merely so many families plunged into mourning; but

---

7   10 September 1870, The *Daily Telegraph*; 10 September 1870, *Liverpool Daily Post*; undated (September 1870), from Coles Papers, National Maritime Museum, Greenwich, folio CCC/3.

a large part of those families are actually deprived of their living.'[8] *The Broad Arrow* naval and military gazette announced its 'deepest regret that an event has occurred for which no parallel can be found since the loss of the *Royal George* [in 1782], adding that it was 'too painful to think that this is a fate to which ironclad ships of war are especially liable.'[9]

Among the notable casualties was Leonard Childers, a son of the First Lord of the Admiralty (Hugh Childers); Arthur Napier Thomas Baring, the younger son of another member of Gladstone's government, Lord Northbrook, Under-Secretary State for War (and a future First Lord of the Admiralty, 1880-1885); William Reginald Herbert, third son of Lord Herbert (former Secretary of State for War) and brother of the 14th Earl of Pembroke; and Lord Lewis Gordon, second son of the 10th Marquess of Huntly. The Superintendent of the Royal Laboratory at Woolwich Arsenal, Colonel Edward Boxer, lost his only son. And the former Controller of the Royal Navy, Admiral Sir Baldwin Wake Walker (1st Baronet), not only lost his second son (Charles Sinclair) but his brother-in-law—Captain Burgoyne of the *Captain*—who had received the Victoria Cross during the Crimean War, and was the only son of Field-Marshal Sir John Fox Burgoyne (himself a son of General 'Gentleman Johnny' Burgoyne of the American Revolutionary War, who surrendered his army to George Washington following the defeat at Saratoga). But most dramatically, of course, was the loss of Coles himself; the sensational inventor, gone down in the ship nominally of his design. As *The Illustrated London News* quoted one of his friends, 'when [Coles's] whole heart was not on his wonderful ship creations it was at home with his wife and little children.'[10] A writer to the Editor of the *Hampshire Chronicle* likewise shared a letter from Coles to a close relative three weeks earlier; it was the third cruise of the *Captain* and she had crossed the Bay of Biscay five times. 'Her success is now complete in every way in which it can be tested', Coles offered cheerily. The day before they had passed over the spot off Cape St. Vincent where the previous HMS *Captain* of 74-guns was commanded in battle by Horatio Nelson, and Captain Burgoyne and all of the ship's officers and crew had 'insisted on drinking my health—which was very complimentary, but I felt very shy about it.' Here the writer also thought it was probably for the best that Coles had gone down with his ship, since both his 'feeble frame and "wounded spirit" would have succumbed to such a blow as this, if it had not been fatal to him at the moment.'[11]

---

8   12 and 15 September 1870, The *Daily News*. An article of March 1871 by Captain Edmund Robert Fremantle noted '116 left widows, the mothers of 199 fatherless children…it has been ascertained that about 120 fathers, mothers, or relatives of the seamen drowned owed their subsistence to their exertions'; 'The Loss of H.M.S. *Captain*', *Fraser's Magazine*, New Series, Vol. III, NO. XIII, 68-83.
9   12 September 1870, *The Times*; 10 September 1870, *The Broad Arrow*.
10 17 September 1870, *The Illustrated London News*.
11 17 September 1870, *Hampshire Chronicle* (letter by 'A.C.B.' dated 16 September).

Once people absorbed the shock of such news, and the reality of what had happened, the burning question *why* it occurred swiftly fanned across the country—with few people willing to accept it was a random natural disaster, beyond anyone's control. On 15 September, the *Daily Telegraph* noted a letter from Captain Sherard Osborn which blamed the topsails of the *Captain*, which 'threw her on her beam ends, and the fate of that gallant ship and crew ends in a melancholy way' because of 'the mania for sailing all our fleet, and endangering valuable ironclads, and still more precious lives, by manoeuvring under canvas, as in the days of Benbow.'[12] The *United Service Gazette* was disgusted how quick some of the press and partisan elements in the Royal Navy were willing to suggest the whole affair was due to 'defective design', and how two 'out of the whole number of daily journals have, by inuendo, if not by direct assertion, endeavoured to lead their readers to such a conclusion, and no doubt that impression will be carefully fostered, by those who have already shown how unscrupulous they can be, in getting up a case against an invention which has demonstrated the utter worthlessness of their own designs.' At fault was not necessarily the *Captain*'s low-freeboard, but how the 'necessity of enabling his ship to keep her station under sail with the fleet was earnestly pressed on Captain Coles, and his enthusiasm and eagerness to make his ship at least equal to his rival's induced him heavily to overmast and over-canvas her'.[13] As the wide-spread, deeply-felt controversy unfolded that autumn and indeed well into the following year, *The Times* realised that the British were faced with 'a most unhappy and perplexing story.' The mighty Royal Navy had lost 'a great ship, and with her a host of gallant men':

> This ought not to have been. There was rivalry between Mr. Reed [the former Chief Constructor of the Navy] and Captain Coles. Had there been agreement instead of dissension, the daring genius of one and the trained skill of the other might have spared the nation this dire calamity. Doubtless Captain Coles had his faults, and Mr. Reed may have been put upon his mettle. But we believe that in days to come the turret-ship will be a leading feature in the navies of the world, and the name of Cowper Coles will be cherished as identified with a type of war ship rendered needful by the massive and destructive armaments of modern times.[14]

---

12   15 September 1870, The *Daily Telegraph*.
13   17 September 1870, *The United Service Gazette*.
14   5 and 10 October 1870, *The Times*.

Introduction

'In deference to public opinion'

Commenting wryly on the human condition, the French philosopher Paul Virilio observed: 'The invention of the ship was also the invention of the shipwreck.' The following examination into the great 'turret vs. broadside'-debate in mid-Victorian Britain is also about the price often paid for progress, or perhaps the tragic limits of ambition—not just of the key actors involved like Coles, Edward James Reed or Robert Spencer Robinson (the Controller of the Navy for much of this period, the 1860s)—but a host of other individuals, all connected in one degree or another: Admiralty officers, civil servants, and other authorities at Whitehall; statesmen and heads of state; and various civilian, political and naval-military players, of the professional institutes, the press, and Parliament. In those days of stovepipe hats and crinoline dresses, newspapers were cheap and three out of four adults could read them. Less than one in seven adult males were entitled to vote, but everyone seemed to 'know their place' and be content striving for their own 'respectability'. Crowded city-streets were dimly illuminated at night with gas-lights, which were also replacing oil-lamps in homes and businesses. Electric telegraph lines were stretching out across the British Isles and around the world.[1] Yet despite the advent of steam-powered machinery, daily life largely depended on animals to move goods and people. Horses had to be fed and cleaned up after. People were often sick, and for long periods. Cholera pandemics were common. The infant mortality rate was such that one out of every four children born never survived past the age of five, and this rate in turn affected the overall average life expectancy of the population in the 1860s: 40-years old. Science and technology promised relief. More comfort, less pain, longer lives.

---

1   See for example Iwan Rhys Morus, '"The nervous system of Britain": Space, Time and the Electric Telegraph in the Victorian Age', *The British Journal for the History of Science*, Vol. 33, No. 4 (December 2000), 455-75; and Daniel R. Headrick, *The Tools of Empire: Technology and European Imperialism in the Nineteenth Century* (Oxford: Oxford University Press, 1981), 157-64.

Prosperity, it was believed, fed Progress; and prestige cultivated prosperity.[2] But neither was the nature of these events strictly British; events and personalities from abroad—particularly the United States—factored heavily in decision-making: which ships to build, what naval strategy to implement, when to boldly assert Britain's interests in the international arena, and how. Our characters were at turns proud, selfish, ruthless; brilliant, brave, patriotic. They were also brash, touchy, dishonest, cunning—greedy and determined. They proved to be both remarkably worldly on the one hand, amazingly ignorant on the other. They passionately believed that they were in the right—and others wrong—and they would 'save the nation from folly and ruin', even if it meant their behaviour in doing so was anything that of gentlemen.

This examination also finds that the sinking of HMS *Captain*, as representing an abysmal climax of the ongoing turret vs. broadside-debate, was hardly 'inevitable'. The subsequent court martial of inquiry, from 27 September to 8 October 1870, concluded that the experimental sail-and-turret ironclad capsized not just due to 'the pressure of sail, assisted by the heave of the sea', but because the ship was not 'endowed with a proper amount of stability.' She had been 'built in deference to public opinion as expressed in Parliament and through other channels, and in opposition to the views and opinions of the Controller of the Navy and his department'. Ruminating on the verdict of the court martial, and the finger-pointing now rampant across Britain, *The Times* thought the case 'against the *Captain* herself, as an experiment in naval architecture, comes out worse than was ever anticipated; in fact, the question seems to be, not whether the ship was a mistake, but whether she was not a mistake so gross as to carry her condemnation on her very face.'[3] Indeed, the court martial went further in noting that 'before the *Captain* was received from the contractors a grave departure from her original design had been committed, whereby her draught of water was increased by about two feet, and her freeboard was diminished to a corresponding extent, and that her stability proved to be dangerously small, combined with an area of sail, under these circumstances, excessive; the Court deeply regret that, if these facts were duly known and appreciated, they were not communicated to the officer in command of the ship; or, that, if otherwise, the ship was allowed to be employed in the ordinary service of the Fleet before these facts had been sufficiently ascertained by calculations and experiment.'[4] Although it was unlikely, given the sequence of events, that the *Captain* would have been conceived and designed very differently, she might well have been built and then deployed differently. She and the souls aboard might have survived, never to suffer such a fate. The errors in her design, perhaps in her

---

2   As noted by Andrew Porter, 'Prestige, especially in India, joined economic ties as vital bulwarks to survival as a Great Power', Andrew Porter (ed.), *The Oxford History of the British Empire: The Nineteenth Century* (Oxford: Oxford University Press, 1999), 6.
3   11 October 1870, *The Times*.
4   See 10 October 1870, *The Times*; and *Parliamentary Papers, Minute by the First Lord of the Admiralty with Reference to H.M.S.* Captain *with the Minutes of the Proceedings of the Court Martial and the Board Minute Thereon* (London: Harrison and Sons, 1871).

handling, were ones of degree only—and other ships of war, built better, succumbed to the sea, before and after—while others even more inherently 'unseaworthy' never sank.[5] As other histories have suggested, there is, therefore, the peculiar quality in this story of a multitude of factors (some intentional, some by chance) coming together in just such a way, a time and place, to create a catastrophe. It's all too easy to blame Coles, for example, and when Childers attempted to blame Robinson and Reed, the elderly Burgoyne wrote to him how 'the same awful calamity has brought grief on both of us, by one of those fearful casualties of the service in which our poor sons were engaged, and such as I am satisfied are occasionally unavoidable, in the spirited course of action necessary for its improvement; and it is cruel now to attempt to attach responsibility to those who worked zealously for their country, for results, the extent of which never was, nor could be, anticipated.'[6]

If the design of the *Captain* was not absolutely the cause of her own destruction in 1870—and Coles was not strictly responsible for either her design, her fitness as completed as an oceangoing cruiser, or her ready deployment in exercises with the rest of the ironclad battlefleet—then much of the history of these events has nonetheless condemned the ability of Coles to get her built anyway.[7] Two years later, in 1872, a *Times* correspondent with a combined squadron off Portland admired the sailing broadside-ironclads ('magnificent and costly men-o'-war') 'without a thought of the turret-ships in the background, a thought which is comforting or uncomfortable according to the way we take it. We may congratulate ourselves that these vessels, noble as they are and invincible as they seem, are not entirely trusted with the fortunes of England, and that we have another string to our bow which is, perhaps, better...' Two weeks later, and with the touring fleet now at Spithead, the correspondent was more definte, thinking that England surely 'never had a fleet which looked a better "safeguard to our Sovereign and her dominions"...They may not be mechanically

---

5   Colin Jones argued in his comparison of Reed's high-freeboard sail-and turret HMS *Monarch* with the low-freeboard *Captain*, for example, that the latter ironclad 'was the result of trying to establish an impossible compromise: a turret ironclad of radically modern design that would also be a good sailing ship', but he was not clear how the error in construction—resulting in an extra submersion of nearly two-feet—had condemned the overall design or not; '*Monarch* and *Captain*', in John Jordan (ed.), *Warship 2009* (London: Conway, 2009), 117-24.
6   Spencer Childers (ed.), *The Life and Correspondence of the Right Hon. Hugh C. E. Childers 1827-1896*, 2 vols. (London: John Murray, 1901), 1: 194.
7   See most recently, for example, Don Leggett, *Shaping the Royal Navy: Technology, Authority and Naval Architecture, c1830-1906* (Manchester: Manchester University Press, 2015), especially 126-64, stressing 'the ability of Coles to mobilise an influential group in Parliament that lobbied on his behalf' which in turn 'mobilised to encourage the then Liberal government to consider, fund and expedite trials with turret-ships.' How Coles was able to forcefully convince MPs of the necessity of his ideas, and their willingness to entertain them versus those of the Admiralty spokesmen, remains at issue. Not all political lobbies succeed, and neither Palmerston, Russell nor Gladstone were helpless in the art of politics or managing public opinion through the press the other way.

invincible, but sixteen stronger ships no nation can show.' Here, as long as the 'skill and courage of those who command them be impregnable,' rationalised *The Times* reporter, taxpayers could rest content that their money was well spent, and both the honour of their Queen and the lives of their sons at sea were safe. 'It is no good putting the captain in an iron beehive and the gunners in a plated battery, unless the captain and the gunners are men of the same stuff as those who stood exposed on the decks of the fleet that followed Nelson, and we may be certain that in battle personal skill and prowess would still go for a great deal, and might even make up for a deficient inch or two of iron plating.'[8] As laughable as this defence of one type of ironclad less fully-protected than others was (since, after all, men of Nelsonian talent and courage might command turreted warships as well), the former First Lord of the Admiralty who originally sanctioned Coles to build his version of a perfect seagoing ironclad, the Duke of Somerset, took deep satisfaction. For one, he had never approved of Reed's parting ironclad, the mastless turret-ship HMS *Devastation*, currently preparing for her first commission and undergoing careful inclination tests of her stability at Portsmouth Dockyard. 'As to Captain Coles and his inventions, *The Times* has now come to the conclusion which was rejected for five years, while that contest as to these seagoing turret-ships filled the columns of the newspapers', he wrote to his wife. 'Even now, if the survivors had not escaped to tell the truth, we should be in danger of losing more lives from the obstinate conceit of that unfortunate man.'[9]

In this vein Sir William Laird Clowes, in his popular seven-volume history of the Royal Navy published in 1903, was quick to extol the virtues of HMS *Monarch*, the high-freeboard sail-and-turret ironclad designed by Reed, while the *Captain* 'was the production of an amateur.' Equally influential navalist John Frederick Thomas Jane (of the *Jane's Fighting Ships* series) agreed in 1912, calling 'Coles' ideal turret-ship…an impracticable sort of ship' and tracing the decision to build the *Captain* to the 'perfect "turret craze"' which gripped the country following news of the duel between the *Monitor* and the *Merrimac* (CSS *Virginia*) at the Battle of Hampton Roads (9 March 1862).[10] By 1931 seapower was one of steel ships fuelled by oil, and the fateful course of the 'turret vs. broadside'-debate of the previous century, of iron ships powered by both sail and coal, was widely attributed to growing pains in the evolution of modern naval architecture and professionalism, with Admiral George A. Ballard calling the 'Parliamentary and Press agitation' in favour of seagoing turret-ships with lower

---

8   10 and 24 August 1872, *The Times*.
9   18 September 1872, Somerset to wife, in William Hurrell Mallock and Helen Guendolen Seymour Ramsden (eds.), *Letters, Remains, and Memoirs of Edward Adolphus Seymour Twelfth Duke of Somerset* (London: Richard Bentley and Son, 1893), 387-8; for the *Devastation*'s tests see for example *The Times*, 12 September 1872.
10 William Laird Clowes, *The Royal Navy: A History from the Earliest Times to 1900*, 7 vols. (London: Chatham Publishing, 1997 reprint of 1903 original), 7: 26-7; Fred T. Jane, *The British Battle-Fleet: Its Inception and Growth throughout the Centuries* (London: Conway, 1997 reprint of 1912 original), 188.

freeboard as advocated by Coles an 'irresponsible intervention...absolutely without parallel in British naval history.' In this interpretation, the problem at work in the Admiralty which led to the *Captain* disaster of 1870 lay with the Board's civilian not naval element, and Childers (not Robinson) was castigated by Ballard as 'a man of autocratic temperament, notoriously given to differences with his naval colleagues and subordinates'. Two years later, James Phinney Baxter's monumental treatise on *The Introduction of the Ironclad Warship* (1933), similarly emphasised how 'in his long struggle to persuade the Admiralty to install his turrets on seagoing ships, Coles showed a dogged persistence and an irascible temper which remind one of Ericsson.'[11] But it was Arthur Hawkey's dramatic account of the sinking of HMS *Captain*, first published in 1963, and later republished in 1999 as *Black Night off Finisterre*, which cemented the roles of Coles as simply 'The man who was wrong' and Reed as 'The man who was right'—inasmuch as the latter was (practically in Reed's own words) 'a man of science, object of criticism both in and out of Parliament and in the Press for his opposition to the revolutionary views of Captain Coles on ship design'.[12] Nicholas Rodger widened the analysis, pointing out that the *Captain* 'was in effect the Liberal's answer to Tory naval architecture; designed, built and supported by Childers's political friends...intended to show the naval world the enlightened spirit of scientific progress at sea.'[13]

But these accounts became increasingly specialised forms of (naval) history in their own right, concerning the evolution of British naval power on the one hand or the modern capital ship on the other. As a result, they respectively distanced themselves from the exact nature of the 'craze', among other factors, which fuelled the 'turret vs. broadside'-debate to the point where broadside-ironclads were largely condemned by both the British public and naval professionals. So while Nicholas Rodger rightly emphasised in 1975 that the *Captain* had been built 'in response to political pressure', and that Childers was pressing for even more seagoing turret-ships 'on explicitly political grounds', it was not explicit how or why the 'political' had taken primacy 'over the professional outlook'. The Admiralty was traditionally a fairly conservative institution whose secular authority was not just respected but expected by the British public—and while the administrative reforms of Childers perhaps crucially eroded the civil-military functionality of the Board from 1869, the *Captain* had been ordered and approved three years earlier over the course of two governments, one Liberal (under Russell) the other Conservative (under Derby); neither could Somerset nor Pakington be considered especially reform-minded First Lords. 'Childers's scheme

---

11 G. A. Ballard, 'British Battleships of 1870: The *Captain*', *The Mariner's Mirror*, Vol. 17, No. 3 (1931), 244-69; also *Black Battlefleet*, 99-113; James Phinney Baxter, *The Introduction of the Ironclad Warship* (Cambridge: Harvard University Press, 1933), 329.
12 Arthur Hawkey, *HMS* Captain (London: G. Bell and Sons, 1963); *Black Night off Finisterre: The Tragic Tale of an Early British Ironclad* (Annapolis: Naval Institute Press, 1999), 136.
13 N. A. M. Rodger, *The Admiralty* (Lavenham: Terence Dalton Limited, 1979), 110-11.

was embodied in the Order in Council of 14 January 1869', but the *Captain* was launched at Birkenhead just two months later. The real battle which ensued was between Childers and Robinson, and this stemmed in no small degree from the professional (not the politician) becoming Controller *and* Third Naval Lord on the Board. Childers had in fact given Robinson too much power, not too little, something which other sailors as well as civil servants in the Admiralty thought was bound to lead to trouble.[14] As C. I. Hamilton wondered in his 1982 survey of recent works on 'The Victorian Navy', HMS *Captain* was 'all the more impressive as evidence of civilian influence' in major warship construction.[15] Stanley Sandler likewise stressed the loss of HMS *Captain* could be traced directly to the Lords of the Admiralty fatally altering their policy 'in deference to public opinion'. Attacks in the British press and Parliament became too much to bear. The political liability of incessant controversy had to be contained. Yet as this book will highlight, the decision in 1865 to build Reed's *Monarch*, a seagoing turret-ship, was the real major turning point. There couldn't have been a *Captain* without the *Monarch*. The Admiralty should never have built her. Robinson and Reed did not want her. If the judgement of history is that the *Captain* was built in 'deference to public opinion', then so was the *Monarch*. But it remains unexplained how discussions of mere weapons and tactics could incite either newspaper editors or MPs this way, and this indeed went all the way back to the blinkered conclusions of the original court martial.[16]

* * *

As for the face of British naval power itself, as epitomised by the Royal Navy's first-class battleships, Sandler felt bound to chart 'steady improvements' from Reed's central-battery ironclads like *Bellerophon* and *Hercules*—jumping right over the *Monarch* and *Captain*—'that culminated in the [mastless, relatively low-freeboard] *Devastation*.' In fact, Reed was manifestly a proponent of the central-battery form of ironclad, even after he was ordered to design this British (i.e., breastwork) version of a seagoing monitor. His sail-and-broadside *Hercules* was as much of a 'dead-end' in naval architecture as the sail-and-turret *Captain*. Clearly, something else intervened

---

14 N. A. M. Rodger, 'The Dark Ages of the Admiralty, 1869-85 Part I: 'Business Methods', 1869-74', *The Mariner's Mirror*, Vol. 61, No. 4, 331-44. As Rodger noted, 'Robinson had some reluctant admirers in the Admiralty, but no friends' (other than Reed); 'The Design of the *Inconstant*', *The Mariner's Mirror*, Vol. 61, No. 1 (1975), 9-22.
15 C. I. Hamilton, 'The Victorian Navy' review-article, *The Historical Journal*, Vol. 25, No. 2 (1982), 471-87. See also Don Leggett's analysis, 'Neptune's New Clothes: Actors, Iron and the Identity of the Mid-Victorian Warship', in Don Leggett and Richard Dunn (eds.), *Re-inventing the Ship: Science, Technology and the Maritime World, 1800-1918* (Farnham: Ashgate publishing Limited, 2012), 71-92.
16 Stanley Sandler, '"In Deference to Public Opinion": The Loss of HMS *Captain*', *The Mariner's Mirror*, Vol. 59, No. 1 (1973), 57-68.

on this evolutionary timeline to produce 'the prototype of the modern battleship.'[17] As this study of the 'turret vs. broadside'-debate in Britain from approximately 1860-1870 reveals, the pressure to build the *Captain* stemmed in no small part from the expressed desire to marry the tactical perfection represented by the low-freeboard, mastless, double-turreted monitor USS *Miantonomoh*—which toured the British Isles in the summer of 1866—with the strategic range and speed of the first-rate broadside-ironclads. By cleverly playing up the latent threat posed to U.S. sovereignty in 1861 by Britain's giant new iron-armoured screw-frigate HMS *Warrior* (even before the *Trent Affair* that November-December), John Ericsson was able to clinch final authorisation to build his radically experimental USS *Monitor*.[18] And it is similarly difficult to imagine Coles's *Captain* ever being sanctioned by a reluctant Board of Admiralty in 1866 without the lingering spectre of the *Monitor* (lost at the end of 1862); the diametric opposite of *Warrior* on this revolutionary spectrum in ironclad design. Reed's brother-in-law and successor as Chief Constructor of the Navy, Nathaniel Barnaby, at least, did not mince words. Ericsson's USS *Monitor* and the Union Navy's subsequent wholesale development of low-freeboard, mastless turret-ships mounting the heaviest guns and armour-plating possible was, in his estimation (made in 1904), 'not a contribution of any value in shipbuilding, or in marine engineering, but it was the most striking illustration of enterprise and resourcefulness which is presented in the whole story of naval development during the century.'[19]

That sentiment provided a clue to the forgotten significance of the 'turret vs. broadside'-debate, for at its heart lay a hidden paradox—and previous estimations of Coles and the *Captain*, panning the 'hysteria' of the British public who saw fit to intervene in such a discussion, have rather overlooked the forest for the trees. Reed, after all, was hardly free of design errors or bad ideas. His decision to do away with wing passages as longitudinal bulkheads in the hull of the *Audacious*-class central-battery ironclads of 1867 helped ensure the sinking of HMS *Vanguard* when accidentally rammed on 1 September 1875.[20] Shortly after this Reed quietly left

---

17 Stanley Sandler, *The Emergence of the Modern Capital Ship* (New Jersey, Associated University Presses, Inc., 1979), 247-9.
18 See for example, Howard J. Fuller, 'The *Warrior's* Influence Abroad: The American Civil War', *International Journal of Naval History*, Vol. 10., No. 1 (October 2013).
19 Barnaby, *Nathaniel Barnaby, Naval Development in the Century (Toronto: The Linscott Publishing Company, 1904)*, 92. 'The *Devastation, Thunderer, Dreadnought, Inflexible, Ajax, Agamemnon, Colossus* and *Edinburgh* are all of the monitor type and grew out of the American system. Low-freeboard, thick armour, a few heavy guns and no secondary armament are the notes of the system. Regarded as a part of the naval centre plan much may be said for them, and they may wait for the eventual and certain acceptance of that plan. As parts of a fleet of fast ships engaged in naval tactics, they are obsolete', 83.
20 With enough water quickly entering the engine-room that pressure for the pumps was lost. See for example the analysis by Oscar Parkes in *British Battleships, 'Warrior' 1860 to 'Vanguard' 1950: A History of Design, Construction and Armament* (London: Seeley Service & Co., Ltd., 1970), 152-9; also Chris Thomas, *Lamentable Intelligence from the Admiralty:*

the country, touring Russia. At Nikolaev, a Ukrainian shipyard forty miles up the Bug River from the Black Sea, he witnessed the launching of a completely circular, mastless ironclad designed by Russian Admiral Andrei Popov. Armoured by 18-inch thick iron plating all around, this drew thirteen-feet of water and was propelled by six screws, with a pair of very heavy guns mounted in an open barbette. Reed was openly and stubbornly enamoured with the design and wanted to see versions of it the Royal Navy, much to the loss of his professional reputation.[21] In a letter to the Editor of *The Times* on 2 November 1864, 'Z' demanded that the turrets of the converted wooden line-of-battle ship HMS *Royal Sovereign* be tested under fire. 'Upon the result our maritime supremacy may depend.' Here the writer excused himself and the British public, which 'care naught either for Captain Coles or M. E. J. Reed, or, indeed, for any other inventor; but so long as ships of war are indispensable it is determined that they shall be the best possible.' What was infuriating was how Whitehall kept deferring the question—the real question—which was at stake. 'The notion is pretty generally entertained that the Admiralty, from some cause or other, are not anxious for the success of the turret system...The British public will sooner or later insist upon knowing the truth in this matter, and the Admiralty would show their wisdom by timely concession.'[22]

As this book explores, the mid-Victorians felt that the 'turret vs. broadside'-question left their ideal of Great Power status teetering precariously between two vast extremes. Such a sensation, like the dark uncertainty of the future itself, was an unpleasant one. The past, one of bloody Nelsonian victories and dangerous Palmerstonian interventions, seemed much safer if only because it was recognisable. As Palmerston argued forcefully in the House of Commons in August 1860, 'if there be one thing which more than another tends to endanger the continuance of peace, it is when a wealthy nation like England—the object of a natural rivalry and jealousy in

---

The Sinking of HMS Vanguard *in 1875* (Dublin: Nonsuch Publishing, 2006), especially 44-6, 90-7, 101-2, 110-11, with Reed admitting that effectual watertight subdivisions against ramming were reduced in order to accommodate greater engine power with larger boilers, and that future ironclads had improved compartments. Parkes also noted that greater firepower and sail area were maximized in *Audacious*-class at the cost of safety—the same essential flaw attributed to the *Captain*'s design philosophy.

21 E. J. Reed, *Letters from Russia in 1875* (London: John Murray, 1876), 1-25, 33-5, 68-75. See also Reed's 4 February 1876 RUSI paper 'On Circular Ironclads', *Journal of the Royal United Service Institution*, Vol. 20, 1877, 85-109, where he was ridiculed for even referring to these floating-battery platforms as 'ships'. In the audience, Robinson attempted to defend his former colleague's advocacy of them by declaring, without a trace of irony, that it was 'worth while to consider every point of this new armoured vessel most carefully, and to see whether it does or does not contain the elements of that very great success which Mr. Reed has shown it possibly may contain', and noting that aside from mere coastal defence or assault, Reed saw 'no limit to its application'. *Punch* lampooned Reed and Popov with its own 'Warship of the (Remote) Future': a colossal floating breech-loaded gun which was itself a mastless ironclad; 20 November 1875.

22 2 November 1864, *The Times*.

the case of other Powers—leaves herself open to attack and insult without having the means of repelling the one or avenging the other.' Less than two years later, following the *Trent* Affair, he admitted that had the U.S. not acquiesced to Britain's ultimatum 'we should have been bound to extort by the usual means, as far as we were able to do so, that compliance which had been refused to a courteous application.' Here the real issue was not the maritime legality of the case or even whether the incident was authorised by Federal authorities; it was 'the courage to insult the British flag' as shown by the (dangerously enfranchised) people of the Northern States. Watching this mob-nation then bow its head before the fleet of wooden ships-of-the-line sent to reinforce Britain's North America and West Indies Station was the supreme moment of Palmerston's whole career as a British statesman, and was immensely gratifying to the mid-Victorian public. Others were not so afraid, observing that wars and constant threats of war were an unnecessary source of tension in their own right (or wrong). Genuine, sustained peace was the 'undiscovered country', and as Shakespeare's young Hamlet reflected, why should they be afraid? It did not necessarily require 'supremacy' or 'sovereignty' to feel safe, or proud, just as the modern world itself since at least the 17th-century seemed to totter between a 'naturally' egalitarian order, ultimately, or a strictly hierarchical one. In denouncing Palmerston's pre-emptive military and naval mobilisation against the U.S., Radical leader John Bright warned 'for ten, twenty, or thirty years hence, whether the Union be restored or not, the Northern States will probably continue to increase as rapidly as they have ever increased, in population and in power.'[23] Thus, fifteen years after the American Civil War ended, the 76 year-old Duke of Somerset condemned in his treatise on *Monarchy and Democracy* (1880) the 'philosophic complacency' of his former cabinet colleague, Gladstone, in predicting both the pre-eminence of the United States in the global economy and the sinking of Great Britain 'into a subordinate position': 'As Venice and Genoa yielded to other nations the primacy of mercantile greatness and naval power, so also Britannia is, we are told, doomed to let fall the sceptre of the seas, and we ought to prepare for the day of our affliction.'[24]

* * *

---

23 2 August 1860, 'Second Night' (debating coastal fortifications), *Hansard*, Vol. 160, 485-588; 17 February 1862, 'Correspondence in Case of the "*Trent*"—Observations', *Hansard*, Vol. 165, 380-94. 'In their rejection of power and preferred identification with powerlessness, British and American liberals were suspicious of a Pax based on naval predominance, and often pictured the Royal Navy as an obstacle to world peace', Bernard Semmel, *Liberalism and Naval Strategy: Ideology, Interest, and Sea Power during the Pax Britannica* (London: Allen & Unwin, Inc., 1986), 178-81.
24 The Duke of Somerset, *Monarchy and Democracy: Phases of Modern Politics* (London: James Bain, 1880), 189-90.

It is not the intention of this work to offer a full technical exposition of the various ships involved, such as Britain's original seagoing broadside-ironclad HMS *Warrior* or the Union Navy's first turret-ship, USS *Monitor*; let alone other important ironclads of the period like *Gloire, Royal Sovereign, Bellerophon, Miantonomoh, Devastation*—even the *Captain*. Such details can be found in numerous other published works, in records, and on websites with varying degrees of accuracy. Any errors in detail, as such—there and herein—are usually (and hopefully) not too far from a true conception of what these vessels were like, what their respective capabilities—and flaws—were. More often it's about how the facts are represented; the thinking that's brought to bear. An ironclad might be forgiven for being slow by one advocate, for example, in emphasis of other qualities argued to be more important. The reverse was then argued equally well. It still is. What this volume does, however, is bring more primary source-based evidence as well as analysis to bear; to provide greater historical context, along with some added details. Despite many technical explanations on the one hand and broad references to naval history or strategy on the other, there is still much to be said on the how and why of this overall story. History is very much about not just reminding but remoulding the significance of the past. Based on the consideration of additional evidence, what did these events *signify*?

For an enigma has remained subtly embedded in the literature. As Peter Burroughs suggested for *The Oxford History of the British Empire* (1999), 'despite incidents and alarms, no foreign powers were able to challenge Britain's maritime mastery; indeed they acquiesced in British overseas pretensions and self-appointed policing role, made the more palatable by the shared benefits of free trade. The result was an exceptional period of international peace when Britain's pacific approach to global trading relations, backed by industrial muscle, commanded general acceptance. What was later dubbed *Pax Britannica* reflected an unwillingness on the part of European competitors to question one nation's unassailable naval supremacy.'[25] Taken *a priori*, this easily reduces the European 'Balance of Power' and the whole course of the nineteenth century worldwide as one dictated by British foreign policy interests—backed directly by fear of British seapower on the one hand and the lure of free trade-globalisation (networked through the City in London) on the other. But examined *a posteriori*, this is soon exposed as a rather rose-tinted conception of the past.[26] By taking into account the 'turret vs. broadside'-debate, crowned by the *Captain* disaster of 1870, and the revolution not just in naval technology or tactics but in wider socio-political and geostrategic affairs in the mid-nineteenth century, one sees British foreign policy (peacefully) adapting to the progressive retreat—not confident assertion—of

---

25 Peter Burroughs, 'Defence and Imperial Disunity', in Porter, *Oxford History*, 320-45.
26 See for example, Muriel E. Chamberlain, *British Foreign Policy in the Age of Palmerston* (London: Longman Group Limited, 1980), 89-90; and Muriel E. Chamberlain, '*Pax Britannica*'? *British Foreign Policy 1789-1914* (Harlow: Longman Group UK Limited, 1988), 6; 123.

Britain's 'unassailable naval supremacy'. In truth, the period between '1860-1870' was dominated by three wars of national unification, the American Civil War, the German Wars of Unification (leading to the Second Reich), and the unification of Italy; whereby the map of not just Europe but the world was re-ordered. Likewise, although France signed a free-trade treaty with Britain in January 1860, the U.S. threw up the protective Morrill Tariff in March 1861, with Germany and Russia following suit as part of their own industrialisation efforts (versus Britain) in the 1870s-1880s. As will be shown, that Britain played no part in these events was not for a perceived lack of strategic interest or ends, but in means.[27] The subsequent course of history was not so much about what Britain could do to other powers, but what she couldn't; not about the international peace which she (clearly had not) enforced, but the peace of her own isolation. Indeed, the ultimate symbol of trying to assert British interests if not 'primacy' in world affairs was HMS *Warrior* in 1860 but then HMS *Captain* in 1870. Inconveniently wedged in between these two stately Victorian capital ships was an ugly, diminutive 'machine': the USS *Monitor*. As *Punch* lamented in 1866:

> If the loss of prestige has pain in it,
> In our case there's this salve for the sore,
> That we might, in attempting to win it,
> Have both lost it and also much more.
> And prestige is a consideration
> Of small weight as compared with expense.
> But let no cost be spared by this nation
> That it needs to insure its defence.[28]

---

27 'Having failed to throw back Russia into the mid eighteenth century, and also having come to see how reluctant his countrymen were to quarrel with the United States, Palmerston took a more modest view of Britain's ability to assert herself internationally… Even the world's biggest navy might be frustrated by a power which was prepared and able to sacrifice its seaborne trade and its coastal cities', wrote C. J. Bartlett. 'The truth concerning the limits of British influence in Europe did not become apparent until the Polish and Danish crises of 1863 and 1864', *Defence and Diplomacy: Britain and the Great Powers 1815-1914* (Manchester: Manchester University Press, 1993), 68-9.
28 20 October 1866, 'Poor John Bull's Prestige', *Punch*.

1

'If we were the defendants of Cronstadt I should laugh at any attacking force'

As with much in history, the casual link or chain of events culminating in the foundering of the experimental low-freeboard, sail-and-turret HMS *Captain*, in September 1870, begins well before '1860'—or say the launch of Britain's equally experimental seagoing broadside-ironclad, HMS *Warrior* (on 29 December 1860). Indeed, even HMS *Devastation* of 1871, being mastless, steam-powered and screw-propelled, had much in common with the Royal Navy's first ironclads which were, however, designated 'floating batteries' and whose designs were based directly on those supplied by the French Ministry of Marine in 1854—during the Crimean War (1853-1856).[1] In many respects, this was not the type of great 'maritime war' that many in either Britain or France had expected since the end of the Napoleonic Wars. First of all, such a conflict was not being waged against one another, given that between 1702 and 1815, England had been at war with France in greater or lesser degrees for approximately sixty-five years.[2] Now they were allies against the Russian Empire which was, despite its powerful navy—typically ranked third behind that of the 'maritime powers'—very much a continental power. Since the Congress of Vienna in 1815, an ongoing concern for Britain had been with the 'Sick Man of Europe': propping up the Ottoman Empire 'to save India from the Tsar'. British, Russian and French powers had intervened in the Greek revolts of the early 1820s, culminating

---

1   Although major fighting effectively ended with the Russian victory at the Siege of Kars (28 November 1855), peace negotiations did not begin until the following month, with the Treaty of Paris signed on 30 March 1856. As J. B. Conacher points out, 'the Russian success made it easier for the Czar to agree to peace negotiations' hoping that it would serve as a counter bargaining chip to the humiliating loss of Sevastopol in early September, *Britain and the Crimea, 1855-56: Problems of War and Peace* (London: Macmillan Press, 1987), 133. For the early Crimean War battery designs (specifying a draft of less than 9-feet) see for example, Baxter, *Introduction*, 71-80.
2   Or 'Great Britain' since the Act of Union in 1707. For a long-term view of modern French naval power see for example, E. H. Jenkins, *A History of the French Navy: From its Beginnings to the Present Day* (London: Macdonald and Jane's, 1973).

in the naval battle of Navarino (27 October 1827) which rolled back earlier Moslem victories and secured the independence of Greece from Ottoman rule. But this was also done to create a buffer against Russian expansion at Turkey's expense, leading to the London Straits Convention of 1841 which likewise prevented Russian warships from penetrating into the Mediterranean. These actions prevented a war between the Great Powers but did not resolve the prevailing strategic issues—especially the crowding of rival Russian and British interests in the region. Meanwhile the 'Great Game' between these two powers over hegemony in Central Asia had begun in earnest, with British East India Company forces invading Afghanistan in 1839, and disastrously routed in 1842. When the bubble finally burst in 1853, first with Turkey's declaration of war against Russia, and then the annihilation of a Turkish squadron by the Russian Black Sea Fleet at Sinope, it was understood that the main Anglo-French thrust would be against the main Russian naval-arsenal of Sevastopol, in the Crimean Peninsula.[3]

The campaign was marked by uncertainty, however. It was not clear whether or not the formidable Russian Black Sea Fleet would seek an open battle, and by concentrating a far larger and more technologically-superior (steam-powered) naval force in the vicinity, the Allies perhaps unwittingly forced their enemy to shelter behind Sevastopol's modern sea-fortifications and play a waiting game. Finally, by the 1850s it was considered dangerous in the extreme to risk 'wooden ships against stone forts' especially when the latter were armed with shell-firing guns (high velocity projectiles which could penetrate wooden bulwarks and then explode).[4] Ships could be set on fire and sunk, forts could not. So despite a massive qualitative as well as quantitative advantage by sea in September 1854, the Allied fleets of wooden ships-of-the-line and support vessels were obliged to anchor well out of range of Sevastopol's guns. Any thought of blasting past forts Constantine and Alexander through the main ship channel to sink the Russian fleet in place and bombard the dockyard facilities was also dismissed when the Russian naval commander decided to scuttle a portion of his own ships-of-the-line across the harbour entrance. This line of obstructions was then shielded from any demolition attempts by the outer forts.

---

3 See for example, Norman Rich, *Why the Crimean War? A Cautionary Tale* (New York: Mcgraw-Hill, Inc., 1985), especially 89-132; also David M. Goldfrank, *The Origins of the Crimean War* (Harlow: Longman, 1994), especially 184-6, 234-5, and 271-82.

4 As noted by the Captain Ducie Chads of the Royal Navy's gunnery school, HMS *Excellent* at Portsmouth naval base, forts might simply be out-ranged by ships armed with long-range shell-firing guns. But this assumed enemy forts were not similarly armed, and that fire at extreme range from rolling ships would be effective. He also outlined the threat posed by a landing force which could march to a position from which to shell a crowded dockyard like Portsmouth or Devonport; see Montagu Burrows, *Memoir of Admiral Sir Henry Ducie Chads* (Portsea: Griffin and Co., 1869), 31-5. Chads later helped establish the ordnance testing grounds at Shoeburyness (Essex), on the Thames Estuary.

If the issue was the destruction of Russian naval power in the Black Sea and beyond, then the only way to do this was to land a large expeditionary force beyond the harbour forts (at Eupatoria), marching around Sevastopol to set up a bombardment of the base from the landward side. But the crews and guns of the scuttled Russian men-of-war were used to augment the firepower of the shore forts as well as arm a new line of field fortifications defences on the south side of Sevastopol, brilliantly engineered in haste by General Edward Todleben. Although Russian attempts to disrupt the Allied movement to hem them in failed at the costly battles of the Alma (20 September), Balaclava (25 October), and Inkerman (5 November), neither were the combined Anglo-French battlefleets able to silence the sea forts in their attempt of 17 October.[5] The costly, desultory Siege of Sevastopol then characterised the rest of the contest as one of attrition. In the Baltic, the application of Allied sea power proved even more problematic, especially without the assistance of a major field army. The main Russian naval base of Cronstadt was on Kotlin Island, twenty miles from St. Petersburg, at the end of the Gulf of Finland. By 1854—and throughout most of the nineteenth-century—the shallow waters around Cronstadt helped make it the best defended port on earth, with multi-tiered, granite-faced fortifications channelling enemy ships into successive lines of interlocking fields of fire, at close range. Still, the British despatched a powerful force of steam-powered, screw-propelled line-of-battle ships under the command of its most celebrated admiral, Charles Napier. Perhaps the Russian Baltic Fleet might come out and fight—and be destroyed. Perhaps the Russian capital could be taken by a naval *coup de main*, and the war ended. But once Napier's forces surveyed what they were up against it became quickly obvious that very little could be done offensively against the Russian other than blockade.[6]

5   See for example D. Bonner-Smith and A. C. Dewar (eds.), *Publications of the Navy Records Society, Vol. LXXXIII, Russian War, 1854—Baltic and Black Sea, Official Correspondence* (London: Navy Records Society, 1943), 336-40, 357-8. William Laird Clowes notes total British losses from the 17 October 1854 naval attack on Sevastopol's defences as 44 killed and 266 wounded, with French warships suffering a further 212 casualties during the action. The 90-gun HMS *Albion* and the frigate *Arethusa* were sent to Constantinople for serious repairs. HMS *Agamemnon* was struck at least '240 times', *The Royal Navy*, 6: 440-5. Russian losses were a fraction of this, damage to the forts was 'negligible' and British naval authority David K. Brown suggested only 23 of Fort Constantine's 94 guns, for example, actually faced the British fleet; David K. Brown, *Before the Ironclad: Development of Ship Design, Propulsion and Armament in the Royal Navy, 1815-1860* (London: Conway Maritime Press, 1990), 142. See also David K. Brown, 'Shells at Sevastopol', *Warship* 3 (1979), 74-79. Albert Seaton credits the Russians with firing some 16,000 shot and shell in return, *The Crimean War: A Russian Chronicle* (London: B. T. Batsford Ltd., 1977), 133.
6   As the First Lord of the Admiralty, Sir James Graham, wrote to Napier on 1 May 1854, 'I by no means contemplate an attack either on Sweaborg or on Cronstadt. I believe them to be all but impregnable from the sea, and none but a very large army could co-operate by land efficiently in presence of such a force as Russia could easily concentrate for defence of the approaches to her capital', from Charles Stuart Parker (ed.), *Life and Letters of Sir James Graham*, 2 vols. (London: John Murray, 1907), 2: 231.

What was needed was a coastal assault flotilla of shallow-draft gunboats which could engage with Russian shore batteries at effective range on the one hand, and out-range Russian smoothbores with rifled guns and mortars on the other. The Royal Navy did not have such a force on hand. In any event, it was not until 30 September 1854—six months *after* Britain joined France in declaring war against Russia—that the Admiralty petitioned the Treasury for a 'supplemental credit of £550,000' to build mortar-vessels, gunboats and armoured-batteries. This was not only a 12 percent increase beyond the navy estimates for 1853 ('£6,235,493'), it tapped most of the expected surplus the government had painstakingly built-up in the national budget, during peace, and amidst Liberal mid-Victorian calls for 'retrenchment'. A year later, and with war imminent, Chancellor of the Exchequer William Gladstone was pleased to announce that the national revenue had been roughly £1 million more than expected while expenditure was roughly £1 million less—indicating an 'overplus at the present time at £2,854,000.' But as £2,840,000 was now expected above normal to pay for war preparations in all the services, Gladstone could only lament how peace would have meant a sizeable profit to the country—and still the Navy was about to hit him for half a million more for entirely new weapons which 'may contribute powerful aid to the speedy and honourable conclusion of this War'. The Admiralty could only try to sweeten the offer by adding that 'the Means of attack, which we now propose to provide, will at all Times be most useful and available for the defence of our own Shores and Harbours.'[7]

Napier quietly returned from the Baltic before the winter ice sealed off the region; *Punch* depicting him as a cowardly lion, pathetically armed with a tiny pistol. As Conservative leader of the Opposition the Earl of Derby jibed, 'never did a mighty force—one of the most powerful armaments which this country has ever sent forth— sent, too, with no little amount of self-laudation—accomplish so little.'[8] Indeed, the British Lion's inability to tame the Russian Bear quickly enough in 1854 saw Napier and the First Lord of the Admiralty, Sir James Graham, attacking one another in the press and Parliament for the navy's incapacity in the Baltic.[9] Sensing 'no confidence'

---

[7] 18 April 1853, *Hansard*, Vol. 125, 1423-4, and 6 March 1854, vol. 131, 360; 30 September 1854, Admiralty to the Treasury, British National Archives (Kew), 'TNA', ADM (Admiralty) 1/5632.

[8] 1854, 'The Return from the Baltic!!', *Punch*, vol. xxvii, 117; 12 December 1854, 'The Queen's Speech', *Hansard*, vol. 136, 31-2. *Punch* had also suggested 'New Names for the Navy', suggesting that instead of bellicose titles for new ships such as 'the *Bulldog*, the *Terrible*, the *Vengeance*, or the *Fury*…The peaceful war policy of our present Government would…be indicated far more correctly by such names as the *Lamb*, the *Reluctant*, the *Forbearance*, the *Harmless*, and our ships would thus no longer be sailing under false titles, as seems to be the case, especially in the Black Sea', 100.

[9] See for example, 13 March 1856, 'Operations in the Baltic', *Hansard*, vol. 141, 48-119; and 4 April 1856, 'Sir Charles Napier at Acre', *Hansard*, vol. 141, 480-522; also Arvel B. Erickson, *The Public Career of Sir James Graham* (Oxford: Basil Blackwell, 1952), 370-2.

in his war-time coalition government of Whigs and Peelites, Lord Aberdeen[10] resigned as Prime Minister at the end of January 1855 and was eagerly replaced by Lord Palmerston. 'The public is judging, and we are partly judging *ex post facto* which is not just', wrote the new First Lord, Sir Charles Wood, to Lord John Russell (as Secretary of State for the Colonies). 'Nobody thought that the Russians would fight as they have done.'[11] But when Napier's successor, Rear-Admiral Sir Richard Saunders Dundas, returned to the Baltic with another fleet in the spring of 1855, it was not much better equipped. Wood described to his wife how he couldn't help being impressed with the sheer pageantry of British naval power which he witnessed departing from Portsmouth that April, including the flagship HMS *Duke of Wellington*, a burly new 131-gun screw-propelled first-rate. '19 Sail of the Line in two lines, such a sight has never been seen since 1815 & 6 or 8 paddle steamers besides. It was a glorious sight.'[12] But Dundas was soon writing to the First Lord that what was needed was more light-draft gunboats, not battleships whose size prevented them from entering the northern channel off Kotlin—the only potential weak spot of Cronstadt unanticipated by Russian defence planners and which Napier had identified the year before.'[13]

The only technology that might salvage Britain's reputation, at least by sea, were now the shallow-draft, screw-propelled iron-armoured floating batteries. Even then their approach in such narrow, confined waters would be hazardous. Dundas thought they 'might at least be got to the edge of the barrier in 10 feet of water, and they might be got a little further in if we could remove the barrier…but I cannot help thinking that without an active moveable force within the barrier they might positively be boarded and carried by a numerous flotilla. Is our moveable force to enter by one small opening and is it to retreat in case of need in presence of a larger force through that same opening?'[14] By the end of June 1855, Wood confided to Rear-Admiral Sir Frederick Grey that Dundas 'will make nothing of it' against Cronstadt, which seemed 'stronger than we thought at first, on closer inspection.' Had the Royal Navy been equipped with enough gunboats the previous year, however, 'we might probably have burnt the place.'[15] When the first of the armoured batteries were deployed against Kinburn on the Black Sea (17 October 1855), the three French versions seemed 'perfect…the shot struck against them in many places, but simply indented the iron a trifle, and shell

10   George Hamilton-Gordon, 4th Earl.
11   7 December 1854, Wood to Russell, Halifax Papers, British Library, London ('British Library'), Add. Ms. 49531, Vol. 1.
12   4 April 1855, Wood to his wife (Mary), Hickleton (Halifax) Papers, Borthwick Institute (University of York), A2/43.
13   See for example the annotated chart appended to 9 January 1856 (plan for attacking Cronstadt with armoured mortars, dated October 1855) in TNA ADM 1/5677; also 2 May 1855, Dundas to Wood, Halifax Papers, British Library, Add. Ms. 49533, Vol. 3.
14   4 June 1855, Dundas to Wood, Halifax Papers, British Library, Add. Ms. 49533, Vol. 3.
15   25 June 1855, Wood to Grey, Halifax Papers, Borthwick Institute, A2-70. Grey was a relation by Lady Mary Wood, daughter of Second Earl and Countess Grey.

broke against them like glass', wrote Captain William Mends from aboard the new flagship of the British Black Sea fleet, HMS *Royal Albert*; another massive, 121-gun, screw-propelled ship-of-the-line. Exactly one year before his previous command, HMS *Agamemnon*, had been 'well-hammered' by Sevastopol's coastal forts. 'It has been a good experiment; now Cronstadt and Sweaborg are doomed; nothing can save them. If they are not destroyed before this time next year, it will be a disgrace to us.'[16] Iron might overrule stone, just as Russian forts had routinely negated wooden sea power. But the ironclad floating batteries at Kinburn were neither solely nor even primarily responsible for the Russian surrender there. The official report of Rear-Admiral Edmund Lyons (C-in-C of the Black Sea fleet) was one of allied combined operations. After waiting several days for the weather to provide smooth enough water for the armoured batteries, mortars and gunboats, the bombardment soon proved overwhelming to the Russian defenders, completely outflanked on their thin spit of land by ships from the rear and troops on land blocking off reinforcements.[17]

* * *

The problem was that ironclads, just like any other men-of-war, were not 'unsinkable' weapons-platforms. It did not help, as critics pointed out in the House of Lords in the spring of 1855, that they were built in war-time haste as copies from experimental French designs. Since there was 'a question involved which affected the finances of the country', could they be certain 'the science of the country had been applied to the construction of these vessels'?[18] As a rule they were underpowered the lighter they were—the less seaworthy they were. Less power in the engine room meant less control at the helm. And if ironclads ran aground off Cronstadt they were all but lost, or worse, captured by the enemy. Both the early British and French ironclads likewise revealed the fatal design compromise which affected all battleships of the modern era: relatively weak deck armour, as well as no protection below the waterline. This meant they were especially vulnerable to high angle plunging shot as well as to explosions under their keels. Clusters of such vessels, creeping forward slowly, would be much easier to hit with concentrated Russian mortar fire. 'A Floating Battery at long range would, or at least ought to have great resisting power against horizontal fire,' wrote Dundas to Wood, 'but being larger than Mortar Boats and less active than small Gunboats it would be more liable to injury by vertical fire...'[19] One British report from 1860 suggested vertical fire alone could stop ironclads in their advance against fortified ports, since 'the fall of two or three 13-inch shells upon the deck of any vessel

16   From Bowen Stilon Mends, *Life of Admiral Sir William Robert Mends, G. C. B.: Late Director of Transports* (London: John Murray, 1899), 166-70, 302.
17   23 October 1855, Lyons to Board, TNA ADM 1/5654; see also Brown, *Before the Ironclad*, 158.
18   1 May 1855, 'Floating Batteries', *Hansard*, vol. 137, 2037-42.
19   2 July 1855, Dundas to Wood, Halifax Papers, British Library, Add. Ms. 49533, Vol. 3.

would probably destroy it'.[20] With their overall design emphasis upon shallow-draft to allow them to engage shore defences at the closest range possible, the unavoidable trade-off in design meant a perilous dearth of reserve buoyancy. If they struck a mine, for example, they would sink faster than deeper vessels with greater hulls.[21]

Meanwhile, the Russians were expending all of their remaining energies upgrading the guns on their forts. Having inherited an unwanted war from his father (Nicholas I), Tsar Alexander II had warned that if Britain and France 'were bent on humiliating Russia' he would 'would resist their unjust aggression with all the vigour which the resources of his Empire and the patriotism of his People placed at his disposal', as relayed by the British ambassador at Stockholm to the Foreign Office in December 1855 (i.e., three months *after* the fall of Sevastopol). One report from Todleben called for over five-hundred new guns of larger calibre for the Cronstadt forts. Heavier mortars were also ordered. A covert report from one correspondent in Brussels, dated 12 January 1856 supplied details of the French floating batteries. Smuggled copies of *The Times* provided detailed lists of the warships built and building for the Royal Navy against Russia.[22] The Russians had been hard at work on building a new flotilla of light-draft, steam-powered, screw-propelled gunboats since the war began. Forty were ready, with possibly another '72' by the spring thaw of 1856. British intelligence reports found these vessels 'small and remarkably well built' though their armament remained unknown. 'Practical' war-time experiences, however, indicated that heavy Russian guns could reach '3,400 or 3,600 yards'.[23] Massive Russian manpower reserves, some 30,000 workmen, were called in to complete the wooden stockade and pilings in the shallow channels north and south of Kotlin Island. Behind them, older line-of-battleships 'strengthened by Iron plates' would act as sentinels to protect

20 July 1860, *Report of the Committee appointed by H.R.H. the General Commanding-in-chief to revise the Confidential Circulars of 1853 on the Equipment of Coast Batteries*, in TNA WO (War Office) 33/09, 2.
21 During the Crimean War, the Royal Navy ordered three wooden-hulled Aetna-class floating batteries (*Aetna, Thunder* and *Meteor*), two slightly larger versions, *Glatton* and *Trusty*, and the iron-hulled *Thunderbolt, Erebus* and *Terror*. *Aetna* inauspiciously caught fire upon her building slip and slid into the Thames, a wreck, though Wood declared he was not interested in iron-hulled replacements; 17 November 1855, Wood to Peter Bolt, Halifax Papers, British Library, Add. Ms. 49565, Vol. 35, Letterbook Vol. 11.
22 1 January 1856, Russian National Archives, St. Petersburg, RGAVMF (Russian State Archive of the Navy), fond 19, op. 1, *Papers of Alexander Sergeyevich Menshikov*, St. Petersburg National Archives; delo 358; also RGAVMF, fond 317, op. 1, delo 288. British newspapers as a source of Russian intelligence can be found in delo 365. Secret papers from French sources are in delo 673. See also A. A. Rasdolgin and Y. A. Skorikov, Кронштадтская крепость, *The Fortress of Cronstadt* (Leningrad: Stroyizdat, 1988), especially 198-221.
23 16 April 1855, 'Extracts of a Memorandum', TNA ADM 1/5659.

the barrier from any demolition attempts.[24] The vessels themselves would be the first ironclad warships in Russian history.[25]

For the added protection of the shallow channel north of Cronstadt Russian engineers also devised iron-armoured pontoon-rafts. Fourteen of these were laid down from an order dated January 1856 by the Grand Duke Konstantin (younger brother of Tsar Alexander II and head of the Imperial Russian Navy). A working prototype was first completed in the spring while the others were prepared with the assistance of a private contractor, S. G. Kudryavtsev, for the hulls and Meingard in St. Petersburg to produce the iron plating. If peace was concluded in Paris the rafts were to remain unassembled and stored in special sheds for a future date.[26] These were steady weapons-platforms of very shallow draft, to be towed into position by steam tugs. They each mounted four of the heaviest naval guns in Russian service behind a vertical iron shield 4½-inches thick backed by at least fifteen inches of wood, on top of a sloping base-glacis more lightly armoured with 2-inch thick plating which protected the semi-submerged pontoons. Other plans indicated they might also mount 7.7-inch calibre mortars. Of course, there is no way to gauge how effective these revolutionary naval units would have been, combined with the other warships, forts and mines constituting the Russian defence of Cronstadt.

Perhaps the real significance of their construction is that few if any (non-Russian) works today note their existence, nor do they appear in any British Admiralty or Foreign Office reports.[27] Dundas would have found them a nasty surprise had peace

---

24   23 April 1856, from the Foreign Office, in TNA ADM 1/5677; Russian gunboats built in a hurry 'with such rotten materials' were by 1859 considered 'unseaworthy', see 29 June 1859 'Memorandum on Russian Steam Navy' in Sir Alexander Milne Papers, National Maritime Museum, Greenwich, MLN 142/3; 25 June 1855, Richard Dundas to Admiralty, in TNA ADM 1/5647. See also John Tredrea and Eduard Sozaev, *Russian Warships in the Age of Sail, 1696-1860: Design, Construction, Careers and Fates* (Barnsley: Seaforth Publishing, 2010), 228, who describe at least three 74-gun battleships and three heavy frigates employed as floating batteries off Kotlin Island and boasting broadside armaments of twenty-four 60-pounders. Descriptions of various Russian gunboat classes can be found on pages 425-7, drawing less than 8-feet and armed with three 68-pdr shell-firing guns.
25   See for example, N. Monasterev and L'Serge Terestchenko, *Historie de la Marine Russe*, translated by Jean Perceau (Paris: Payot, 1932), 198-9.
26   Russian National Archives, RGAVMF, fond 921, op. 2, delo 26. Detailed descriptions of the armoured rafts dated 27 January 1856; letter on raft storage dated 22 March 1856. Seventy newer, heavier sea mines were also ordered to be stored in readiness. Fond 164 also discusses the construction of the armoured rafts, dated 26 February – 18 March 1856 under the supervision of naval engineer Colonel Sl. Cherniavsky, a pioneer of the early Russian ironclad programme of the 1860s.
27   The author has found only one printed reference in English: Jack Greene and Alessandro Massignani, *Ironclads at War: The Origin and Development of the Armored Warship, 1854-1891* (Pennsylvania: Combined Publishing, 1998), 31. For detailed Russian descriptions see for example, R.M. Melnikov, V.Yu. Gribovsky, I.I. Chernikov (eds.), *The First Russian Ironclads, Articles and Documents* (St. Petersburg, 1999). Melnikov notes for example that

negotiations failed in the early part of 1856 and a third British fleet returned to Cronstadt later that summer. An encounter between his screw-propelled batteries and the Russian armoured-rafts might have gone down as the first fight between iron-armoured craft in history (not the duel between the USS *Monitor* and the CSS *Virginia*/'*Merrimac*' on 9 March 1862.) Once again, the Russians proved capable of anticipating the Allies' next move just in time. Although these armoured rafts made the most of 'modular construction' techniques and could be mass-produced relatively quickly, they were retrograde technology and their deployment, probably anchored in lines to protect the minefields and engage British ironclad batteries at short range, may have only succeeded in delaying the inevitable. But if they proved difficult to knock out (British 95-cwt, 68-pounders[28] would not have penetrated 4½-inches of wood-backed iron unless making successive hits at point-blank ranges), the 1856 campaign may have stalled or even been called off.[29] That would be good enough for Russia.

Even worse than ironclads, the Russians had no qualms about employing underwater threats or 'infernal machines'; secret British reports indicated dozens perhaps hundreds of 'submarine mines extending in every direction around Cronstadt'. Mid nineteenth-century naval warfare had no viable technology much less established practice for sweeping these or obstructions.[30] They had been diabolical enough for Napier's fleet in the Baltic before places like Sweaborg (guarding Helsinki) and outside Cronstadt. And even though their blasting charges were found to be enough to damage ships rather than blow them out of the water, the technology itself was clearly present, including mines detonated offshore by electric wire.[31] Not surprisingly, another

    the armour plating of each raft weighed 52.6 tons, 20 percent of the total tonnage of each raft. Napier noted these armoured rafts when he visited Cronstadt after the Crimean War in July-August 1856; see for example *The Sydney Morning Herald*, 1 December 1856. 'Against such defences Admiral Dundas, had he come out in the beginning or middle of July, would not have accomplished a single thing,' commented Napier, 'even had he brought double the number of mortars. As the weather was bad, the probability is that many of his ships would have been swamped.'

28 The 'cwt.' is the old 'long hundredweight' of approximately 112lbs, meaning the 95-cwt. 68-pounder, shell-firing smoothbore weighed nearly five tons.

29 Wood noted to Dundas that the floating batteries at Kinburn 'were not exposed to any severe trial—32- and 24-pound shot at 800 yards made little or no impression on them', 6 November 1855, Halifax Papers, British Library, Add. Ms., Vol. 34, Letterbook Vol. 10. Post-war Russian tests against their own 4½-inch thick iron plates proved that even at 300 yards it took 158 hits by 60-pounders before one of their fourteen floating batteries could be silenced, with only five shots actually penetrating; Russian National Archives, RGAVMF, fond 16, op. 1, delo 40, report by I.F. Likhachev, 13 August 1858.

30 See for example 13 November 1854, 'submarine blasting apparatus for clearing a navigation passage into the Harbour of Sevastopol', one of many similar offers made by private contractors to the Admiralty, in TNA ADM 3/265.

31 That the Admiralty took Russian mines seriously enough was indicated by early samples of the explosive used in them recovered forwarded to Professor Michael Faraday for analysis; 3 July 1855, Board to Faraday, TNA ADM 13/7. The Russians referred to their

report dated 4 February 1856 reached the Admiralty of 'a new infernal machine of much greater power and destructiveness than those hitherto employed', designed in Bavaria and built under a Swedish engineer's supervision at the Lichtenberg works at St. Petersburg. Writing to the Admiralty from his vantage point in command of the wooden screw ship-of-the-line *Exmouth* off Cronstadt, Rear-Admiral Michael Seymour therefore found little 'at all encouraging … on the relative position of Russia and ourselves'.[32] Unknown to the Allies, the Russians were also experimenting with long-range rockets to knock out mortar vessels.[33]

Indeed, British public scrutiny had become a potent force in and of itself as a result of the war. No one in public office was safe, from the Prime Minister down, and everyone was on edge. 'I will not guarantee you against being attacked' in the press, Wood wrote to Dundas. 'Who would guarantee any man in a public situation now a days?' The First Lord himself, like everyone else representing the government in Parliament, had become 'case hardened and could almost rival our floating batteries.'[34] But neither had the situation abroad improved. 'We are, it cannot be denied, sinking instead of rising in Public estimation in Europe in regard to our Power and Position as a Nation', Palmerston warned Lord Clarendon (Secretary of State for Foreign Affairs) even after the Russian defeat at Sevastopol. The dénouement of the great siege was how French troops had taken the Malakoff while British ones failed to capture the Redan. The costliness of the siege itself and the widely-publicised instances of British generals' 'incompetence', Allied squabbling, and the inability of the Royal Navy to 'take Cronstadt' did not help. Britain therefore had to be careful not to truckle over Austria's latest plans for brokering a settlement with Russia. Peace might favour

   mines as 'Shutiha' ('Squibs'), with at least a double-row of them sown in the northern fairway as well as in the Neva River at St. Petersburg; Russian National Archives, RGAVMF, fond 317, op. 1, delo 11.
32 For various British reports on Russian 'infernal machines' see Sir Charles Napier Papers, TNA PRO 30-16, 5; 4 February 1856, TNA ADM 1/5674; 23 February 1856, Foreign Office to Admiralty, TNA ADM 1/5677 (information clandestinely supplied via the Swedish Minister at St. Petersburg, General Nordin); 7 July 1855, Seymour to Alexander Milne (Fourth Naval Lord), in Milne Papers, Greenwich, MLN 165/11. Desperate for any solution to the problem of naval mines and obstructions, Palmerston wished First Lord of the Admiralty Sir Charles Wood to explore shipbuilder John Scott Russell's radical proposal for a 'submarine vessel, or locomotive Diving Bell', 17 December 1855, Halifax Papers, A4-63. For Russian descriptions of mine networks around Cronstadt and in the Gulf of Finland (including those developed by Alfred Nobel for the Russian government) see Russian National Archives, RGAVMF, fond 224, op. 1, *Letters of Konstantin Nikolaevich*, delo 289.
33 Russian National Archives, RGAVMF, fond 317, op. 1, delo 286. The 'missile commander', Colonel Konstaninov, withdrew from the project in February 1856 due to serious illness. See also RGAVMF, fond 317, op. 1, delo 251 and 17; the latter specifying twenty-two new embrasures at Fort Alexander for rockets as early as March 1854.
34 19 November and 25 September 1855, Wood to Dundas, Halifax Papers, British Library, Add. Ms. 49564, Vol. 34, Letterbook Vol. 10.

France as well as Russia (both exhausted by the war effort) but leave Britain short on esteem. The question then was how much Palmerston's government might be tempted to overcompensate by actually expanding the war with Russia, as well as exacerbating relations with other powers, namely the United States.[35] Even the Queen and the Prince Consort were in a 'great fuss about Pam', noted fellow cabinet member Lord Granville to Clarendon. 'They are determined to behave well and with confidence to him, but the old mistrust haunts them, and they suspect him as likely to make a sudden splash before they know where they are…There is no doubt that success makes him dangerous in these respects.'[36] Then again, Clarendon had written to Wood that he could conceive 'nothing so likely to lead to war with the U.S. as meetings in this country against it, and nothing so likely to prevent war as shewing the Yankees that we were not afraid of them': thinking very much in line with Palmerston's own. Given the country's enormous naval preparations, consensus was also growing that a 'real campaign in the next Baltic next year will double up Russia.'[37]

* * *

By mid-December Austria had dispatched an ultimatum to St. Petersburg to accept the Allies' peace terms, including the controversial Black Sea clauses which prevented Russia (and Turkey) from building naval bases or fleets there. This was despite the surrender of the fortress-city of Kars in eastern Anatolia to Russian forces on 28 November. The alternative was Austria's entry into the war and the opening of another front against Russia. As far as Clarendon was concerned, this was 'very satisfactory', especially given the French government's 'reckless haste for peace on any terms.' The 'political importance' of the forthcoming Allied war council in Paris—and the continuation of Britain's naval and military mobilisation—therefore 'cannot be exaggerated', he wrote to Wood, 'for once a plan is settled we shall hold the Emperor fast.' The Foreign Secretary stressed the same to Palmerston that same day: the need for 'some settled plan of our own to bring forward together with full

---

35 8 November 1855, Palmerston to Clarendon, Palmerston Papers, Broadlands, GC/CL/719-732.
36 15 September 1855, Granville George Leveson-Gower, 2nd Earl Granville, to Clarendon, from Herbert Maxwell (ed.), *The Life and Letters of Earl of George William Frederick, Fourth Earl of Clarendon*, 2 vols., (London: Edward Arnold: 1913), 2: 92.
37 15 November 1855, Clarendon to Wood, Halifax Papers, Borthwick Institute, A4/57. Palmerston had already outlined to the French ambassador in London, Count Persigny, his intention to 'extend the Theatre of war to the Baltic and drive the Russians out of Finland which should go back to Sweden; and also do whatever Else might appear practicable in those Quarters', whilst Allied troops were 'driving the Russians out of Georgia and Circassia and making a Barrier for Turkey in that Direction'; 26 October 1855, Palmerston to Clarendon, in Winfried Baumgart (ed.), *Akten zur Geschichte des Krimkriegs*, Series III, *Englische Akten zur Geschichte des Krimkriegs*, Band 4, (Vienna: R. Oldenbourg, 1988), 249-50.

information as to our means of giving effect to our intentions and to what we can do in aid of the French.'[38] Without it the Anglo-French alliance might falter, Russia would likely reject the Austrian ultimatum, and worse, Britain would suddenly be obliged to carry on the war alone; no one trusted Austria to risk its long exposed border against Russia's armies stationed near Galicia without French military support. Firm plans for offensive operations in 1856 would also be an indispensable bargaining chip in any future peace negotiations with Russia if she did accept the Allied terms.

But the Admiralty was not sure exactly what to do with the massive littoral strike force it was building—or the likelihood of its success against Russian defences at Cronstadt. Despite the suppositions of previous historical studies, a clear margin of certainty or confidence was never achieved. British numerical advantage in gunboats and heavy naval guns behind iron plating was about 60 percent overall. By January 1856, the Admiralty had already discounted the notion of Anglo-French combined forces in a Baltic campaign, given all of the joint command and operational issues which manifested during the previous two years in both the Black Sea and Baltic theatres. Perhaps a small force of 10,000 troops might be transported to the Baltic and put to good use in essentially raiding operations intended to divert Russian forces. But Wood was certain 'it would be far better that they be English troops', Dundas complaining of 'embarrassment and confusion' otherwise, and Wood agreeing that 'anything which tends to impair the complete unity of command and action is an evil which may, and it has, prove fatal to any energetic action.'[39]

Likewise, there was still no solution how to safely demolish the barrier in the north channel. Captain Bartholomew Sulivan, a surveyor from the Hydrographer's office, tried to convince the Admiralty that he could personally (with his brother George) plant a massive charge against the underwater obstructions before he went numb or drowned in the icy waters, trusting 'to their swimming powers, clad in oilskin dresses, lined with wool to resist the cold, with pockets for holding small sounding-lines and lead.'[40] This implied the entire operation, involving thousands of men in hundreds of ships, might stall if something went wrong with Sulivan.[41] Alternative schemes

---

38   16 December 1855, Clarendon to Wood, Halifax Papers, Borthwick Institute, A4/57; 16 December, Clarendon to Palmerston, Palmerston Papers, Broadlands, GC/CL/750-776.
39   8 January 1856, Wood to Lyons, Halifax Papers, British Library Add. Ms. 49565, Vol. Vol. 35, Letterbook Vol. 11.
40   Henry Norton Sulivan and Sir George Henry Richards, *Life and Letters of the Late Admiral Sir Bartholomew James Sulivan, K.C.B., 1810-1890* (London: J. Murray, 1896), 181.
41   Perhaps not surprisingly, although Brown thought the 'plan outlined by Sulivan for an attack on Kronstadt [was] an impressive preview of a Second World War assault using a combination of all arms,' he also found it 'far from clear as to the extent to which Sulivan had obtained acceptance of his plan', *Before the Ironclad*, 208. Even a relatively recent history of *The Crimean War at Sea: The Naval Campaigns Against Russia 1854-56* by Peter Duckers (Barnsley: Pen & Sword, 2011) is baffled there is 'little evidence that plans for a renewed Baltic campaign were ever fully formulated for 1856', 143-4. See also D. Bonner-

were no less exuberant, and chancy. Palmerston along with Prince Albert favoured reputable shipbuilder John Scott Russell and Sir Charles Fox's plans for submarines (or 'locomotive diving bell') which could strike the stone barrier with explosives: a suicide mission.[42] The joint war councils held in Paris that January produced nothing specific or encouraging regarding plans for attacking Cronstadt either. Their report could only conclude that 'although success might be hoped for by means of a flotilla decidedly superior to that of the enemy, everything must depend on the increased means of defence which may be, and which probably will be, adopted by the enemy.'[43] After questioning the results of recent tests which defeated the 4½-inch plates of the floating batteries ('Why should we not add more?') Palmerston then turned to second-guess Dundas as proper leadership material for the 1856 Baltic campaign, based on an anonymous letter he had received—presumably from a rival naval officer. At any rate, the admiral's letters to Wood the previous summer did not impress the Prime Minister with their sombre if not defeatist sentiments regarding the inherent difficulties of any naval assault upon Cronstadt's combined defences. Perhaps Lyons would make a better choice than someone who would 'never do anything anywhere but keep his ships safe and maintain a Blockade.' Wood replied firmly: while he admitted that Dundas was not an especially 'enterprising officer', he nevertheless went beyond the maintenance of the blockade, 'for he completely destroyed all that was valuable in Sweaborg and as he could not have landed he could not have done more good.' That Dundas did not press for an extended attack of Helsingfors was understandable for a variety of sound military and naval reasons, but also the fact that the 'Finlanders are not hostile. And we should have increased much odium and gained little by bombarding an open town.' Surely the British would complain, 'and justly', if the French did the same to Brighton, for example. Having spoken with Dundas since his return, the First Lord was fully satisfied that if he ordered him to

    Smith (ed.), *Russian War, 1855: Baltic Official Correspondence* (London: Navy Records Society, Vol. 84), 4-6, who notes the closest remnant of Sulivan's 'plan' (of which evidently only six copies were made) is reprinted as a supplement in this volume. Sulivan noted the factors of fog, disease and the necessary presence of at least '50,000' troops and the expenditure of 10,000 shells *per day* to completely crush Sweaborg's defences; 382-98.

42 See for example, 24 November, 1855, Berkeley to Wood, Halifax Papers, Borthwick Institute, A4-74; 5 and 12 December, 1855, Palmerston to Wood, Halifax Papers, Borthwick Institute, A4-63; 2 January, 1856, Board to Sulivan, TNA ADM 13/7, 9 January, 1856, Prince Albert to Palmerston, Palmerston Papers, Broadlands, RC/H/59-84; 31 January, 1856, Wood to Prince Albert, Halifax Papers, British Library, Add. Ms. 49565, Vol. 35, Letterbook 11; and 19 March, 1856, Wood to Palmerston, Palmerston Papers, Broadlands, GC/WO/66-83; also 21 November 1855, Benjamin Disraeli to Lord Derby, in M. G. Wiebe (ed.), *Benjamin Disraeli Letters, Volume Six 1852-1856* (Toronto: University of Toronto Press, 1997), 453; and George S. Emmerson, *John Scott Russell: A Great Victorian Engineer and Naval Architect* (London: John Murray, 1977), 85-7, 97.

43 14 January 1856 committee report (No. 342), in Baumgart, *Akten zur Geschichte des Krimkriegs*, 599.

make the attack—even in the south channel—it would be done 'as well as it can be done with his arrangements and the officers and force he has under him':

> But we must not be led away by thinking it a very easy or very practicable measure. If we were the defendants of Cronstadt I should laugh at any attacking force, and the Russians at Sevastopol have taught us not to despise them too much. They have abundance of men. They can afford to sacrifice hundreds with the certainty of replacing them in 6 hours or less. They will fight under their Emperor's eye and we must be prepared for a stubborn and devoted resistance. We may triumph, but it will be a very doubtful battle …
>
> I say all this that we may not entertain an unreasonable expectation of success. It is no reason why the attempt should not be made and we may succeed and I hope that we may, but we must not set down the operation as a certain one and everybody who doubts it as a fool. The Baltic officers who know most about the place and are most anxious to try do not see their way very clearly and all admit that much depends on what the Russians do before spring.[44]

In the meantime, news had arrived that Tsar Alexander II had accepted the Austrian terms; emergency councils summoned by the Tsar in late December 1855 and early January 1856 had pointed to strategic isolation and economic exhaustion as the deciding factors.[45] Despite Britain's naval build-up, Clarendon also admitted to

---

44 14 January 1856, Palmerston to Wood, Halifax Papers, Borthwick Institute, A4-63; 16 January 1856, Wood to Palmerston, Halifax Papers, British Library, Add. Ms. 49565, Vol. 35, Letterbook 11. Clarendon relayed to Wood the failure of Sweaborg to impress Napoleon III, who dismissed reports 'of the total destruction of Sweaborg' from Lord Cowley in Paris as 'another sailors' lie', 9 September 1855, Halifax Papers, Borthwick Institute, A4/57. Dundas later wrote that both Cronstadt and Reval were far too well-defended to risk an attack, whereas 'Sweaborg was built to be shelled and this is the secret of the havoc which we have really produced there', 21 August 1855, Dundas to Wood, Halifax Papers, British Library, Add. Ms. 49533, Vol. 3.

45 See for example the letters and council minutes by Russian diplomat Peter Meyendorff, in Peter von Meyendorff and Otto Hoetzch (eds.), *Peter von Meyendorff, Ein russicher Diplomat an den Höfen von Berlin und Wien*, vol. 3. (Berlin: Walter de Gruyter, 1923), 210-17, 415-16; also Winfried Baumgart, translated by Ann Pottinger Saab, *The Peace of Paris 1865: Studies in War, Diplomacy, and Peacemaking* (Santa Barbara: ABC-Clio, 1981); 20 November 1857, A.V. Golovnin, 'Report of the Real state councillor M.Kh. Reitern to General-admiral Grand Duke Konstantin Nikolaevich on the financial condition of Russia', Russian National Library, Department of Manuscripts, Collection 208, File 67; and William Blackwell, *The Beginnings of Russian Industrialization 1800-1860* (Princeton: Princeton University Press, 1968), 183-7, who surmises the war cost Russia 'well over a billion rubles.' Following the loss of Sevastopol, Tsar Alexander informed Field Marshal Paskevich to prepare 'for a long war' with 'new enemies', the long border with Galicia being his major concern; Russian National Archives, Russian State Historical Archive (RGIA), fond 1018, op. 7, 'Correspondence with Emperor Alexander II'. Cronstadt

Granville during the subsequent peace negotiations in Paris that 'whatever Palmerston in his jaunty mood may say, we could not have made war alone, for we should have had all Europe against us at once, and the United States would soon have followed in the train...'[46] Hence, when the Foreign Secretary as well as Britain's chief negotiator finally met with his Russian counterpart, Count Orlov[47], on 24 February 1856, they both met as 'old friends' but ready to bluff one another if possible. The Russian began by stating that the Tsar was perfectly sincere in his acceptance of the Four Points as put forward by Austria, but since then the capture of Kars had clearly altered Russia and the Allies' opposing balance of victories and defeats in the war. Clarendon waved this way; Russia would be obliged to give up *all* her gains in the war, just as the Allies were prepared to abandon Sevastopol and the coasts. He then countered by asking Russia to give up the Aland Islands—and in reference to this he 'took occasion to mention the great naval preparations [Britain] had made for the next campaign.' But Orlov in turn waved this away:

> ... he was well aware but that on the other hand the Russians had not been idle, that they had now 40,000 Men at work at Cronstadt and the vicinity and that they should be at least 4 times as strong as they were last year, when we certainly might if we had chosen have done them great injury, but the best way perhaps, he added, of making Peace was to be well prepared for War and when two Nations respected each other they were more likely to come to an agreement.[48]

Not only was there the perceived danger of alienating France, which at least Palmerston's Cabinet and the Crown recognised, but it would clearly drive up the costs of Britain's war-time economy. In the wake of the 23 April (St. George's Day) naval review at Spithead in 1856, of the standing Blue Water battlefleet with the emergency Brown Water flotilla called into existence by the war against Russia, *The Times* assuaged its readers that unlike 'the exhausting influences of which have been felt and confessed alike by our enemies and our allies, we are able to give to ourselves and the world so signal and decisive a proof of unabated strength and unexhausted resources ... We have now the means of waging a really offensive war, not only against fleets but harbours, fortresses, and rivers,—not merely of blockading, but of invading and carrying the warfare of the sea into the very heart of the land.'[49] Yet Britain's

was never mentioned. See also Valerii L. Stepanov, 'The Crimean War and the Russian Economy', *Russian Studies in History*, Vol. 51, No. 1 (Summer 2012), 7-34.

46 12 March 1856, Clarendon to Granville; Maxwell, *Life and Letters*, 118-19; see also 3 March 1856, Clarendon to Palmerston, in Baumgart, *Akten zur Geschichte des Krimkriegs*, 825-8.
47 Prince Alexey Fyodorovich, a veteran of both the Napoleonic Wars and the Turkish War of 1828-9, was thirteen years Clarendon's senior in 1856.
48 25 February 1856, Clarendon to Palmerston, TNA FO (Foreign Office) 27/1168.
49 24 April 1865, *The Times*.

national and naval power manifestly had practical limits, and the force-multiplier of high technology in international power-politics often worked two ways. By the time all sides concerned had agreed to peace, in the spring of 1856, Clarendon wrote Lord Cowley, the British ambassador in Paris, that even Palmerston was 'not only pleased… but is extremely doubtful whether our army might not have been destroyed by disease if we had attempted an expedition to Asia Minor, and whether we might not have been beaten on our own element at Cronstadt, so there is no discontent in that quarter, and the cabinet generally are satisfied.'[50]

Certainly, the American military delegation, appointed by the U.S. Congress to report on the 'Art of War in Europe' as a result of the Crimean War, was impressed by the new potential for both coastal assault *and* defence. At least in terms of 'Sea-Coast and Harbor Defenses', it felt the U.S. had 'less to learn from the Europeans than of any other part of the art of war.' The way in which Russia held off the great maritime powers with her forts was encouraging; and the quality of American granite 'was not surpassed by [that] at Cronstadt.'[51] During the Crimean War, Palmerston was obsessed with the notion that American filibustering in Central America would try to take advantage of British 'preoccupation' against Russia and thereby sweep aside British interests all over North America. Instead, the war-time mobilisation of British naval forces should be used aggressively against the Americans. 'The U.S. have no navy of which we need be afraid,' he pointed out, '& they might be told that if they were to resort to privateering, we should however reluctantly be obliged to retaliate by burning all their Sea Coast Towns.'[52] Although successive governments

---

50 Undated, probably April 1856, from Henry Richard Charles Wellesley (ed.), *The Paris Embassy during the Second Empire: Selections from the Papers of Henry Richard Charles Wellesley 1st Earl Cowley, Ambassador at Paris 1852-1867* (London: Thornton Butterworth, Limited, 1928), 94-5. In many respects, the war had been won economically; as Prince Albert adroitly observed in May 1854, 'the victor in the long run will be the one with the biggest purse, no matter how it is in the beginning with the force of the army…Russia is not to be conquered, but financially she can be ruined', in Hector Bolitho (ed.), *The Prince Consort and His Brother: Two Hundred New Letters* (London: R. Cobden-Sanderson Ltd., 1933), 145-6. He had previously described the Allies' enemy as 'a vast and ponderous mass, upon which blows on the few spots where they can be planted will make no deep impression', 24 January 1854, to Stockmar, in Kurt Jagow (ed.), *Letters of the Prince Consort 1831-1861* (London: John Murray, 1938), 207. See also Brian Connell, *Regina v. Palmerston: The Correspondence between Queen Victoria and Her Foreign and Prime Minister 1837-1865* (London: Evans Brothers Limited, 1962), 192-3; Donald Southgate, *'The Most English Minister…' The Policies and Politics of Palmerston* (London: Macmillan and Company Limited, 1966), 386-9.
51 Major Richard Delafield, *Report on the Art of War in Europe in 1854, 1855, and 1856* (Washington: George W. Bowman, 1860), 2, 24-6, in 36th Congress, 1st Session, Senate, Ex. Doc., No. 59.
52 Memorandum dated 10 September 1854, from Kenneth Bourne, 'Lord Palmerston's "Ginger-beer" Triumph, 1 July 1856', in Kenneth Bourne and D. C. Watt (eds.), *Studies in International History* (Hamden: Archon Books, 1967), 148-50.

in Washington D.C. disavowed (often pro-slavery) filibustering by private citizens/mercenaries, the strategic issues surrounding overland isthmus trading routes and what would eventually become the Panama Canal flared into sharp diplomatic crises such as at Greytown, Nicaragua; a British protectorate. By 1856 both the First Lord of the Admiralty and the British Foreign Secretary had few qualms 'with respect to sending out a powerful fleet' to overawe 'these Yankee Bullies'. But even more powerful factions in Parliament were aghast at the thought of a third Anglo-American conflict disastrous to all concerned. By the mid-nineteenth century the manufacturing interests of 'Lancashire' threatened to topple any British government which pushed the containment of America too far as well as too little.[53]

---

53   4 June 1856, Clarendon to Wood, Halifax Papers, Borthwick Institute, A4/57.

2

'We are only copying the French'

The outbreak of the Indian Mutiny the following year (1857) along with renewed hostilities against China laid bare other strategic priorities which interfered with a sustained policy versus America. Cries of 'Retrenchment' in proudly Liberal Britain—temporarily muzzled during the Russian war—had to be considered in times of peace, even as the Empire was at war simultaneously against various enemies around the world. The Crimean War helped erode the Anglo-French alliance, as Napoleon III intervened in Italy against Austria (1859) and Palmerston feared the worst; a resurgent French army dominating the continent and backed by a large, steam-powered navy.[1] The war against Russia also underscored the apparent vulnerability of maritime nations' bases of power to naval attacks—unless well-defended. Despite the traditional command of the English Channel by a powerful British home fleet, a memo from the Inspector-General of Fortifications, General Sir John Burgoyne, in July 1857 outlined a scenario 'either from a sudden combination of powers, or from other circumstances, we might, for a time at least, be deprived of that superiority.' An invasion of the British Isles by the old enemy, France, would surely follow.[2] The resulting Anglo-French naval arms race, signified by the launching of the French ironclad-frigate *Gloire* in 1859 and the British *Warrior* (a tense year of 'invasion panic' later), further alienated the great 'maritime powers' from one another.[3] Russian

---

1   For analyses of Louis Napoleon's aims see for example, Imbert de Saint-Amand, *Napoleon III at the Height of His Power* (New York: Charles Scribner's Sons, 1912); A. R. Allinson (ed.), *Intimate Memoirs of Napoleon III, by the Late Baron D'Ambes* (Boston: Little Brown, and Company, 1912); F. A. Simpson, *Louis Napoleon & the Recovery of France 1848-1856* (London: Longmans, Green and Co., 1923); and J. P. T. Bury, *Napoleon III and the Second Empire* (London: The English Universities Press, Ltd., 1970); and J. P. Parry, 'The Impact of Napoleon III on British Politics, 1851-1880', in *Transactions of the Royal Historical Society*, Sixth Series, Vol. XI (Cambridge: University Press, 2001).
2   20 July 1857, *Memorandum by the Inspector-General of Fortifications*, TNA WO 33/05.
3   The leading account remains C. I. Hamilton, *Anglo-French Naval Rivalry 1840-1870* (Oxford: Clarendon Press, 1993); see also Baxter's detailed account in *Introduction*, 92-

diplomacy played on this development as much as possible, while Prussia prepared its own plans for expansion at the expense of any lingering 'Concert of Europe'.

Part of the explanation for this mounting sense of strategic frustration in the mid-Victorian era was technological. The Great Exhibition of 1851 showcased British invention and industrial resources harnessed to global imperial and economic ambitions. But neither could it be denied that Britain was not alone in these pursuits. Money, for one, could buy technology as need be. Inventions at home or abroad could be mass-produced so that long-held assumptions the military balance-of-power were suddenly at risk. Steam power was a great enabler for British commerce, but it also represented destabilisation if an enemy could use it to 'bridge' the English Channel or prey upon that commerce worldwide. Railroads helped Britain mobilise national resources for war, although it quickly became obvious that British coastal raids could be met by enemy railroads networked from military 'interior lines' to any threatened periphery. The same then went for the telegraph. Much of the succeeding debate of the era was dominated by first the 'ships vs. forts' question in the age of steam and iron, followed by the 'guns vs. armour' race with the advent of early ironclads. 'The improvements in projectiles, the great improvements in shipping, have altogether altered the relative position of countries so near to each other,' Palmerston had warned the House of Commons in May 1857, and there was 'now at Cherbourg the means for collecting a large naval force. The ships which we now build are of such magnitude that whereas formerly only a few hundred men could be transported by one ship now more than 1,000 or 1,200 can well be embarked in a single vessel. It is impossible now for this country to rely entirely for its defence upon its naval means.'[4] At the same time, British imperial defence mandates were exactly that: defensive. In 1860, Palmerston insisted not upon a standing coastal assault armada of shallow-draft ironclads but stationary defences on land and sea (particularly in the Solent).[5]

Both the British and French navies during and following the Crimean War had meanwhile carried on with their building programmes of steam-powered, screw-propelled ships-of-the-line; an Admiralty memo of March 1858 noting the Anglo-French balance of power at sea was only 42 to 37 in favour of Britain, but with commensurate pressures on manpower since British first-rates required crews of nearly a thousand sailors and gunners. A subsequent memo by Surveyor of the Navy Sir Baldwin Wake Walker in July outlined the need to covert more sailing ships-of-the-line to steam-power, since 'although a few years ago we were far ahead of them...they are now for the first time equal to us and unless some extraordinary steps are taken to expedite the building of Screw Ships of the Line, the French at the close of next year will be actually superior to us as regards the most powerful Class

---

180.
4   25 May 1857, 'Supply—Army Estimates', *Hansard*, vol. 145, 843-99.
5   See for example, Michael Stephen Partridge, *Military Planning for the Defence of the United Kingdom, 1814-1870* (New York: Greenwood Press, 1989).

of Ships of War.'[6] Yet since the Crimean War, the brilliant French naval architect Dupuy de Lôme was certain that iron armour plating thick enough to resist the heaviest naval guns in service could be safely mounted to a seagoing screw-frigate for service anywhere in the world. At the beginning of 1857 he had been appointed as the Director of Matériel in the French Navy, and by September 1858 orders had been issued for no less than four large ironclads (*Gloire*, *Invincible*, *Normandie*, and the iron-hulled *Couronne*).[7] Napoleon III had meanwhile told Palmerston during a visit to Paris that he had become convinced that naval warfare was on the verge of a revolution—one of iron armour shielding—and that he had ordered the navy to stop building wooden ships-of-the-line.[8]

The Admiralty was forced to reply in kind, quickly. The Board members thought wooden-hulled armoured-frigates of 36-guns would match the *Gloire*. But the Surveyor was far more ambitious. Because iron was stronger than wood it allowed for an overall savings in weight which could be applied to things like larger engines, coal capacity and gun battery. As Isambard Kingdom Brunel's monstrous *Great Eastern* steamer (launched in January 1858) had recently shown, iron hulls could be made far larger than any comparable wooden structures—and they allowed for water-tight compartments to ensure safety in case of grounding or damage during combat.[9] Concentrating the extent of 4½-inch armour plating to the central portion of the ship, sealed off fore and aft by thick iron transverse-bulkheads, would also help insure superior seaworthiness and speed to the French versions.[10] Thus, early British ironclads such as HMS *Warrior* were designed to operate on the high seas and at great ranges if need be; to meet threats in any ocean. As Walker stressed, while the French *Gloire* was fully-armoured from stem to stern, and thus boasted more 'security from Shot and Shell', the *Warrior* (and her sister-ship *Black Prince*, ordered in October 1859) were all the more 'seagoing' and that much better suited

---

6 Memo by Sir John Pakington (as First Lord of the Admiralty under Derby's Conservative Ministry of February 1858 to June 1859), March 1858, in Milne Papers, Greenwich, MLN 142/2; 27 July 1858, Walker to Board, TNA ADM 1/5705. For the evolution of Britain's steam-powered wooden capital ships see for example, Andrew Lambert, *Battleships in Transition: The Creation of the Steam Battlefleet 1815-1860* (London: Conway Maritime Press, 1984); also Brown, *Before the Ironclad*, 44-173.

7 See for example, Baxter, *Introduction*, 97-101. Admiral Ferdinand Hamelin was the French Minister of Marine at this time (April 1855 – November 1860).

8 Wellesley (ed.), *The Paris Embassy*, 166; also Jasper Ridley, *Lord Palmerston* (London: Book Club Associates, 1970), 484.

9 See for example David Brown's analysis in *Before the Ironclad*, 204-5.

10 See 27 January 1859, Walker to Board, TNA ADM 1/5729; also 28 April 1859, where Walker informed the Board that his own department's design (for the *Warrior*) was better than those submitted by all the leading private commercial firms. The Surveyor's original warning about the need for iron-armoured-frigates was dated 28 June 1858, as noted by Parkes, *British Battleships*, 11.

'for general service.'[11] What that actually meant was not so vitally important as the status symbol *Warrior* was intended to be, as the largest, fastest, most powerfully-armed warship in the world. During the Crimean War the heaviest service ordnance in the Royal Navy was the 8-inch, muzzle-loaded, shell-firing, relatively high-velocity 68-pounder smoothbore. This was a big, tough gun with good range and could still be handled by a reasonably-sized gun crew with traditional block-and-tackle on the broadside. Britain's first seagoing ironclad would boast twenty-six of these, as much as an entire flotilla of the Crimean War gunboats. Talented engineer and inventor William Armstrong had also successfully developed heavy rifled breechloading guns, first for the British Army, and then a 40-pounder for the navy. By 1861 the Board of Admiralty agreed to mount ten of Armstrong's new 7-inch 110-pounder rifled breechloaders, both in broadside and on the open top deck of the *Warrior*.[12] These experimental guns with their conical projectiles could range nearly 4,000-yards with much greater accuracy, making them the weapon of choice for shore bombardment, for example.[13] Her long, spacious gundeck provided an ideal environment for delivering an efficient, sustained rate of fire, while her gunports were higher out of the water than the French broadside-ironclads—meaning that she might be able to safely fight better in rough seas. Huge Penn trunk engines would generate over 5,000 indicated horse-power (when the latest screw ship-of-the-line on the stocks—HMS *Victoria*—boasted 4,300 IHP), and hopefully a steam-speed of fifteen knots; when first-rates (and the *Gloire*) were never expected to exceed thirteen. An unprecedented coal bunkerage of over 800-tons, along with a full ship's rig of masts and sails, helped guarantee this majestic behemoth's strategic reach.

As such, no one imagined a fleet of such vessels to convey the message of industrial Britain's naval power to every corner of the globe. She was herself a fleet in being. British sea power had arguably never been so magnificently embodied in a single man-of-war. But as many critics both within the Admiralty and in the public sphere remarked, such a statement came at a large price. At over £250,000 *Warrior* was one of the most expensive—and risky—investments ever made by the Royal Navy. Because the royal dockyards were not experienced with iron shipbuilding and were fully occupied at any rate completing screw ships-of-the-line, the Admiralty had little choice but to turn to private contractors to lead the way in Britain's naval revolution.[14]

---

11 10 January 1861, Walker to Board, TNA ADM 1/5774. Robert Napier and Sons of Glasgow was awarded the contract for *Black Prince*.

12 Armstrong was knighted in 1859, having signed over his patent (and profit) rights to the War Office that January, while taking upon a lucrative contract position as ordnance engineer for the army, then as Superintendent of the Royal Gun Factory at Woolwich; 1 May 1860, report on the history of the Armstrong gun, TNA WO 33/09.

13 See for example, 3 October 1859 War Office to Admiralty, TNA ADM 1/5708.

14 See for example, David Evans, *Building the Steam Navy: Dockyards, Technology and the Creation of the Victorian Battle Fleet 1830-1906* (London: Conway Maritime Press), 2004; also Ian Johnston and Ian Buxton, *The Battleship Builders: Constructing and Arming British*

Yet as experienced as Thames Ironworks and Shipbuilding was, HMS *Warrior* also quickly proved to be their most difficult contract ever. Soon the company ran over cost, with delays further sinking Thames to the point that emergency financial relief was necessary in order to complete the vessel. Even before this, it became apparent that as powerful as she was in many crucial respects, she was also acutely weak in others. Only half her sides were protected by armour, implying the other half was a write-off in combat. Her crew would have to huddle in the central citadel while the rest of their vessel was perforated by shot and exploding shell, set on fire or flooded. And with such an unprecedented length (some 380-feet between perpendiculars; 420-feet overall) her steering and manoeuvrability proved as poor as her speed and range were great—yet her unarmoured stern also featured a large rudder openly exposed to damage. Thus, HMS *Warrior* literally had an Achilles Heel. She would have to keep her enemies at arm's length; the closer a floating opponent got in the smoke and confusion of battle, the more her weaknesses could be mercilessly exploited. Likewise, her iron hull prohibited the customary use of coppering to control marine growth or 'fouling'; she would have to be docked and cleaned far more regularly than wooden-hulled ironclads.[15] Yet she was too big to be accommodated anywhere in Britain except at Portsmouth, tides permitting. No base in the Mediterranean or the rest of the world could help keep her running efficiently or repair any serious damage.[16] The last thing the Admiralty wanted to do was risk such a costly, high-profile vessel on any extended cruise.

Because of these doubts, and the intense feeling of *experiment* involved with armour-plating any seagoing capital ship, a new Board of Admiralty (from June 1859) insisted upon two smaller—presumably safer—and more economical versions: *Defence* and *Resistance*. These featured the same armour thickness in a similar, concentrated configuration, but with a necessarily smaller armament of 68-pounders and Armstrong BL-guns. Walker objected to these compromises with the new First

---

Capital Ships (Barnsley: Seaforth Publishing, 2013). For a detailed, document-based assessment of Portsmouth Dockyard during this period see especially C. I. Hamilton (ed.), *Portsmouth Record Series, Portsmouth Dockyard Papers 1852-1869: From Wood to Iron* (Winchester: Hampshire County Council, 2005).

15 See for example David Brown's Appendix 7 in *Before the Ironclad*, 202.
16 There are many accounts of the legendary HMS *Warrior*, but some of the most comprehensive and authoritative include Andrew Lambert, *Warrior: The World's First Ironclad Then and Now* (London: Conway Maritime Press, Ltd., 1987); John Wells, *The Immortal Warrior: Britain's First and Last Battleship* (Emsworth: Kenneth Mason, 1987); Ballard, *The Black Battlefleet*, 49-59; Parkes, *British Battleships*, 11-24; David K. Brown, *Warrior to Dreadnought: Warship Development 1860-1905* (London: Chatham Publishing, 1997), 12-14, but especially *Before the Ironclad*, 174-87; and his articles 'H.M.S. *Warrior*—The Design Aspects', *Royal Institution of Naval Architects*, 129, (Spring 1986), and 'Developing the Armour of HMS *Warrior*', *Warship*, No. 40 (October 1986); also Ernest F. Slaymaker, 'The Armament of HMS *Warrior*', parts 1-3, *Warship*, No. 37, (January 1986), No. 38 (April 1986), and No. 39 (July 1986).

Lord, the Duke of Somerset; they would be no faster than a wooden-ship-of-the-line, nor have the same range as the big ironclad frigates. Yet they would be just as vulnerable. Significantly, despite all their high hopes by the end of the Crimean War how iron-armoured floating batteries might prove useful in projecting naval power ashore like never before, neither the French nor British navies during this period were especially interested in further developing a standing force of improved versions—either for defensive or offensive purposes. British military authorities like Burgoyne opposed precious resources being invested in them as opposed to permanent defences like coastal forts. The *theoretical* ability of mastless, shallow-draft, armoured warships to force passages under fire and subject targets like naval dockyards or arsenals—or commercial port-cities—to bombardment was over-rated; 'sufficient consideration is not always given to the ultimate result; thus, it is frequently treated as to be expected that they would even run into a harbour; or other *cul-de-sac*, to effect a given amount of destruction, and then return; but how difficult may that return be in the exhausted and partially damaged state of the ships, and at periods not selected as most favourable, but probably forced; the very knowledge of having so desperate an undertaking as that of the return alone would lead to very few making the attempt.' Likewise, there was by now every indication that ordnance was going to become larger and more powerful, and at a much faster rate of development than ever experienced before. Therefore, it made little sense building a large amount of armoured ships designed to float a set thickness of iron plating—which might then be penetrated by new guns. Better to put the new guns into forts which didn't have to worry about added size or weights of armament.[17] Besides, the best defence of the country against invasion was a seagoing fleet which commanded the English Channel. But these types of objections still didn't address how such a fleet might press against an enemy's coast in turn, especially if defended by floating batteries which—like the older blockship concept—trimmed down sea-keeping capabilities in favour of greater defensive powers and armament.[18]

Hence, even by 1860, the geopolitical balance-of-power more and more favoured the strategic defence. Britain, Russia and the United States invested heavily in 'bricks and mortar'. But this also meant that continental expansion on the part of the two great land powers could proceed fairly safe from at least direct attacks from the

---

17   27 January 1860, and 12 May 1860, Sir John Burgoyne, printed memoranda; also 2 February 1860, 'Confidential Minute on the Report of the Commissioners appointed to inquire into the Defences of the United Kingdom', by Sir Howard Douglas; in *Papers respecting National Defences* in Palmerston Papers, Broadlands, ND/A/26-36, National Defence, 1859-60.
18   See for example, 8 May 1857, Captain E. Gardiner Fishbourne, 'On the forms of ships with relation to naval gunnery', in *Journal of the United Service Institute*, Vol. 1 (1858), 78-92; also an early recommendation for converting ships-of-the-line and frigates to screw propulsion, and using the weight saved in masts, sails and long-range provisions to heavily arm both broadsides and the ends of the trimmed down 'block-ships' for coast defence; 4 November 1844, in TNA WO 55/1409.

'Mistress of the Seas'. Their inward-looking drives for an ocean-to-ocean 'manifest destiny' similarly fed into rising nationalism in the nineteenth-century. British seapower in turn became more of an economic deterrent and less of a military one. This strategic shift allowed Russia to securely recover from the Crimean War, even so far as risking the emancipation of millions of serfs in 1861. As such, when fifty-one backbench MPs reminded Palmerston that the country had been at peace since 1856, yet military and naval defence estimated kept rising, the First Lord of the Treasury barked that the 'true meaning of the Memorial is that we should have no more rifled muskets, rifled cannon, Iron ships, or defensive works, that we should have no sufficient army or navy, that we should cease to be an influential Power in the world... that our Commerce shall be shut out from the Mediterranean, that we should hold our existence as a nation at the good will of France and Russia, and that we should sink down to be the object of contempt and derision to the nations of the world.'[19] He had similarly lectured Gladstone (still Chancellor of the Exchequer); that the ironclad revolution now meant additional costs to the nation, on top of those for building new coastal fortifications—to defend against ironclads. This was because 'the Command of the Ocean will still be with the Power that can fit out the strongest Fleet of Line of Battle ships.' And that fleet would take many years to convert from wood to iron. There was simply no question that such 'Command' equalled security—and he could only assume that it still meant influence. Likewise, Palmerston thought that smaller vessels 'may be useful as auxiliaries in the narrow seas or defend Coasts & Colonies, but the heavy Battery of a First or Second Rate will always be too much for smaller vessels.'[20]

* * *

The Admiralty had already committed to building more seagoing (broadside) ironclads, given that the French in June 1859 had laid down two more of much greater tonnage, *Magenta* and *Solferino*; fully-armoured again, yet featuring a double-decks of guns and prominent spur or ram bows. Rear-Admiral Walker (now known as the 'Controller' of the Royal Navy) still insisted that the primary trait desired was superior speed— which his architects maintained required hulls of 'extraordinary length' thus also built of iron. With dockyard upgrades, Chatham might now accommodate one of these improved *Warrior*s, with armour coverage extended along the sides and waterline. 'Ships of such magnitude and character are necessarily very costly,' he admitted, 'but it is more than questionable whether, in the end, a far greater sum would not have

---

19 From T. A. Jenkins, *The Liberal Ascendancy, 1830-1886* (London: Macmillan Press, Ltd., 1994), 93-4.
20 25 and 29 November 1859, Palmerston to Gladstone, in Philip Guedalla (ed.), *The Palmerston Papers: Gladstone and Palmerston, being the Correspondence of Lord Palmerston with Mr. Gladstone 1851-1865* (London: Victor Gollancz, Ltd., 1928), 113-14. For spring 1860 the naval estimates reached a fantastic peacetime height of £12,800,000.

to be expended, if any indecision were now manifested by this Country.'[21] This new ironclad would eventually take shape as HMS *Achilles*. 'We cannot allow ourselves to be inferior to the French in Iron cased Ships', Somerset acknowledged to Palmerston, on 14 December 1860, 'though what is the best Model to take seems to be still a Doubtful Question.' It was true that the smaller French ironclads with their wooden-hulls would take to the seas sooner, and in greater numbers. But neither did the First Lord want to leap into the dark in a panic, committing to 'great numbers of this class of Vessels without some clear knowledge of what description of Build is best calculated to attain the object we have in view.' Palmerston admitted that he was one of those unsatisfied by the *Warrior*'s practical defensive powers versus the French ironclads plated with 4.7-inch iron from stem to stern. And as he privately relayed to Sir Charles Wood, although news had arrived from Paris that the French desired peace with Britain (despite recent tensions over the Franco-Austrian War of 1859, and France's acquisition of Savoy and Nice), it was now confirmed that 'our Friend the Emperor has just ordered Ten more Iron cased Ships like the *Gloire*.'[22]

This prompted another debate in the Admiralty. The Board wanted smaller, perhaps more practical seagoing ironclads, but with greater armour protection, good for at least coast defence. Designs poured into Whitehall in the latter half of 1860 from private British firms and inventors, some more unfeasible than others. Awkwardly-masted versions included one with an armoured casemate angled 40-degrees to the horizon to deflect shot—and a submission by Captain Cowper Phipps Coles for a ship armed with revolving 'shields' in the form of truncated cones. During the Crimean War he was one of many British naval officers obsessed with finding a way of bringing effective fire ever closer to the Russian shore. His 'Lady Nancy' of 1855 even featured in *The Illustrated London News*: a steady wooden raft floating upon casks and supporting a single 32-pounder. He then proposed mounting the gun on a turntable, itself covered over with an iron dome: a turret.[23] But since the advent of armoured seagoing frigates, his thinking now expanded into improving upon the *Warrior* concept not by adjusting the hull or armour coverage so much as the nature of the armament itself: instead of heavy guns mounted through fixed broadside-ports on a large, unwieldy vessel, his plan called for nine revolving turrets mounted along the centreline of

21   28 September 1860, TNA ADM 87/77.
22   14 December 1860, Somerset to Palmerston, Palmerston Papers, Broadlands, D/RA/A/2A/256; 9 and 21 January 1861, Palmerston to Somerset, Somerset Papers, Aylesbury, D/RA/A/2A/37; 11 January 1861, Palmerston to Wood, Halifax Papers, Borthwick Institute, A4/63. At the time, Wood was in the sensitive new post of Secretary of State for India, following British suppression of the Indian Mutiny (or 'Sepoy Rebellion') in 1858, the disestablishment of the East India Company, and the formal absorption of India by the British Crown.
23   5 December 1860, 'Papers found in Mr. Large's Drawers—Armour Clad Ships—Designs submitted and reported on about December 1860—Mr. Abethell's, Captain Coles's, Mr. Jones's, Mr. Chatfield's, Mr. Cradock's, Mr. Turner's, Mr. Henwood's, Mr. Robinson's, Mr. Large's', TNA ADM 87/77; 11 August 1855, *The Illustrated London News*.

the deck. Because less guns would be needed because they were themselves more manoeuvrable, a smaller, handier vessel could be had with just as much firepower per given ton—and at less cost. 'One shield-ship equal to cope with and destroy three 3-deckers...requires only one-fifth of a 3-decker's compliment of men', he proclaimed in a pamphlet of 1860.[24] As intriguing as these ideas were, Walker's team rejected the Coles submissions as unworkable. All of the necessary impediments of 'steam funnels and casings, masts, bitts, capstans, and other appliances' would limit the turrets' field of fire, and it was unclear whether his plan made for a steadier gun platform (as he had asserted). Working guns within a turret might prove safer for the gunners but it was doubtful they would be handled more efficiently—even if on a turntable—than in an open gundeck.[25]

Somerset and Lord Clarence Paget, the Admiralty Secretary, meanwhile pressed Walker for suitable alternatives. However much the *Warrior* was the perfect embodiment of Britain's 'mastery of the seas'—and the pride of the Controller's Department—they were still concerned of losing a numbers game against the French. 'It is a perfect disgrace to our country, and particularly to the Admiralty, that we can do no more than hobble after the French, turning up our noses proudly at their experiments and improvements,' wrote Prince Albert to Lord Russell (now the Secretary of State for Foreign Affairs in Palmerston's second ministry), 'and, when, they are established as sound, getting horribly frightened, and trying by wasting money to catch up lost time, and all the while running serious risk of our security.' Having been personally taken with Coles's ideas for turret-armed ironclad warships, the Prince Consort urged the First Lord two days later, on 10 December 1860, to 'give the order to build one of Captain Coles's ships *at once*, with such modifications as may be suggested by him':

> I quite agree with you that it would not be prudent to restrict ourselves to vessels of this novel construction, but we should give the country the benefit of possessing some such. We are only copying the French, and that only after having for a long time declared their schemes quite impracticable. Should Captain Coles's plan succeed, his ships will be vastly superior in a great many points to those we are building; and the responsibility on the part of the Government is very great, in incurring periodically an enormous expense to get up a large force of a kind of ships just going to be superseded.[26]

---

24 Captain Cooper[sic] Phipps Coles, *Shot-Proof Gun-Shields, as Adapted to Iron-Cased Ships for National Defence* (1860).
25 5 December 1860, Somerset to Controller; 5 December 1860, 'Papers', TNA ADM 87/77.
26 8 December 1860 Albert to Russell, and 10 December 1860, Albert Somerset, in Theodore Martin (ed.), *The Life of His Royal Highness The Prince Consort*, 5 vols., (London: Smith, Elder, & Co., 1879), 5: 256-8.

On 10 January 1861 Walker forwarded the dimensions of the subsequent *Hector* and *Valiant* of 7,000-tons (25 percent less displacement than *Warrior*), noting that iron plating would now stretch from 4½-inches on the sides to 2½-inches tapering around the ends, while it was considered prudent to leave the waterline un-armoured within thirty-feet of the stem and thirty-five feet of the stern (to five-feet below the waterline). 'But it will scarcely be questioned that this amount of security against injury from Shot and Shell is not to be obtained without compromising important qualities of seagoing ships', he added. Such vessels would surely pitch to such an extent that they would be 'unsuited for general service'.[27] Disgusted when the Board approved the plans anyway, Walker resigned his post—having steered shipbuilding policy in the Royal Navy since 1848. For the Admiralty, it was now becoming obvious that a technological revolution was underway; an increasingly complex interplay between steam and sail, and wood and iron—mixed with a deadly new array of naval guns (smoothbore and rifled, muzzle- and breech-loaded), and an astonishing variety for not just armour-plating vessels great and small, but in the structure of vessels themselves. But more than this, the issue of somehow *controlling* these developments was paramount, especially when naval innovations and naval *inventions* crossed lines; naval professionals, public servants and private entrepreneurs all having a vested interest in the success of the 'one' design which would enshrine Britain's prestige (and perhaps their own) the best. As such, when Walker left under an angry cloud—taking up a post as C-in-C of the distant Cape of Good Hope and West Coast of Africa Station—the Admiralty replaced him with Rear-Admiral Robert Spencer Robinson on 8 February, taking care to initially appoint him for a fixed five-year term only.[28]

Before the month was out, the Institution of Naval Architects, formed the previous year in 1860 (and with Edward James Reed as its Secretary), intensely debated ironclad designs for three days following shipbuilder Charles Lungley's paper 'On a New Mode of Constructing Shot-Proof Ships of War'. Here, Coles announced his commitment 'to the great problem which has to be solved', and that since the Crimean War he had 'devoted much time and labour in endeavouring to overcome the many difficulties that necessarily arise in the construction of these novel engines of war.' He firmly believed that his shield ships 'could circumnavigate the world as well, if not better, than any ships in Her Majesty's Navy.' Sulivan regretted that the French floating batteries of 1855 had been sent to the Black Sea, attacking Kinburn, rather than to the Baltic, for he was sure 'that Admiral Dundas would have tried it, and I have no doubt that the floating defences, large and small, would have been driven back or destroyed… The only question, then, was to give these ships a form to make them seagoing.' But fellow veteran Captain Sherard Osborn also expressed how in the Black Sea he saw 'the critical condition at which our naval supremacy had arrived.' The real strategic phenomenon at stake was how fortified naval bases allowed an enemy to safely gather

27 10 January 1861, Walker to Board, TNA ADM 1/5774.
28 See 11 February 1861, TNA ADM 3/269.

his invading fleet 'and soldiers brought down for an attack upon this country'. Surely ironclad warships of some form could reverse this trend. 'When you build a huge thing like the *Warrior*, she may be a splendid sea boat', he noted, 'but when she is sent into the Baltic, God help the man in command of her.'[29]

By May 1861, the Board of Admiralty issues a series of memos outlining the threat posed by the seagoing ironclad fleet of France (with *Gloire* already in commission for over a year, three others launched and completing, *Magenta* and *Solferino* due to launch the next month, and ten improved *Provence*-class ironclads with even thicker, 6-inch armour laid down); against which the Royal Navy had 'afloat and plating' *Warrior*, *Black Prince*, *Defence* and *Resistance*, with *Hector* and *Valiant* only contracted in January, and one improved super broadside-ironclad (the *Achilles*), 'the keel of which is not yet laid'.[30] Robinson agreed with the Board that work on any more wooden ships-of-the-line begun by his predecessor had to come to an end. Likewise, the stubborn preference for iron-hulled ironclads—while it played to Britain's strengths in the commercial iron and shipbuilding industries—had taxed the capabilities of private firms far more than expected. Everyone was new to the iron-hulled ironclad business. Armour plate manufacturers in particular would take some time before new planing and rolling facilities were in place for large orders, once the promise of sustained work was there. Some of the screw wooden ships-of-the-line on the stocks would have to be converted immediately if the British Navy was to avoid serious embarrassment over the next few years. The Controller pointed to the second-rate, 91-gun *Royal Oak* as a prime example, which could very feasibly be cut down from two decks to one, and be armoured from bluff stem to rounded stern with 4½-inch iron-plating. While she would not be as world-ranging as the *Warrior*-class, she could certainly cruise 'to the Mediterranean if required' and be a match for at least the *Gloire*.[31]

This the Board approved, along with the conversion of the *Triumph* (later named *Prince Consort*), *Caledonia*, *Ocean* and *Royal Alfred*. Somerset added on 23 May that by saving money on the naval estimates in this way before Parliament—anxious about the French ironclad frigates on the one hand, and the costs of Britain's own on the other—it might prove easier to ask for more money for additional iron-hulled ironclads, provided every other 'source of expenditure' had been carefully

---

[29] 26 February 1861, Charles Lungley, 'On a New Mode of Constructing Shot-Proof Ships of War' (with extended discussion on 28 February and 1 March), *Transactions of the Institution of Naval Architects*, Vol. II (London: 1861), 37-91. For a general history see K. C. Barnaby, *The Institution of Naval Architects 1860-1960: An Historical Survey of the Institution's Transactions and Activities over 100 Years* (London: George Allen and Unwin Limited, 1960). By April the Admiralty was willing to conduct initial tests of an angled Coles 'shield' with glacis fitted to the floating battery *Trusty* at Woolwich Yard, at a cost of £300; 3 April 1861, Woolwich Superintendent to Board, TNA ADM 1/5764.
[30] See for example, 23 May 1861, TNA ADM 1/5765.
[31] 2 and 8 May 1861, Robinson to Board, TNA ADM 1/5774.

pruned first.³² Initially the talk was for 'ten' more *Warrior*s, possibly only six. But when Robinson presented the Board with the designs drawn up by Isaac Watts (the *Warrior*'s chief designer) and his assistants it soon became clear that only three could be managed. This *Minotaur*-class broadside monster exceeded 10,000 tons, with an incredible array of five masts to help push its iron hull at 14-knots, armoured stem to stern with 5½-inch plating (though with less teak backing than on *Warrior* and her immediate follow-ons.) Only a few iron shipbuilders in the country could attempt to build such vessels, and eventually contracts were awarded to Thames for the *Elephant* (later named *Minotaur*), Laird, Son & Company for *Agincourt*, and Mare & Company for the *Northumberland*.³³

U.S. policy according to the Monroe Doctrine of 1823 had been one of non-intervention in Europe and zero-tolerance of European interference in the western hemisphere. But with the outbreak of civil war between the Northern and Southern States in April 1861, the strategic temptation by Great Britain to intervene in favour of British long-term geopolitical interests was never greater before or since, especially under Palmerston's leadership. For him and many other British ruling elites, it was better for domestic tranquillity at home that the American 'experiment' in popular self-government and republican democracy end in a resounding failure for everyone to see.³⁴ 'The History of the World shews that Power in the hands of the Masses throws the Scum of the Community to the surface and that Truth and Justice are soon banished from the Land', Palmerston wrote to Russell in October 1862. 'We should all fare in the same way under the sway of [John] Bright and

32 23 May 1861, Somerset memo, TNA ADM 1/5765. Dundas added in his own (undated) memo that at this point 'even a wrong decision' in terms of speed and seaworthiness versus armour protection, yet 'certain progress' would be better than no decision at all—especially since other foreign powers were beginning to lay down armoured ships of their own.
33 See 31 May and 1 and 31 August 1861, Robinson to Board, TNA ADM 1/5774. Mare went bankrupt trying to complete the *Northumberland* and the task was taken up by Millwall Ironworks. All three ships were bound by contract to incorporate changes in the armour plating configuration up to three months after contract without extra charge, with a £5,000 penalty to be imposed if not finished in time. However, *Minotaur*, while launched at the end of 1863, was not completed until December 1868; *Agincourt* was not launched until 1865, though completed in 1867; and *Northumberland* was not launched until 1866 and ready for service in October 1868—seven years after being laid down; see for example Howard J. Fuller, '"Seagoing purposes indispensable to the defence of this country": Policy-Pitfalls of Great Britain's Early Ironclads', *The Northern Mariner/Le Marin du nord*, Vol. 13, No. 1 (January 2003), 19-36.
34 See for example, R. J. M. Blackett, *Divided Hearts: Britain and the American Civil War* (Baton Rouge: Louisiana State Press, 2001), 61; also R. B. McDowell, *British Conservatism 1832-1914* (London: Faber and Faber, 1959), 75-84. British laboring classes were divided on their views of the Union cause; see Jonathan Rose, 'Workers' Journals', in J. Don Vann and Rosemary T. Van Arsdel (eds.), *Victorian Periodicals and Victorian Society* (Toronto" University of Toronto Press, 1994), 303.

his associates.'[35] At the same, however, there was little doubt that Britain would formally declare its neutrality in the conflict—even after President Abraham Lincoln's government announced a naval blockade of all the rebel ports in the recently proclaimed 'Confederate States of America'. Indeed, Southern politicians in Congress had boasted for years that depriving British textile mills of cotton imports (from slave-states below the Mason-Dixon Line) for three years would be enough to see Britain economically 'topple headlong and carry the whole civilized world with her, save the South.'[36] While Northern industrialization and protectionism irritated British merchants and politicians alike, the Free Trade relationship between Britain and the American South had been especially lucrative; so much so that the new Confederate Constitution shrewdly prohibited protective tariffs and industrial development on the one hand while enshrining slavery—for the production of cotton and other raw materials for export to Britain and France—on the other.[37] As King Leopold of Belgium explained to his cousin, Queen Victoria later in 1862, 'your Government admits that the two fractions are *belligerents*; recognising this implies already that the Southern States are independent, as no fraction of States could make war on the remainder in this regular way without being independent of the other. The point of most vital importance to England is, that there should be two great Republics instead of one, the more so as the South can never be manufacturing, and the North, on the contrary, is so already to a great extent, and actually in many markets a rival'.[38]

* * *

By the end of 1861, cotton exports to Britain had dropped by 99 percent—due as much to an informal Southern embargo to strong-arm Britain into formal diplomatic recognition of the Confederacy than as a result of the Union blockade, which was still mobilising.[39] Only a surplus of such imports the previous years prevented a serious crisis from developing in Lancashire mills and other affected industries. But it was

35 28 October 1862, Palmerston to Russell, Russell Papers, TNA PRO 30-22, 14D.
36 According to South Carolina Senator James Henry Hammond in 1858 (declaring 'Cotton is King'); see for example Frank Lawrence Owsley, *King Cotton Diplomacy: Foreign Relations of the Confederate States of America* (Chicago: 1959), 16.
37 Article 1, Section 8 of the Confederate Constitution specified 'no duties or taxes on importations from foreign nations be laid to promote or foster any branch of industry.'
38 20 November 1862, in George Earle Buckle (ed.), *The Letters of Queen Victoria, Second Series 1862-1878*, 2 vols. (London: John Murray, 1926), 1: 47-8.
39 See for example, James M. McPherson, *Ordeal by Fire: The Civil War and Reconstruction* (New York: McGraw-Hill, 2009), 238-9; also David G. Surdam, 'The Union Navy's Blockade of the Confederacy: Tradition-Bound or a Betrayal of America's Birthright', in Peter N. Stearns (ed.), *The American Civil War in a Global Context* (Richmond: Virginia Sesquicentennial of the American Civil War Commission, 2015), 36-55, and more generally, David G. Surdam, *Northern Naval Superiority and the Economics of the American Civil War* (Columbia: University of South Carolina Press, 2001).

clear that the American Civil War was turning into a short fuse on a powder keg of Anglo-American relations, waiting for just the right incident to set it alight. It did not help that on 31 October 1861 the Spanish, French and British empires had agreed in a convention hosted in London to despatch a joint naval task force with 10,000 troops to Mexico—to force the civil war-ridden republic to repay on defaulted loans as well redress a host of violations against European nationals. Although Spain and Britain soon withdrew their forces from Vera Cruz, more French troops poured into the country, intent upon regime change.[40] On 8 November the screw-frigate USS *San Jacinto* intercepted the British Royal Mail packet paddle-steamer *Trent* between Cuba and the Bahamas. On board were two Confederate emissaries, bound for Europe to open foreign relations with Britain and France. The Union commanding officer, Captain Charles Wilkes, forcibly removed the Southern agents then left the *Trent* to carry on her business. When news of the incident reached London Palmerston was outraged, as was much of the British press and Parliament.[41] A Yankee warship had dared to apprehend a ship flying the British flag. For the first time the Prime Minister found his Cabinet in agreement that a demand should be issued to Washington for the immediate release of the two Southern emissaries—or suffer the consequences. Thousands of troops were quickly dispatched to reinforce the imperial garrison in British North America; naval units were likewise sent to bolster the forces of the North America and West Indies Station, headquartered at Bermuda under the flag of Rear-Admiral Sir Alexander Milne.[42] Palmerston had already toyed with the notion of sending the *Warrior* and *Black Prince* across the Atlantic. 'Their going could produce no bad Impression here,' he wrote to Somerset, 'and depend upon it as to Impression

---

40 As depicted, for example, in a full-page spread of *Harper's Weekly* (21 December 1861). On the Mexican intervention see for example, Percy F. Martin, *Maximilian in Mexico: The Story of the French Intervention (1861-1867)* (New York: Charles Scribner's Sons, 1914); Jack A. Dabbs, *The French Army in Mexico 1861-1867* (Hague: Walter De Gruyter Inc., 1963); Alfred Jackson Hanna and Kathryn Abbey Hanna, *Napoleon III and Mexico: American Triumph over Monarchy* (Chapel Hill: University of North Carolina Press, 1971); Jasper Ridley, *Maximilian and Juárez* (London: Phoenix Press, 1992); Michele Cunningham, *Mexico and the Foreign Policy of Napoleon III* (New York: Palgrave, 2001); Erika Pani, 'Law, Allegiance, and Sovereignty in Civil War Mexico, 1857-1867', *Journal of the Civil War Era*, Vol. 7, No. 4 (December 2017); and Christina Carroll, 'Imperial Ideologies in the Second Empire: The Mexican Expedition and the Royaume Arabe', *French Historical Studies*, Vol. 21, No. 1 (February 2019).
41 See for example, Norman. B. Ferris, *The* Trent *Affair: A Diplomatic Crisis* (Knoxville: University of Tennessee Press, 1977); and Gordon H. Warren, *Fountain of Discontent: The* Trent *Affair and Freedom of the Seas* (Boston: Northeastern University Press, 1981). As described by Kenneth Bourne, the *Trent* Affair was 'the most dangerous single incident of the Civil War and perhaps in the whole course of Anglo-American relations since 1815', *Britain and the Balance of Power in North America 1815-1908* (London: Longmans, Green and Co. Ltd., 1967), 251.
42 See for example, Kenneth Bourne, 'British Preparations for War with the North, 1861-1862', *The English Historical Review*, Vol. 76, No. 301 (October 1961).

in the United States the Yankees will be violent and threatening in Proportion to our local weakness and civil and pacific in Proportion to our increasing local strength.'[43]

A fairly blunt ultimatum from Palmerston and Russell to Washington demanding the release of the two Southern prisoners, as well as a formal apology from America to Britain, was only softened by Prince Albert—as he lay on his deathbed in December 1861—suggesting tactfully that Wilkes must not have been acting under deliberate orders from his superiors, and therefore his actions should be disavowed by the U.S. Government. This was eagerly taken up by Lincoln, although Britain's peremptory military and naval preparations for war genuinely startled him. 'The English didn't give us time to turn around,' he later noted. 'It was very humiliating at the time, but we had one big war on hand and we didn't want two at the same time. England in the end will be the only one hurt.' International maritime law was sketchy whether or not Wilkes had the legal right to board the neutral vessel and apprehend the two rebels as 'contraband of war'. Later it was agreed the *Trent* should have been captured and sent back to a U.S. prize court to determine the case, rather than sending her back on her way (in an effort to avoid further embarrassment). But the British captain, James Moir, and his crew already knew they had violated the Queen's Proclamation of Neutrality in even taking James Mason and John Slidell, and their families, on board as honoured guests. They knew they were headed to represent the Southern cause to Britain and France, respectively, seek formal recognition of the Confederacy, arrange arms shipments through the Union blockade and eventually secure open military alliances against the United States. Thus, when intercepted by the American warship in international waters and called to heave to, the British ship refused. Then the *San Jacinto* fired a wide shot across the *Trent*'s bow. Moir carried on. Only when a second shot was fired, much closer, did the British captain order his vessel to come about, yet when he was asked for his passengers list by the respectful but firm executive officer of the Yankee man-of-war, Moir angrily denied Mason and Slidell were on board and denounced him as 'a damned impertinent, outrageous puppy'. When the U.S. officer insisted, and stated he was legally obliged to also search the ship, Moir flew into a rage. A retired Royal Navy commander serving on board as the *Trent*'s mail agent, Richard Williams, had already hidden the official credentials and state papers of the Southern emissaries in the mail room under lock and key. Then he came up on deck to loudly threaten 'the British navy would retaliate within a few weeks by destroying the entire Northern blockade'. Typically, President Lincoln reduced it to parable, 'of an incident which occurred out west. Two roughs were playing cards for high stakes, when one of them, suspecting his adversary of foul play, straightway drew his bowie-knife from his belt and pinned the hand of the other player upon the table, exclaiming: "If you haven't got the ace of spades under your palm, I'll apologize."'[44]

---

43   23 June 1861, Palmerston to Somerset, Somerset Papers, Aylesbury, D/RA/A/2A/37.
44   See Ferris, *The Trent Affair*, 19-26; Carl Sandburg, *Abraham Lincoln: The War Years*, 4 vols. (New York: Harcourt, Brace & Company, 1939) 1: 364-5.

Palmerston nonetheless delighted in this successful political show of naval force—his last. 'Diplomats and protocols are very good things,' he had written to Rear-Admiral Charles Napier in 1847, 'but there are no better peace-keepers than well-appointed three-deckers.'[45] The blustering of the U.S. Secretary of State, William H. Seward, at the beginning of the Civil War (suggesting a war with European Powers in a desperate effort to re-unite the South with the North) had particularly annoyed the British.[46] Now the Premier had forced him to 'eat the leek'.[47] But the *Trent* Affair, while ruthlessly exposing the Union's vulnerability to British naval power at that critical juncture, also highlighted the limits of that force by 1862.[48] Despite their undeniable presence, the more deep-draft, screw-propelled ships-of-the-line the Admiralty despatched to Milne the more apprehensive he became. The 101-gun HMS *Conqueror* ran aground in the Bahamas on 13 December 1861; a total loss. Instead he pleaded for more shallow-draft paddle-steamers, like those in use for the Union Navy. Indeed, it was the lighter craft of the Yankees which proved better adapted for warfare in American waters. As he later wrote to Vice-Admiral Sir Frederick Grey, the First Naval Lord:

> If it had been war the great want would have been Frigates and Corvettes. By my letter to the [First Lord of the Admiralty] you would see the large service I had in view, and the Line of Battle ships would never have stood the gales and sea off the American coast. Every one of them would have been disabled, in fact I don't see of what service I could have employed them. As to attacking Forts it must never be done by anchoring ships but by ships passing and repassing in

---

45 Undated (autumn 1847), Palmerston to Napier, in Noel Williams (ed.), *The Life and Letters of Admiral Sir Charles Napier, K.C.B.* (London: Hutchinson & Co., 1917), 222; see also C. J. Bartlett, *Great Britain and Sea Power 1815-1853* (Aldershot: Gregg Revivals 1993 reprint of 1963 original), 58.
46 See for example, Norman B. Ferris, *Desperate Diplomacy: William H. Seward's Foreign Policy* (Knoxville: University of Tennessee Press, 1976), especially 6-13, 60-2, and 91-2.
47 26 January 1862, Palmerston to Laurence Sulivan (his brother-in-law), from Kenneth Bourne (ed.), *The Letters of the Third Viscount Palmerston to Laurence and Elizabeth Sulivan 1804-1863* (London: Royal Historical Society, 1979), 319. The reference is from Shakespeare's Henry V, Act V, Scene 1, where Captain Fluellen, the honourable Welshman in the King's service, savagely beats Pistol (the 'lousy knave' who had mocked him) until he eats the leek which Fluellen wears as a badge of honour. Only the surprise use of force places Fluellen over the humiliated Pistol, who in turn vows 'All hell shall stir for this.' A comical scene for Elizabethan audiences, the character of Gower nevertheless reminds Pistol that by repeatedly taunting his superior on a point of honour he had it coming.
48 See for example, Francis M. Carroll, 'The American Civil War and British Intervention: The Threat of Anglo-American Conflict', *Canadian Journal of History*, Vol. XVVII (Spring 2012), quoting Palmerston's assurance to Queen Victoria that 'Great Britain is in a better state than at any former time to inflict a severe blow upon, and read a lesson to the United States which will not soon be forgotten.'

rotation so as not to allow a steady object to the Enemy. Ships with larger draft of water are unfit for this mode of attack you need not build any more. Their days are numbered except [against] France … if she ever gets up a Navy.[49]

Furthermore, as with all of Britain's ships-of-the-line, of the 91 guns of HMS *Agamemnon* (launched in 1852, and reinforcing the British naval base at Bermuda from Gibraltar) no more than a third of these were 68-pounders, the rest being 32-pounders in use since the Napoleonic era.[50] There were few if any of the new Armstrong 110-pounder rifled guns, yet Milne had to express his surprise at seeing a heavy Parrott rifle gun on the visiting USS *Keystone State* (a converted merchant paddle-steamer).[51] Many U.S. warships were also typically armed with 9-inch Dahlgren guns firing 90lb solid shot and 73lb exploding shells. Bermuda's capability to act as a war-time base of operations for a large force against the American coastline—700 miles from Hampton Roads, Virginia—also troubled Milne. Coal would have to be continuously shipped over from the British Isles, 2,800 miles away from Halifax; 3,400 miles from Bermuda. That meant long, unprotected supply lines, or mobilising large elements of slow, outdated wooden vessels (and their crews) for escort.[52] In terms of defences, there were no troops assigned to man the forts, while he complained to Grey how it was 'painful to think that in our principal sea coast defences here 24 pdr-guns should be still mounted.'[53] But neither was Milne about to rush into a coastal bombardment of New York City or Boston. One ambitious report at the time from the British naval Hydrographer, Captain John Washington, suggested New York might be attacked, but only if the floating batteries from the Crimean War were mobilised, safely made it across the Atlantic, and were accompanied by all of the navy's armoured-frigates available—four of them at best. But even here these were only partially-armoured, and the slow, unwieldy iron batteries had no deck armour and were thus extremely

---

49 10 March 1862 and 17 January 1862, Milne to Grey, Milne Papers, Greenwich, MLN 116/2. 'I certainly for active service would prefer Frigates and smaller Vessels that I could substitute on the Station', he wrote to the First Lord of the Admiralty, 'as I cannot send the larger Ships to cruize in the West Indies or to American Ports,' 15 May 1862, in Somerset Papers, Aylesbury, D/RA/A/2A/34.
50 See David Lyon and Rif Winfield, *The Sail and Steam Navy List: All the Ships of the Royal Navy 1815-1889* (London: Chatham Publishing, 2004), 185, 189.
51 25 December 1861, Milne to Grey, Milne Papers, Greenwich, MLN 116/2. Described as a '32-pounder', possibly a 4.2-inch Parrott rifle, firing a 29lb. shell.
52 Milne warned the Admiralty 'every 8 to 10 days we must replenish coal'; 'so you see by this nearly a *double* set of ships as relays in the Blockades will be required', 25 December 1861, Milne to Grey, Milne Papers, Greenwich, MLN 116/2.
53 2 January 1862, Milne to Grey, Milne Papers, Greenwich, MLN 116/2. The other major British naval base on the station, Halifax, was approximately 600 miles from New York. See for example, Roger Willcock, *Bulwark of Empire: Bermuda's Fortified Naval Base 1860-1920* (Princeton: Roger Willcock, 1962), 47-52.

vulnerable to plunging shot from forts on high ground and mortar fire.[54] 'It is stated by the American papers that the *Warrior* could not enter New York Harbour on account of her great draught of water, and therefore she would be unable to take any part in engaging the forts', *Colburn's United Service Magazine* complacently observed in January 1862. 'As there is little probability that any American frigate would have the temerity to engage her in single combat at sea, the *Warrior* would not be found to be of much service in an American war.' All this was regrettable since 'we ourselves have heard several persons, not members of Mr. Bright's bloody-minded aristocracy, but sober-minded citizens belonging to the middle classes express regret that England was not able to go and thrash the Yankees and pay them off for their innumerable insults to this country.' Here the author admitted that 'most of us feel a kind of pride and satisfaction in having by threats of immediate war compelled these bragging Americans to give in to our demands.'[55]

54 *List of the Chief Ports on the Federal Coast of the United States, showing the Shipping, Population, Dockyards and Defences as far as known; also how far accessible or vulnerable to an Attack, as far as can be gathered from the Charts. With an approximate Estimate of the Number of Vessels required to blockade the several Ports and Rivers* (London: HMSO, 1861); copy found in Milne Papers, Greenwich. See also Bourne, *Britain and the Balance of Power in North America*, 240. Washington may have based much of his information in turn on the pre-Civil War alarmist pamphlets of Major J. G. Barnard of the U.S. Corps of Engineers; namely *Dangers and Defenses of New York* (New York: D. Van Nostrand, 1859) and *Notes on Sea-Coast Defense* (New York: D. Van Nostrand, 1861), which specified the importance of the new Rodman 15-inch gun in checking the ascendancy of armored batteries over fortifications; on the latter work see pages 27-8, 44-8, 56-60. British military professionals had already pointed to heavy seacoast mortars as a powerful antidote to slow-moving floating batteries weak on deck armour; see for example 22 May 1857, Admiral Sir Edmund Lyons to Lieutenant General Sir John Pennefather, TNA ADM 1/5682; Captain Thomas Spratt to Rear-Admiral Sir Houston Stewart, dated May 1856, enclosed in 7 March 1859, Vice-Admiral Sir Arthur Fanshawe to Admiralty, TNA ADM 1/5682; and especially 13 November 1860, Captain Bartholomew Sulivan (Board of Trade) to Admiralty, in TNA ADM 1/5763. A February 1859 memorandum from Burgoyne, foresaw 'a time, and at no distant period' when vertical bombs would 'crush all ordinary artificial bomb-proof cover…and by their explosions, ruin ramparts, and even overturn escarps', TNA WO 33/07.

55 'Theseus, Late R.N.', 'England's Naval Resources', *Colburn's United Service Magazine and Naval and Military Journal*, January 1862, Part 1 (London: Hurst and Blackett), 219. *Warrior* and her sister-ship *Black Prince* drew nearly 27-feet of water while the two smaller partially-armoured-frigates *Defence* and *Resistance* likewise drew 26-feet. This meant any attempt to force the Narrows would be limited to the ability of a good pilot fairly intimate with New York Harbor, manoeuvring slowly through a narrow passage, under fire. *Warrior* herself was, for all her innovations, a remarkably traditional man-of-war turned monstrous by her prodigious iron-framed bulk; some 600 men out of a total crew of 700 were required to heave up her two-bladed screw for sail-only cruising on the high seas (with 100 men needed to raise the anchors), and she was unable to turn an extreme angle at her rudder helm beyond 18 to 25-degrees in less than 1.5 minutes with forty men on relieving tackles; see Parkes, *British Battleships*, 16-24.

The *Trent* Affair, while it did not end with the Anglo-American war which the Confederacy at least desperately hoped for, did succeed in ratcheting up the mobilisation of the North's war machine—now against the British Empire as well as the rebel South. As reported by Gideon Welles, the U.S. Secretary of the Navy, on 2 December 1861, the Union's force afloat had gone from 'forty-two vessels, carrying five hundred and fifty-five guns' before the Civil War began in March 1861 (with another sixteen frigates and sloops which had been called up out of reserve and placed in commission) to a powerful new armada 264-strong, mounting 2,557 guns and manned by over 22,000 seamen. The following year, 1 December 1862, Welles reported a collective mobilised strength of 427 men-of-war (323 of them steam-powered) mounting 3,268 guns, with 54 ironclads built and building.[56] In a special report to Congress on 4 July 1861, Welles had indeed recommended a special board of naval officers be convened to review plans for 'Iron-Clad Steamers or Floating Batteries', with submissions from the private sector. Publications like *Scientific American* had already been warning that 'we have not a single first class war steamer—one that can compete with the most recently built French and British ones…we mean the iron-cased war wolves.'[57] In August, the brilliant Swedish-American engineer-inventor John Ericsson penned a letter to the White House warning that because forts could no longer be relied upon to stop warships which were clad in iron, civilian targets like New York City were likewise 'quite at the mercy of such intruders, and may at any moment be laid in ruins' by European-built varieties carrying 'Armstrong Guns'.[58] Presented in this way, the problem of how to stop oceangoing ironclads from projecting power against continental powers like the United States—especially during the domestic turmoil of a major civil war—was the greatest geo-strategic threat facing the nation in 1861. After the ignominious defeat of the largely volunteer Union Army at Bull Run (or Manassas, 21 July), the Navy remained the only viable deterrent while the U.S. military now took care to mobilise and train masses of recruits more properly.

At the same time, Congress was urged by Welles on 3 August to appropriate $1.5 million for ironclad construction.[59] Intelligence had arrived that the Confederates at Norfolk, Virginia had raised the scuttled remains of the steam-frigate USS *Merrimack* and were covering the largely intact engines and hull with an iron-armoured fort which would be invulnerable to gunfire. When launched, the Confederate Secretary of the Navy (Stephen Mallory) hoped that it would act like a wolf amongst sheep. Given the North's overwhelming naval superiority in wooden warships, the South *had* to have armoured men-of-war; 'to enable us with a small number of vessels comparatively to keep our waters free from the enemy and ultimately to contest with

---

56 2 December 1861, *Report of the Secretary of the Navy*, 37th Congress, 2nd Session; 1 December 1862, *Report of the Secretary of the Navy*, 37th Congress, 3rd Session.
57 12 January 1861, 'New War Steamers', *Scientific American*.
58 29 August 1861, Ericsson to Lincoln, John Ericsson Papers, American-Swedish Historical Foundation, Philadelphia, Box 2.
59 Equivalent to £300,000, or the approximate figure for one *Warrior*-class ironclad.

them the possession of his own.'[60] After reviewing a multitude of design submissions from private shipbuilders and naval architects, the U.S. Ironclad Board awarded contracts in October 1861 for three widely different, experimental concepts: a wooden-hulled broadside-ironclad drawing just over fifteen-feet and partially armoured with 4½-inch plating (USS *New Ironsides*); a smaller armoured sloop with 2½-inch plating but drawing only eleven-feet (USS *Galena*); and a submission from Ericsson for a completely steam-driven, iron-hulled, shallow-draft vessel armoured on the sides with 5-inches of iron plating. In the middle of the completely flush 1-inch thick iron deck rose a gun turret 8-inches thick and rotated by internal steam machinery. Of course the board members were highly incredulous of his design; most of the craft was submerged below the waterline, with the upper 'raft' like portion of hull only showing 18-inches above the waterline—to say nothing of a turret-based armament of only two heavy guns (11-inch caliber Dahlgren smoothbores). It was utterly unlike any other warship in the world. Treating his theoretical battery as more of a floating steam-machine than a traditional ship, Ericsson had to literally lecture the naval officers on the physics involved with low-freeboard buoyancy, and the mathematical certainly that his vessel simply would not sink to the bottom when launched. But his proposal nevertheless offered a means of providing the thickest armour protection of any other ironclad afloat—whilst drawing only ten-feet. Unlike the other contractors, only Ericsson could promise to have his 'battery' completely built—by a form of modular construction—and ready for combat within '90 days' (it took 117 from the date of the contract). It was also half a million dollars less expensive than *New Ironsides*. 'All I have to say is what the girl said when she put her foot into the stocking,' remarked Lincoln when shown the small cardboard model of Ericsson's ironclad: '"it strikes me there's something in it."'[61]

---

60   See William N. Still Jr., *Iron Afloat: The Story of the Confederate Armorclads* (Indianapolis: Vanderbilt University Press, 1971), 10-17.
61   An interesting story, told many times; see for example, James Tertius DeKay, *Monitor: The Story of the Legendary Civil War Ironclad and the Man Whose Invention Changed the Course of History* (Pimlico: Random House, 1999), 76. See also John Ericsson, 'The Building of the *Monitor*', in Robert Underwood Johnson and Clarence Clough Buel (eds.), *Battles and Leaders of the Civil War*, 4 vols. (Edison: Castle Books, 1956, reprint of 1884-88 original series), 1: 730-44.

3

'Such a proceeding on our part is simply impossible'

Before 1861 was out Congress had passed a bill for another twenty armoured 'gunboats', though it was still unclear which type of ironclads would be favoured.[1] Improved coastal and harbour fortifications, with improved armaments, were also called for. Yet by the time his vessel was ready to launch in January 1862, Ericsson had settled on name for her: 'Monitor', partially on the basis that 'Downing Street' and the 'Lords of the Admiralty' would be 'startled and admonished by the booming of the guns from the impregnable iron turret'.[2] This was in direct response to the current *Trent* Affair, and the British threat of war spelled out so clearly by *Blackwood*'s in February:

> The Americans have been coerced into an act of justice, which they performed with the worst possible grace; and we are frankly assured that a time is coming, when they mean to take ample vengeance for present humiliations. It appears, then, that a war with the Federal States of America is only deferred. If not imminent, it is pretty sure to come sooner or later… How shall we prepare for such a contingency and conduct the war when it comes?
>
> There are two modes of carrying on war with America—one aggressive, the other defensive. We shall probably adopt both. We shall assail their harbours, burn their fleets, destroy their commerce, and keep their whole seaboard in a state of constant alarm; and we shall give employment by these means to no inconsiderable portion of the half million of men whom they boast to have under arms. But we shall have a defensive war likewise to provide for, on the side of Canada.[3]

---

[1] As noted by Baxter, the Bureau of Ship Construction and Repair favoured high-freeboard turret vessels, with revolving towers similar to those of Coles; *Introduction*, 250-2; 263-4; 275-6.

[2] See for example, Howard J. Fuller, *Clad in Iron: The American Civil War and the Challenge of British Naval Power* (Westport: Greenwood, 2008), 44-56, 78.

[3] February 1862, *Blackwood's Edinburgh Magazine*, 228.

Ericsson had already assured the Secretary of the Navy that he could quickly build six more of his shallow-draft, turreted-ironclads as need be. They could make the most of the North's existing industrial facilities—and limitations—like no other ironclad design could. And thanks in part to their low-freeboard design they did not require the import of solid 4½-inch armour plates—from Britain of all places—as the high-freeboard design worked up by the U.S Navy's Bureau of (Ship) Construction and Repair.[4] By February 1862, the Senate Committee on Naval Affairs reminded Welles about the ironclad-gunboats. His reply was evasive; the number of new ships to be contracted for now hovered around 'ten or twelve' in the next six months, 'and probably double or three times that number within a year.' But as the *Monitor* was gearing up for an inevitable confrontation with the rebel ironclad-ram at Norfolk—now christened the CSS *Virginia*—the Navy Department had decided to 'avail itself of the experience which will be gained in the construction of those now going forward, one of which will soon be tested in actual conflict.'[5]

Sure enough, on the morning of 8 March 1862, the *Virginia* finally crept out of her base and proceeded straight for the five powerfully-armed Union frigates which were anchored in Hampton Roads at Newport News (near Fort Monroe, on the Virginia Peninsula). But the point-blank broadsides of both the USS *Congress* and USS *Cumberland* merely glanced off the rebel ironclad's 4-inch iron-armoured casemate—sloped at an angle of 36-degrees.[6] The *Virginia* then ploughed into the *Cumberland*, sinking her almost instantly, while Confederate shellfire turned the *Congress* into a floating inferno. Hundreds of Union sailors were dead and wounded, in the worst defeat of the U.S. Navy until the surprise Japanese attack on the Pacific Fleet anchored at Pearl Harbor on 7 December 1941. The USS *Monitor*, with a crew of 58 officers and men, had meanwhile been hurriedly despatched from the Brooklyn Navy Yard south to Hampton Roads two days before. In what was essentially her shakedown cruise she encountered heavy seas which critically exploited leaks in the vessel, with enough water entering to impede the steam-powered blowers to the boiler fires, which then produced a flood of carbon dioxide gas in the engine room, while the pumps also failed. Only after the *Monitor* was towed closer to shore were the engineers able to re-fire the boilers and restore power to the semi-submerged vessel. On the night of 8 March she stood in towards the *Minnesota*, which had run aground (along with the *St. Lawrence*, while the USS *Roanoke* had been waiting for engine repairs). The next morning the *Virginia* reappeared, prepared to finish off the rest of the Union squadron—only to spot the peculiar form of the Federal ironclad slowly steaming out from behind the *Minnesota* to intercept her.

4   See for example, 31 January 1862, Daniel B. Martin to Commodore Joseph Smith, U.S. National Archives, RG 19 (Bureau of Construction and Repair), Entry 61, Box 1.
5   Fuller, *Clad in* Iron, 76-7.
6   See for example the account by A. B. Smith, 'Statement of the Pilot of the *Cumberland*', in Frank Moore (ed.), *The Rebellion Record: A Diary of American Events*, Vol. 4 (New York: Putnam, 1862), 272-3.

For four hours the two mastless ironclads, one casemated the other turreted, engaged each other at point blank range. The *Monitor*'s two 11-inch Dahlgrens were fired with low charges since even their designer hadn't imagined using them against armoured vessels and feared the result of their bursting in the confines of a crowded turret. The *Virginia*, in turn, was rarely able to bring her ten guns to bear against her low-profile antagonist, which was also slightly faster and distinctly more manageable than the hulking broadside vessel. Shots against the Yankee ironclad's turret bounced off harmlessly, leaving only dents.[7] In the end, it was the 21-foot draft of the Confederate vessel which obliged her to retreat back to Norfolk, once the spring tide began to fall again. It was the first clash between armoured-warships in history, and it was tactically a draw. But strategically the victory went to the North by default. The blockade had been preserved. The rebel's best warship—which had so shocked the country with its ruthless destructive powers and apparent invincibility on 8 March—had been dramatically checked the very next day by the comparatively diminutive 'Ericsson Battery'. Union General George B. McClellan had meanwhile reformed Union forces massed in Washington, D.C. into the 'Army of the Potomac'. With this he planned to launch a huge amphibious campaign on the Virginia Peninsula, landing near Fort Monroe, with the intention of advancing along the James River and capturing the Confederate capital at Richmond from the rear. Now that the '*Merrimack*' had been driven back to its lair, the invasion could proceed. Within two months Union troops occupied Norfolk, forcing the crew of the *Virginia* to scuttle their own vessel; she was too deep to ascend the James towards Richmond, and too unseaworthy to flee anywhere else.

Welles had meanwhile written to the chairmen of both the House and Senate naval committees that a full $30 million was needed to put the country on a proper war footing at sea—not just against the Confederacy but with an eye on possible intervention by foreign powers (Britain and France). The allocation of $1.5 million in 1861 was to test different types of ironclads, broadside versus turret, and now his Department was certain that Ericsson's monitor-ironclads were needed more than any other class. It was painfully clear that without armour protection wooden steam vessels could make 'but feeble resistance' against ironclads, and as the Union Navy could not at the moment 'successfully contend against a Power employing iron clad vessels', it could not meet the requirements of the country.' Likewise, only a whole fleet of ironclads would be 'commensurate with the great interests at stake', and the best designs for ironclads would be those which would 'secure to our country equality if not pre-eminence in naval construction.' That sort of quantitative and qualitative edge could only be had with superior technology—starting with new guns 'sufficiently heavy and powerful to break and destroy the armature now placed upon vessels' (i.e., 4½-inch iron plating, as was covering British and French seagoing broadside-ironclads). Hence, orders had already been placed for 15- and even 20-inch

---

7   S. Dana Greene, 'In the 'Monitor' Turret', in Johnson and Buel, *Battles and Leaders*, 1: 723.

calibre guns, and $500,000 was needed immediately to equip the Washington Navy Yard for their production. As the *gun* was now determining the type of ironclad, the Department proposed to contract for 'a class for harbor defence, and to operate upon the Atlantic coast and in the Gulf of Mexico, which shall be as far as possible invulnerable, each armed with 15 inch guns, and finally it proposes to attempt an ocean steamer possessed of the same sailing and armoured properties, armed with guns of 20 inches calibre.'[8]

This was an extremely bold undertaking. That Congress largely approved the money, and its stated purpose, had much to say for the historic chain of events that made such a radical commitment imaginable let alone possible: the Civil War, the *Trent* Affair, and then the Battle of Hampton Roads. The decision also steamrolled over the preferences of John Lenthall, the Chief of the Bureau of Construction and Repair since 1853, and the talented Engineer-in-Chief of the Navy, Benjamin Isherwood. On 17 March 1862 (eight days after the ironclad battle at Hampton Roads), they urged Welles to consider that Ericsson's monitors would hardly 'constitute a navy or perform its proper functions.' Only proper high-freeboard, seagoing ironclads could do that, as demonstrated by the great maritime powers, Britain and France. All things being equal in the dawning ironclad revolution, now was the time to join in on that race. 'Wealth, victory and empire are to those who command the Ocean, the toll gate as well as the highway of Nations; and if ever assailed by a powerful maritime for, we shall find to our prosperity, if ready, how much better it is to fight at the threshold than upon the hearthstone.' But this grandiose vision also meant asking Congress to also invest in a massive overhaul of Federal dockyards for the production of the largest possible steam-powered warships and their armour-plating. Perhaps more to the point, the government men were suspicious of private contractors and 'men of genius' like Ericsson, however wildly popular they were becoming, they grumbled, thanks to the chance happenings of the war going on around them. In their experience these people were profit-driven as they were publicly unaccountable.[9]

Yet Ericsson was hardly a war-profiteer or mercenary. As he had told Lincoln in 1861, he was already well within his means from the rights and sales of his caloric engines before the war. Everyone who knew him saw a frugal Swedish immigrant living a rather reclusive life in his modest home in New York City; a fiery though fiercely patriotic inventor who was totally uninterested in wealth (though not fame), and who tended to pour any profits from one project into the next experiment. 'There cannot be the slightest objection to your ordering copies to be made and distributed of the plans and specifications which I have presented to the Department', Ericsson

---

8   25 March 1862, Welles to John P. Hale and Charles B. Sedgwick, US National Archives (Washington, D.C.), Record Group (RG) 45, Entry 5.
9   17 March 1862, Lenthall and Isherwood to Welles, US National Archives, RG 45, Letters Received; see also 13 May 1862, Ironclad Board (Lenthall, Isherwood and civilian naval architect Edward Hart) to Welles, RG 45, Letters Rec'd.

wrote to Welles in April 1862. 'No charge whatever has been contemplated on my part for those plans and specifications.' The uniquely compact and low-profile vibrating-lever engine of his design would feature in the new improved monitors (of the *Passaic*-class) at a rate of 'one per cent on the contract price'. For their use in the subsequent *Canonicus*-class single-turret monitors the rate was ⅜ percent of the contract price.[10] Ericsson's boldness was also well known, writing directly to Secretary of State Seward on 23 April how 'the state of the naval defenses of the country being so intimately connected with its inter-national relations, I deem it my duty to report to you that under orders from the Secretary of the Navy, keels for 6 vessels of the Monitor class of increased size and speed have already been laid'. Their real significance was in the unprecedented 'amount of mechanical force now concentrated on the work': machines would both build and characterize America's naval power, to a far greater extent than the sailing fleets of the Old World Powers. As such, news of the latest developments in Britain were quite encouraging since even the latest (12-ton) experimental Armstrong gun would not be enough against monitors with sides only 18-inches above the water, 'a circumstance which converts their decks into bulwarks supporting the armor plate with resistless force. Our turrets, too, are absolutely impregnable as we now make the same 11¾-thick—all iron.' On the other hand, none of the *Warrior*-class follow-ons nor the converted wooden-hulled broadside-ironclads featured armour plating and backing which would be able to resist the 450-pound solid shot of the new 15-inch guns. It was reported that the Royal Navy had also commenced a trial Coles turret-ship converted from a wooden screw-liner. But Ericsson assured Seward this was also a 'serious blunder' on the part of England, since the higher-freeboard sides of the hull below the turrets would only be protected by plating as thick as any of the broadside vessel. 'The British Admiralty, it would appear, can only see in the *Monitor* a revolving turret (erroneously supposed to be of English origin),' he concluded, 'forgetting that without the peculiarly constructed hull of the *Monitor*, her cupola Ships will stand no chance in a conflict with this country.'[11]

Indeed, Charles Francis Adams, the U.S. Ambassador to Great Britain had already noticed a sea change in Anglo-American relations since the first reports had arrived of the sensational events at Hampton Roads. 'In December [during the *Trent* Affair] we were told that we should be swept from the ocean in a moment, and all our ports would be taken', he wrote to his son, Charles Francis junior. 'They do not talk so now. So far as this may have a good effect to secure peace on both sides it is good'.[12]

10   16 April 1864, Ericsson to Rear-Admiral Francis Gregory, Ericsson Papers, Library of Congress (Washington, D.C.), Manuscript Division; also 24 April 1862, Ericsson to Welles, Ericsson Papers, Philadelphia, Box 4.
11   23 April 1862, Ericsson to Seward, Ericsson Papers, Philadelphia, Box 7. See also William Conant Church, *The Life of John Ericsson*, 2 vols. (New York: Charles Scribner's Sons, 1890), 2: 5-6.
12   4 April 1862, Charles Francis Adams to Charles Francis Adams, Jr., from Worthington Chauncey Ford (ed.), *A Cycle of Adams Letters, 1861-1865*, 2 vols. (Boston: Houghton

For *The Illustrated London News* this 'Naval Revolution' was absolutely front-page material—the mastless armoured *Virginia* ramming into the wooden *Cumberland* with spectacular violence.[13] It wasn't so much the shock of point-blank, shell-firing, ramming tactics, or even the invulnerability of the two ironclads when squared off against one another on the second days' fighting; it was how two large, finely-built men-of-war had been blown to pieces, burnt and sunk within minutes on that first day. Entire capital ships were destroyed. There was no question whether their decks had been so reduced, or their motive power stripped away by a successive battering of gunfire, that they might strike their colours and be captured—soon incorporated into the victor's navy. The British now contemplated how their once stout and majestic floating fortresses of oak would be ripped to shreds by monster guns, their hulls smashed in, sinking so fast that most of their crews would go down with their ships. Before, their inherent vulnerability to gunfire was counterbalanced by their ability to offer superior counter-fire. But against an armoured foe this was suddenly irrelevant, and even a first-rate ship-of-the-line might be mercilessly overpowered by a much smaller vessel which had rather turned its strengths against it. This was of course the argument played up by Coles, in his letter to *The Times* of 31 March 1862. Only by employing his invention of revolving 'shield' ships—perhaps converted from wooden ships-of-the-line themselves—could Britain's shores be defended against broadside-ironclads. All of the money being spent upon coastal fortifications was money wasted. That same day, Sir Frederic Smith rose in the House of Commons to renounce his faith in the four proposed island-forts for Spithead, in the Solent. 'If the *Warrior* had met the *Merrimac*,' he ventured further, 'it was a matter of grave doubt whether the angular-sided vessel would not have overcome her vertical-sided antagonist; but if the *Warrior* and the *Monitor* had met, there was little doubt that the smaller vessel would have plunged her shot into the unprotected parts of the *Warrior*, and would, in fact, have overcome the pride of the British navy.'[14]

* * *

The problem which seemed unique to Britain was that, given her preference for the biggest, fastest—best—ironclads in the world—they were taking the longest to complete. Forgings of the massive iron slabs for their armour were in themselves Victorian feats of strength. As described by the First Lord of the Admiralty to his wife:

Mifflin Company, 1920), 1:123.
13 5 April 1862, 'The Naval Revolution, *The Illustrated London News*.
14 31 March 1862, *The Times*; 31 March 1862, 'Iron-Plated Ships—Observations', Hansard, vol. 166, 263-89. At 72, Lieutenant-General Sir John Mark Frederick Smith, Conservative MP for Chatham, was also Colonel-Commandant of Royal Engineers.

We then went to the works [of John Brown and Company, Sheffield] to see the rolling of some large armour plates by means of some new machinery, the largest as yet used for this purpose. One large plate rolling was very interesting; the mass of iron red-hot was so heavy the workmen could hardly drag it out, and then it was a question whether the rollers would not break. There was a check for a moment, and great excitement; at last the men and machinery prevailed, and the mound of red-hot iron was drawn through the rollers, coming out duly shaped on the other side; the workmen, strong-limbed, and black with smoke and dirt, then gave immense cheers. We waved our hats, and Mr. Brown's wife was so excited at his triumphant success that she could not help kissing him in the midst of us ...[15]

The rest of the world was, meanwhile, hardly going to wait. Armies were on the move. 'I hope you will stir up the slow and steady Admiralty to some vigour about Iron Ships', Russell thus wrote to Palmerston on 31 March 1862. 'The French have long been before us and in six months the United States will be far ahead of us unless our builders in the Navy Department exert themselves.' This was because the bold new designs of American ironclads—mastless, turreted, and heavily armoured—were also cheaper and quicker to produce than the gargantuan, oceangoing specimens advocated by Watts and the Controller's Department the year before. It was astonishing to think that Ericsson's high-tech ironclad steamer had been built and launched within one-hundred days, and cost one-sixth the price of the *Warrior*, which took a year and a half to launch, let alone complete. What's more, the Federal turret-ships were armed with much bigger guns than any conceived for European broadside-ironclads. 'Only think of our position,' Russell sighed to Palmerston, 'if in case of the Yankees turning upon us they should by means of iron ships renew the triumphs they achieved in 1812-13 by means of superior size and weight of metal.'[16] The next day *The Times* went further, claiming that it was now 'quite impossible to dissemble the fact that nine-tenths of the British Navy have been rendered comparatively useless.' The only hope was that in a new world of ironclads or nothing, at least the *Warrior* was a superior class of ironclad than the crude American version which had fought at Hampton Roads. *The Illustrated London News*, however, had its doubts:

> Is the *Warrior* itself a match for the *Monitor*? It is useless now to talk of speed and magnificence. We don't want our war ships to run away successfully, or to be looked at admiringly, but to fight. How would the *Monitor* deal with the *Warrior*? The guns of the first send shot of 170lb; the guns of the second, shots

---

15 Mallock and Ramsden, *Letters, Remains, and Memoirs*, 318-19.
16 31 March 1862, Russell to Palmerston, Palmerston Papers, Broadlands, GC/RU/691-716.

of 100lb…Again, the *Monitor* is practically invulnerable to existing artillery: is the *Warrior* the same?'[17]

Meanwhile at Bermuda, Milne was fairly certain what the implications now were for the Anglo-American balance-of-power on his station. 'If these ships of the line now here were cut up into small vessels, they would be of use to me', he wrote from his bravura flagship, the 91-gun *Nile*, 'but except for Demonstrations clear of *Merrimac* and *Monitor*, they are no use'.[18]

After the successful trial of Coles's turrets on the *Trusty*, the Admiralty had little reason not to trial at least one purpose-built turret-ship—now especially given the British public's furore over the American ironclads (with Coles expressing to Paget his 'deep mortification…at the Americans' taking away the Palm of the invention from this country.'[19]) On 4 April, the Board relented into cutting down of the giant, 121-gun screw ship-of-the-line *Royal Sovereign* into a mastless ironclad vessel topped with five revolving turrets, housing 68-pounders and Armstrong 110-pounder rifled guns. This was later reduced to four turrets at Coles's urging to accommodate Armstrong's experimental 12-ton '300-pounders'.[20] Not satisfied with this expedient, however, Watts also produced a design for an iron-hulled coast defence turret-ship—to be named in honour of Prince Albert—with four turrets and drawing no more than twenty-feet fully-loaded. But these were distinctly understood to be floating batteries—not prestige vessels. When informed by Reed (as Chief Constructor) over a year later that the *Royal Sovereign* was 'in no way to test the merits of a sea going ship', Coles was more than disappointed, absolving himself of 'any responsibility for disaster that may occur from the *Royal Sovereign* having no topworks.'[21] Before the end of April 1862, Robinson also informed the Board that if they wanted smaller,

17 1 April 1862, *Times*; 5 April 1862, *The Illustrated London News*, 328
18 From Regis A. Courtemanche, *No Need of Glory: The British Navy in American Waters 1860-64* (Annapolis: Naval Institute Press, 1977), 153. See also Hamilton, *Anglo-French Naval Rivalry*, 92, who observes that after Hampton Roads 'it was patently obvious that all battleships had to be armoured. The British parliament and press realized that the country's screw-liner fleet was obsolete and that recent shipbuilding policy had been purblind and wasteful.'
19 31 March 1862, Coles to Paget, in 11 April 1862, Robinson to Board, TNA ADM 1/5802.
20 See 8 July 1862, Coles to Paget, TNA ADM 1/5791, with Robinson's marginal comment that the 'greatest possible inconvenience is felt both as regards the *Royal Sovereign* and the *Prince Albert*, from the want of the Drawings of the Shields which Captain Coles was requested to furnish in April and May last.'
21 5 September 1863, Coles to Paget, TNA ADM 1/5827; and 21 August 1863, Robinson to Board, TNA ADM 1/5841, with Reed's enclosed letter to Coles dated 21 August 1863. Coles had already complained that no seagoing turret-ship had been contemplated by the Admiralty in early July 1862; see for example, 15 July 1863, Coles to Paget, TNA ADM 1/5827. Coles wrote the year before that if the guns of the *Royal Sovereign* were to be muzzle loaders then the cupolas would have to redesigned as cylindrical turrets rather

handier ironclads then the best proposal he had seen had come from naval architect Edward Reed, educated at the Mathematical School at Portsmouth. This was more specifically for converting smaller wooden warships to fully-masted ironclads with an armour belt along the waterline (and running several feet below), and a central armoured box housing a small but heavy battery—which would also allow for fore and aft fire from traversing guns. It was unusual that a Controller/Surveyor would endorse a design from outside his own team of qualified (and seasoned) naval constructors, but Somerset agreed that it represented a viable response to mounting public criticism over the monster ironclads of Watts approved the year before. The resulting trial conversion of the sloop *Circassian* into HMS *Enterprise* was Reed's first central-battery ironclad. Yet provided the test didn't altogether fail, his concept could be theoretically applied to any sized vessel.[22]

Thus, while the U.S. Navy committed itself to a largely coastal turret-ship force in the spring of 1862, the Admiralty's ironclad building programme had splintered into different—soon to be fiercely competitive—directions. How this would affect Britain's foreign policy decision-making was first indicated later that autumn. At the ferocious and costly Battle of Antietam (17 September 1862), neither Confederate General Robert E. Lee's Army of Northern Virginia nor McClellan's Army of the Potomac managed to drive the other from the field, though Lee was at least compelled to withdraw his invading forces from Maryland back into Virginia. For Lincoln this was the moment he had been waiting for; a tide of 'victory' in which to issue an Emancipation Proclamation as Commander-in-Chief—freeing the slaves in rebel states, and inviting them to make their way across the lines to join the ranks of the Union Army. Given the scorn heaped upon his war-time administration by the European press, Lincoln also assumed that adding emancipation as a 'Cause' would appease the anti-slavery British in particular. But given the string of Union defeats at the hands of Lee and other Confederate generals, and the increasing scale and slaughter of American campaigns, both France and Britain considered Lincoln's act nothing more than a frantic attempt to win the war by inciting 'servile insurrection' on the Southern home front (Palmerston's cabinet in particular had the racial atrocities of the Indian Mutiny fresh in their minds).[23] Napoleon III quickly saw this as an

---

than cones; 6 September 1862, Coles to William Romaine, the Admiralty (Permanent) Secretary between 1857-1869, TNA ADM 1/5791.

22   14 April 1862, Robinson to Board, TNA ADM 1/5801, with Robinson noting that Reed should be paid £600 for his work; see also Parkes, *British Battleships*, 82-92.

23   See for example 4 October 1862, Russell to Palmerston, Palmerston Papers, Broadlands, GC/RU, with Gladstone's printed memo dated 25 October 1862. 'Is the name of Lincoln ultimately to be classed in the catalogue of monsters, wholesale assassins and butchers of their kind?" asked *The Times*. 'When blood begins to flow and shrieks come piercing through the darkness, Mr. Lincoln will wait until the rising flames tell that all is consummated, and then he will rub his hands and think that revenge is sweet', 21 October 1862.

opportunity to suggest an offer of joint 'mediation' with Britain: if the irresponsible political leadership in Washington rejected it then the Great Powers would have every moral right to formally recognise the Confederate States. Seward, had, in the meantime, threatened such a move as tantamount to a declaration of war against the United States.[24] Hence the only question that mattered in the series of lengthy memos which circulated in the British cabinet that October and November was whether the country was willing to ignore this risk as happily as it was the previous December. While Gladstone was eager to intervene in the American Civil War on humanitarian grounds, the military ministers were not convinced this was enough. By the time of the *Trent* Affair the Northern States had only begun to mobilise. Now the situation at sea—the arena which mattered most in terms of British capabilities—was far more problematic. As Secretary of State for War Sir George Cornewall Lewis had to remind his colleagues, in the event of hostilities with the United States 'the wooden ships of Europe would encounter the small iron-cased steamers of America, which, though not seagoing ships, would prove destructive in the ports and rivers.' This was an especially bitter pill to swallow, since during the *Trent* mobilisation less than a year before he had assured a friend that 'We shall *iron the smile* out of their face.'[25] Somerset had already confided to him his concern that the French Emperor was manipulating events, having already despatched the ironclad *Normandie* across the Atlantic to Mexico, 'which has no fleet and no fort to be taken. If they mean to recognise the South, it is well to have such a vessel in those waters, otherwise the ship is ill-suited to that climate and station.'[26] Palmerston was also concerned of an Anglo-American conflict especially in the winter, when 'Communications with Canada would be cut off, and we have not there a Garrison sufficient for War Time.' The French by contrast had 'no Point of Contact with the Americans, and their Naval Force is stronger than that of the Americans while they have less commercial navy to protect or to lose.' The best policy therefore remained 'to go on as we have begun, and to keep quite clear of the Conflict between North and South.'[27]

---

24 See for example, Howard Jones, 'History and Mythology: The Crisis over British Intervention in the Civil War', in Robert E. May (ed.), *The Union, the Confederacy, and the Atlantic Rim* (West Lafayette: Purdue University Press, 1995), 34.
25 7 November 1862, Sir George Cornwall Lewis, printed memo: *Recognition of the Independence of the Southern States of the North American Union*, TNA WO 33/12, 2; 5 December 1861, Sir George Cornewall Lewis to Edward Twisleton, from Gilbert Frankland Lewis (ed.), *Letters of the Right Hon. Sir George Cornewall Lewis, Bart. to Various Friends* (London: Longmans, Green, and Co., 1870), 406.
26 16 October 1862, Somerset to Lewis, Somerset Papers, Aylesbury, D/RA/A/2A/256. See also Charles S. Williams and Frank J. Merli (eds.), 'The *Normandie* shows the way: report of a voyage from Cherbourg to Vera Cruz, 4 September 1862', *The Mariner's Mirror*, Vol. 54 (1968), 153-162.
27 18 October 1862, Palmerston to Russell, Palmerston Papers, Broadlands, GC/RU/1136-1148. Granville also shared with Russell his concerns that if it came to war with the United States, 'whether the French went with us or not, it is not unlikely that

The same week that Lewis highlighted the strategic problem which shallow-draft turret-ships now presented for any serious consideration of trans-Atlantic operations against the Union, the Admiralty received an alarming intelligence report from a British naval officer of the Royal Defence Commission of Canada, just returned from a tour of U.S. facilities. All across the North, steps were being rapidly taken to prepare for a major war with the British Empire. A U.S. Defense Committee in April 1862 had recommended to Congress upgrades to the Erie and Hudson Canal and the canal network connecting the Illinois River and Lake Michigan, so that 'the Lakes might be swarmed with [warships] built in security on the Ohio, Mississippi, Missouri, Illinois, Hudson &c to be withdrawn perhaps during the winter to act on the Atlantic coast and Gulf of Mexico.' This sort of strategic consolidation would be further facilitated 'by an efficient network of railways', so that 'a large amount of men and material of war' could be concentrated 'to any important point on the Northern frontier in a short space of time.' There were many thriving commercial port-cities on the Great Lakes such as Chicago, Cleveland, Toledo, Detroit, Newport and Buffalo. Sackets Harbor on Lake Ontario (in New York state), for example, 'was perfectly protected', with an old line-of-battle-ship on the stocks; this 'might be made available (by repair and partial re-construction) as a plated turret vessel.' Indeed, there were foundries and machine shops 'of every description exist at all the important places, many of which, now employed in the manufacture of Agricultural implements and Railway rolling stock, could, in the event of hostilities, be employed in the construction of Marine Engines and iron cased Vessels.'[28]

On the other hand, he considered U.S. government dockyards (Boston, Portsmouth, Brooklyn, Philadelphia and Washington) 'inadequate to either the construction or maintenance of a large fleet. Private yards partially supply the defect. The work done by contract is reported to be unsatisfactory and the expense to Government much greater than it would be if the public yards were on a more extended scale.' Some thirty-eight ironclads of various descriptions were under construction, with a flotilla of light-draft armoured gunboats already performing hard duty in the West, on the Mississippi River. The partially-armoured-frigate USS *New Ironsides* had been launched in May and was also in commission. As for ordnance and forts, he had interviewed Captain John A. Dahlgren (Chief of the new Bureau of Ordnance) at the Washington Navy Yard, who informed him that he was currently designing a smoothbore gun of 20-inch calibre, and 'spoke of adopting a plan which has been submitted to him of a gun with a 36 inch bore.' Perhaps more startling, Dahlgren had now come around to the idea—advanced by Ericsson—that 'for the protection of rivers and harbours the gun would soon be the principal part and the vessel only its

---

circumstances might arise which would enable the Emperor more freely to adopt any Foreign Policy either in Italy or elsewhere which might suit him', undated (presumably October 1862), Granville to Russell, Granville Papers, TNA PRO 30/29 18/7.
28   8 November 1862, Captain John Bythesea to Paget, TNA ADM 1/5791.

carriage.' American granite forts were meanwhile faced with iron plating, 'two plates of four inches thick being laid on the sides of the embrasures.' Boston harbor's Fort Warren was set to mount 330 guns with a garrison of 1,500 men. Over 300 guns from four large stone forts commanded the Narrows leading into New York Harbor, while any hostile warship attempting to force the entrance to Portland, Maine 'would be exposed to the combined fire of the Forts [Scammel and Preble] for about 6,000 yards [3.5 miles] of her passage. She could then lay above the bridge about 4,000 yards from the fort on Hog Island ledge [Fort Gorges]—the only one which could then bear on her.'[29] Thanks to massive funding contracts from Congress since the *Trent* Affair, nearly all the labourers in the area 'who could be advantageously employed were engaged upon the works at Portland.'[30] It was the greatest mobilisation of continental-scale human and natural resources in American history. 'We are not, it is true, in a condition for war with Great Britain just at this time', Welles reflected in his diary on 11 August 1862, 'but England is in scarcely a better condition for a war with us.'[31]

* * *

The immediate problem for the U.S. Navy, however, remained how to subdue the Southern Confederacy. After a six-day preparatory bombardment by 13-inch mortar schooners (which proved largely ineffective), a wooden squadron by Union flag officer David G. Farragut dashed past the forts below New Orleans on the night of 24 April 1862 and placed the South's largest city directly under its guns the next day. Two enormous Confederate casemated broadside-ironclads (*Louisiana* and *Mississippi*) which might have turned the tide of the battle lay unfinished and had to be scuttled. The Assistant Secretary of the Navy, Gustavus Vasa Fox, now envisaged deploying the new turret-ironclads in a coastal assault role against other fortified Southern ports. As Charleston, South Carolina was where the Civil War began, with rebel shore batteries firing upon Federal Fort Sumter in the middle of the harbor (12-13 April

---

29   Begun in 1857, Fort Gorges was a two-tiered, six-sided casemated work nearly as large as Fort Sumter (Charleston, South Carolina). During the Civil War she was initially armed with 10-inch Rodman guns, firing a 100lb. shell with a 15lb. charge up to 4,800 yards at 30-degrees elevation. See for example, Jeffrey M. Dorwart, *Fort Mifflin of Philadelphia: An Illustrated History* (Philadelphia: University of Pennsylvania Press, 1998), 109-31, Nelson H. Lawry, Glen M. Williford, and Leo K. Polaski, *Portsmouth Harbor's Military and Naval Heritage* (Charleston: Arcadia Publishing, 2004), 39-46, and Leo Polaski and Glen Williford, *New York City's Harbor Defenses* (Charleston: Arcadia Publishing, 2003), 15-34. See also Warren Ripley, *Artillery and Ammunition of the Civil War* (New York: Van Nostrand, 1970), 71-85.
30   8 November 1862, Captain John Bythesea to Paget, TNA ADM 1/5791.
31   Journal entry dated 11 August 1862, in Howard K. Beale (ed.), *Diary of Gideon Welles: Secretary of the Navy under Lincoln and Johnson*, 3 vols. (New York: W. W. Norton & Company, Inc., 1960), 1: 79.

1861), this 'hotbed of Secession' would be an especially valuable prize for propaganda as well as strategic reasons.[32] To test the notion, the Navy Department ordered the USS *Monitor* south to attack Wilmington, North Carolina in company with the newly commissioned monitors *Passaic* and *Montauk*. She had already attempted to drive up the James River as far as Richmond in May 1862, but her progress was blocked eight miles short of the Confederate capital by obstructions and heavy plunging fire from Fort Darling which riddled the USS *Galena*. On the night of 30 December, the *Monitor* encountered a fierce gale off Cape Hatteras, on her way to being towed to Beaufort, North Carolina. Contrary to Ericsson's instructions, the crew had packed oakum under the base of the turret (his design made the juncture watertight by the sheer weight of the iron turret, 160-tons, set on a brass ring in the deck).[33] Rather than cast loose her hawsers, the *Monitor* was also dragged through mountainous waves by her pitching paddle-wheel escort so that one line snapped and the low-freeboard vessel became unmanageable. Soon flooding dampened the coals, gained on the pumps, and by 11pm the order was given to abandon ship. A few hours later 'Ericsson's Folly' sank to the bottom. Sixteen of her crew perished, while forty-seven were successfully rescued from the freezing, tumultuous sea. The loss of the *Monitor* was treated as a national disaster, but the exact circumstances of her sinking were attributed more to chance than inherent unseaworthiness of the low-freeboard design. Both the *Passaic* and *Montauk* encountered the same storm and survived, the latter because her commander ordered her hawsers cut. Three weeks later, sister-ship USS *Weehawken* likewise encountered a 'hard gale' with seas '30 feet high' on her voyage south to Port Royal. But casting loose her tow and properly battened down, the monitor 'rode it like a duck', as her commanding officer later wrote to his wife. No other Union monitors were lost at sea during the Civil War (although many high-freeboard vessels were).[34]

---

32 See for example 13 May 1862, Welles to flag officer Samuel Francis Du Pont, US National Archives, RG 45, Entry 15.

33 For the *Monitor*'s sinking see for example the account by Francis P. Butts, 'The Loss of the *Monitor*', in Johnson and Buel, *Battles and Leaders*, 1: 745-8; also the description by Donald L. Canney, *The Old Steam Navy Volume Two: The Ironclads, 1842-1885* (Annapolis: Naval Institute Press, 1993), 29-34; for the *Montauk*'s voyage see Samuel T. Browne, *First Cruise of the Montauk, Personal Narratives of Events in the War of the Rebellion*, No. 1, Second Series (Providence: The N. Bangs Williams Co., 1880), 15-24. There was also speculation that the sharply angulated upper and lower hulls of the original *Monitor* (unlike those in the finer ship lines of the subsequent *Passaic*- and *Canonicus*-classes, for example) started to separate at their juncture, due to the enormous force of the waves pounding the vessel on her final voyage. Archaeological evidence does seem to offer any clues, but neither did the upper and lower hulls separate on her maiden voyage through stormy seas 7-8 March 1862.

34 22 January 1863, John to Anne Rodgers, Rodgers Family Papers, Library of Congress, Manuscript Division, Box 22. See W. Craig Gaines, *Encyclopedia of Civil War Shipwrecks* (Baton Rouge: Louisiana State Press, 2008). The *Weehawken* sank at anchor off Charleston on 6 December 1863 when her trim was made too low by the bow, while a forward hatch was accidentally left open during a moderate swell. As water quietly poured

By the beginning of April 1863 the Union Navy had amassed outside Charleston Harbor seven *Passaic*-class monitors, *New Ironsides*, and another experimental ironclad, USS *Keokuk* (a low-freeboard ram with two fixed towers mounting one 11-inch Dahlgren gun each, but armoured with a layering of iron bars and wood to less than 6-inches total thickness.)[35] The ironclad squadron's commanding officer, Rear-Admiral Samuel Francis Du Pont, was sceptical of his own ships' ability to withstand the heavy gauntlet of fire which Confederate engineers had carefully devised for two years—from the outer defences centred upon Fort Sumter (a large two-tiered casemated structure on a man-made island in the middle of the main ship channel) to the city's wharf batteries.[36] A line of obstructions stretched from Sumter to Fort Moultrie on Sullivan's Island, with two formidable Confederate steam-rams with angled-armour 4-inches thick lurking beyond. Du Pont had no clear idea if the obstructions were also laced with explosive torpedoes, or how to clear them effectively while under fire at less than 1,000 yards from multiple directions. His goal seems to have been only to silence Sumter first by pressing his monitors as close as possible, while his deeper-draught flagship *New Ironsides* poured in supporting fire.[37] The subsequent attack on the afternoon of 7 April was soundly repulsed. The broadside-ironclad could barely stem the tide and bring her guns to bear, while the monitors bunched before the line of obstructions, firing their ponderous 15-inch Dahlgrens as best they could through the thick smoke and roaring hail of fire which the rebels rained down upon them. Finally, the admiral signalled a retreat, but the *Keokuk* had been penetrated so many times that she sank in shallow water the next morning. All of the monitors had absorbed an incredible amount of hits—four of them were disabled in one degree or another—but neither had Sumter been seriously damaged.[38]

into the vessel undetected, dragging the bow below water and the screw out, the pumps were unable to reach the flooded compartments until it was too late.

35 For the USS *Keokuk*, see for example S. Kirby, 'USS *Keokuk*' in John Roberts (ed.), *Warship Volume VII* (London: Conway Maritime Press, 1983), 244-50.
36 See for example 26 December 1862, 'Circular of instructions from the commanding general at Charleston, S.C., *Official Records of the Union and Confederate Navies in the War of the Rebellion* ('*ORN*'), Series 1, Vol. 14, 102-5.
37 'Order of battle and plan of attack upon Charleston, South Carolina' in *Report of the Secretary of the Navy in Relation to Armored Vessels* (Washington: Government Printing Office: 1864), 60-1.
38 See for example Rear-Admiral C. R. P. Rodgers, 'Du Pont's Attack at Charleston', in Johnson and Buel, *Battles and Leaders*, 4: 37; also Robert Erwin Johnson, 'Ships Against Forts: Charleston, 7 April 1863', *The American Neptune*, Vol. 57, No. 2 (Spring 1997), 123-35. For the operations of the South Atlantic Blockading Squadron see Robert M. Browning, Jr., *Success Is All That Was Expected: The South Atlantic Blockading Squadron During the Civil War* (Washington, D.C.: Brassey's Inc., 2002). For a vivid account of the assault generally see Ivan Musicant, *Divided Waters: The Naval History of the Civil War* (Edison: Castle Books, 2000, reprint of 1995 original), 368-408. USS *Weehawken*'s turret jammed when struck between the base of the turret and the deck, while *Passaic* had her turret base bulged in enough to jam one of the gun slides; *Patapsco* was meanwhile struck

Du Pont refused to risk his ships in any further attack, and then blamed the Navy Department for pressuring him to pit ships against forts with 'machines' rather than proper ships.

A major press scandal and Congressional inquiry followed. Either Welles and Fox had foolishly placed too much faith in John Ericsson, or Du Pont had mis-used the national resources entrusted to him—or something else. As early as September 1862, Ericsson had warned Fox that 'that the number of 15-inch guns rather than the number of vessels will decide your success against the Stone forts.'[39] While Fox waited anxiously in Washington for news of the assault, Ericsson was more certain of failure than success, precisely because he was 'so much in the habit of estimating force and resistance'. Seven monitors only floated fourteen guns while Charleston's defences bristled with hundreds of them. At best (i.e., provided there were no obstructions), the low-freeboard, heavily-armoured vessels might run the gauntlet straight to Charleston and hopefully compel the rebel stronghold to surrender. Any broadside-rams which opposed them could be quickly blasted out of the way by the big, armour-crushing guns of the monitors. But a standup duel against the forts themselves? 'A single shot will sink a Ship', Ericsson pointed out, 'while a hundred rounds cannot silence a fort.' The only thing that concerned him was 'that the contest will end without the loss of that prestige which your Iron Clads have conferred on the Nation abroad.'[40]

Even as Du Pont rallied the support of influential friends in Washington, his case was undermined by the Confederates themselves. Believing that the recent repulse at Charleston had proven the Yankee monitors were far less powerful than the Northern press had played them up to be, they sortied out from Savannah on the early morning of 17 June in their newest ram, the CSS *Atlanta*. With a spar-torpedo projecting forward from her armoured ram bow, she would quickly sink any monitor which got in her way, then proceed to roll up the Union blockade of wooden vessels. But two monitors had been waiting for her to emerge at Wassaw Sound, and at 300 yards a 400-pound cored-shot fired from the 15-inch gun of the *Weehawken* with a 30lb charge smashed through her 4-inch armoured casemate (sharply angled at 30-degrees to the horizon)—scattering the interior with iron splinters and jagged shards of wood, and concussing nearly everyone on the gundeck. It was the single most powerful blow ever inflicted upon a warship up to that time. Another 15-inch shot ripped off the top of the *Atlanta*'s armoured-pilot house, 'wounding two pilots and stunning the men at

---

at least 47 times; *Nahant* 36, *Nantucket* 51, *Catskill* 20, and *Montauk* 14; see the individual battle/damage reports in *ORN*, Series 1, Vol. 14, 10-24. The most serious damage to the ironclads was inflicted by the four 10-inch smoothbore Columbiads and two 7-inch Brooke heavy rifled guns of Fort Sumter and the five 10-inch Columbiads of Battery Bee, near Fort Moultrie; see 'Return of guns and mortars at forts and batteries in Charleston Harbor, engaged April 7 1863, *ORN*, Series 1, Vol. 14, 83.

39 30 September 1862, Ericsson to Fox, Ericsson Papers, Library of Congress.
40 10 April 1863, Ericsson to Fox, Ericsson Papers, Philadelphia, Box 6.

the wheel.'⁴¹ Within minutes the Confederates ran up a white flag; the battle was over. Not only did this go far in redeeming the U.S. Navy, it spelled doom for all of the other Confederate rams under laboured construction throughout the South. Ericsson typically analysed the after-action reports of the monitor captain and the engineers assigned to inspect the captured *Atlanta*: the 15-inch shot didn't just defeat 4-inches of armour plating backed by 18-inches of oak and pine. Having struck at a compound angle of 22-degrees meant that 'independent of deflection, the shot must pass through nearly five feet of obstruction—namely, eleven inches of iron and four feet of wood.' Thus it also 'proved that the 4½-inch vertical plating of the magnificent *Warrior* of nine thousand tons—the pride of the British Admiralty—would be but slight protection against the 15-inch monitor guns'.⁴² When Du Pont was later replaced by Dahlgren in command of the South Atlantic Blockading Squadron, his successor was instructed by Welles not to attempt a reckless thrust into Charleston Harbor, or an open, prolonged duel with the outer forts: 'the Department is disinclined to have its only iron-clad squadron incur extreme risks…Other operations of great importance on our southern coast are pending, and in case of a foreign war, which has sometimes seemed imminent, these vessels will be indispensable for immediate use.'⁴³

Little did Welles know, but by the beginning of 1863, the Controller of the Royal Navy agreed that the monitors had conferred 'enormous defensive power…a power which I believe renders the Americans practically unassailable in their own waters.' Since the Battle of Hampton Roads, Milne's officers had been assiduously gathering intelligence (mostly gleaned from Northern newspapers) about the various Union ironclads. In forwarding these to the Admiralty on 12 December 1862, Milne remarked how the Americans had given prominence to 'the power of using their Guns ahead and on the Bow, which, I consider for vessels of every class, but more crucially in the smaller clad Vessels, is an absolute necessity'. Robinson thought, however, that 'there appears to be no novel or important principle elucidated by these constructions.' The *New Ironsides* was no better than the *Gloire* or the *Royal Oak*-class of wooden broadside-ironclads. And the low-freeboard turret-ships were 'mere Rafts carrying very few heavy guns propelled at moderate speed, and though perfectly well adapted for the Inland waters of that great Continent, and most formidable as Harbour Defences, [were] not in any sense sea going Ships of War.' As such they were not a direct threat to Britain. 'If again, Admiral Milne means that we have not yet an Iron plated Flotilla capable of going into the inland waters, rivers and Harbours

---

41   17 June 1863, John Rodgers to Du Pont, *ORN*, Series 1, Vol. 14, 265-6.
42   Captain John Ericsson, 'The Early Monitors', in Johnson and Buel, *Battles and Leaders of the Civil War*, 4: 30-1.
43   9 October 1863, Welles to Dahlgren, Welles Papers, Library of Congress. 'May you for a moment lose sight of the passing necessity of fighting forts,' Ericsson wrote to Fox, in his argument for a single turreted USS *Puritan*, with thicker armour and heavier guns than a double-turreted version could float; 5 August 1863, Gustavus Vasa Fox Papers, New York Historical Society Library Manuscripts, New York, Box 6.

of the United States, and when there, able to fight an Action on equal terms with the description of Vessels which will be found awaiting us, he is perfectly right and it will be only necessary to observe that such a proceeding on our part is simply impossible.'[44] There was no provision for such a force in the latest estimates, and even if there was it was not clear how to bridge the divide which the (unseaworthy) turret-ships had now made of the Atlantic Ocean.

As 1863 rolled on, this became an increasingly serious concern. In January insurgents in the Russian vassal-state of Poland made an armed bid for independence, encouraged by the Tsar's defeat in the Crimean War and the wave of nationalist movements in both Italy and the American South. Russia responded swiftly and harshly, determined to make an example of the Poles lest other portions of the vast Russian Empire followed suit. Reaction in Liberal Britain, controversially at times a champion of the 'right' of self-determination of peoples, was dead-set against the brutal, oppressive policies of Tsar Alexander II. 'The British subject is a citizen of the world. He has to do with all nations, and is interested in them', proclaimed *The Times* on 2 April 1863. 'He wishes for them what he wishes and obtains for himself. His Government carries out his wish.' But this leader was commenting on Palmerston's speech at a banquet in Glasgow that day before; where he declared his wish that his government could indeed 'decide the destiny of that noble people' (of Poland). However, after extolling the virtue of the Crimean War as having at least brought England and France together like never before, he could only 'presume that even the most enthusiastic admirers of that noble Polish nation would hardly, under the circumstances of the times, expect or ask that any forcible intervention should by this country be undertaken.' The same went for the American Civil War, for 'any interference on the part of the nations of Europe, so far from extinguishing the flame, would, in all human probability, have only made it burn fiercer and with greater heat.'[45] Yet later that same week, Scottish Lord Napier, writing from St. Petersburg as British Minister to Russia, warned that the Tsar's government feared the British might nevertheless be drawn, 'by their connections with France, by the force of circumstances & popular feeling into War, without deliberate premeditation.' Defensive preparations were therefore now underway. 'The works of Cronstadt are being hastily furnished with Guns, and iron plates are being sent down to be applied as armour for some of the Vessels there, or as some say to be used as clothing for the Granite Fortresses before the Harbour.'[46]

---

44 30 January 1863, Robinson to Board, TNA ADM 1/5840.
45 2 April 1863, *The Times*. See also Tytus Filipowicz (ed.), *Confidential Correspondence of the British Government Respecting the Insurrection in Poland 1863* (Paris: Librairie H. Le Soldier, 1914).
46 5 April 1863, Napier to Russell, forwarded from the Foreign Office to Admiralty in TNA ADM 1/5851; Francis Napier, 10th Lord Napier, was formerly the British Minister to the United States between 1857-1859. The Russian Navy also committed to laying down a squadron of *Passaic*-class monitors, the plans of which had been forwarded by the U.S.

There was talk of world war.[47] From the beginning of the internecine conflict in America, Russia was alarmed at the potential demise of the United States; the only other geo-strategic counterweight in the mid nineteenth-century to the meddlesome 'maritime powers', Britain and France.[48] As tensions heightened over Poland the Russian Navy sent a squadron of screw-frigates to the Union on a 'diplomatic visit'— to avoid being bottled up in Cronstadt by a British blockade in the event of war, and to be used as commerce raiders against the British Empire. When Milne made his own goodwill tour of the Northern States in September 1863, he was surprised to find five Russian warships anchored in New York Harbor. They were armed with Dahlgren-like 60-pound smoothbores, reportedly 'going to the Pacific', and were packed with surplus crewmembers in case fast American steamers needed to be purchased on the spot and commissioned as Russian cruisers (as had been done with Confederate raiders built in Britain like the CSS *Georgia*.)[49] Palmerston was not especially concerned. 'The Russians might imagine that in such a case [war] they could intercept our Gold Ships from Australia, or prey upon our Commerce elsewhere,' he wrote to Russell, 'but their Ships would be sure to be overtaken and taken at last.' Yet in advising Russell on his diplomatic addresses to the Great Powers about the possible detachment of a kingdom of Poland from Russia, the Premier thought it unwise to mention 'a possible war with the United States. It would not be well to tell the French that we could not

Navy Department; see for example, Stephen McLaughlin, 'Russia's "American" Monitors: The *Uragan* Class', in John Jordan (ed.), *Warship 2012* (London: Conway, 2011), 98-112.

47 See for example, 3 September 1863, 'Russia and America', The *Philadelphia Inquirer*.
48 See for example, Frank. A. Golder, 'The American Civil War Through the Eyes of a Russian Diplomat', *The American Historical Review*, Vol. 26, No. 3 (April 1921), 454-63. *Punch* (24 October 1863) ridiculed how 'Extremes Meet'; Lincoln and Alexander II shaking hands as war-mongering despots ruthlessly suppressing their respective rebellions (though ignoring their wide-spread liberation of slaves and serfs). 'Come to my arms, and let us be allies!' declares 'Abe'. 'We'll squelch John Bull, and scuttle Britain's isle; but let us go and liquor up meanwhile.' See also William C. Fuller, Jr., *Strategy and Power in Russia 1600-1914* (New York: The Free Press, 1992), 266-73, 286-9.
49 18 October 1863, Milne to Admiralty, TNA ADM 1/5821. For Russo-American relations at this time see for example 5 February 1866, *The Times*; Charles Boynton, *The Four Great Powers: England, France, Russia and America; Their Policy, Resources, and Probable Future* (Cincinnati: C. F. Vent & Co., 1866); James Morton Callahan, 'Russo-American Relations During the American Civil War', *Diplomatic History*, Series 1, No. 1 (January 1908), 1-44; Norman E. Saul, *Distant Friends: The United States and Russia, 1763-1867* (Lawrence: University Press of Kansas, 1991); Frank A. Golder, 'The American Civil War Through the Eyes of a Russian Diplomat', *American Historical Review*, Vol. 26, No. 3 (April 1921), 454-63; Robin D. S. Higham, 'The Russian Fleet on the Eastern Seaboard, 1863-1863: A Maritime Chronology', *American Neptune*, Vol. 20, No. 1 (January 1960), 49-61; Howard I. Kushner, 'The Russian Fleet and the American Civil War: Another View', *The Historian*, 34: 4 (August 1972), 633-49; and C. Douglas Kroll, *'Friends in Peace and War': The Russian Navy's Landmark Visit to Civil War San Francisco* (Washington DC: Potomac Books, Inc., 2007). For Milne's tour see for example Courtemanche, *No Need of Glory*, 119-24.

carry on war in Europe as well as in America. They might take advantage of such a Hint if ever we became embroiled with the Americans.' On the other hand, even without Austria's support, Britain and France if 'really determined' could probably force Russia to give up Poland. In such a case, Palmerston even thought Sweden 'would probably give us effective assistance'; another scheme from the Crimean War days. But here too there was no point in advertising all of the practical and strategic considerations for not engaging in such a conflict.[50] At the same time, the death of King Fredrick VIII of Denmark (15 November 1863) and the issue of his succession led to renewed tensions between Denmark and the German Confederation over the fate of the duchies of Schleswig and Holstein. This presented the ambitious Prime Minister of Prussia, Otto von Bismarck, with an opportunity to galvanise German nationalism under Prussian leadership by not only supporting the military occupation of Holstein but invading north (with the support of Austria) into Schleswig as well. How the other Great Powers might react was uncertain. 'I think this country has passed through the warlike phase of its character…and could never again support a great war', wrote the Editor of *The Times*, John T. Delane, to cabinet member Sir Charles Wood. 'You must', he urged, 'keep us out of war as we shall soon lose that great fictitious reputation on which all our power is based. We might manage one in India, but in Europe or America we should soon see our real weakness exposed.'[51]

---

50 19 October, 29 September and 2 October 1863, Palmerston to Russell Papers, TNA PRO 30-22, 22.
51 18 October 1863, Delane to Wood, from E. D. Steele, *Palmerston and Liberalism, 1855-1865* (Cambridge: Cambridge University Press, 1991), 245.

4

'We should be laughed at if we stood by'

Indeed, it was partially because of Britain's less than ideal experience of war against Russia—a sense of tarnished prestige—that naval and military forums like the Royal United Service Institution had thrived. 'I think that the want of some arena in which professional questions can be calmly and dispassionately discussed is most strongly felt, particularly since the commencement of the present Session of Parliament', declared Vice-Admiral Sir Frederick Grey—the First Naval Lord of the Admiralty—in the opening address of RUSI's 32nd Anniversary meeting of 14 March 1863. 'I think no person present who has heard or read the debates which have taken place on the House of Commons during the present Session can have failed to be struck with the unfitness of such an assembly for discussing professional questions.' Given the paucity of members with any 'scientific knowledge' it was no wonder that the public—including *The Times*—was so often misinformed. But eleven days later this notion was complicated by a well-attended and much-anticipated presentation on 'Iron-Clad Seagoing Shield Ships', by Captain Coles, who had only the month before published a pamphlet comparing *Iron-Clad Ships with Broadside Ports, and Ships With Revolving Shields*.[1] The day after the lengthy discussion which followed, Coles also appeared 'with extreme diffidence' at the Institution of Naval Architects 'to answer

---

1   14 March 1863, *Journal of the Royal United Service Institution*, Whitehall Yard, Vol. VI, 1862-3 (London: W. Mitchell and Son, 1863), xiv; *A Comparison between Iron-Clad Ships with Broadside Ports, and Ships With Revolving Shields* (Portsea: James Griffin, February 1863); Robinson objected to the main points set forth in this pamphlet in his 24 February 1863 letter to the Board, TNA ADM 1/5840. He later rejected a proposed seagoing ironclad with two-turrets submitted by Coles—the 'third or fourth' one so rejected—the Controller noted to the Board on 16 April. Despite the complaints received by Coles, Robinson insisted there had only been 'an opposition to crude and impracticable ideas, which it was right and proper should be offered by those who have the responsibility of spending the Public Money and whose business it is to see that, Ships which can only carry certain weights are not burdened with double the amount their flotation will support'; 20 April 1861, TNA ADM 1/5840.

the attack…upon my principle of arming and protecting guns and their crews in ships of war'—which had been made by Reed in a paper the day before. Here Coles noted the authority of the members, while he was only 'a man who passed the best part of his life at sea'. Yet Reed had chosen to compare HMS *Defence* with an 'imaginary shield-ship', while Coles showed that in relation with the actual *Prince Albert* building the turret-armed ironclad would boast a much heavier weight of fire from its larger (though fewer) guns. He did not, however, note that *Defence* carried full masts and sails, whereas *Prince Albert* was destined for two-pole steadying sails only, other than that 'a small portion of the great difference of tonnage would be ample to allow for masting and seagoing qualities.' This, as Reed and Robinson had already pointed out, would complicate the fields of fire enjoyed by the *Prince Albert*, *Royal Sovereign* and the American turret vessels. But Coles persisted in comparing Reed's new central-battery HMS *Favorite* (to be armed with four Armstrong 110-pounder rifled breechloaders) with a hypothetical sail-and-turret-ship of equal tonnage on his system (calling it, somewhat facetiously, the '*Naughty Child*'), armed with three 300-pounders and using his system of 'tripod' masts which helped alleviate obstruction of the top deck. Reed then replied that the imaginary Coles turret vessel ('as I prefer to call her, the *Very Naughty Child*') would not actually be able to mount two turrets with such weight, and indeed he would 'not admit any proposition of any gentleman who is not a naval architect on a naval architectural question.' In rough seas, however, he had little doubt that his *Favorite*, with her 6-foot bulwark, would be a drier ship and able to fight her guns better. Of course, he was speculating as much as Coles: there were neither central-battery nor sail-and-turret ironclads anywhere afloat to really know either way; only the various figures in play and one's understanding of the sea. But the real worry, he concluded, was that 'the Board of Admiralty will be used as a weapon to overthrow scientific knowledge, and to goad naval designers into the adoption of plans to which the laws of nature are essentially and unalterably adverse.'[2]

Were Robinson's rejections of the various plans submitted by Coles personal? When similar suggestions came in the Controller was equally clear what he wanted to see. Captain C. S. Dowson of the Royal Fusiliers was told that the problem with his plan for six 300-pounders on turntables in the centre of the ship, run out through armoured broadside ports, was that 'Ships intended to carry a small number of guns of the greatest calibre and weight should have those guns more concentrated than he

---

[2] 27 March 1863, 'On Iron-Clad Seagoing Shield-Ships', *Transactions of the Institution of Naval Architects*, Vol. IV (London: 1863), 99-117. Chairing the session, the President of the Institution, former First Lord of the Admiralty Sir John Pakington, teased this was 'one of those cases which we find in most private families, where the favorite is very apt to be the naughty child.' Perhaps Pakington's own irony was that he was First Lord when Boards of Admiralty ordered the *Warrior* as well as HMS *Captain*. Likewise, Reed's later design for HMS *Monarch*, his own high-freeboard sail-and-turret ironclad with centrally grouped turrets (which Coles condemned), bore a remarkable resemblance to the enclosed diagrams of the *Naughty Child* envisaged by Coles, though with tripod masting.

has shewn in his drawing, so as to render it practicable to increase the thickness of the armour plating as required'.[3] In other words, the greater the guns, the more protection they should have. Likewise, the smaller the vessel the more concentrated the armour scheme and thus thicker armour plating. Robinson's report to the Admiralty coincided remarkably with one submitted that same day in early 1864 to the Board from the far side of the Atlantic. Here, Captain James Goodenough wrote of his recent arrival in the United States, visiting Lord Lyons in Washington. Before this he'd spent six days in Boston and was met 'with great courtesy from the Commandant of the Navy Yard by whose permission I visited the ships under construction consisting of a double turret-ship half finished[,] three light draft Monitors in various stages[,] and two of the new sloops of 3000 tons.' The British naval attaché had already sketched how the Union monitors' turret guns were operated and their friction gear yet was hoping for 'better drawings at this ordnance department.' He'd also met with Major Thomas Rodman of the U.S. Army, who invited him to witness the casting of one of the Yankees' mammoth 15-inch smoothbores.[4] There could be no doubt that the Americans were fully sold on the idea of 'monster guns' mounted in heavily-armoured revolving turrets. These could destroy any ironclad afloat—while the fast new sloops were clearly intended to sweep the high seas of enemy (probably meaning British and/or French) merchant vessels. By contrast, two days later (on 6 January), the Board noted that new flagship for the North America and West Indies Station, the wooden screw ship-of-the-line HMS *Duncan*, was to have a crew of no less than 900, manning some one-hundred relatively light (65cwt) 8-inch shell-guns and 32-pounders.[5]

Yet around this time the War Office informed the Admiralty it had just accepted Sir William Armstrong's offer to build two 8-inch (7-ton) and two 10-inch (12-ton) guns for experiment, suggesting that the future of naval hegemony indeed belonged to ships armed with the heaviest possible ordnance. Captain Sir Astley Cooper Key on HMS *Excellent*, however, noted there were practical limits to consider. 'An Armour Plated Ship should certainly be armed with guns capable of penetrating her own side at a certain limited distance', he informed the Board. 800-yards was a reasonable range for this, given the likelihood of hitting a moving target from a moving platform. He thought 6½-tons was the likely limit of guns which could be 'worked in a sea way',

3   4 April 1864, Robinson to Board, TNA ADM 1/5889.
4   4 April 1864, Goodenough to Secretary of the Admiralty, TNA ADM 1/5879. See also Lothar W. Hilbert, 'The Early Years of the Military Attaché Service in British Diplomacy', *Journal of the Society for Army Historical Research*, Vol. 37, No. 152 (December 1959), 164-71. Goodenough refers to the double-turreted USS *Monadnock*, commissioned in October 1864; probably the *Casco*-class monitors *Casco*, *Nausett* and *Squando*; the *Contoocook*-class screw-sloop USS *Pompanoosuc* (whose keel had just been laid but was never completed); and possibly the 3,800-ton screw-frigate USS *Ammonoosuc* (launched in July 1864); see Stephen P. Carlson, *Charlestown Navy Yard Historic Resource Study*, Volume 3 of 3 (Boston: National Park Service, 2010), 1159-71.
5   6 January 1864, Special Minutes, TNA ADM 3/271. The 8-inch smoothbore weighed nearly 3½-tons and fired a spherical shell weighing 49 pounds.

while heavier guns were bound to be so difficult to handle that they 'should be used for rare and special service only.'[6] As for mounting such weapons in revolving turrets, Robinson revealed a certain ambivalence. The Belgian government requested details of target tests against Coles towers which were to be used in the new British coastal forts—in exchange for information it had on the new heavy Krupp guns. But the Controller could only reply to the permanent Admiralty Secretary, William Romaine, that his department knew nothing about the tests or an intention to use Coles towers in this fashion.[7]

Meantime, the Admiralty happily endorsed the establishment of a College of Naval Architecture, to replace the School opened at Portsmouth in 1811 but closed in 1832. This would be open to the public, useful to the merchant service as well as the navy, and its graduates 'would be eagerly sought after and appreciated.' Already the issue of proper naval architecture (or not) had become a public one. Enclosed in the Admiralty's deliberation on the proposed College was a 1863 pamphlet on *Our Dockyards: Past and Present State of Naval Construction in the Government Service* by Sir William Snow Harris, forwarded to Robinson by Paget as a form of warning, since they would 'probably be interrogated' by Parliament over what types of ironclads the Royal Navy was going to introduce next. 'How comes it that the most powerful naval and commercial country...is absolutely without any public establishment for the cultivation of that science upon which its glory and its influence in the scale of nations so mainly depends', asked the pamphlet? Recent warship-building in Britain, it went further, could be 'figuratively represented as the departing rays of a setting sun.' Reed's appointment as Chief Constructor, in July 1863, was all the more suspect (even 'rather despotic') since he was appointed from the private sector over the heads of established master shipwrights in the various government yards. The core problem was 'administrative'—a shot across the bows of the Controller's Department currently under Robinson. And the primary case in point were the cupola or turret-ships of Coles, where 'a sufficient amount of inductive philosophy has not been brought to bear upon the question and propriety of the construction of such ships.' The converted *Royal Sovereign*, though still far from complete, was manifestly a failure—at least if the Federals' experience against Charleston Harbor (7 April 1863) with their own turret vessels could be considered a guide. What the country needed were more armoured-frigates, not unwieldy floating gun platforms pitted against forts.[8] *The Times* seemed to echo this judgment in early 1864 by pointing to events across the sea. In the combined operations-siege of Charleston, South Carolina, the Union Navy had 'failed in the part assigned to it, and how complete the failure has been the American

6   8 January 1864, Key to Admiralty, TNA ADM 1/5905 (from War Office).
7   11 January 1864, Robinson to Romaine, TNA ADM 1/5889.
8   13 January 1864, Admiralty, 'College of Naval Architecture', TNA ADM 1/5882; Sir William Snow Harris, *Our Dockyards: Past and Present State of Naval Construction in the Government Service* (Plymouth: 1863), 4, 20, 25. Successful graduates of the former School included Isaac Watts, who went on to design *Warrior*.

public has only just discovered. The truth has long been suspected from the inaction of the fleet of ironclads throughout the summer and autumn.'[9]

Nor was the anti-monitor sentiment entirely an English (or 'anti-Yankee') one. The U.S. Secretary of the Navy's long-awaited, controversial *Report* on armoured vessels, published late in the spring of 1864, was obliged to cite the opinion of Rear-Admiral Louis M. Goldsborough, for example, who thought the turret vessels over-specialised. Ironclads as a specie of warship ought 'to be made to answer as many naval purposes as possible, and their cost alone,' he added, 'is enough to determine this question.' While the Union Navy's monitors perhaps invoked a sense of 'charm of novelty in construction, or quaintness in appearance', he doubted their ultimate utility outside of inland waters; the contested zones of the Civil War itself. 'Popular opinion is not always right on such subjects,' he concluded, nor was it likely to be correct 'when it runs counter to popular naval opinion'—the latter being associated with actual naval professionalism.[10] Tasked with taking Charleston at all costs with his South Atlantic Blockading Squadron, Dahlgren's assessment of the monitors, however, started with their endurance; eight of them had absorbed 1,030 hits from weapons like the Army's coastal 10-inch Columbiad[11], often under 1,000 yards, in the operations against Morris Island. The *Passaic*-class USS *Montauk* was struck 214 times; her sister-ship *Weehawken* 187. But the real question at stake was 'turret vs. broadside', or as Dahlgren identified, the 'desire for comparison which rages just now'. Here the monitors came out on top against the *New Ironsides*, which drew too much water and exposed her unarmoured ends to enemy fire at awkward moments when the channel tide proved unmanageable—unable to fire her guns in return:

> Keeping in view the peculiar exigencies of the case, which required light draught and great ordnance power, it appears that the selection of the department could not have been more judicious in preferring a number of Monitors to operate from a heavy frigate as a base; and if the intent of the department could have been carried out in regard to numbers, we should now have been in entire possession of the coast from the capes of Virginia to New Orleans, including Wilmington, Charleston, Mobile, & c.[12]

9 14 January 1864, *The Times*.
10 *Report*, 26 February 1864, 571-9.
11 This 7½-ton, hollow-cast, shell-firing smoothbore fired a solid shot weighing 128-pounds. 'The force of the 10-inch shot must be experienced to be appreciated', noted Dahlgren, who at times accompanied the monitors into action, and was 'nearly shaken off my feet in the pilot-house when engaging Moultrie'; ibid., 28 January 1864, Dahlgren to Welles, 585. See also Alexander L. Holley, *A Treatise on Ordnance and Armour* (New York: D. Van Nostrand, 1865), 106-21.
12 *Report*, 28 January 1864, Dahlgren to Welles, 579-88.

But even Russell confided to Somerset days earlier that although Washington D.C. was probably sharpening its anti-British rhetoric 'before the next Autumn Election of President', he hoped again that Milne's replacement as North America and West Indies Station C-in-C, Rear-Admiral Sir James Hope, 'will be very cautious.' The First Lord thought that while the American state of feeling was 'unsatisfactory' neither was it 'fair towards this country after all we have lately done.' This was in reference to Russell ordering earlier that October that the two turreted ironclad 'Rams' built by Lairds in Liverpool be seized by government officials—before they could slip out, join the Confederate Navy, and wreak havoc against the Union blockade of the South.[13] But unlike the press, British officials could not afford to complain too loudly.

As Russell noted to Lord Lyons, this was also because of the nation's current preoccupation with Prussia and Denmark.[14] The Foreign Secretary had been repeatedly warned by Somerset about dispatching the Channel Squadron to Danish waters—possibly to intervene in the conflict there. This included sending the ships from their current position at Gibraltar back to readiness at Plymouth or Portsmouth, where disease would inevitably affect sailors on shore leave, resulting in a 'large proportion of men on the sick list.' Possible operations in the North Sea by British heavy ironclads had to now be considered carefully since there was 'no fleet at present to oppose them, and they are less suited to purposes of blockade, if such measure should be resorted to, than lighter wooden vessels.' At this time of year, the weather in those waters also meant 'great risk...for the mere purpose of a demonstration.' When Russell demurred, the First Lord assured him that he had not countermanded any order to the Fleet. Although intended to bolster forces in the Mediterranean, the converted wooden-hulled broadside-ironclad HMS *Royal Oak* had been detained, with two more ironclads being commissioned that very day (11 January). 'This is the most formidable force taken all together', he pointed out, 'which has ever been afloat.' It was left for the Cabinet to decide what to do with it.[15] In a private letter to Sir

13   24 January 1864, Russell to Somerset, Somerset Papers, Aylesbury, D/RA/A/2A/53; 25 January 1864, Somerset to Russell, TNA Russell Papers, PRO 30-22, 26. On the other hand, Lyons admitted his relief to Milne that the U.S. government had not seemed to notice, as Milne previously reported, that H.M. Dockyard at Bermuda had been used to repair vessels running the Union blockade, 10 January 1864, Lyons to Milne, TNA ADM 1/5871.
14   January 1864, Russell to Lyons, TNA Russell Papers, PRO 30-22, 97. For Britain and the Second Schleswig War (February-October 1864), see for example, Keith A. P. Sandiford, *Great Britain and the Schleswig-Holstein Question 1848-64* (Toronto: University of Toronto Press, 1975); and Adolphus William Ward and George Peabody Gooch (eds.), *The Cambridge History of British Foreign Policy*, 1783-1919, 3 vols., Volume II: 1815-1866 (Cambridge: Cambridge University Press, 1923), 2: 522-82.
15   10 and 11 January 1864, Somerset to Russell, TNA Russell Papers, PRO 30-22, 26. As Oscar Parkes notes, *Royal Oak* was the first British wooden-hulled (oceangoing) ironclad; *British Battleships*, 51. The two other ironclads noted by Somerset were HMS *Hector*, an improved *Defence*-class, although drawing 25-feet—only a foot less than *Warrior*—and

Charles Wood (Secretary of State for India), Earl Grey feared a war 'which we shall sooner or later be involved.' At the same time, for all their threats against Prussia, Russell and Palmerston had foolishly admitted Britain would 'not support our words by acts'—'And in certain circumstances we must act', he added. Who else would intervene to help weaker states in Europe from aggression if not the British? Grey agreed with the former First Lord of the Admiralty 'that a blockade of Hamburg would be little likely to do any good'. Yet he also considered that weather permitting in a few months, gunboats might serve in defensive operations in Danish waters— perhaps in support of a British land force.[16]

That same day (15 January), Somerset reported to Russell that the earliest Britain could move into the Kattegat and the Belts which divided Denmark, and then reach Kiel, would be mid-March. Since Prussian troops would command the Elbe with river batteries, however, 'the only possible operation here would be a blockade'. Likewise with the Eider, 'which would render operations in that river impossible for small wooden ships, and the depth of water would not admit our iron-clad ships.' But the Admiralty was confident that a seagoing ironclad 'or two' might reach Cuxhaven and with gunboats in support could blockade the entrances there, while British troop landings might be possible if Denmark held certain key strategic points. 'This is a rough sketch of the coasts', Somerset concluded, 'and shows the difficulty of any effective action for two months, in case such action were deemed desirable.' In any event, no help could be expected from the French, who had at least refrained from making idle threats against Prussia.[17] Obviously, what the Royal Navy needed was a ready flotilla of light-draft ironclads—and no mention was made of attempting to deploy the Crimean War batteries, for example. So British naval power projection could only penetrate so far. How the presence of Austro-Prussian naval forces in the vicinity might complicate affairs was also left out. In March 1864, the War Office listed five armoured screw frigates in the Austrian Navy, laid down in 1861-2 (*Kaiser Max*, *Don Juan D'Austria*, *Prinz Eugene*, *Drache* and *Salamander*), with two more building at Pola. A wooden 92-gun screw ship-of-the-line (*Kaiser*), 2 screw frigates and corvettes, and 1 sailing frigate had been ordered to the North Sea. Not long

---

HMS *Prince Consort*, a sister-ship to *Royal Oak*, drawing as much as *Warrior* and therefore at greater risk in close operations along the North Sea and Baltic German coasts. During inclement weather the new Channel Squadron of experimental ironclads was routinely kept in port; see for example TNA ADM 50/330, reports of Vice-Admiral Sir S. C. Dacres, KCB, Commanding Channel Squadron.

16   15 January 1864, [Henry George Grey, 3rd Earl] Grey to Wood, Halifax Papers, Borthwick Institute, A4/55-4.
17   15 January 1864, Somerset to Russell, TNA Russell Papers, PRO 30-22, 26; 26 January 1864, Somerset to Russell, TNA Russell Papers, PRO 30-22, 27.

afterwards the British Charge d'Affairs at Hamburg noted a Coles double-turreted ironclad (the *Arminius*) was being built by Samuda in Britain for the Prussian Navy.[18]

Even here, another double-turreted 'Danish Monitor', the *Rolf Krake*, had already been laid down by Napier and Sons in 1862, launched in May 1863, and seen action against Prussian forces on 18 February.[19] This represented the first trial by combat of a Coles tower. As reported by the British press, the *Rolfe Krake* was first tasked with destroying a Prussian pontoon bridge into Broager. Here she met stiff resistance and was soon enveloped in 'a constant fire from the land batteries on three sides for nearly two hours' yet withdrew from action fully operational. What prevented the Coles turret-ship from actually accomplishing her mission, however, was her 23-foot draft; 'the water being so shallow she could not get near enough to see the bridge' and obliging her to fire 'at random'.[20] One report forwarded to the Admiralty noted how Prussian gunners were certain they'd struck the Danish ironclad repeatedly—to no apparent effect—though 'She showed extraordinarily little above water.' Nevertheless, a Danish officer on board the *Rolf Krake* later recounted she was struck along her exposed freeboard 66 times. 'The towers were hit several times; 16 shots went through the funnel, one through the steampipe, two through the foremast, one through the mainmast, two through the mizen, and 60 to 70 through the bulwarks, small boats, sails, and rigging.' All of this was done by Prussian field artillery, not heavy coastal or naval guns.[21] What was awkward for Britain was that turreted ironclads were being combat tested abroad by foreign powers, while the Royal Navy's own specimens stuttered forward hesitantly. After two years' converting at Portsmouth, HMS *Royal Sovereign* was finally launched on 8 March 1864. The Admiralty had it 'now in their power to bring the "turret" principle to a practical test within the space of a few weeks,' *The Times* urged, 'and thus solve the great question of the day—i.e., whether the turret or broadside gun ships carry the most powerful ordnance, for that, after all,

---

18 All of the armoured screw-frigates featured solid 4½-inch iron plates. Confidential, *Strength of the Navies of Denmark, Prussia, and Austria, 1864*, Second Edition (War Office, March 1864), TNA WO 33/13, 7. All of the armoured screw-frigates featured solid 4½-inch iron plates. Confidential, *Strength of the Navies of Denmark, Prussia, and Austria, 1864*, Second Edition (War Office, March 1864), TNA WO 33/13, 7; 1 September 1864, forwarded report, in TNA ADM 1/5903. *Arminius* was launched in August 1864, drew 24-feet, and was armed with four steel 8.2-inch rifled Krupp guns firing 218-pound projectiles; see for example, K. R. Crawford and N. W. Mitiukov, *Identification of the Parameters of Naval Artillery* (Prague: Vědecko vydavatelské centrum, 2013), 25-8

19 See Arnold A. Putnam, '*Rolf Krake*: Europe's First turreted Ironclad', *The Mariner's Mirror*, Vol. 84, No. 1 (February 1998).

20 2 March 1864, *The Times*.

21 The heaviest Prussian artillery used against *Rolf Krake* were 24-pounders. 7 March 1864, Foreign Office to Admiralty; enclosed reports from Berlin dated 21 February 1864, TNA ADM1/5901; 9 March 1864, *The Times*.

is the real question at issue.'²² Moreover, the Admiralty could hardly afford to remain aloof if British foreign policy threatened action against those same navies, fighting for control not just of sea lanes, coastlines and deep ports but shallow waters.

* * *

All of this in turn complicated an ideal implementation of Palmerstonian foreign policy. 'What turn events may take in the North of Europe, it is impossible to see,' the Premier tried to assure Earl de Grey and Ripon, the Secretary of State for War on 2 February, adding vaguely, 'but whatever line the course of events may lead the British Government to adopt, I am convinced that we shall not be found deficient in the means necessary to give effect to the policy which we may think the best.'²³ Yet by 6 February, Russell confided to Lord Lyons in Washington that as 'the peace of Europe must be paramount', Denmark was likely going to have to sacrifice some of its 'reputation and power'; the implication being there was little either Britain or France would—or could—do to prevent it. The Foreign Secretary could only hope in the meantime that the U.S. presidential election later that year would 'not require much more abuse of England than we have had to bear already.' As neither Russia nor Italy were bound to be sympathetic to British interests, Lyons was to also try and insure that they were not chosen as arbitrators in the ongoing Anglo-American dispute over the San Juan Islands.²⁴ The sooner the British squadron arrived from Lisbon the better, Palmerston therefore wrote to Somerset; 'its arrival here will have a good political effect'. The Prussians and Austrians probably wished to dictate terms from Copenhagen, as Napoleon Bonaparte had done from Vienna and Berlin. 'We should be laughed at if we stood by, and allowed this to be done', he warned. The First Lord replied that *Warrior*, *Black Prince*, *Defence* and *Prince Consort* were now available for the defence of Copenhagen—HMS *Hector* being finally completed after some delays that same day (22 February). Two more ironclads were to be left in the Mediterranean (*Royal Oak* and *Resistance*), keeping an eye on Austria. But he foresaw there would be 'some difficulty in protecting Copenhagen from attack, while the Danes pursue and seize all German ships at sea.' Additionally, a naval war with Prussia and Austria meant that Britain 'must expect that *Alabama*s will be fitted out

22   10 March 1864, *The Times*. Of the thirteen 10½-inch, 12-ton Armstrong guns available in the UK, five had been appropriated to arm the *Royal Sovereign*, noted the War Office on 29 February 1864; TNA ADM 1/5905.
23   2 February 1864, Palmerston to Ripon (George Robinson, 1st Marquess of Ripon), in Lucien Wolf (ed.), *Life of the First Marquess of Ripon*, 2 vols. (London: John Murray, 1921): 1: 205.
24   6 February 1864, Russell to Lyons, Russell Papers, TNA PRO 30-22, 31. Russell and Palmerston had made it clear that unless acting with French (military) support over Denmark 'no useful result could be hoped for', 14 April 1864, Clarendon to Russell, Russell Papers, TNA PRO 30-22, 26.

in America and elsewhere to prey on our Commerce.'[25] This was daily manifesting itself as a serious peril in the age of steam-powered warfare on the high seas. 'Every maritime Power requires for its service not only a strong fleet,' lectured *The Times*, 'but a vast number of vessels of all descriptions.' The U.S. Navy was in the process of building many *Alabama*s of its own, and the Admiralty spokesman in Parliament (Paget) recently announced the Navy's intention to build a new class of comparable versions, and these it was hoped 'will serve efficiently to carry us through the period of transition' to small, high-speed armoured cruisers which someday would replace the wooden frigates, corvettes and sloops which constituted the bulk of the British fleet worldwide.[26]

Although Palmerston was loathe to admit culpability for the escape of the '290' and the subsequent destructive career of the CSS *Alabama*, Lord Argyll's memo of 18 February warned the Cabinet to consider the dangers of prestige unbound. 'No man can doubt the supreme interest which England has in limiting as narrowly as possible the precedents which will be founded on the *Alabama*. Every right conceded to her is a right conceded to the future enemies of England.' Perhaps within the strict letter of municipal law the British weren't guilty of not just building but manning much of the Confederate Navy. But it was surely up to the Government 'to look at the whole series of transactions as one operation, performed in contempt of its sovereignty, and in a manner affronting to its dignity.'[27] The matter of the Laird Rams also needed to be settled quickly and quietly. Russell thought buying them up as additions to Britain's own ironclad force the neatest possible solution. The First Lord worried the two vessels were 'not good for much'.[28] The Admiralty's naval experts soon relayed their estimation that the sail-and-turret ironclads were indeed not the best examples of the latest technology, and hardly worth their new '£300,000' asking price. At any rate, he wrote to the Foreign Secretary on 22 March, the Navy 'could not purchase them even at £200,000 except by some arrangement with the Treasury.' But Russell replied the next day that Palmerston, Grey and other Cabinet members 'were at my house when the opinion was unanimous that something more than base value should be offered for the Iron-clads.'[29] As *The Times* had recently opined, a series of recent

---

25 20 February 1864, Palmerston to Somerset, Somerset Papers, Aylesbury, D/RA/A/2A/40; 22 February 1864, Somerset to Palmerston, Palmerston Papers, Broadlands, GC/50. Russell accepted that 'Our trade would suffer, but would be protected by our Navy', 21 June 1864, Russell to Ripon, in Wolf, *Life of the First Marquess of Ripon*, 1: 209.
26 2 March 1864, *The Times*.
27 18 February 1864, Confidential *Memorandum by the Duke of Argyll Respecting the "Alabama"*, in Russell Papers, TNA PRO 30-22, 26; see also 6 March 1864, Palmerston to Russell, ibid., PRO 30-22, 27.
28 18 February 1864, Russell to Somerset, Somerset Papers, Aylesbury, D/RA/A/2A/53; 18 February 1864, Somerset to Russell, Russell Papers, TNA PRO 30-22, 26.
29 22 March 1864, Somerset to Russell, Russell Papers, TNA PRO 30-22, 26; 23 March 1864, Russell to Somerset, Somerset Papers, Aylesbury, D/RA/A/2A/53; Sir George Grey, 2nd Baronet, the Home Secretary since July 1861.

spectacular debates in Parliament were triggered by the Tory Opposition's efforts 'to get this country into a war with somebody':

> They are indignant because we are not ready to fight Russia for the sake of Poland, or the United States for the sake of Mr. Laird and his Steam Rams, or Austria and Prussia for the sake of Denmark. Taunts, sneers, and sarcasms are hailed upon the Government and its supporters, because they have succumbed to the dictation of one Power, yielded to the violence of another, or swallowed the insolence of a third.

None of these potential conflicts were in England's best interests, *The Times* loudly rationalised. 'We can afford to leave to others the glory of being the champion of the human race…and to show by our unwillingness to take offence how sincerely we are in favour of that peace which we continually, if sometime vainly, preach to others.' *Punch* portrayed a matronly Britannia giving Lord Russell a swat on the head for writing one 'troublesome' dispatch after another.[30] But these sentiments must have crushed the hopes of the Poles, Danes, and Confederates in turn. It also left many in Britain and abroad wondering why Palmerston—whose reputation as a leading liberal interventionist was rather notorious—seemed so unnaturally restrained as the 1860s wore on. Though subjected to a 'grand bombardment' by critics in Parliament, it had 'not done any harm' to the aging Prime Minister's 'fortifications', Russell blithely wrote to Lyons, '& the bombarding force has sheared off leaving Poland a deserted a wreck on the shore.'[31]

Ironically enough, the sticking point in all of this was very much the perceived strength of the Royal Navy. On 4 April 1864, the Admiralty complied with Parliament's request for particulars on the widespread failure of the Armstrong 110-pounder breechloading rifle at Kagosima the previous August. Rear-Admiral Sir Augustus Kuper's after-action reports of five of his vessels engaged with the combined Japanese defences all noted vent-pieces broken, handles and hammers blown off when the heavy Armstrongs were fired—in pouring rain—at a range of 4,000 yards. By contrast the 68-pounder smoothbores were all reported on favourably. Accidents continued to crop up around the world, in peacetime. On July 26th, HMS *Princess Royal* reported how on just the third round of target practice the whole of the centre part of a 7-inch Armstrong's vent-piece 'was blown through the breech screw, passed between the legs of the powder boy, and broke the leg of the captain of the fore-top,

---

30   27 February 1864, *The Times*; 27 February 1864, 'John in a Mess', *Punch*. As leader of the Conservatives, Disraeli wrote privately that an 'English Government that, in its wisdom, goes to war with Germany, must make France the Mistress of Europe', 20 January 1864, to Sir George Sinclair, in M. G. Wiebe, *et. al* (eds.), *Benjamin Disraeli Letters, Volume VIII 1860-1864* (Toronto: University of Toronto Press, 2009), 336.
31   27 February 1864, Russell to Lyons, Russell Papers, TNA PRO 30-22, 97.

who happened to be passing on the opposite side of the deck.'[32] Coles meanwhile quoted to Richard Cobden a *New York Times* article ridiculing Reed's new pride and joy ironclad now building at Chatham, since '"a turret Vessel of adequate speed may keep close to the stem of the *Bellerophon* or pass her sides for 60 feet without being molested with her guns. Let us imagine the [USS] *Dictator* with her power to direct her entire Battery over the bow placed as we have stated, how long would this 'Monster' endure the raking shot from the 15 inch Gun which would plow through from end to end."' Yet, Coles observed, Reed's experimental central-battery ironclads *Research* and *Enterprise* had been fast-tracked into completion and were already undergoing sea trials. This was well after the orders to convert the *Royal Sovereign* had been given by the Admiralty, while men engaged in building the *Bellerophon* likewise received 'encouragement money'.

Even so, the Board was at least 'anxious' enough to urge the War Office 'to obtain an effective rifled gun for Turret-ships', and it would be 'glad to have the 13-ton of 9.22 calibre sent to Shoeburyness as soon as possible'. Somerset also agreed with the proposal by Lord Lyons in Washington, forwarded by Russell, to appoint a naval attaché to the United States, agreeing that 'knowledge of the innumerable inventions brought forward in the States'—especially in terms of firepower—'would be of great interest to us'. His projected tally that July was that by the following April 1865, the Navy might have seven 9-inch '300-pounder' rifled 12-ton guns, thirteen 10.5-inch 12-ton smoothbores, and fifty 9-inch 6-ton smoothbores on hand, as part of a major projected overhaul of Britannia's ordnance afloat.[33] Whether this would be enough remained to be seen, since both Lieutenant-Colonel William Jervois of the Royal Engineers and Vice-Admiral Hope considered Bermuda and Barbados quite vulnerable to an attack by heavily armed and armoured American warships. Some '£500,000' was need needed to shore up the defences Barbados alone, and 'one or two' turret vessels like the *Royal Sovereign* and 600-pounder Armstrong guns (if they could be had) would help ensure Bermuda's safety. By July 1864 the Admiralty practically wrote off the notion of defending Antigua. 'I fear a good deal of money has been spent—even during the last two or three years and is still spending here,' Hope then complained to Somerset about Halifax's defences, 'on works which will be of little or no use for Sea defence against armour-plated ships.' As far as he was concerned, the

---

32 4 April 1864, *Parliamentary Papers*, Session 1864, Paper 145, Volume XLII, 25, 'Admiral Kuper's Official Report of Performance of Armstrong Guns in Action at Kagosima'; 1 August 1864 Minute 12,923, 'Failures and Accidents', *Abstracts of Proceedings of the Ordnance Select Committee, for the Quarter ending 30th September 1864*, TNA WO 33/14, 407.

33 8 April 1864, Coles to Cobden, Cobden Papers Collection, Chichester, West Sussex Record Office; 21 May 1864, Admiralty to War Office, TNA ADM 1/5883; 23 May 1864, Somerset to Russell, Russell Papers, TNA PRO 30-22, 26; 'Cannon—July 1864', Somerset Papers, Devon Archives Record Office (Exeter), Box 19, A1-5. '20' 7-inch, 6-ton rifled guns were also noted as possibly available by December 1865.

engineer officers sent out from Britain seemed 'by no means alive to the comparatively short ranges at which guns of the heaviest calibre can be made effectual against plating of 5½-inches in thickness and that they must devise some means of mounting them and some mode of protecting the gun crews, less expensive and more efficient than those they now resort to.'[34]

But in late July 1864 Robinson rejected a request from the Iron Plate Committee for additional 4½-inch plating to restore the *Lord Warden* Target and resume testing. Both ironclads of the class, *Lord Warden* and *Lord Clyde* were now too far advanced to permit serious changes in the armour configuration (more iron for less wood), he observed. If the Admiralty wanted further tests conducted to see 'the effect of the splinters from thin iron when penetrated by heavy shot', the Controller and his team had no objection—provided they were quietly done at Portsmouth by the Navy, since at Shoeburyness 'many of the trials that take place is frequently misunderstood and misrepresented.'[35] By August the Controller must have been glad to see the back of the Iron Plate Committee, now dissolved. Yet the British public still took pride—and ownership—of the latest advances in the 'guns vs. armour' race which had transpired, and which affected the image of the Navy far more than it did those who were building Palmerston's coastal fortifications. Top-hatted civilians and military officials crowding around to measure every crack and hole made on a '*La Gloire* Target' was a featured cover-scene of the 20 August 1864 issue of *The Illustrated London News*. After all, as *The Times* relayed, since 1860 'both the Ordnance Select Committee and the Iron-plate Committee have been steadily at work, the former perfecting our means of attack in guns, the latter improving our system of defence in armour-plates, and, as was to be expected, the former have gained the advantage.' Naval warfare had been reduced to a mathematical equation, a question of physics, whereby larger guns firing steel shot 'can as easily pierce any system of armour-plating that can reasonably be expected to float at sea as if it was so much wood. In plain terms, this is really the result at which all the Shoeburyness experiments have at last arrived':

> Wooden ships are relatively stronger against 68-pounders than are iron-clads against the 150-pounder and 200-pounder shunt guns. We have quite reached, if needed experience does not show us that we have over-passed, the limit of armour weight which such ships as the *Lord Warden* and *Bellerophon* can safely carry in a heavy sea. Yet these two vessels, which with the American ship *Dictator* are the strongest and the thickest plated known to exists, are also

---

34 27 April 1864, Hope to Admiralty, TNA ADM 1/5872, the enclosed memo by Jervois is dated 4 February 1864; 24 June 1864, War Office to Admiralty, with Admiralty reply dated 5 July 1864, TNA ADM 1/5905; 6 July 1864, Hope to Somerset, Somerset Papers, Aylesbury, D/RA/A/2A/29.
35 28 July 1864, Robinson to Board, TNA ADM 1/5891.

known to be almost as vulnerable to the heavy guns at Shoeburyness as wood is to the 68-pounders.[36]

As for which types of ironclad were best suited to carry the best armaments, Reed's central-battery *Research* was condemned by Pakington in Parliament when compared with the Danish *Rolf Krake* and its twin Coles towers; each vessel armed with only four guns. When Cobden publicly joined the fray on a point of naval economy if not efficiency, Reed objected in a letter to *The Times*. 'It suits the objects of some persons to set up a fancied rivalry between Captain Coles and myself', he declared, though it hardly mattered whether heavy guns were mounted in 'square boxes vs. round boxes'. A leader in the same issue then took aim at Cobden's views on modern war generally, since 'the stern logic of facts compels even the Apostles of peace to admit that war is, that war will be, that it may be any day, that we must provide against war, and that war will be all the more destructive, ruinous, and implacable for our not being prepared for it.' The United States was the prime example of that tragic truth, fighting as it was for its very survival in part because it had been proudly basking in its relatively peaceful, unarmed state before. Cobden's fault was thinking 'that war can be done in the same cheap and regular fashion as the works of peace' and that government officialdom was the natural enemy of the people as represented by private industry. Instead, the 'Thunderer' argued, 'There is no greater mistake than that which supposes that the higher you go the worse men become.' Yet Cobden's suggestion about Reed was hardly naïve either; as he wrote to Reed privately (later reprinted in *The Times*), 'I said that unless you were an angel you would prefer to forward your own inventions to those of a rival. Is it derogatory to you to admit that this principle applies to you as well as other men?' It was likewise axiomatic that 'when an office of the Government is at the head of a construction of manufacturing department, and at the same time virtually at the head of the contract or purchasing department, he cannot fulfil the two functions satisfactorily to the public or the private producer, whatever may be the satisfaction he gives himself.'[37] It would therefore benefit Reed, Robinson or the Admiralty very little to appeal to false civilities any more than resort to disingenuous platitudes; the only thing that mattered was whether the turret or broadside system proved *better*. The mid-Victorian readership was intensely interested in these questions, and increasingly impatient with mere (official) excuses.

* * *

Robinson was wholeheartedly in support of the popular notion that Britain's naval prominence depended upon utilising the heaviest guns possible as soon as possible—on seagoing warships. His 23 August 1864 memo to the Board of Admiralty outlined

---

36 6 August 1864, *The Times*.
37 Ibid., 21, 25 and 29 July 1864.

the goals for 1866: the combination of 110-pounder breechloading Armstrong rifles and 68-pounder smoothbores were to be phased out in favour of muzzle-loading 6¼- and 12-ton guns. Half of all the lighter weapons were to be rifled. At least forty-three 12-ton guns were needed immediately, with another twenty-five by the end of 1866. The whole face of British seapower would be divided between its core fleet of oceangoing ironclads and a new generation of fast, powerfully-armed wooden cruisers for commerce defence.[38] Yet this overriding sense of prudence failed to satisfy many when it came to Britain's first turret ironclad, the *Royal Sovereign*. Was she intended to be a heavily armed and armoured replacement for the older floating batteries after all or something more? As reported on 1 August, her heavy guns were fired with 40lb charges without inconveniencing the turret crews with concussion or smoke. *The Times* therefore thought 'it must be admitted…by every unprejudiced mind that the English turret principle has been fairly tested and has proved a decided success; and this may be asserted without entering any further into the somewhat foolish controversy of "central v. broadside ships' batteries" than to observe that the 12-ton 10½-inch gun has been fired in the Channel from a central-battery on board a ship, whereas it has not from a ship's broadside battery.' As a coastal vessel for shallow waters, however, the *Royal Sovereign* suffered from deep draft—more the obvious fault of the Admiralty than Coles—and since her smoothbores could not presently be rifled safely her relative efficiency was indeed shrunk 'to a very narrow compass.'[39] Moreover, within six weeks her commanding officer, Captain Sir Sherard Osborn, reported that wood carriages for her 12-ton guns were 'a mistake, they should be of iron. Most of them are already defective, and one not safe to fire with.' More mechanisation was needed for running them in and out of the turret ports than block and tackle. Ventilation was inadequate and vulnerable to destruction from fire on the one hand and leaks on the other. 'Skylights, Hatchways, and Turret flaps all leak, and we are very damp indeed when it rains.' Rather than lowering her target profile, Osborn thought the raised bulwarks a 'very great comfort' and wished they were fully six feet in height with a deck still higher out of the water. Reed took note of this for future reference, while Lord Palmerston, after his own inspection of the *Royal Sovereign* the previous month, only saw a broad-beamed platform slowly moving through narrow waters and thus vulnerable to a boarding party. Moving quickly, they would likely dodge the main guns firing shrapnel and then lob hand grenades 'into the Tops of the Turrets'.[40] The experimental vessel was soon taken out of commission to effect necessary repairs and modifications.

38 29 August 1864, Robinson to Board, TNA ADM 1/5891.
39 1 August 1864, *The Times*.
40 23 September 1864, Robinson to Board, TNA ADM 1/5801 (Osborn's enclosed report is dated 13 September 1864); 2 August 1864, Palmerston to Somerset, Somerset Papers, Aylesbury, D/RA/A/2A/40.

Recognising that the trials might not be the spur that he had hoped for, Coles begged Somerset in early September 1864 to reconsider the idea of building a first-class seagoing turret vessel, 'of the utmost importance to me and to the reputation of my invention'. Many in Whitehall were sympathetic, and Robinson relented that it was 'quite true that H.M. Navy does not possess a single cupola ship adapted for the Navigation and Police of the high sea, and the reason is obvious, since no design has yet been prepared by anybody which has realised such an idea…' He promised the Board that he would *now* confer with Coles 'as to the design for a seagoing cupola ship, which shall embrace all the requirements of a seagoing Armour Plated ship of war, in which the crew can live in health and comfort, and which could be sent across the Atlantic without risk of foundering.'[41] But within days the British press resumed its attack on the Admiralty and throughout the rest of the autumn. 'The cupola principle has now been before the world for nine years', noted *The Times*, and yet 'we learn to our astonishment that the [*Royal Sovereign*] is to be paid out of commission and placed out of sight in the steam reserve…If Sir William Armstrong's newest gun had been sent out to Bermuda as ballast, the proceeding would have been hardly more unaccountable.' Just because the American monitors were 'not good specimens of the class' in terms of their seakeeping should experiments cease in the Royal Navy. The Admiralty's subsequent explanation that the ship needed alterations—and that as an ironclad she was never intended to be more than a low-lying, mastless floating battery—was all the more galling. The British public had been rather misled since 'Nobody doubted that a turret-vessel might serve well enough for a guardship.' Why all the dithering, when ironclads like the *Achilles*, *Minotaur* and *Bellerophon* were built as fast as possible, for world-ranging commissions if need be? 'It could hardly have required the conversion of a fine three-decker, the employment of a distinguished commander, and the adoption of a new principle of armament, to make a vessel fit to be paddled about a harbour as a shot-proof raft.'[42]

Cobden sighed it was indicative of a broader fault in British defence policymaking. 'The whole of this scheme of inland fortifications is the offspring of these old men's brains whose united ages amounted to about 240 years, viz. Palmerston, Howard Douglas, and Burgoyne', he wrote to Coles. 'If an enemy is our Master at Sea, so as to be enabled to land an army and keep open his communications, he is capable of blockading us and starving us into subjection. He would therefore be a fool to land an army at all.' At least Coles was able to get someone distinguished like Osborn to trial the *Royal Sovereign*; 'his report must enable us to revolutionise the navy some day. But these old men of 80 stop the way.' Who in the Royal Navy could be relied upon to reach someone of prominence in the government like Chancellor of the Exchequer Gladstone? Coles agreed, thinking 'we shall never make security and economy the

---

41   7 September 1864, Robinson to Board, TNA ADM 1/5891. Coles' enclosed letter to Somerset is dated the 'United Service Club', 5 September 1864.
42   5 and 8 October 1864, *The Times*.

base of our expenditure until it is brought about by some lamentable war and disgrace that will whip us into the right path—and bid our old men of 80 stop at home and sip their tea.' Gladstone had already been given a tour by Coles of the turret vessel and was impressed by her relatively small crew manning extra-large guns—like Lincoln when he visited the original USS *Monitor* in the spring of 1862. Surely this sense of cost-effectiveness *and* greater power was the spirit of the age rather than attempting to 'keep up these herds of seamen.' As with Ericsson's vision of a semi-automated navy of semi-automated warships, Coles confided that Britain's 'Engines of war must be made as much as possible self acting with few men—and the *Royal Sovereign* is the nearest approach to that of anything we have had as yet.' He then followed this up with a letter to *The Times* which attacked 'the anti-turret party'. As with other novel inventions of the age, 'no sooner are one set of objections disposed of than others are set on foot, some real, some imaginary, by engineers, shipbuilders, practical, unpractical, scientific men, friends and foes.' Yet given the severe (though unpublished) tests of the *Trusty*'s turret under fire, and the actual combat experience of both the *Rolf Krake* in Denmark and the monitors of the Union Navy (which, according to Rear-Admiral Dahlgren's recently printed report, had sustained no less than 128 hits each on average with no turrets jamming), it was difficult to fathom why the Admiralty would hedge its bets by quickly paying off its only experimental turret vessel. If more tests were needed, fine, Coles insisted, but 'let it be done quickly, and do not let us potter over the *Royal Sovereign* for another 12 months.'[43] And while Cobden thought Coles fought his press battle 'manfully', he feared 'red tape' would prove too much for him.[44]

In the meantime, in order to comply with the Admiralty's directive for designs of a seagoing turret vessel, Coles had requested the Controller's Department to send him the plans for Reed's smaller central-battery ironclad under construction since late 1863, the *Pallas*. By the end of October nothing had arrived.[45] The Chief Constructor objected that he was not given the order to supply both the plans and a professional draughtsman to assist Coles until 12 October, and that once he had received them from Woolwich two weeks later he duly forwarded them on to Whitehall two days later, to be transmitted to Coles. However, no draughtsman was forthcoming; the Admiralty thought Coles would choose his own after consulting with the Admiral Superintendent at Portsmouth; Coles explained to Romaine on 5 November that he could not be expected to choose his own, especially since he had been told his previous calculations had been wrong. The Board would have to assign someone they regarded as suitably competent. The plans for the *Pallas* he had eventually received also omitted

43 30 October 1864, Cobden to Coles, and 9 November 1864, Cobden Papers, Chichester; 12 November 1864, *The Times*.
44 12 November 1864, Cobden to Coles, Cobden Papers, Chichester.
45 10 October 1864, Coles to Paget, TNA ADM 1/5879, and 2 November 1864, Reed to Robinson, TNA ADM 1/5892, with Coles' enclosed letter to Romaine dated 29 October 1864.

recent changes including 'another deck added'. Reed in turn complained that the information sent to Coles was admittedly incomplete, 'because it was understood that in modifying the Design it was proposed that Captain Coles should simply deal with the portion of the Ship above the water; I have now, however, caused as many of the particulars which he enumerates on the paper annexed as are on record in this Office to be filled up, but', he added defensively, he saw 'no necessity for taking the draughtsmen under my orders off urgent work for the purpose of calculating such particulars as I have left blank, because they are not essential to the Designing of ships in this Office. Moreover, they may be calculated from the Drawings already in the possession of Captain Coles if they are really required.' At any rate, the changes to the *Pallas* were indeed significant, adding height to the bulwarks at the cost of 70 extra tons and further draught by three inches. The Chief Constructor then countered with the real question at stake in all this tiresome correspondence: it was well understood that Coles could not actually *design* a seagoing turret himself—had he not told the First Naval Lord (Sir Frederick Grey) as much?—yet he assured the Board that he was '"perfectly ready to Design a vessel representing my views"'. It was unclear how and to what extent the Royal Navy was to help Coles help the Royal Navy. Accordingly, because of this 'slight discrepancy' and 'to prevent any misunderstanding', their Lordships requested Coles to 'inform them whether he is prepared to design a seagoing vessel wholly and entirely for the purpose of carrying one or more Turrets, or whether he would prefer a Vessel being designed in the Office of the Controller of the Navy capable of being adapted to the Turret Plan.'[46] It hardly mattered. Within weeks Reed and Robinson headed off this renewed drive for a turret-armed cruiser by quietly proposing a light-draft (16-feet), twin-screw ironclad corvette armed with four 300-pounders—configured as a central-battery and mounted broadside. These guns, they assured the Board, would be capable 'of firing within 15° of the fore and aft line, both ahead and astern.'[47] Coles might get another turret 'experiment' out of the Admiralty to help quiet the British press and Parliament, but the Controller's Department had no intention of relinquishing control over its real policy when it came to types of ironclads and their scheme of armament.

---

46   10 November 1864, Reed to Robinson, TNA ADM 1/5892. Parkes, on the other hand, curiously wrote that Reed 'was quite agreeable for the plans of the *Pallas* to be loaned', *British Battleships*, 127.
47   5 December 1864, Robinson to Board. TNA ADM 1/5892. When Coles complained on 6 December that the Controller's Department was stonewalling the dispatch of a suitable draughtsman, Robinson replied testily, 'As Captain Coles has more than once referred to delays in answering his letters, and thrown something like imputations on the motives of the Controller's Department, I beg leave to point out that the delay in answering his letter of the 5th November and on the appointment of this competent Draughtsman did not take place in this Office', 6 December 1864, Coles to Paget, TNA ADM 1/5879; Robinson's margin reply is dated 8 December. Reed, however, confirmed three days later that a draughtsman had finally been assigned, '*notwithstanding the inconvenience to the Service which will result from so employing him*' [italics added], TNA ADM 1/5892.

These heated exchanges also failed to address the proverbial 'elephant in the room': Britain's ongoing foreign policy about-face, and the risk of declining stature at a time when it was needed most. It wasn't just about the larger, ancillary costs of upgrading Britain's naval power, from wood to iron. The Royal Commission on Dockyards in August 1864 was 'struck with a remark by Admiral Sir Alexander Milne...that two [wooden] frigates were lately sent home for repairs in consequence of there being no Government dock in any of Her Majesty's colonies on this station in which those ships could be docked.' Heaving down on careening wharves could no longer be safely applied to ships whose delicate steam machinery might be deranged, and in their absence from the station the costs of wages, victuals, coals, and wear and tear were a 'dead loss'. How much worse would it be with iron ships, 'as it is necessary to dock them for the mere purpose of cleaning their bottoms at least four or five times in the course of the ordinary duration of a commission'?[48] Indeed, on 13 December, Robinson presented the Board with 'General Remarks on the Classification, Distribution and Construction of Armour Plated Ships'; his programme for shipbuilding into 1865 and beyond. Like many historical documents, its significance is marked not just by what it contained but what it ignored. By spreading contracts and construction around, the Controller's Department suggested, three more central-battery ironclads of the *Bellerophon*-class—not turret-armed capital ships—would bring the Royal Navy's ironclad numbers up to sixteen, 'and by these means our superiority would be unquestionable; as in the event of war [with France] we should have in addition to a Fleet equal to theirs, a squadron of six of the fastest and most powerful ironclads in the world, capable of bringing on an action and of deciding it favourably.' The Board assented to this projection as well as to Robinson's preference for ironclads 'a little larger than the *Favorite*'-class central-battery ships as flag-ships on foreign stations ('to mount eight heavy guns on broadside, armour-plated with six-inch iron at the water-line and battery'). The key features here would be to offer 'a seagoing ironclad, fast, powerfully armed, and possessing the qualities of a good cruiser, so that if any maritime power detached an iron-clad across the ocean, there should be one ship on the spot which would not be driven off, and could maintain the honour of the Flag.' Yet even though the Controller considered it 'very desirable to provide a number of small single-turreted ships', they were to be deployed strictly 'for the mouths of our rivers, and for the defence of our harbours, which would also be able to prevent any landing on any unprotected beach or harbour on our coasts'. In this role they were a low priority, not to be 'commissioned except in war-time', and 'gradually built, year by year.' If the whole package was accepted, he promised that Britain would 'not be taken at a disadvantage if forced into a war,' adding only 'the one exception of the protection to be given to our commerce from privateers and enemy's

---

48 See 12 August 1864, *The Times*.

fast-sailing wooden cruizers.'⁴⁹ But all this said nothing about actually waging war against other Great Powers such as the United States (as in 1862), Russia (in 1863), or even Germany (1864). A struggle for 'command of the sea' against France remained theoretical on the one hand and increasingly irrelevant on the other. It was also perhaps unnecessarily expensive, as Gladstone complained to Somerset that same short, cold day in December. 'The amount of Naval force, including the Reserve, is greater at this moment, when the public mind is tranquil, and no cause of danger is near at hand, then it was in 1860, when the public mind was agitated and excited by the expectation of a French invasion,' he recounted, 'and when the absence of a reserve was always pleaded as the reason for the maintenance of a vast force at an enormous cost.' The various station-squadrons around the world might be justified, like global police, as helping to keep the peace but the historical record also suggested how a monopoly of violence (and intimidation) also tended to 'multiply causes of quarrel and dispute.' Of course it was understood that the ironclad revolution meant a large bill for new types of ships, but the 'turret vs. broadside'-debate meant 'it was very far indeed from having been as yet demonstrated or brought to a state of reasonable certainty' that ironclads themselves needed to be large to be powerful.⁵⁰ As it turned out, by the time Britain could finally rest assured of its ability to win a Trafalgar-type clash far from land, in 1870, France's own 'line-of-battle force in ironclads' proved to be essentially useless in its life-or-death fight with Prussia.

49   13 December 1864, *General Remarks on the classification, Distribution and Construction of Armour-Plated Ships*, TNA ADM 1/5892.
50   13 December 1864, Gladstone to Somerset, Somerset Papers, Aylesbury, D/RA/A/2A/15.

5

'We must go back very much to the recognized forms, the recognized proportions, and the recognised shapes'

It was the immediate future, moreover, that had gradually become a problem for a sense of British naval supremacy, and its efficacy. Back in April, Palmerston fancied sending the fleet to the Baltic, 'to protect the retreat of the Danish army'. If France and Russia agreed, maybe the German powers could be given the threat of sending the Fleet 'to execute such orders as we may think fit to give it', he advised Russell. 'Public opinion in this Country would be much shocked if we were to stand by and see the Danish Army taken Prisoner and Denmark thus laid prostrate at the feet of Germany.' But the Queen was alarmed by this prospect; the Danes should be told to accept Austro-Prussian terms and that their blockade of Prussia would prove ineffectual.[1] Dissatisfied with this stance, and with the 'timidity and weakness' of his Cabinet on the subject, Palmerston decided 'to make a notch off my own Bat', as he described to Russell on 1 May. Earlier that day the ageing Prime Minister had summoned the Austrian ambassador, Count Rudolf Apponyi, and blithely informed him that while British intervention by land was not feasible, given the time of year and the comparative smallness of British forces in a potential struggle 'with all Germany by Land', by sea the situation was quite opposite; 'we are strong, Germany is weak and the German ports in the Baltic, North Sea and Adriatic would be greatly at our command.' Blockade was a given, but perhaps the inference was that naval bases like Pola would suffer the same fate as Sevastopol. Apponyi could only assent that an Austrian squadron attempting to enter the Baltic would probably 'run the Risk of a Catastrophe' if pounced upon by a fleet of British ironclads or 'Humiliation' by altering course back home.[2] While Russell was delighted by this blunt approach, reflecting Palmerston's belief that seapower gave Britain the ability (if not the right) to act unilaterally, within days he was scolded by Granville that the rest of

---

[1] 22 April 1864, Palmerston to Russell, Russell Papers, TNA PRO 30-22, 15B; 30 April 1864, Stanley to Russell, Russell Papers, TNA PRO 30-22, 26.
[2] 1 May 1864, Palmerston to Russell, Russell Papers, TNA PRO 30-22, 15B.

the Cabinet—even including Clarendon—strongly opposed the 'language of Lord Palmerston' and any mention of sending the fleet in official diplomatic correspondence with Prussia or Austria. The obvious risk was of committing Britain to a war without land power allies, namely France, and calling Palmerston's bluff that the Royal Navy could somehow sufficiently counterweigh the immediate advantages of the Prussian army in the field against Denmark. Importantly, the First Lord of the Admiralty was not optimistic of forcing a result which itself was 'not worth fighting for'. Holstein would not remain united with Denmark given half a chance. Hence, however strong Britain was by sea, the country would 'only lose credit by struggling feebly for an unattainable result.'[3] Annoyed, the Foreign Secretary replied to Granville on 6 May that the Cabinet should then consider formulating an alternative policy, leaving Palmerston 'to consider whether he can be responsible for that policy' if and when the Austrian Fleet appeared. When Victoria demanded that all such despatches 'will at once be stopped', Russell politely refused. Palmerston's 'Confidential' despatch promising naval retaliation would not be communicated he told her, but it was 'impossible to conceal that the appearance of the Austrian Squadron in the Downes in the North Sea has irritated the House of Commons and the Country in a degree that would hardly have been believed three months ago.'[4]

As spring turned to summer, the divisiveness over British naval power and foreign policy continued. On 11 June, Russell complained to Somerset that he had taken pains 'before asking officially for the return of the Channel Fleet, to ascertain that there would be no objection on the part of the Admiralty.' It was politically useless at the moment, on its test cruise off Gibraltar. Not sending it to Danish waters now 'would make the Germans indulge more than ever in their sneer at our pacific bluster, and the harmless roar of the British Lion.'[5] To the Queen he protested that no one 'was more averse to War' than he was. But if Prussia was determined to make extreme demands upon Denmark then surely 'an equitable peace' was impossible. In the event of Anglo-German hostilities he promised that 'the Measures probably adopted' would only be a 'blockade of the German Ports in the North Sea and in the Adriatic', and German merchant ships would be left unharmed. He also conceded to Somerset that 'respecting the practicable operations of the Navy in the North of Europe', 'we should leave the work of blockade chiefly to the Danes, and only interfere to protect them—in short to cover the blockade as an army covers a siege.'[6] The First Lord in turn did his best to assure the Foreign Secretary that if need be, an overwhelming naval force consisting of *Warrior, Black Prince, Prince Consort, Hector,*

---

3   5 May 1864, Granville to Russell, Russell Papers, TNA PRO 30-22, 26; 5 May 1864, Somerset to Russell, ibid., PRO 30-22, 27.
4   Ibid., 10 May 1864, Phipps to Russell, and 10 May 1864, Russell to Queen, PRO 30-22, 15B. See also Connell, *Regina v. Palmerston*, 338-53.
5   11 June 1864, Russell to Somerset, Somerset Papers, Aylesbury, D/RA/A/2A/53.
6   13 June 1864, Russell to Queen, Russell Papers, TNA PRO 30-22, 15C; 16 June 1864, Russell to Somerset, Somerset Papers, Aylesbury, D/RA/A/2A/53.

Defence, Research and *Enterprise* as well as wooden, screw-propelled line-of-battle ships could be summoned. 'We could easily send 20 gun-boats to sea at once in addition to the above…Other vessels could be brought forward in a few weeks.'[7] Their presence would be crucial, but as Robinson warned the Board later in August, the Crimean War-era gunboats on the China Station at least 'have shewn signs, more or less, of Rot, and in many instances the decay has been found so extensive as to make it undesirable to undertake even partial repairs, where the probability existed of having to rebuild the vessels altogether.'[8] Despite Russell wanting to intervene against Prussia on behalf of Denmark more than ever, he wrote the Queen, 'the more evident does it become that that assistance will be insufficient unless France joins in.' All talk of what Britain could unilaterally compel Austria or Prussia to do had quietly fallen by the wayside. 'But then comes the Question,' the Foreign Secretary continued, 'What will France require as the price of her alliance with England in checking the ambition of Germany and is it the interest of England to pay that price.' Somerset thought Britain's bargaining position so weak by early July, and Prussia so manifestly unwilling to countenance British threats seriously enough, that no further 'advice' should be offered. 'Why should we take any responsibility in this last humiliation of Denmark?' The rest of the Cabinet agreed, and Palmerston had already admitted that while any '*fearful* consequences of a war with Germany' probably only existed 'in the Queen's imagination', still, the 'want of ultimate success in accomplishing our purpose…would be an evil, to be weighed against those attending an opposite course.' Political cartoonist John Tenniel meanwhile captured the mounting frustration in the 2 July edition of *Punch*: 'Blow it, Bill!' a Royal Navy sailor exclaims to his shipmate, gesturing to a flabby 'German' in the background with a nautical telescope casually tucked under his arm. 'We can't be expected to *fight* a lot o' lubberly swabs like him. We'll *kick* 'em if that'll do.'[9]

Damage control was now the order of the day. On 23 August 1864 Palmerston addressed a large public crowd at Tiverton, his Parliamentary borough seat since 1835. His purpose above all was to defend British foreign policy over the past few years, and somehow explain how the mightiest navy in the world failed to intimidate foreign powers nowhere near as advanced or prosperous as Great Britain. The previous year, he stated, the concern was over Poland's treatment by Imperial Russia. 'We might have

7   17 June 1864, Somerset to Russell, Russell Papers, TNA PRO 30-22, 26.
8   9 August 1864, Robinson to Board, TNA ADM 1/5891.
9   23 June 1864, Russell to Queen, Russell Papers, TNA PRO 30-22, 15C; ibid., 3 July 1864, Somerset memo to Cabinet, PRO 30-22, 27; 20 June 1864, Palmerston to Ripon, in Wolf, *Life of the First Marquess of Ripon*, 1: 208; 2 July 1864, *Punch*, 'Jack on the Crisis'. Victoria likewise noted in her journal entry of 21 June 1864 that Palmerston 'entirely agreed with me that it was very doubtful whether we could do anything, for nothing but naval assistance could be given, and that only for three months. Would not that therefore be more humiliating for England than doing nothing at all?' Connell, *Regina v. Palmerston*, 353.

embarked in war, and with great acquiescence in popular feeling'. But unfortunately, no other power in Europe could be enlisted to take 'moral and political action'. As for intervening in the American Civil War, Britain 'could have nothing to gain, and we should only have added thousands of our own sons to the hecatomb of victims which that calamitous and bloody slaughtering war has sacrificed.' The only remaining hope was that the Northern States would realise their own 'slight hopes of success' and sue for peace with the Southern Confederacy. Then there was the Danish question. Here the Prime Minister was certain that 'every Englishman who has a heart in his breast and feeling of justice in his mind, sympathises with those unfortunate Danes... and wishes that this country could have been able to draw the sword successfully in their defence.' But how exactly? British forces were purposefully minimal compared with those of continental nation-states. No one was going to risk their defeat against '300,000 or 400,000 men whom the 30,000,000 or 40,000,000 of Germany could have pitted against us.' As for the role of the vaunted Royal Navy, Palmerston blamed geography and the weather. 'To have sent a fleet in midwinter to the Baltic every sailor would tell you was an impossibility'. More to the point, had the powerful Channel Fleet been despatched, Palmerston admitted that 'it would have been attended by no effectual result'; implicitly a lesson from the Crimean War campaigns of 1854 and 1855. Yet he was not prepared to go into specifics. 'Ships sailing on the sea cannot stop armies on land,' he offered, 'and to have attempted to stop the progress of any army by sending a fleet to the Baltic would have been attempting to do that which it was not possible to accomplish.' This deliberately ignored the option of blockading or bombarding German coasts in the North Sea, Baltic or Adriatic in the same way that he had threatened the Austrian ambassador three months earlier. Instead, Palmerston switched tack by suggesting that Britain was at least 'amply sufficient to defy attack from whatever quarter it may proceed.' From this perspective, it was not so much about drawing the sword to defend other countries as how the fleet 'was growing every year, adapting itself to the modern requirements of naval warfare, and fully adequate for the defence of the country.' All talk of (Palmerstonian) intervention the past few years was now to be forgotten. 'Our object is defence—not aggression', he declared. And it was because of this that the country could not 'undertake vast operations beyond its confines'. The problem with Denmark (and Poland, and the American South), finally, was that its cause was 'not considered as sufficiently British, and as sufficiently bearing on the interests and the security and the honour of England, as to make it justifiable to ask the country to make those exertions which such a war would render necessary.'[10]

That left the United States. In his February 1864 assessment of the defence of Canada in the event of an Anglo-American rupture, Jervois warned that the United States 'must now be ranked amongst the great military nations of the world', and that even though the Union was still preoccupied with the Civil War, 'it seems most probable that if the war be prolonged, the superior resource so the North must

---

10   See 24 August 1864, *The Times*.

ultimately prevail.' The British Empire would then be faced with a fully mobilised industrial power at its doorstep. Back in late 1861, during the height of the *Trent Affair*, 'no doubt one reason why it did not suit the States to go to war...was, that the fixed and floating defences of their coast were not in such a state as to enable them to hope to successfully to resist attacks upon their sea-ports; Portland, Portsmouth, Boston, New York, Philadelphia, and Washington were all to a greater or less extent open to sea attack.' Since then, however, enormous efforts had been made to right that deficiency. Now Britain was sorely deprived of its own ability to strike back with the strong arm of its naval power. Even smaller Northern sea towns like Salem, Marblehead, Gloucester, Newburyport, and Plymouth were defended by temporary earthworks mounting heavy guns all pointing to sea—in preparation for war.[11] Jervois was the Deputy-Director of Fortifications and naturally considered that only improved fixed defences at Quebec, Montreal, Toronto and Kingston would offset the relatively small number of British imperial troops and local militia operating in Canada against the vast, battle-hardened Union Army with its now veteran corps of field officers and sophisticated logistics. Yet the total forces required, as agreed by a reviewing Defence Committee in early 1865, was no less than 150,000 men—and this assumed 'that the works of fortification which have been recommended were constructed—the communications improved as suggested—the Lower St. Lawrence commanded by a naval force—and the shore of Lake Ontario protected by such vessels as might be rendered available, acting in conjunction with the fortifications'. Both the Committee and Jervois specified at least six ironclads for Lake Ontario, but his initial estimate of '£300,000' for these, as they were informed by Grey of the Admiralty, was that 'more powerful, and consequently more expensive, vessels would be required'. At any rate, all of these preparations (especially the notion of turning Kingston into a major naval station on Lake Ontario) had to be undertaken immediately, during peace, if they were to have any hope of countering American shipbuilding on the Lakes.[12] After consulting with the Chief Constructor, Robinson suggested in February 1865 that twin-screw, double-turreted monitors 'superior in every respect to the *Monadnock*' might be constructed in Britain which drew only 8½-feet yet mounted four 20-ton guns[13] behind 8-inches of armour. But here the Controller had to warn the Admiralty that 'this outline will convey some slight idea of what really is required to obtain and keep command of the Lakes, and as these vessels must be numerous, of the prodigious

11 February 1864, *Report on the Defence of Canada and of the British Naval Stations in the Atlantic, Part I—Defence of Canada*, Carnarvon Papers, TNA PRO 30-6, 168. The cover letter of Jervois is dated Pall Mall, 24 March 1864. He had toured Bermuda, the Northern States, and British North America for three months.
12 Confidential 1865, *Memorandum by the Defence Committee on the Report of Lieutenant-Colonel Jervois on the Defence of Canada*, TNA WO 33/15. See also 'Navigation to Lake Ontario' (1864), Somerset Papers, Devon, Box 19, A1-5.
13 Possibly referring to Armstrong's massive 22½-ton, shunt '600-pounder'; a rifled muzzle-loader known in the British press as 'Big Will'.

cost which must of necessity be incurred in doing so.'[14] How long it would take to produce such a flotilla and convoy it safely across the Atlantic, while the Americans carried on with their own building programmes and weapons development was also left an unspoken issue.

In summer 1864, Lieutenant-Colonel T. L. Gallwey of the Royal Engineers and Captain H. J. Alderson of the Royal Army also reported to the Under Secretary of State for War on the *Military Affairs of the United States of America* as well as on the 'probable operations of the United States Forces in case of a war with this country'.[15] These were detailed equivalents of U.S. Corps of Engineers Major Richard Delafield's 1860 printed *Report on the Art of War in Europe in 1854, 1855, and 1856*, with extensive appendices, U.S. reports and physical specimens shipped back overseas for close examination back in London. They did not recommend for British service monster smoothbore guns like those of Rodman or Dahlgren, nor Captain Robert Parrott of the U.S. Army's scheme of cast iron rifled guns reinforced at the breech with wrought iron bands (which 'has the advantages of cheapness and facility of production…but little endurance').[16] Nevertheless, a growing arsenal of such weapons daily reinforced U.S. coastal fortifications, and places like New York Harbor, they reported, saw works being constructed 'on every point which offers a convenient defensive position.' The mile-wide Narrows leading to America's richest city was guarded by Fort Hamilton and auxiliary shore batteries on the (eastern) Brooklyn side, with Fort Lafayette off shore; on the Staten Island side stood Fort Tompkins to landward and Fort Richmond on bluffs overlooking the new four-tiered Battery Weed (later Fort Wadsworth) and more shore batteries. In fact, most of the inner harbour bristled with gun emplacements, although the British officers thought heavy guns mounted *en barbette*—on the tops of the brick and granite casemated forts as well as in earthworks—were too crammed for their own good and needlessly exposed. They even conjectured that they might be 'silenced from a distance of two miles', presumably from ironclads anchored safely off Sandy Hook firing rifled Armstrong guns. But accuracy would be difficult at that range especially without any form of local spotting, and there would still be the problem of rifled Union counter-battery fire as well as interference from enemy ironclads. Indeed, they noted, 'the Monitor fleet would render great service to the defence of the harbour, and extensive use would also be made of floating obstructions and torpedoes.' This was the coastal defence (or 'ships vs. forts') principle confirmed during the Crimean War, and which was playing out yet again during the American Civil War: 'that ships cannot contend with forts when the conditions are anything like equal. If an iron-clad fleet can run past one or more forts, and take up a position

---

14   22 February 1865, Robinson to Board, in Milne Papers, Greenwich, MLN 124/1.
15   See 27 May 1864, Gallwey to Lyons, TNA FO 115/426. See also Michael Somerville, *Bull Run to Boer War: How the American Civil War Changed the British Army* (Warwick: Helion & Company Limited, 2019).
16   Gallwey and Alderson, *Report upon the Military Affairs of the United States of America* (War Office: 1864), in TNA WO 33/14, 34.

between them and the place defended, with impunity from attack, and further be a match for any auxiliary floating defences, it can only be said that that particular system of defence is defective, and not that forts are not a match for ships.'[17] Unfortunately for Great Britain in 1864, despite some flaws in design and execution of their ships, forts and guns, the Americans were now able to hold up a more than adequate defence. So in that strategic posture, the age-old maxim played out in their favour. Capturing and occupying these places would now be 'extremely difficult'.[18]

* * *

Russell could only hope in the summer of 1864 that Grant's Overland Campaign in Virginia would fail, with the Yankees thus 'beaten into patience and calmness'. Otherwise he worried there was 'no saying what degree of gumption they may reach if they are inflated with victory'. Maybe the Federal debt would be enough to dampen any thoughts of 'incurring a new debt' by indulging in their long-promised war of revenge against Britain. To Lord Lyons in Washington he suggested it might even be useful to send a formal British 'Civil or Military Agent or Commissioner' to Richmond, just in case.[19] By August, the Army of the Potomac had indeed suffered enormous losses— some 100,000 casualties—in its relentless attempts to crush Lee's Army of Northern Virginia. The two battered forces were now locked into siege at Petersburg, a vital supply hub for not just the rebel capital but the beleaguered Confederacy's entire war effort. After the disastrous attempt by the Union Army's IX Corps to tunnel under Lee's trench-lines culminated in the ghastly 'Battle of the Crater' (30 July 1864), *Punch* felt buoyant enough to suggest that 'Lord Pam' might just go ahead and recognise Confederate President Jefferson Davis after all.[20] On 28 August, the Prime Minister privately expressed to the King of the Belgians his wish that Mexico, now occupied by French imperial troops, would eventually embrace the Austrian archduke Maximilian as its Emperor, since a monarchy would not only be 'a real blessing to Mexico, but a great advantage to Europe.' As for the Monroe Doctrine and the anger of the United States to a Napoleon III-backed puppet-government south of its border, Palmerston

17 Ibid., 9-13. 'Unless there be some weak points in construction or mode of armament,' Gallwey and Alderson concluded, 'a ship must be destroyed if she enters into an engagement with a fort.'
18 19 July 1864, Foreign Office to Admiralty (forwarding from Lyons the report 'on the probable operations of the United States Forces in case of a war with this country'), TNA ADM 1/5902. Here Gallwey also noted 'that strenuous efforts would be made to produce wrought-iron guns in case of war with France or England; and it would be therefore advisable to watch the future progress of the U.S. in the manufacture of Heavy Artillery.'
19 21 May, 4 June and 23 July 1864, Russell to Lyons, Russell Papers, TNA PRO 30-22, 97.
20 27 August 1864, 'Very Probable', *Punch*.

was confident that Lincoln's administration 'have come to the conviction that they are unable to prevent it and had better therefore say as little as possible on the subject.'[21]

But by the autumn it was more apparent how ill-equipped the U.K.—not the U.S.—was for backing up any diplomatic threats. Somerset had already assured the Foreign Secretary on 6 September that British naval ordnance was not so far behind that of foreign powers, as suggested by the 19 June duel between the *Alabama* and the USS *Kearsage* (whose 11-inch Dahlgren guns had apparently 'mortified' Napoleon III). Here it wasn't so much about their calibre as their overall weight. The First Lord of the Admiralty hoped to have over one hundred of the new 6-ton guns ready by 1865. These were strong enough to penetrate any French ironclad afloat. 12-ton guns were also coming but he believed they were 'inconveniently heavy' for general service and therefore he'd asked for a 9-ton version instead, adding that even those wrought iron guns for forts and ships deemed 'most immediately requisite' would add considerably to the army estimates for 1865.[22] The key problem of course was not one of money but time, as astutely observed by Palmerston. At the moment neither the British nor the French ironclad fleets carried guns which could sink the other, 'unless we go to a size beyond the Capacity of a seagoing Ship to carry', he wrote to Somerset. As for the Americans, he was still optimistic that 'we shall find Means to send across the Atlantic and into the St. Lawrence Guns strong enough to send their floating batteries to the Bottom, the heavy Guns would go in one Ship and another would go light and be ready to receive the heavy Guns when in the St. Lawrence, or at Halifax.' Yet in the meantime, the U.S. would surely 'send out a Swarm of fast Steamers not armour-plated, and not meant for fighting, but speedy enough to escape from our Cruisers, and strong enough to capture any Merchantman.' Something had to be done soon to address this contingency—in preparing 'for a Storm which as far as political Forecasting goes has been foretold as likely to follow the Conclusion of Peace between the Federals and Confederates.' Somerset could only repeat what he'd told Russell three days earlier; that 6-, 9- and 12-ton guns were on order, to replace

---

21 28 August 1864, Palmerston to the King of the Belgians, Palmerston Papers, Broadlands, MS62, Private Letterbox. Union General Ulysses S. Grant indeed considered the establishment of 'a European monarchy upon our continent…as a direct act of war against the United States … and supposed as a matter of course that the United States would treat it as such when their hands were free to strike.' But even though he broached the topic to Lincoln and Seward more than once, he 'never heard any special views from them to enable me to judge what they thought or felt about it', Elizabeth D. Samet (ed.), *Annotated Memoirs of Ulysses S. Grant* (New York: Liveright Publishing Corporation, 2019), 927-8. See also 4 January 1866, Bruce to Clarendon (as Foreign Secretary), expressing his belief that 'the Mexican people are at present incapable of appreciating a republican form of government, and that the United States have the most direct interest in seeing a firm and orderly Government substituted for the anarchy which has hitherto prevented the development of the resources of Mexico', TNA FO (Foreign Office) 5/1062.

22 3 September 1864, Russell to Somerset, Somerset Papers, Aylesbury, D/RA/A/2A/53; 6 September 1864, Somerset to Russell, Russell Papers, TNA PRO 30-22, 26.

the British fleet's current armament of 68-pounder muzzle-loading smoothbores and 110-pounder breechloading rifled Armstrongs (seriously prone to mishap, as it turned out). Fifty 6-ton guns, unrifled, were 'now nearly ready' and these would be duly tested in various broadside-ironclads over the next year. There were also the carriages and friction gear for all this new, experimental heavy ordnance to work out. But these assurances rather missed the point, Palmerston complained to the Secretary of State for War two days later, 'as it is all about what is to be.' If rifled ordnance firing steel shot were the order of the day then these needed to be pressed forward immediately, no matter the cost, since only guns 'which would smash and sink the Monitors' could be relied upon to keep the St. Lawrence River open.[23]

It was now a race between how soon the North could finally subdue the South versus British readiness for any Anglo-American war to follow. The Admiralty therefore pressed the War Office to re-arm all of its ironclads in commission along with those which might be ready for 1865-6. 'In the event of any pressure from the probability of War,' the Board added, 'an increased number would be necessary.'[24] And while Somerset tried to mollify Palmerston that upcoming ships like the armoured corvette *Pallas* and the *Amazon*-class of wooden sloops (fitted as rams) might serve well in a commerce war later in 1865, the Royal Navy was wholly deficient in vessels like the Americans' fast, heavily-armed, 'double-ender' paddlewheel-steamers which had been proving their worth along the Southern coastline. How to attack places like New York Harbor or Washington D.C. also remained problematic in the extreme. 'On the breaking out of a Foreign war,' reported U.S. Major Barton Alexander to Brigadier General Richard Delafield (Chief of Engineers), effective obstructions could be placed in the Potomac River 'in a few days' if need be, since both modern military theory and recent combat experience had demonstrated that 'if we can detain a hostile fleet for a single hour under the close fire of powerful shore batteries, that we can either destroy it, or so cripple it that it cannot advance to another attack'.[25] Yet the ranking British naval officer on the scene, Vice-Admiral Hope, had been instructed by the First Naval Lord to economise the North America and West Indies Station, part of a general trend 'of reducing the Force abroad with the view of increasing

---

23 6 September 1864, Palmerston to Somerset, Somerset Papers, Aylesbury, D/RA/A/2A/40; 9 September 1864, Somerset to Palmerston, Palmerston Papers, Broadlands, MS 62, GC/50; 11 September 1864, Palmerston to Ripon, Palmerston Papers, Broadlands, MS 62, Private Letterbook, April 1862 to March 1865.

24 24 September 1864, Admiralty to War Office, TNA ADM 1/5885. In addition to eighty-five 6½-ton rifled 7-inch guns already ordered for 1864-5, a further 243 was required for 1865-6. But the guns were to be rifled 'on such principle as may be determined on, when the experiments now in progress have been completed.'

25 12 September 1864, Somerset to Palmerston, Palmerston Papers, Broadlands, MS 62, GC/50; 11 November 1864, No. 371, 'Reports relative to the United States Vessel of War *Tallapoosa*', TNA ADM 1/5873; 17 September 1864, forwarded by Goodenough's successor, British naval attaché Captain John Bythesea, to the Foreign Office; TNA ADM 1/5992. Alexander also noted laying down electrically-fired torpedoes (mines).

that at home.' The timing was poor. The U.S. Congress was ready to abrogate the Reciprocity Treaty which had formally governed trade with British North America since 1854. But worse than this, on 19 October 1864 Confederate agents operating from Canada robbed banks in St. Albans, Vermont, killed a civilian, and tried to burn the town down before fleeing back across the border. Under intense U.S. pressure, Canadian officials arrested the men and returned what money they could but claimed that British neutrality in the American Civil War prevented them from extraditing the prisoners (who were later released). Angry and frustrated, the White House now gave new thought to withdrawing from the Rush-Bagot Treaty of 1817 with Great Britain, which limited naval forces on the Great Lakes to a tiny handful of 100-ton vessels armed with 18-pounders. Although Federal authorities were more likely to introduce small ships 'for Police purposes' only, Hope wrote to Somerset that even if they began construction of ironclads on the Lakes, he 'should deprecate anything in the shape of a building competition with them, but would recommend the adoption of their own policy of allowing their neighbours to build to their heart's content and when [they] come to a stop, then providing some means of offence so much more formidable as to render their previous preparations comparatively useless':

> But the real question is, can we in the face of the great natural advantages possessed by the Americans, obtain this superiority—and if so would the cost both in men and money not be so great as to render it much more serviceable to the Country to spend it elsewhere.
>
> I should view any such attempt as a drain and a most unwise one on the resources of the Country in no degree inferior to that occasioned to Russia by the Siege of Sebastopol.[26]

The alterative, however, was hardly more palatable. As *The Times* bemoaned earlier in that year, it was all too tempting to behave like Imperial France, 'enforcing her views by a resort to arms'. Unleashed, the Royal Navy 'could sweep the seas with our fleets', shutting down the Mediterranean and the Baltic if need be, blockading 'any port of any maritime country.' A British army corps of 30,000 men could be projected anywhere in the world, and 300,000 allied troops could be subsidised from stuffed British coffers. But all this would literally come at a cost, in the form of 'largely increased taxations, and deficits after all', and even £20 million 'would not cover our Navy Estimates on these principles of foreign policy, nor would any amount of armaments answer the purpose without actual war now and then.' And while the same degree of perpetual war-readiness, war-mongering and warfare could be applied to any power in the world—with perhaps the United States (formerly a relatively benign and provincial second-rate power) serving as the prime example in 1864—this *choice* was something Britain had clearly eschewed. Once again, defence was one

26   27 December 1864, Hope to Somerset, Somerset Papers, Aylesbury, D/RA/A/2A/29.

thing, Palmerstonian interventionism another. Britain had proved willing to pay for the former, but only offer lip-service in support of the latter. Now the consequences were plain to see. 'When a man who will not fight except under irresistible pressure interferes in a quarrel, and wishes the combatants to accept his judgment, we know what words he is likely to get. But this "humiliation," such as it is, is the inevitable incident of such a policy as we have chosen.'[27] By the end of the year, *The Times* could exclaim some measure of relief that most of the other major powers had not gone mad—headlong into world war. If anything, more money was being invested into their self-preservation than aggrandisement. Russell murmured in October that if the Americans thought they could grab Canada 'they must look to a fight with us', but on 19 November he confided to Lyons his doubt that the U.S. Government had 'any ill intentions towards us,' nor that their unprecedented mobilisation would be used 'to add a war with us to their existing difficulties.' That same day, the American *Army & Navy Journal* noted the new massive iron casemates, building in Britain by Millwall, to modernise the already imposing granite forts of Cronstadt. These were to house '600-pounder' Krupp guns of the latest design and were to be ready by early 1865. The sheer magnitude of such monster guns protected by such 'impregnable' shielding, as featured on the cover of the 19 November *Illustrated London News*, was the quintessence of isolationist Russia herself.[28] How was the Royal Navy supposed to cope? *The Times* thus considered how glad it was Britain had not been 'drawn into a war with Russia for such a chimaera as the regeneration of Poland', for no other reason than the prospect of Russian commerce raiders issuing from American ports to attack British sea-lanes around the world, making Britain 'feel the evils of the conflict in the most sensitive place and in the severest manner.'[29]

As Palmerston had suspected, Somerset was not in favour of naval cutbacks for the immediate future. Withdrawing ships and their crews from the North American and West Indian Station would only invite further transgressions from 'private ships in blockade running' thereby exacerbating Anglo-American tensions. 'I think also it would have the worst effect in Canada,' he added, 'if they heard that our force on the station were largely reduced.'[30] On the other hand, the Northern States surely no longer felt as 'threatened' by the presence of Her Majesty's Ships of War off their coasts. Gladstone therefore had to concede two months later that although the Cabinet expressed sharp differences in opinion on the nature and necessity of naval force, 'the feeling was generally against me' and he was therefore willing to agree to

27 12 March 1864, *The Times*.
28 20 October and 19 November 1864, Russell to Lyons, Russell Papers, TNA PRO 30-22, 97; 19 November 1864, *Army and Navy Journal*, 197-8; 12 November 1864, *The Illustrated London News*; see also the full two-page illustration of the battery in the 1866 *L'Univers illustré*. The shield structures were described as 43½-feet wide by 10-feet high and reinforced with wrought-iron bars 12 x 12-inches thick.
29 17 September 1864, *The Times*.
30 14 November 1864, Somerset to Palmerston, Palmerston Papers, Broadlands, GC/50.

the Naval Estimates.[31] Yet he might have taken some comfort as well that other voices in Britain, such as Cobden's at Rochdale on 23 November 1864, struck a chord of truth: 'that we achieved a revolution in our foreign policy.' The impotence of bellicose Tory Lords like the 74 year old Earl of Ellenborough was revealed not just by his sharp critique of the Queen for refusing to support a war against Prussia and Austria over Denmark, but by his frustration that 'the whole people' of Britain were seduced by '"others…who appealed to more common things, to love of repose, to love of quiet, but, above all, to the love of money, which has now become the engrossing passion of the people of this country."' Cobden now called for British public speakers and the press 'to treat foreign questions in a different spirit to what they have done', especially since 'we come to have a proper and due opinion of how little we can really do to effect any change abroad'.[32] Palmerston's chief concern over naval reductions going into 1865, 'in the face of all the warnings we have of contingent Hostility on the Part of the Federal States of North America', was how it would force 'upon ourselves a very dangerous Responsibility', and Somerset anticipated more questions than it answered: 'why were these reductions not made last year? Are the Federal states less inclined to make demands on our forbearance? Are the blockade-runners less troublesome? Is the question of the island of St. Juan happily settled? Are there no troubles in the Pacific? Is Japan so quiet and comfortable that our squadron can be recalled? Is New Zealand so secure that not only the Army but the Navy also may be withdrawn? Are these measures of economy proposed to meet the position of affairs abroad or to meet eventualities expected at home? Are the estimates framed only for the general election? Are the reiterated professions of national defence and maritime security to be suddenly forgotten? If the policy of the last five years was good; why is it now to be abandoned?'[33]

* * *

What Sir John Pakington, President of the Institution of Naval Architects, told his distinguished listeners at their annual meeting of 29 March 1865 therefore shouldn't have come as much of a shock. Although it was announced that Edward Reed was now going to be made a Vice-President, the two main questions to be considered over the next week of papers and discussions, as far as Pakington was concerned, was 'How far it is possible to apply iron armour to a man of war without injuring her seagoing

---

31 28 January 1865, Gladstone to Palmerston, from Guedalla, *Gladstone and Palmerston*, 320.
32 See *The Times*, 24 November 1864. See also A. J. P. Taylor, *The Trouble Makers: Dissent Over Foreign Policy 1792-1939* (London: Pimlico, 1993 reprint of 1957 original), who goes so far as to argue that 'Cobden was the real Foreign Secretary of the early eighteen-sixties', 64-6.
33 30 November 1864, Palmerston to Somerset, Somerset Papers, Aylesbury, D/RA/A/2A/40; 1 December 1864, Somerset to Palmerston, Palmerston Papers, Broadlands, GC/50.

qualities? And secondly, How far it is possible to apply that new mode of arming men-of-war by the revolving turrets which have been invented by Captain Cowper Coles?' Both the Institute and Britain had cause to celebrate, since a School of Naval Architecture had now been opened, its first session taking place earlier that November with sixteen students, including four from the private trade (and with a curriculum very similar to the pre-existing school of naval architecture in France.) Yet if the Admiralty could be blamed for anything lately it was not for transforming the British fleet from wood to iron too slowly but not cautiously enough; by not 'ascertaining, as far as possible, the real bearings of this question before a very considerable number of costly ships were so covered with armour as to make it questionable whether they are fit to cross the Atlantic.' This was a stinging rebuke of not just Robinson's emergency expedient in 1861, of converting wooden ships-of-the-line into fully-armoured broadside-ironclads like the *Royal Oak* and her sisters, but possibly also Reed's central-battery alternative, the *Bellerophon*. Assuming that ironclads armed with turrets meant both an even greater concentration of armour and economy of weight, the President confessed his 'wish that the experiment had been tried sooner. It has been fairly tried upon ships which are admirably adapted for coast defence, but it has not yet been tried upon ships to go to sea, and I think the Admiralty would have given it a much fairer test if they consented to Captain Coles's proposal three years ago, and had constructed an experimental ship, to see whether or not this important principle could be applied to cruising vessels.'[34]

Ironically enough, the issue of whether or not such a question could be scientifically assessed by naval professionals without the trouble and expense of building an entire ship was not addressed. Instead, on 6 April, Admiralty naval constructor Nathaniel Barnaby presented his findings of 'An investigation of the Stability of HMS *Achilles*', which stressed the importance of the relation between the metacentre of a ship and its centre of buoyancy. Vice-President J. Scott Russell then commented that this 'third ship of the *Warrior* class' was probably as far as a seagoing ironclad could be safely loaded up with armour plating without making the vessel inherently unstable, while Reed differed from Barnaby 'that we are altogether unable to find the place of the centre of gravity in a ship'; only not '*precisely*'. In any case, Barnaby felt that if the watertight compartments on the ends of the *Achilles* were flooded that 'she would be quite safe, but if they were in the middle we might say of her, as of every iron ship, that it is very doubtful whether she would not sink.'[35] Against weapons like the Armstrong 9-inch 12-ton RML or the American 15-inch smoothbores this placed an obvious premium upon a stronger belt of waterline armour than that of the *Achilles* and all the

---

34 *Transactions of the Institution of Naval Architects*, Volume VI (London, 1865), xx-xxii.
35 Nathaniel Barnaby, 'An investigation of the Stability of H.M.S. *Achilles*', *Transactions of the Institution of Naval Architects*, Volume VI (London, 1865), 1-12.

current British ironclads afloat.[36] Rear-Admiral Sir Edward Belcher then argued in a different paper that because 'no reasonable thickness of iron plate...can be expected to withstand the heavy ordnance which it is contemplated to use for service afloat,' that the latest British ironclads, with their 5½- and 6-inch plating were 'virtually inefficient as rapid, handy, and active cruisers'. Surely the trend for a proper oceanic navy should be for less, not more armour? Scott Russell added his concern: 'Shall we abandon altogether a ship-shape ship, and merely consider that what we have to provide is a floating gun carriage?' British ships must be made 'capable of making long voyages, such as are required for the protection of our country, ships which have to remain a long time at sea, and to follow an enemy wherever he pleases to go'. The obsession over heavier guns vs. thicker armour was warping the evolution of the capital ship in dangerous directions. The creator of the original *Warrior* therefore considered 'we must go back very much to the recognized forms, the recognized proportions, and the recognised shapes.'[37]

Reed was bound, of course, to respectfully disagree. All of the large ironclads in service were proving themselves as oceangoing cruisers, 'and all, excepting the very long ships, are as handy under the helm as the ordinary wooden vessels, turning the same circle in the same time.' There was actually nothing to suggest that proper sea-keeping was inherently incompatible with adopting thicker armour protection—it was all a matter of proper design. What's more, while British warships certainly needed to fulfil their classic obligations to both national and imperial defence, neither could the Admiralty ignore the technological changes—and challenges—going on around the world, and what those meant for British prestige. Thus, 'it appears to me, and has all along appeared to me, that the obvious policy of this country, with all its enormous resources, is to go on with armour plating; but when we lay down a new ship to see if we cannot make her superior to the ships already laid down, and so keep up the competition with other Powers, into which we have been driven, but which we did not seek, so that we may have at least one or two ships, or as many as we can afford to build, manifestly superior to those of other nations.' Here was the candid origin of Britain's future 'fleet of samples', a strategic curiosity in the long

---

36 Including the turret-ships *Prince Albert*, and *Scorpion* and *Wivern*, with their 4½-inch thick side plating, and *Royal Sovereign*, armoured with 5½-inch plates along the beam tapering to 4½-inches on her ends. Reed's *Bellerophon*, with 6-inch plating on her sides amidships from the upper deck to 6-feet below the waterline, was not launched until the end of the following month (26 April). By early 1865 the most strongly armoured British ironclad was the Reed-designed, ram-bowed *Lord Clyde*, with her 24-inch thick (unseasoned) oak hull covered by 1½-inch iron plates, and another strake of 6-inch oak supporting the main armour plating of 5½-inches, which was then covered by a final 4-inches of outer oak planking—a combined thickness of 41-inches (although her wooden hull had neither watertight compartments nor armoured bulkheads). See Parkes, *British Battleships*, 94; and Ballard, *Black Battlefleet*, 76-8.

37 Edward Belcher, 'On the Construction of Armour-Clad Ships of War', *Transactions of the Institution of Naval Architects*, Volume VI (London, 1865), 74-100.

annals of British naval history, and one which would continue for at least another generation. As one exasperated Board of Admiralty member wrote in April 1874, 'What is required for a Channel Squadron…is that the ships composing it shall be of the same type, so as to manoeuvre together, turning the circle in about the same time, and able to cruise under canvas. At this time we have four distinct Classes in a Squadron consisting of six ships, viz., *Agincourt, Sultan, Triumph* and *Resistance*.'[38] It was not just the continual 'turret vs. broadside' or 'gun vs. armour' questions which drove Reed and Robinson into this direction—as close to a 'policy' as the Admiralty in this period ever consciously developed—nor was it simply about keeping up with the French. It was how the even more classic, fundamental divide between Blue and Brown water spheres of influence was playing itself out in recent years; to the apparent disadvantage of Britain as a Great Power, precisely because so much of her identity was invested in her maritime empire and global interests. Of course, Reed assured his colleagues that 'we have no reason, with the immense advantage which iron give us, to fear our power to carry a limited but effective defence of 11 inches of armour, if necessary.' The Admiralty's latest 'response', inasmuch as he was allowed to reveal it publicly and even semi-officially, was going to be a seagoing, central-battery-ironclad with truly unparalleled defensive strength (the *Hercules*). But shipbuilder Charles Lamport doubted even Reed's boasted 'foot of solid armour plating' would be enough, because the 'very clear line' at stake in these deliberations was 'between those vessels which are seagoing, and have to keep at sea a considerable time, and those vessels which are for the defence of our shores.' The Chief Constructor thus had no reply when asked 'whether he would like to send the *Warrior*, if plated to the extremities as she ought to be, to the American coast to maintain a blockade there?' Either she would be safe from the sea *or* from the monster guns of (even more heavily armoured)

---

38 Ibid., 88; (10 April 1874) *Letter from Rear-Admiral G.T.P. Hornby, Commanding the Channel Squadron, to The Right Hon. George Ward Hunt, M.P.*, enclosed minute dated 13 April 1874, from Vice-Admiral Sir John W. Tarleton (Second Naval Lord), in Milne Papers, Greenwich, MLN 144/2. See also C. J. Bartlett, The Mid-Victorian Reappraisal of Naval Policy', in Kenneth Bourne and D. C. Watt (eds.), *Studies in International History* (Hamden: Archon Books, 1967), 189-208; Antony Preston and John Major, *Send a Gunboat! The Victorian Navy and Supremacy at Sea, 1854-1904* (London: Conway, 2007 reprint of 1967 original), 39; and Stanley Sandler, *Battleships: An Illustrated History of Their Impact* (Santa Barbara: ABC-CLIO, 2004), 44, 67, 89-90. John Beeler argues that while the British ironclad fleet evolved into a '"miscellaneous collection of bizarre and ill-sorted designs"…yet it is difficult to see what alternative policy might logically have been pursued. To have settled on one design, especially in the absence of any consensus regarding the future of naval warfare, risked at the same time getting left behind technologically and being saddled with a fleet of obsolete vessels,' *British Policy in the Gladstone-Disraeli Era, 1866-1880* (Stanford: Stanford University Press, 1997), 258. Significantly, he adds, 'Any ship intended for a global role had to carry sails until at least 1885.'

enemy floating batteries, but not against both. Chairing this evening's session, fellow Vice-President Sir Isaac Watts, architect of the original *Warrior*, was likewise silent.[39]

The year had already begun with more sensational news from America. Confederate Fort Fisher, guarding the approaches to Wilmington, North Carolina, had finally been captured (13-15 January) by three Union assault divisions closely supported by a massive naval bombardment from 58 ships. Not only was Wilmington the last protected base for blockade-running operations on the eastern seaboard of the continent, its increasingly vital imports supplied—some 250 miles away—General Robert E. Lee's Army of Northern Virginia, entrenched at Petersburg, Virginia since early June, and the beleaguered Confederate capital of Richmond. The largest coastal fortification designed by Southern engineers throughout the course of the Civil War, Fort Fisher's defenders had long boasted it was the 'Gibraltar' of the South. With the Cape Fear River on one side and the Atlantic on the other, its heavily armed bastions ran over a mile long and were anchored at Fisher's southern tip by a huge, 60-foot high packed-earth and sand Mound Battery likened to the Russians' infamous Malakoff Tower of the Siege of Sevastopol. *The Times* couldn't help but be impressed with the terrible magnitude of a single continuous barrage whereby some '25,000 shells' had been expended, and 'we much doubt whether any single fort in the world has ever been subjected to so tremendous a fire.'[40] More than this, the Union broadside-ironclad USS *New Ironsides* and four monitors (the double-turreted *Monadnock*, and single-turret *Canonicus*, *Mahopac* and *Saugus*), it was admitted, 'lay for five days within 800 yards of Fort Fisher and received no material injury.'[41] The Foreign Office meanwhile made sure to forward to the Admiralty Porter's printed report to Secretary of the Navy Welles, which directly compared the merits of the *New Ironsides* with the *Monadnock*. The former's 11-inch Dahlgren guns, firing at a much greater rate than the monitors' 15-inch smoothbores, played a singular role in supporting advancing Union troops as they advanced from traverse to bloody traverse, while the Union rear-admiral was certain the *Monadnock* was 'capable of crossing the ocean alone (when her compasses are once adjusted properly), and could destroy any vessel in the French or British navy, lay their towns under contribution, and return again (provided she could pick up coal) without fear of being followed.

---

39 Belcher, 'On the Construction of Armour-Clad Ships of War', 89-92.
40 Porter estimated '115 rounds per minute' were fired by his fleet against Fort Fisher during the initial 24 December 1864 bombardment; 26 December 1864, Porter to Welles, *ORN*, Series 1, Vol. 11, 254-60. The subsequent Union naval one of 15 January 1865 was the largest of its kind until the Second World War; see Michael Clodfelter, *Warfare and Armed Conflicts: A Statistical Encyclopedia of Casualty and Other Figures, 1492-2015* (Jefferson: McFarland & Company, Inc., 2017, 4th ed.), 293-4.
41 1 February 1865, *The Times*.

She could certainly clear any harbor on our coast of blockaders in case we were at war with a foreign power.[42]

Coles was annoyed with these latest taunts issuing from America (which echoed his own). Yet he took the wrong lesson from the engagement. Whereas Porter observed that the heavy guns of his turret-ships were 'not at all calculated to silence heavy batteries, which require a rapid and continuous fire to drive men from the guns', Coles wrote to Cobden sighing that while turret-ships were 'gradually making their way', they would be 'too late to save the vast expenditure on these monster Broadside Ships of 6000 tons', and that in the perennial question of 'ships vs. forts', 'Fort Fisher has proved to a great extent that my theory is right'. Both men at the time were seriously ill, yet 'if we live,' he continued, 'I fear that after spending all this money on the forts, we shall be able only to look at them as monuments of folly.'[43] Palmerston was also pained to observe to Somerset earlier, on 18 January, that British possessions in North America including Bermuda were clearly even more vulnerable against a great Union combined operation. 'The warnings of eventual hostility on the part of the United States are not to be disregarded,' he wrote, 'and the Irish Fenians in North America would give us trouble in Ireland if we had War with America.' As always—and despite the objections of Gladstone on the one hand and Cobden on the other—'the best security for Peace lies in defensive strength, and the Cost of Defensive works and arrangements is nothing compared with the expenses of the most quickly successful War.' Perhaps even more significantly, while the Union monitors played a conspicuous role in the reduction of Fort Fisher (unlike their efforts before Charleston), the ageing Premier added his disapproval that, 'As to Turret-ships, we have not yet, as I understand the matter, succeeded in making a good Sea Going Ship of that kind.'[44]

Indeed, Robinson and Reed had already come to the conclusion that just as the U.S. Navy had come to reply upon shallow-draft turret-ships for both strategic defence and offensive operations against the South, monitors would be the best possible type of ironclad warships for the defence of Canada. In a long memo to the First Lord of the Admiralty, in the dark early days of 1865, the Controller was adamant there was no hope of matching the Americans in the local production of ironclads for operations on the Great Lakes once war had already been declared, for the simple fact that the Northern States had already been mobilising for full-scale war by land and sea for nearly four years. 'WE never could under such circumstances be ready to commence

---

42   6 February 1865, Foreign Office to Admiralty, TNA ADM 1/5952; 28 January 1865, Porter to Welles, *ORN*, Series 1, Vol. 11, 453, and 15 January 1865, Porter to Welles, *ORN*, Series 1, Vol. 11, 600-2.

43   18 March 1865, Coles to Cobden, Cobden Papers, Chichester. Within two weeks (2 April) Cobden indeed succumbed, age 61, to the acute bronchitis which had plagued him for years: his last attempt to speak in Parliament was over the issue of Canadian fortifications; see for example 8 April 1865, *The Illustrated London News*.

44   18 January 1865, Palmerston to Somerset, Somerset Papers, Aylesbury, D/RA/A/2A/41.

hostilities as well prepared as THEY would be: in fact, the disproportion of Naval force at the commencement of a War, would be as 3 to 1 in their favour':

> If again, we are not so superior in Naval Force, at the outbreak of hostilities, as to be able to assail the establishments they will form (directly a war breaks out) in these Lakes, with every prospect of destroying them, they would from their very superior resources rapidly gain command of the inland waters and keep down our attempts to have a naval force equal to their own…It is however clear to my mind that, whenever, both parties commence the preparations of War Vessels on these Lakes, the American will beat us in the proportion of two to one, at least. What they have already done in the way of armoured gun boats and in constructing war vessels adapted for inland navigation, is proof of this; we might build better vessels, but we should be longer about it, and the expense to us would nearly twice as much per ton as to them…they would probably repudiate the debt, which both of would contract in performing these operations.'
>
> 'No one in looking at these questions can forget that the Naval Force possessed by the United States for <u>defensive</u> purposes is four or five times larger than that of any European power, and that the possibility of making serious assaults by sea against any of their towns is in consequence very limited indeed. It is clear that what was quite possible in 1861 is no longer so in 1865.'

For the command of the St. Lawrence River between Quebec and Montreal, the Royal Navy could produce twin-screw turreted-ironclads of wood and iron construction which would not draw more than 16-feet, with engines powerful enough to manage 'the rapidity of the stream'. And while they could not be constructed in the Mother Country and sent safely across the Atlantic, the architects in Robinson's department were confident they could be 'partly prepared in England and built at Quebec.' Not acting for their defence in this way might actually make the Canadians question their loyalty to the Crown, Robinson warned, even if it was necessary to call upon them to help pay for such efforts and consider forming a colonial naval force of their own (though commanded by RN officers). Somerset, however, was inclined to proceed cautiously in the face of such a blitz. 'This suggestion opens a large question[:] a new navy for the lakes of Canada under a new commander in chief', he minuted. 'Such a plan could hardly be undertaken without the direct sanction of Parliament', he affirmed, otherwise it would mislead the Canadians how much Britain was prepared to pay on their behalf. At any rate, before the Admiralty planted a flag which might redefine the imperial relationship between the British and Canadian governments, the Colonial Office must also be consulted.[45]

---

45   9 January 1865, 'Defence of Canada', TNA ADM 1/5931.

Yet even if strategic contraction was the order of the day, Whitehall was nonetheless inundated with reports of rival states expanding their own defensive capabilities, if not ambitions. Prussia was fast at work fortifying Kiel dockyard and equipping it for the construction of large ironclads. The Germans were intent upon an armoured force of no less than ten ironclad frigates and ten monitors, all operating from well-defended ports.[46] By September Russian defences at Cronstadt mounted some two-hundred of Krupp's breechloading, 9-inch steel guns. *The Illustrated London News* had already graphically described an 11-inch, 14-ton RML Blakely gun, firing 500-pound shot, and mounted on an iron carriage and slide, as part of the Russian defences in the Gulf of Finland. More worrying, the Russian Government had since determined 'to order no guns from abroad, but to manufacture all they require at their own establishment at Alexandroffski, under the direction of General Aboukoff.' Russian steel was claimed 'to be the finest in the world. Its superiority is ascribed to the excellence of the Siberian ore, and to its being smelted with charcoal.'[47] Palmerston also wondered how Somerset expected to upgrade British government dockyards' accommodation even within fifteen years, as noted earlier in Parliament. 'This Period seems an Eternity, in Times when Every Thing and Every Body are moving at the double quick.' By contrast, the British naval attaché in Paris, Captain Edward Hore, reported that at Toulon 'the last and largest of the 3 new docks is now nearly ready for use' and a new basin was completing rapidly 'large enough to berth 30 vessels of the size of the *Solferino* broadside on to the quays leaving sufficient space between them'. Plans were meanwhile underway for blocking the entrance to the harbor with a combination of chains and three lines of torpedoes during wartime, while the French Navy moved ahead with an experimental twin-screw, single (fixed) turret ram (the *Taureau*) with 7-inch iron-plating along the waterline of a sharply sloping hull and armed with a 313lb rifled gun. And even as Robinson scrutinised disapprovingly the plethora of ironclads, great and small, building in private British shipyards for foreign powers, French firms were turning out armoured rams and gunboats for Italy, Turkey and Brazil. One private contractor, whose establishment (the Société Nouvelle des Forges et Chantiers de la Méditerranée) employed some 3,000 workmen and which

---

46   18 February 1865, Foreign Office to Admiralty, report of Acting Consul in Hamburg, TNA ADM 1/5952; 25 April 1865, Foreign Office to Admiralty, TNA ADM 1/5953.
47   4 September 1865, *Abstracts of Proceedings of the Ordnance Select Committee, for the Quarter ending 30th September, 1865* (London: George Edward Eyre and William Spottiswoode, 1865), 594, in TNA WO 33/15; 8 April 1865, *The Illustrated London News*. See also the 1866 pamphlet *Recent Experiments with Heavy Rifled Guns in Russia* (Woolwich: Royal Artillery Institution), in Somerset Papers, Devon, Box 20, PPP 7-11. The Russians had also established a large iron foundry and armour-plate manufacturing facility at Kolpino, St. Petersburg; see also Blackwell, *Beginnings of Russian Industrialization*, 70-1, 183-7, 251, 389-401; and, very recently, G. N. Shumkin, '"The continuous experimentation of our artillery scientists have yielded magnificent results": The Creation of Armor-Piercing Coastal Artillery in the Mid-Nineteenth Century', Voenno-istoricheskii zhurnal (*Military History Journal*), 2020, No. 4, 33-40.

had just completed the 7,000-ton, iron-hulled, broadside-ironclad *Numancia* for Spain, happily offered to build an ironclad for the British Navy if need be![48]

Britain's problems by this time also concerned the guns as much as the ships. When Robinson returned in late February to the subject of armoured vessels for service in Canada, he had repeat to Somerset his conviction that 'nothing that could be sent from this side of the water, capable of navigating across the Atlantic, would be of any avail. Looking to the system of railroads, and the far denser population on the American shores, as compared with that on the British side of the Lakes, there is little doubt that they could bring at very short notice, a formidable fleet of Ironclads, specially adopted for the work, into any of the Lakes and that they could either build or transport all such instruments of war at a far less cost, and far more quickly than we can.' Again, the only feasible option was to 'build on the spot the kind of vessel required,' and 'the American Monitor would be the most suitable for that particular service.' Reed's plans for twin-screw double-turreted monitors would be far less expensive than a deep-draft, seagoing (broadsided) ironclad, at £150,000 each including the contracted engines, but a substantial surcharge would be added by their shipping to and reconstruction in Kingston (eastern Ontario), 'where skilled labour is much dearer than in this country'—and Kingston itself was a frontier dockyard which would have to be re-tooled with its own factory and specialist personnel, as well as re-fortified (the later alone estimated at £400,000). A flotilla of such vessels might therefore require a Parliamentary naval supplement in the millions of pounds.[49]

And yet this said little for their armament. Indeed, the 'advantage that the Americans appear to possess in the matter of heavy guns', Captain Key of the *Excellent* dourly observed in March 1865, 'is that they have the guns, and have certainly learnt to use them at Sea.' Robinson was obliged to concur that 'on the necessity of considering the Armament of a Ship before designing her, and on the importance of considering a Ship as mainly designed to carry Guns', as stressed by Key. But he also had to remind the Admiralty 'that at this very moment there are more Ships fitted to carry large guns than there are guns ready to put into them.'[50] By mid-March 1865, Robinson observed that of the 135 guns of 12- , 9- and 6½-ton weights ordered in

---

48 11 June 1865, Palmerston to Somerset, Somerset Papers, Aylesbury, D/RA/A/2A/41; 7 June 1865, Hore to Admiralty, TNA ADM 1/5953, also 14 June 1865, Hore to Admiralty, TNA ADM 1/5954; 10 March 1865, Robinson to Board, TNA ADM 1/5941. These firms included, just on the Thames River, Thames (in Blackwall), Millwall, Samuda Brothers, and Green's (in Poplar). The following month, Robinson noted the construction by Atlas Works in Sheffield of a large Coles turret building for the Belgian Government, for land batteries at Antwerp, 5 April 1865, TNA ADM 1/5941. See also Theodore Ropp, *The Development of a Modern Navy: French Naval Policy 1871-1904* (Annapolis: Naval Institute Press, 1987), 13, 16-18.

49 22 February 1865, Robinson to Somerset, TNA ADM 1/5766; see also the copy in Milne Papers, MLN 124/1.

50 29 March 1865, Robinson to Board, TNA ADM 1/5941; Key's enclosed report is dated 21 March 1865.

1864, only fifty smoothbores had been supplied, with the remaining eighty-five to be rifled. Two-hundred more guns were ordered for the fiscal year 1865-1866, 285 total as rifled guns. But in terms of the heaviest firepower available, thirty-two 12-ton guns were required for 1865, and unless twenty-two were supplied by June then the *Agincourt*, *Bellerophon*, *Wivern* and *Prince Albert* would be left high and dry.[51] 'I do hope that we are making progress with our 300 and 600 pounders for we should have ample employment for them', Vice-Admiral Sir James Hope meanwhile nervously wrote to Somerset from Barbados. The latest news from Britain was serious talk of a likely U.S. 'war of revenge' against Perfidious Albion as soon as the Confederacy surrendered, which was expected any day now.[52]

---

51 16 March 1865, Robinson to Board, TNA ADM 1/5941.
52 7 April 1865, Hope to Somerset, Somerset Papers, Aylesbury, D/RA/A/2A/30.

Henry John Temple, 3rd Viscount Palmerston (1784-1865). (CDV courtesy of the National Portrait Gallery)

John Russell, 1st Earl Russell (1792-1878). (CDV courtesy of the National Portrait Gallery)

Sir Charles Wood, 1st Viscount Halifax (1800-1885). (CDV courtesy of the National Portrait Gallery)

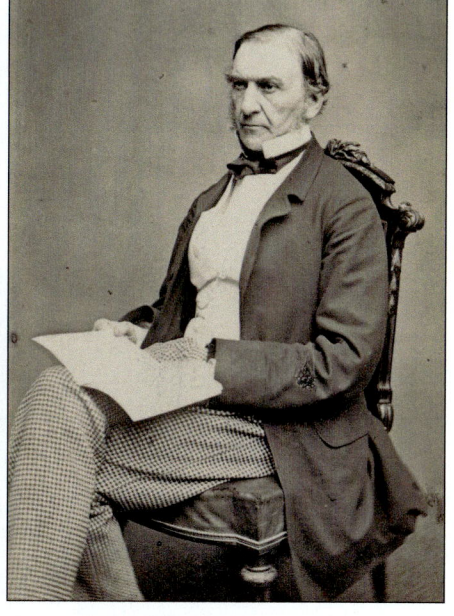

William Ewart Gladstone (1809-1898). (CDV courtesy of the National Portrait Gallery)

II Turret versus Broadside

The combined Anglo-French fleet engages Russian harbour defences at Sevastopol during the Crimean War (17 October 1854) The *Illustrated London News-supplement, 14 April 1855.* (Author's collection)

The heavily fortified Russian naval arsenal of Cronstadt: home of the Russian Navy in the Gulf of Finland, and guardian of the seaward approaches to the Imperial Russian capital of St. Petersburg (shown in the distance). Cronstadt defied two successive British naval campaigns in the Baltic between 1854 and 1855, and was preparing to check a third in the summer of 1856, had the war continued. (Author's collection)

IV   Turret versus Broadside

French floating ironclad-battery *Foudroyant* (*Dévastation*-class), laid down in August 1854 and launched the following June. Armed with sixteen shell-firing smoothbores protected by 4.3-inch iron armour-plating, the mastless, screw-propelled vessel drew only nine-feet of water and posed a serious threat to coastal fortifications wherever she could be safely deployed. (Author's collection)

The emergency Russian response to armoured floating batteries versus Cronstadt's defences was a flotilla of heavily armed pontoon rafts capable of floating in three-feet of water and partially-armoured with solid 4-inch-thick iron plates. (Author's collection)

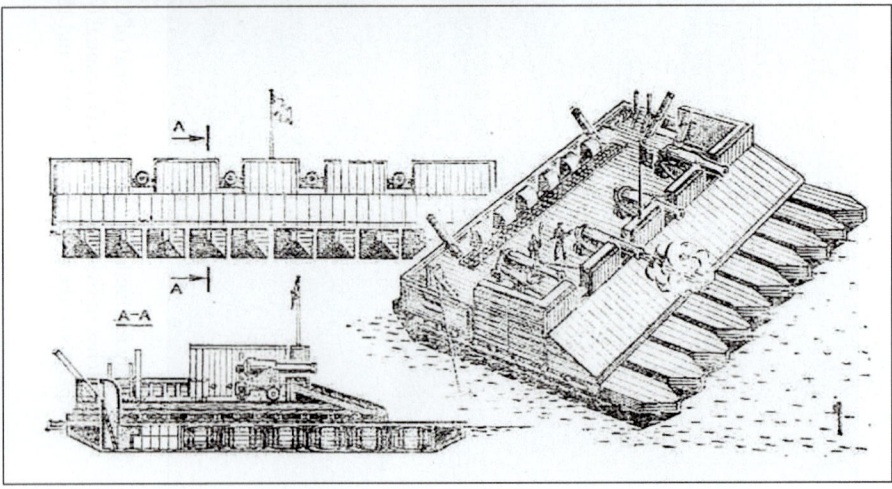

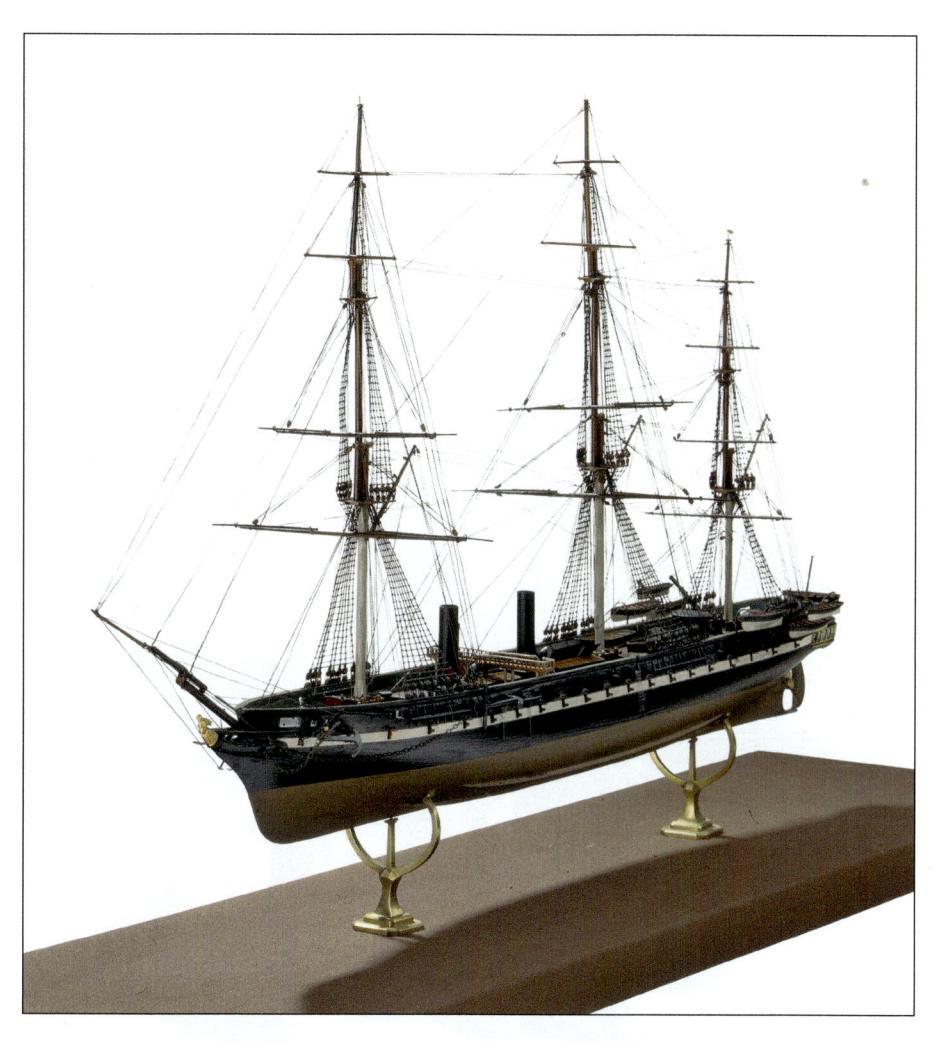

Model of HMS *Warrior*, laid down in 1859 as a response to the French iron-armoured screw-frigate *Gloire* (begun a year before). She was the Royal Navy's first seagoing ironclad, and the world's first iron-hulled armoured capital ship. Despite her impressive speed and firepower, *Warrior*'s extreme size and cost were controversial, along with her partial armour-configuration which left her stern and rudderhead exposed to a potential enemy. (Image courtesy of the National Maritime Museum, Greenwich)

VI   Turret versus Broadside

PUNCH, OR THE LONDON CHARIVARI.—March 16, 1861.

JACK'S "NAVY ESTIMATE."

Mr. Bull. "DEAR, BLESS ME! WHAT A PRICE I PAY FOR MY NAVY!"
Jack. "AX PARDON, YER 'ONOUR, TAIN'T ALONG O' WE FIGHTIN' BEGGARS, IT'S THEM **THINKIN'** BEGGARS."

The Admiralty's decision to invest in the largest, fastest, most-powerfully-armed ironclads possible in the emerging naval arms race with Imperial France came at a heavy price—and only private firms could do the work. Thames Iron Works and Shipbuilding required financial relief to avoid bankruptcy in constructing the novel *Warrior* over two and half years (and still retain a '12½-percent' profit margin). 'Per ton' of iron, the subsequent *Defence* and *Resistance*—though much smaller—were even more expensive. All of Britain's early seagoing broadside-ironclads went over-budget and took substantially longer to complete than contracted for.

The Mid-Victorian public was fascinated (and disquieted) by the remarkable changes in naval architecture underway in the early 1860s.

The baroque armoured bow of HMS *Minotaur*, a 10,500-ton super broadside-ironclad, shown here drawing 27-feet. Although laid down in September 1861, she was not fully completed with a revised armament until 1867—by which time her 5-inch-thick iron-plating was long considered inadequate against the latest ordnance. (Image NH 71224 courtesy of Naval History and Heritage Command, Washington, D.C.)

VIII   Turret versus Broadside

Rare likeness of Edward Adolphus Seymour, 12th Duke of Somerset (1804-1885). (William Hurrell Mallock and Helen Guendolen Seymour Ramsden (eds.), *Letters, Remains, and Memoirs of Edward Adolphus Seymour Twelfth Duke of Somerset* (1893))

John Ericsson (1803-1889). (Image NH 305 courtesy of Naval History and Heritage Command, Washington, D.C.)

Edward James Reed (1830-1906). (CDV courtesy of the National Portrait Gallery)

Cowper Phipps Coles (1818-1870). (CDV courtesy of the National Portrait Gallery)

PUNCH, OR THE LONDON CHARIVARI.—December 7, 1861.

LOOK OUT FOR SQUALLS.

Jack Bull. "YOU DO WHAT'S RIGHT, MY SON, OR I'LL BLOW YOU OUT OF THE WATER."

Britain's popular response to the *Trent* Affair of November-December 1861 was brutally simple: either President Abraham Lincoln's administration would bend to Lord Palmerston's ultimatum to release two captured Confederate emissaries or face a hostile dose of British naval power. As the Prime Minister assured Queen Victoria, 'Great Britain is in a better state than at any former time to inflict a severe blow upon and read a lesson to the United States which will not soon be forgotten.' At the time the Royal Navy was still dominated by wooden steam-powered, screw-propelled ships-of-the-line. Both the Union Army and Navy was still mobilising for war.

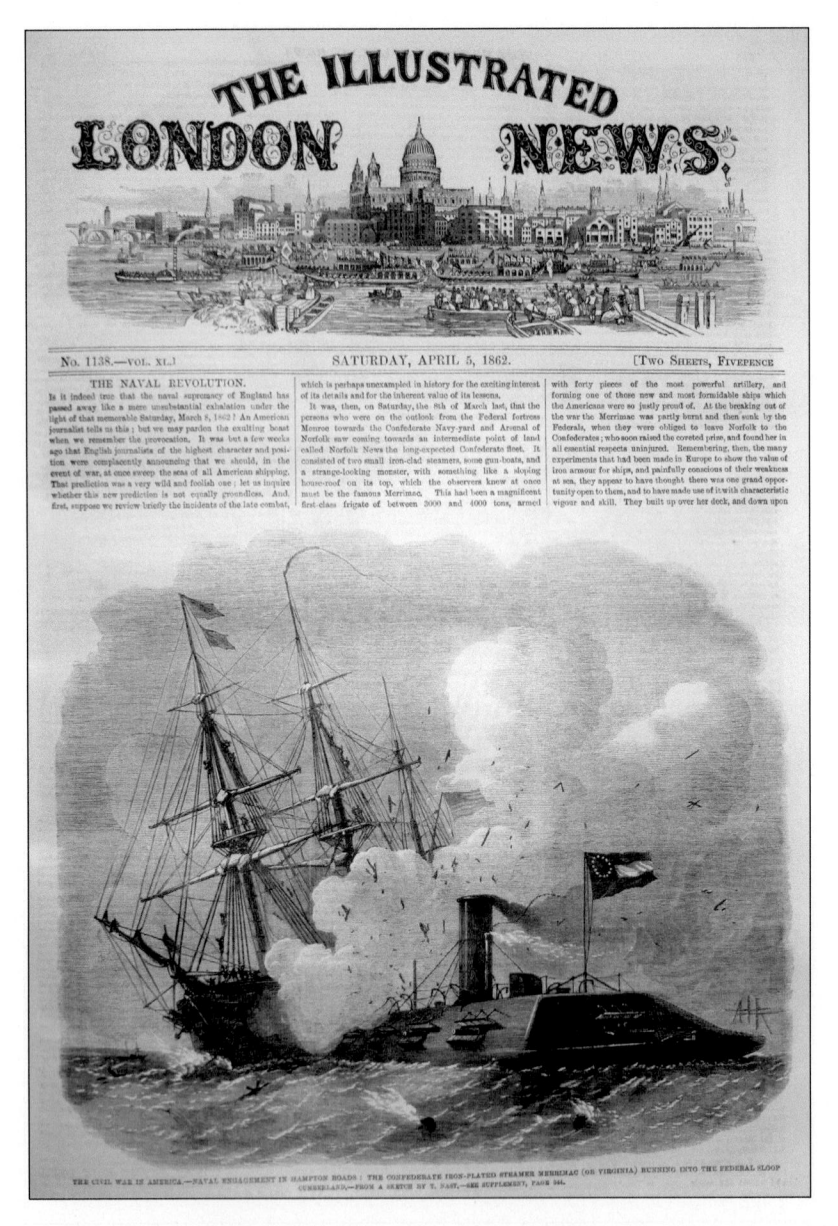

Scarcely four months after the *Trent* Affair, news reached Britain of the Confederate Navy's spectacular attack against the Union blockade anchored at Hampton Roads, Virginia. The 'Naval Revolution' as depicted here was the obvious invulnerability of armoured warships to point-blank broadsides from powerfully-armed wooden men-of-war. The next day, the U.S. Navy responded to the CSS *Virginia*'s attack with a small turreted vessel, the *Monitor*, which John Ericsson named to 'startle and admonish' 'Downing Street' and 'the Lords of the Admiralty' as well as 'the leaders of the Southern Rebellion.' The implications for British naval power were brutally simple.

Monitor vs. Virginia, by Lukasz Kasperczyk – The Battle of Hampton Roads (8-9 March 1862) was not just the first battle between armoured warships, but a turret vs. broadside duel. Here the effectiveness of the deep-draft casemated ironclad in coastal waters was limited by the ebbing tide—and the Confederate giant ran aground at a critical moment during the battle. (Image courtesy of Lukasz Kasperczyk)

XII   Turret versus Broadside

Although the ironclad action at Hampton Roads was technically a draw (neither vessel was sunk), the Union blockade was preserved. The Northern States also made the most of the geopolitical implications of Ericsson's monitor-form of ironclad, which promised to reverse the humiliating resolution of the *Trent* Affair three months earlier. Britain's wooden navy was now clearly vulnerable against ironclads, and the Royal Navy's new seagoing broadside-ironclads were likewise at risk against mastless, low-freeboard, turretted 'machines'. This sort of love-hate rivalry dominated Anglo-American relations throughout the nineteenth-century. (Author's collection)

Photographic Section 1   XIII

(Above Right) *Punch*, 31 January 1863; as a result of the Battle of Hampton Roads and the success of the USS *Monitor*, both Ericsson and Coles were idolized as inventors of state-of-the-art turret-ships which magnified the technological scope—and strategic limitations—of the ironclad revolution.

Armstrong 8-inch caliber, 150-pounder, rifled muzzle-loader—captured at Fort Fisher in January 1865, and now a prize of the U.S. Military Academy at West Point, New York. Contrast the above with the Dahlgren 15-inch, 450-pounder smoothbore below, now at Filipstad, Sweden—one of a pair given by John Ericsson to his native country in 1865, to arm her first *Passaic*-class monitor. These are believed to be the sole remaining 15-inch Dahlgrens in the world. (Author's collection)

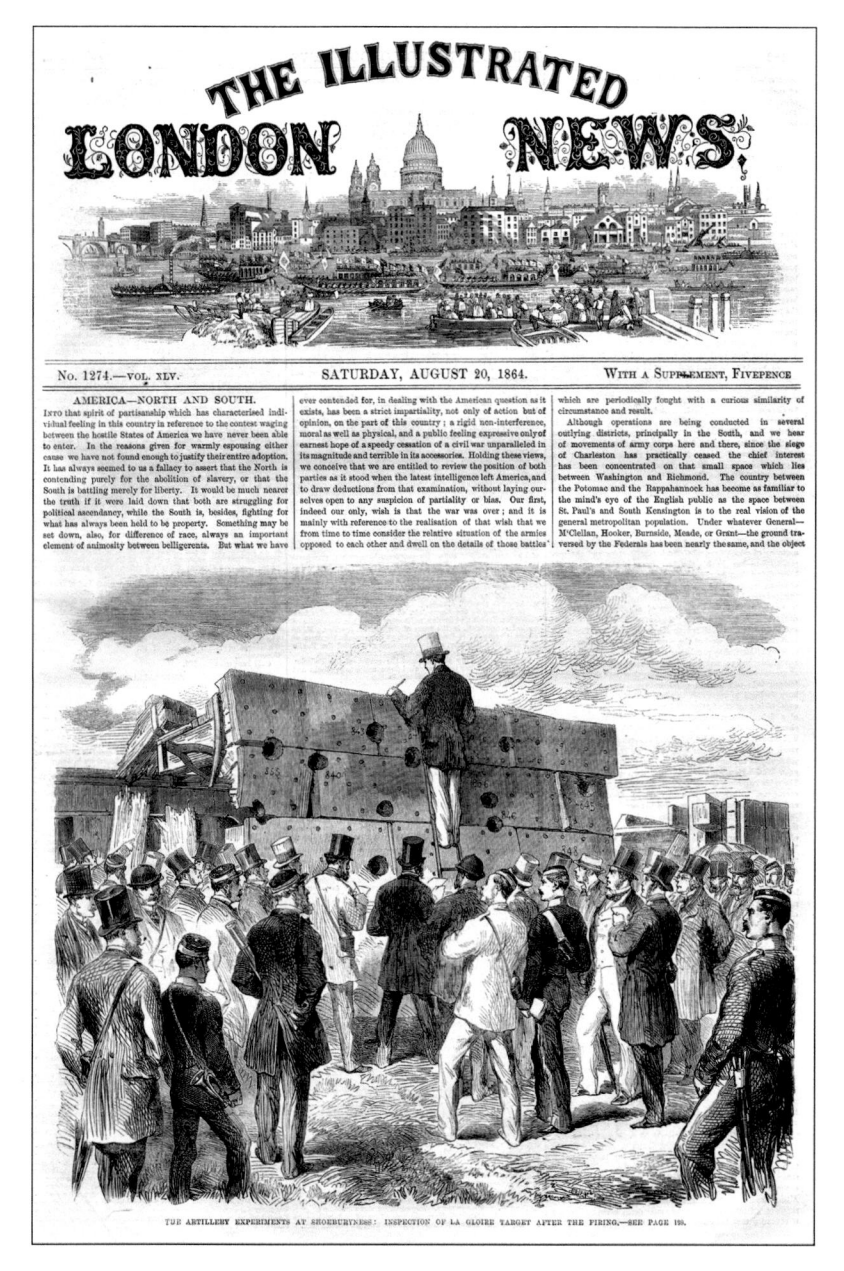

The 'guns vs. armour'-contest in the 1860s was front-page news and intertwined with both the 'turret vs. broadside'-debate and the larger, long-term question of 'ships vs. forts'. Many elements of British public and professional society had a vested interest in the outcome of increasingly elaborate and expensive trials of experimental guns and armour configurations for ships and coastal forts. Here a *Gloire* Target' resisted both the 68-pounder smoothbore and 110-pounder Armstrong rifled breech-loader at 200 yards but succumbed to the new '300-pounder', 12-ton 'shunt' gun muzzle-loader.

Model of HMS *Wivern*, originally contracted by Confederate agents to be built by John Lairds & Sons (Birkenhead, Merseyside) in April 1862. The Battle of Hampton Roads also suggested that ironclads with a turret main armament would be cheaper and quicker to build than larger broadside-ironclads, as well as being capable of carrying heavier (though fewer) guns. The ship displaced only 2,750-tons and drew 17-feet for coastal operations. Other innovations included in the design were a ram-bow, and tripod masts to minimize rigging which might otherwise interfere with the training of the guns when the hinged bulwarks were lowered for action. The two 'Laird Rams' were considered a deadly threat to the Union blockade, which consisted mostly of wooden warships. Under intense pressure from the U.S. minister to Great Britain, the vessels were seized by Palmerston's government before they could escape from Liverpool and were then incorporated into the Royal Navy. The Admiralty was not enthusiastic, however. The pioneering ironclads were underpowered compared with larger broadside-armed versions, and the whole concept of combining masts and sails with open deck turrets seemed inefficient and contradictory. Their cruising abilities were likewise impaired by the combination of rolling at sea with a relatively low freeboard.

Coles and his supporters (both in and out of the navy) instead emphasised their tactical advantages as well as economy and argued that larger versions would be both faster and more seaworthy. (Image courtesy of the National Maritime Museum, Greenwich)

6

'Were we at war with America or France, the right thing would be done instantly'

The Ordnance Select Committee, in reviewing a copy of the annual printed *Report of the Chief of the* [U.S.] *Bureau of Ordnance* (1 November 1864), were 'much struck with the proof this report affords, that the Americans have overcome the preliminary difficulties attending the introduction of guns of 10 to 22 tons into the fleet, and have the guns, the carriages, the ammunition, and the service of the magazines in a state of working order. They are in this respect much in advance of us.' Indeed, the *Report* cited an increase of 1,522 cannon of different calibres into naval service since the beginning of 1861.[1] No wonder the British public was dismayed by this state of affairs; on 25 March 1865 *Punch* depicted 'Vulcan in the Sulks', with Britannia prodding her brawny yet brooding armourer to help her 'resist Mars', a lanky but fully armed Lincolnesque figure striding in their direction.[2] Yet like their French professional counterparts, the Committee members roundly condemned the Yankee cast-iron smoothbore 11- and 15-inch muzzle-loaders themselves, taking comfort in the belief that the latter gun was 'probably not superior' to British wrought-iron weapons like the (10½-inch) 12-ton Armstrongs—even though they had to admit they were 'the only ones we really have afloat, and those in very limited numbers.'[3] Captain Key of HMS *Excellent* also tried to assure the Admiralty that quality might yet prove as important as quantity; the Americans appeared 'very far behind us in knowledge as to the best mode of constructing guns; having only now begun experimentation with wrought-iron'—even though American casting techniques were acknowledged as very

---

[1] 27 February 1865 ('Report No. 3645'), *Abstracts of Proceedings of the Ordnance Select Committee, for the Quarter ending 30th September 1864*, TNA WO 33/15, 114-15; *Report of the Chief of the* [U.S.] *Bureau of Ordnance* (1 November 1864), 5.
[2] 25 March 1865, 'Vulcan in the Sulks', *Punch*.
[3] 27 February 1865, *Abstracts of Proceedings of the Ordnance Select Committee*, 114.

refined, yielding heavy guns with amazing endurance, while 'the life time of our 68 pdrs. has lately been about 250 rounds.'[4]

As far as they were concerned, raw numbers did not necessarily speak for themselves. In this sense it was perhaps all too easy for mid-Victorians to suspect how war-time public officials in a messy overseas 'republic' were especially bound to overstate matters for political and propaganda purposes. For years, the generally accepted impression, as expressed by *Punch* at the beginning of 1862, was that America was a 'despotism of tyrannous democracy', with its citizens 'governed by Rowdies, whom nevertheless they make no effort to dethrone.' At the beginning of 1863, the popular British satire pictured the smiling ghost of King George III prodding the not-so-happy ghost of George Washington: 'Well, Mr. Washington, what do you think of your fine republic now, eh?—What d'ye think? What d'ye think, eh?'[5] On the same day that *Punch* decried the Empire's defensive readiness against possible American aggression in 1865, *The Times* expressed its amazement how the smallest of Union victories was soon magnified into a massive defeat of Confederate forces and was quickly endorsed by no less than the U.S. Secretary of War (Edwin Stanton). But shortly after, when 'the true state of the case was made known[,] no one appeared to be disappointed, or to be particularly angry with Mr. Stanton for giving official currency, not for the first or hundredth time, to a gross exaggeration.' Even the new U.S. Vice-President, Andrew Johnson, *The Times* correspondent added with contempt, was anything but a gentleman, being 'brutally' drunk at his own inaugural.[6] Two days later, the Conservative *Morning Post*'s own correspondent in America sneered that if there 'was one characteristic more than all others that journalists in this country are noted for,

---

4   21 March 1865, in 29 March 1865, Robinson to Board, TNA ADM 1/5941. The American cast-iron 15-inch Rodman (Army) gun was cast hollow and cooled from the interior; the cast-iron 15-inch Dahlgren (Navy) was cast solid, cooled from the exterior and bored out; see for example, Warren Ripley, *Artillery and Ammunition of the Civil War* (New York: Van Nostrand: 1970), 78-80, 97-100. The Chief of the Bureau of Naval Ordnance, Captain Henry A. Wise, testified to a U.S. Senate Committee on heavy ordnance on 28 January 1865 that 36 of the Navy's 15-inch guns had been cast on the Rodman plan, 'Report on Heavy Ordnance', 23. The first Rodman-cast 15-inch Navy gun had been test-fired up to 900 times, with charges up to 60lbs of normal black powder (versus Rodman's own 'mammoth' powder, consisting of very large granules compressed into a cartridge or 'cake'), 23; see also Seymour H. Mauskopf, 'Pellets, Pebbles and Prisms: British Munitions for Larger Guns, 1860-1885', in Brenda J. Buchanan (ed.), *Gunpowder, Explosives and the State: A Technological History* (Aldershot: Ashgate Publishing Limited, 2006), 303-40.
5   11 January 1862, 'Who is an American?' *Punch*; 10 January 1863, 'Latest from Spirit-Land', *Punch*.
6   25 March 1865, *The Times*; 27 March 1865, The *Morning Post*. The Duke of Somerset, like Palmerston, condemned British Radicals politicians precisely because they 'believed that the Americans owed their property to their Republican form of government'. See also Mallock and Ramsden, *Letters, Remains, and Memoirs*, 460.

that characteristic certainly is prophesying.'[7] Like Palmerston, the First Lord of the Admiralty admonished British Radical politicians who sought the vote for all adult males, regardless of their station, precisely because they 'believed that the Americans owed their prosperity to their Republican form of government.' In a political tome comparing *Monarchy and Democracy* (1880), the aging Duke of Somerset quipped how 'few Europeans settle in America, unless driven there by lack of money or of character', while educated Americans 'gladly escaped from the vulgar monotony of a community absorbed in money-making, to [Imperial Paris] which, after many convulsions, still retained traces of its traditional culture and refinement.' Indeed, the 'whole construction of the American Constitution', he argued, 'seems calculated to maintain a low standard of moral integrity.' The last thing Britain needed was a government of the people, by the people, and for the people.[8]

Hence, the Ordnance Select Committee had 'only to observe that considering the opportunities afforded by the present war in America for the exercise of individual ingenuity and professional talent,' it was 'a matter of some surprise that, with all the resources of the country, American ordnance has not attained a higher standard of excellence'—perhaps reflecting not just natural or technological factors but political and social failings rather endemic to their cousins across the Atlantic. When it came to their monster guns' terrible power and efficiency in four years of combat, therefore, American military and naval professionals were not to be taken at their word. For one thing, the Federals had obviously only been fighting against poorly armed—and armoured—rebels. So even though Bureau Chief Henry Wise quoted the Southern captain of the (British built, armed and manned) CSS *Alabama*, to demonstrate the immense power of exploding shells from the *Kearsage*'s two 11-inch Dahlgren pivot guns, it was his subsequent comment how the engagement had taught both the 'English and French navies...a lesson in practical gunnery and seamanship, which they will not soon forget' which rankled those in London even as it delighted readers in Washington, D.C. There were facts, and there were feelings. When Wise summarised that the experience of both American battlefields and ordnance and iron target testing grounds had rather proven that 'spherical shot for smoothbores [were] immeasurably superior to the elongated rifled shot in every form', he was bound

---

7   27 March 1865, The *Morning Post*. The correspondent's report is dated 'New York, March 10'. The following day, Sherman's forces captured and destroyed the Fayetteville arsenal in North Carolina, which had been a major source of Confederate small arms, gun carriages and ammunition. Three weeks later, Union forces under Grant occupied the Confederate capital of Richmond, Virginia, as the tattered remnants Confederate General Lee's Army of Northern Virginia fled westward towards Appomattox.

8   Paraphrasing Lincoln's Gettysburg Address of 19 November 1863; Somerset, *Monarchy and Democracy*, 64, 72-5. He went on to conclude that 'inasmuch as the extension of the franchise will include a lower class of voters, it must be expected that political morality will deteriorate rather than improve', 176. See also Mallock and Ramsden, *Letters, Remains, and Memoirs*, 460-7.

to elaborate what this meant for the Anglo-American balance of power in North American waters, since 'no manner or thickness of iron or steel armor that could be carried on the hulls of seagoing ships will resist the impact of solid spherical shot fired from the heaviest calibres of the navy, at close range, with appropriate charges of cannon powder.' Because American cast-iron shot was itself 'made from the best charcoal iron', tests suggested it was as strong as steel shot; 222 consecutive blows from an eight-ton steam hammer failed to break up a solid cast-iron 15-inch specimen.[9]

The British found these claims both unbelievable and absurd, the obvious result of American war-time expediency and haste—and flying in the face of years of careful experimentation and deliberation undertaken in England. 'The Americans have evidently made their experimental steel shot of very inferior quality,' assumed Captain Key, 'as they find equal penetration through iron plates with cast iron shot, and greater effect.' It was inconceivable that their manufacturing process had made cast iron shot 'as tenacious an unyielding as good steel.' By retaining cast iron, their heavy banded Parrott rifles had also proven unreliable (an alarming number of them had burst in firing upon Fort Fisher, accounting for more causalities in Porter's fleet than from enemy guns). As a result, Key deduced that the Americans had been rather 'compelled to be satisfied with heavy smooth bore ordnance', and these gave an enemy armed with rifled guns a marked advantage at longer ranges.[10] Although it was known that the Confederates had indeed fielded their own heavy (Brooke) rifles, these were not winning the war for them against Union smoothbores because they were probably inferior to Armstrongs.[11] The Ordnance Select Committee felt the same: Wise's comparison between cast-iron and steel shot 'must be accepted with reserve', and his assertions could 'only be accounted for by the supposition that the iron plates against which they were tested, were either of inferior material or of insufficient thickness.' And it was only because 'the Americans are entirely committed to the use of that metal' that there were 'good grounds for believing that in America much greater attention is paid generally to the quality of cast-iron used for projectiles than is the case in the Government establishments in this country.' As for U.S. iron targets explicitly, the Committee again could 'only infer that the experiments upon which Commodore Wise's assertions are based were conducted against a very inferior quality of iron plating, and that a very different effect would be produced on the soft tough material now supplied.' Gallwey, one of the Committee's members, had already reported after

9   *Report of the Chief of the Bureau of Ordnance*, 15, 17.
10 21 March 1865, in 29 March 1865, Robinson to Board, TNA ADM 1/5941.
11 See for example 17 December 1863, *The Times*; and 16 May 1864, R. A. E. Scott, 'Progress of Ordnance Abroad Compared with that at Home', *Journal of the Royal United Service Institution*, Vol. 8, 1864, 449-50. Brooke defended his rifles' reputation, since two (possibly double-banded) 6.4-inch guns had withstood 1,500 rounds each in action on James Island, South Carolina (20 February 1864, Journal entry); by 1 April 1864 one of them had burst with a 6lbs powder charge and 65 lb rifle shell, having fired '1,700 times' (1 April 1864 report); in Brooke, *Ironclads and Big Guns of the Confederacy*, 176-7, 180-1.

his fact-finding tour of U.S. facilities (and capabilities) in 1864 that successful test-fires of the 15-inch gun against crudely fashioned iron-plated targets were 'carried on at 60 feet distance from the target.' For as much as Britannia's 'Vulcan' might have seemed like Achilles sulking in his tent, British ordnance experts had 'perused' their overseas rival's swagger with self-proclaimed 'satisfaction' if not complacency.[12]

But Gallwey's own published *Report* admitted that his information had come second-hand. They had been refused permission to board the Union monitors before Charleston, 'and so we were unable to speak of the powers of resistance of that class of vessel from personal observation' (while it had proved relatively easy to find disgruntled Union naval officers willing to disgorge their own disapproval of both monitor-ironclads and monster smoothbores). The British military officers had seen 15-inch Rodmans test-fired a few times, but never against an object, 'so that we were unable to judge of their accuracy.' Still, when they were allowed to take an iron sample from the moulding of a large gun on Rodman's technique (hollow-casted and then water-cooled from the core barrel-interior outwards), their own test confirmed it was 'of unusually high tenacity.' They had also never witnessed the target-tests or examined the iron plates themselves. What the Ordnance Select Committee (and perhaps also Gallwey) failed to note was that not only was the cited '60 feet' target penetrated from a ludicrously point-blank distance, but it was itself a combination of eight 1-inch, one 4-inch, and another six 1-inch plates to a preposterous total thickness of '18-inches of iron backed with 30-inches of oak.'[13] Significantly, most of the sixty or more American targets constructed since 1862 consisted of limited numbers of sample plates from various iron manufacturers, which therefore restricted the overall area of the target surface—necessitating closer firing ranges than the '200 yard' standard practiced by British ordnance officers. American civilian critics like Alexander Holley, in his detailed *Treatise on Ordnance and Armor* (published in 1865), warned that the 'resistance of a ship's side to this kind of assault cannot be truly ascertained by firing at small targets. The large mass has the greater inertia and presents the greater resistance to fracture when the blow is slow enough to allow the surrounding elasticity and tenacity to be called into service.'[14] Yet unlike British targets at Portsmouth or Shoeburyness, U.S. iron targets (mostly built by the Navy Department at the Washington Navy Yard) were packed against a solid hillside bank of clay which absorbed most of the force of impact from heavy projectiles. Federal authorities had at least spared no expense importing the very best *British-* and *French-*made iron plates to carefully test their 11- and 15-inch smoothbores against. Thus, 'Target 61' consisted of a single 18-foot long, 39-inch wide slab of 5-inch thick, rolled

---

12   27 February 1865, *Abstracts of Proceedings of the Ordnance Select Committee*, 115-16.
13   Gallwey and Alderson, *Report upon the Military Affairs of the United States of America*, 9-10, 40, 49, 57-8. Rodman himself had specified the iron must have 'an average tenacity of from 33,000 to 35,000 lbs, and density 7.21. If below 30,000 lbs, the gun is rejected', 49.
14   Holley, *A Treatise on Ordnance and Armor*, 158-9.

iron plate from John Brown & Company of Sheffield (backed by 20-inches of oak and an inner 1-inch plate of iron). From the sure-fire distance of '169 feet' the American 15-inch gun not only struck the target dead-centre with a 435lb cast-iron shot with a 60lb charge, but completely penetrated the plate, shattered the backing and embedded ten feet into the clay bank, 'where it was found unbroken'. On the same day, 20 September 1864, a 7-inch thick iron plate from the leading French iron forger Pétin and Gaudet, 8 feet long and 38-inches wide—comprising 'Target 62'—was penetrated by a 15-inch 480-pound steel shot with a 50lb charge. Perhaps more importantly, such tests of the giant Yankee smoothbore recorded an initial velocity from 60lbs charges at 1,572 feet per second, greater than any rifled gun on either side of the Atlantic. Earlier that summer, one of the powerful 7-inch Brooke rifles from the captured ironclad-ram CSS *Atlanta* failed to penetrate 'Target 57' (another sample 5-inch plate purchased from John Brown) with a 120lbs wrought iron, steel-faced projectile with 16lb charge. 'All of which proves very conclusively', the U.S. naval officer superintending the experiment added laconically, 'the usual exaggeration of the Rebels and their sympathizers ... made in reference to this gun.'[15]

The question for Lord Palmerston's government in 1865, therefore, was just how far the fortunes of the British Empire had become hopelessly entangled with the nightmarish fate of the Southern Confederacy, bled white on the battlefield and finally succumbing to a pitiless combination of mass starvation and simultaneous invasions from every direction. The blasé evaluations of U.S. 'standards of excellence' by British military and naval authorities meanwhile offered scant assurance and only seemed to bristle with their own insecurities. For one thing, they admitted to having neither the military or naval means at hand, nor had they expressed any clear strategic ends in the event of an Anglo-American conflict.[16] Talk was cheap, and false pride potentially catastrophic. Gladstone was still firm in his belief, as he wrote to the Secretary of State for War, Earl de Grey and Ripon, that 'to commit the honour of England and of the British Navy to the defence of any one of the American Lakes against the United States is one of the gravest questions ever submitted to a Cabinet', at least until the Canadians themselves demonstrated they would fight for their independence

---

15   US National Archives, RG 74 (Bureau of Ordnance), Entry 98, 'Reports Concerning Target Practice on Iron Plates, 1862-64, 2 vols.', 2: 27, 45-68. These include detailed drawings and colourised photographs. Some of these imported iron plates—one 8-inches thick with a 15-inch iron shot embedded in it—still exist on the display grounds of the Washington Navy Yard (Washington, D.C.) off the Anacostia River. According to one contemporary British naval pundit, 'Mr. Brown [of Sheffield] can roll plates such as no ships afloat can carry comfortably, and such as no artillery yet known to science can penetrate', P. Barry, *Dockyard Economy and Naval Power* (London: Sampson Low, Son, and Co., 1863), 255. For a listing of British iron targets at Shoeburyness since 1862 see the memo-table ('11344/66') in TNA ADM 1/5595.

16   See for example, Howard J. Fuller, ' "The absence of decisive results": British Assessments of Union Combined Operations', in Craig Symonds (ed.), *Union Combined Operations in the Civil War* (New York: Fordham University Press, 2010), 115-34.

from their southern neighbour 'in the same spirit in which the South has fought.'[17] In Parliament, former Cabinet minister Baron Lyveden was embarrassed how the reports by Colonel Jervois on the defences of Canada had 'disclosed a state of things which ought to have been kept from the public eye until some steps had been taken to remedy it', he told his peers.[18] Now that the reigning government had chosen to publicise the matter, the leader of the Conservatives, the Earl of Derby, could only wonder why the Queen's Speech earlier had omitted it—especially given the potential costs to the nation? How was it that the Royal Navy seem so powerless to intervene? Trying to downplay the nature of Anglo-American tensions themselves, Russell only made matters worse by reiterating his 'opinion at the commencement of the civil war, that on the part of the North it was a contest for empire; just as I believe our contest in 1776, which we continued till 1783, was a contest for empire and for nothing else. I believe, as we acted then, the United States have acted now; and had our position been similar to theirs, we should have acted much as the Northern States have done.' He then did his best to back-track the whole affair the following month, on 23 March, given how the debate had spilled over into the Commons as well.[19]

Here the Foreign Secretary was totally at a loss to account for any failing in the maintenance of good relations between the two countries, even during the *Trent Affair*—when John Bull pointed his naval gun at Uncle Sam's head. But even in this he admitted that the pre-emptive ultimatum prepared by Palmerston and himself (when the Royal Navy enjoyed a massive wooden steam fleet second to none with at least one operational ironclad frigate) was 'too abrupt', if not 'unfriendly and uncourteous', softened only by the last-minute personal intervention of the dying Prince Consort. Without alluding to the fact that the U.S. Navy now boasted over 600 warships, most of them purpose-built to control the waters of all North America, with a new cruiser fleet building to act as fast commerce raiders if need be, Russell blamed the exacerbation of international tensions since then not on Government policy, which had been 'of a pacific and friendly character' all along, but 'on the one side by those partisans of the North who were constantly stating that we were acting in a manner hostile to the North, and, on the other, by those [like Laird] who were as constantly violating the neutrality which Her Majesty had proclaimed in the pursuit of their own private ends.' Four days later, the Government shifted responsibility even further as Somerset confirmed in the second reading of the Colonial Naval Defence Bill that 'its object was to enable several of the colonial possessions of Her Majesty to make better provision for their own maritime defence', adding that they had 'lately received a proposal from the colony of Victoria for building vessels in this country of a large

---

17 10 May 1865, Gladstone to Ripon, in Wolf, *Life of the First Marquess of Ripon*, 1: 200-1.
18 Robert Vernon, 1st Baron Lyveden; 20 February 1865, 'Defences of Canada—Reports of Colonel Jervois—Question', *Hansard*, Vol. 177, 416-40.
19 23 March 1865, 'Relations with the United States—Observations', *Hansard*, Vol. 178, 68-75.

class as well as of smaller vessels on the turret principle to enable them to defend their harbours.'[20]

* * *

Of course, not everyone was convinced by all of this. 'The House of Lords was the scene, the other day, of a somewhat undisguised display of panic on the subject of an American war', chided Oxford Professor Goldwin Smith in *Macmillan's Magazine*. 'The Peers when thus fluttered scarcely correspond to the aristocratic ideal.' It was true that the end of the Civil War in America was finally at hand, leaving Americans with 'a large, veteran and victorious army under good generals, and a fleet formidable in its number of vessels, and commanded by brave officers, though hastily, and as competent judges think, not durably built, and, as to the bulk of it, rather adapted for the coast service on which it has been engaged than for ocean war.' So why all the acrimonious panic and accusations? For all the swagger and war spirit of certain American officers and the popular press, 'pandering to the most violent among the passions of the hour', it was also understood that they 'will not be allowed to act against the national interest' by the great mass of the people.[21] They had recently re-elected President Lincoln and thereby endorsed his policy, as expressed in his Second Inaugural Address, as 'malice towards none…to bind up the nation's wounds…to do all which may achieve and cherish a just, and a lasting peace, among ourselves, and with all nations.'[22] The British press was thus no less guilty of fanning the flames, Smith continued, and 'wild cries of alarm are sure to aggravate any danger that may exist':

> The English people need no goading to make them feel, in case of need, that they are Englishmen. They are as ready as ever they were, perhaps readier, to fight for the safety and honour of their country, though they may not be so ready as they once were to fight for the exclusive interest or the antipathies of a class. Nor is England defenceless: on the contrary, never in the course of her

---

20   Ibid., and 27 March 1865, *Hansard*, Vol. 178, '(No. 39) Second Reading', 272-3.
21   Goldwin Smith, 'The Danger of War with America', April 1865, *Macmillan's Magazine*, Vol. 11, November 1864-April 1865 (1865), 417-25.
22   4 March 1865; see for example, David S. Reynolds (ed.), *Lincoln's Selected Writings* (New York: W.W. Norton & Company, 2015), 364-8. Commenting in the *Die Press* on 12 October 1862, Karl Marx extolled Lincoln as 'not the product of a popular revolution. This plebeian, who worked his way up from stone-beaker to senator in Illinois, without intellectual brilliance, without a particularly outstanding character, without exceptional importance—an average person of good will—was placed at the top by the interplay of the forces of general suffrage unaware of the great issues at stake. The new world has never achieved a greater triumph than by this demonstration that, given its political and social organization, ordinary people of good will can accomplish feats [Lincoln's Emancipation Proclamation of 22 September 1862, following the costly Battle of Antietam five days before] which only heroes could accomplish in the old world!' ibid., 396.

history has her power been so great as if put forth in a cause that united all her sons, and wielded by the man, not by the shadow, it would be now.[23]

Russell seems to have mollified his views about the likelihood of war, though not Yankee integrity, over the past couple of months, corresponding to news from America. On 11 February 1865 *Harper's Weekly* proudly depicted the double-turreted *Monadnock* and reminded its readers that 'the Monroe doctrine declares that the United States will drive every European power from our neighborhood'. Yet it also warned that the issue of France's imperial occupation of Mexico, 'demands the utmost sagacity and not the least swagger. There is nothing in the world easier than to strike an attitude and cry hands off. But before defying any of the Great Powers to mortal combat upon such a point it is well to calculate every chance.' That same day Russell wrote to Lyons' temporary successor in Washington of his hope that 'Mr. Seward will be willing and able to moderate the violent impulses of the Congress', who not only wanted some form of reparation from Britain for the losses inflicted by the CSS *Alabama* and other British-built commerce raiders upon the U.S. merchant marine, 'but they want it before it can possibly be given.' Four days later he wrote to Palmerston: there was, at last, 'a gleam of peace from America'. The passing by Congress of the Thirteenth Amendment, abolishing slavery once and for all, was meanwhile 'grand[,] tho' this blessed country no longer cares about it.'[24] Once Union victory was undeniable, by April, he attributed the North's success not to any moral superiority but to superior numbers, which were 'too much for the gallant men who have fought for Southern independence.' Now he ventured to admit to Palmerston he had become 'very sanguine of maintaining peace both with France and America.' Indeed, he was willing to go so far as to suggest it might be time to abolish the Income Tax; 'a most convenient weapon for a government in danger of foreign war, but I think its abolition with a power of revival would be a proof of power and confidence in our means which would

---

23 Smith, 'The Danger of War with America', 424-5. As Secretary of State William H. Seward wrote to Charles Francis Adams, U.S. Minister to Great Britain, on 22 April 1864, 'the insurgents manifestly have a bold, vigorous, and effective party in both houses of Parliament and in the British press, which party is confessedly influential in the general administration of public affairs...There is, moreover, a marked habit prevailing in Great Britain of comparing British resources and achievements with American resources and achievements, and this is done so unnecessarily, and often in a spirit so illiberal, as to indicate a sense of rivalry', *Papers Relating to Foreign Affairs Accompanying the Message of the President to the Second Session of the Thirty-Eighth Congress, Part I* (Washington: GPO, 1865), 'Diplomatic Correspondence', No. 917, 638-9.

24 11 February 1865, Harper's Weekly; 11 February 1865, Russell to J. Hume Burnley, Russell Papers, TNA PRO 30-22, 97; 15 February 1865, Russell to Palmerston, Palmerston Papers, Broadlands, GC/RU. Lyons was reposted, departing New York on 14 December 1864; see for example Mark Jenkins, *Lord Lyons: A Diplomat in an Age of Nationalism and War* (Montreal: McGill-Queen's University Press, 2014), 234, 245-8.

greatly satisfy our own people and astonish our enemies abroad.'[25] This was the same day, 6 April, that Barnaby at the Institution of Naval Architects certified the stability of HMS *Achilles*—though not if her 4½-inch armour was penetrated at the waterline amidships—and Reed attempted to assure his colleagues that an oceangoing ironclad powerful enough to prevent this from happening, though without turrets, was not only possible but already under consideration.

This placed all the more importance upon the various peacetime tests undertaken in Britain. Could the Royal Navy float an armoured vessel for 'general service' which could withstand the latest ordnance or not? Some critics not only doubted armour would ever hold out against guns, but the process of British experimentation itself which highlighted growing civil-military tensions. In *Shoeburyness and the Guns*, published in the spring of 1865, journalist and naval commentator Patrick Barry cautioned his readers that 'gunnery instruction is in a much less satisfactory state in the Royal Artillery than is generally supposed.' Worse, he considered American gunnery practices 'as greatly in advance of the French as the French are in advance of us.' Over the years he had witnessed the evolution of target tests, and his judgment (shared by increasingly many) was that both the Ordnance Select and Iron Plate committees had been nothing more than 'pettifogging empires—men who have neither satisfied themselves, the inventors, nor the public...Science has been seldom scandalised by more impudent and unfit pretenders.' Here the army and navy service professionals were at odds with private inventors, who themselves waged 'perpetual and harassing war against their enemies' (and against each other) and were thus 'not particular about the weapons. The contest is with the knife and to the knife.' Like Barry's previous exposé, *Dockyards and Naval Economy* (1863), this struck a chord with a mid-Victorian readership accustomed to being leery of government mismanagement and bureaucratic inefficiency, of petty official fiefdoms and professional cliques operating behind closed doors—all at the taxpayers' expense.[26] But his advocacy of big smoothbore guns also ran against the grain, which was for scientific progress yielding technological superiority. Neither the French nor Americans guns were as advanced as the intricately 'coiled' and 'hooped' wrought-iron Armstrong rifle, clever as Rodman's casting technique was. And this fed in turn the much deeper mid-Victorian impulse for greater individual status as well as global supremacy.[27] The British system of heavy ordnance delivered

---

25 1 April 1865, Russell to Sir Frederick Bruce (the new official British Envoy to the United States), Russell Papers, TNA PRO 30-22, 97; 6 April 1865, Russell to Palmerston, Palmerston Papers, Broadlands, GC/RU.

26 P. Barry, *Shoeburyness and the Guns: A Philosophical Discourse* (London: Sampson Low, Son, and Marston, 1865), 22, 26, 41-55, 66-70.

27 See for example, in a vast body of scholarship, Asa Briggs, *Victorian People: A Reassessment of Persons and Themes 1851-67* (London: Penguin Books Ltd., 1990 reprint of 1955 original), 104-6; W. L. Burn, *The Age of Equipoise: A Study of the Mid-Victorian Generation* (New York: W. W. Norton & Company Inc., 1965), 21-3, 70-1, 83-7, 253-67; and more recently, Albert D. Pionke, *The Ritual Culture of Victorian Professionals: Competing for*

heavy projectiles which could sustain a higher velocity over a greater range. Surely the ability to open fire upon an enemy vessel or fort first, and for longer, with at least equal penetration to smoothbores firing at close range only, was the future of warfare at sea. Fresh from their ordeal by fire, American ordnance experts like Dahlgren poked holes in this theory: in the heat of combat rifled guns and their projectiles, being more complex, were more prone to mishap like jamming especially during rapid fires. The inner rifled grooves themselves were delicate, frequently fouled, and relatively high charges meant shorter lifespans than smoothbores. In terms of accuracy, the slightest roll of a ship upon a wave disrupted a gunner's aim, and the further away the target the more the rifled shot simply veered off course. Unless firing at a large stationary target like a coastal fortification, ranges beyond even 1,000-yards during a naval battle were generally pointless, a waste of precious ammunition—which also degraded the life of the rifled gun.[28] There was pioneering, and there was practical; the distant future and the present moment.

But for ironclads themselves it was Columbia not Britannia which boasted a cutting-edge advantage, in the form of steam-powered rotating gun turrets. To drive this point home during the Civil War years, John Ericsson commissioned a colour lithograph for public and professional distribution which showcased '*Ericsson's Monitor of 1854*', his original designs submitted to French Emperor Napoleon III during the Crimean War (when the Allies were seeking a way of getting past the heavily-armed granite forts guarding the Russian fleets at Sevastopol in the Crimea and Cronstadt in the Baltic.) This graphically described a fully steam-powered, screw-propelled, semi-submerged, iron-hulled craft with forced ventilation, and sporting a six-inch iron armoured 'globular' or dome-shaped revolving turret. 'This new system of naval attack will place an entire fleet of sailing-ships, during calms and light winds, at the mercy of single craft', the inventor promised. 'Of what avail would be the "steam guard ships" if attacked on the new system? Alas for the "wooden walls" that formerly "ruled the waves"!' Subtitled *America, Not England, Its Birth-Place—Ericsson, Not Coles, Inventor of the Revolving Cupola*', Ericsson's poster attacked the 'absurdity of Captain Coles' claim' and ridiculed British technology since his rival's '"gun-shield

---

Ceremonial Status, 1838-1877 (Abingdon: Routledge, 2016 reprint of 2013 original); also Edward Beasley, *Mid-Victorian Imperialists: British Gentlemen and the Empire of the Mind* (Abingdon: Routledge, 2005); John M. MacKenzie (ed.), *Popular Imperialism and the Military 1850-1950* (Manchester: Manchester University Press, 1992), 1-24, 109-138; C. C. Eldridge, 'Sinews of Empire: Changing Perspectives', in his edited volume *British Imperialism in the Nineteenth Century* (London: Macmillan and Publishers Ltd., 1984), 168-89; and Robert Kubicek, 'British Expansion, Empire, and Technological Change', in Porter (ed.), *Oxford History*, 247-69.

28 See (25 January 1864) 'Report on Heavy Ordnance', 113-25. Dahlgren's testimony submission, forwarded by Welles to the Senate committee chairman, is dated 15 April 1864. 'If the objects were at rest, afloat, or ashore, the power of inflicting certain damage, total or partial, might be extended to 2,000 yards, and, with some few exceptions, I should be inclined, from present experience, to limit artillery fire to this distance', 124.

and revolving platform'" was 'turned by manual power only.'[29] Indeed, the Union's monitor-ironclads were heavily politicised as quintessentially superior because they were, after all, *American*. Published in 1867, the semi-official *History of the Navy During the Rebellion* considered the North's progressively gigantic (and ruthless) war effort against the South 'the first great national American act', and it was almost to be expected that since the U.S. Navy's ironclads and their guns were the 'creations of fresh and independent thinkers' they had been 'rudely criticised, ridiculed, and condemned as visionary or imbecile, because their thoughts were beyond, or outside, the common range of mind and of professional experience.' As such, the clash between the original *Monitor* and the Confederate '*Merrimac*' was one of the most important naval battles in *world* history because the turret and broadside ironclads represented not just a contest between North and South, for control of Hampton Roads, Virginia, 'but between European and American thought...to determine whether Europe or America should control this Western Continent.' Nothing expressed so clearly how America had been 'thinking ahead of Europe, had indeed out-thought the world' during its civil war than in the 'construction and armament of ships'. This fed into the myth that the New World model republic was itself not only an improvement upon the British political, economic and social structure in particular (against which the Thirteen Colonies originally had declared their rebellion in 1776) but also, as Lincoln expressed at the appalling Gettysburg battlefield-cemetery, the 'last, best hope of earth'. Given the horrific *costs* of such an ordeal it was perhaps only natural for the Americans to magnify what surely must be its benefits—even in terms of naval prestige. 'God was leading this nation to the position of the world's teacher in the application to political and social life of those principles upon which the progress of the race depends,' and the four-hour trial by combat between rival ironclad systems at Hampton Roads 'demonstrated that she has the power needed for a great leader among

---

29 See the copy at the U.S. Navy Art Library, Washington Navy Yard. See also *The Revolving Turret Not the Invention of Captain Cowper Phipps Coles, R.N., but of Charles Wentworth Forbes* (London: Dorrell & Son, 1865), in Somerset Papers, Devon, Box 20, PPP 3-6; and Baxter, *Introduction*, 181-95. An even more advanced steam-powered gun turret was designed by shipbuilder-engineer and inventor James B. Eads for the four double-turret river monitors of the *Winnebago-* (or *Milwaukee-*) class. This 134-ton, eight-inch armoured turret also revolved by steam, but used machinery to run two 11-inch Dahlgren guns in and out, open and close the armoured port-stoppers, and lower and raise the entire gun platform below deck for reloading; see for example, Arnold A. Putnam, 'The Eads Steam-Powered Revolving Turret', *Warship International*, Vol. 42, No. 3 (2005), 302-17. But during the Battle of Mobile Bay (5 August 1864), the Eads turret on the USS *Winnebago* frequently jammed, forcing the commander of the monitor to pivot his vessel to get a shot on the CSS *Tennessee*; see 6 August 1864, Commander T. H. Stevens to Rear-Admiral David G. Farragut, and 7 October 1864, Lieutenant W. F. Shankland to Welles, *ORN*, Series 1, Vol. 21, 496-7 and 489-501.

the nations; and that Europe, so far from checking the progress of our Republic, must herself yield to the force of American thought.'[30]

Coles, of course, had been thinking along similar lines. It was his own 'invention', the armoured gun turret for naval warfare, which was the best expression of not just a British identity which was innovative and enterprising but of Britain's unquestioned pre-eminence at sea. Ericsson had clearly been able to capitalise on the extraordinary, even wild, circumstances of the Civil War to get his novel ideas past institutional conservatism and bureaucratic obstruction—steaming into glory and immortality as his luck as well as skill literally helped 'save the nation'. 'Were we at war with America or France, the right thing would be done instantly,' mused Barry, an impression shared by many of his contemporaries, 'but, until that good time comes, if the expression may be allowed, the probability is that official incapacity, misrule, and corruption will hold their own.'[31] Coles thought the latest Naval Estimates presented to Parliament (Committee) that March 'pretty well showed the profligate waste that is going on.' For 1865-66 Lord Clarence Paget had outlined a bill for £10,392,224, of which £2,930,654 (or 28 percent) was for stores and shipbuilding, claiming a savings of £460,179 (or 14 percent) from the previous year on the same count. The Royal Navy could eventually count on thirty ironclads of various shapes and sizes, including nineteen 'armour-plated ships-of-the-line'. While the Admiralty Secretary declared he did not want to be drawn 'on the present occasion enter into the controversy of "turret versus broadside," as we shall have time for discussion upon that point hereafter', he then proceeded to describe the newly-projected champion ironclad of the fleet, the central-battery *Hercules*. But 'Vote 10' allocated £120,000 towards a £240,00 final sum in future for at least one privately contracted ironclad—and this might be a seagoing turret-ship. The problem, he stressed, was that no suitable design for one had yet been received by the Admiralty by Coles, despite ships' plans and the assistance of a Navy draughtsman. Nevertheless, Sir John Pakington rose to deliver a long and devasting critique of the disordered character of the broadside ironclads themselves, a perfect menagerie of opposing sea-keeping abilities, speeds, armaments and armour configurations. The *Prince Consort* had nearly foundered in the Irish Channel (at the end of October 1863), he surmised, because of the mistaken emphasis upon all-round armour-plating. Last-minute alterations by the Controller's Department only added to the confusion and delays. The converted, and re-converted, *Royal Alfred* was, to quote *The Times*, 'a monstrous burlesque upon what will then be considered a first-class iron-clad'. It was inexcusable that the *Minotaur*-class *Northumberland* was still incomplete—and wouldn't be ready now until closer to '1867'—and that Paget had laid the blame entirely upon the Millwall Shipbuilding Company. Reed's

---

30 Charles D. Boynton, *History of the Navy During the Rebellion*, 2 vols (New York: D. Appleton and Company, 1867), 1: 14-17. The author was listed as 'Chaplain of the United States House of Representatives, and Assistant Professor at the U.S. Naval Academy'.
31 Barry, *Shoeburyness and the Guns*, 88.

'experimental' ships, *Enterprise*, *Research* and *Favourite*, were patent failures; neither especially well-protected nor good seaboats. Hiring him as Chief Constructor, the former First Lord of the Admiralty was now 'pained' to state publicly, was itself a mistake, even as dissenting talents like Isaac Watts had been quietly pushed out of the way or had quit 'through disgust'. Such vessels were the product of 'the vacillation and the weakness of the Admiralty, and in their not knowing or being unable to decide on what principle they are to act in building these iron-covered ships.' As for the Admiralty's working relationship with Captain Coles, Pakington wondered why it was only now that a proper seagoing turret-ship was being seriously considered? Why stutter forward with the coastal defence versions, the *Prince Albert* and the (apparently abortive, since quickly decommissioned) *Royal Sovereign*? 'I am afraid there is some ground for the suspicion widely entertained that there is a secret influence at the Admiralty, which is opposed to the turret principle,' he surmised, 'which found that principle more successful than it liked, and which accordingly procured the paying off of a crew [of the *Royal Sovereign*] that will not soon be got together again.'[32] As awe-inspiring as Britain's ironclad fleet was becoming, no amount of Admiralty spin could divert attention away from just how professionally and politically divisive its development had become too.

* * *

With the Admiralty clearly on the defensive, Coles penned his reply to Paget two days later, in *The Times*. The nation still had no seagoing turret vessel, despite his 'humble efforts to assist in solving the great problem of ironclad ships.' But neither could he be held responsible for the delays, precisely because had 'never attempted to become either a shipbuilder or a naval architect.' The working relationship between himself and the Controller's Department was not clear. He could provide working gun turrets, but the actual platform upon which they floated—the ship—was not his to design. The speculative drawings he had done for the sail-and-turret-ship '*Naughty Child*', which he presented to RUSI in 1863, for example, were strictly that: speculative and drawings, not complex plans with draught and displacement calculated, and so forth. 'However, time rolled on, and I asked if there were objections to those various designs, that I might be allowed to know them, so that they might be remedied; but I was

---

32 18 March 1865, Coles to Cobden, Cobden Papers, Chichester; 6 March 1865, 'Supply—Navy Estimates', *Hansard*, Vol. 177, 1146-1201. The U.S. *Army and Navy Journal* likened the 'over-laden' *Prince Consort* to a 'fatigued beast of burden; in sea-phrase she had no life in her, and did not rise to the sea.' Things became so bad for the British ironclad that the depth of water in the hold exceeded seven feet, and was within inches of putting out her fires—and therefore the pumps 'throwing out two hundred tons of water per hour'; 28 November 1863, *Army and Navy Journal*, 218.

told that it was not customary to give such information to *inventors*.'³³ Robinson was incensed by this latest piece of adverse publicity, and the more Coles resorted to the press the less trusting the Controller felt he was obliged to be. When Coles asked for plans for Reed's *Bellerophon* at the beginning of the year, to help him work a practical design for a turreted ironclad with the same hull, Robinson questioned to the Board of Admiralty 'How far is it right to furnish all these particulars to irresponsible persons?' He could not forget that Captain Coles, the pamphleteer and public lecturer, had only ever harassed Admiralty policy with 'a total want of candour and fairness—nor that he has expressed strong personal feelings against the Chief Constructor.' The result was that the British people were now 'prejudiced' against the Controller's Department and the reputations of those who designed Her Majesty's ironclads were 'damaged'. Yet a month later, 25 February, both Reed and Robinson pressured the Board to accept the in-house design of a twin-screw ironclad corvette drawing only sixteen feet nine inches, with a central-battery armament of eight (9-ton) eight-inch guns behind six inches of iron armour—and to forego the usual practice of calling forth competitive designs from the private trade. Perhaps the last thing they wanted was a turret-ship version coming from Lairds, for example. It could also be built at the government yard at Pembroke. As such, Robinson argued there were 'very great objections to building ships (which are necessarily in some sense experimental), altogether by contract, and as the proposed vessel is urgently wanted for foreign stations, it is necessary that no time should be lost in proceeding with this [central-battery] design.'³⁴

Now Robinson set out to discredit Coles in a printed, twenty-seven-page chronicle of correspondence between the inventor and the Admiralty stretching back to September 1861. Methodical and caustic, the Controller portrayed an ambitious, unscrupulous and egomaniacal officer who was, unfortunately for the Royal Navy, also rather incompetent. Gripped by indecision, his 'designs' were often assessed by professional naval architects as hopelessly unrealistic, often piling on weights a vessel couldn't float safely. Still, the Board had politely asked Coles to furnish revised plans, time and again. Departmental constructors in the meantime had deduced that even a trimmed-down dual-turret 'cupola' vessel armed 'with only four guns' was considered too expensive, 'and that the cost in such a case, whether calculated by gun or by ton, was far in excess of any other mode of arming a ship.' Following news of both the penetration of a *Warrior* Target by the new Armstrong 150-pounder gun and the Battle of Hampton Roads, Coles wanted fewer turrets for his trial ship if they could mount the heaviest ordnance possible, 'and for the delay thus occasioned the

---

33 Letter to the Editor dated 11 March 1865, printed in the 16 March edition of *The Times*; original *emphasis*.
34 24 January and 25 February 1865, Robinson to Board, TNA ADM 1/5941. Even though the *Penelope* would feature 6-inch armour along her sides, the box plating fore and aft was 4½-inches thick and therefore more susceptible to raking penetration from heavy guns. At 4,400-tons she was less than half the displacement of HMS *Achilles*, for example, and 14 percent larger than the *Pallas* yet drawing 2½-less feet of water.

Admiralty was certainly not responsible', observed Robinson. In his rush for the most powerful ironclad possible, Coles wantonly threw away 'what had already been ascertained by experiment to be possible and useful' and even before 'the working drawings for a plan which had been successful were ready, he was urging changes and improvements depending upon guns not in existence, and without drawings of which he always represented that he could not construct his improvements.' It also did little good for Coles to complain that either the *Prince Albert* or *Royal Sovereign* were left mastless—and therefore never considered to be more than harbour or coast defence vessels—since those decisions had been made from the outset, and no one was willing to risk turrets on a fully-rigged capital ship, at least at first.[35]

Robinson and Reed's closely jointed vehemence went too far, however. Not just Coles but anyone who questioned their shipbuilding programme and preferences was attacked in progressively lengthy, methodical memos to the Board seemingly intended to annihilate opposition. The Controller maintained a professional feud with Rear-Admiral Sir Sydney Dacres, commanding the Channel Squadron, requesting that a separate officer be assigned to make sure the C-in-C and his ship captains kept more 'accurate' records. When Dacres understandably took offense, and Robinson denied he had 'made no insinuation against anybody', Grey intervened since 'there would be no advantage in continuing the controversy'; the whole matter was simply a misunderstanding.[36] Shortly after the debate in Parliament over the Naval Estimates, the former Secretary of the Iron Plate Committee, Royal Army Captain A. Harrison, presented a paper for the Royal Artillery Institution—'On the construction of our Iron-clad Fleet, and a few remarks on iron shields for Coast Batteries'. When this was forwarded by the War Office to the Admiralty for comment before possible publication, Robinson found objection 'to the whole tenor of his remarks', beyond his detailed breakdown of every paragraph for inaccuracies, declaring 'the M.S. really goes far beyond the mere record of facts, and enters into collateral discussions concerning the course officially pursued by the Admiralty in the execution of its duty, and suggests, if it does not directly express, opinions calculated to reflect injuriously upon the manner in which their Lordships and their officers have performed their duty.' Indeed, practically anything coming from the former Iron Plate Committee, if not the Army, was quite unwanted and uncalled for. But Somerset and Grey were obliged to be more diplomatic, and simply trying to suppress publication altogether might invite a lengthy 'inter-service' debate (inevitably publicised) which everyone was keen to avoid. 'We should not wish to get into another controversy with Captain Harrison which a discussion of the different points might lead to,' the First Naval

---

35 'Confidential', 'Captain Coles and the Admiralty' (1865), in Somerset Papers, Devon, Box 20, PPP 1-2.
36 21 July 1865, 'Rolling of Ships', TNA ADM 1/5942; see also 5 and 11 November 1864, Dacres to Board, TNA ADM 1/5867; 19 November 1864, Robinson to Board, TNA ADM 1/5892.

Lord minuted on 14 March, 'but the corrections might be accompanied with such explanations as might be required for the information of Lord de Grey.' Robinson replied that was 'unable to comply literally with Sir F. Grey's minute, by furnishing the corrections and explanations on separate papers, owing to the magnitude of the alterations which appear to be necessary, and which no mere modification of words or phrases can in some cases effect.'[37] But his fact-checking precis was duly forwarded, and Harrison's paper published in the *Proceedings of the Royal Artillery Institution* later that year. Whatever the 'tone' of the original draft, this was a fairly mild analysis, which the author hoped would be 'useful in enabling any officer, who is interested in the subject, to acquaint himself with what has been doing regarding the reconstruction of our navy, and towards obtaining the requisite protection, for our guns and gunners, from the large projectiles which will undoubtedly be used in all future warfare.' As for Coles and turret-ships, Harrison noted only that there 'seems no longer to be any dispute of the value of turret-ships for harbour and coast defence…The difference of opinion is now narrowed to the relative value of turret and broadside ships as seagoing vessels.'[38]

On 3 April Coles finally submitted his own version of a seagoing *Pallas*-type ironclad (the plans for which had been grudgingly supplied by Reed). This substituted the central-battery casemate arrangement of four 6½-ton guns and two 110-pounder Armstrong breechloaders as pivot guns for a single turret-armament of two 20-ton '600-pounders', and with due hull weights and displacements properly re-calculated and certified by a draughtsman supplied by the Admiralty.[39] At last, the Royal Navy *could* have a sail-and-turret ironclad—which could cruise anywhere, operate on foreign stations, and stand up well tactically against potential ironclad enemies. But the Chief Constructor and the Controller now took turns throughout the rest of the month treating the Coles schematic as an abomination. Robinson's preliminary report of 8 April was itself fourteen pages long; Reed's of 11 April was forty-three; and Robinson's follow-through another nineteen: seventy-six handwritten pages of technical fault-finding and scorn for the Board of Admiralty to digest. Reed's report alone was a masterpiece of obdurate dissection, leaving one to wonder had *he* been

---

37 21 March 1865, Robinson to Board, TNA ADM 1/5941; Robinson's enclosed memo concluding 'there can be no advantage to the Public Service in permitting Captain Harrison to publish statements of the character I have just described' is dated 11 March.
38 Captain A. Harrison, R.A., 'On the construction of our Iron-Clad Fleet, and a few remarks on iron shields for Coast Batteries', *Minutes of the Proceedings of the Royal Artillery Institution, Vol. IV* (Woolwich: Royal Artillery Institution, 1865), 415-54. The War Office defended its reports on iron targets against the accusations made by the Controller that they contained 'certain errors'. In most cases the errors 'are merely apparent and arise from different modes of expressing the same thing', 5 April 1865, War Office to Admiralty, TNA ADM 1/5956.
39 Joseph Scullard, Chief Draughtsman of Portsmouth Dockyard; as Parkes notes, upon request Coles was also sent the plans for Reed's (iron-hulled) *Bellerophon*; *British Battleships*, 127.

assigned to assist Coles in the plan as a professional naval architect, would many of the imperfections have been worked out well in advance in the process of design? As it was, none of their comments could be considered constructive criticism. More to the point, they assaulted the whole utility of a turret armament in any respect; even if it meant necessarily thinner armour protection per gun overall, they argued, a central-battery 'box' was still superior to smaller, more thickly-plated turrets since there would be more guns to knock out—even when this sort of rationale clearly undermined Reed's whole 'improvement' upon the long broadsides of the *Warrior* and her sister-ships with a much smaller armament of heavier guns behind thicker armour in the first place. And although the same might be said for his own experiments, from *Enterprise* to *Hercules*, Reed ridiculed Coles for having 'greatly embarrassed the consideration of his Design by submitting not a fixed and settled Design for such a ship as he would like to see built, but alternative proposals on points of great importance concerning which he, as a seaman and as the advocate of the Turret system, might fairly be expected to have settled opinions.' The key to this double-standard came in his conclusion, since 'if, notwithstanding the objections pointed out, their Lordships should consider it desirable to build the ship,' Reed promised he would 'spare no pains, of course, to render her as perfect and successful as possible.'[40] The Navy could have its seagoing turret-ship, provided that the Chief Constructor operating within the suzerainty of the Controller's Department provided the actual design.

In any case, nowhere in all this vitriol was there a political consideration how Coles and other turret-ship advocates, now spread far and wide indeed, would react or how that reaction might be managed. The situation was now only going from bad to worse. As featured in a full-page spread of *The Illustrated London News* earlier that weekend, the newly completed HMS *Minotaur* seemed more of a bloated, 10,600-ton dinosaur than clever 'ship of the future'; a stupendous iron wall gliding implacably along at sea. *The Times* commented that 'handsome as she undoubtedly is in her hull, she is certainly unsurpassed for ugliness in her spars and rigging aloft, where her five masts, 12 crossed yards, and compound tracery of rigging seem to have been designed for the special purpose of affording a certain mark to an enemy's shot in action, and an equal certainly of fouling the screw of the ship when knocked away

---

40   8 April 1865, Robinson to Board, TNA ADM 1/5941. Both Reed and Robinson also demurred at the thought of two 600-pounders as a main armament, Reed preferring two 300-pounders instead, and the Controller remarking they were overkill when lighter guns 'will pierce even 6-inch armour plates' (though any ship approved in 1865 would not be ready for service until at least 1867). At any rate, such guns were too 'experimental'—certainly requiring machinery to operate efficiently—and would probably have a lower rate of fire than lighter guns. The Chief Constructor even speculated that 'if two 600 pounders are placed within a turret they will so far fill it as to leave little room for the Turret to suffer without injury to them, and still less room for remedying any derangement that may happen.'

and overboard.'[41] Given the trend of not just Coles and the popular press but also Robinson and Reed's escalating defensiveness, the Board realised it was unprepared to resolve the matter even on its own authority. 'A careful and un-prejudicial inquiry into the advantages and disadvantages of this design by a committee will be desirable', Somerset minuted: a slap on the wrist as well as administrative sleight of hand.[42] Tasked to 'obtain the unbiased opinion of practical naval officers whether a ship built and armed as proposed would be equal or superior to any other vessel of equal tonnage and speed that could be designed and whether she would possess those qualities and those powers of offence and defence which are essential to a good ship of war', the reviewing committee was chaired by Vice-Admiral Sir Thomas Maitland[43], with Rear-Admiral Sir Hastings Yelverton, Captain Henry Caldwell, Captain John James Kennedy, Captain Henry Bouchier Phillimore, and Secretary Arthur Price.[44] When it asked on 2 May for copies of various ship designs and other correspondence between the Admiralty and Coles, Robinson bristled at the intrusion. The explanatory cover letter from Coles which came with his submission was already no longer in his office and must be 'in the Record Office'; some of the naval reports, like those made by Dacres on the performance of the Channel Squadron at sea, or Osborn's report on the trial of the *Royal Sovereign*, were either too secret for dissemination or must be accompanied with his own comments upon them; and at any rate his department was too busy and had neither the time nor the funding to make the necessary copies. Yet if 'their Lordships think proper to give them,' he stipulated that 'the Committee should be prohibited from making them public, the more so as their Lordships have always refused to give publicity to the reports of the Iron Plate Committee and disapproved of the Armaments lately proposed for H.M. Ships being sent even to the Dockyards, except confidentially.'[45]

As a fellow inventor, Reed was no less protective and suspicious, and as Chief Constructor of the Navy perhaps even more. When the Committee also asked for the plans of *Pallas* and *Bellerophon*, he objected they were not subject to public scrutiny because they were *his*. 'This understanding has been departed from by Captain Coles, who has used as many of my ideas and plans as he has pleased and departed from them in other respects at his own will and pleasure. The proportions of the Turret-ship

---

41 8 April 1865, *The Illustrated London News*; 25 April 1865, *The Times*.
42 8 April 1865, Robinson to Board, TNA ADM 1/5941; Somerset's marginal minute is date 12 April 1865.
43 11th Earl of Lauderdale.
44 Kennedy had recently returned from the North America and West Indies Station, where he commanded the screw-corvette HMS *Challenger*; Phillimore had been promoted to captain the previous April and was only 32 when he served on the Admiralty-appointed committee reviewing the Coles turret-ship proposal.
45 8 April 1865, Robinson to Board, TNA ADM 1/5941; enclosed letter from Price is dated 2 May 1865, with Romaine's reply dated the same; 4 May 1865, Robinson to Board, TNA ADM 1/5942.

are, nevertheless, substantially those of the *Pallas*, while the structure of the Hull is substantially that of the *Bellerophon*.' This was a sensitive issue since Reed's own 'Bracket Plate' system of hull framing construction utilised in these ships allowed for greater strength at less weight, for less cost, and less time in construction. Robinson, of course, attempted to back his colleague to the Board. But by now such petulance on all sides was becoming tiresome indeed, and the Board replied there was in fact 'no reason to believe that the Committee have in any way departed from the line pointed out in their instructions which confine them to a consideration of the design submitted to them and they will take care that no act in any way unjust or prejudicial to Mr. Reed shall receive their Lordships sanction.' They also saw fit to clarify that 'the drawings of Ships which have been constructed for H. M. Service can no longer be considered as private property and they cannot admit any claim on Mr. Reed's part to object to their Lordships making any use of them which they may deem necessary for the good of the service.'[46] The Committee, at least, did not dwell upon the mass of documentation and testimonies of expert witnesses called upon, submitting its report to the Admiralty on 28 June.

Fate, however, had already intervened, since Coles was so debilitated over the spring that he missed his chance for explaining his ideas and defending his design rationale directly, in person. When the Committee sent him a long list of thirty criticisms compiled from various witnesses (but mostly from Reed and Robinson), on 5 June, Coles declined in writing to address them unless he was also given the full transcript of each testimony as well. Above all, the Committee members noted the inherent vulnerability of the high-freeboard turret-ship from penetration of the side armour, thereby wrecking the entire offensive power of an ironclad with just two guns. This in turn stemmed from 'constructing a seagoing ship armed on the turret system, so as to have her upper deck of sufficient height above the water to render the ship a good sea boat, and afford adequate protection for the health and comfort of the crew under all circumstances, but more especially when forcing the ship against a head sea, trade wind, monsoon, or strong periodical winds met with in all parts of the world, and which ships are liable to encounter when making a passage.' Here they had to observe that American monitors were free of this weakness since, as harbour and coast defence vessels only, they could enjoy the tactical strengths which low-freeboard

---

46 22 May 1865, Robinson to Board, TNA ADM 1/5942. As Reed testified to the Committee on 23 May, 'the designs of the *Pallas* and the *Bellerophon* were prepared by me while I was a private individual, and not a servant of the Government, and offered to the Government for their use, and accepted by the Admiralty,' 28 June 1865, *Report of a Committee of Naval Officers Appointed to Examine the Design of a Seagoing Turret-Ship Submitted to the Admiralty by Captain Cowper C. P. Coles, R.N.*, in TNA ADM 268/97, 61. For an exposition of Reed's innovations as a shipbuilder see 12 December 1866, Reed to Robinson, in 13 December 1866, Robinson to Board, TNA ADM 1/5983, in a discussion over Reed's salary as Chief Constructor of the Navy; also E. J. Reed, *Shipbuilding in Iron and Steel* (London: John Murray, 1869), especially 110-34.

('semi-submersion') gave them. If for any reason a single turret monitor's guns were knocked out of action, it could retreat back to its base nearby, whereas the consequences would be dire in the extreme if a seagoing single turret-ship, fighting upon the high seas or against an enemy's coastline, suffered similar damage. Perhaps a monitor could cross the Atlantic, as some American officers (and Ericsson) had boasted, but no one on the Committee was willing to regard such vessels 'as seagoing cruizing ships.' The French showed no interest in adopting them for this role, and the political controversy over monitors even within the U.S. Navy was well known. Yet despite the attempts of the Controller and Chief Constructor to quash a turret-based armament at all, the Committee did consider it 'most desirable that a conclusive trial should be given to the system in a seagoing ship to be armed with two turrets, capable of carrying two 12-ton guns in each turret, or if necessary one 22-ton gun in each; as we think it very possible that such guns as those of 22 tons may be required at sea ere long, and it is not improbable that the French, when considering the subject some time ago, did not contemplate the necessity of carrying such heavy guns.' Even if the completed vessel failed as a seagoing ironclad, it added, 'the two-turreted ship would still be a most useful and formidable vessel for coast defence.'[47]

---

47 Ibid., *Report of a Committee of Naval Officers Appointed to Examine the Design of a Seagoing Turret-Ship Submitted to the Admiralty by Captain Cowper C. P. Coles, R.N.*, 7-8, 14. Robinson testified on 19 May 'there are other modes of armament which, taking the same weight of materials as are now used in the turret-ship of Captain Coles, would give you a superior armament', 51. But the Committee ultimately disagreed, as 'the advantages of the turret system of armament appear in many respects to be so great, and the facilities which it affords for carrying the heaviest description of ordnance are so evident, that...the matter should be no longer left in doubt, and that a trial should be given to the system in a seagoing ship, armed with two turrets', 14.

7

'Wherever these Monitors manage to get, we should have vessels of equal fighting powers'

While this verdict might have seemed a personal vindication for Coles, the problem remained that the all-powerful Controller's Department was openly against his ideas—at least as they came from him, professionally. When asked by Captain Caldwell of the Committee if he had any 'decided objection to such a vessel being constructed for special purposes, and not as an ordinary cruiser', Reed replied that the question was very much about economies. 'My own feeling has always been that it is very desirable that the best seagoing turret-ship which can be produced should be produced, and sent to sea for some months, and reported upon for the guidance of their Lordships and others.' But incredibly this was only because he thought that 'the thorough trial of such a vessel on sea-service would tend considerably to the settlement of the difference of opinion that exists on the adaptability of the turret system to seagoing purposes.' Given Reed and Robinson's predilection for central-battery, broadside-ironclads, it was rather assumed that a seagoing turret-ship would 'fail' in some form or another, and if it took an enormous amount of public investment to make that finally unquestionable then perhaps it would be worth the experiment after all. This was partially due to the fact that 'the authority of the naval architect comes in…stating what qualities are and what qualities are not practicable in a ship', even though Reed declared that 'the opinions of naval architects as to the value of ships for seagoing and fighting purposes are quite subordinate to the opinions of naval officers.' Yet the Chief Constructor was also careful in adding that, in his estimation, 'the Admiralty already have the means of giving a fair trial to all the doubtful points of this design in the vessels which they already possess, and that it is extremely undesirable for a public department in a country like this to evade the responsibility which belongs to it in deciding a question of this sort, by expending large sums of the public money on so-called experiments, unless they have reason to believe that great and decided advantage would result from that expenditure.' The Controller was even more adamant that 'the box principle…is the best principle which can be acted upon.'[1] Critically, however, when he returned for more questioning on 1 June, Robinson testified being equally certain 'that for the defence of harbours, rivers, inland waters, and for coast defences in fine weather, I consider a modified turret-ship superior to all others, however much I may object to the particular design of Captain Coles' before me.' Following a successful test of the 12-ton gun mounted on the broadside of HMS *Minotaur* the next month, Captain Key also declared there were no practical reasons 'why a heavy gun should not be worked on a broadside with the same security as in a turret; and I am satisfied that there is no difference between the two systems in this respect' (in fact, initial practice suggested the rate of fire of the 12-ton Armstrong was slightly faster than on the *Royal Sovereign*.) Thus he also concluded that while 'for harbour defence and short voyages for the purposes of attacking a fortified position, the turret would prove of great value,' he did not consider 'we could retain that superiority at sea which is necessary to our existence as a first-rate power, if we armed our fleet for ocean service in all parts of the world entirely on the turret-system, as its inferiority under the varied circumstances in which a ship of war must necessarily be placed would prove to be very decided.'[2]

But the distinctions drawn here seemed ambiguous: how could a turret armament be best for operating on coasts or against enemy forts only, while a broadside was better everywhere else, against enemy ships? 'For service on an enemy's coast, and more especially for attacking batteries,' nothing was better for the Royal Navy than the wooden-hulled, fully-armoured broadside-ironclads of the *Royal Oak*-class, wrote the mastermind behind Baltic operations in 1855 (and those projected for a 1856 campaign) against Russia, Rear-Admiral Bartholomew Sulivan, in a letter to *The Times*. The only exception he foresaw was 'off a port on an exposed coast', in which case partially-plated ships like the *Warrior*- or *Defence*-classes would be the safest bet. To what extent did masts and rigging undermine a seagoing turret-ship's effectiveness against the blind-spots associated with even a central-battery form of broadside vessel, and was there room in this comparative margin of error for making the turret-ship every bit as seaworthy? For all the vulnerabilities Robinson highlighted for a more mechanised heavy armament—rotating gun turrets—in a seagoing ironclad (jamming of turrets, limited numbers of guns overall, top decks lower in the water and susceptible

---

1   Ibid., Reed's second day of testimony, 25 May 1865, 64-7; Robinson's first day of testimony dated 19 May, 50 and his second on 1 June 1865, 50, 77; 11 July 1865, *Report of Trial of Turrets and Guns of the Royal Sovereign*, TNA ADM 1/5943.

2   Ibid., Robinson's second day of testimony, 1 June 1865, 77; 11 July 1865, *Report of Trial of Turrets and Guns of the Royal Sovereign*, TNA ADM 1/5943; letter dated 11 March, printed 13 March 1865, *The Times*. Key noted that while rotation of the *Royal Sovereign*'s turrets was done with 'but little manual labour', 'To run the gun in…requires great power', with training tackle requiring eighteen men, and the use of winches also making the operation 'very slow and tedious and would be attended with danger in a sea-way. Powerful winches such as those fitted in [*Wivern* and *Scorpion*] and which have for some time been preparing for the *Royal Sovereign*, should be supplied without delay.'

to penetration on the one hand, and frequently awash from the sea on the other), the same faults applied to light-draft monitors with even lower freeboard. On 3 July 1865 a *Times* leader did its best to distinguish between the American monitor form of turret vessel and the more ambitious roles advocated by Coles. The former, 'though an ingenious design, was a practical mistake', at least in terms of its seaworthiness, while the advent of Armstrong's new heavy guns meant that while the British 'do not want even a "turret-ship" for itself, but it does seem as if we might most urgently want a ship in which the armament could be carried centrally, and that brings us to a turret-ship in some form or other.' It was the Admiralty's policy, therefore, that was conceptually flawed 'with regard to Captain Coles's proposals', and its officials 'seem to have been scandalized at the idea of making a British frigate like Mr. Ericsson's Monitor.'[3]

The Board now tasked the Controller—not Coles—with carrying out the Committee's recommendation for a double-turreted seagoing ironclad. And while Robinson couldn't resist noting Key's report ('a remarkable confirmation of all the reports and submissions I have made to their Lordships on the subject of Turret-ships'), he replied on 13 July that by considerably reducing the space between the two turrets a more concentrated, central armoured-citadel could be had for their protection, even though this would considerably reduce the turrets' unobstructed fields of fire. A reply was slow in coming, 9 October, but the Board was willing to give up clear fore and aft firing arcs 'to obtain a good seagoing vessel' by allowing for 'fixed bulwarks forward and aft combined with a Forecastle and with or without a Poop.' Light chase guns might be substituted on the ends, though they would be relatively exposed. The turrets themselves had to be no less than fourteen-feet from the waterline; there could be no question of their being able to operate in all seas, even if the higher freeboard meant a diminution of armour thickness amidships, perhaps no more than 5½-inch iron-plating.[4] This was HMS *Monarch*. It was hoped this would be good enough to satisfy *The Times* and other Coles supporters; a proper seagoing turret-ship and not a makeshift, hybrid conversion like the *Royal Sovereign*—too deep for littoral operations in shallow waters yet not seaworthy enough for much else. But she was not going to be a Coles invention as another credit to Reed's creativity and engineering skill. The parameters of the design were, as with all ironclad warships, a tortuous exercise in compromise. Soon enough, however, Coles and his supporters suspected the Admiralty of playing it too safe in terms of the *Monarch*'s sea-keeping even if meant that the 'turret system' would be thereby discredited for the British people to witness. Only a conservative institution operating largely behind closed doors could produce something so ridiculous in a government yard—unless of course

3   3 July 1865, *The Times*.
4   7 July 1865, Board to Controller, TNA ADM 3/272; Coles was informed the same day that the Board was not accepting his design, though they proposed 'to give their immediate attention to this important subject', TNA ADM 3/372; 13 July 1865, Robinson to Board, TNA ADM 1/5942, with enclosed letter from Paget to Robinson dated 9 October 1865.

the secret intention all along was to build (another) turret-ship 'failure' so that a fleet of central-battery broadside-ironclads could be further justified while adverting the far greater risk of a fleet of Coles-designed turret-ships?

Robinson indeed pressed on with the *Hercules*, also to be built at Chatham. Not without irony, the flaws of the future *Monarch* were anticipated in Reed's final modifications which now promised 'every point around the ship is commanded by the fire of a protected Gun', though it meant fewer of them. To further wet the Board's appetite, the armour thickness and wood backing were beefed up, even if it meant sacrificing an armoured pilot house; the Chief Constructor seriously suggesting that an ironclad 325-feet long might be steered in battle from within its fore-gunports. As the design specified ten 12-ton 300-pounders, the Admiralty urged the War Office to speed up production of an experimental iron carriage for immediate testing at Portsmouth.[5] Coles, in the meantime, had recovered sufficiently to reply to the thirty objections (with their evidence-testimonies) forwarded to him by the Committee. Only rather than submitting his full rebuttal to the Board, he chose to publish them in another pamphlet. This served to defend his turret-ship system as well as attack the whole concept of Reed's latest champion, the *Hercules*. Worst of all, Coles challenged Robinson and Reed of not just nit-picking but applying a double-standard from their privileged positions: 'Let me ask, what would have been the fate of the *Research*'s and *Pallas*'s designs if they had been submitted to a Committee of naval officers?' While he stated his indifference who actually designed the dual-turret-ship recommended by the Committee, he emphasized that 'it would be advisable to stipulate that the naval architect to whom the designs are entrusted, is not opposed to the Turret system, and should ensure a higher rate of speed than that which the *Pallas* or any other square box ship yet tried possesses, or than we may even anticipate from those building.' In other words, anyone but Reed.[6]

What *was* true, everyone could agree, is that no acceptable solution to the vexing riddle of how to combine the tactical perfection presented by Ericsson's 'Monitor' with the sea-worthiness and global reach of the *Warrior* had yet been found. Two days after Robinson repeated to the Board how he was 'desirous as the most uncompromising advocate of the Turret system, to find a solution of the problem which shall be satisfactory', *The Times* simply pronounced that 'a perfect ironclad is an imperfect sea-boat'.[7] The Americans, by contrast, seemed quite content with their turret-ships, for in their everyday vernacular 'ironclad' had become synonymous with all things safe and secure, from household commercial brands to penny tokens struck with an

---

5   1 August 1865, Robinson to Board, TNA ADM 1/5942; 8 August 1865, Minute, TNA ADM 3/272.

6   *Letters from Captain Cowper Coles to the Secretary of the Admiralty on Seagoing Turret-Ships* (12 August 1865). In response to the complaint that crew working sails in his turret-ship would be exposed to enemy fire during combat, for example, Coles only had to ask why steam power would not be used, 27.

7   Ibid., 1 November 1865, *The Times*.

image of 'Our Little Monitor'. Southerners who wished to join the reconstituted United States of America only had to swear an 'Ironclad Oath of Allegiance'.[8] 'Those iron-clads which *The Times* has handled so severely, the Monitor *Monadnock* among the rest, are intended for coast and harbor defense', Ericsson avowed for the influential U.S. *Army and Navy Journal* in March 1865. 'It is not proposed to send these vessels after the *Bellerophon*s or *Minotaur*s, but at the same time it may not be prudent to send these unwieldy craft after them. Our trans-Atlantic cousins are welcome to wring by their sophistical reasoning, whatever conclusions they please…but they must use thicker armor, have lighter draught and more manageable vessels, and equip them with more powerful guns, if they expect to meet with success in any act of aggression on our harbors or coasts. We are surrounded by a wall of iron, within which we intend, unmolested, to develop our national strength.'[9] Until they could devise a fleet of powerfully-armed turret-ships of their own—yet roving far beyond the horizon—the mid-Victorian British considered themselves, and their global interests, only more or less 'armoured'. Their ironclads, along with everyone else's, were more vulnerable the more seafaring they became. Their shipbuilding choices entailed more compromise, more serious calculations of risk. As this suggested that 'perfect' national defence was at odds with an 'imperfect' imperial one—or assertive foreign policy—such a lingering technological and strategic dichotomy was profoundly unacceptable. In a proudly progressive age of 'self-made' men and 'self-help', nothing else quite explains the how and why of the eventual *Captain* disaster better.

This feeling was only worsened, of course, with the death of Lord Palmerston on 18 October 1865. Following both the surrender of Confederate General Robert E. Lee at Appomattox Courthouse (9 April) and the brutal assassination of Abraham Lincoln five days later, Russell wrote to Sir Frederick Bruce in Washington D.C. that while this 'brought out…the real feeling of this nation of sympathy with the United States', yet he feared that 'in the US themselves the cry of vengeance which had been kept low by President Lincoln will now be very loud and menacing.' On 27 May he reiterated his suspicion 'that the American people are usually easily excited, and their recent successes, ending with the capture of Jefferson Davis, are enough to make them wild.'[10] But that summer both the French and British ironclad fleets toured

---

8 See Anna Gibson Holloway and Jonathan W. White (eds.), *"Our Little* Monitor*": The Greatest Invention of the Civil War* (Kent: The Kent State University Press, 2018), 87-112; and Mark E. Neely and Harold Holzer (eds.), *The Union Image: Popular Prints of the Civil War North* (Chapel Hill: The University of North Carolina Press, 2000), 109-28, who note most representation of the original USS *Monitor*, for example, still tends to ignore the ship's heroic commanding officer during the Battle of Hampton Roads, Lieutenant John L. Worden, emphasising either the faceless technology itself or the ironclad's 'genius' inventor, Ericsson; for the 'Ironclad Oath' see for example, Susanna Michele Lee, *Claiming the Union: Citizenship in the Post-Civil War South* (New York: Cambridge University Press, 2014), 13-14, 17, 55.
9 18 March 1865, 'The XV-Inch Gun', *Army and Navy Journal*, 473.
10 29 April and 27 May 1865, Russell to Bruce, Russell Papers, TNA PRO 30-22, 97.

each other's home ports, to great popular fanfare in both countries, and with *Punch* quipping that both countries would have saved much money spent on ironclads had their politics 'only been in jolly earnest'. Now Russell hoped 'the good sense of the American people will teach them that while they have so tremendous a task before them as that of reconstituting the society of ten of their states they will do well to avoid a foreign war. If not of course their pugnacity will lead to a similar pugnacity on the part of England and France who have had so much experience in fighting one another that they know how.'[11] Palmerston was quick to observe to Somerset the real value of the Anglo-French fête, not just for peace between the world's two greatest maritime powers, but for the 'most wholesome effect in Yankee Land, where they will be taken as indications of a closer union then in Fact really exists, and they will thus tend to disincline the Yankees from aggression upon us.' In one of his last despatches to a First Lord of the Admiralty, 'Old Pam' wrote on 2 September how the welcomed presence of French ironclads at Portsmouth 'cannot fail also to produce a wholesome impression upon all other Nations and most especially the Yankees, who will no doubt see in these Meetings…a stronger Disposition between the Two Countries to coalesce against a common Enemy than is really at the Bottom of the Whole Thing; and the Yankees will be all the less likely to give Trouble either in Canada or in Mexico.' Indeed, such a geostrategic alignment was necessary, given the remarkable solidarity shown between the U.S. and Russia—the world's two greatest continental powers—during the American Civil War. As for the French, Palmerston remained incorrigible: their army hated the British 'with a Bitterness proportionate to the National Humiliation which our Military victories have inflicted on them', while the superiority of the British Navy 'has been from the Beginning an established and admitted Fact, and their defeats by Sea, though as invariable and as complete as any of their Defeats by us by Land, were looked upon, so much as matters of course that they excited no Resentment though much regret.'[12] With such a stalwart icon of British

---

11 See for example 3 June 1865, Foreign Office to Admiralty, TNA ADM 1/5953, and 3 August 1865, minute, TNA ADM 3/272; 26 August 1865, 'The Moral at Cherbourg', *Punch*; 5 August 1865, Russell to Bruce, Russell Papers, TNA PRO 30-22, 97. Russell added 'I satisfy myself with thinking that the [US] ship will right itself and be 'great, glorious and free' tho not 'first flower of the earth', and that Europe will remain much as it is—England free, France half-free, Prussia and Russia not free at all.'

12 27 August and 2 September 1865, Palmerston to Somerset, Somerset Papers, Aylesbury, D/RA/A/2A/41. On other hand, the Assistant Secretary of the Navy, Gustavus Fox, wrote that 'we should not hesitate to send a Fleet of [monitors] across the ocean to take part in any contest requiring their presence. None of our naval Captains would hesitate to attack the combined iron fleets now at Portsmouth with the last four double turreted Monitors now building [*Kalamazoo*-class] which are fourteen inches thick in their side armour, fifteen inches in the turrets, and three inches on deck. This is not a boast; it is the teaching of the war and the confidence we feel in the wonderful production of that great Swede, John Ericsson', 12 September 1865, Fox to Captain Axel Adlersparre (Swedish Navy), Fox Papers, New York, Box 10.

nationalism suddenly dead, the mid-Victorians couldn't escape not just a sensation of grief but hollowness, which had been building for some time. His name, proclaimed *The Times*, 'once the terror of the Continent, will long be connected in the minds of Englishmen with an epoch of unbroken peace and unparalleled prosperity'. But the question of his later years—of his government's recent foreign policy—begged a satisfactory answer. For 'in the eyes of our neighbours,' *The Times* continued five days later, 'his patriotism had latterly taken a safe and cautious line, instead of the sharply-defined foreign policy of earlier days…The policy of England has latterly, some of them say, become weak and indistinct.' To this, all that could be offered was that the Prime Minister and his ilk were, of course, 'gentlemen'. Lord Palmerston had not been made impotent at the end so much as 'patient and forbearing'.[13]

It was then left for Russell, as his successor, to pick up the pieces. While he agreed with Somerset that it was unwise to consider 'any considerable diminution of our naval force which is the force that is our vital strength', he also admitted to 'agree with Gladstone in thinking that in our present favourable circumstances we ought to have a progressive reduction of our military and naval force.' Somerset in turn, while he couldn't say 'what that force must be', feared that Gladstone sought 'larger and more immediate reductions than I could agree to, and I should be sorry to embarrass you at the commencement of an administration which must meet many difficulties'.[14] In the meantime, it wasn't until 6 December 1865 that Reed submitted two different plans for a dual-turret, seagoing ironclad to Robinson, with the Board of Admiralty secretly approving the larger, faster and more expensive version (the eventual 8,300-ton *Monarch*) the following day. This was as much 'in deference to public opinion'—and against the wishes of the Controller and the Chief Constructor—as the subsequent *Captain* was, though not quite in fulfilment of Pakington's wishes at the beginning of the year, for example. Nor did it to serve pacify Coles, more alienated from Admiralty decision-makers than ever, and for whom the First Naval Lord saw 'no reason' in allowing a clerk.[15] For in another letter to *The Times*, dated 13 December, Coles acknowledged that while recent tests on board the *Minotaur* suggested Armstrong's 12-ton gun might now be mounted safely on the broadside, it remained questionable whether a '6,000-ton' ship was the best, most cost-effective way to do it; 'the great merit claimed for my inventions is the power of carrying and fighting efficiently the heaviest ordnance on a *minimum* tonnage with a *maximum* speed', he stressed. 'Truly, you remark that no real seagoing turret-ship has yet been built.' Even the former 1,800-ton Laird Rams built for the Confederate States Navy, the *Scorpion* and

---

13 19 and 24 October 1865, *The Times*.
14 8 October 1865, Russell to Somerset, Somerset Papers, Aylesbury, D/RA/A/2A/54; 20 October 1865, Somerset to Russell, Russell Papers, TNA PRO-30-22, 15F.
15 6 December 1865, Robinson to Board, TNA ADM 1/5943. As Robinson wrote to Romaine, 'I asked the Duke whether I should leave the letter and drawings he said no! but I think he did not see that it would be right to have an official record of what had passed'; 9 December 1865, Grey minute, TNA ADM 3/372.

Wivern, he argued, could wield four turret-mounted 12-ton 300-pounders against the *Minotaur*'s two on each broadside ('a target of 8,800 square feet, with numerous open port-holes [versus] a target of only 1,140 square feet'). To ram home his point, as always, Coles pointed to the Americans:

> The *Monadnoc* [sic], we hear, is going to the Pacific, and although I do not admit that the American turret system can be compared with mine for seagoing purposes, let me ask what vessels have we out there that can cope with her in open fight with her 15-inch guns and low sides? Wherever these Monitors manage to get, we should have vessels of equal fighting powers than can be sent to meet them; and for this reason I have so long and so earnestly tried to persuade their Lordships to build one experimental seagoing turret-ship, from which in case the time ever should come that we want them we may have learnt what vessels are best adapted and most economical, not only to carry but to fight the heaviest ordnance in any part of the world where England's honour and trade have to be protected.[16]

* * *

As one of Coles' closest navy supporters, Rear-Admiral Edward Halsted, submitted to Somerset, it had been five years 'since Captain Coles publicly declared his System capable of producing a ship as large, as sea-worthy, and as fast as the *Warrior*, but full-armoured instead of semi-armoured, and with far more destructive and defensive powers.'[17] Instead, professional journals like *The Engineer* had loudly denounced any inclination of Britain to adopt the American monitor form of ironclad, and in its 5 January 1866 article on 'Broadside and Turret-ships' went further in reminding its readers 'that the agitation in favour of turrets has chiefly proceeded from irresponsible officers of the navy, who may well be supposed to be less competent judges of the real merits and difficulties of the question than the mechanical officers of the Admiralty.' The Chief Constructor had, in the meantime, gifted the nation with the magnificent central-battery *Bellerophon*, with more excellent versions to follow as soon as possible. Turrets, being far more radical in nature than belt-and-battery designs, simply meant

---

16 15 December 1865, *The Times*. Reed and Robinson subsequently did their best to dismantle Coles's comparisons before the Board; claiming greater armour protection for the *Minotaur*, in terms of pounds per square foot, but ignoring the thicker plating of the *Scorpion*'s and *Wivern*'s turrets as well as the fact that only six-feet of (4½-inch plated) of their freeboard was exposed to fire. They also felt that HMS *Research* was even better value for money than the turret-rams, though carrying only four 6¼-ton guns and less armour, because she had comparable speed, drew one-foot less water, and offered 'excellent accommodation for her Officers and Crew', 20 December 1865, Robinson to Board, TNA ADM 1/5943.

17 8 January 1866, Rear-Admiral Edward Pellew Halsted to Somerset, in 17 January 1866, Robinson to Board, TNA ADM 1/5980.

that more caution (therefore time) was required by the Admiralty 'before they could venture to order a large and costly seagoing ship on so novel and experimental a principle.' The next day, *The Illustrated London News* featured a half-page portrait of Edward Reed, at 36, with the same issue devoting a full-page depiction of his newly completed HMS *Pallas*: 'It is not true, we believe, as is often represented, that Mr. Reed is an opponent of turret-ships. Although he certainly has not advocated their introduction, this is chiefly on account of the great cost by which he believes the construction of such ships will be attended, armour for armour and gun for gun.' The article further hinted that Reed had been asked to stand as MP for Greenwich and Pembroke, which he had modestly declined, but that his address to Greenwich 'seems, however, to point to the probability of his desiring to enter Parliament at a future time.'[18]

Perhaps sensing that Reed's rising star was now rapidly eclipsing his own, with each large central-battery ironclad slipping down the ways, Coles now launched a direct attack upon the Admiralty—and 'Mr. Reed's ships'. In a letter to *The Standard* published 10 January 1866, he compared twelve broadside ironclads built for the Royal Navy with twelve turret-ships which had been built in Britain 'under all the disadvantages attending new inventions', mostly for foreign powers. Reed's *Research* and *Enterprise*, the only two central-battery ironclads which had actually been to sea, had been judged poor sailors with worse speeds, while *Pallas* and *Bellerophon* had likewise failed to meet their lofty design expectations. A year had gone by since their launch, while Reed and the dockyard shipwrights tinkered with these ironclads (including having to redesign the *Bellerophon*'s bow and stern), offering extra pay and feverishly pushing on the work night and day. But what really irked Coles, he wrote to the Editor, was the lack of 'fair play'. 'Give me a hundredth part of the encouragement and assistance Mr. Reed is given, and I think we could turn out a seagoing ship with as much despatch as *Pallas* or *Bellerophon* and ensure her being as great a success in her way as the *Royal Sovereign* has been in hers.' Again, he didn't 'care' who designed such a ship, but as to Reed's *Monarch* Coles couldn't say; he had not been shown the drawings.[19]

The same day that Coles's letter was published, he wrote to Romaine reminding him that four months had passed since the Admiralty had asked him for any observations he may have upon Reed's design—even as Robinson finally forwarded them to the Board.[20] In doing so the Controller struck an unusual tone in comparison with other submissions of proposed ironclads. He was 'quite aware it is open to considerable objections; objections belonging to the nature of a turret-ship intended for seagoing

18 5 January 1866, *The Engineer*, see the copy in TNA ADM 1/5980. Reed subsequently denied the charge made by Coles that he had authored the article; 6 January 1866, *The Illustrated London News*.
19 10 January 1866, *The Standard*. Coles's letter was dated 6 January.
20 10 January 1866, Coles to Romaine, TNA ADM 1/5970.

purposes, and which it has not been possible entirely to obviate.' Its defensive armour was inadequate, the turrets could be disabled by shots where the turret met the deck (and those penetrating the high-freeboard sides below them). The turrets were bunched together in the ship's centre since placing them closer to the extremities 'would in all probability destroy the seagoing qualities of the ship.' Perhaps worst of all, a permanent forecastle, armoured to carry a 7-ton rifled gun in the bow, replaced any collapsing bulwarks which might otherwise offer greater arcs of fire to the forward turret. But this would at least secure the anchor gear better and offer the crew better shelter from heavy seas. As it was, the turrets were fourteen-feet out of water, as the Board had prescribed, yet to make them even more secure on the high seas, at sixteen-feet, the Controller noted this would only make for an even bigger vessel requiring more armour, more powerful engines, and more cost, 'besides presenting a much larger target to shot.' In closing he assured the Board that 'every person in this office has given me all the assistance possible in working out this design, on which in their several departments they have shown the same zeal and application in overcoming difficulties which they have always done when employed on other designs'—this he stated 'to meet the objections which have already been made' (by Captain Coles).[21]

But of course, the main complaint of Coles was precisely that his design proposals had never enjoyed the same resources, much less 'zeal and application in overcoming difficulties'. In this sense, it had never been about whether the turret or broadside was superior, since the Controller's Department could clearly make either type of ironclad when ordered to; it was about how Reed and Robinson had personally co-opted the Admiralty's shipbuilding policy with whatever designs they preferred, better or not. As the Secretary to the Admiralty, Lord Clarence Paget, attested later, it was because of this pressure that he decided to quit the government at the first opportunity in 1865 and take up a command at sea (as C-in-C of the Mediterranean Station, in March 1866). Indeed, to help stem Robinson and Reed's growing domination of Britain's ironclad programme and even naval strategy and policy, he proposed reviving the old Navy Board, since the 'construction of ships and the management of the dockyards would be under a responsible department, in connection with but not under the Admiralty':

> On this particular point I must say the present system is extremely faulty. The controller—formerly surveyor—is responsible, not to the public, like the old Navy Board, but to the Admiralty, and shelters himself under their wing. He proposes a plan of a ship to the Board, or rather to the First Lord, who sends for any member of the Board into his room, after perhaps half an hour's discussion, a vessel, to cost nearly half a million of money, is decided on, and the plan comes into the board-room for official signature and seal. This I affirm has been

---

21 See 10 January 1866, Robinson to Board, in *Navy (Turret-ships), Parliamentary Papers*, return ordered 1 March 1866, and printed 6 July 1866, 177-9.

the whole consideration given to the plan of construction of the fleet of amour ships built during the last seven years. Nor could the First Lord act otherwise, since he has no machinery but the Board to help him. But these gentlemen are charged with, I may say, enormous duties…so that they cannot possibly give adequate attention to this matter. For of what vast importance it is that a vessel of war should be thoroughly studied in design before she is called into existence? She is not, so to speak, a single vessel; she is the representative of a class …

This was what made his position, as formal presentative of the 'Admiralty's policy', having to defend first broadside then central-battery ironclads, an increasingly odious one between 1859 and 1866. Paget himself admitted the class of vessels 'may admit of doubt.' But the turret system of Coles—and the vociferously public means with which he advocated them—had been equally contentious. 'His injudicious conduct towards the department, who really have treated him like a spoilt child,' Paget concluded, 'has doubtless been detrimental to a full and fair exposition of the merits and demerits of this system.'[22]

Thus, as much as Coles hit the mark in this letter to *The Standard* of 10 January 1866 like never before, it also woefully backfired. The Board was pricked by his sharp accusations, and Robinson could no longer conceal his outrage against public accusations from a naval officer who was supposed to be serving, not damaging, the reputation of the Admiralty and his brother officers: he should be immediately dismissed from their Lordships' service. This they proved more than willing to do, with a draft minute dated 13 January which 'regretted' that after many warnings, and 'instead of cordially cooperating with the Controller of the Navy in the endeavour to solve a most difficult problem', Coles had 'preferred to appeal to the public press and to publish disingenuous statements and reflections on the Officers employed under the Board of Admiralty.' He would no longer be allowed to review the Chief Constructor's plans for the *Monarch*, nor would they 'sanction his employment in connection with the construction of a seagoing turret-ship'. Any extra funds aside from his half-pay as navy captain were also suspended. Indeed, the 'tone and spirit' of his published letter attacking Reed suggested he was practically more an enemy now of the Admiralty than an ally. Even if everything that Coles had said in regard to Reed's ironclads were

---

22   Arthur Otway (ed.), *Autobiography and Journals of Admiral Lord Clarence Paget* (London: Chapman & Hall, 1896), 360-2, 'Appendix II: Remarks on the Board of Admiralty'. Paget also noted that Robinson's predecessor, Rear-Admiral Sir Baldwin Walker, was perhaps no less domineering and 'like most naval men, had a high and perhaps overstrained sense of honour, and a very susceptible disposition [to criticism]'; while David Brown observed that the former Chief Constructor (or Assistant Surveyor), Sir Isaac Watts, 'seems to have been an autocrat—as are most successful designers', with few master shipwrights willing to question his designs; *Before the Ironclad*, 177. See also Brown's analysis, 'British Warship Design Methods 1860-1905', *Warship International*, Vol. 32, No. 1 (1995), 59-82.

true (which they weren't), Robinson argued, it did not automatically follow that the turret versus broadside issue had been really resolved one way or the other.[23]

A pitched battle now ensued. After waiting for confirmation from Coles directly that the letter in *The Standard* was indeed his, and with Coles affirming so on 16 January, Robinson pressed the Board for his dismissal which they did three days later. Coles had replied that not only was his letter in 'reply' to a leader in *The Times* of 1 January which had incorrectly compared the merits of turret versus broadside ironclads, and therefore disparaged himself as the inventor of the turret system, but 'to demonstrate to the public that the strongest reasons exist to justify the expenditure to be incurred in building the sea going Turret-ship which from the public journals I understand has been ordered by their Lordships.' Ignoring his personal attack on Reed, Coles attempted instead to press home his position, as 'a national question of the greatest importance', by referring to documents he had lately received from St. Petersburg. These charted Imperial Russia's investment in a whole flotilla of shallow-draft, mastless turret-ships (monitors of the *Passaic*-class). Their combined weight of broadside 'from 300-pounders' he then compared, again, to the 'latest designs' of British ironclads, 'which are publicly acknowledged as adapted in rivalry to my principles, including the *Bellerophon*'. Now the Gulf of Finland was implicitly closed off to any foreseeable British campaign against Russia, again. As far into the Baltic that her monitors might venture, Russia's power would expand, and Britain's power would diminish. As one early 1866 pamphlet argued, the whole world was now crawling with monitors. British-built turret-ships were something enjoyed mostly by foreign powers, observed the *Nautical Magazine*.[24]

But to this Robinson repeated his indignation; such statements by Coles, 'based on most erroneous statements, are untouched by anything I have read.' Reed had also confirmed, in writing, that he had neither written the article in *The Times*, nor those in the *Engineer* or *Engineering* which Coles had enclosed as proof of Reed's own anti-turret partisanship—although 'I beg leave to state that at the solicitation of the Editors of those Journals I gave them my version of the questions which they have discussed, and I do not think they have hesitated to adopt in the main my views, how closely they may have adopted them I am not prepared to state from memory.'[25]

---

23   10 January 1866, Robinson to Board, TNA ADM 1/5980; 13 January 1866, Paget to Coles, in *Navy (Turret-ships), Parliamentary Papers*, 179.

24   Anonymous (but presumably British shipbuilder John Bourne, a close correspondent with John Ericsson), *Captain Coles and the Admiralty, By the Son of An Old Naval Officer* (London: Longmans, Green, and Co., 1866), 22; 'Turret-ships at Home Abroad', *The Nautical Magazine and Naval Chronicle for 1866—A Journal of Papers on Subjects Connected with Maritime Affairs* (London: Simpkin, Marshall and Co., 1866), 123-32. See for example, Stellan Bojerud, 'Monitors and Armored Gunboats of the Royal Swedish Navy: Part 1', *Warship International*, Vol. 23, No. 2 (1986), 167-80; also Daniel G. Harris, 'The Swedish Monitors', *Warship*, Vol. 18 (1994), 22-34.

25   19 January 1866, Robinson to Board, TNA ADM 1/5980. The enclosed letter, with clippings, from Coles is dated 16 January, and Reed and Robinson's replies 18 January.

Five days later, facing professional suicide, Coles attempted to put the Board on the defensive. He had never received 'any intimation of their disapproval of my writing in the public journals on the subject of Cupola Ships', indeed his written agreement with the Admiralty from 7 August 1862 gave him 'free liberty by means of lectures, models, publications and otherwise to prove the great utility, value and economy of his invention of shield ships'. He could only assume that meant responding to perceived attacks on his system in the press.[26] The Board replied that it did not deprive Coles of the right to defend his views, but to attack those of 'the Officers of the Controller's Department', which only gave 'injury to the public service'. Coles retorted on 30 January that his letter of the 16th had specified 'should their Lordships think that I have overrated the arguments in favour of Turrets, or wish for any correction, I should have great pleasure in considering their view.' Robinson, in his exasperation, had only referred them to the book of armaments in regards to the weight of broadsides in question as well as the published steam trials of Reed's ironclads. The comparison with Russian monitors was pointless, having 'no bearing on the controversy between Broadside and Turret armaments for seagoing Ships', while acknowledging 'that floating batteries are perfectly unrestricted in their power of carrying the heaviest Artillery'. But Coles also repeated his 'regret' for causing offence, and that his published statements 'should have been misunderstood as meaning to attack, or to reflect on the Officers of the Controller's Department.' The Board was unmoved: his contracted expenses were not tied to his half-pay but to his patent allowing them to use his turrets for an extra fee each time one was built, and as for his arguments in the press they had 'nothing to add to their answers to his previous letters.' Robinson was only prepared to reconsider engaging Coles if he made 'a suitable acknowledgement of the errors of conduct and of judgement into which he had fallen', perhaps even a public recant.[27] In the meantime, the Controller was pleased to accept the Board's renewal of his office and authority for another five years.[28]

The Royal Navy's history with Captain Cowper Coles might have ended there, leaving Rear-Admiral Robinson and Edward Reed free to pursue their shipbuilding policy without any interference from at least within the Admiralty, as such. The *Monarch* would presumably have been built, but then effectively side-lined as a potential model for any more seagoing turret-ships, while improved central-battery ironclads great and small continued to dominate the fleet. But the larger 'turret vs. broadside'-debate was far from over, as Coles, angrier and more determined than ever,

---

26 24 January 1866, Coles to Romaine, TNA ADM 1/5970, with enclosed Board response dated 26 January.
27 5 February 1866, Robinson to Board, with enclosed letter from Coles to Romaine dated 30 January and the Board's approved minute dated 7 February; and 18 and 19 January 1866, Robinson to Board, TNA ADM 1/5980. Coles had been receiving three pounds-three shillings per day-allowance as a turret consultant, a considerable sum in the 1860s.
28 2 February 1866, Somerset minute, TNA ADM 3/272, and 7 February 1866, Romaine to Board, TNA ADM 1/5980.

rallied his supporters and took legal advice on his connection with the Admiralty. On 10 February he wrote to Romaine that the original written agreement with the Admiralty 'did not stipulate that the allowance, which has now been withdrawn, was to be considered as part remuneration for my Patent'. It was also expected that his employment would continue for '14 years', provided that his inventions continued to perform well, which they had. The attorney who negotiated his contract confirmed in writing that Coles had declined 'to part with the Patent unless the £3 per day were definitely given.' The Board stressed the agreement 'plainly shews that the pay and allowances was to be the remuneration for his services when employed—adding that it would have 'no difficulty in replacing Captain Coles in the employment in which he was engaged'; he must declare that he would never attack the Controller's Department like that again. In this Grey was convinced that Coles had little choice to bend to their will for the sake of his precious invention. 'I think it will not be difficult on this letter to write him a reply which will put him in his place for the future, if the Board are inclined to give him a further trial.' Indeed, Coles in his letter forwarding his counsel's testimony, not only again 'deeply' regretted that his publications and correspondence had been regarded as personal attacks on officers in the Controller's Department (namely Reed), but avowed that had he known his communication with the press would be objected to by the Admiralty, he would 'have abstained from exercising in that way, the right of free publication which I believed I possessed.'[29] Despite Pakington in the House of Commons declaring that Coles had still not been given a 'fair trial' of his system, and that it was 'notorious that the present Chief Constructor of the Navy, Mr. Reed, has himself adopted a rival system', Coles wrote to Romaine two days later (28 February) he had 'no hesitation' in assuring the Board he would refrain from 'attacking the Officers of the Department'. But there was a caveat: if his services were to be renewed, he was to retain the right to disapprove 'of any designs for sea going Turret-ships which [he] might consider not calculated to giving that System a fair trial'. Otherwise he would be obliged to decline 'so embarrassing a position' if it really meant nothing more than buying off his silent submission. Indeed, a leader in *The Times* that same day hoped that Earl Russell's teetering Liberal government would not see him replaced by the relatively obscure Duke of Somerset, who had made a rather poor showing as First Lord of the Admiralty. His dubious policies, as reflected in the recent debates in Parliament over the Navy Estimates were more or less centred around the issue 'of turret-ships, or, in other words, that of the treatment received by Captain Coles at the hands of the Admiralty.' Coles had not had a 'fair trial…and it would be very hard to convince the world that the fault was not on the side of the authorities. One single experiment conducted according to Captain Coles's own discretion, and tried with expedition and goodwill, would have silenced this controversy for ever.' The Board thus agreed

---

29   10 and 21 February, Coles to Romaine, with enclosed letter dated 20 February 1866 from F. G. Davidson to Coles, and Grey's minute dated 22 February, TNA ADM 1/5970.

on 1 March to renew its working association with Coles—it could hardly ignore his apologies, for one, with so much public scrutiny as well—promising in turn that the Controller's Department would not only furnish him with the plans for the *Monarch* to review but offer 'every encouragement and assistance'.[30]

* * *

That same day, back in the Commons Committee on the Naval Estimates, Sir Morton Peto deplored 'the harassing and vexation which poor Captain Coles had had to endure.' It was meanwhile startling to learn that the Admiralty's plans for a seagoing turret-ship armed with four heavy guns in two turrets—the *Monarch*—would be no less than 5,000 tons. Peto had just returned from a visit to the United States, where he was allowed to inspect the (3,300-ton) *Monadnock* before she departed for the Pacific. 'He would admit that she was not a good seagoing vessel; but for harbour defence she was scarcely to be equalled, because she exposed so small a mark to an enemy's guns, while able to inflict great mischief with her own.' A sharp back-and-forth then broke out between Paget and his immediate predecessor as Secretary to the Admiralty, long-standing Conservative MP Henry Lowry-Corry, who argued it was incomprehensible that the Admiralty had chosen to entrust the design of the *Monarch* to 'Mr. Reed, the avowed enemy of the turret system.' When Paget objected to this designation, Corry stated he wished no offence, 'but, at all events, Mr. Reed was the advocate of a totally opposite system of his own. That was very much like requiring an allopathic doctor to treat a patient upon homoeopathic principles, an experiment which would not be likely to produce a very satisfactory result.' Reed at the same time had been hired as Chief Constructor with no shipbuilding experience himself, and his ironclads were every bit as experimental (and prone to trial-and-error alterations) as the turret-ships which he condemned. Paget soon found himself ground down by his more experienced colleague in Opposition, who finally brandished a letter in his hand 'from his hon. Friend the Member for Birkenhead (Mr. Laird)…in which he also expressed the opinion that a seagoing turret-ship could be built of 3,500 tons, to carry four 600-pounders with great speed, and with ample accommodation for her crew; and his hon. Friend maintained, moreover, that a ship carrying such an armament would be more powerful than any vessel afloat.'[31] Not long after, there was another torrent of

---

30 26 February 1866, 'Supply—Navy Estimates', *Hansard*, Vol. 181, 1160; 28 February 1866, Coles to Romaine, TNA ADM 1/5970; 28 February 1866, *The Times*; also *Parliamentary Paper*, July 1866, *Correspondence relative to Navy (Turret-ships) between the Admiralty and Captain Cowper Coles, and Papers relating thereto*, 5-7.

31 Sir Samuel Morton Peto, 1st Baronet, 'Liberal' Member for Finsbury (1859-65); 1 March 1866, 'Supply—Navy Estimates', *Hansard*, Vol. 181, 1322-68. Corry served in Peel's Admiralty between 1841-6, and as First Secretary again between 1858-9 during the Earl of Derby's Conservative ministry. When completed, HMS *Monarch* was in excess of 8,300-tons—far more than *Bellerophon*'s 7,600-tons, or HMS *Captain*'s (over-weighted) 7,800-tons. Captain Bythesea noted before the Parliamentary Committee of 1871 that

debate in the House of Lords—this time not in connection with the navy budget for the next year, but exclusively on the relationship between the Admiralty and Coles. Here, Somerset could only agree to have all of their correspondence published, as well as the full report of the 1865 committee on the Coles turret-ship proposal. 'There is no denying that the Admiralty, unfortunately perhaps, but not unnaturally, has been adhering throughout to old principles in the face of new systems', *The Times* observed.[32]

This was not what Reed himself had promised, four years earlier. Following the sensational news from America of the duel between the strange, mastless 'ram', the '*Merrimac*' (CSS *Virginia*), and the even stranger U.S.S. *Monitor*, the talented young Secretary to the Institute of Naval Architects wrote of 'The Great Naval Revolution' for *Cornhill Magazine*. The trap, he said, was for the British to be lured 'from our glorious course in the last Continental war, and to concentrate our thoughts and energies upon coast defences.' The proposal to convert the three-decker *Royal Sovereign* down to a multi-'cupola' vessel on the plan of Captain Coles was clearly a mistake, since none of its guns would be able 'to fire even a single shot in our favour anywhere save on our own coasts.' At least as a wooden sailing battleship she served 'all purposes of naval dominion or power abroad'; now that would be lost. Four years later, in the spring of 1866, with the threat of war with both France and America largely subsided, it was unclear to the British public how this had all happened—peace instead of war—and whether it could still be assumed it was due to British supremacy at sea after all. 'It is very easy to build a turret-ship so that she may be perfectly able to go round the world, and yet not be fitted to cope with another vessel,' admitted the First Lord of the Admiralty to Parliament on 12 March 1866. 'It may be said that we have made [the *Monarch*] unnecessarily heavy. But what is the use of comparing her with vessels like the *Scorpion*, when if you send her to distant parts of the world she may have to meet ships armed like the *Monadnock*?' But neither was it certain how a sail-and-turret ironclad with fourteen-feet of freeboard would fare against a local turret vessel with less than four-feet, either. At any rate, what was certain was that nothing that Reed

---

the *Monadnock*'s sister ship, the USS *Miantonomoh*, floated 1,225 tons, 'old measurement' ('Builders') before the Moorsom System but still in use in the U.S. until 1864; testimony dated 13 February 1871, *Report of the Committee Appointed by the Lords Commissioners of the Admiralty to Examine The Designs Upon Which Ships of War Have Recently Been Constructed with Analysis of Evidence* (Parliamentary Paper 1872), *Evidence, Appendix, and Index*, 35.

32 12 March 1866, 'Question—Motion for an Address', *Hansard*, Vol. 182, 1-14; 10 March 1866, *The Times*. Aside from the added work involved, Robinson objected to having to supply copies of all their correspondence with Coles (and the reports on the performance of the Channel Squadron at sea), because it would not provide him an opportunity to defend himself; 'the object is clearly (after what has passed there can be no doubt of it) to find fault', 28 March 1866, Robinson to Board, TNA ADM 1/5974. These were submitted, however, on 11 April 1866; Robinson to Board, TNA ADM 1/5980.

had built or was building for the Royal Navy—the *Monarch* included—was likely to command the St. Lawrence.[33]

It was at this point that a third party interjected in the Coles-Reed, 'turret vs. broadside'-debate. In private collaboration with John Ericsson, British shipbuilder and engineer John Bourne's pamphlet on *Captain Coles and the Admiralty, By the Son of An Old Naval Officer* (1866) also condemned the Coles ideal of combining a fully-masted, (necessarily) high-freeboard ironclad with a turret armament. What he implored the Admiralty to do was 'look the facts of the American experience fairly in the face and to resolve that neither in power of guns nor in efficiency of armour we shall remain inferior to any nation in the world.' The Royal Navy needed an oceangoing *Dictator*, not a *Monarch*.[34] But when Bourne attempted these same arguments at the Institute of Naval Architects, on 23 March 1866, Reed had only to observe that an Ericsson monitor being semi-submerged (or 'sub-aquatic'), he 'should very much like to hear some opinion expressed by naval gentlemen, because it seems to me that the deck is very low for the upper deck of a ship, and that one might not quite like being locked up for many days together, in making a voyage, down below there, with artificial light and artificial ventilation, and without the slightest sight of the heavens or the sea.' This was truly the 'revolution' at stake: a submarine lifestyle, making daily human survival in a hostile environment (below water) entirely dependent upon the efficiency of machines for the first time in history. As Reed cleverly implied, this was simply asking for too much. It had been difficult enough over the past four decades, in the gradual transition from sail to steam, getting old salts to place any faith in engineers and their 'infernal machines'—but to ask them to suddenly place their lives in the hands of an eccentric 'genius' inventor? To live *in* a Machine—to service it day and night as a matter of life and death—rather than skilfully working a Ship through winds and riding upon the waves? Bourne's reply that life on board a monitor at sea was more about security than comfort ('a sentimental affliction with which I do not pretend to deal') missed a larger point: unlike the American one, the British Navy was

---

33 'The Great Naval Revolution', *Cornhill Magazine*, Vol. 5 (January to June 1862), 550-59; 'On a Further Reconstruction of the Navy', *Cornhill Magazine*, Vol. 4 (July to December 1861), 715-24; 12 March 1866, 'Question—Motion for an Address', *Hansard*, Vol. 182, 1-14.

34 Bourne, *Captain Coles and the Admiralty*, 19-22. As Bourne wrote to Ericsson in January 1866, 'I have the same sympathy with Mr. Reed that I have with you, for he is a man of practical ability who has been placed in an onerous position, heretofore occupied by amateurs or pretenders, and he has the full diapason cry of that class against him. He is fighting the battle of practical men against party intrigues, family interest, and other such things imported so commonly into public affairs', Church, *Life of John Ericsson*, 2: 81. Ericsson forwarded copies of the pamphlet to Fox, thinking the author 'has somewhat overshot his mark by wounding John Bull's pride and by making a martyr of Coles, as was evinced by the cheers in the House of Commons during the debate on the Navy Estimates, when Lord C. Paget stated that he had forgiven Coles' offence', 22 March 1866, Ericsson to Fox, Ericsson Papers, Philadelphia, Box 6.

a large, standing naval force deployed all over the world, existing most of the time in a state of peace, with its sailors spending much of their lives on board their ships; hence another reason why 'cruisers' were so important versus floating batteries.[35]

To help him pitch his ideas to Britain's maritime and engineering trade community (and the Admiralty), Ericsson had provided Bourne with a detailed cross-section of his own pride and joy, the single-turret 'ocean vessel' *Dictator*.[36] This would have been the first engraved schematic of a Federal monitor that Bourne, Reed or indeed anyone in Britain would have ever seen, and Reed above all could appreciate the attention to form and detail, as one professional engineer and warship designer to another. Ericsson had originally conceived the mastless ironclad as a 'swift, impregnable turret carrier' within days of the Battle of Hampton Roads.[37] She had a sharp ram bow capping off a 312-foot long hull whose lines were so fine one American shipbuilder described them as 'beautiful as a woman's leg'. Drawing only twenty-feet compared to *Warrior*'s twenty-six, and with than less than half the British ironclad's displacement, Ericsson confidently expected her to make 16-knots. This was in spite of her 6-inch armoured raft overhang ('upper hull' or 'shelf'), capped off with a 1½-inch thick armoured deck and 24-foot diameter revolving gun turret, with fully 15-inches of iron armour plating, and protecting two 15-inch Navy Dahlgrens.[38] To make life a bit more bearable for her officer and crew, an eight-foot tall, iron-grated hurricane deck or 'promenade' was fitted abaft the funnel per Fox's request, so 'Jack could take his cigar'.[39] She would be, Ericsson had promised Fox in the spring of 1862, 'the new Ocean Monarch'.[40]

---

35   John Bourne, 'On the American System of Turret-ships', *Transactions of the Institution of Naval Architects*, Vol. VII (London: 1866), 131-43. For the ironclad monitor as a 'machine', requiring its crew to live below the waterline for the first time, see for example, David A. Mindell, *War, Technology, and Experience aboard the U.S.S.* Monitor (Baltimore: John Hopkins University Press, 2000). 'The departure shown in the foreign vessels from the simple monitor idea of single-turreted battery, designed for fighting purposes alone, was a necessary concession to nautical ideas', observed Ericsson's biographer. 'A complete adherence to the type, even in our own navy, was only possible so long as Ericsson had control', Church, *Life of Ericsson*, 2: 92.
36   See 6 February and 1 June 1866 Ericsson to Bourne, Ericsson Papers, Philadelphia, Box 4.
37   See for example 13 March 1862, Ericsson to Fox, Fox Papers, New York, Box 3; also Fuller, *Clad in Iron*, 92-6, 101-1, 118-24.
38   Canney, *The Old Steam Navy*, 89-91. Ericsson specified to Fox on 24 March 1866 that USS *Dictator* weighed a total of 3,478 tons: 3,099-tons 'without turret, guns, pilot-house, gearing coal, water in boilers, stores and ammunition'; Ericsson Papers, Philadelphia, Box 6.
39   18 March and 15 April 1862, Fox to Ericsson, Fox Papers, New York, Box 5; and 16 April 1862, Ericsson to Fox, Fox Papers, New York, Box 3.
40   1 April 1862, Ericsson to Fox, Ericsson Papers, Philadelphia, Box 6. For the USS *Dictator* see for example, Christopher C. Wright, 'The New London Naval Station: The First Years 1862-1885', *Warship International*, Vol. 30, No. 2 (1993), 112-33.

Yet given Anglo-American tensions which had only recently begin to subside, why send the plans to the British of all people? What did Ericsson (and later Gustavus Fox, the Assistant Secretary of the U.S. Navy) have in mind? For one thing, even if the *Dictator* had proven to be as fast and trouble-free as his calculations indicated she would be, where could she go? There was no discussion of sending American monitors to the Mediterranean or the Far East, and for all the casual boasts (or threats) during the Civil War years of sending a monitor to 'dictate terms' on the Thames itself, these were not the same as a 'cruise' or long-term deployment. Perhaps as 'floating fighting machines', as Ericsson liked to refer them, their usefulness was at best in performing precise, targeted 'missions'. So when the French-built, single-turret ram *Stonewall* was finally given over to the Confederate Navy, and loosed upon the Atlantic, Welles responded by despatching the *Monadnock* and the single-turreted *Canonicus* to intercept her in Havana, which they did.[41] But the U.S. had no permanent colonies, trading posts or coal depôts in the Caribbean like the British Empire did. There was no *reason* for the American monitors to stay; and it would have been quickly difficult for them to do so. Their mission accomplished, the machines went straight back to Norfolk and New York.[42] 'Monitors, like ours, will yet defend the English coast', Ericsson wrote to Fox in early March 1866. 'Please stick a pin here.' Fox imagined selling the ideas of monitors to Britain, offering the keys to a new type of naval power that became stronger the closer to home it was. As he recounted in May 1870, the *Monitor* 'enabled a weak or economical nation to arm itself with superior powers of offence and defence', and Ericsson's latest experiment, a locomotive torpedo, 'emasculates all attacking power from the mechanical force of such a country as England.'[43] Yet in May 1866, the irascible Swedish-American inventor-engineer

---

41 See 16 May 1865 (telegram), Welles to Rear-Admiral Sylvanus W. Godon, Gideon Welles Papers, Library of Congress, Manuscript Division; also *ORN*, Series 1, Vol. 3, 518; and 22 and 31 May 1865, Godon to Welles, 525-6, 535-6. 'I think it proper under all circumstances to remain here a certain time', write Godon. 'The effect of our presence among our friends on the island is to confirm them in their good will and to impress upon those differently affected the vitality and vigor of our nation, with its monitors floating about from point to point. The 15-inch gun seems to have its weight in that direction.' Having now seen the dreaded *Stonewall*, he thought the *Canonicus* 'would have crushed her, and the *Monadnock* could have taken her beyond a doubt.'
42 In May 1867 Welles was opposed to Seward's plan of purchasing Denmark's islands in the West Indies for $7,500,000. In peace-time he saw no need of a station. 'We are now as well accommodated as if we owned St. Thomas', he wrote in his diary. 'In case of a war with either of the great powers,—British, French, or Spanish,—we could seize the islands', entries dated 21 and 23 May 1867, in Beale, *Diary of Gideon Welles*, 3: 95-8.
43 2 May 1870, Fox to Ericsson, Ericsson Papers, Philadelphia, Box 1. See also Edwyn Gray, *Nineteenth-Century Torpedoes and Their Inventors* (Annapolis: Naval Institute Press, 2004), who notes Ericsson's experiments with both pneumatically-propelled and electric-powered torpedoes; 89-94. Welles noted in his diary on 6 May 1867 a delegation of Japanese hosted by Seward: 'They wanted monitors but had learned it was difficult handling and navigating them. I told them we could well spare some monitors, but it would be scarcely

also stated he had offered his plans for the *Dictator*—and his services—'free of charge, merely from a motive of being useful to England, without the friendly aid of which, my native country [Sweden] will sooner or later become a Russian province.' As for the Russians themselves building ten of his monitors, he thought 'the more the merrier', probably knowing that Russia's overriding strategic concern was defending the Gulf of Finland from British or French ironclads. Thus, Ericsson also wrote to Bourne that while the Assistant Secretary of the Navy (facing retirement) hoped to build a 'Monitor Fleet' for Prussia, it was doubtful that he 'ever entertained the absurd idea of building anything in the way of ships for the great Mechanical Island Nation' since British industry and resources, far more than America's at present, could 'build these vessels as they ought to be built.'[44] That the Royal Navy never actually built monitors to anywhere near the same degree—or with the same sense of urgency—as the Union Navy had during the American Civil War was something which Ericsson had already predicted. 'England—ingenious, mechanical England—like a certain animal deeming himself safe providing his head is protected,' he wrote to Bourne, 'spends millions after millions, adding inch after inch to the thickness of armor-plates, for the purpose of producing towering, impregnable iron castles, placed upon, not "sand" as the fable relates, but upon a thin bladder that may be pricked in a thousand ways':

> Their Lordships have unintentionally done the right thing, in my opinion; for already the introduction of iron-clads has, by throwing out of the count England's mighty fleet of ships of the line, rendered her voice only half as potent as it used to be. If now her sons set to work elaborating the subaquatic system of warfare, build and carry into practice, so that her enemies may learn—that they may be fully convinced that there is no mistake about her iron-clads too being worthless—then, what little influence Albion yet possesses will be diminished in proportion to the success of the proposed device.
>
> ... Once more, do not be in a hurry to do anything tending to disturb the present balance by showing that there is no such thing as *maritime* power. The truth will leak out some day, but I trust not until its promulgation will be harmless to that country to which mankind is mainly indebted for the enjoyment of its liberty.[45]

---

possible to get them to Japan. Any vessels which we could spare I would be glad to have them possess', Beale, *Diary of Gideon Welles*, 3: 91.

44 2 March 1866, Ericsson to Fox, Fox Papers, New York, Box 11; 11 and 1 May 1866, Ericsson to Bourne, in Church, *Life of Ericsson*, 2: 83-4 and 87; 27 July 1866, Ericsson to Bourne, Ericsson Papers, Library of Congress.

45 1 May 1866, Ericsson to Bourne, in Church, *Life of Ericsson*, 2: 88-9. 'It is obvious that it was Ericsson's purpose to drive fighting men from the ocean; not to make them comfortable there', added Church, 'and there was an inevitable antagonism between his point of view and that of the naval officer.'

That high-tech might serve as a military equalizer between nations, great and small, and thereby end the phenomenon of the 'naval bully', was very much a mid-nineteenth century dream. Large armaments being too costly to maintain, and modern wars themselves too costly to wage, peace would inevitably emerge as the only sane alternative. Science would, in its own way, eventually force political leaders to outlaw war.[46] Tensions in early 1866 had already been mounting between Prussia and Austria over their partitioning of Schleswig and Holstein from Denmark, with mobilisations begun on each other's borders that March.

---

46 'The art of war as I have always contended is positively in its infancy—when perfected man will be <u>forced</u> to live in peace with man', Ericsson wrote to Bourne on 21 December 1866. 'This glorious result which has been the cherished dream of my life will unquestionably be attained before the close of the present century', Ericsson Papers, Library of Congress.

8

'If the American shipbuilders are right ours must be wrong'

In terms of warship design the 'science' was still very new. In April 1866 Robinson, now promoted to vice-admiral, wanted copies of John Scott Russell's massive three-volume treatise, *The Modern System of Naval Architecture for Commerce and War* (August 1865), distributed to the dockyards, if only to emphasise that theory was converging with practical experience when it came to the issue of adding progressively more armour to ironclads without necessarily affecting their seaworthiness.[1] But the day before, 17 April, Coles submitted his analysis of Reed's plans for the *Monarch*. 'The great point which remains to be further developed in my invention,' he began, 'is its enabling the heaviest ordnance that would destroy any iron-clad in existence, to obtain an all round fire, and being efficiently carried on a minimum beam and tonnage, with a maximum speed, at the same time showing the minimum area above the waterline to be plated, that can be given to ensure safety to the Vessel at Sea, and render her habitable for the crew in all climates.' Implicit here was that no broadside ironclad could fulfil these conflicting requirements; only a turret vessel could. Indeed, 'the Americans in this feature of showing the least possible area of Vessel as a mark to be fired at, have gone to the extreme, the Monitor presenting not more than two feet side above the water'. Yet there had been many reports that with proper care taken, the monitors could safely weather gales, and recently the *Monadnock* had gone to the Pacific. Because of their shallow draft and low-freeboard, the turret system of Ericsson exposed a much higher tower above the deck than Coles did in his system, which also allowed for higher freeboard. He was certain that he could offer a design which offered all-round fire from the turrets, as currently denied in plans of the *Monarch*. Because

---

[1] 18 April 1866, Robinson to Board, TNA ADM 1/5980. See also George S. Emmerson, *John Scott Russell: A Great Victorian Engineer* (London: John Murray, 1977), especially 168-74, and 180-2. On the 'present state of seakeeping knowledge as it is applied to surface warships', see for example, David K. Brown, 'Seaworthy by Design', *Warship International*, Vol. 24, No. 4 (1988), 341-52, who also concluded the simplest answer to rolling at sea was 'to make ships bigger. A big ship will always behave better in a random sea than a small one.'

of the addition of a forecastle and permanent stern bulwarks, guns had to be mounted here to compensate for the blocked turret guns, and therefore armour was needed to protect the fore and aft guns as well. This added weight on her ends, therefore, must surely detract from her sea-keeping qualities. Of course, he noted, only broadside ironclads had to wrestle with these considerations given their inherently limited arcs of fire. The armoured pilot house was also badly positioned; before the fore turret, further blocking its fire, and not abaft as in the *Royal Sovereign* and other turret-ships already constructed. Coles would reduce not just the armour above the waterline at the ends but lower the height of the turrets above water from seventeen- down to fifteen-feet, thus also saving on displacement (his estimate was 458-tons). This in turn 'would produce a Vessel considerably smaller, cheaper, and requiring less crew.' She might also be faster. By lowering the turret-ship's freeboard Coles thought she would not be as 'top heavy'. 'A good sea boat does not altogether depend upon height out of water,' he ventured, 'but upon form and the extremities of the ship being kept light in proportion to their displacement.' Finally, he acknowledged that without the assistance of a draughtsman, and the full particulars of the *Monarch*'s design at that point, his assessment might be in error. But for now he could not (publicly?) declare this turret-ship represented 'my views of a sea going Turret-ship, nor can she give my principle a satisfactory and conclusive trial.'[2]

This conspicuously opened the way for yet another unpleasant debate and negative exposure to the Admiralty. Grey's attached minute of 21 April thought Coles's wording 'to have been written rather with the view of its appearance in a [Parliament-ordered, government] Blue Book, as a complaint against the Admiralty than with any idea of assisting by his advice in the construction of a sea going Turret-ship.' Robinson could only comment that the designs his department had produced indeed met those stipulated by the Board on 13 October 1865, 'as essential for a satisfactory seagoing Turret-ship'. Now he effectively washed his hands of the matter by stating these were 'evidently questions which the Board of Admiralty will decide, and on which they do not require any further information from me.' If so, the First Naval Lord thought there seemed to be only one way left to avoid running into another storm of controversy: 'Should he not be allowed to prepare his own design of a sea going ship of not less than two turrets and send it in for consideration of the Board[?]' This was the political genesis of HMS *Captain*. Somerset minuted the Board should express its 'regret to find that Captain Coles considers that the *Monarch* will not fairly represent his views of a sea going turret-ship nor give his principle a satisfactory and conclusive trial.' This was, however, in the 'absence of any reasons on which this opinion is founded', and as it still wasn't clear to the Board from what Coles had written 'what the essential conditions for a sea going turret-ship are', orders were to be given to the Controller to proceed with the *Monarch* as she was. At the same time,

2   24 April 1866, Robinson to Board, TNA ADM 1/5974, with enclosed letter from Coles to Romaine dated 17 April 1864.

Coles was indeed going to be given 'the opportunity of reducing to practice his own views of what a seagoing turret-ship should be,' authorising him to submit a design to be constructed from an enclosed list of private shipbuilding firms (including Thames, Samuda, Millwall, Wigram, Laird, Palmer and Napier). There would be no more independent reviewing committee. If Coles agreed, the Board would reserve for itself the right to enter into a contract—if the conditions they considered 'indispensable' were met in his design: 'namely the efficient protection of the ship from heavy shot, the comfort of the crew, sufficient speed, and the seagoing qualities of a cruiser' (something which Reed's design for the *Monarch* had arguably already done).[3] Three days later, the Board informed Admiral Hope that 'in the course of the summer' HMS *Scorpion* would be sent to relieve the old Crimean War floating battery *Terror* at Bermuda, and Paget resigned his post as Secretary to the Admiralty.[4]

In the meantime, Robinson was obliged to submit another *Return of Correspondence relative to Navy (Turret-ships)*, including Captain Osborn's reports on the trial of *Royal Sovereign*, for public scrutiny by Parliament. Annoyed with this and having failed in his efforts to exclude Coles from Admiralty decision-making, the Controller had reminded the Board of the 1865 Turret-ship Committee's recommendations for a 'practical' test of Coles' turrets. His suggestion was for brutally subjecting the *Royal Sovereign* to live-fire from a 12½-ton gun, as mounted on board Reed's central-battery *Bellerophon*. Coles immediately objected. His turrets on the *Royal Sovereign* had been designed years before to withstand the lighter ordnance of the day. The Board tried to reassure him: 'My Lords do not propose to fire at the *Royal Sovereign* for the purpose of instituting a comparison between naval systems but solely with the view of testing the resisting power of the Turrets as constructed in the *Royal Sovereign* in order that in future turret-ships any defect that may be brought to light may as far as practicable be remedied.' But couldn't the same be said for central-battery armaments? Why not fire upon the *Bellerophon*'s casemate ports in turn?[5] On Friday, 15 June 1866, a

---

3   Ibid., Robinson's enclosed comment is dated 20 April 1866, and the Board's letter to Coles was dated 24 April. Somerset also specified that the terms of contract on any proposal from Coles 'would be fair and reasonable', that the 'complement of such a ship must be fixed at a number sufficient to handle her with ease and to keep her in the order required for an efficient ship of war[,] and that she must have not less than two turrets carrying the heaviest gun.' On 8 May 1866 Coles confirmed his selection of Laird Brothers to help him prepare a design; see Parliamentary Paper, *Return of Correspondence relative to Navy (Turret-ships)*, 11. The Board, however, did not formally award the tender to Lairds until 1 February 1867; see 'Captain Coles Correspondence', TNA ADM 1/6009.

4   27 April 1866, Board to Hope, in TNA ADM 128/23; 27 April 1866, Minute, in TNA ADM 3/272.

5   See for example, 17 May 1866, Coles to Baring, TNA ADM 1/5970; and 25 May 1866, Minute, TNA ADM 3/272. Robinson specified that the gun to be used in the test was not a '300-pounder', as Coles claimed, since this was not a 10½-inch, rifled 12½-ton gun from 1863, but a 1866 9-inch rifled 12½-ton gun throwing a 240lb. shot; the original '300-pounder' having been found 'deficient in endurance, and too light to fire so heavy

large crowd at Southsea watched the surreal exhibition of a towering British central-battery ironclad—recognised as the Admiralty and Reed's pet favourite—blasting away at the Royal Navy's odd, mastless, yet clearly formidable ironclad converted upon Coles' 'turret system', at a range of 150 yards. The press described it as nothing less than a 'great duel', and despite the severe damage inflicted upon the aft turret of the *Royal Sovereign* it did not jam as expected and continued to operate successfully. 'All honour, therefore, to Captain Coles', proclaimed *The Times*, 'for his persistent advocacy of a system of mounting ordnance on board a ship that will, at any rate, add a power to our fleet of ironclads equivalent in nature and force to the siege artillery of an army before the famous Venetian Quadrilateral!'[6]

Since the telegraph wire had signalled the previous day (14 June) the outbreak of war between Prussia and Austria, this reference took on special meaning. In the Commons it was noted that France, having sniffed an imminent aggrandisement of territory at either Prussia or Austria's expense, had encouraged Italy 'to arm and remain armed' in the expectation of some portion of new territory herself. The Emperor had recently also publicly derided the Vienna Settlement of 1815.[7] Once again, the Continent was up in arms, and the 'Concert of Europe' unmasked as a charade.[8] As Foreign Secretary Lord Clarendon wrote to Lord Cowley in Paris, the Queen had been 'horribly put out, as the thought of war haunts her night and day.' But at the same time he had warned Her Majesty that aside from the Austro-Prussian quarrel affecting 'neither English honour nor English interests…in the present state of Ireland, and the menacing aspect of our relations with the United States, the military and pecuniary resources of England must be husbanded with the utmost care.' That was on the last day of March. When the Queen appealed again on 6 May—including whether Britain could not 'threaten or remonstrate' against Prussia—Clarendon stressed it was pointless without the cooperation of France, and that 'any demonstration of our

---

a rifled projectile as 300 lbs with large charges of power continuously'. He thought it obvious that since it was 'the use of this gun in Turrets that Captain Coles claimed the great superiority of a Turret armament over broadside armament' that his turret could resist fire from the same; 1 June 1866, Robinson to Board, TNA ADM 1/5970; see also 27 October 1865, Robinson to Board, TNA ADM 1/5943.

6   16 June 1866, *The Times*.
7   The Austro-Prussian War (June-July 1866), sometimes referred to as the Seven Weeks War; 1 June 1866, 'State of Europe—Question', *Hansard*, vol. 184, 117-76. Emperor Napoleon III had indeed promised Italy the long-held Austrian province of Venetia if she joined Prussia, in the expectation of a more balanced (and therefore longer) German conflict which would eventually leave France in a position to turn the scales either way, possibly for the agreed price of the Rhine provinces or even Belgium; see for example A. J. P. Taylor, *The Struggle for Mastery in Europe 1848-1918* (Oxford: The Clarendon Press, 1954), 158-66.
8   See for example, Paul W. Schroeder, *Austria, Great Britain, and the Crimean War: The Destruction of the European Concert* (Ithaca: Cornell University Press, 1972), especially 392-427.

fleet…would not be sufficient if we acted alone, and we had weakened ourselves so much by a threatening policy without its being supported by deeds.'[9] As British naval power was not supreme enough to leverage peace, the British Lion had best remain silent. 'The thunders of Albion are no longer backed by lightning charges', Bismarck had remarked contemptuously the year before, 'even children do not fear them.'[10]

Within a week of the Germanic powers going to war with one another, Russell's government also collapsed, failing to push even a moderate Reform Bill through Parliament in the face of both 'Adullamite' (reactionary) Liberals who opposed any extension of the franchise to the 'ignorant' working classes and Tories led by Disraeli who saw this as a golden opportunity of checking the rising popularity of Gladstone if nothing else.[11] Defeated in the House on 18 June, 315 votes to 304, Russell told the Queen his intention to resign, despite her protests. Conservative Lord Stanley noted in his diary how the government ministers were mostly surprised by the result, and that Gladstone 'especially seemed, not angry, but perplexed and disconcerted.' This was unknowingly confirmed by Gladstone's own journal entry that same evening: 'With the cheering of the adversary there was shouting, violent flourishing hats, & other manifestations which I think novel & inappropriate.'[12] By Tuesday, 26 June the Liberals were out and Lord Derby reluctantly agreed to form (a minority) Government in close collaboration with Disraeli. 'Oh! For one hour of Palmerston who would

---

9   5 May 1866, Clarendon to Cowley, in Wellesley (ed.), *The Paris Embassy during the Second Empire*, 302; 31 March 1866, Clarendon to Queen Victoria, and 6 May 1866 Memorandum by Queen Victoria, in Buckle, *Letters of Queen Victoria*, 1: 314-15, 325-6. The 30 March 1866 extract from the Queen's Journal noted sending a memorandum to Lord Russell 'showing the absolute necessity of our attempting to do something, in conjunction with France, to arrest the misfortunes a war would entail,' 1: 314. See also Anna A. W. Ramsay, *Idealism and Foreign Policy: A Study of the Relations of Great Britain with Germany and France, 1860-1878* (London: 1925); Ward and Gooch, *The Cambridge History of British Foreign Policy, op, cit.*, Volume III: 1866-1919 (New York: The Macmillan Company, 1923), 3: 3-16; and W. E. Mosse, 'The Crown and Foreign Policy: Queen Victoria and the Austro-Prussian Conflict, March-May, 1866', *Cambridge Historical Journal*, Vol. 10, No. 2 (1951), 205-23.

10 From Raymond James Sontag, *Germany and England: Background of Conflict 1848-1894* (New York: W. W. Norton & Company Inc., 1969), 88.

11 'If the Reform Bill passes,' Disraeli warned Henry George Liddell (Lord Eslington, 1874, 2nd Earl of Ravensworth from 1878, MP for Northumberland South), 'the aristocratic settlement of this country will receive a fatal blow from which it will not easily recover… It is our only chance of defeating a measure which will shatter both Whigs & Tories, & utterly destroy the present Conservative organisation', 15 June 1866, in Michel W. Pharand, Ellen L. Hawman, Mary S. Millar, Sandra Den Otter and M.G. Wiebe (eds.), *Benjamin Disraeli Letters Volume Nine 1865-1867* (Toronto: University of Toronto Press, 2013), 86.

12 (15th Earl Derby) 18 June 1866 entry, in John Vincent (ed.), *Disraeli, Derby and the Conservative Party: Journals and Memoirs of Edward Henry, Lord Stanley 1849-1869* (Hassocks: The Harvester Press, 1978), 253; 18 June entry, in H. C. G. Matthew (ed.), *The Gladstone Diaries, Volume VI: 1861-1868* (Oxford: Clarendon Press, 1978), 444.

settle this matter in a moment without a jot of danger to the Government', exclaimed the Liberal Party Whip, Henry Brand.[13] Indeed, in mid-June 1866 a perfect storm of naval, diplomatic and political volatility had been forming, intensifying a long-term, underlying feeling of uncertainty and vulnerability in much of British society. And it was during this precise moment that the double-turreted monitor USS *Miantonomoh*—sister ship to the celebrated *Monadnock*—dropped anchor at Spithead.

In the context of the wearisome 'turret vs. broadside'-debate—and the fateful design of HMS *Captain*—the timing couldn't have been worse.[14] In his last letter to Russell as First Lord of the Admiralty, dated 17 June, Somerset assured him that despite the alarming article forwarded to him from the *Mechanics' Magazine*, the average speed of Britain's seagoing ironclad fleet was at least a good 12-knots (aside from 'your old friends the Liverpool-rams'). 'As to guns we are better off than the French. The seven ton gun, which will soon be our smallest fighting gun, will pierce the French ironclads; we have tried it, while they have not yet a gun in their service to pierce our ironclads. As to armour plating they have wooden ships only partially protected by armour in many cases, whilst ours are more heavily plated.' The French advantage was in having more broadside ironclads of a class, able to steam together better. But that was the inevitable result of British efforts to construct ships with ever heavier armour protecting ever heavier guns. 'The French are perfectly aware of our position in regard to ships and guns; we have not so many as would be desirable in the event of an emergency but we are now advancing steadily', he concluded. 'I think the Americans have more to cope with us than the French have.'[15] Now the presence in British waters of a bona fide Yankee ironclad, floating 20-ton guns with ease behind 10-inches of turret armour, and with such a low-freeboard, threatened the Admiralty's composure. On 16 April 1866, Russian Tsar Alexander II narrowly escaped an assassination attempt, and a month later the U.S. Congress passed a resolution expressing its 'deep regret' of the attempt, in acknowledgment of Alexander's emancipation of the serfs in 1861—which echoed the Emancipation Proclamation in 1862 by former President Lincoln (and who had been murdered the previous April). Russia had also been the only Great Power openly supportive of the Union cause during the Civil War, and given the ostentatious naval display of Anglo-French solidarity in the summer of

---

13 23 June 1866, Brand (1st Viscount Hampden, 1884) to Wood, Halifax Papers, Borthwick Institute, A4/94. See also Gertrude Himmelfarb's classic analysis of the subsequent Second Reform Act of 1867 as 'perhaps *the* decisive event in modern English history', *Victorian Minds: A Study of Intellectuals in Crisis and Ideologies in Transition* (Chicago: Elephant Paperbacks, 1995 reprint of 1968 version), 333-92, with Michael Bentley referring to it as 'the strangest story in the modern history of party politics', *Politics Without Democracy 1815-1914: Perception and Preoccupation in British Government*, 2nd ed. (Oxford: Blackwell Publishers, 1996), 126.
14 Although the Foreign Office had been alerted by Bruce in Washington; 15 May 1866, Bruce to Clarendon, TNA FO 5/1065.
15 17 June 1866, Somerset to Russell, Russell Papers, TNA PRO 30-22, 16C.

1865, Congress wanted a copy of the Resolution conveyed to Russia by the Assistant Secretary of the Navy, 'in a national vessel'. Commissioned in September 1865 the *Miantonomoh* was a natural choice to Fox, and to save coal and provisions she would be escorted by two paddlewheel steamers. Welles meanwhile officially assigned him to take advantage of his tour to Russia and Europe to 'obtain all information that is attainable relative to the means which are possessed by the principal naval powers for building, repairing, and laying-up naval vessels, and whatever may be useful in regard to their navy yards and navy establishments.'[16] In turn, Fox also invited the British naval attaché, Captain Bythesea, to personally evaluate the monitor's performance at sea by joining him on the trans-Atlantic voyage to the American squadron's first point of call, Great Britain. In his diary, Welles confided that Fox was 'bewildered' going to Europe as a high-ranking representative of the United States, and that he was 'sorry to see so much self-glorification.' But Fox was being pressed to flaunt America's newfound naval prestige by Secretary of State Seward and Senator James W. Grimes (Chairman of the Senate Committee on Naval Affairs), amongst others. Pushing the issue of 'turret-ships' so overtly this way, abroad—especially given all of their controversy at home during the Civil War—the Secretary considered rather selfish and 'wrong'. President Johnson also thought the mission contrived, when demobilisation and reconstruction was the order of the day.[17] Others were more concerned about tipping America's hand and wilfully throwing away the hard-won technological edge the country possessed—perhaps not for very long, given the drastic post-war funding cuts to the army and navy. There were tensions with France over Mexico; with Britain over Fenian raids into Canada (from Maine and New York); and a potential ironclad duel had brought Spain and the U.S. to the brink of war at Valparaiso earlier that year.[18] The *Miantonomoh* was to be commanded by Commander John C. Beaumont, but her previous commander, Commander Daniel Ammen, now warned General

16 John D. Champlin (ed.), *Narrative of the Mission to Russia, in 1866, of the Hon. Gustavus Vasa Fox, Assistant-Secretary of the Navy, from the Journal and Notes of J. F. Loubat* (New York: D. Appleton and Company, 1873), 9-21; Welles' letter to Fox is dated 26 May 1866.
17 Entries dated 12, 17 and 21 May 1866, from Beale (ed.), *Diary of Gideon Welles*, 2: 506, 509, 511-12.
18 Between the Spanish broadside-ironclad *Numancia* and the monitor USS *Monadnock*; see for example, Howard J. Fuller, 'Chilean Standoff: Ironclad-Monitor U.S.S. *Monadnock*, Naval Power-Politics & the Spanish Bombardment of Valparaiso, 1866', *Naval History*, June 2011 (25: 3), 58-65. For the *Numancia*, see for example, Christian de Saint Hubert, 'Early Spanish Steam Warships with Special Emphasis on Screw Frigates and Armoured-frigates and Corvettes (1834-70), Part 1', *Warship International*, Vol. 20, No. 4 (1983), 338-67, and Christian de Saint Hubert, 'Early Spanish Steam Warships with Special Emphasis on Screw Frigates and Armoured-frigates and Corvettes (1834-70), Part 2', *Warship International*, Vol. 21, No. 1 (1984), 21-45 (especially 'Section IV'); for the *Miantonomoh* see for example, Canney, *The Old Steam Navy*, 64-70. See also, R. B. Mowat, *The Diplomatic Relations of Great Britain and the United States* (London: Edward Arnold & Co., 1925), 199-203, 206-20.

Grant who in turn urged Johnson 'about the impropriety of allowing the *Miantonomoh* to go abroad'. On 20 July, following news of the monitor's sensational embrace by the London *Times* and other British journals, Ammen wrote Grant it was 'all painful and we may doubt if ever before the great interests of a Country have been so betrayed.'[19]

* * *

It had taken the mastless ironclad—the first to cross an ocean—ten days ten hours to arrive at Queenstown from St. John's. Fuel was the major anxiety, not 'seaworthiness'. *Miantonomoh*'s flat-bottomed, wooden hull was 249-feet long and drew only fifteen feet, limiting her coal bunkerage to 350-tons. A temporary crib on deck and bags of coal stored in the turrets brought this up to 400-tons. But even at an economy speed of seven knots the twin-screwed monitor still consumed nearly 40-tons of anthracite coal per day, necessitating a tow by the USS *Augusta* for 1,100-miles of the journey. Over the North Atlantic the *Miantonomoh*, with her two-inch armoured top deck only 31-inches from the waterline, rolled an average of five-degrees while her high-freeboard escorts rolled 18 and 24. As Fox later reported, 'Head to the sea, she takes over about four feet of solid water, which is broken as it sweeps along the deck, and after reaching the turret it is too much spent to prevent firing the fifteen-inch guns directly ahead...In the trough of the sea her ports will be liable to be flooded, if required to use her guns to windward.' Bythesea's own report included a copy of the vessel's log and another copy of the *Monadnock*'s voyage to the Pacific. In February 1871, in the wake of the sinking of HMS *Captain*, he testified before the special Admiralty committee on ships designs that there were three pairs of engines supplying the monitor's artificial ventilation, which was 'exceedingly good', and that even though only one of these was required it had to be kept running even when the ship was at anchor, otherwise the air below deck became 'stuffy and nasty' quickly. But he contradicted Fox's assertion about fighting her guns (only 6½-feet from their axis to the water) in a headway, noting that for the two days the *Miantonomoh* experienced a half gale on her port-quarter with a north-westerly wind, 'she could not have opened her ports with safety; the sea was rushing on board and half way up the turret.' On the other hand, there was nothing to prevent the guns from being loaded while the turret was facing away and, rotating back on the weather side, 'snatching the opportunity' to fire. Below deck life was 'perfectly comfortable' (the captain's cabin was even fitted with its own pump-flushed toilet), and as long as the two-inch iron hatchways flush with the deck were kept secure, the monitor preserved her limited buoyancy exceedingly well—even though she was washed over by waves almost continuously, 'the sea came on board forward, and went off again immediately. It was not held on the deck in

---

19 29 May 1866, Grant to Ammen, and 20 July 1866, Ammen to Grant, in John Y. Simon (ed.), *The Papers of Ulysses S. Grant, Volume 16: 1866* (Carbondale: Southern Illinois University Press, 1988), 210-211. During the Civil War Ammen had also commanded the *Passaic*-class monitor USS *Patapsco*.

any way.' This did not mean that mastless, low-freeboard turret vessels might replace high-freeboard ironclads; as the only officer in the entire Royal Navy who ever sailed in a Union monitor, he could attest that 'as vessels for coast defence they might be made more efficient than broadside ships. But the opinion I formed of them was that they never would be independent ships, or efficient cruisers.'[20]

By the time the USS *Miantonomoh* arrived in Ireland she had only forty-tons of her stores left and had lightened by ten-inches. Here she presented a striking contrast to the two lofty broadside ironclads stationed there, HMS *Black Prince* and HMS *Achilles*. When Fox presented himself to the British naval commander-in-chief (Rear-Admiral Charles Frederick), he was found on a bluff overlooking the harbour, observing the American monitor through his telescope. 'Did you cross the Atlantic in that thing?' he asked. When Fox answered proudly that he had, Frederick—the former Third Naval Lord of the Board of Admiralty between 1861 and 1865—snorted 'I doubt if I would!'[21] Five days later, fully provisioned, the *Miantonomoh* steamed for Portsmouth, arriving two days later, on Saturday morning, 23 June 1866. In the meantime, Italy had also declared war against Austria (20 June), and the British people were currently waiting for a functioning government. The 'Thunderer' wasted no time, announcing later that same day that 'a real Monitor has just crossed the Atlantic, and is now lying in British waters.' As the peculiar vessel was 'literally a floating gun carriage, and nothing more', her significance in the context of the 'turret

---

20   See 20 June 1866, Bythesea to Clarendon, in TNA ADM 1/5992. 'The entire Deck where not occupied by the turrets is covered with three thicknesses of Iron plate ¾-in. thick making an aggregate of 2¼-inches,' noted Bythesea, 'these plates are protected from the weather by a wooden planking 3-inches thick secured by screws and caulked.' He also claimed *Miantonomoh*'s turrets were 12-inches thick, the vessel displacing 3,706.3 tons. There were two pairs of horizontal back-acting (Benjamin Isherwood-designed) engines, each pair driving a screw independently. The *Monadnock* used Ericsson patent vibrating lever-engines. Despite the wooden hull, the Union monitor had watertight compartments with watertight doors. Bythesea calculated a fuel consumption of 7,000 lbs (over 3-tons) of anthracite coal per hour, giving a full (1,700-horsepower) speed of 10¼ knots per hour. Even with extra coals loaded, this gave the monitor barely five days' steaming at maximum speed, perhaps a range of 1,400 miles; or just enough for a return voyage from Newport News, Virginia to Bermuda; *Report of the Committee* (1872), *Appendix*, 34-41. David K. Brown misquoted Bythesea's evidence, claiming that 'a two-man boarding party with hammers and wedges could put [the turret of the *Miantonomoh*] out of action' (*Warrior to Dreadnought*, 56), when in fact Bythesea stated: 'A couple of wedges and a couple of sledge hammers, one on each side, was sufficient to lift the turret.' When asked by the Committee, Bythesea further added his opinion that the American arrangement was 'a very good one; the wedges were easily knocked out, and the turret could be lowered or raised in five minutes.' Brown also (inexplicably) stated that 'it was claimed that [the Ericsson turret] could turn through 90° in one minute, a claim which [Bythesea] saw as dubious' (*Warrior to Dreadnought, 56*); but here too Bythesea actually testified 'As far as I can recollect it was something under a minute; at any rate it was done very quickly', *Report of the Committee* (1872), *Appendix*, 37.
21   19 June 1866, *The Times*; Champlin (ed.), *Narrative of the Mission to Russia*, 32-3, 37.

vs. broadside'-debate—loudly punctuated a week earlier when the *Bellerophon* test-fired upon the *Royal Sovereign*, near where the American double-turreted monitor was now anchored—was how she had carried 20-ton guns across the Atlantic. It had also been reported that the Americans had already cast guns twice this weight (20-inch Dahlgren smoothbores, weighing over 40-tons and firing 1,000-pound solid shot), for a single-turreted monitor, USS *Puritan*. Since recent news from Callao suggested 'the repulse of the Spaniards was due to the few heavy guns mounted on the Peruvian batteries', *The Times* concluded that either 'the advantage does not belong exclusively to the largest gun, or that advantage does not belong to us.'[22]

But this was only the beginning of a mounting tidal wave of irate public opinion. For the next two months the British press, closely followed by Parliament, commented upon the 'portentous spectacle' of the *Miantonomoh* almost daily.[23] Along with Vice-Admiral Sir Thomas Pasley, the C-in-C at Portsmouth, hordes of people from the mainland and the Isle of Wight visited the American ironclad that first weekend in June. By contrast, the Royal Navy ironclads *Bellerophon*, *Pallas*, *Hector* and *Royal Sovereign* were in the harbour. *The Times* now applied another curious logic: for since the U.S. Navy clearly relied upon monitors to exert its power, 'it follows almost inevitably that if the American shipbuilders are right ours must be wrong'. Not only was it simply unacceptable that the Americans could be right, and the British wrong, but that the circumstances of either were the same (which clearly they weren't). And yet the semi-submersion principle seemed to bear investigation, especially if newer monitors were now being edged out further and further abroad while still retaining their minimal low-freeboard, and thereby presenting 'no broadside at all'—when the Admiralty was only willing to risk turret-ships with the highest broadside possible. 'As a war machine for close heavy fighting she appears to be perfect', proclaimed another leader the next day (28 June). This seemed especially the case for harbour and coast defence, or attack. Below deck, *The Times* reporter was struck with the sensation of life in a futuristic machine-world powered by seventeen separate steam engines of various sizes and functions, six of which could drive the blowers, and with fresh air supplied from the nine-foot high armoured pipe above deck through shaftings all over the ship. Still, he thought the *Royal Sovereign* 'very much more habitable'.[24]

22   23 June 1866, *The Times*. On 2 May 1866, a Spanish fleet's attempt to bombard Callao (which was heavily defended with modern coast defences) was anything but a success. The Spanish admiral was wounded, *Numancia* suffered damage from an Armstrong 300-pounder, and with both ammunition and coal running low, the Spanish fleet withdrew never to return; see for example the later British reports, 3 December 1866, Powell to Board, TNA ADM 1/5970; also 23 June 1866, Foreign Office to Admiralty, with enclosed newspaper reports from the *Madrid Gazette*, TNA ADM 1/5992.
23   See for example, 17 July 1866, *The Times*, commenting further that the *Miantonomoh* at Sheerness was as a 'wolf in the fold, and the whole flock was at its mercy.'
24   25, 27 and 28 June, *The Times*.

The following afternoon, Friday, with the weather clear and pleasant with a light breeze from the northeast, Fox and Bythesea returned to the monitor to host a visit from the Board of Admiralty, Robinson, and Coles. Captain Key of HMS *Excellent*, who had just written to Pasley that unless an effective way could be fire heavy guns fore and aft 'ships armed on the broadside must gradually give place to turrets', accompanied them on board the Royal Yacht *Osborne* out to see the Federal monitor. After touring the entire ship everyone returned topside to the iron hurricane deck to watch the aft turret keyed up, rotated, and watch a test-fire of its 15-inch guns. At extreme elevation with a 35lb charge 'and a deep hoarse roar' a shell was blasted out landed 3,500-yards out to sea in a slow arc. The second discharge, a 450-pound cast-iron solid shot, was sent ricocheting off the water for greater accuracy—something which elongated rifled projectiles could not do. But while Somerset politely remarked to Fox that no cast-iron guns in Britain could withstand powder charges like that, the *Miantonomoh*'s inexperienced gunners failed to properly secure the compressors and the recoil from both guns cut off their rear guides. Fox remained unflappable before his discerning guests at this critical moment, and as *The Times* later recounted, the Assistant Secretary of the Navy declared 'that if the experiment could be made without exciting ill-feeling on either side, he would allow the whole ironclad fleet of England to open fire on the *Miantonomoh*, and continue it for two days, provided that the *Miantonomoh* might afterwards be allowed to have ten hours' firing at our ships in return.'[25]

The Board returned to London that evening. The next day an unusual summer hailstorm pelted the city, as *The Illustrated London News* devoted two full pages to the spectacle of the *Bellerophon* firing upon the *Royal Sovereign*, the mangled Coles turret, and the 'Arrival of American Ships of War' in the same issue.[26] On Monday, 2 July, *The Times* returned to bid farewell to the *Miantonomoh* which had hauled off to visit Cherbourg, promising to return in a week. Again the fundamental trade-off presented seemed to be one of tactical prowess versus a ship whose crew 'might have to keep the sea for months, or possibly years'. Yet it was also known that the Americans divided such responsibilities in their own fleet, with fast wooden cruisers complementing what were still, in essence, floating batteries. This made the potential

---

25 30 June, and 2 and 16 July 1866, *The Times*; 28 June 1866, Robinson to Board, TNA ADM 1/5980, with enclosed letter from Key to Pasley dated 27 June 1866. See also Champlin (ed.), *Narrative of the Mission to Russia*, 43. I have been kindly assisted here by Carter Beaumont Refo, a distant family namesake of Commander John C. Beaumont, who allowed me to use the unpublished 200-page personal journal which Beaumont kept of his mission to Russia in the USS *Miantonomoh*; page 58 noted the recoil malfunction.
26 30 June 1866, *The Illustrated London News*; the caption of the scene depicting the *Miantonomoh*, *Augusta* and *Ashuelot*, in contrast to the *Achilles* in the background, is mislabeled as 'Arrival of the American Ships of War in Cork Harbour': 'Our View of the *Miantonomah* [sic] and her escorts in Queenstown Harbour is from a drawing by Mr. R. L. Stopford, of Cork.'

of turret-ships all the more tantalising, 'if Captain Coles had been allowed free scope for the development of his system.' What the Royal Navy now needed was monitors of its own, but with greater depth of hull for more supplies, 'and better accommodation for the officers and crew in hot climates': the imperial mandate. A far-ranging British turret-ship should also have as low a freeboard as possible, *The Times* even suggesting 'giving her the means of submerging her hull to any required depth on going into action by the admission of water to the wing passages, &c.' But what was indisputable was how the Americans, for better or worse, had at least pressed on with the ironclad policy they thought best, while 'we do not pretend to regard our experiments or performances with confidence.' A Letter to the Editor from Lairds Brothers on a different page reminded the British public that their firm had launched three seagoing turret-ships just within the past year (*Huascar*, *Bahia* and *Bellona*); so if there was any issue over turret armaments for the navy the problem was with the Admiralty, not the private sector. It seemed no longer a question of whether or not turret armaments would characterise British naval power as well—but when. Later that same evening, a large 'mob' of Reformers descended upon Trafalgar Square, with speeches decrying how 'those who talked of putting down the working classes relied upon bayonets for support'. The next day, the Prussian Army smashed the Austrians at the Battle of Königgrätz.[27]

After nearly a week at Cherbourg, where she was visited by thousands of curious French civilians and naval and military officials, the *Miantonomoh* headed back to Britain, anchoring off Sheerness on Sunday evening, 8 July. The next day she was toured by Vice-Admiral Sir Baldwin Walker, the C-in-C at the Nore, and former Controller of the Navy who had ordered Britain's first generations of sailing broadside-ironclads including the *Warrior*. Not fully satisfied, Walker returned four days later for another inspection. The following day, 14 July, the American Minister at the Court of St. James's, Charles Francis Adams, came on board to host a royal visit from the Prince of Wales and his suite, including the Duke of Edinburgh, at 2pm.[28] It had been a busy week: on 5 July Somerset's departing Board of Admiralty expressed their thanks to the several navy departments, singling out Robinson and Reed's services in meeting 'the difficulties constantly arising in the construction of new descriptions of vessels made necessary in consequence of increased experience in the use of iron in building and plating Ships of War.'[29] A new Board of Admiralty was now headed by Pakington. Grey resigned as First Naval Lord; knighted, a full admiral, and wanting very little to do with the endless 'turret vs. broadside' controversy. The new

---

27   2 and 3 July 1866, *The Times*.
28   John C. Beaumont diary, 62-3; Albert Edward (later King Edward VII, 1901) was 25 when he toured the American monitor-ironclad at Sheerness. He had achieved notoriety in 1860, age 19, when he toured North America and the United States. As a newly minted Duke of Edinburgh, Queen Victoria's second son, Alfred, was 22 at the time and a captain in the Royal Navy.
29   5 July 1866, Admiralty memo, TNA ADM 1/5976.

First Lord of the Admiralty entreated Vice-Admiral Sir Alexander Milne to replace him.[30] Days before, Somerset had also written to his predecessor as First Lord of the Admiralty (1855-58), Sir Charles Wood (now 1st Viscount Halifax). Pakington was bound to ask Parliament for an increase in navy estimates, 'when the fact will come out, that Clarence Paget had asked for sanction to build some small wooden ships for reliefs, when an angry debate ensured, and Palmerston finally promised to build no wooden ships that year. This concession, which *The Times* then approved as a triumph over the Admiralty, has led to some inconvenience, but the blame rests on those, Pakington amongst others, who then would have nothing but iron-clads to cope with the French'.[31]

As for the armaments of the huge sail-and-broadside ironclads insisted upon since 1859, Robinson had already warned the outgoing Board in early June 1866 that 'the present armament of these ships is, with rare exceptions, wholly inefficient against other Iron Clads, an is in many respects so complicated as to present most serious inconveniences.' His suggested shopping list included a simplified array of 7-inch 6½-ton and 9-inch 12½-ton rifled guns: twenty-six of the former for the *Warrior*, eighteen of the same with four 12½-ton guns for the *Minotaur*-class; *Valiant*, *Hector*, *Defence*, and *Resistance* and all of the *Royal Oak*-class ironclads to be re-armed with 6½-ton guns; as a converted central-battery ironclad *Royal Alfred* was projected to have ten 12½-ton and four 6½-ton guns; *Zealous* sixteen 6½-ton guns; *Bellerophon* ten 12½-ton and three 6½-ton guns; *Hercules* would have eight massive 18-ton rifles with two 12½-ton guns; and *Penelope* eight 12½-ton guns. Only four ironclads, he added, 'have guns on board capable of certainly piercing even 4½-inch armour plates. They are the *Lord Clyde*, the *Pallas*, the *Favorite*, and the *Prince Albert*. The remaining twelve have a most composite armament, and yet such as it is, no gun on board is really capable of dealing with an armour-plated ship, unless those in the *Royal Sovereign* and *Wivern* (12½-ton smooth bore guns) may be considered on exception.' The Controller followed this up three days later with another memo outlining a 'New Scheme of Armament' for ironclads of the Royal Navy, noting here, however, that only the turret-ship *Monarch* would be armed with four monstrous '22-ton' guns—the largest in the fleet for the foreseeable future.[32]

---

30   2 July 1866, Pakington to Milne, Milne Papers, Greenwich, MLN 165/10; 10 July 1866, TNA ADM 3/272.

31   11 August 1866, Somerset to Wood, Halifax Papers, Borthwick Institute, A4/126.

32   4 and 5 June 1866, Robinson to Board, TNA ADM 1/5980; 8 June 1866, TNA ADM 1/5975. Long dissatisfied with its relationship with the War Office for the supply of its ordnance, the Admiralty announced on 27 August 1866 the appointment of Sir Astley Cooper Key as 'Acting Director General of Naval Ordnance', with the rank of Rear-Admiral. 'He will be placed in constant and immediate communication with the Director of Ordnance, the Controller of the Navy and the member of the Board of Admiralty on whom devolves the superintendence of Gunnery Questions.' In collaboration with the Director of Ordnance, Key was to help determine new target tests, either on ship or at Shoeburyness, with evidence then being supplied to the Ordnance Select Committee.

* * *

In terms of stemming the tide of public disappointment with 'the state of the navy', however, this all seemed a matter of too little, too late. *Punch* depicted 'Captain Coles and His Turret-Ship'; a sprawling cartoon farce with sailors haplessly playing with a 12½-ton gun (including lobbing a shell onto a pleasure yacht), a turret-ship 'with Captain Cowper Coles upon it (only he wasn't)', and a clutch of clueless British admirals in the centre of it all—'My Lords turning their backs upon Captain Cowper Coles'.[33] Whereas before, outspoken criticism of Admiralty ironclad shipbuilding policy had been tempered by a sense of relative insularity—the French fleet of largely broadside-ironclads being the only direct point of comparison—now the advocates of the Coles 'Turret System' only had to point to the American monitor at Britannia's gate as proof how dilatory British naval and military professionals had been developing the nation's ships and guns. The Royal Navy had clearly rested on its laurels for far too long, while the rest of the world forged ahead with superior warships carrying heavier guns at lighter tonnage. *The Times* lamented that 'we learn slowly in England. We are slow to form new ideas, and what is far worse, we are slower still in abandoning old ones.' The Admiralty should feel ashamed of itself. Despite the proof positive example of low-freeboard ironclads before their eyes, it would still likely require a war before old British sailors would ever really change their ways. 'But how many ships and how many noble crews that no money can replace may be sent to the bottom before Admirals can be brought to reason! It is the public, not the service, that will lead the way'. Naturally, John Laird echoed this sentiment in the House of Commons on Friday, 20 July; 'that one cause of the great outlay for the navy, and of its present inefficiency, arose from the determination of the old Board of Admiralty to resist the introduction of the cupola system.' Lord John Hay, on the other hand, didn't think that England need feel 'humiliation or alarm' in comparison with the U.S. Navy since that force had been built up for operations along its own coast. That was what its turret-ships were for. A recent article in the *Edinburgh Review* reminded its readers that 'it was not in England or France alone that official men mistrusted their ever being fitted for sea service.' Little did MPs know that at that very moment, the

Captain Sherard Osborn was also appointed in Key's place as a member of the Ordnance Select Committee; 27 August 1866, Board to Under-Secretary of State for War, TNA ADM 1/5976.

33 7 July 1866, 'Captain Coles and His Turret-Ship', *Punch*. *Punch* returned on 28 July that it was 'Ready, Aye Ready' for the Royal Navy to be reconstructed after the pattern of the *Miantonomoh*, 'to be a match for the Americans', but it added caustically that by the time this was done the Americans would have likely moved on to new inventions, and 'will perhaps buy the idea of those contrivances of an Englishman who will have had the offer of it rejected by his own.'

Austrian and Italian fleets (including some twenty ironclads) were battling to the death near the eastern shore of the Adriatic, off the island of Lissa.[34]

John Bourne decided now was the time to court the new Board of Admiralty with Ericsson's ideas directly, writing to Pakington on 23 July that only a monitor-form of ironclad could offer 'side armour 18 inches thick[,] furnished with sufficient power to propel them at a speed of 16½ or 17 knots[,] and carrying a single turret 24-inches thick, armed with two wrought iron 20 inch guns'; an astounding concentration of armour and firepower. Anything less than this, he urged, 'would fail to advance us into equality with foreign nations which you have signified your intention to achieve.' Truly, it had become paramount for Britain's government needed to evince bold, firm policies on every score; that same day, some 200,000 Reform demonstrators overwhelmed 1,500 policemen and troops in Hyde Park. Milne at least was willing to agree with Bourne's suggestion that any man-of-war plated with even 6-inches of iron would now be 'useless', and Rear-Admiral George Henry Seymour, as Third Naval Lord, concurred that 'handy ships with thicker sides would be more useful in action than the long ships like the *Achilles* built for great speed'. But Dacres (as Second Naval Lord) thought that while American-style monitors would surely be ideal for coast defence, it was also imperative that the Royal Navy had 'highly manoeuvrable vessels of great speed brought forward to protect the Commerce.' More crucially, Reed as Chief Constructor wrote that he was 'unable to concur with the Writer's opinion that "nothing short of considerably thicker armour and considerably heavier guns than have already been introduced can be of the least avail in maintaining our Maritime position," because it is certain that the ships now built and building would be of very considerable avail in accomplishing that object if necessity arose.' At least by now he was willing to entertain the viability of artificial ventilation in ships, which he felt would inevitably feature in at least Britain's own monitors of the future. Officially at least, this was as far as the *Miantonomoh*'s visit to Britain, as the *Scientific American* muttered, was 'counselling our enemies'.[35]

---

34 14, 16 and 17 July 1866, *The Times*; 20 July 1866, *Hansard*, 'State of the Navy—Observations', Vol. 184, 1187-1217; 'The American Navy in the late War', *Edinburgh Review*, Vol. CXXIV (July-October), 1866, 185-227. The article also noted that newer monitors were far less prone to mishap in combat, and more seagoing; the *Miantonomoh* 'is at Spithead at this moment, and she does the greatest credit to the American flag, since it must be confessed that there is not a vessel in the British navy which could destroy her by gunnery, or which she could not destroy', 226.

35 31 July 1866, Robinson to Board, TNA ADM 1/5981, with Reed's enclosed letter to Robinson dated 31 July, and the Board's enclosed remarks dated 2 August. Reed rather skewed the facts here, since unlike the smaller 'citadel' portion of his own sail-and-turret *Monarch*, eighty feet of the *Captain*'s waterline armour, abreast of the two gun towers, was plated with 8-inch iron, the space between them plated with 7-inches, and the rest of the beam tapering to 4-inches of iron plating on the ends—still less than *Hercules* overall (with 9-inches along the central battery, then 8-inches tapering to 6-inches on the ends)—but with more than 1,000-tons less displacement, and four 12-inch '25-ton'

Coles had meanwhile perceived not just the advantageous—not dangerous—low-freeboard of the American monitor but agreed with Laird that twin screws for his model seagoing turret-ship were also best. 'I certainly consider that the proposed ship will be an effective Man of War', he wrote to Romaine, 'and as regards the design I am not only ready to accept any joint responsibility which may fairly belong to me but should be ready to take the sole responsibility of strongly recommending their Lordships to build this ship as designed.' Yet as for 'contracts, prices, or any matters other than the design itself, the responsibility, of course, with rest with Messrs. Laird.' Once again, Coles was emphatically not a shipbuilder.[36] In the meantime, Robinson in turn rejected the prediction by Laird to the Admiralty that the *Bellerophon* would fail her speed trials, and his recommendation that the bows of both that ironclad and the *Monarch* be altered. The failure of the small sail-and-turret 'rams' *Scorpion* and *Wivern* in either speed or sea-keeping the Controller considered proof enough the other way, despite the safe passage of the *Huascar* to South America. 'It is therefore but fair to allow this department to show what sort of authority Mr. Laird is as to the designing of ships and how far his opinions are entitled to be accepted as indisputable truths.'[37] This then complicated the critique made by Robinson and Reed of Laird's suggestion to the Board that the *Captain* would easily attain fourteen-knots—soon to be the fastest steaming ironclad in the British fleet. Even if this turned out to be true, the Chief Constructor protested it would not be due to any fault of his own, much less credit to the private shipbuilder: 'I beg leave to observe that the Design for a Turret-ship which Mr. Lairds's sons have lately submitted to their Lordships is throughout, from Keel to gunwale, an unconcealed imitation of the many novel structural combinations which were first introduced in the *Bellerophon*, and which form a most prominent and important part of those systems of designing and shipbuilding adopted by the Admiralty for the last three or four years which Mr. Laird's letter calls in question.'[38]

Yet in light of recent events this sort of civil-military squabble only served to further erode the trust of the British public. Tenniel recrafted Richard Brinsley Sheridan's

guns in 9-inch armoured turrets faced with 10-inch plating, as opposed to eight 10-inch 18-ton guns; see for example Parkes, *British Battleships*, 120-4, 130-8. At any rate, Reed concluded he was of opinion 'that the ships we are now building, and which are about to be built (except the *Hercules*), however valuable for some purposes, will not be fit to encounter the larger Vessels of the American Navy, owing to the comparative weakness of their armour.'

36 24 July 1866, Coles to Romaine, TNA ADM 1/5970.
37 22 August 1866, Robinson to Board, TNA ADM 1/5981; for the *Huascar*'s speed trials at the measured mile and her subsequent passage overseas, as noted by Lairds, see 20 August 1866, *The Times*.
38 28 August 1866, Laird Brothers to Board, TNA ADM 1/5997. Reed's enclosed letter to Robinson is dated 28 July 1866. Robinson defended his Constructor in an enclosed letter to the Board of the same date, calling Laird 'a gentleman whom I must consider neither responsible nor impartial.'

satire *The Critic* from 1779 with a foppish English Admiral informing the outraged figure of Tilburina, 'The British Fleet thou canst not see—because—it is not yet in sight!' The same 18 August 1866 issue of *Punch* further mocked the Admiralty with not just one but two poems on successive pages, with 'The Queen of the Sea' declaring 'Other nations have navies of steel; iron-clads we have got two or three', and 'Though our solus are with business engrossed, Yet ten times seven millions have we In experiments spent; Goodness knows how it went'; while 'The Fleet of the Future' chimed that only when 'the great case of Coles v. Reed has been tried, Cupola principle versus broadside…When all these questions and scores beside (That my Lords to come will have to abide), Are docketed, pigeon-holed, red-tape tied, The wonderful fleet we then shall see, Will that "The Fleet of the Future" be?' *The Times* noted that even the President of the British Association recently judged the Royal Navy's ironclads as 'costly mistakes, and of our guns he could say nothing better.' After seven years of converting its naval power from wood to iron, Britain only seemed less positive with each new armour-plated ship being launched. 'We were convinced of the need of ironclads, but we built them so slowly, so distrustfully, at such heavy cost, and after such protracted experiments, that other Governments, with less money but more confidence, succeeded in doing more than we did':

> The only question, therefore, is whether we should not have employed greater energy in building these new vessels and shown less fastidiousness in the selection of patterns. One nation, and one only, has adopted this policy. The Americans made up their minds upon the question with singular decision. After rejecting the principle of an ironclad force for some years, they were at length so influenced by the action in Hampton Roads that they rushed headlong into the new system. They took the *Monitor* as their model and built Monitors as fast as they could. It must also be added that they are perfectly satisfied with the result. They alone, of all the people in the world, possess a Navy which in numerical strength is amply sufficient, and which in excellence of pattern they believe to be unapproachable. Whether we, under similar circumstances, should be equally contented must admit of some doubt. The Americans, however, entertain no doubts on the question.

On this overarching issue of *confidence*, the question really came down to one of turret vs. broadside. For in terms of the latter type of armament, *The Times* was certain its readers would agree that 'our ironclads are probably better than those of any other country.' The problem remained, however, 'that we have so few of them, and that the Navy of Great Britain no longer exhibits its old superiority of force and power.'[39] At the same time, the British press avoided the underlying issue at work in both the 'turret vs. broadside' and 'guns vs. armour' debates; how the Royal Navy had kept its *sails* in

---

39   18 August 1866, *Punch*, '"The Critic" (Slightly Altered)'; 25 August 1866, *The Times*.

the projection of British naval force and power but had lost its 'old superiority'—and thus the nation's poise—on a point of numbers including weight of guns and armour. The Americans had scores of ironclads precisely because they weren't going very far. As such, even by September 1866 *The Times* gloomily pronounced there could be 'no doubt, indeed, about our relative weakness as a Naval Power at the present moment'—and yet was comforted that 'We are still probably the strongest maritime Power in Europe.' This seeming contradiction between naval and maritime power supremacy could only be worked out in the form of a sail-and-turret ironclad, thus continuing Britain's 'striving after excellence in individual specimens rather than numerical strength.' Until that time, a naval force like America's remained larger and more powerful in important aspects, even if her heavy guns, for example, were not so 'perfect'.[40]

Key was grappling with this conundrum, for example, in his memo to Vice-Admiral Pasley of 11 August. 'A weak Maritime power should therefore construct vessels of great defensive strength,' he wrote, 'while powerful nations, wishing to command the sea, must look primarily to the offensive power of their fleets.' Because seagoing ships had to sacrifice more armour not just for their general seaworthiness but also because of the increased penetrating power of naval ordnance, they should actually float less in the way of shielding and more in the way of (unprotected) heavy guns. That would be the only way to possibly dominate weaker powers again. If anything, the latest ironclad heavies put out by Reed were going in the wrong direction, obsessed with high speeds and piling on more armour at the expense of other qualities. 'Naval History teaches us that ships were rarely captured in consequence of the number of men killed on either side, but usually by masts falling, or [the] rudder being disabled, the ships thus becoming unmanageable; or by being sunk or carried by boarding.' Lissa had quickly devolved into a smoke-filled, point-blank melee, fought at ranges (and even with similar tactics) as the Battle of Trafalgar. The American-built Italian flagship, the broadside-ironclad *Re d'Italia*, had her exposed rudder-head shot away first, leaving a her a sitting duck to a fatal ramming blow from a similar vessel, the Austrian flagship *Erzherzog Ferdinand Max*. Key argued that only British ironclads built on these principles should 'form the Fleet which is to command the Seas; for I imagine it cannot be disputed that England exists as a first rate power, solely by her maritime supremacy, which is not to be maintained by a defensive fleet.' Not surprisingly, Robinson disagreed, joined by Sir John Dalrymple-Hay that 'we must endeavour to get an Iron-Clad Fleet capable of going about 14 knots at the measured mile.' Likewise, if other powers were designing fast ships which protected their gun crews, so must Britain; 'we are not free agents'.[41]

40   4 September 1866, *The Times*.
41   11 August 1866, Key to Pasley, enclosed with 5 September 1866, Robinson to Board, TNA ADM 1/5981. For contemporary British assessments of the Battle of Lissa see for example 2 August 1866, Major General G. Cadogan to H. Elliot, and 11 August 1866,

Nonetheless, when the Board of Admiralty requested the Controller to report on the current state of the navy, he noted that in an effort to economise the needs of the fleet while devoting significant resources towards ironclad construction, older wooden vessels on foreign stations were repaired as best as possible, with only one new class of wooden cruiser (*Amazon*) being introduced in the previous administration, and another—swift and heavily-armed (*Inconstant*)—was designed to meet the threat of the over-engined American sloops of the *Wampanoag* and *Pompanoosuc* classes. The result was that 'the lives of the wooden ships, some of considerable age, others constructed of green timber, during and after the Crimean War, rapidly ran out'. Scores of older paddlewheel sloops and frigates had meanwhile been sent to the breakers.[42] Robinson then followed this up two weeks later with *A General Outline of the Wants of the Navy at the present moment with reference to Ships* (23 August). This reiterated the three main types of naval threats facing the British Empire: invasion of the home islands, attacks upon imperial possessions worldwide, and the destruction of the merchant marine. The first challenge was one of local command of the seas, and that meant countering the rival ironclad battlefleet of Imperial France. At the present moment the ratio was 19-16 in Britain's favour. He also noted, however, the absence of harbour and coastal defence ironclads, recommending four double-turreted, twin-screw iron-hulled monitors 'by the 1st of April, 1869'—a proposition which Milne noted as 'questionable'.[43] Almost as if to make the Controller's suggestions seem more reasonable, Romaine added his own memo to Pakington six days later, on 19 September, which was nothing if not extravagant. At present estimates, he advised, French ironclads by the end of the following year would all be armed with heavy guns as powerful as those intended for British service. Yet a naval defeat did not 'seriously affect the position or security of France. To England a defeat at home unless she is prepared with a reserve capable of immediately taking the sea, means ruin to her commerce, stoppage of food and supplies, and of intercourse with India and her colonies.' French naval power was 'a luxury and a vanity', whereas British supremacy at sea was 'a question of Life or Death.' Given this premise, it was imperative that the Royal Navy field no less than '63 Ironclads of the First class and 31 Ironclads of inferior qualities and sizes', with at least thirty stationed as a Home Fleet, fifteen in the Mediterranean, six in America, ten in Australia and the rest scattered in every station around the world. These figures were necessary just to absorb the first shock of hostilities, he concluded, 'but to afford complete protection'

    forwarded reports translated into French, in TNA ADM 1/5992; 8 September 1866 (collection of documents), TNA ADM 1/5977; 2 and 8 August 1866, *The Times*; and P. H. Colomb, 'Lessons of Lissa', *Journal of the Royal United Service Institution*, Vol. 11 (1868), 104-26.

42 8 August 1866, *Programme of Works, 1866, 1867—State of Work at the Yards in August, 1866*, in TNA ADM 1/5981.

43 See Milne's annotated copy of this printed memo in Milne Papers, Greenwich, MLN 143/2.

the numbers should be increased still further to eighty-four First Class ironclads and forty-one Second Class—an immense ironclad armada blanketing the earth.[44]

---

44   19 September 1866, Romaine to Pakington, TNA ADM 1/5977.

Photographic Section 2   XVII

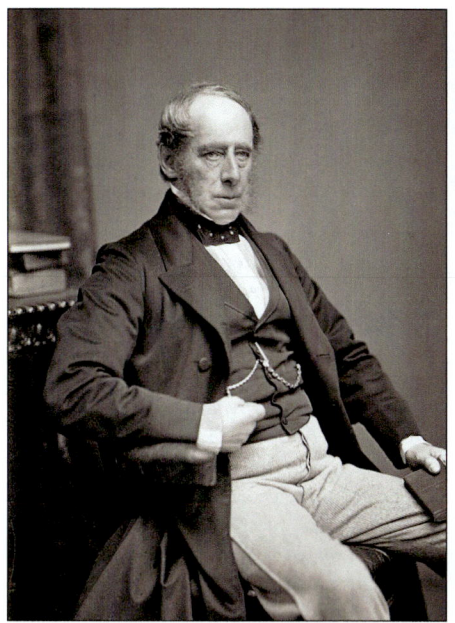

John Somerset Pakington, 1st Baron Hampton (1799-1880). (CDV courtesy of the National Portrait Gallery)

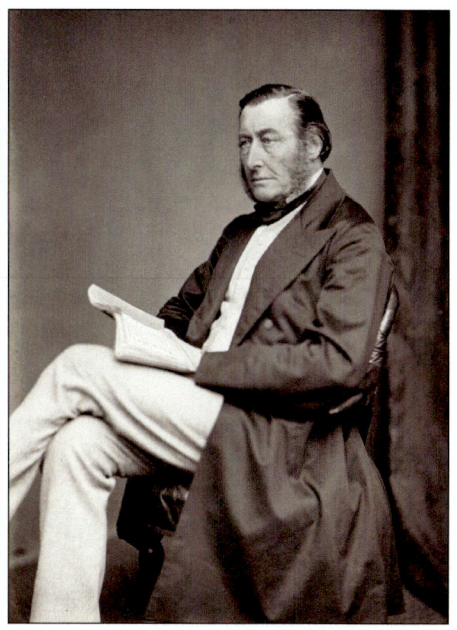

Henry Thomas Lowry-Corry, (1803-1873). (CDV courtesy of the National Portrait Gallery)

Hugh Culling Eardley Childers, (1827-1896). (CDV courtesy of the National Portrait Gallery)

Sir Alexander Milne, 1st Baronet (1806-1896). (Author's collection)

XVIII   Turret versus Broadside

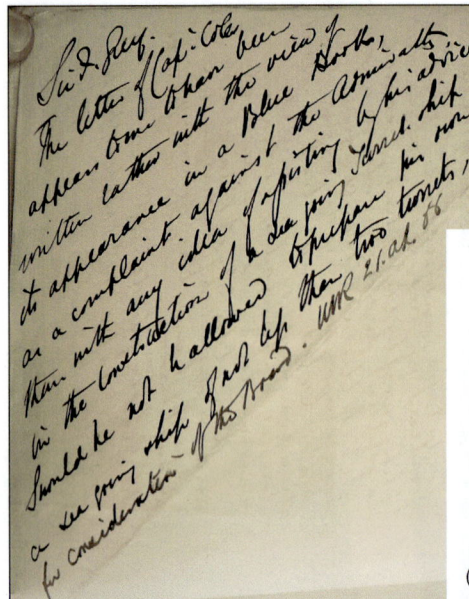

[Sir Frederick Grey, First Naval Lord, minute]:
'The letter of Cap. Coles appears to me to have been written rather with the view of its appearance in a Blue Book, as a complaint against the Admiralty, than with any idea of assisting by his advice in the construction of a sea going Turret ship. Should he not be allowed to prepare his own design of a sea going Ship of not less than two turrets, and send it in for consideration of the Board[?]' - 21 April 1866. (The National Archives, Kew, ADM 1/5794)

As a major source of national prestige, Britain's ironclad fleet was subject to intense scrutiny by respectable, tax-paying Victorians, worried that the Royal Navy would prove of an inferior status to those of rival powers. (Image courtesy of the National Maritime Museum, Greenwich)

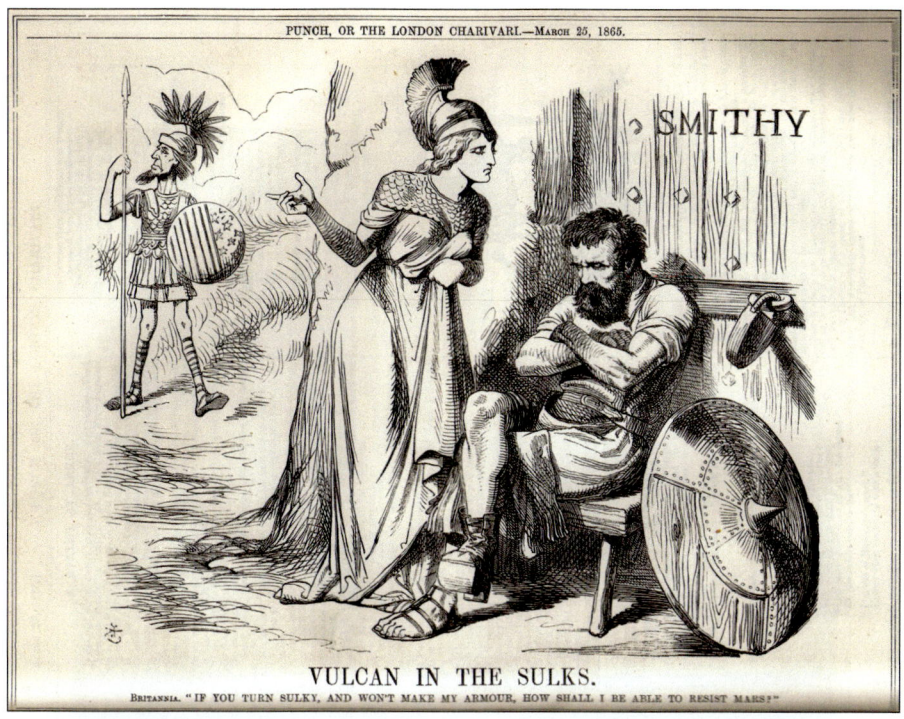

U.S. 'Target No. 61 Sept 20 [1864]': a rolled 5-inch-thick iron plate from John Brown & Company (Sheffield) backed by 20-inches of oak, penetrated by a solid 438-pound cast-iron shot fired by a 15-inch muzzle-loaded smoothbore with a 60lb charge. (U.S. National Archives, RG 74 (Bureau of Ordnance, Entry 98))

MAY 17, 1872.   THE ENGINEER.   345

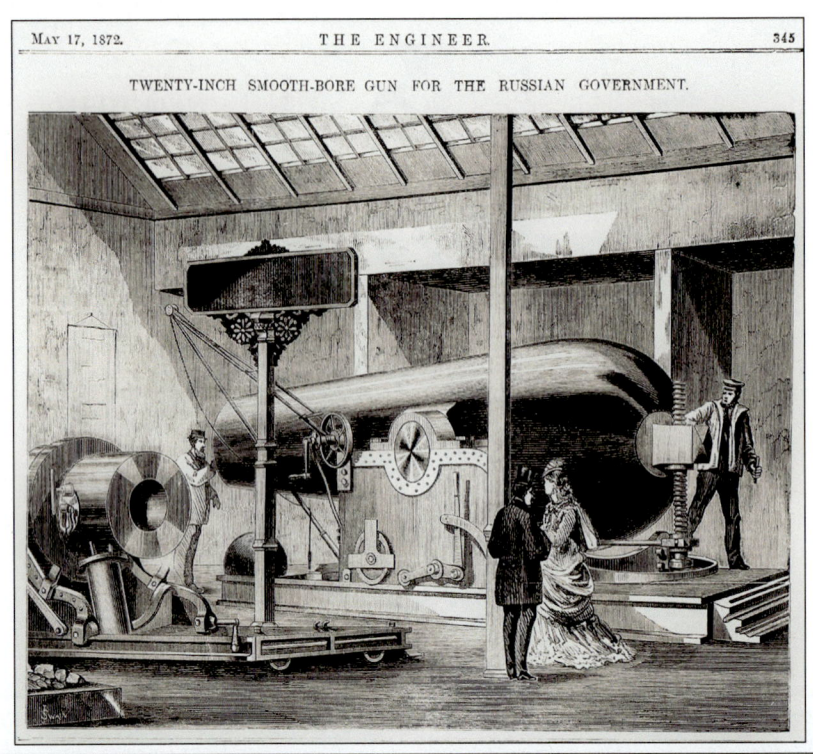

TWENTY-INCH SMOOTH-BORE GUN FOR THE RUSSIAN GOVERNMENT.

THE MONITORS "MONADNOCK," "CANONICUS," "MAHOPAC," AND "SAUGUS" AT ANCHOR NEAR FORT FISHER DURING A GALE. (AFTER LITHOGRAPH BY ENDICOTT & CO.)
Their commanders were surprised to find that not one of the turret vessels dragged its anchor, while the remainder of the fleet was in great danger owing to the inability of the ground tackle to hold out against the pressure of the wind on the top hampers, from which the monitors were free.

The American turret-ship experience during the Civil War offered mixed lessons, easily misinterpreted. Monitors, with their small numbers of very heavy guns, proved deadly against Confederate ironclads like the *Atlanta*, *Tennessee* and *Virginia II*, but were of correspondingly limited value in subduing fortifications. If battened down properly they were exceptionally seaworthy, but their lack of sails and small coal bunkers prohibited their use as long-range cruisers (never mind their long-term habitability). (John Ericsson, 'The Monitors', *The Century Magazine*, November 1885 to April 1886, Vol. XXXI, New Series Vol. IX)

Like Coles in Britain, Ericsson took pains to promote his invention to the American public. But the argument over who made the first turret-armed man-of-war in history overlooked a vital distinction in how the ships themselves were conceptualised. Whereas Coles always had a seagoing cruiser in mind, only armed with turrets rather than broadside-mounted guns, Ericsson envisaged a more radical 'machine'—a modern weapons system—where the ship was merely a platform for carrying a supreme, ship-killing gun. (Image courtesy of Navy Art Collection, Naval History and Heritage Command, Washington, D.C.)

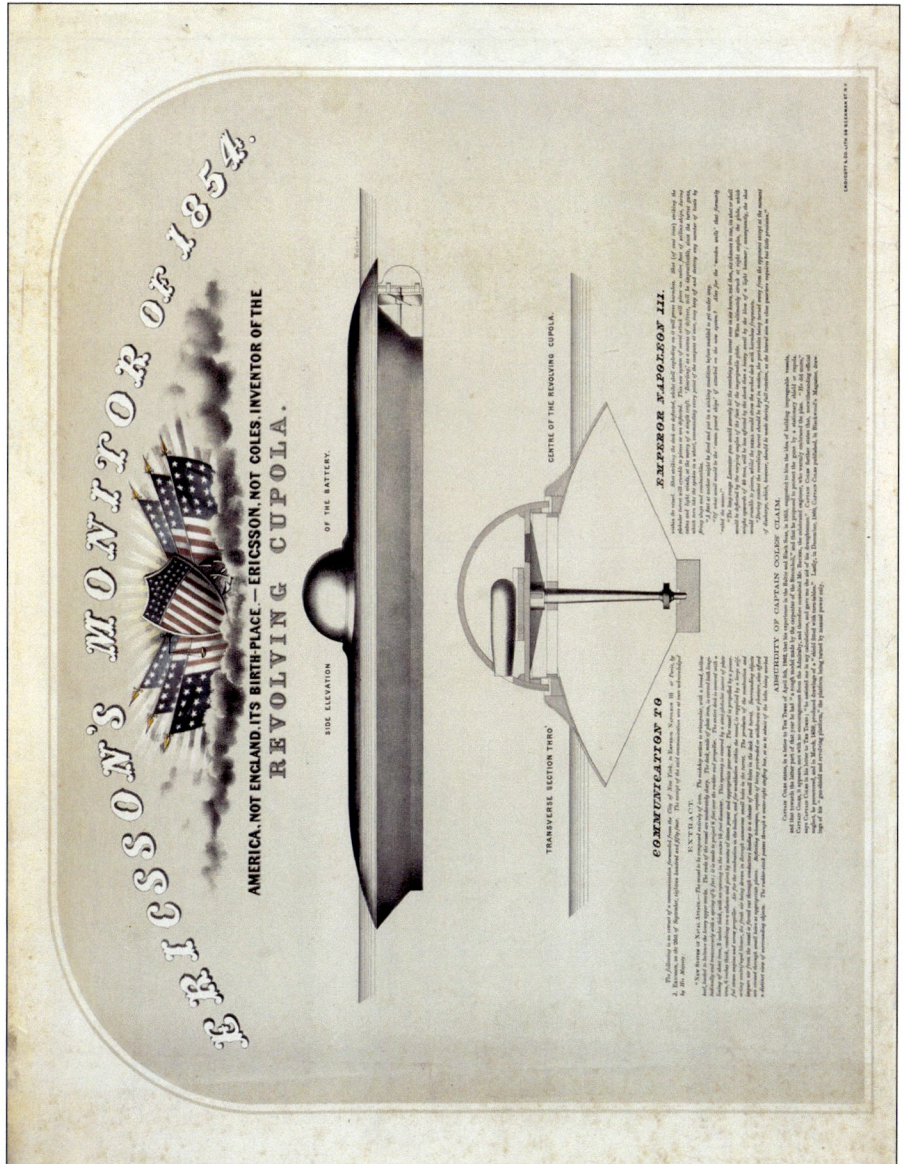

XXII Turret versus Broadside

Extent of Armour on the Sides of Iron Cased Ships, 30 April 1866, and signed by Robert Spencer Robinson (Admiralty Controller) Contrast the partial armour protection scheme of *Warrior* and *Defence* to that of *Valiant*, then *Achilles* and the *Minotaur* class. Only the *Caledonia* and other *Royal Oak* class conversions featured full protection for their size. After that the tendency was clearly towards more concentrated, thicker armour schemes protecting fewer though heavier guns until the 'central battery' profiles themselves resembled American monitors and rams, though with full masts, sails, and extensive surrounding superstructures. (Image courtesy of the National Maritime Museum (Greenwich)

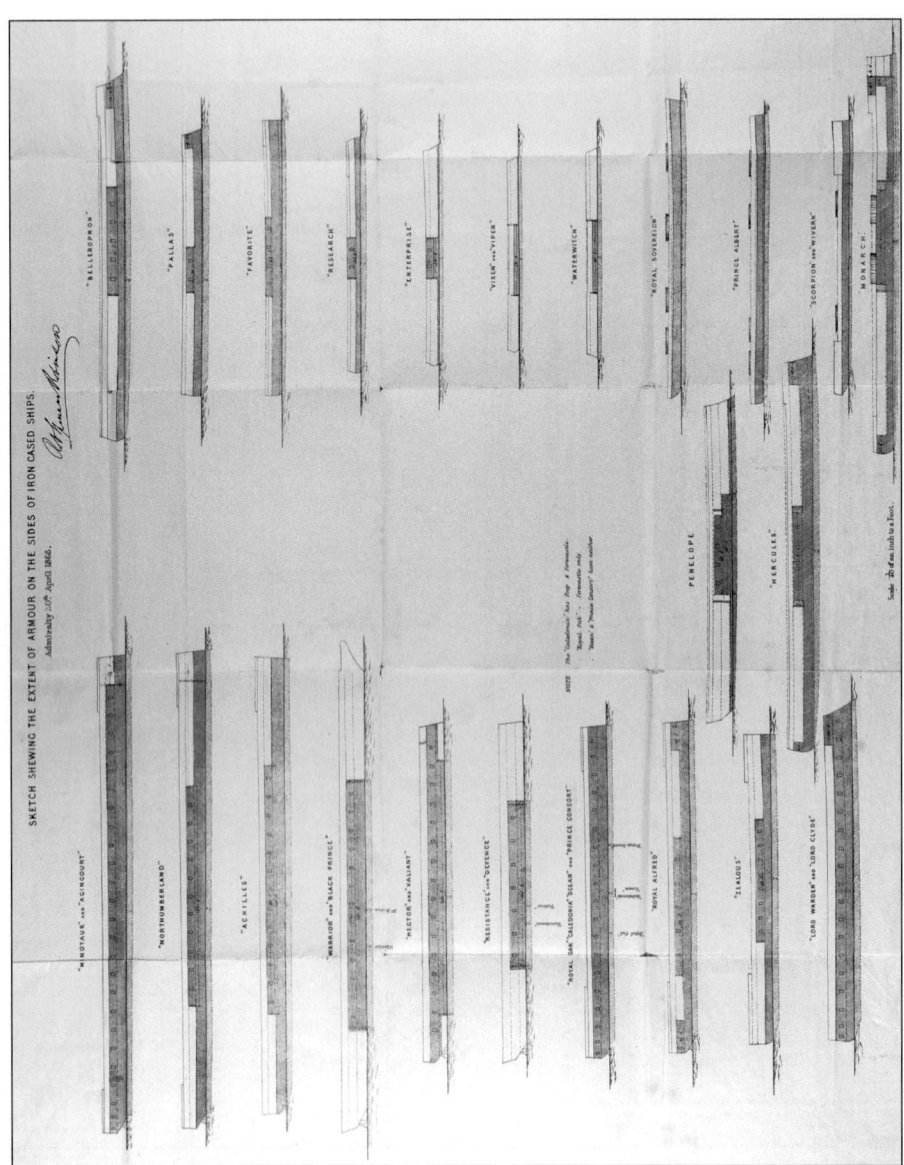

EXPERIMENTAL FIRING OF THE BELLEROPHON AT THE ROYAL SOVEREIGN AT SPITHEAD.—SEE PRECEDING PAGE.

XXIV   Turret versus Broadside

The 'Turret vs. Broadside'-debate in Britain reached its peak in 1866, when Coles was sacked, rehired, and finally offered a chance to build his own 'perfect' sail-and-turret ship (HMS *Captain*); but also when the Controller's Department carried out a brutal test of turret armaments under fire, with Reed's central-battery ironclad HMS *Bellerophon* blasting away at HMS *Royal Sovereign*, a wooden line-of-battle ship cut down in 1862 and armed with Coles turrets. Meanwhile, the U.S. Navy despatched its newest monitor, the double-turreted USS *Miantonomoh* (shown here at St. John's, Newfoundland), on a goodwill tour of Europe and Russia. (Image NH 105802 courtesy of Naval History and Heritage Command, Washington, D.C.)

The *Miantonomoh*'s to Britain in the summer of 1866 caused a wave of public indignation with Admiralty shipbuilding policy. Almost all of the Royal Navy's ironclads featured high-freeboard broadsides which could be penetrated by the American monitor, while none of their guns could retaliate. Although the Board had already taken steps to rectify this embarrassing situation, with new ships under construction mounting heavier guns behind thicker armour-plating, Coles and his supporters were now convinced that a low-freeboard sail-and-turret ironclad was practicable.

XXVI   Turret versus Broadside

THE RECENT ATTEMPT TO LAUNCH THE NORTHUMBERLAND.—from photograph page.

HMS *Northumberland* plagued her original builders (Mare & Company) who transferred their contract to Millwall Ironworks in 1863. Millwall also went bankrupt in 1866 trying to complete the vessel. Her armour was added while she was still on the stocks, and upon launch she stuck halfway down the ways, straining her hull integrity. Repeated attempts to pull the *Northumberland* loose failed. The Admiralty was then called in to help, at an additional cost to the public of £20,000. The April 1866 crisis cast further doubt upon broadside-ironclads, when just launching such behemoths was considered a triumph. (The Illustrated London News, 14 April 1866)

[July 3, 1868.] THE ENGINEER. 27

THE MONITOR DE TYGER, FOR THE DUTCH GOVERNMENT.
BUILT BY MESSRS. NAPIER AND SONS, GLASGOW.

GLASGOW.
No. II.

We have a word or two to add to our notice of the Fairfield Works before describing one of Messrs. Napier's most recent productions, which we this week illustrate.

The new setting-plates and drawing-loft come close to those heretofore in use, and form altogether probably the largest surfaces in any existing yard for tracing the lines and shaping the frames of iron ships. The process of setting the angle irons to the precise angle required at different sections of the ship has always been a tedious one, from the fact that not only do most of the frames differ in set from their fellows, but each frame itself, especially those near the stem and stern of the ship, vary considerably throughout their length in the angle which the web must make with the side of the vessel. The method of bending cold in a punching machine, employed by Messrs. De Burgh in bridge work, could not easily be applied by the iron shipwright, as it is scarcely applicable to any but straight work. Messrs. Randolph, Elder, and Co., are, however, now trying an experiment which will, if successful, greatly facilitate the setting process. Beside their new plate and between two pairs of reverberatory furnaces they are fixing side by side five small steam hammers, the anvil and hammer of each of which are fitted with a series of cast iron dies corresponding to the various sets of different sized angle iron required in their class of work. When in operation each hammer can have a die with a different angle for the same scantling of bar, so that the same bar can receive five variations of set, or if a number of bars require to be set each to a uniform but different angle to the others, they can each have their appropriate dies under a separate hammer. The arrangement was not quite completed when we had the pleasure of visiting these works, but we have no doubt Messrs. Randolph, Elder, and Co. will soon have acquired such experience with this new adaptation of the steam hammer as will enable them to pronounce authoritatively on its economy and usefulness.

THE GOVAN YARD AND LANCEFIELD FACTORY.

Messrs. Robert Napier and Son's fine establishments are at present almost exclusively occupied in the construction of ironclads for our own and the Dutch Governments. For the former they have at present on the stocks two of the class to which the Invincible belongs, from Mr. Reed's designs, on which we have already commented, whilst two turret ships for the Dutch Government were launched lately and are now about to be handed over to the King of Holland's inspectors. The first of these vessels is the De Tyger, whose preliminary cruise we chronicled in a recent number, and the construction of which we now illustrate from drawings kindly furnished to us by Messrs. Napier, who were themselves the designers of both vessels. Before proceeding to describe this vessel we wish to correct a typographical error which appeared in our notice of her cruise—the statement that "on easing the speed of the starboard screw the vessel contrived to pay off to port" should read "continued to pay off to starboard." The circumstance of the cruise occurring immediately before our day of publication prevented the possibility of correction by the writer.

The principal dimensions of the De Tyger are:—Length, 187ft.; breadth, 44ft.; depth moulded, 11ft. 6in.; tonnage (builder's measurement), 1613 tons.

This vessel is built in compartments with water-tight doors, and has a double bottom—it being intended that the space between the outer and inner bottoms shall be filled with water when preparing for action so as to sink the vessel to her fighting draught, which will be about 9ft. 6in., thus leaving only about 2ft. of the topsides exposed to the enemy. Under ordinary circumstances, however, the draught will be 12in. less than this, thereby adding to the comfort and seaworthiness of the ship.

The armour-plating on sides of vessel is 5½in. thick having a backing of teak 10in. thick, and an iron inner skin supported by strong iron girders and frames.

The turret, on Captain Coles' plan, is protected with armour 12in. thick at the ports, and 10in. in rear of the guns, supported by teak backing 12in. thick, with an iron inner skin and frames similar to vessel's sides. The armament will consist of two 300lb. 12½-ton Armstrong guns, having the most improved iron slides and carriages,

---

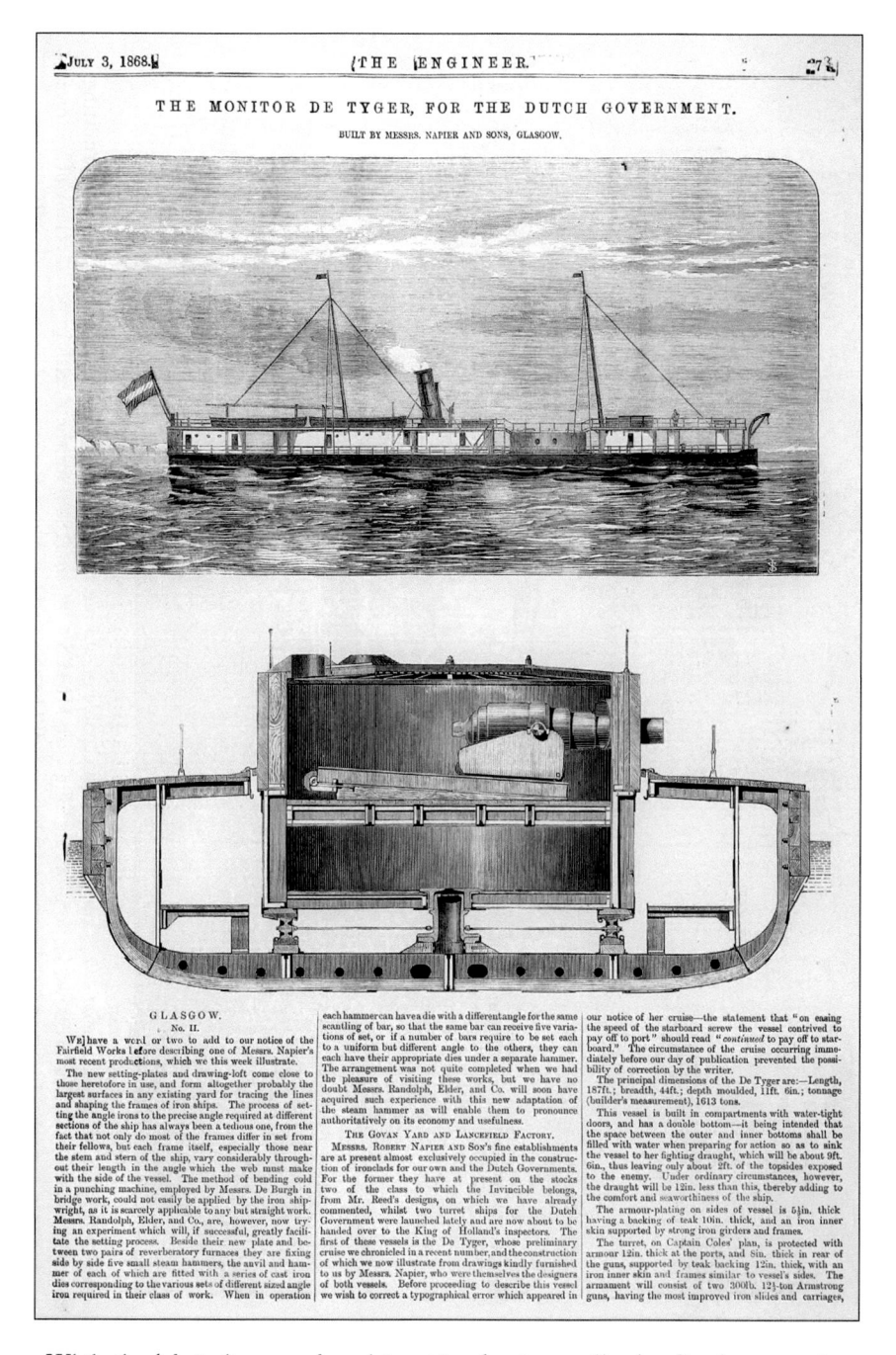

While the Admiralty seemed recalcitrant in adopting smaller, handier, less expensive and more powerfully-armed and armoured turret-ships, private British firms carried on developing a variety of shallow-draught, sail-and-turret and low-freeboard monitor-type ironclads for foreign powers.

XXVIII Turret versus Broadside

Reed's response to the American *Miantonomoh* as an apex ironclad capable of sinking any ironclad she could encounter—range permitting—was the 'coastal defence', mastless 'breastwork-monitor', starting with HMVS *Cerberus* (1868) for the British imperial colony of Victoria, Australia. Today her wreck—sunk as a breakwater in 1926—can still be seen in Half Moon Bay, near Melbourne. (Image courtesy of Lukasz Kasperczyk)

Photographic Section 2 XXIX

USS *Miantonomoh* – laid down 1862, launched 1863. (Author's collection)

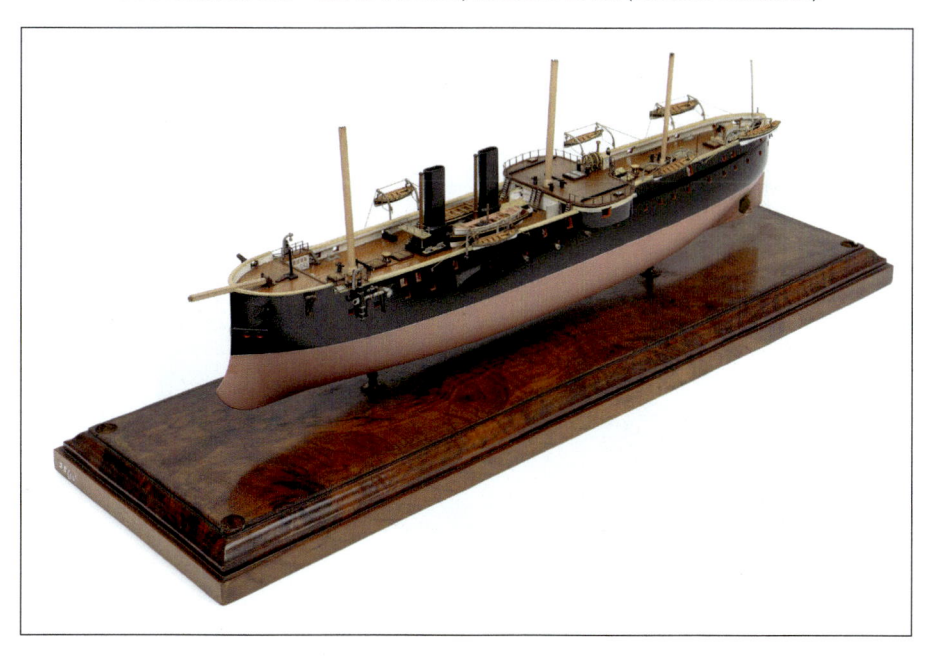

HMS *Sultan* (central-battery ironclad) – laid down 1868, launched 1870. (Image courtesy of the National Maritime Museum, Greenwich)

HMS *Devastation* - laid down 1869, launched 1871. (Image courtesy of the National Maritime Museum, Greenwich)

HMS *Captain* - laid down 1867, launched 1869. (Image courtesy of the National Maritime Museum, Greenwich)

The Age of the Ironclad began when traditional 'Blue Water' naval power, in the form of oceangoing battlefleets of capital ships, proved unable to effect much against Russia during the Crimean War (1853-1856), obliging the French and British to fashion shallow-draft, iron-armoured floating-batteries which could engage coastal forts with a reasonable prospect of success. The American Civil War (1861-1865) subsequently gave rise to low-freeboard turreted ironclads which could sink broadside-batteries either defending Southern ports or threatening Northern ones. In a coastal *assault* role they required close coordination with land forces—combined operations—to achieve victory against strongholds such as Charleston or Fort Fisher. While the Mid-Victorian public was clearly fascinated by these developments, both the British and French navies persisted in developing ironclad fleets which could 'command the sea'. The Franco-Prussian War (1870-1871) subsequently demonstrated again the limits of deep-draft seagoing ironclads against a continental power; a disaster for France, and a warning to Britain. 10 April 1869, 'The Volunteer Review at Dover: View of Dover from the Sea—The Naval Squadron Attacking the Forts'. *Illustrated London News* (Author's collection)

XXXII   Turret versus Broadside

Captain Hugh Talbot Burgoyne, (1833-1870). (Author's collection)

'The only Survivors of H.M. late Ship "CAPTAIN" in the same Clothing they wore on landing at Finisterre.' No other ship has shared her name since then. (MLN/161/4, Milne Papers, National Maritime Museum, Greenwich)

9

'We must not relax our efforts ... however great the expense'

Even then there was no guarantee of perfect security, at least in terms of quality. Towards the end of that turbulent summer of 1866, Rear-Admiral Yelverton in command of the Channel Squadron (ironclads *Caledonia*, *Achilles*, *Hector*, *Lord Clyde*, and *Pallas*) had sortied for an experimental cruise where he encountered 'high westerly winds and a rough sea, of which every advantage has been taken to test the stability and sea going qualities of the Ships, as also their capabilities of working their heavy guns broadside on to the sea'. Rolling at 10- to 12-degrees, both the *Caledonia* and *Pallas* shipped 'considerable quantities of water' through their main deck broadside ports, handled by their scuppers, but both *Caledonia* and *Hector* dipped enough that the cartridges in their broadside guns were drowned.[1] In company with Rear-Admiral Frederick Warden, Yelverton was sent out by the Admiralty again in September, this time to comparatively test much more thoroughly the qualities of *Caledonia*, *Achilles*, *Bellerophon*, *Lord Clyde*, *Ocean*, *Hector*, *Pallas*, *Research*, and *Wivern*, with particular emphasis on the sail-and-turret ironclad's 'capabilities as a cruising vessel; and whether in a seaway she can use her weather Guns, and if she is considered in her present state a safe Ship for her Crew.' This time he was far more specific. 'For special service, or a long voyage where a quick and certain passage is the object,' he reported, 'the *Achilles* is far superior to any of our finest Frigates, and from what I have seen of her in blowing weather, I have no hesitation in saying that she is a safe and good sea-boat':

> We must not however lose sight of the fact, that with all her good qualities the *Achilles* is from her great length, most difficult to handle, and this defect in action, more especially if engaged with a Turret-ship, might be her ruin. It is perhaps going beyond the bounds of what is probable, but I feel certain that this ship might, and probably would have to go out of action to turn round, thus

---

1   23 August 1866, Yelverton to Admiral Sir Charles H. Fremantle (C-in-C Devonport), in TNA ADM 1/5963; also 7 August 1866, Yelverton to Admiralty, TNA ADM 1/5968. The Channel Squadron cruised at sea between 3-13 August.

exposing herself in almost a defenceless position to the fire of more than one of the enemy's ships.

Did that suggest a turret-ship of equal tonnage could have performed any better? Warden, writing his own report from the *Lord Warden* on 27 October, believed so, since broadside-ironclads seemed unable to open their main deck guns unless head to sea, while the trials also practically emphasised their limited arcs of fire. 'It follows, therefore, that if a Turret-ship had taken up a position in either bow or quarter of [*Lord Clyde*], there would have been a radius of 4 or 5 points on either bow or quarter, which would be points of impunity, or she would, at the worst, only have to contend with one Gun.' Yet even if the turret-ship was in an angle to be fired at by the broadside ironclad, he continued, 'the result would be, that the Main deck of this Ship, and the upper deck of the Turret, would be both flooded alike, but the advantage would, as I think, still remain with the latter. The Sea might, and probably would, wash right over the deck of the Turret-ship, but the water would be got rid of, whilst here it is not at all clear that it could be got rid of, and certainly not as fast as it would accumulate.' Whether the admiral was imaging an encounter between a low-freeboard monitor or a sail-and-turret ironclad, however, wasn't clear, even with the addition of a drawing which he enclosed of a small single-turret ironclad exploiting the starboard quarter blind-spot of a large broadside-armed opponent.[2]

Robinson and Reed now set to work mitigating—if not over-writing—the damning conclusions of these reports. The Controller did not agree with Yelverton's suggestion to convert more wooden ships-of-the-line on the plan of the *Royal Oak*-class, despite his original suggestion in 1861 to do just that. They would roll as badly as the French ironclads; yet if they converted them on the plan of the *Zealous*, as central-battery ironclads, 'we leave wooden unarmoured extremities fearfully liable to be set on fire by shells, a catastrophe which happened to the Italian ship *Palestro* at the battle of Lissa.' As the *Hector* was contracted before he took office, Robinson could only quote Walker's initial warnings about building cheaper versions of the *Warrior*, which despite waterline armour protection on their ends would be 'unsuited for general service'. As for the *Wivern* and *Scorpion*, Robinson entirely agreed with Yelverton, but unlike him did not hold they were even 'well adapted for Coast defence, but I entirely concur in thinking that it is the only use to which they can be put.' But even though both Yelverton and Warden thought powerfully-armed turret-ships would have the advantage over lumbering broadside-ironclads even in a battle on the high seas, the Controller offered that 'the reports of the two Admirals as a whole' had

2   See 11 September 1866, 'Proposed Instructions for Rear-Admiral Yelverton', TNA ADM 1/5977. Yelverton reported sailing between 20 September and 1 November 1866; see 10 November 1866, Yelverton to Admiralty, TNA ADM 1/5968. His subsequent report was dated 10 November 1866. See also the detailed individual reports by the squadron's ironclad captains in 7 December 1866, 'Channel Squadron—remarks on Rolling', in TNA ADM 1/5983.

proved 'the Iron Clad Fleet satisfactorily fulfilled what it was designed to perform': prove seaworthy at all.³

Pakington's Board of Admiralty was already at odds, and Robinson's plans for the future of the navy were at the heart of the debate. At the end of September, the First Lord wrote to his senior naval adviser, Milne, that it was imperative for them to see eye to eye. 'We are engaged in working what I confess I regard as a very clumsy machine, and I think the best, if not the only way to work it successfully, is for those who are so engaged to act together in the most frank and friendly spirit.' Milne was agreeable as well as professional, much to Pakington's relief. In the meantime, he confided, 'I do not weep over the misfortunes of the Channel Fleet—on the contrary, I have just written to Romaine that I am glad they found what they went to look for.' Whatever anxiety Yelverton's reports may inspire, Pakington felt 'it will quiet us much in settling our programme.' As for the contentious wooden second-rate (90-gun) *Repulse*, the Board agreed to adopt the Chief Constructor's proposals to finish her as a relatively inexpensive, uncomplicated central-battery ironclad with eight 8-inch, 9-ton guns protected by 6-inch armour, and unused Penn engines lifted from the first-rate *Prince of Wales*. Milne considered this would give the navy a 'serviceable ship' which could bolster foreign stations.⁴ But she neither would she be a turret-vessel which might better cope with monitors.

For this, Robinson and Reed unveiled in November what they thought the best possible compromise. In a printed memo on *New Designs for Ships* the Controller

3   December 1866, 'Remarks on Admiral Yelverton's Report on the Cruse of the Channel Fleet', TNA ADM 1/5968. As for the wooden ironclads as a whole, Reed advised Robinson these needed to be deployed on foreign stations as soon as possible—before they rotted beyond their serviceable life spans. 'I am aware that the *Lord Clyde* is having 9-ton Guns prepared for her,' he wrote, 'but her present armament is a powerful one, comprising a complete Main deck battery of 6½-ton Guns, and my firm conviction is that the existence of our more perishable ships will prove too brief to justify their detention in and about our Harbours year after year for the purpose of undergoing repeated adaptations to new Armament as they arise', 27 October 1866, TNA ADM 1/5982.
4   30 September and 3 October 1866, Pakington to Milne, Milne Papers, Greenwich, MLN 165/10; 3 October 1866, Reed to Robinson, TNA ADM 1/5982, with Milne's attached comments dated 5 October. *Prince of Wales* went on to serve as the new *Britannia* training school at Dartmouth. As Parkes astutely observed, because 4½-inch armour plating—like that of Reed's central battery conversion of the 2nd-rate 90-gun *Zealous* (1864)—was no longer considered sufficient in naval warfare by 1866, Reed's plan for converting *Repulse* was to further contract her armoured battery from 103-feet of the side of *Zealous* down to 70-feet on *Repulse* to allow for 6-inch plating as well as increasing the calibre of the rifled muzzle-loaders from 7- to 8-inches, though reducing their number from sixteen protected guns down to eight. 'Hence, as this entailed 33 ft. more of main deck timber being exposed on each side, the *Repulse* became more vitally committed to destruction by gun fire than had ever been anticipated when thinner armour ensured immunity from shell fire. That she should not be exposed to ordeal by battle through conflict with her peers was more or less assured by despatching her to the Pacific station', *British Battleships*, 146-7.

offered more detailed choices for the Board to consider than in August and September. Only the first-class ironclads would feature high-speeds, though in the smallest possible package, since only in 'ships of unrestricted dimensions' were greater speeds obtainable. And of the two enclosed designs, one central-battery the other two turreted, Robinson 'should myself prefer the broadside ship' though they would cost the same (estimated at £410,000). This improved *Hercules* would have an 8-inch armoured box with a main deck six feet above the water protected by 2-inch plating, but its belt would feature prodigious 10- to 12-inch thick iron at the waterline. Armament was projected as eight '22½-ton' guns within the central citadel and a further six 9-ton guns on the exposed upper deck. 1,736-tons of the massive ship's displacement ('9,624' tons) would be just in iron armour slabs, along with 300-tons of teak backing, inner iron skin and deck plating. The first-class turret-ship ('with light upper deck') had essentially the same hull and armour. Its deck would be augmented, however, by a platform under the twin turrets and giving a freeboard of fourteen feet. Reed thought this design would preserve, 'to the fullest extent possible, the system of commanding the whole horizon by means of the turret guns, an advantage which I regret to see sacrificed to a very large degree in the *Captain*, without the compensation of the protected bow fire ahead provided for in the *Monarch*.' Given the same rig as the central-battery ironclad (though with less guns), the ship's compliment would be 525 men, and the 10-inch armoured turrets mounting 22½-ton guns would be operated by steam machinery. But Reed had also devised a 'First Class Monitor Turret-ship', which was mastless. The saving in weight would allow for 12-inch thick amour 'everywhere, excepting the lower strake, which is ten inches, the deck being made of uniform height throughout, and plated with 2-inch iron as before…the top of the deck being as before 6 feet above the water.' In the absence of a rig, she would be manned by nearly half the crew of the central-battery ship (350 versus 600 men) and be propelled by twin-screws each driven by its own 600 horse-power engine. In order to undertake long sea voyages the turret vessel would stow fifty percent more coal than the central-battery ship. All three major ironclad capital ships would draw twenty-six feet of water and should obtain a speed of fourteen-knots. In addition to these, Reed's team had worked up plans for an improved *Penelope* central-battery 'frigate' with increased spread of canvas and a better designed hull with double bottom against ramming attacks, and a double-turreted, twin-screw 'Coast Defence Monitor' of 2,107 tons with 350 dual horse-power engines making nine knots.[5]

In forwarding these designs to Robinson, Reed noted his consultation with Milne while the Controller was touring naval armaments in France and Italy. As time was of the essence, the Chief Constructor stressed that he was only able to offer these proposals 'embracing a vast number of calculations, and the production of many finished drawings, besides many more of a temporary and sometimes of a tentative

---

5   20 November 1866, *New Designs for Ships*, in TNA ADM 1/5982; see also Milne Papers, Greenwich, MLN 148/2.

character, in addition to much other work' thanks to 'the liberality of their Lordships in authorising the employment of six additional draughtsmen, and placing all the Draughtsmen upon extra time and pay.'[6] Again this unintentionally highlighted the enormous differences of professional resources which had been available to Reed versus Coles over the years.[7] Reed also acknowledged the Board's specific desire now for monitor ironclads for coast defence, leaving him 'free, to a certain extent, with reference to the sea going Iron Clads.' He couldn't resist pointing out that his department considered small seagoing turret-ships which were also fast as being impracticable—and that Coles' attempt the previous year, rejected by the independent reviewing Committee, 'practically admitted the impossibility of producing small 14-knot two-turreted ships carrying heavy armour and armament to say nothing of the small 15- and 16-knot vessels which have sometimes been imagined or thought of outside of the Admiralty.' What's more, he argued, 'the great delay that has taken place in the production of a seagoing Turret-ship' was not the fault of the Admiralty but the turret-ship advocates themselves, who had insisted that heavy armour and firepower could be combined with small size (i.e., a monitor) and yet be fully rigged and seaworthy. But while he didn't think the broadside principle could be improved on— or condensed—any further, and that the high-freeboard turret-ship notion remained insoluble, his first-hand experience with the American monitor had intrigued him. As it was, Reed informed Robinson that he was not 'fully satisfied' with his enclosed design for a first class monitor, that previous work commitments had prevented him from fully working out his ideas, and he mysteriously alluded to having 'just now invented or devised certain methods by which I can hope to accomplish the object on dimensions that will not appear preposterous. I have now, however, put such a design in hand, and expect to get it in a presentable form before Christmas.'[8] This was the 'breastwork' concept, which added the height of an extra deck to bring the turret guns higher away from the water, and which replaced the iron lattice hurricane decks and thickly-armoured ventilation shafts of the *Dictator* and *Monadnock* classes of Federal monitors with a solid superstructure. Because this doubled the target surface area, however, requiring dense armour protection to shield the Coles towers below the surface of the top gun-deck, less weight was free for even thicker armour and heavier guns than in a 'pure' monitor. Hence, when Ericsson was forwarded a rough sketch

---

6   20 November 1866, *New Designs for Ships*, with Reed's enclosed letter to Robinson dated 17 November, TNA ADM 1/5982. Parkes noted that during this time the Constructor's Department regularly employed three Assistant Constructors (including Barnaby), a Surveyor of Contracts, a Secretary to Reed, and ten draughtsmen, *British Battleships*, 153.
7   See for example 13 November 1866, Coles to Romaine, requesting that Scullard be assigned to assist him with plans for the *Captain*, as well as a clerk. Prior to this Reed had assigned Coles a draughtsman from Devonport unfamiliar with his turrets and too far from Coles's residence to facilitate faster work; TNA ADM 1/5970.
8   20 November 1866 ('New Designs for Ships'), Robinson to Board, TNA ADM 1/5982, with Reed's enclosed letter to Robinson dated 17 November 1866.

of Reed's initial plans for the eventual *Cerberus*-class of dual-turreted, twin-screw coastal defence monitors (mastless, but with an added armoured deck or breastwork), which the Chief Constructor showed to Bourne at the end of July 1866, the inventor of the original USS *Monitor* wrote he was disgusted with the British constructor's 'modification', calling it a 'barbarous mutilation' of his own ideas.[9]

But the question also remained: why not build this far more seagoing turret-ship far earlier? Why not work *with* Coles to make it happen? It took the visit of the *Miantonomoh* in the summer of 1866 on the one hand, and the irresistible pressure of Coles and his supporters in the British press and Parliament on the other, to finally get Reed (and then also Robinson) to really put their minds to resolving the monitor—not just 'turret-ship'—issue. Engine improvements aside, other reports had already come around to the idea that sea battles would be fought in moderate water at worst (and probably close to land); that 'great speed' was not as important as firepower and protection; and that turret-ships might operate safely enough over great distances with 'escorts'—like an armoured Knight with a trusty Squire[10]. It was only when Edward Reed felt obliged to work out the problem that a potential solution was reached—as naval historians have referred HMS *Devastation*: the first oceangoing, mastless capital ship armed with revolving gun turrets. As an article in *Blackwood*'s on 'The British Navy' exclaimed in March 1871, 'if these views had only prevailed at an earlier date, we should not now be boasting of thirty-six broadside ironclads, of which no more

---

9   16 August 1866, Ericsson to Bourne, Ericsson Papers, Philadelphia, Box 4. When asked by the 1871 Committee on Ship Designs to imagine 'a ship too be constructed of precisely the same proportions as the *Miantonomoh*, but of the same displacement as the *Devastation*,' Barnaby calculated that the armoured breastwork added 884 tons (i.e., which might otherwise have been applied to increased side armour, turret thickness and/or weight of guns in an American-style monitor); 11 February 1871, *Report of the Committee* (1872), *Addendum*, 205. Clearly perturbed, David. K. Brown thought it 'interesting that *Miantonomoh* was very highly rated by the public and many seamen whilst the greatly superior *Cerberus* was seen as second rate', *Warrior to Dreadnought*, 57. But his comparison was itself rather disingenuous: the 10-inch, 18-ton guns of Reed's breastwork-monitor were not ready for service until early 1868, whilst the 15-inch guns which armed the *Miantonomoh* were first mounted in Union monitors by the end of 1862—and capable of penetrating the four-foot high-freeboard of *Cerberus*, armoured by 6-inch plates outside the central citadel. Given the low internal reserve buoyancy of the *Cerberus* as with any shallow-draft monitor (flat-bottomed and drawing 15-feet as with *Miantonomoh*), flooding of the fore or aft compartments would have dangerously threatened her stability. Parkes also notes that the Coles turrets of *Cerberus*—which was launched in December 1868—were operated by hand (*British Battleships*, 168), versus the steam-powered Ericsson turrets of the older American monitor (launched in 1863); something which Brown ignored.

10 With a nod to George Ballard, who likened Reed's slow breastwork monitors to 'full-armed knights riding on donkeys, easy to avoid but bad to close with', *Black Battlefleet*, 219.

than fourteen (if so many) could with any prudence be commissioned to fight in line of battle against a squadron of well-armed Monitors':

> In the face of the troubled state of Europe, with interests and political objects that clash in the East and in the West—in the midst of the armed rule and misrule that now agitate the nations—it is with mingled feelings of remorse and relief that we survey the condition of the British Navy. With remorse we contemplate the wasted time, the lost opportunities, the lavished treasure, which a few self-willed and mistaken men have spent in the creation of our broadside ironclad fleet. With relief we recognise that before it was quite too late a new course was taken, sound principles enunciated, a different type selected, and a class of vessels commenced to which we can with confidence and security intrust the honour of the British flag.[11]

* * *

As for Reed, he was awarded a pay rise a month after his submission of new designs for ironclads in mid-November 1866. When he was first appointed as Chief Constructor, on 9 July 1863, his salary was £900 per year, and after 8 January 1866 this was increased to £1,000, and then again to £1,200 the following month. Here it was noted that Sir Baldwin Walker had been £1000 per annum to start, raised to £1,300 by the time he was replaced in 1861. Reed would now receive £1,500 'from 24 February 1870'; in recognition that his work had been increasingly detrimental to his health, that as a civilian he could expect no pension, and that marine engineers tended to be paid more in the private sector.[12] Yet the Board of Admiralty, in reviewing the extraordinarily new proposals for ironclads coming from Reed that year, proved more inclined to err on the side of caution. In a memo that December, Milne did not think it 'expedient' to risk building any large new turret-ship until the *Monarch* and *Captain* had been tried first. 'The *Wivern* and *Scorpion* of 1857 tons', he added, 'are not sea going Ships. It might be expedient to construct a Ship of about 2500 to 3000 Tons,

---

11 'The British Navy – What We Have, and What We Want', *Blackwood's Edinburgh Magazine*, Vol. CIX, January-June 1871, 357-74; possibly authored by Thomas Brassey (1st Earl, 1886), when he was 35. The article quotes at length Robinson's testimony to an 1868 committee, where he advocated Reed's plans for large breastwork-monitors of the *Devastation*-class; 'He explained that the ships were specially designed as powerful seagoing ships; not so much as cruisers for the ordinary protection of commerce, as engines of offence, capable of being sent to the Baltic or Mediterranean, across the Atlantic, to the West Indies, or to the Cape of Good Hope.' Here Robinson then cited the seaworthiness of the *Miantonomoh* as proof that low-freeboard, mastless turret-ironclads now constituted the mainstay of British naval power projection. The *Monarch* and *Captain*, by contrast, were dead-ends.
12 12 December 1866, Reed to Robinson, in 13 December 1866, Robinson to Board, TNA ADM 1/5983. Reed would have been allotted a pension of £140 per year.

but I doubt this Class of Ship so low in the water ever becoming serviceable cruizers, although well adapted for special purposes of attack and defence of Harbours.' But given the unique defensive requirements of the British Empire, when so many other nations were arming themselves with ironclads as quickly as possible, the First Naval Lord thought 'we must not relax our efforts...however great the expense', suggesting at least one first-class ironclad, twenty of the second-class, and one turret-ship of 2,700 tons. Dacres agreed that a £400,000 first-class turret-ship 'I would never build until the excellency of one, or the contrary, as a cruizing ship had been proved.' In recognition of a lack of coastal defence ironclads, however, 'and for many reasons', he thought 'it would be expedient to build a first class Monitor Turret-ship, even if only an experiment.'[13]

As for Coles, the initial designs for his model ironclad had been drawn up in conjunction with Lairds earlier that year and forwarded to Pakington's new Board of Admiralty on 14 July. Reed took less than a week to denounce them. The *Captain* of Coles would only be superior to his *Monarch* by virtue of her smaller size—obtained by lowering the freeboard from fourteen- to eight-feet. Had the previous Board stipulated eight-feet to the Chief Constructor the previous year, on dimensions of his *Bellerophon* like the *Captain* was, he would of course have done so (so why resort—and relent—to Coles at all?) On 23 July Coles was informed that he was allowed to proceed with his ship, 'on the entire responsibility of yourself and Messrs. Laird, but the works will be carried on under the usual Admiralty inspection as to workmanship and materials.' He was not cautioned about the *Captain*'s freeboard, at least at eight-feet, nor was it clear how the Admiralty might intervene if the finished product departed radically from the proposal. Reed's concern was that Coles was allowed to build a sail-and-turret ironclad that would be lighter, cheaper and just as fast as the *Monarch*, with more powerful guns on a lower target profile: proof of the Chief Constructor's incompetence in fashioning the best possible men-of-war for the Royal Navy, never mind a victory for Coles, his supporters, and similarly marginalised British shipbuilders, engineers and inventors in the 1860s. As such, when asked by the Board to report further on design particulars of the *Captain*, on 24 July and 2 August (given the unprecedented arrangement as to accountability for the warship's success or failure), Reed stated that the hull 'appears to me to be somewhat heavily designed in places, and the weight

---

13   December 1866, 'Proposed New Ships', in Milne Papers, Greenwich, MLN 143/2, with annotation by Dacres dated 1 December 1866. As Ericsson wrote to Bourne on 19 October 1866, it was obvious in terms of the 'Monitor System' that 'Reed now understands the question perfectly[,] but he knows that his occupation is gone as soon as a single Monitor has been added to the British Navy, and hence he will oppose you to the last', Ericsson Papers, Philadelphia, Box 4. Two months later, and Ericsson's doubts over Reed's initial courting of Bourne and Ericsson's plans were complete: '[Reed] has no intention of giving you a chance to profit by planning or constructing anything for the Government', he wrote Bourne on 21 December 1866, 'And when he has obtained all the knowledge from you which he needs he will assuredly cut you', Ericsson Papers, Library of Congress.

allowed barely sufficient', yet 'if any suggestions of mine led to increased weight, occasion might thus be afforded for a transfer to this department of a responsibility which does not belong to it, in the event of the ship proving too deeply immersed.' Not only was he washing his hands for any potential failure—perhaps disaster?— Reed was making this eventuality, perhaps a likely one even at that stage, a rather positive one for the sake of the Admiralty and the Controller's Department. How could the Captain *not* failing not be in the best interests of the service in this respect? Similarly, when Reed expressed his concern that the centre of gravity might prove too high in the vessel, taking into account extras like steam machinery for rotating the turrets and a large array of sail, it was only to be transmitted to Lairds as 'advice', and that they 'be requested to thoroughly satisfy themselves on this point'. If they altered their design accordingly, Reed could later claim with some degree of truth that any supposed improvements upon the *Monarch* were later rejected after all, and that the Admiralty and the nation had clearly wasted its time and money upon Coles. The subsequent letter by the Board to Laird, of 10 August, explicitly set the parameters for success or failure, victory or defeat, and in these terms the labour of building a perfect seagoing turret-ship was indeed 'Herculean'—that is, an impossible task contrived by a jealous king to humble a presumptuous mortal (annoyingly favoured by the gods): 'it is in contemplation to place on you and Captain Coles the entire responsibility of the design, the efficient construction of the ship, and the satisfactory accomplishment of your undertaking to complete her as an effective seagoing man-of-war, bearing two turrets with four 600-pounders, and attaining a speed under steam of not less than 14 knots when in all respects ready for sea.'[14]

Within months Coles was seriously ill again and wrote the Admiralty on 19 November that he was unable to exercise his full powers as a veritable 'Controller of the Navy' in overseeing the construction of the *Captain* so far north in Birkenhead (from his residence in Southsea, Portsmouth). Again, he was at most the ship's designer. Robinson then wrote to the Board four days later that in an effort to avoid delays and complications in finishing the *Captain* that the contract be altered replacing every reference to 'Captain Coles' with 'Controller of the Navy', and the same power given to him which Robinson used to oversee the construction of HMS *Agincourt*, also built by Lairds. 'I am fully aware how difficult and onerous such a position would prove. However careful I may be, and however painfully anxious to cause the ship to be built according to Captain Coles' wishes, the experience of five years has taught me how small a chance I have of succeeding, or of avoiding most unpleasant communications.' But this also meant that any attempt made by Coles and Lairds to alter their original design for the *Captain* would have to be approved by Robinson (and Reed) again; hence the Board's stricture of 4 December 1866 that 'any modifications or alterations of any nature whatsoever in the design of the ship while building, whether made at

---

14 26 September 1870, *Summary of Correspondence relating to the Design and Construction of the late 'Captain'*, in TNA ADM 1/6159, 4-6.

Captain Coles' suggestion, or approved by him, which will occasion any extra expense, or in any way prevent delivery of the ship by the time agreed upon, must be submitted for their Lordships' approval'. Coles and Laird might have objected that few if any of the ironclads built in the Royal dockyards were built without any modifications, cost overruns or delays, and that by exacerbating the approval process for any necessary changes the Admiralty was in fact unnaturally binding the *Captain*'s designer and builders to a first-draft effort only, with no margin for error, and practically in the full expectation of inevitable mistakes. Reed's central-battery creations, by contrast, had been continually, and in some cases drastically, modified during and after their construction to hastily transform embarrassing failures into public triumphs. Indeed, having already accepted the challenge to do what the Controller's Department couldn't—or wouldn't—do, Coles was sharply warned by Robinson that any attempt to change the specification 'which rules the weight of the hull' was a change of design, and this would not be permitted. 'His design and specification are put forward on his responsibility, and if the ship is built according to that design, it must be built on that specification, and he must be held responsible for both.' Since Reed had already declared the year before that the *Captain* could be considered a failure in many fundamental respects, Robinson was clearly determined to see this through to the bitter end and prevent Coles from escaping the inexorable consequences of questioning proper authorities.[15] Again, the *Captain* had to do everything that Coles had promised: prove superior.

Coles could only reply, on 8 December, that when the Board accepted his design in their letter of 23 July it included 'the specification so far as weight goes, and if the specification by Messrs. Laird had been so incorrect as to weights as to necessitate any alteration of design, I submit that the Department officers [namely Reed] should have pointed this out, before the design was accepted by the Board, after full consideration had been given to it by the officers of the Controller's Department.' Robinson waved this charge away, reminding the Board that the design was approved 'on the entire responsibility of Captain Coles and Messrs. Laird'; it didn't matter if the ship design was correct or not, only who was *responsible* for it (being incorrect). As ruthless as Coles was, as a naval officer he couldn't believe the inference here that the Controller and Chief Constructor of the Royal Navy were blithely willing to watch an entire first-class warship be constructed at great effort and public expense, in the baited expectation that its failure would finally see the ruin of Coles. That was ruthlessness of another order of magnitude. Robinson went so far as to add his personal scorn of the Lords of the Admiralty as well for humouring Coles in the first place, when their predecessors had a chance to be rid of him at the beginning of the year. Now they were just as locked into the fate of the *Captain* as Coles and Lairds. 'Their Lordships are quite aware that neither the design nor the specification met with my entire approval, and accepted both with that knowledge', he wrote the Board on 11 December. 'I

---

15   Ibid., 6-7.

do not therefore think it necessary to give them any further trouble on this matter.' Even when Coles pleaded for the sail-and-turret *Captain* to feature a crew of 400 men, rather than '500' as originally stipulated, since 'one of the important advantages which in my opinion would result from the adoption of Turret instead of Broadside ships would be the saving of expense consequent upon (amongst other items) the diminished complement which would be required', the Board's initial reaction was to reject the proposed change, drafting a terse reply on 26 December that 'without entering into a discussion whether 400 Men is sufficient or not My Lords consider the general Duties of a Ship of War of the Captain's Tonnage requires 500 men which is to be her compliment.' The draft response was then cancelled, Milne noted, because the Controller thought it 'advisable to leave the question as it is or difficulty might arise in regards to the plans of the ship.'[16] When Coles again tried to question how the contract for the *Captain* allotted responsibility, on 5 January 1867, Robinson snapped that Coles was only stalling, and that 'energetic measures should be at once taken to get on with the construction of that design.'[17]

On 15 January 1867, Bourne tried one final time to convince his peers (at the Institution of Civil Engineers) of the perfect soundness—the mathematical certainty—of Ericsson's 'Monitor System' for the British Navy. Addressing 'the nation at large' on the 'proper construction of Ships of War', he began by pointing out the vulnerability of Britain's broadside ironclads from *Warrior* to *Bellerophon* to the latest heavy ordnance. Indeed, because the 'guns vs. armour' race had in fact become a numbers game 'only vessels built on the Monitor system of Ericsson', he argued, were ultimately 'capable of carrying sufficient thickness of armour to resist modern ordnance'. Carrying this principle to extremes, with an eye on developing ironclads which would also be future-proofed against ordnance for the next few years, Bourne suggested that the Admiralty should immediately invest in large monitors with side armour no less than '18 inches thick backed by 4 feet of oak, and a turret 24 inches thick, carrying two 20-inch wrought-iron guns.' Only low-freeboard monitors could accommodate such titanic figures, while their proven seaworthiness, he stressed, was no longer in doubt. 'Nevertheless, such is the intractability of naval prejudice in this country, that, up to the present moment, while there is an abundance of frail antediluvian arks—powerless for offence and equally powerless for resistance—there

---

16   21 December 1866, Coles to Romaine, TNA ADM 1/5970. Within a week of the *Captain* being launched (27 March 1869), Coles relented that working such heavy masting as his low-freeboard turret-ship featured, and her 'being likely to cruise as such with other vessels also, makes me wish that her complement should be such as to place her under no relative disadvantage'—500 men would therefore be necessary. As Frederick K. Barnes of the Constructor's Department noted at the time, this would indeed further increase the vessel's draught (on top of the expected increase of thirteen-inches already), if only by another 1½-inches; Parkes, *British Battleships*, 141.

17   26 September 1870, *Summary of Correspondence relating to the Design and Construction of the late 'Captain'*, in TNA ADM 1/6159, 8-9.

is not a single Monitor in the Royal Navy. The fact is, the art of maritime war has entered upon a phase with which naval men, as a rule, are but little qualified to deal. It is a question of a preponderance of forces; and the Monitor is the engineering solution to that problem.'[18]

What undermined Bourne's stated preponderance of logic, however, was his unwillingness to propose monitors for British service without also providing a strategic rationale for their use; a mistake common to all too many other engineers, inventors and shipbuilders at the time. Just within the course of those four subsequent evenings of discussion in early January 1867, three of the commentators not only criticised the merits of the 'American Monitors' but suggested in turn their own ideal of a perfect ironclad, each more impractical than the last. Civilian professionals might design perfectly good ships, but they were still civilians and hardly in a position to also design British naval strategy. Navy men in turn only made it worse by suggesting warships without having to realistically calculate opposing weights for their speed, armament or armour let alone their sail and fuel capacity, hull strength or seaworthiness. As was often the case during the 1860s, this only added to the din, crowding out Bourne's ideas in the process, and leaving audience members like Reed and Barnaby safely in place as the only naval officials in the room actually in charge of designing Her Majesty's ironclads and thereby steering in their own way British warship-building policy if not naval strategy.[19] Indeed, Reed was tactful in agreeing that many of Bourne's notions were worth serious consideration. Yet he doubted whether ships as large as Ericsson's *Dictator* or Reed's own *Bellerophon* could operate effectively with only sixteen-inches of freeboard. Coles-type towers would have to be raised higher out of the water to avoid flooding, and here the Chief Constructor took over the discussion by publicly unveiling his plans of a seagoing breastwork-monitor. 'With regard to carrying masts and sails with this large amount of armour, his opinion was,

18 John Bourne, 'Ships of War', *Minutes of the Institution of Civil Engineers*, Vol. XXVI (Session 1866-67), 1867, 166-242.
19 Formalised 'strategic planning' at the Admiralty was problematic, especially given the absence of a standing naval staff dedicated to formulating in peace-time well-prepared strategies for winning the next war. An 1871 Committee on the Board of Admiralty confirmed that no mechanism existed in the same way that Prussia's formidable General Staff had been largely responsible for Germany's fast and efficient victory over Imperial France. Here Robinson confirmed in his testimony (of 13 March 1871) that 'there was hardly ever a discussion at the Board of Admiralty upon anything'; 'I think that in 90 cases out of 100 there was never any discussion whatever', *Parliamentary Paper, Report from the Select Committee of the House of Lords on the Board of Admiralty; Together with the Proceedings of the Committee, Minutes of Evidence, and Appendix, Session 1871* (1871), 54. When considering 'How will this country wage war with one or more maritime Powers?' in April 1874, Robinson also commented that 'indeed, all the time I was at the Admiralty, I never heard it referred to or examined in a large or comprehensive spirit—it [naval strategy] always appeared to be too vast and too difficult to be seriously grappled with', (10 April 1874) *Letter from Rear-Admiral G.T.P. Hornby*, 18.

that a ship with duplicate screws, quadruple engines, and an abundant supply of fuel, would be in a better position in stormy weather on a lee-shore than an iron-clad under canvas, in the event of accident to her machinery. He expected to hear great opposition to that view; but in these ponderously armoured vessels, it was far better to trust to good engines and plenty of fuel than to the winds.' Barnaby rather confirmed his belief, shared by other navy constructors, that American monitors 'behaved badly in a seaway', nor could they 'maintain an independent existence on the sea.' Once they were then fitted with masts and sails they became 'the English type of turret-ship, which could carry not heavier armour than a broadside ship.' If Bourne wasn't talking about seagoing ships of war, then Barnaby felt that his paper failed to address 'the real question at issue between broadside and turret principles in England.'[20]

Even while this ostensibly 'civil engineering' debate was underway on Great George Street in London, a short walk away at the Admiralty Milne wrote to Pakington: the navy was caught between the earlier proposals outlined by the Controller for ensuring parity with the French ironclad fleet and the more recent call for economy, reducing the numbers of new ships to be built. Including Robinson and Dacres, they could not 'in justice to the positions we respectively hold as your Naval Advisors' agree to the latter course. Replacing wooden frigates on foreign stations with second-class ironclads meant less ships for home defence and/or in the event of a war, and at the moment there were 'only two vessels of this class in the service adapted for this special purpose'.[21] Reed had meanwhile advanced his plans for British monitors drawing fifteen feet—to be deployed for the defence of Bombay and later also Melbourne. Low submersion the Chief Constructor now considered to be essential, as HMS *Royal Sovereign* and even the Coles turret-ship *Arminius*, built by Samuda Brothers for the Prussian Navy, were more vulnerable by virtue of their higher freeboard.[22] Coles at the same time attempted to interest the Admiralty in an array of multi-turreted ironclads based on his past designs for foreign powers as well as Britain. As with his earliest submissions of 1861, 1862 and 1863, these were nothing more than coloured 'sketches' with rudimentary calculations of weight. Nevertheless he added it was 'obvious and it is I believe now generally admitted that by lowering the freeboard to the minimum (which is practicable only by adopting central armament) the following advantages are obtained':

1. A steadier gun platform, and incidentally less risk of being struck below plating whilst rolling in a sea way.

---

20 Bourne, 'Ships of War', *Minutes of the Institution of Civil Engineers*, 166-242.
21 16 January 1867, Milne to Pakington, Milne Papers, Greenwich, MLN 165/10.
22 See 25 February 1867, Robinson to Board, TNA ADM 1/6017, with Reed's enclosed report dated 21 February 1867; also 26 March 1867, Robinson to Board, TNA ADM 1/6018; and 8 August 1867, Robinson to Board, TNA ADM 1/6019.

2. Diminution of area to be plated makes smaller Vessels and thicker plates practically available.
3. Diminution of target and increased thickness of plates, both incident to lowering of freeboard, seem the only effectual means of resisting the advances of modern guns and projectiles.

Coles also suggested that use of a hurricane deck between and above turrets would help obviate any 'discomfort to the ship's company'. All of his profiles showed variations on the *Captain*; that is, significantly lower freeboard than previous turret-ships yet retaining masts and sails. Robinson remarked that while he could still only offer rough plans which others would have to work out as practicable or not, it was 'no discredit to Captain Coles' remarkable ingenuity that his original proposal for Turret armour plated ships were widely different from those he now puts forth.' The addition of the American-inspired hurricane-deck was clearly a step forward (and something which Reed had also incorporated into his own designs.) But neither did Coles address the problem of waves threatening the safety of the low-freeboard turrets where they passed through the deck, 'and which no contrivance has as yet kept nearly watertight.'[23]

* * *

At the beginning of May, however, Coles, Robinson and Reed exchanged fire point-blank on the occasion of the turret-ship champion's paper at the Royal United Service Institution—on 'The Turret versus the Broadside System'. The Board of Admiralty had already invited tenders to leading private shipbuilding firms for a second-class seagoing ironclad, either turret or broadside-armed, with Robinson specifying that any turret-ship must be double-turreted mounting four 18- or 23-ton guns, not exceed 3,500- to 3,800-tons displacement, and draw no more than twenty-two-feet, six-inches. Furthermore, it was 'essential that an all-round fire, either by guns in the Turrets, or outside of them, should be practicable.' Freeboard was not listed, only that the height of the guns out of water 'must be carefully considered', but sail power was specified at 4.4-feet of canvas per ton of displacement and speed no less than 13½-knots. All designs submitted would be vetted by a 'Committee of Naval Architects' for review before being sent to the Admiralty for consideration, although officers of the Controller's Department would decide which design had fulfilled 'the various objects required to be obtained.'[24] Now Coles opened his evening address by stating even its title was out of date, 'since it is now generally admitted that the turret principle for fighting purposes is the right thing, and it only remains to be decided

---

23   9 March 1867, Robinson to Board, TNA ADM 1/6018, with enclosed letter and six sketches from Coles dated 2 February 1867.
24   12 April 1867, Robinson to Board, TNA 1/6018.

which is the best description and class of vessel for carrying and fighting these turrets under all circumstances for the protection of our country, of her vast commerce, and of her colonies.' The contest was who could come up with the better light draft turret-ships, and Coles presented illustrations of an 'Improved *Prince Albert*' and a triple-turreted version—all with a monitor's low-freeboard yet with a permanent hurricane-deck over the turrets with which to work a light sailing rig. The rest of his presentation resorted to minute comparisons with Reed's broadside-ironclads, especially the *Bellerophon*. Pound-for-pound, his forthcoming *Captain* would be a better ironclad. It would also roll less than a high-freeboard broadside ship, and here Coles could not resist quoting from Yelverton and Warden's recently published reports on the Channel Squadron's sailing and fighting capabilities from the previous autumn. More than this, he critiqued Robinson's remarks on their reports. 'They argue in favour of this broadside fleet, and conclude by trying to disparage the advantages which the Admirals consider a *good* turret-ship would have. The Controller says "the seagoing turret-ship has shown as much disposition as her broadside consorts to roll;" but this remark must be taken with the correction, that no seagoing turret-ship was in company with them, or even possessed by the *British Navy*.' The Laird Rams, as Coles had pointed out more than once, were never intended to act as cruisers. Robinson's further rationale that sea battles were unlikely unless in a moderate weather also played into Coles' hands, since a low-freeboard turret-ship with thicker armour would surely have 'decisive advantages' over broadside-ironclads even in calm waters. 'The Controller thus advocates his broadside guns as gallantly as he would fight them if he were in command, but when he is forced by the Admiral's reports to rely on the argument that Naval actions will only be fought *in a moderate sea*, surely it may be said in all good humour that he is reduced to his last cartridge!'[25]

Reed was the first to reply, awkwardly invited as a leading example of 'the "anti-turret party"' by the chairman (Captain E. Gardiner Fishbourne). Instead, the architect of much of Britain's 'broadside fleet' declared 'I have always been a great advocate of the turret system'. That itself was 'ill-fated' in Britain, however, because of the way Coles himself tended to misrepresent the facts in his 'undue enthusiasm'. Humiliating the Controller was, in turn, '*ex parte* and irresponsible'. When the discussion was resumed the following evening Vice-Admiral Robinson addressed the large meeting 'with extreme diffidence'; the room was filled with many Coles supporters. 'However amusing it may be, and however advantageous for the moment it may be, in discussing such questions as these,' he admonished them, 'to make use of a personal argument, or to give a home-thrust to an opponent, the cause of truth... suffers in the end from the temporary triumph anybody may obtain by a good hit and a smart thrust.' But like Reed he also swore that he was 'the oldest, the most consistent, and the most persistent advocate of the turret system—yes of the turret system, for

---

25   1 May 1867, Coles, 'The Turret versus the Broadside System' and 'Adjourned Discussion', *Journal of the Royal United Service Institution*, Vol. 11 (1868), 434-62, 462-84.

that which it is capable of doing'. He then proceeded to argue strenuously that while low-freeboard monitors were perfect for littoral warfare, only high-freeboard vessels should carry turrets at sea. As for the merits of broadside-ironclads, much credit was due to Reed for daily improving them, so that many foreign visitors 'believing that we were a pack of old women, and that we had no Navy, and were ready to be eaten up' came away admitting that Britain was 'unrivalled in her constructions at sea—unrivalled.' Robinson shared intelligence he had received about the Assistant Secretary of the U.S. Navy 'at a diplomatic dinner the other day' (in Russia), giving his opinion that the French had little chance of toppling British supremacy at sea. As for Russia's prospects against British naval power, Fox told his hosts '"You have got the finest line of defence on the waters in the world. Nothing can attack you, and your defence is perfect; but if you attempt to go to sea, if you attempt to cross the ocean, you would not be six months, before you would be swept away completely. You have not got a single iron-clad seagoing ship in your whole Navy."' As far as the Controller was concerned, he told his audience, 'the great opponent of the turret-system, as applied to seagoing ships, sits in that chair'—pointing to Coles. 'He has refused to accept, as a principle of a good seagoing turret-ship that her guns should be high out of the water. He has contended that the true principle of a seagoing turret-ship us to have her guns low in the water.' Only mastless monitors could manage that, enabling them to act as 'a piece of siege artillery' in coastal operations. But seagoing turret-ships had to contend with waves if they were to be considered proper cruisers.[26]

Coles responded to all of these points in equally convincing thoroughness if nothing else. With no small amount of sarcasm he was now 'glad' that everyone concerned openly agreed with the merits of the turret system. How much freeboard would suffice in seagoing turret-ships was therefore only 'a matter of degree', and only time would tell.[27] The *Daily News*, however, thought the Coles had practically won this 'turret vs. broadside' argument. The wonder was that it was 1867 and the Royal Navy still did not have a single seagoing turret-ship afloat, when other countries had already benefited by those built for them in Britain. Having Reed and Robinson state their objections in public had only exposed the Admiralty's 'shallowness' of their 'professed reasons for this state of things'. So Reed thought Coles had not been 'impartial'; but that was not an excuse for the Admiralty's rejection of other admirals and captains on the subject, nor an explanation why the Royal Navy was dominated by his ships, while Coles had been denied a single fair chance. 'Mr. Reed in one sentence protests that he is a sincere friend of the turret system, and in the next breath he warns his hearers that officials have their sentiments of honour, and if much badgered will refuse to budge!...Mr. Reed defends Admiral Robinson's honour and devotion to his duties, when the charge is not of dishonour but of prejudices, and not of laziness but of wrongheadedness.' The *Daily News* thought Robinson's arguments were more refined,

26 Ibid.
27 Ibid.

but he was 'by no means a more successful apologist than his coadjutor.' One had to admire the vice-admiral's boldness in declaring himself the turret system's champion and Coles its worst enemy. Yet declaring low-freeboard turret-ships the most perfect devices for coastal operations also neglected to explain why the Royal Navy had none, except perhaps the two Laird Rams (originally built for the Confederate Navy). What had clearly been at work in the country was nothing more than 'official jealously' against Coles, while Reed had been allowed to build and then refine a whole fleet of broadside ships, sparing no expense, and benefiting from 'every official indulgence and protection, so long as he would stick to fixed boxes in place of revolving turrets.' Captain Coles had no such sponsorship from Robinson, 'who sits up aloft to twist the report of every seaman who calls for turrets as preferable to boxes into evidence that seamen don't understand their business'. This scathing analysis was then reprinted by the *Nautical Magazine* approvingly, who reframed the issue as one of 'Monitors versus Ironclads':

> The curious fact still remains before the world, that a naval officer of this country produces an invention which is carried off to America, and perfected by that Government as the most formidable means of Naval warfare; which is also reproduced in this country (although not to the extent that it is in America) at the desire of several foreign Governments, to carry on their little wars, and to add to their own navies; while our own Government, hesitating and doubting, and even denying its efficiency at length allow the inventor to build one. Our rolling ironclads are laughed at. The Americans laugh at the idea of any vessels blockading their ports in the face of the Monitors which they have obtained from ourselves, of course improving on the principle.[28]

It was true that nothing aggravated 'turret vs. broadside' rivalries quite like Britain and America's active taunting of one another throughout the period. The same could be said for the unremitting competition between guns and armour. On 15 October 1866, Bruce sent to Lord Stanley (the Secretary of State for Foreign Affairs since the

---

28   3 May 1867, The *Daily News*; 'Monitors versus Ironclads', *The Nautical Magazine and Naval Chronicle for 1867—A Journal of Papers on Subjects Connected with Maritime Affairs* (London: Simpkin, Marshall and Co., 1867), 306-11. For Robinson and Reed's continued challenges over reports from Channel Squadron and other British ironclad cruises at this time see *Parliamentary Paper, Navy (Channel Squadron)*, 30 March 1867 (called for by Laird in the House of Commons); 14 June 1867, Robinson to Board, TNA ADM 1/6018 ('*Prince Consort* and *Royal Oak*—Remarks on Performances'); 5 August 1867, Robinson to Board, TNA ADM 1/6019 (with Reed's enclosed defence of *Bellerophon*'s steaming dated 2 August 1867); 23 October 1867, Reed to Robinson, TNA ADM 1/6020 (complaining of 'very great discrepancies' in Admiral Warden's trial reports of *Achilles*, *Bellerophon*, *Lord Clyde* and *Minotaur*); 25 October 1867, Reed to Robinson, 'Proceedings of Channel Squadron—Remarks on Admiral Warden's Report of 16 Oct. 1867', TNA ADM 116/7; and 20 November 1867, Robinson to Board, TNA ADM 1/6020.

fall of Russell's government in July) a letter published in the American *Army and Navy Journal* criticising the U.S. Navy's monitors and their armaments. 'It confirms the opinion I have ventured to express that the U.S. are destitute of Vessels intended to compete at open sea with the ironclads of our Navy', he wrote with satisfaction. 'The criticisms on even their best monitors show that they are not so generally admitted to be invulnerable as it is supposed in England.' When passed on by the Foreign Office to the Admiralty, Sir John Dalrymple-Hay on the Board commented the article proved that American turrets were not strong enough next to even the older Coles versions on the *Royal Sovereign*; yet just because 'the first crude and hasty efforts of the Americans do not possess all the perfection which may be desired' did not mean that Britain could not improve on the design in respect of speed, armour-plating and heavy rifled guns. But even before these reports circulated in London a spirited reply from 'E' (Ericsson) appeared in the very next issue of the *Army and Navy Journal*, which Bruce also forwarded with some bemusement. 'Its pages are open to rival investors who, though entitled to little confidence when praising schemes they advocate, may be read with profit when picking holes in schemes they oppose!' Indeed, while Ericsson pointed to the *Monadnock*-class monitors and the improved *Kalamazoo*s as capable of crossing the Atlantic, he admitted that 'our laminated 12-inch turrets could not stand firing from the 15-inch guns, and that the constructor did not plan these turrets to resist ordnance which had no existence when the monitors were first built.' Yet like Dalrymple-Hay, he thought this 'in no manner effects the questions whether the Monitor system is superior to the European broadside system. The great fact remains unchanged that, upon our system, we can protect our guns and gunner by 15-inch thick iron, in the large vessels, and 12-inch in the smaller class, with side armor of from 10½ inch to 14-inch backed by several feet thickness of wood in the large classes...all we have to do is to remove the outer plating of our small turrets and apply solid plates to insure impregnability against the formidable ordnance and projectiles possess by our maritime rivals.'[29] Earlier that summer (in 1866), Ericsson also passed

---

29 29 October 1866, Foreign Office to Admiralty, TNA ADM 1/5992. The enclosed *Army and Navy Journal* article was dated 6 October 1866; 5 November 1866, Foreign Office to Admiralty, TNA ADM 1/5992, with enclosed letter from Bruce dated 22 October, and enclosed published letter to the Editor of the *Army and Navy Journal* of 5 November 1866. As Ericsson repeated in the 13 October 1866 issue of the *Army and Navy Journal* ('Woolwich Guns and American Monitors'), 'we advise our maritime friends not to calculate on finding laminated armor only to practice against, should unhappily a conflict ever occur. The Monitor turret is purposely put together that its plating may be readily removed and changed. So with regard to the side armor; it forms no part of the hull and may be detached and replaced at any time. The entire armor backing and plating of the *Passaic* class of Monitors were in some instances applied in little over a month. Thanks to the disinclination of Congress to enable the Navy Department to provide means of taking care of the Monitors, we shall soon want new side armor.' Before the year was out, Bruce wrote Stanley his conviction that while the U.S. was 'without armoured vessels fitted for cruising at sea and that they are "unprepared" even for their construction', yet 'they are

judgment on the Coles 'turret system' as represented by the test firing upon the *Royal Sovereign*. A 15-inch solid shot from the *Miantonomoh* would have easily penetrated the stern of the British turret-ship and knocked out more than one of the Coles towers from below. 'The fact is,' he wrote in the receptive *Army and Navy Journal*, 'a turret mounted on an ordinary high-sided ship is about as poor a contrivance as can well be conceived. The Monitor is the only vessel fit to carry such a revolving tower.'[30]

Tired of endless boasts of the power of American monitor guns, and eager to justify the War Office investment in heavy Armstrong rifled guns against British critics in particular, the Ordnance Select Committee confirmed in December 1866 that it was purchasing a 15-inch Rodman gun complete with iron carriage and slide, ammunition and a thousand pounds of American large-grain powder charges for testing in the UK.[31] On Wednesday, 17 July 1867, this 20-ton import was finally tried against an eight-inch iron-armoured '*Warrior*-backed' target at Shoeburyness: even at seventy-yards and fired with a 'battering charge' of 60lbs of American powder ('equal to 50lbs of English powder'), the vaunted Yankee smoothbore failed, crowed *The Times*. 'The plate was not pierced, the backing was not reached, the skin was intact.' The initial muzzle velocity was calculated as 1,170 feet per second. At a longer 200-yard range the 9-inch 12-ton gun, firing a 250lb shell with a maximum charge of 43lbs, was certainly able to inflict more damage. 'Can anyone doubt the issue of combat between the two systems of artillery? The smooth-bores look very big and threatening, and can doubtless make a great noise when their shot strike the outside of a vessel; but the life of a ship is in its interior.'[32] Thus it was the *tenor* of the trans-Atlantic exchange in particular that resonated the most. 'Our learned contemporaries, the [British] *Engineer* and *Engineering*, are having fine congratulatory festivity over what they call the 'failure' of the big American smooth-bore at Shoeburyness', wrote Ericsson in the *Army and Navy Journal*. '*Engineering*, after the twenty tons of iron have now been removed from its stomach, breathes quite freely again, and is as happy as a man escaped from a horrible nightmare':

> 'We have at last,' says the editor, 'had a trial of the 15-inch American cast-iron gun against 8-inch solid armor, with the *Warrior* backing, and we are glad to say that the gun has been thoroughly defeated.' Glad to say! In that note of exultation we see relief from the oppression which has so long weighed upon British authorities. Visions of stacks of useless ordnance, and other stacks of

---

amply supplied with monitors available for coast and harbour defences. They are powerful for defensive but far less so for offensive purposes', 19 December 1866, in TNA ADM 1/5992.
30 7 July 1866, *Army and Navy Journal*.
31 14 December 1866, Minute (20,640), *Abstracts of Proceedings of the Ordnance Select Committee, for the Quarter ending 31st December, 1866* (London: George Edward Eyre and William Spottiswoode, 1867), TNA WO 33/18.
32 26 July 1867, *The Times*.

vulnerable iron-clads, and of fresh budgets of millions upon millions of pounds, to make up for the huge heaps of iron which it was feared must be turned into the scrap-heap—all these are dissipated. But, a few lines further on, as if fearful lest his oracular judgment might be somewhat overdrawn, the writer cautiously observes that the big gun 'has not quite done its best.' We should think not.'

It is, indeed, really for the interest of America to have the English make all the fun they please of the former's style of ordnance. It was against our interest that they saw our monitors, and that they stole our heavy gun-carriage, without which they would be popping away at monitors with 68-pounders... But if both facts and figures [of U.S. official records] are correct, then the commentary of the whole British press on the late trial is mere stupidity, and, instead of ridiculing the American gun, the British artillerists had better see what it is made of.[33]

Stung by these insolent challenges (as well as sarcasm)—that the controversial gun could not only safely handle 100lb charges but that these would crucially add 'about sixty-three per cent' greater force of impact—the Ordnance Select Committee had no choice but to publicly test the 15-inch Rodman again as called for. This time the target was not only penetrated but *wrecked*. "For seven days after the shot from the 15-inch American gun destroyed the 8-inch solid plate and *Warrior* backing at Shoeburyness, the London *Times* preserved a silence of stupefaction', Ericsson teased in the *Army and Navy Journal* again. 'Before then…*The Times* instantly sent up such a note of triumph that the world was astonished at its exultation.' With a 100lb charge an initial muzzle velocity in excess of 1,500 feet per second (Mach 1.37) had been attained, '200 feet per second faster than the swiftest rifled shot—the 9-inch— upon which England's naval power now rests.' The Rodman meanwhile showed no signs of wear or tear. It was therefore ridiculous to refer to American ordnance as 'large and slow' and the British principle as being 'light and fast', he contended. Likewise, the monster smoothbores were not meant for 'racking' or slowly crushing an enemy ironclad's armour frame versus cleanly penetrating them, as British (and

---

33 24 August 1867, *Army and Navy Journal*. Ericsson challenged the British to fire the 15-inch Rodman gun with '83⅓ lbs English powder', considered equivalent to 100lbs of American 'mammoth' powder. For Ericsson's claim that the British 'stole' his compressor and carriage system for heavy naval guns see for example TNA WO 33/15, 26 May 1865, minute by the Ordnance Select Committee ('Wrought-iron carriages and platforms'): 'the wrought-iron carriage and casemate platform which has recently been constructed in the Royal Carriage Department for the 13.3-inch rifled gun of 22½ tons weight, they thought it desirable as a preliminary measure, to fire a few rounds from it at the proof but, to test generally the strength of the structure and the sufficiency of the compressor (which is on the American principle), to keep the recoil within reasonable limits.' This was to test the Armstrong 600-pounder. Ericsson's carriage and compressor having succeeded, 'the Committee believe that the platform and carriage, light as they appear to be, compared with some other structures of the same sort which they have had the opportunity of examining, will be found abundantly strong enough for the service.'

some American) ordnance experts had tried to distinguish the two systems; 'both shots from the 15-inch gun completely pierced the target and drove the punched-out portions a long distance beyond. That the shot also broke up the target, in a way to cause terrible destruction on shipboard, and that the fragments it scattered would have destroyed everything living on an opponent's gun-deck, is also true.' That was the essential difference to the damage created by penetration from a 9-inch calibre elongated shell fired from the British rifled 12-ton gun, 'because the hole made by the 15-inch is a great, rough hole, which cannot be plugged, from the hopeless way in which it tears the object which it penetrates.'[34] It was perfectly feasible that a few such blasts—torpedo-sized holes—would be enough to quickly sink even the largest ships.[35] Of course timing here was everything. The Admiralty did have ironclads in the works with even thicker, more concentrated armour plating (including turrets) and which would mount considerably bigger guns. Despite the proven ability of the American 15-inch smoothbore to smash through solid eight-inch plating, backed by eighteen-inches of teak and an inner-iron skin-plating of 1½-inches, this was not quite the same as the Admiralty-built *Hercules* Target which in 1865 had defied 'Big Will', Armstrong's experimental 22½-ton, 13.3-inch calibre '600-pounder' shunt-rifle. As Reed confidently declared before the Institution of Naval Architects in March 1866, 'the *Hercules* target may have to encounter American vessels upon which an enormous thickness of armour has been placed, and the intention in the *Hercules*, as in the turret vessel *Monarch*, is that she shall be a vessel fit to go alongside of a vessel of any other nation, and fight an action through.'[36]

34 19 October 1867, 'The "Impregnable" Target Smashed by the Fifteen-Inch Gun', *Army and Navy Journal*.
35 19 October 1867, 'The "Impregnable" Target Smashed by the Fifteen-Inch Gun', *Army and Navy Journal*. Former monitor-ironclad engineer Alban C. Stimers also calculated that based on tests of the 15-inch Rodman conducted at Fortress Monroe (on 8 January 1867), the 453-pound solid shot fired with 100lb. charges would strike a target at 500 yards with a velocity of 1,400 feet per second; 30 July 1867, 'Rodman Guns', *The New York Times*.
36 The Ordnance Select Committee described the 1865 *Hercules* Target as follows: 'The upper half of the target is faced with 9-inches of iron, the lower half with 8-inches, behind both plates is 12-inches of horizontal timber divided by 4 horizontal iron plates, then a skin consisting of two ¾-inch plates; the whole being secured to the ribs which are 10 inches deep filled in between with vertical timber. Behind the ribs are two linings of horizontal timber 18 inches deep, not bolted, but confined by 7-inch iron ribs inside all. Thickness at bottom exclusive of the 7-inch ribs, 47¼-inches, at top 51-¼inches. The bolts are 3-inch; those on the left section are of Major Palliser's design; those on the right are of the ordinary form', from 3 January 1866 (Minute 17,682), *Abstracts of Proceedings of the Ordnance Select Committee, for the Quarter ending 31st December, 1865* (London: George Edward Eyre and William Spottiswoode, 1866), 815, TNA WO 33/16; E. J. Reed, 'On the *Bellerophon, Lord Warden* and *Hercules* Targets' (22 March 1866), in *Transactions of the Institution of Naval Architects*, Vol. VII (London: 1866), 13-27. Reed noted that in the *Hercules* 'we had to provide for resisting the shot of 20-ton guns', and that the shots fired by the Armstrong 600-pounder were with 100lb. charges—penetrating the target only when two successive shots hit in the same location.

10

'Making our experiments with scrupulous care, and wasting nothing on methods which cannot succeed'

But any lead the Americans might have still had against the British in 1867, in terms of weight of guns afloat and thickness of armour, was already being lost. The *Report of the Secretary of the Navy* for that year estimated a budget of $47.3 million for the fiscal year ending 30 June 1869, with some $65 million 'returned to the treasury'; 'evidence that the business of the department has been conducted with economy'. There were now only fifty-six warships mounting 507 guns in squadron service. By contrast, the U.S. Navy commanded $140 million for the fiscal year ending 30 June 1865, Welles reporting in early December 1865 that at the beginning of the year there had been 471 men-of-war in the various blockading squadrons with 2,455 guns.[1] The United States in the meantime was engulfed in political and social turmoil of its own, with President Johnson engaged in an increasingly rancorous duel with Congress. Here, the controlling Republican party was bent on a more punitive Reconstruction of the South while ensuring rights to freed African-Americans (the Civil Rights Act of 1866 was passed only after Congress overrode Johnson's presidential veto of it; the first time in American history). On 5 February 1867, Fox wrote to Welles how the threats of impeachment issued by Congress against President Johnson 'and uncertainties at Washington' were having 'a disastrous effect upon the country…dragon's teeth are sown for the future.'[2] Two weeks later, Fox could only update Ericsson that the *Puritan* would be 'proceeded with during the spring and summer when work is slack at the yard.' Nearly two million dollars had been invested in her already. By May he was still dreaming how a low-freeboard monitor of equal displacement to *Hercules*

---

[1] 2 December 1867, *Report of the Secretary of the Navy*, 40th Congress, 1st Session; 4 December 1865, *Report of the Secretary of the Navy*, 39th Congress, 1st Session. Welles reported a peak strength of 671 warships (including 71 ironclads of various descriptions mounting 275 guns) comprising the Union Navy in December 1864; 5 December 1864, *Report of the Secretary of the Navy*, 38th Congress, 2nd Session.

[2] 5 February 1867, Fox to Welles, Welles Papers, Library of Congress.

or *Monarch* (pushing 9,000-tons) would float 25-inches of side armour and a turret 'with two XXX-inch guns'.[3] But Ericsson had to reply he'd 'not received any distinct instructions from the Department about the completion of the *Puritan*' in either a private or government dockyard (and which he estimated would require at least another $50,000 of 'raw materials' in either case), and 'such are the demands of our workmen that if you offered $500,000 to complete the ship ready for service with the XX-inch guns I would not dare to accept your offer.' When Fox pressed him for a proposal which he could take to Welles, in finishing 'the most formidable vessel in the world', Ericsson responded that the government should be able to complete the work in its own yard for $250,000. In order to 'inspire due respect abroad' the (15-inch thick) turret should also be completed with solid wide slabs of armour 'between the two plate shells'.[4]

In the end nothing was done—and no one was really 'laughing' at John Bull. The momentum of the frenzied, no holds barred-mobilisation of the Civil War was long gone, and the primacy which the Union Navy enjoyed following the Battle of Hampton Roads and the crash ironclad-building programmes of 1862-1863 was plainly being outdone. The *Hercules* would defeat the 15-inch gun, and while the 20-inch gun would likely defeat the *Hercules*, Uncle Sam by 1868 had no other aces up his sleeve. Instead of buying newer weapons programmes in 1867, America bought Alaska from Russia—over half a million square miles of new territory on the Pacific for $7.2 million.[5] Even the concerns since 1861 of French violation of the Monroe Doctrine (in Mexico) had by then disappeared. Napoleon III bent to U.S. pressure immediately following the Union victory in 1865 and withdrew his forces the following year—leaving Emperor Maximilian I to his fate (executed by Mexican nationals on 19 June 1867). The ominous threat of foreign intervention no more than a distant memory,

---

3   20 February and 1 May 1867, Fox to Ericsson, Ericsson Papers, Library of Congress.
4   23 May 1867, Ericsson to Fox, Ericsson Papers, Philadelphia, Box 11; 25 May 1867, Fox to Ericsson, Ericsson Papers, Library of Congress; 31 May 1867, Ericsson to Fox, Ericsson papers, Philadelphia, Box 11. Laid down in 1862 and launched in 1864 as a double-turreted '*Dictator*', *Puritan* was longer at 340-feet but she was never completed. Delays were due in part to the debate over whether to scrap the second turret in favour of one armed with the new 20-inch guns (which Ericsson preferred, and Fox eventually relented to). *Puritan* then had a single 15-inch thick turret (24-feet in diameter, housing two shortened 20-inch guns) and 6-inch side armour similar to that of USS *Dictator*. Ericsson estimated a coal-carrying capacity of 900 tons, and there is some suggestion that with a single turret deck plating was increased to three-inches; see for example 10 August 1863, Ericsson to Fox, Fox Papers, New York, Box 6, and 14 February 1865, Gregory to Fox, Fox Papers, New York, Box 10.
5   'It could not, from its intrinsic value, be worth anything to anybody', commented the London *Times* on 9 April 1867. But as opposed to the fairly disinterested Russian occupiers, Americans would now 'represent an energetic, pushing race, indefatigable in colonizing, greedy of territory, and conscious of a great political mission', likely placing British interests in the Pacific at risk. See also Glyndon G. Van Deusen, *William Henry Seward* (New York: Oxford University Press, 1967), 537-49.

America had not laid down in a new ironclad for years, and no one bothered to offer new designs for one. This contrasted sharply with the steady ironclad shipbuilding trajectories of Britain and France throughout the 1860s and beyond. 'The British *Army and Navy Gazette* makes some sarcastic comments on the contrast between the increase in clamor, by a part of the American Press, "for prompt reparation from England," and the steady decrease in the fighting condition of our navy', brooded *The New York Times* in January 1868. '"It is remarkable," says the paper just quoted, "that the American do not build more monitors ..." The prestige of America is admitted; but a good and efficient navy in existence is a great help to diplomacy.'[6]

Milne had already complained to Pakington of the Conservative government's decision to reject the Admiralty's calls for newer, more powerful armoured-frigates. More investment was needed and even then would be 'only sufficient to place the Navy on an equality with France and required for the defence of the country.' Risking national security as such would be surely prove politically inexpedient, when the balance of power-numbers came up again in Parliament.[7] Yet in October 1866, Disraeli proved immune to Pakington's pressures, stating that the proposal 'of a second supplemental estimate is so highly irregular, that it can only be justified by an emergency.' Money was tight, and in terms of first-class ironclads, the Royal Navy's position was already 'more than respectable'.[8] Since then, Derby and Disraeli had indeed been preoccupied with a Tory version of a Second Reform Act, somewhat tentatively proposed in February 1867, but still considered outrageous enough that Jonathan Peel resigned as Secretary of State for War, with Pakington taking up his Cabinet post in March and Henry Lowry-Corry replacing him in turn as First Lord of the Admiralty. With popular demonstrations increasing across Britain throughout the spring and summer, added provisions to the Bill now expanded the British electorate far more than even Gladstone had thought reasonable and Bright had ever dared.[9] In such times of uncertainty, post-Palmerston, the inviolability of Britain as 'Mistress of the Seas' needed affirmation more than ever; a symbolic eye of calm in the hurricane.

By 26 July Robinson and Reed felt ready to present the Board with plans for a seagoing mastless turret-ship of 5,947-ton displacement, 280-feet long, with a hull below water identical to that of the recent *Audacious-* (or *Invincible*) class approved for foreign stations. This was, they felt, the only way to maximise the power of guns and armour to meet potential threats at home and abroad. Robinson also suggested that aside from the ongoing debate between guns and armour, or turret and

6   21 January 1868, 'The Navy and the National [*Alabama*] Claims', *The New York Times*.
7   23 July 1866 (though labelled '1867'), Milne to Pakington, Milne Papers, Greenwich, MLN 165/10.
8   30 October 1866, Disraeli to Pakington, in Pharand *et al, Benjamin Disraeli Letters Volume Nine 1865-1867,* 194-5.
9   See for example, Maurice Cowling, *1867—Disraeli, Gladstone and Revolution: The Passing of the Second Reform Bill* (Cambridge: Cambridge University Press, 1967).

broadside-armaments for ships, in the ongoing question of 'ships vs. forts', mastless monitors were Britain's best chance for success in helping to defend or assault the latter. Yet even raising the turret gun deck to ten feet out of water (and at least retaining all-round fire), might still make for a wet vessel, warned the Controller. 'In all Turret-ships, designed for seagoing Cruizers this dilemma appears unavoidable.' But he left such questions to be decided by the Board members, noting finally that 'the design produced is probably as good as can be made.' This was consciously done, Reed also admitted, as an alternative to the impending designs for new ironclads from private shipbuilders called for by the Admiralty earlier that spring.[10] Those started to come in the very next day, and by 7 September the Chief Constructor had carefully inspected them all and submitted his report for the Controller, who forwarded this with his own analysis three days later to the Board for their decision. Of all the proposals from leading British firms including Thames, Samuda, Palmer and Millwall, Reed thought only the Lairds 3,764-ton turret-ship—a second-class though improved *Captain*—worthy of serious consideration. This featured fore and aft pivot 7-ton guns protected in a large forecastle and poop, all connected by a bridge 23-feet wide over the two turrets mounting 600-pounders. But Reed's team calculated the vessel, though very similar in dimensions to his *Invincible*, would likely be heavier by 271 tons (and therefore deeper, if even by '3 inches') than called for. 'With the same power,' he added, 'the speed of this ship would be less than *Invincible's*', though he could not specify by how much. Likewise, while the turret guns would be ten-feet out of water, the deck height out of water was given as seven-feet six-inches, so Reed anticipated 'even in moderate seas would no doubt be completely swamped.'[11]

But the problem with these evaluations was obvious: could Reed be expected to 'impartially' judge rival ironclad designs? 'I think it unfortunate that my original proposal to refer these competitive designs to an independent committee of scientific gentlemen, who would not be suspected of partiality could not be carried out', minuted Corry on 17 September. 'For, whatever confidence the Admiralty may justly place in their professional advisors, it can hardly be expected that the Public can participate in it. The opinion of a rival is seldom considered to be conclusive, and in the whole of the remarks in the accompanying papers the *Invincible* and the Turret design of July are set up as the standard of comparison.' Still, he had to acknowledge that both the tone and content of both the Chief Constructor's and the Controller's remarks seemed impartial enough, 'and that their only object is the production of the best possible ship for the Navy'. Whether the faults they had identified could not be communicated back to the various builders for corrections, was another matter. He agreed, moreover, that until the sail-and-turret *Monarch* and *Captain* were fully tried at sea that it would be imprudent to contract for another—as a cruiser—and 'if not applicable for foreign

---

10   26 July 1867, Robinson to Board, TNA ADM 1/6018, with Reed's enclosed letter to Robinson dated 25 July 1867.
11   10 October 1867, Robinson to Board, TNA ADM 1/6013.

stations, there can be no doubt but that they would be formidable adjuncts to the Channel Fleet—the fleet on which we depend for national defence and which in former wars it has been necessary to maintain at least ⅓ of the whole naval force of the Country. I should not therefore hesitate to add a third turret-ship to the two now building—such ships would at least be thoroughly serviceable for the Channel and into the Mediterranean.' Milne agreed with Robinson's critique that by adding a forecastle and poop Lairds had again sacrificed the innate advantage of any 'pure' turret-ship, its all-round arc of fire. Dacres also thought that a seagoing turret-ship was a contradiction of terms. The Board should wait until the *Captain* had been tried. 'As yet I have had no reason to alter my opinion that a Broadside ship carrying guns of the largest calibre that can be trained and worked in a port of moderate size will best fulfil all the conditions of a Man of War…for we are not strong enough in Iron Clads to build ships that are only fit for half the service we may require of them.' The original intention of appealing to private industry for ironclad designs was to see what British entrepreneurs could come up with if indeed given a full, fair chance; 'that we might find some great advantage, or perhaps startling novelties.' None of these designs offered that, at least compared with those already prepared by the Controller's Department. Yet while their criticisms 'seemed eminently fair', noted Dalrymple-Hay, 'the Admiralty in making it the judge of the seven competing designs must have intended to exclude it from the public competition'. Therefore, if the Lairds submission was considered best, then that firm should at least be invited to build 'a broadside ship of the *Invincible* class'. Pressing ahead with a large breastwork-monitor instead was considered too radical and too risky—at least for now—and the ability to destroy forts was a low priority for a peace-time navy, just as it was the army's burden, in turn, to make Britain's coastal and imperial forts impregnable against the latest heavy ordnance.[12]

12 10 October 1867, Robinson to Board, TNA ADM 1/6013; Corry's two enclosed minutes dated 17 and 21 September 1867; Milne's 15 September; and the enclosed 'September 1867' by Dacres is undated. See the very interesting collation made by the War Office in March 1918, 'A Summary of the policy and work of coast fortification in Great Britain during the past 60 years', TNA WO 32/5528; contemporary reports around this time include, for example, *Parliamentary Paper, Malta—Papers relating to the Proposed New Dock in the French Creek; and to the Extension of the Great Harbour* (1865); 'Memorandum with reference to Experiments on Granite Casemates with Iron Embrazures at Shoeburyness, May 18th 1865', in Somerset Papers, Devon, Box 20, PPP 7-11; 24 June 1868, 'Experiments at Shoeburyness on Iron fronted casemates and shields for Fortifications', TNA ADM 1/6083; William Jervois, 'Coast Defences, and the Application of Iron to Fortification', *Journal of the Royal United Service Institution*, Vol. 12 (1869), 548-69; 5 May 1869, *Memorandum upon the Development of Iron Shields during the last ten years, and the present Position of the Question with reference to supplying the Iron Shields for our Fortifications*, signed Wm. F. Drummond Jervois, TNA WO 33/20; and a collection of 1869 newspaper clippings on coastal fortifications in both Britain and the U.S., TNA PRO 30/40, Papers of Major General Sir John Charles Ardagh (fortifications engineer).

On 3 December 1867, Robinson submitted another memo on 'New ships required to be built'. If the Board's directives from that August were to be taken in hand, with some 17 ironclads 'constantly in commission' then 'we must have 34 afloat, and in addition, if 3 are to be in Reserve we must maintain 37 afloat.' This assumed that small ironclads whether broadside (like *Research* and *Enterprise*) or turret (*Wivern* and *Scorpion*) were not to be included in this main force, leaving only twenty-two ironclads afloat and eight of those were currently refitting. Eight more of various types were on order—including four of Reed's new central-battery ironclads of the second-class (*Audacious, Invincible, Vanguard* and *Iron Duke*)—but none of these would be ready for at least another year. There was also a host of unarmoured wooden corvettes, sloops and gun vessels required, as well as thirty-six new gunboats if '51' were to be constantly in commission (102 total). As for completing the work in the dockyards, the Controller thought that 'if even no more of our ships wore out or were lost, or had to be replaced from any cause, it would take 4 years and 9 months from the 1st of next April to complete this Programme, allowing the same number of Artificers to work at new ships as have been employed during the current financial year.' Thus, private firms would have to be called upon, even to help complete the ironclads.[13] The Board attempted to clarify its position in a memo of 18 December, with Robinson confirming on the 27th that the dockyards could build one of the first-class ironclads and one of the third-class ('Rams') which given its novel design should be done under direct government control and not by a commercial shipbuilder. But as the First Lord complained to Milne on 28 December, it was clear that now was not the time to cut costs any further, if Britain was 'to maintain her position of having a Navy superior to that of any other European Power.' Even if everything in the most recent memos were granted, 'it would provide for a relative superiority very far less than that, until the introduction of armour clads, it was considered imperative that we should maintain.' An economic slump combined with the costs of the punitive expedition to Abyssinia (which Disraeli proved more than willing to undertake), would, however materially influence the Cabinet in determining the amount to be allotted to the ordinary services for the coming year.' Yet while it was undeniable that the various foreign stations needed new reliefs in the form of unarmoured wooden vessels, Corry thought that 'above all things it is necessary in the present most alarming condition of our armour clad Navy, in comparison with that of France and the aggregate of the other European Navies, to appropriate every farthing.'[14]

* * *

---

13 3 December 1867, Robinson to Board, TNA ADM 1/6020.
14 27 December 1867, Robinson to Board, TNA ADM 1/6020; 28 December 1867, Corry to Milne, Milne Papers, Greenwich, MLN 165/11.

On 10 February 1868 Reed's 8,600-ton architype, HMS *Hercules*, was finally launched at Chatham dockyard. As with the smaller *Penelope* (launched eight months earlier), experimental recessed gunports on the four quarters of her central armoured casemate were to further reduce any dead-angles which an enemy's fire could exploit.[15] And her eight 10-inch 18-ton rifled muzzle-loaders were protected by nine-inch side armour-plating. The equally large sail-and-turret *Monarch* was set to launch in May, though *Captain* was still a year away from completion. But the British press at least was far from satisfied with these developments. 'There never was a time when the Board of Admiralty stood more in need than they do at the present moment both of wisdom in council and energy in administration', declared *The Times* four days later. 'There never was a time during the last 20 years when the ruling powers at Whitehall were less in favour both with the naval profession and with the general public, or when the public at large were, from various causes, more enlightened and alive to the faults and defaults of Admiralty administration.' The main issue at stake, of course, was in the shape of Britain's ironclad fleet. Aside from charges of endemic dockyard inefficiency and waste, it was disgraceful that foreign stations consisted of small (and wooden) ships which had to 'cut and run' if a big ship (iron-clad) challenged them. Better to adopt the 'flying squadron'-strategy advanced by Childers and reduce the standing naval commitment to foreign stations—if not the number of foreign stations themselves. Just as ironclads had been increasing their strength by consolidating their offensive and defensive powers more and more, so should the British Empire. With monitors building to permanently guard key strategic points in India and Australia (and largely paid for by colonies themselves), 'we shall be freer to move our squadrons from place to place as the emergency calls.' Unless the Admiralty could prove itself capable of both reducing costs—especially in terms of numbers of obsolete ships and surplus sailors—and improve defence with a more resourceful grand strategy then a new administration was necessary. The Board indeed consulted with the Foreign Office about the 'possibility of making reductions of the Naval force employed on some of the Foreign Stations'. Lord Stanley, in consultation with Commodore Geoffrey Hornby, thought the squadron on the west coast of Africa could be trimmed and saw no reason adding to the one operating in the north Pacific.[16]

Robinson, however, was chafing at the motions by Laird in the Commons to produce all the correspondence on the Channel Squadron's reports, which he found 'extremely painful'. He must be allowed to edit the reports by adding his own annotations, otherwise 'the Department is unfairly treated, and the public is misled.' Yet by doing so he would also reveal (at his hands) 'the incompetence of an Officer in a high position,

---

15 Parkes credits Nathanial Barnaby (husband to Reed's sister and acting as Reed's chief of staff) with many of the innovations in *Penelope* and then *Hercules*; *British Battleships*, 115-17.
16 14 February 1868, *The Times*; 20 February 1868, Foreign Office to Admiralty, TNA ADM 1/6072.

and thus Officers in the public service are put into a most disagreeable and unnecessary antagonism to each other.' All reports by ironclad squadron officers should now be scrutinised by the Controller (and the Chief Constructor) first, then their analysis as well as the reports be 'digested' by the Board before Parliament became involved. Such a 'careful analysis of the recorded facts' was surely preferable than the 'crude opinions of a man perhaps quite new to the subject, combated by another who may not be impartial'—on the issue of which armoured ships were best for the Royal Navy. Of course this meant that Robinson and Reed expected their views to prevail; they only wanted the Board's official backing and approval of them versus anyone, naval officers or otherwise, who might disagree.[17] On the other hand, Robinson complained to Milne of the recent Parliamentary Select Committee headed by Liberal industrial tycoon Charles Seely (MP for Lincoln) to examine dockyard practices and Admiralty accounts. 'It appears as if everything that has been done at the Admiralty for the last six years will be the subject of their enquiry. It completely paralyses my department.'[18] By the end of May the record of testimony from witnesses was so damning to the present and previous administrations that the Controller advised the Admiralty to 'obtain the assistance of a well-qualified barrister to watch the proceedings on the part of the Admiralty.' At stake was the whole issue of the mid-Victorian public's ability to question the practices of professional naval administrators—just as they, in turn, questioned the views of professional naval officers.[19]

This was exemplified the next day, 28 May, when the Controller objected to the further suggestion by Admiral Halsted for an independent committee of naval officers and architects 'to examine and report on his system of combined turrets and broadside navies'. He had previously advised the admiral to supply his office with more detailed plans 'which could then be subjected to a thorough investigation of their properties', by Reed and Robinson, but as Halsted had refused to submit anything which would allow 'any professional person to judge of the qualities of the proposed warships', the Controller could not see the point of wasting everyone's time (and the Navy's budget)

---

17   21 February 1868, Robinson to Board, TNA ADM 116/7. Robinson noted the same day that Admiral Warden's Channel Squadron reports were 'incomplete': 'I notice these circumstances because to come to a conclusion as to the comparative merits of different types of ships with different engines, armaments and armour plating; systematic, well considered, and searching trials are required, in which every circumstance that has any bearing upon a result, should be carefully recorded and weighed.' Particularly objectionable, he continued, were Warden's comments that the *Achilles* was a 'finer' ironclad than Reed's converted *Lord Warden* or *Bellerophon*, 21 and 27 February 1868, Robinson to Board, TNA ADM 116/7.
18   6 April 1868, Robinson to Milne, Milne Papers, Greenwich, MLN 165/11. The Controller was eager to prove that ironclads built in government dockyards were more cost-effective than those built in private yards which were subject to inflationary wages and profit margins; see for example 26 May 1868, Robinson to Board, TNA ADM 1/6080.
19   27 May 1868, Robinson to Board, TNA ADM 1/6080.

with a committee. But what was implicit here was just how much the admiral did not trust the Controller or his officers to offer impartial advice, next to other officers and architects. It wasn't about professionals and non-professionals as how professionals had become politicised by their own views as a result of the ironclad revolution: more people everywhere were becoming more critical, defensive, uncompromising, and paranoid; all within the wider context of political and social instability. The Board once again took Robinson's adroit advice, and informed Halsted there would be no committee.[20] Yet in one sense this only deferred the problem and made more enemies of the Controller's Department than friends. When the influential Ordnance Select Committee requested later that summer 'detailed information in regard to Armour and Equipment of ships for the Navy recently built or in course of construction and of ships to be in future laid down, in order to enable them to deal more efficiently with questions frequently before them…also to give authority to comparisons drawn between different structures', Robinson likewise thought this 'very undesirable'. Such information should not be given to any organisation over which the Admiralty—meaning himself—'have so little control…and I submit that the chances of these designs being improperly used would be very considerable if such information as is here asked for were so freely given.' Even in response to Parliamentary inquiry, or 'Mr. Laird's Return' as Reed derisively referred to it, the disclosure of any information of ironclads built or building by the Admiralty to his department's designs was now portrayed by the Chief Constructor as a threat not just to the reputation of the Board of Admiralty and the Navy but to the security of the British nation itself, since 'the publication of such information, brought down to the latest date, would be most objectionable and injurious to the State in a high degree in the event of war, especially at a period like the present when peculiarities of armament, if not made generally known, would give so skilful and able officers immense advantages in an engagement.'[21] Here the interests and safety of the State and Reed were one.

Yet long before this it had become clear to Reed that his views about ironclads were being increasingly more, not less challenged with each passing year; the wolves were closing in. Even as more central-battery ironclads were successfully launched and the Admiralty persuaded to place still more under construction, it was obvious that this hardly pacified rather than antagonised Reed and Robinson's opponents. At the same time, the central tenets of turret over broadside-based armaments were being more, not less, confirmed validated within the context of the 'guns vs. armour' race. Each new heavier and more powerful Armstrong gun (an incredible 35-ton gun was already being contemplated beyond even the experimental 25-ton guns for *Monarch*

---

20 28 May 1868, Robinson to Board, TNA ADM 1/6080. On 25 February, Stanley announced in the Commons that the Earl of Derby was resigning due to serious health concerns, with Disraeli becoming Prime Minister two days later.
21 17 August 1868, Robinson to Board, TNA ADM 1/6073; 11 September 1868, Reed to Robinson, TNA ADM 1/6081.

and *Captain*) threatened to finally make fixed-ports obsolete—and ruin the reputation of those who clung to them. Perhaps Reed recognised that gracefully disengaging from the one system, after all that had been said and done, to then successfully dominate the other (and against the same opponents, especially Coles) would be impossible. No one's authority in the current anti-establishment climate could survive such a contradiction, politically or professionally. Hence his paper delivered at the Institution of Naval Architects on 4 April—'On the Stability of Monitors Under Canvas'—did not go down especially well, since he also used it to promote his own double-turreted, mastless breastwork-monitor building for the defence of Melbourne. Critics like Halsted who had advocated cutting down wooden line-of-battle ships to low-freeboard turret platforms only saw someone who was known to have made mistakes in his own ships as well as errors in calculation. 'Figures are about as easily manipulated as the English language is.'[22]

Not long after this, Reed threatened to leave his post. As recounted by Childers in Parliament in 1872, the ostensible reasons for this were not about quarrels over ironclad designs but money. At the end of 1866 the Chief Constructor applied for an increase of pay and also some form of gratuity in recognition of his bracket plate shipbuilding innovations which had made British ironclads more cost-effective. This included his working 'day and night' coming up with the plans for the *Enterprise* before he was actually salaried as Chief Constructor. Pakington and the Board told Reed on 7 February 1867 that his petition would receive due consideration—just before Corry became the new First Lord of the Admiralty. A year had gone by. Reed then informed Robinson that he'd had enough. To Milne he explained on 20 April 1868 that he would indeed 'act as if I were to remain here, in order to prevent embarrassment.' It was, however, now up to the Controller to determine the best time for him to be quietly replaced, and as Robinson was himself currently 'absorbed in the Account business', he did not want to press him. 'The Admiralty have, in my humble opinion, made a grave mistake in not giving me proper recognition and support', he added. 'It is of supreme importance in these times that the principal executive and professional officer should be strengthened as much as possible; for his weakness, or apparent weakness, weakens the Government in a corresponding degree.' Milne implored him not to submit his letter of resignation just yet, having always 'maintained a high opinion of your ability and zeal'.[23] But others had their doubts. Grieving for his wife at the end of March, the First Lord of the Admiralty began to wonder how the more powerful men like Reed and Robinson became the more likely they were going to drag the government down with them, not help prop it up. He didn't appreciate

---

22 4 April 1868, E. J. Reed, 'On the Stability of Monitors Under Canvas', *Transactions of the Institution of Naval Architects*, Vol. IX (London: 1868), 198-217.
23 18 March 1872, 'Admiralty Organization—Navy Estimates—Resolution', *Hansard*, Vol. 210, 130-213; 20 April 1868, Reed to Milne and 20 April 1868, Milne to Reed, Milne Papers, Greenwich, MLN 165/11.

Reed's sense of 'good taste and judgment' in forcing him to consider such issues, Corry wrote to Milne, and he would not be able to review the case at any rate until his return to London. Given all the recourse to public talks, journals and newspapers, he wasn't sure if it was really up to the heads of the department 'fighting his battles…for him.' Reed was a specimen of a breed of 'self-seeking', 'pushing gentlemen'.[24]

The same went for Robinson. With Gladstone and his supporters bearing down in an imminent general election, Corry had to stress how politically vital it was just then to both the Government and the Admiralty that naval expenses be kept 'within the Votes…and this must be done at all hazards <u>even at the loss of efficiency</u>'. Any extras beyond the amount granted by the Treasury would be 'an intolerable breach of faith'. Yet as he confided to the First Naval Lord in early October, 'You cannot conceive what difficulty I had in getting statistics in a clear and intelligible form for my estimate speech'—all of which had to come from the Controller's Department. He had always thought it 'a great mistake' of the Duke of Somerset to yield so much to Robinson, 'for he has either too much power or not enough—and the latter is what he himself thinks.'[25] This explained much of what had happened with Coles over the years, for even that August, when he asked the Controller's department to furnish him with details of Scott's gun carriages and slides to be fitted into the turrets of HMS *Monarch*, the Controller was chary. The fact that Coles needed them now made it clear 'that he is wanting of something which he cannot himself supply', he wrote to the Board, suggesting the turret-ship advocate's incompetence—even though the Navy needed Scott's help as well, who in turn was informed by the American carriages, slides and compressors. But Robinson went much further in noting that (apart from obviously trying to furnish the turrets for HMS *Captain*) Coles was known to be working with Napier and Lairds in designing turret-ships for foreign governments as well. Supplying him with such plans might only serve to arm Britain's enemies—yet four months earlier, Thames Ironworks shipyard had launched the *Konig Wilhelm* for the Prussian Navy, a 9,600-ton seagoing central-battery ironclad designed by Reed to be even more powerful than the *Hercules*.[26] When Robinson later pressed to be a made a full Member of the Board (yet still as Controller), with 'full and independent

---

24 Undated, possibly early April 1868 and 28 August 1868, Corry to Milne, Milne Papers, Greenwich, MLN 165/2. Lady Harriet Anne Ashley-Cooper died 25 March 1868.
25 4 October 1868, Corry to Milne, Milne Papers, Greenwich, MLN 165/2.
26 22 August 1868, Robinson to Board, TNA ADM 1/6081, with enclosed letter from Coles to Lennox dated 19 August 1868. Both Milne and Dacres agreed with Robinson not to supply the plans and also with Romaine's suggestion that Coles be asked to confirm if he was engaged to design turret-ships for foreign powers, and that if he answered affirmatively that his pay be stopped. The *Konig Wilhelm* was originally contracted for the Ottoman Government in 1865 (and which was later unable to pay for the vessel), with Derby's Cabinet rejecting the asking price from Thames, even though it was known that Prussia was highly interested. 'How can we avert the humiliation of allowing ['the *Fatikh*'] to go to Prussia, because England cannot afford to buy her!' Pakington wailed to Milne on 25 October 1866; Milne Papers, Greenwich, MLN 165/10.

power and authority over the Dockyards and Ships', Milne was disquieted. He understood that such a measure might make close management of the dockyards more practicable—and thereby satisfy the urge for greater centralisation of administrative power as a means of insuring greater cost-effectiveness. But surely the Controller had power over the dockyards already, Milne noted, while as Senior Naval Lord, he confessed he had 'no power or authority to order any repairs or refit or expenditure except by reference to the Controller.' They had already differed on matters of naval etiquette, for example, and if Robinson was given supreme power it was 'very evident that the Senior Naval Lord and Controller could never act together. In fact, Admiral Robinson wishes to place the Controller of the Navy in a position of greater power and Authority than the Board of Admiralty.' The long-serving Admiralty ('Second') Secretary, Romaine, was in agreement here, and he had once written a confidential memo to Somerset to that effect. The Controller must be subservient to the Board, or there was no 'Board'. Instead, Robinson wanted 'to be its Master'. He had occupied a position of singular power for so long that he could not now be expected to work well with others, as equals, being extremely adept at withholding and manipulating information as it suited him, in the name of the 'Navy'. Indeed, Romaine thought Robinson was 'not fitted by temper to take his place at the Board, nor do I see how he could sit there and give the orders and then go and execute them':

> He would in fact be First Lord and First Sea Lord if he is to give orders on important matters in the Dockyard of his own sole authority. The Reports of the Superintendents would naturally only be made to the man who exercised the real authority and the Board would know only as much as he chose to tell them. He is of a very imperious nature and cannot bear the least interference with his views, but the way that he ventures to treat the Board, shews the way in which he would treat the Dockyard Authorities if he had uncontrolled power. The Duke tried him at the Board for a few times, as a regular part of the day's Board meeting. The first day he flatly contradicted Grey—and after a few trials the curtain came to an end. I can fancy nothing more mischievous and unworkable than Robinson at the Board, more powerful than all his colleagues.[27]

It was precisely in this respect that in July 1868 Seely pushed the House of Commons (Committee of Supply) for a 'Scientific Inquiry…to take into consideration the leading characteristics that should be adopted in the future Construction of the Vessels of the Navy', with John Laird adding that 'the question was whether they were to continue building broadside-ships, or go on with the construction of turret-vessels.' Replying

---

27 Undated memos by Milne and Romaine, possibly early December 1868 (Robinson indeed being appointed Third Naval Lord 18 December, with the fall of Disraeli's Government—replaced by Gladstone—and with a new Board of Admiralty headed by Hugh Childers), Milne Papers, Greenwich, MLN 165/11.

on behalf of the Admiralty, Lord Henry Lennox acknowledged that there were 'no plans for turret-ships which they could conscientiously recommend for adoption during the present year.' But the French had not bothered with any either. The First Lord was enthusiastic for having turret vessels for home defence (though these would only cost the nation more than already asked for). The problem remained, however—'namely, that we are not in possession of such information and such a model as would warrant us in building [seagoing] turret-ships instead of broadsides.' Until the *Monarch* and *Captain* were tried at sea over the next two years, the Royal Navy would simply go on building more broadside-ironclads to keep pace with France and other powers. Hugh Childers declared his support of the Board and more specifically to Robinson and Reed; he would vote against the Resolution for any committee which would 'have the effect of divesting the Board of Admiralty of a considerable amount of responsibility, and of casting a reflection upon the ability of eminent men who at present advised the Board.'[28]

Indeed, in order to soothe the Chief Constructor, who had by then announced that he had become a Parliamentary candidate for the borough of Pembroke, Milne assured him on 1 August that not only had Corry and the Board had approved his claims for monetary compensation—in the tune of £5,000 (or nearly £570,000 today)—but that the First Lord had submitted his name 'for the C.B' (Companion of the Bath).[29] When Reed then gave up his candidature, the press smelled a story. 'It is owing to his influence that the present Board have, in spite of their convictions, preserved in the building of broadsides as weak and unsteady as themselves...Shall we be wrong if we ascribe his resignation to a proposal of Mr. Reed's superiors to substitute a turret vessel for one of his broadside ships,' speculated *The Times* on 5 August, 'and his remaining in office to their reversal of the too obnoxious design?' The *Globe* thought 'the real case is extremely simple—it is not Coles versus Reed or Reed versus Coles; the issue raised is in no sense one of personal merit, much less is it a feud of professional jealousy.' If *The Times* was right, and the Chief Constructor wanted to exact his revenge in Parliament, 'so much the worse for Mr. Reed. The pet was puerile, the revenge which he proposed to himself perfectly ridiculous.' But the paper was not convinced that the 'turret vs. broadside'-debate had resolved itself either way, especially since 'Captain

---

28 13 July 1868, 'Resolution', *Hansard*, Vol. 1903, 1111-40. Not long after, Corry affirmed his belief to Milne that both the sail-and-turret-ships were probably failures inasmuch as flying decks between turrets would 'never stand the explosion' yet without them 'how is a low-freeboard turret-ship to be worked?' Relegating them to coast defence would then hardly justify their existence, 'drawing too much water and costing double what a coast defence ship ought to cost.' But he was also 'quite satisfied' with Britain's ironclad force 'relative to the actual strength of other Navies—the French excepted'; 23 and 27 July 1868, Corry to Milne, Milne Papers, Greenwich, MLN 165/2.

29 1 August 1868, Milne to Reed, Milne Papers, Greenwich, MLN 165/11. The Board wrote to the Treasury on 5 August 1868, making its request.

Coles has not submitted to the Board of Admiralty a complete and promising scheme for the production of a safe and good seagoing turret-ship.'[30]

* * *

Reed then submitted his essay, two weeks later, on *Seagoing Turret-ships and Lowness of Freeboard*, and this was certainly intended to foil the Turret-ship party, and further underscore his and Robinson's inimitable authority. As was by now customary, the paper began by flatly denying that the Admiralty had ever been told by them that a 'seagoing turret-ship, with the properties of a cruiser, cannot be built.' Surely the *Monarch* was proof of that, Reed suggested, if not also the *Captain*. But of course, the Chief Constructor and the Controller—if not also Coles—had condemned at least the former vessel since higher freeboard negated the defensive advantages of a true monitor form of ironclad, while the presence of masts and sails interfered with the turret's supposed advantages over fixed (broadside) gunports. As Ericsson had predicted to Bourne, when Reed felt that he was seriously at risk of losing his grip over Britain's ironclad building programme, against mounting criticism in Parliament and the British press, as well as from naval professionals, he proved perfectly willing to jettison the carefully documented and scientific evidence that Bourne had provided him with. Before the Board of Admiralty, Reed now attacked the accounts made in American reports that their monitors had proven seaworthy in the Civil War, eventually weathering gales which drove higher freeboard vessels to port; cherry-picking any recorded faults and ignoring any positive conclusions made by their commanders. In the absence of any negative reports of other (*Passaic*-class) monitors at sea, Reed could only suggest that 'although we have no details of their behaviours, we are bound to conclude that it did not differ much from theirs.' Indeed, he argued, as the original USS *Monitor* sank in a storm at sea, then surely any monitors which followed must also be fundamentally unseaworthy. Even then (and writing of himself in the third person), Reed concluded: 'It is not correct to say that Mr. Reed maintains it is impossible to construct a monitor with two feet of freeboard having stability enough to carry sail. That would be absurd, except when limited by the consideration of keeping with a reasonable breadth to length, and by other considerations.' The danger was in (anyone else) making 'hasty conclusions on the subject'.[31]

---

30   5 August 1868, *The Times*; 5 August 1868, The *Globe*.
31   E. J. Reed, 12 August 1868, *Seagoing Turret-ships and lowness of Freeboard*, 'for the Controller'; in Milne Papers, Greenwich, MLN 148/2; 'Healthiness of Ironclads', in *Report of the Secretary of the Navy, December 4, 1865* (Washington: GPO, 1865); see also Sandra W. Moss, *Edgar Holden, M.D. of Newark, New Jersey: Provincial Physician on a National Stage* (Xlibris, 2014), 92-114; a detailed biography of the surgeon on board the USS *Passaic*. As British shipbuilder Charles Lamport cynically remarked at the Institution of Naval Architects in March 1869, 'it was a misfortune to this Institution,—I am almost inclined to think it a misfortune to the country, that Mr. Reed has such forcible eloquence, such clearness of statement, and the power of making the worse appear the

Despite their sponsorship of the Second Reform Act of 1867, the general election at the end of 1868 resulted in a mass upset for the Conservatives, with the Liberals under Gladstone's leadership sweeping into power for the first time. As Corry had expected, he lost his position as First Lord of the Admiralty and was replaced on 9 December by someone much younger (and in better health): Childers. At only 41 he represented a new wave of leadership indeed, and one of his first major policy decisions was to agree that Robinson as Controller would serve much better as a full Lord of the Admiralty. Before the year was out, directives went forth that Robinson's submissions to the rest of the Board were to be now treated as minutes, along with any submissions from Reed approved by the Controller.[32] Robinson in the meantime had been made a civil Knight Commander of the Bath (7 December). After the Treasury declined the Admiralty's request to compensate Reed, on 28 October 1868, his subsequent appeal to the Board was once again set aside with another change of power.[33] On 24 February 1869 the Chief Constructor pressed the issue with the new Board. Gladstone's Cabinet then suggested on 24 July that rather than receive a full £5,000 gratuity that he should be granted a £500 increase to his personal allowance per year.[34]

Meanwhile, Childers wasted no time in suggesting to Reed that a new turret-ship for the Royal Navy should be worked up; not exceeding 3,000-tons capacity, fast at fourteen-knots, only two guns but perhaps '40 to 45 tons', with enough coal to cross over to Halifax and 'limited sail power': a monitor, or another *Captain*? On 3 February 1869, Reed submitted his analysis, objecting to the tonnage since he had

> better cause…We may with propriety say of Mr. Reed, what was said of our greatest orator—*non tetigit quod non ornavit*—He touches nothing that he does not ornament. But that may be ornamented which is not true and I am afraid that Mr. Reed, with that earnestness which we know carries all clever men and men of genius, in a groove, almost to the extent of absurdity, has, in this instance, been ornamenting that which will not bear strict examination as a correct nautical theory upon which it would be safe to rely', E. J. Reed, 'On Long and Shot Iron-Clads', *Transactions of the Institution of Naval Architects*, Vol. X (London: 1869), 59-91. Nicholas Rodger also noted that in debate, Reed was 'fluent, powerful, and unscrupulous…a man to whom enmity and argument were the breath of life', 'The Design of the *Inconstant*', 13-14.

32   23 December 1868 memo, TNA ADM 1/6082. Instead of four naval lords and one civil lord there would now be three lords: First Naval Lord, Second Naval Lord (Controller) and the Secretary. Dacres replaced Milne as First Lord; Captain Lord John Hay became Third (or Junior) Lord, with Mr. George Trevelyan the Civil Lord. See also the outline of new duties in 11 February 1869, TNA ADM 1/6105.

33   The Board of Treasury's response, dated 28 October 1868, was to counter-propose that Reed's annual salary be increased from £900 to £1,000 and that 'his Superannuation, when he should retire, should be on the highest scale given to Public Officers', in TNA ADM 1/6019. The Treasury noted that Reed had originally been offered—and accepted—£600 for his time designing the *Enterprise* before he received his salary as Chief Constructor.

34   See TNA ADM 1/6109, with the Board's letter of request to the Treasury dated 27 July 1869.

been arguing for years that high speeds were incompatible with small size (to say nothing of heavy guns and thick armour) for seagoing vessels. All first-rate British ironclads up to that point floated at least 4,000- but more often 6,000-tons. Similarly, it 'would not be possible…to put even a moderate spread of canvas upon a ship of the foregoing dimensions and of the general qualities which this vessel must possess, if the deck were very low, without incurring the risk, exact calculations would probably force me to say the certainty of the ship capsizing in a breeze or gust.' An armoured breastwork covering the funnel uptakes, hatchways, ventilators and so forth would be necessary as well as serve to raise the guns higher out of the water. But by adding all the accoutrements a seagoing vessel required, he warned that the 'invisibility of Monitors' would become 'a mere imagination'. Adding up all the basic weights, Reed's team calculated no less than 1,267-tons for the engines needed to work up at least 4,500 horse-power, boilers, anchors and cables, 62-tons for masts and sails, and 180-tons for guns and ammunition; adding another 896-tons of coals needed to cross to Halifax from Cork. That left little for armour: 4-inches thick on average overall, 5½-inches at best.[35]

Robinson's enclosed comments of the same day could only suggest that Reed's numbers must be right, leaving the Admiralty to consider what kind of ship was needed 'for service with a fleet of the present day.' The Controller's own thinking had also been coalescing in a new direction for some time: naval combat had come down to destroying an enemy with the heaviest guns possible, or by ramming. While he had (somewhat notoriously) declared at the end of 1866 that an ironclad fleet action would only likely be fought in moderate seas, he also now contended that 'No great naval battle will be fought at very high speeds'. Hoisting a large amount of sail for cruising or pursuit over many days only weakened the potential power of a ship's armament itself. 'The great maritime Powers with whom alone we should enter on a contest for life and death would be France and Russia' (presumably both powers allied against Britain), yet their relative lack of overseas interests allowed them to build fleets centred around ironclads which were that much more purpose-built for combat and less for cruising. Thus, French ironclads were mostly barque-rigged and from the beginning, fully-armoured from stem to stern. The Imperial Russian Navy had invested in a host of low-freeboard, mastless monitors on the American pattern, making them masters of their own territorial waters. 'A war with America would be of so different a nature that the navy required for that purpose is altogether a thing apart', thought Robinson, 'but if we have to contend for great national purposes with either France or Russia, the contest must be in European waters; the Channel, Mediterranean, or the Baltic, will be scenes of strifes fearful to contemplate.' In this sort of industrialised, hand-to-hand armoured combat only those with the thickest iron shielding and capable of delivering machine-like crushing blows would survive. Thus, the most important quality of the modern English man-of-war should be defensive power. If French or Russian

---

35   3 February 1869, Robinson to Board; TNA ADM 1/6138.

ironclads carried heavy armour 'so must ours'; an 'irrefutable' position, 'though we may admit that no perfect protection against even the guns carried at sea, can, in all cases, be had.' Victory in any future naval conflict was going to go to the power who concentrated their powers the most. The time had come to invest in improved versions of the newly conceived, mastless breastwork-monitor *Glatton* of 4,900-tons (laid down the previous August and boasting 12-inch iron plating and two 25-ton guns) and the heavily-armoured ram *Hotspur* (with a turret structure mounting a single 25-ton gun rotating between fixed ports by a rotating turntable base), laid down in October 1868 with a projected 4,300-tons. 'I have not thought it necessary to describe the fleet which operates in distant seas', Robinson concluded, 'and which will rarely be called on to fight other actions than the duels which in older times shed the brightest lustre on our flag. Of such ships, iron-clads and others, we have a larger number in proportion than of ships qualified to fight fleet actions, while the reverse is the case both with France and Russia.'[36]

All this, of course, represented a significant change in both British naval strategy and capital ship design by the end of the 1860s. Majestic ironclads like HMS *Warrior* now seemed baroque with their 'showy and attractive qualities of excessive speed and large coal-power', wrote the Controller, next to the sort of burly armoured turret-rams devoid of sails and thickly encrusted with iron plating which he and the Chief Constructor had in mind: the only realistic means of coping with the guns and armour race touched off by the likes of John Ericsson and William Armstrong. Taking his cue, Reed responded to Robinson two days later that with a 4,400-ton capacity, a twelve-knot turreted-ironclad could be had with twelve-inch armour plating, two-inch thick deck, dual turrets each protected by twelve-inch plating and fourteen-inches around the gunports and 'either two 25-ton guns, or one 50-ton gun'—deliberations which now echoed those of Ericsson and Fox seven years earlier, an ocean away. This was, at last, the *Devastation*: the one ironclad of the period which might technologically bridge the strategic and tactical gap created by the *Warrior* and the *Monitor*. As noted by Robinson on 15 February the 'outlines of this design were approved at a discussion between the First Lord of the Admiralty, Vice-Admiral Sir S. Dacres, and Vice-Admiral Robinson, and the Chief Constructor of the Navy.' By November 1869, the full plans were in hand and the 9,100-ton mastless turret-ship laid down at Portsmouth dockyard.[37]

---

36 Ibid. At that time only the Spanish iron-hulled broadside-ironclad *Numancia* had circumnavigated the world, while the French wooden-hulled, armoured-corvette *Belliqueuse* (with 6-inch waterline and 4.7-inch central battery-armour) had also set off to cruise around the world in December 1867, returning to France in May 1869.

37 Ibid. As for the United States, a War Office memo of 28 May 1869 still regarded the ability of Canada to defend itself, along a 1,000-mile frontier, and with a population of 4 million against 30 million Americans with their fully developed resources, as practically hopeless—unless key points were heavily fortified, local militia trained up, and Britain devoted significant military and naval assistance. 'An effective defence of Canada is in

But this milestone in the evolution of the modern British capital ship, as such, was not without cost. It would be two years before the *Devastation* was launched, and following changes made in her design following the *Captain* disaster, she was not ready for sea trials until 1873. By then both Reed and Robinson were long gone from the Admiralty; their influence lost, and their places in history forever linked to the fate of their nemesis, Cowper Coles. Indeed, Reed had done his best in the latter part of 1868 and early 1869 to fortify his reputation with *Our Iron-Clad Ships: Their Qualities, Performances, and Cost* ('with Chapters on Turret-ships, Iron-Clad Rams, & c.'), published at the end of the year. Coming from a Chief Constructor of the Royal Navy, this sort of treatise was unusual. Sir Isaac Watts had not bothered, having been 'Assistant Surveyor of the Navy' (as it was known before 1860) since 1848—the same year that Baldwin Walker became Surveyor—and having overseen much of the Royal Navy's transition from sail- to steam-power, paddle- to screw-propulsion, as well as wood- to iron-construction, and being 66 when Reed replaced him in 1863, at age 33. But this only stemmed from an ignorance of the issues at stake. It was understood by those who cared about them the most that Reed had only 'gone public', in the most comprehensive manner that he could, to pre-empt critics of *his* ironclad ships, obsequiously dedicating the volume to Childers, the current First Lord of the Admiralty. The main concern identified by Reed was twofold: 'clinging to any type of ship, or any feature of naval construction, merely because it is old and accustomed...rejecting things because they are new'—hence his changes from long broadsides to central-battery schemes—and yet 'making our experiments with scrupulous care, and for wasting nothing on methods which *cannot* succeed.'[38] This meant combining low-freeboard turrets ships with full masts and sails. Despite Robinson's recent reassessment of Britain's strategic priorities by sea, Reed was proud of Britain's ironclads as they were up to that point only, thinking that 'if we have made a mistake with reference to the introduction into the British Navy of turret-ships, and especially of monitors, that mistake has consisted in adopting them too rapidly, rather than too slowly.'[39]

Despite noting on 11 August 1869 how Reed was a 'Fortunate Official', having his salary recently increased by £500 to £1700 per annum—and granted the full

---

fact only practicable when naval forces can act in conjunction with the troops on land', noted Colonel William Jervois; 'W.F.D.J.', *Considerations on the Military position of Great Britain with respect to the United States*, TNA WO 33/20. Jervois also thought that the current garrison at Bermuda—2,000 men—'should be doubled.' Halifax was in a much better position thanks to recent fortification work, and 'with proper armaments and the application of torpedoes' could block attacks by sea, but unless Britain commanded the seas in question, a force could be landed to attack the base from the landward side and 'burn the shipping, town, and naval establishment from the eastern side of the harbour.'

38 E. J. Reed, *Our Iron-Clad Ships: Their Qualities, Performances, and Cost, with Chapters on Turret-ships, Iron-Clad Rams, &c.* (London: John Murray, 1869), *vi*, original *emphasis*.
39 Ibid., 242, 254.

£5,000 gratuity after all—then taking a few weeks' leave to Paris ('ill from the result of his close attention to his duties at Whitehall', but presumably also from writing *Our Iron-Clad Ships*), *The Times* was delighted with his book. 'Englishmen are justly proud of their ships, and are, perhaps, prepared to spend more money upon them than on any other national object that could be named'. If nothing else, Reed's work had presented its reader with the fact that some forty-seven ironclads had been built during the previous ten years at a cost of roughly £10 million (while £117 million had been spent on the Navy generally). Childers had indeed defended both his reforms of the Admiralty and the Estimates for 1869-70 on the basis that forty-seven ironclads would constitute Britain's ironclad fleet 'carrying 598 guns, of which eighteen are 25-ton, nineteen are 18-ton, and 111 are 12-ton.' But Corry, now in Opposition, questioned whether the *Devastation*-class was a sound investment. Although he had been 'very soundly abused', it had been his intention in 1868 not to lay down any more ironclads for 1869, certainly no more turret-ships until the *Monarch* and *Captain* had undergone sea trials. 'But whether I was right or not a year or two years ago, the matter is in a very different position now, when we are within two or three months of the time when the *Captain* and the *Monarch* will be tried. I do not care whether those ships fail or succeed—that makes no difference so far as this question is concerned. If they fail, there is an end of the matter for the present; if they succeed, a great number of alterations of different kinds will necessarily suggest themselves for adoption.' The present Board of Admiralty's resort to mastless, twin-screwed breastwork-monitors which would nonetheless draw 26-feet was therefore inexplicable. No mastless ironclad could be expected to act as a cruiser, while the report of a Committee 'which sat on the subject, [was] that no vessel for coast defence ought to draw more than sixteen feet water.' Joseph Samuda joined in to remind the Commons that six months before, the Controller of the Navy had 'prevented turret-ships from being built, when proposed by persons outside that Department', yet now 'proposed to build three turret-ships themselves.' How was it fair that the Admiralty 'refused last year to build a vessel of 3,739 tons with 10 feet of freeboard', yet now agreed to build an even larger turret-ship with far less freeboard? 'It should be remembered that, whatever might be the talent at the Admiralty,' Samuda concluded, 'the amount of talent outside could never be compared with, but must greatly exceed, that of a single individual there.'[40] In

---

40   14 February 1870, *The Times*; 8 March 1869, 'Supply—Considered in Committee', *Hansard*, Vol. 194, 863-932. Childers later defended the Board's decision to build the *Devastation* (and *Thunderer*), as improvements on the *Glatton*, which Corry's administration had sanctioned, and as mastless turret-ships 'not designed to serve as coast defenders, but thorough seagoing vessels, capable of traversing the Atlantic or taking part in an action as efficient fighting ships…Besides, now we had experience with reference to ships more similar to those proposed than the *Captain* and the *Monarch*; and that experience enabled us to see what their faults were and how they could be avoided. Two well-known American Monitors, the *Monadnock* and the *Miantonomoh*, were not entirely satisfactory, but we had been able to see in what respect they were not, and to avoid their

the House of Lords the Duke of Somerset stated that he 'had not the least complaint to make against them, for he believed the Controller to be a very able and energetic man, who gave up his whole time to the interests of the service; while the Chief Constructor was originally appointed by himself, and his great ability and skill had been acknowledged both by the late and the present Government; but he was anxious to learn what had occurred to make them regard as a safe seagoing ship one which a few years ago they declared to be unsafe, or at least so uncomfortable that sailors could not be put into it.' Perhaps he recalled that when news of the original USS *Monitor*'s success against the casemate broadside-ironclad *Virginia* reached London in April 1862, and threw the country into something of a panic, the former First Lord of the Admiralty helped break the tension in Parliament by mocking the Union turret vessel as 'something between a raft and a diving bell.' When he had toured the USS *Miantonomoh* in the summer of 1866, one of the U.S. naval officers when asked about life on board confided that it was 'exceedingly disagreeable, that the crew only lived on air which was pumped in, and that if anything had happened to the engine—an accident did, in fact, once occur—they would all have been stifled.' Was the British Navy any more prepared now to have its sailors 'living in a kind of dungeon—for it was, in fact, a dark dungeon under water which we were contriving'—than the American Navy had been?[41]

---

defects'. Having been consulted by the Board on 24 March, Coles (along with the Earl of Lauderdale, Key and others) had also approved of Reed's plans for a mastless turret-ship; 2 April 1869, 'Supply—Considered in Committee', *Hansard*, Vol. 195, 52-123.

41 8 April 1869, 'Question', Vol. 195, 340-52; 3 April 1862, 'Iron-Plated Ships—Question', *Hansard*, Vol. 166, 430-44.

11

'It is very desirable that we should shew our strength well'

In early 1870 many in Britain were now looking to the alternative model of HMS *Captain* to reassert a more comprehensive sense of British naval supremacy, as the classic wooden three-deckers had for so long before. Robinson was eager to test—and perhaps condemn—the *Captain*, especially in direct comparison with Reed's *Monarch*. *The Evening Standard* had been struck by Reed's wilful use of double-standards in his book when it came to the 'turret vs. broadside'-debate, calling the sail-and-turret *Scorpion* and *Wivern* the Royal Navy's 'weakest' ironclads' while pleading for the deficiencies of his own *Pallas* because she was 'little'. Not only were the turret-ships iron-hulled while Reed's was wooden, but they carried far heavier guns. 'The circumstance that the *Captain* is now afloat in the British sea invests this subject with fresh interest' noted the article, and the 'turret-ship controversy is not to be laid at rest by ill-reports of the American monitors [which Reed quoted heavily].'[1] The Coles sail-and-turret-ship had been launched at the end of March 1869 but was not ready for her first trial commission until the end of April 1870, under the command of Captain High Talbot Burgoyne, son of the famous general and a decorated officer in his own right, including the Victoria Cross during the Crimean War. Here there was never any consideration of the new sail-and-turret-ship, with her unexpected freeboard of over six-feet rather than eight-feet, being inherently unstable and unsafe. Instead, on 31 May 1870 the Controller reported that he had accompanied both ironclads for ten days down to their 'rendezvous off Cape Finisterre' with the rest of the Channel Squadron under the command of Vice-Admiral Sir Thomas Symonds. He also promised to make a subsequent analysis later in the year comparing the sailing turret-ships with the *Hercules* and her veritable sister-ship, HMS *Sultan* (launched that same day); and the results even then might be expected, given all previous comparisons made by his department which came down in favour of broadside armaments in every instance. In terms of their firing, Lieutenant Ernest Rice (assigned from HMS *Duke of Wellington*) reported that while standing on the hurricane deck above the *Captain*'s

---

1   2 February 1870, 'Turrets v. Broadsides', *The Evening Standard*.

turret the concussion from the 12-inch guns was not violent, and indeed 'A full bucket of water stood close by me, from which none was spilt.' Robinson thought the *Captain* could be cleared for action as fast as the *Monarch* with her guns enjoying a greater arc of fire; the latter turret-ship being higher out of water was 'an advantage on the side of the *Captain*.' But quoting Rice's observations, the *Monarch*, with her turret guns being higher out of water, 'decidedly has the advantage', while the *Captain* 'during a double reefed topsail breeze certainly had a great deal of water washing over her main deck, but this would not prevent her fighting the guns.' From these the Controller concluded that 'as a fighting ship only (in fine weather), for the inference would not go further, the *Captain* has a superiority over the *Monarch*, that superiority is obtained, and indeed is occasioned by the inferiority of her powers as cruizing ship, and that the solution of the problem how to combine a turret armament in a seagoing cruizing armour-clad has been better solved in the *Monarch* than in the *Captain*.'[2]

More than this, Robinson thought the various imperfections in arrangements found in the *Monarch* could be corrected, and that an improved ship on this pattern (designed by Reed's department)—though with larger tonnage to provide for even thicker armour plating—would 'give the best possible seagoing cruizing armour-clad ship, armed with heavy guns in turrets that can be put afloat.' Yet he wouldn't apply the same rationale for any future versions of the rival sail-and-turret-ship. Indeed, it was 'not easy to point out in what respect the *Captain* could be improved, and more extended trials are necessary to bring to light defects which at present may not have become apparent.' In other words, Robinson was fairly certain that defects could—and would—be found. In the meantime, he was already willing to pronounce that while the *Monarch* had 'fulfilled in every respect the intentions of the designers', the turret-ship which had been subsequently demanded by Coles 'has not; the former has carried her weights exactly as she was intended to do, the latter has been constructed at least 800 tons too small to do so.' Even if the *Captain*'s original design had been altered to accommodate the extra weights, so that 'many points in the ship would have been improved', the Controller was unwilling to suggest these would be improvements enough—at any rate he had already prohibited any substantial changes when the ship was contracted and under construction. An improved ship was not what his department had been counting upon. He also left out any mention of the main points which Coles had originally stressed as superior to the higher freeboard turret-ship—namely thicker armour (at significantly less displacement, and somewhat less cost overall) and a lower target profile providing for greater tactical efficiency. Nevertheless, Robinson maintained that any 'armour-clad turreted Navy' must now consist of only two types, his department's own types: the *Monarch* on the one hand for long-range cruizing, and the mastless, very low-freeboard *Devastation* (or '*Thunderer*')

---

2 31 May 1870, Robinson to Board, TNA ADM 116/143; Robinson noted the 'greatest roll observed in the *Monarch* on wearing was 18-degrees. The *Captain*'s greatest roll by signal was 18-degrees; the waves being about 25 feet high, and about 90 feet apart', 16.

on the other.[3] Although he made sure to initially commend Coles for his advocacy of turrets for warships in general; 'a great idea of a mind highly practical, inventive, and ingenious', still the overall tone of the Controller's comparative report and its conclusions made it unmistakable that the Royal Navy didn't need Coles; it never did, and it never would. HMS *Captain* may as well have never existed.

Yet in another sense this was all part of the larger, longstanding struggle by Robinson for greater command and control over various national resources (including the private shipbuilding industry), cementing the Royal Navy's reputation in British society as well as his own undisputed authority within the Royal Navy. On 4 July 1870, the Foreign Office forwarded to the Admiralty various reports on the American Navy compiled for the Minister to the U.S., Sir Edward Thornton, by Captain William Ward, the latest British naval attaché in Washington. Here the weights and dimensions of older U.S. sailing vessels was found to be incomplete, and though allowed by Admiral Porter to secure the aid of a Navy Bureau to accurately tabulate the figures for all US. warships, Congress later objected to such a report being provided. Porter then apologised to Ward, since 'we want every dollar we can get from Congress and we can't afford to offend them'. Robinson saw this as a cover-up, noting that some of the privately-built ships turned out to be failures because of 'insufficiency of displacement consequent on insufficient dimensions.' This helped explain why many of the American fast-sloops contracted for did not afterwards meet their trial expectations. 'Exactly the same causes have turned out the *Captain* 900 tons too small to carry the weight put into her,' he pointed out, 'exactly the same causes have led to the rejection by the Admiralty of designs put forward by Mr. Henwood, Captain Halsted, the Thames Company, Messrs. Samuda, Messrs. Laird'—in fact, all of the critics of Robinson and Reed's ironclad programme. 'The builders in the U.S. uncontrolled by a central authority had their own way and failed just as Messrs. Laird failed', the Controller summed up. 'These assertions are easily verified and should be publicly stated in Parliament in justice to the Constructive departments.'[4]

Perhaps what he didn't know, or preferred to not to remind the Board of Admiralty, was that most of the Federal warships of the period were not designed by private shipbuilders but the Bureau of Ship Construction and Repair, headed by John

---

3   Ibid., also TNA ADM 136/3, and Milne Papers, Greenwich, MLN 161/16, with annotations, including corrections to Robinson's assertion that the *Captain* was 'darker and altogether more confined' in her lower deck than in the *Monarch* due to the absence of side-scuttles; 'there are side scuttles on that deck, and the impressions of darkness which my visits to the *Captain* left on my mind must have been derived from some other source.'

4   4 July 1870, Robinson to Board, TNA ADM 1/6169. Two weeks later, Robinson forwarded to the Board a French article on rapidly mobilising maritime populations for war. 'There are some excellent articles in this Review, worthy of the attention of all Naval Officers. I wish we had Naval subjects discussed in any periodical with the calmness, the good sense, and the scientific knowledge of which this number gives proof—especially this article on the stability of Monitors and the Masting of Ironclads—which are admirable', 18 July 1870, Robinson to Board, TNA ADM 1/6169.

Lenthall, and the Bureau of Steam Engineering, controlled by the Engineer-in-Chief of the U.S. Navy, Benjamin Isherwood (both of whom personally and professionally despised Ericsson no less than Reed regarded Coles). In the American experience at least, it wasn't necessarily about the superior competence of government institutions over private companies, or institutions over individuals, but about rival professionals— whether in or out of institutions.[5] 'In '61 before Ericsson gave us such an admirable inshore impregnable battery we had nothing, nor the offer of anything', Fox wrote to Secretary Welles in August 1863. 'Isherwood thought iron clads a humbug and Lenthall shrank from touching the subject, just at that period when fatal days and months were passing.'[6] But as one private shipbuilder to another, Ericsson 'candidly' replied to John's Laird's letter to him of 7 June 1870, describing the successful performance of the twin-screwed HMS *Captain* at sea under canvas, that such results took him 'by surprise'. When not engaged the screws would act as a serious drag, especially at lower speeds, while in a deep draft vessel a single screw would consume less coal. 'As to the low-freeboard, that unquestionably ensures a steady platform for the guns; but if made as low as it should to secure the great object in view, protection against shot, it is incompatible with sailing qualities. In fine, the low-freeboard is only applicable to the "fighting machine", the genuine Monitor.'[7]

By then, the summer of 1870, war clouds had gathered over Europe again. Ever since Bismarck's stunningly swift victory over Austria in 1866 tensions between France and Prussia had been at an all-time high, with both their armies kept at full readiness, despite growing economic and social pressures at home. As a democratic gesture to the French people, Emperor Napoleon III held a national plebiscite on his political and legislative reforms of the French Constitution since 1860 (and to endorse his various imperial adventures since then). The overwhelming vote in his favour was congratulated by Lord Lyons, Britain's Ambassador to France since 1867, though the Emperor had been 'a good deal annoyed and disappointed by the tone of the English

---

5 See for example Frank M. Bennett, *The Steam Navy of the United States* (Westport: Greenwood Press, 1896), 56-7, 142-76, 201-422, 514-83; also Frank M. Bennett, *The Monitor and the Navy Under Steam* (Boston: Houghton, Mifflin and Company, 1900), 69-211.

6 15 August 1863, Fox to Welles, Welles Papers, Library of Congress. Porter had written to Fox the year before complaining of 'those miserable apologies for ['90-Day'] gun boats which Lenthall so prides himself on', 9 March 1862, Porter to Fox, David Dixon Porter Family Papers, Library of Congress Manuscript Division, Box 17. Perhaps the most dismal failure of the Union Navy's ironclad programme during the American Civil War was Lenthall and Isherwood's conversion of the screw-frigate *Roanoke*, originally intended to float 'no less than four Coles towers on her, with eight 12- or 15-inch guns', as noted by Donald Canney, as well as retaining her original (weak) engines. Later she was changed to float three Ericsson-type turrets. Too deep, a dangerous roller at sea, and never exceeding eight-knots, she lingered at Fortress Monroe, Hampton Roads as a floating battery; *The Old Steam Navy*, 59-62.

7 8 June 1870, Ericsson to Laird, Ericsson Papers, Philadelphia, Box 11.

Press. After all he has established a Constitutional form of Government more democratic than that which exists in England', and 'the principal security we can have for Free Trade and cordiality between the Countries' was that he remained a popular sovereign ruler. Meanwhile, Lyons thought it unlikely that the French would support Britain 'if we put ourselves in the front rank to resist American encroachments in the matter of the Panama Canal.' While the French experience in Mexico he believed had 'made them timid', he was also glad that Britain in turn had 'never given the Colombians the slightest cause to expect support from us, for I do not see how we are to give it to them'. At any rate, he considered that 'public opinion in England would be far from sanctioning a quarrel with the United States on this matter. We are neither strong nor plucky, it seems to me in American quarters, and therefore all we can do is to keep as clear of them as possible.'[8] Spain's attempts to bolster her national status with imperial demonstrations of naval power abroad, on the other hand, had only backfired, helping lead to a liberal revolution in 1868 and the exile of Bourbon Queen Isabella. Although a constitutional monarchy was now in place, there was no monarch. When Bismarck manoeuvred to have Spain offer its throne to the Hohenzollern Prince Leopold (nephew of Prussian King Wilhelm I), France was outraged—providing the German Chancellor with just the sort of pretext he needed for yet another foreign war which would serve to momentarily quell domestic unrest while further nationalising a united Germany under Prussian leadership. He had already secretly insured that Russia would stay neutral in the event of a war with France, while Louis Napoleon and his advisors mistakenly believed that both Denmark and Austria were eager to avenge their losses under French leadership. No one considered Britain likely to intervene in the event of such a conflict. By 9 July France, conscious of a fatal loss of prestige in European affairs as well as 'encirclement', threatened war if Prussia did not renounce Leopold's candidacy. Although this served to deter Wilhelm and Leopold, who agreed, the French Foreign Minister (the Duke of Gramont) further insisted on 12 July that it be accompanied with a written promise that such a thing would never happen again: seeking open humiliation as well as compliance. When Bismarck doctored the Prussian King's response as a cold refusal and released it to the press, France had no choice but to declare war less than a week later—and appear the spiteful and capricious aggressor.[9]

Even before the infamous 'Ems Despatch' which finally triggered the Franco-Prussian War of 1870-1871, the Admiralty had instructed Milne (now a full Admiral)

---

8   24 May and 23 June 1870, Lyons to Clarendon, TNA FO 361/1.
9   France declared war on 15 July 1870. A vast literature on this conflict, but leading examples are still Michael Howard, *The Franco-Prussian War* (London: William Clowes and Sones, Limited, 1961); and Geoffrey Wawro, *The Franco-Prussian War: The German Conquest of France in 1870-1871* (Cambridge: Cambridge University Press, 2003);
plus Richard Millman, *British Foreign Policy and the Coming of the Franco-Prussian War* (Oxford: Clarendon Press, 1965). See also the succinct analysis by Stephen Badsey in *The Franco-Prussian War 1870-1871* (Oxford: Osprey, 2003).

to link up the Mediterranean Fleet at Gibraltar with Yelverton's Channel Squadron for a combined cruise off the coast of Spain under his overall command. Childers added on 12 July that he had heard no news from the Foreign Office, and while there was 'no present fear of being dragged into the quarrel', it was 'very desirable that we should shew our strength well considering especially what in the event of a French and Prussian war the former will be able to do.' On 20 July Milne was notified that the Cabinet thought it best to have the fleets 'come North rather than remain near Gibraltar', and the following week official orders to Yelverton specified that in addition to *Minotaur*, *Warrior*, *Hercules* and *Monarch* that he also take with him the fast-frigate *Inconstant*, and ironclads *Agincourt*, *Northumberland* and *Captain*. Combined with the *Lord Warden*, *Caledonia*, *Prince Consort*, *Royal Oak*, and *Bellerophon* this was the largest ironclad force Great Britain had ever deployed. Steam was only to be used when Vice-Admiral Milne thought it necessary, and particular attention was to be devoted to the comparative qualities of *Hercules*, *Monarch* and *Captain* (considered by many to be the best-protected, most heavily-armed seagoing ironclad in the world).[10] Although *The Illustrated London News* featured a full-page depiction of the Prussian ironclad fleet, followed by one of a French armoured squadron in the Baltic, Britain's primary concern was whether France would make a play for Belgium. Bismarck again proved himself a more agile manipulator of events than Napoleon III, allowing Delane of *The Times* to publish details of a secret proposed treaty between Prussia and France in 1866 in which the French Emperor would announce his approval of the union of North and South Germany under Prussian leadership, and in return King Wilhelm would acknowledge the absorption of Belgium by France.[11]

While many in Britain doubted the authenticity or even relevancy of the Prussian claims, *The Times* at least held forth that their immediate Continental neighbour was as ambitious as ever and not to be trusted with any opportunity to re-alter the settled map of Europe in 1856 let alone that of 1815. Following her revolution from the Netherlands, Belgium's political independence had been guaranteed by the Great Powers in the London Conference of 1830.[12] As for Earl Granville (replacing Clarendon as Foreign Secretary upon his death on 27 June), Cardwell, the Secretary

---

10 8 July 1870, Board to Milne, TNA ADM 1/6159; 12 and 20 July 1870, Childers to Milne, Milne Papers, Greenwich, MLN 165/1; 26 July 1870, TNA ADM 1/6159. However, Childers also advised Milne 'not to spare a few tons of coal' during exercises. 'We shall not fight under sail, or at low speeds', undated (probably end-July 1870), Childers to Milne, Milne Papers, Greenwich, MLN 165/1.
11 30 July and 13 August 1870, *The Illustrated London News*; see for example, *The History of The Times*, 2 vols, *The Tradition Established 1841-1884* (London: *The Times*, 1939), 2: 423-8; also Dora Neill Raymond, *British Policy and Opinion During the Franco-Prussian War* (New York: AMS Press, Inc., 1967, based on her 1921 doctoral dissertation), 87-106; and Arthur Irwin Dasent, *John Thadeus Delane—Editor of The Times, His Life and Correspondence*, 2 vols. (London: John Murray, 1908) 2: 266-7.
12 See for example J. S. Fishman, *Diplomacy and Revolution: The London Conference of 1830 and the Belgian Revolt* (Amsterdam: Charles E. Vos, 1988).

of State for War (replacing Pakington after the general election in December 1868), and Prime Minister Gladstone, Delane privately complained they 'are indeed a set of clerks, excellent for Parliamentary purposes or the business of administration, but quite incapable of the courage required in such emergencies as these.' But the day before, 16 July, Gladstone had already asked Cardwell to contemplate despatching 20,000 British troops to Antwerp—as if the sovereign state of Belgium was the same as British North America during the *Trent* Affair.[13] Soon after it became apparent that Britain was not in a position to mobilise even for a state of 'secure' neutrality, with Parliament voting by the end of July an emergency £2 million supplement for national defences. £500,000 of that funding was understood as an immediate boost to the navy.[14] On 9 August 1870, with the *Captain* on her way south to continue her trials—and with Coles on board as an invited observer—Robinson wrote to Dacres that (given the restructuring of the Board of Admiralty by Childers) the 'responsibility of giving sound professional advice to the First Lord rests upon us'. £45,000 was to be spent tendering for six iron screw-gunboats of the remarkable new *Ant*-class; mastless, flat-bottomed, drawing only six-feet, but mounting a single fixed 10-inch 18-ton rifled muzzle loader on the exposed bow which could, however, be lowered by hydraulic power below deck for voyages. The Controller also urged the building of four coastal breastwork-monitors of a class he had suggested in 1866; twin-screwed, double-turreted, drawing sixteen-feet and armed with four 18-ton rifled muzzle-loaders (*Cyclops*, *Gorgon*, *Hydra* and *Hecate*). Indeed, these were 'more wanted than any other class of vessel.' Unsurprisingly, Robinson told the First Naval Lord that he did not 'advise that a contract should be entered into for another *Monarch* or another *Captain*, because the Admiralty have publicly declared, to the House of Commons, and to the Country, that they have not been able to come to any opinion or form any judgment as to these two ships'. Their cost would also be considerable and either one would take three years to build. But this did not prevent him from recommending a contract for another *Sultan* central-battery ironclad (although just as expensive and time-consuming given the present crisis). His enclosed memo on the current Anglo-French naval balance of power also noted a discussion on 26 July in which 'three large Iron-Clads were mentioned as necessary', and the ships 'named as most proper

---

13   17 July 1870, Delane to G. W. Dasent, in Dasent, *John Thadeus Delane*, 265-6; 16 July 1870, Gladstone to Cardwell, in John Morley, *The Life of William Ewart Gladstone*, 3 vols. (London: Macmillan and Co., Limited, 1903), 2: 339.

14   See for example, 25 July 1870, Gladstone memo to Queen, in TNA Cabinet (CAB) 41/2/36. As for British neutrality in the Franco-Prussian conflict, days before news reached him of the *Captain*'s sinking, Gladstone responded to the personal appeal from Michel Chevalier (who had worked out the Free Trade treaty with Richard Cobden at the height of Anglo-French tensions in 1860), that it was 'not competent to us to interfere about the war with authority', 6 September 1870, in H. C. G. Matthew (ed.), *The Gladstone Diaries, Volume VII: January 1869 – June 1871* (Oxford: Clarendon Press, 1982), 353-4.

to be ordered were, an improved *Monarch*, a *Fury* [*Devastation*], and a *Sultan*—all department-designed ships with no mention of another *Captain*, which was already regarded as a one-off, a dead-end.[15]

* * *

Reed had by then already made public his own contempt of this ironclad freak, writing in *The Times* that Coles had originally, and for years, maintained that what was needed was a small, fast seagoing cupola vessel:

> But is the *Captain* small? No; she is a 4,200 ton deep-draught frigate…Has she a Monitor's freeboard? No; her side is 6ft. high and would have been 8ft. but for an alarming blunder in calculation—the worst that I have ever known. Does she present a very small target to the enemy? No; every one who has seen her at Spithead during the last few days must have noticed that she stands up as high and as big as any broadside ship of her tonnage…Has she an all-round fire? No; let the world be told that this perfect type of turret-ship, according to Captain Coles's views—this pattern of warlike power and efficiency—is the only ironclad built of late years for the British navy which cannot fire a gun ahead or astern from behind armour! If I had designed and the Admiralty had built such a ship from my design, Captain Coles would have been the first to denounce her as a burlesque upon his system; and she undoubtedly is the direct opposite of all that he once advocated.[16]

This was grossly unfair—and it was unlikely Coles would have ever seen the letter when it was published on 8 August since the *Captain* had departed on her final voyage four days earlier (he certainly proved unable to ever respond).[17] The fact of the controversial ironclad, as a seagoing turret-ship 'cruiser', was that she was a 'better

---

15   9 August 1870, Robinson to Dacres, TNA ADM 1/6159, with enclosed memos dated 6 and 4 August. Dacres also added his own memo, dated 8 August, which concurred with Robinson's suggestions for four improved coastal monitors like the *Cerberus* and another *Sultan*. 'I should be sorry to propose a fourth *Fury* [*Devastation*; along with *Thunderer* and *Fury*] until one is tried, but that would be preferable to a *Monarch* or *Captain* for their capabilities as seagoing cruizers rest too much on self-interest and prejudice to justify such an immense expenditure…If the House of Commons are informed what is proposed with reference to further trials of *Hercules*, *Monarch* and *Captain* the building of four turret vessels would convince the public of our impartiality.'
16   8 August 1870, 'Our Ironclad Navy', *The Times*.
17   Even *The Times* that same issue (8 August 1870) observed how 'The Controller of our Navy … and Mr. Reed, in more than official antagonism, have for years opposed Captain Coles with an animus which is signally shown in the letter which we publish today. If it were wise or patriotic, we could point out hundreds of weak points in all the ships which Mr. Reed, with unlimited scope and skilled assistance, has added to the British Navy.'

fighter' than Reed's *Monarch*. If *Captain* was too large then *Monarch* was even larger. Although not a small target she was significantly smaller than *Monarch*. She did not have all-round fire but could nonetheless train her guns more than *Monarch*. She did not have (small) guns behind armour on her forecastle but she was more thickly armoured than *Monarch* generally. In most respects outlined by Reed, Coles had beaten him with the *Captain*—assuming her speed and sailing qualities were comparable. But of course there were two main problems to consider: how safe would she be with her reduced freeboard (even if she had been completed at eight-feet rather than six), and how far was Reed actually comparing the *Captain* here not with the *Monarch* but with his mastless, large-tonnage *Devastation*? Even if the *Captain* had proved stable enough with a slightly higher freeboard after all, she would not have been tactically superior to the breastwork-monitor. Yet neither was the *Devastation*-class expected to 'cruise'—and the general emphasis was still upon the creation of a 'perfect' ironclad man-of-war which could go anywhere as need be, even without fuel, and fight on the high seas on far better terms than any higher freeboard broadside or lower-freeboard turret-ship could. Robinson and Reed had already considered an improved *Monarch*; one wonders how much better an improved *Captain* could have been—starting with a better distribution of weights and centre of gravity. The initial trial reports of Vice-Admiral Sir Thomas Symonds comparing the two sail-and-turret-ships side-by-side, *The Times* noted, suggested that improving the *Captain*—not the *Monarch*—was where the future of British seapower lay.[18]

This also seems to have been very much on the First Lord's mind earlier that summer—and Reed, while outraged, had already shown that his best arguments (like Robinson's, and no less than those of Coles) were clearly fraught with omissions, inconsistencies and bias. So now the Chief Constructor of the Navy resigned. Rather than feed yet another 'turret vs. broadside'-scandal, the circumstances of his decision were publicly linked to his accepting a lucrative standing offer to go into business with gun manufacturer Whitworths, and not just pursuing a career in politics, or his claims for extra pay. It was also suggested that he quit in protest of one of Childers' recent reforms which saw Robinson prohibited from future sea-service ('after ten years' behind a desk as a flag officer), with the Controller also threatening to resign.[19] 'What is the matter at the Admiralty?' asked *The Standard* on 22 June 1870. Wrangling over economies in the navy was one thing, but 'now the very skies are falling, and a sort of general strike seems coming.' Their initial, and longstanding, suspicion for the cause of the affair was ultimately proven correct. 'As journalists we have not always

---

18 Ibid.
19 See for example 19 June and 4 July 1870, Childers to Gladstone, Gladstone Papers, British Library, Add. Ms. 44,128 (Vol. XLIII), in which Childers (on 4 July) relayed the rumour that 'Sir J. Whitworth will tempt Reed from us. His adherence to Robinson's fortunes was clearly a pretence not creditable to him.' See also the enclosures of the June 1870 exchange between Childers and Robinson on the retirement issue in Gladstone Papers, British Library, Add. Ms. 44,614, DXXIX.

agreed with Mr. Reed. While admiring his talents and industry we have objected to his persistent advocacy of the broadside type of war-ship.' Yet if this was indeed the real issue at stake, and 'the Controller and the Chief Constructor of the Navy are determined not to build the class of ship which modern science shows to be requisite for our naval supremacy there is no alternative but to part with such men, however great their ability may be in carrying out their own plans.' *The Times* was also not satisfied with the official explanation provided by the Admiralty 'of this obscure and lamentable dispute. Why Mr. Reed should threaten to resign because the Controller of the Navy is debarred from future service afloat is a riddle difficult to solve.' But here too Britain's leading press announced that if Reed could not 'cultivate the lowly virtues of a public servant we think he would do better to retire at once from a position for which he is too great. There are many avenues open to him in private life, through some of which, if he is to be always resigning and never resigned, he would do well to select his course... England is the factory of shipbuilding, and contains many able naval architects. We do not wish to lose Mr. Reed, but good ships were built before him, and good ships will still be built if he should unfortunately be compelled, in deference to his own feelings, to retire from the public service.'[20]

By 11 July, with Europe now plunged into crisis, Reed's resignation was confirmed—leaving the British to feel that no one was at the helm of their ironclad navy's development after all. *The Times* was pensive. 'If these two inventors, who were designed to supplement the other's deficiencies, could only have been brought to work together harmoniously in the public service, it is no injustice to declare that formidable as is our Navy at the present time, it would have been more formidable still. That this happy result has not been attained is not the fault of Captain Coles alone.'[21] The next day, *The Standard* went so far as to suggest that Reed was neglecting his patriotic duty when his country needed him most. '*The Times* would have it appear that the golden prospect of the Whitworth partnership was the original cause of Mr. Reed's resignation. This is not a fact...To assert that the reason of Mr. Reed's resignation "is not dissatisfaction with the Admiralty" is a mere assumption.' That Robinson was now

---

20 22 June 1870, *The Standard*; 27 June 1870, *The Times*. Robinson was placed on the Retired List of the Navy on 2 June 1870, his 10-year 'sea-service' being up (as a flag officer at the Admiralty) counted towards retirement; but he was offered to remain on the Active List by Childers two days later—if he took up the C-in-C post at Sheerness. When Robinson protested to Gladstone directly, asking that the Orders in Council be either changed or suspended in his case, the Premier politely refused, assuring him that the decision had no bearing on the high regard the country had for Robinson's services as Controller, and so forth. See Matthew, *Gladstone Diaries, Volume VII*, entry dated 18 June 1870, 310-12. Childers wrote to Gladstone on 27 June that 'you may wish to know that he [Reed] has said nothing to me either in writing or verbally about resignation. My knowledge of his resignation is derived from the letter written to me by Sir. S. Robinson, which I shewed you (immediately) on Friday week, and from his open mouthed statements to half the gentlemen of the office', Gladstone Papers, British Library, Add. Ms., 44,128, Vol. XLIII.
21 11 July 1870, *The Times*.

not going to resign after all had proved to be 'ridiculous contradiction…In the absence of Mr. Reed we cannot conceive what will be the use of Sir Spencer Robinson. Had Mr. Reed continued at the Admiralty there is little doubt that he would have absorbed Sir Spencer into himself and became both Controller and Chief Constructor.' On 18 July, *The Times* quoted the rumour published in the *Army and Navy Gazette* that Reed had tried to retract his resignation—and was refused by the Board. The *Morning Post* then confirmed the explanation of Childers in Parliament for Reed's resignation, 'alleging that he was moved to do so in consequence of the low estimate in which all Governments held scientific and mechanical skill compared with private firms; but that, on hearing of the complications between France and Prussia, he had telegraphed his willingness to continue his services should his retirement cause inconvenience to the Admiralty, and that the offer had been declined.'[22]

But that first week of September 1870, the *Captain* and the rest of the combined British ironclad fleet was busy with naval exercises off the coast of Spain, while Napoleon III personally found himself and the French Army of Châlons (after a month of stunning military reverses) surrounded by Prussian forces at Sedan, on the Meuse River. On 2 September, following a ruinous break-out attempt by his army the previous day, the Emperor surrendered and was taken prisoner along with over 100,000 soldiers. The backbone of the French military was broken, the political leadership of Imperial France captured, and the Franco-Prussian War was effectively ended as quickly as it had begun: the greatest feat of German arms in the nineteenth-century. No sooner had the British public begun to digest news of these extraordinary events then the first telegraphic message from Admiral Milne came into the Admiralty from Vigo, Spain, on the evening of 7 September: 'Her Majesty's Ship *Captain* must have foundered in the night. She was close to this ship [*Lord Warden*] at 2 this morning. Sudden S.W. Gale—very heavy squalls. At daybreak the *Captain* was missing. This afternoon her Boat (or boats) and spars found. All have unfortunately perished.'[23] Overnight, all the future plans and debates over future British naval strength had abruptly come to a stop, as the country's strategic show of force off the coast of Europe turned from triumph to tragedy: the greatest loss of British naval life between 1815 and 1914.[24] Once it was later reported that there were indeed eighteen survivors who had made it to shore in another launch, a court martial was formed in Portsmouth for 27 September, with records of the *Captain*'s

---

22   12 July 1870, *The Standard*; 18 July 1870, *The Times*; 19 July 1870, The *Morning Post*. See also 26 July 1870, Robinson memo, TNA ADM 1/6159, with enclosed letter from Admiralty to Reed dated 28 July 1870, declining his 1 July 1870 offer for any extra information or services in regard to ships under construction.
23   See the collection of first reports and remorseful telegrams of inquiry in TNA ADM 1/6159.
24   See for example W. P. Gossett, *The Lost Ships of the Royal Navy 1793-1900* (London: Mansell Publishing Limited, 1986), 95-125. Likewise, more British sailors were lost in this single ship disaster than during the course of the Crimean War.

previous logs requested from the Admiralty. 'The whole of the Ship's Company, both officers and men, appear according to the statements of the Survivors to have had great confidence in the Capabilities of the Ship', noted a Board-approved despatch for the newspapers in the meantime, with Yelverton writing to Milne that he had the 'consolation of knowing, and we all feel, that you have used every exertion to get at the cause of a misfortune, the prevention of which was beyond your reach.'[25]

As noted by the *Summary* of correspondence on the design and construction of the *Captain* (26 September 1870), the Admiralty had already knowingly failed to take steps which might have averted disaster. On 4 September 1867, Barnaby visited the sail-and-turret ironclad—at that point six months into her construction—and reported 'the work everywhere well and honestly done, but if I were responsible for the weight of the ship, I should be greatly alarmed at the appearance everywhere of extravagance in the use of material. There is no evidence anywhere of economy in either material or labour.' But neither did he feel obliged to share this with Lairds. When the *Captain* was finally completed and floated out of dock a year and a half later, on 27 March 1869, Barnaby wrote to Reed that she had indeed exceeded her estimated contract weight by 427 tons and was down thirteen-inches in the water further than originally expected. With a crew of 500 men her freeboard would be further reduced to 6-feet 9½-inches, Reed relayed to Robinson. This was all they needed to hear, and had been waiting to hear for some time. Thus, when Robinson forwarded the news to the Board, he couldn't resist adding what he had complained about for years; 'that, as a rule almost of universal application, the displacement allowed by the designers of private ship-builders is insufficient for the weights they have to carry.' This of course ignored the errors committed by government officials who designed and built warships for the Royal Navy as well. But the salient factor here, at least as far as the Controller and Chief Constructor were concerned, was that they could now already point to the illegitimate HMS *Captain* as an abortion, and a profound disgrace to the bastard ship's father, Coles. As the official *Summary* observed, 'Their Lordships noted the papers, but did not communicate on the subject with Messrs. Laird or Captain Coles'—again because the ship was not their 'responsibility'.[26]

Nearly a year later, and with the experimental sail-and-turret ironclad completed and ready for trials, Lairds requested the Admiralty to properly determine the stability of the vessel in relation to her centre of displacement by inclining the *Captain* in the steam basin, as had been done on other ironclads of the British navy. Reed, however, counselled to delay the test 'when an opportunity offers and the weather is settled', and was eager for the ship to conduct her steam trials on the 'measured mile' in Stokes

25   14 September 1870, Minute, and 21 September 1870, 'Loss of HMS *Captain*—Court Martial', TNA ADM 1/6159; 7 October 1870, TNA ADM 3/286; undated, presumably 'Saturday' 10 September 1870, Yelverton to Milne, Milne Papers, Greenwich, MLN 165/13. For a list of the survivors by name see Hawkey, *Black Night*, 183.
26   26 September 1870, *Summary of Correspondence relating to the Design and Construction of the late 'Captain'*, in TNA ADM 1/6159, 12.

Bay (the Solent off Portsmouth). These took place on 2 March 1870. Here Frederick Barnes, Assistant Constructor of the Navy, reported that the *Captain* was more like 735 tons overweight. 'The actual height of gunwale is 6 feet 7 inches, with the practical mean draught of 24 feet 10 inches' (not 23 as planned). Two days later he added the ship was down 'at least 22 inches' from her estimated freeboard. 'This large departure from what was intended by the contract of the ship,' he suggested, 'raises the question whether the ship should be accepted in that condition by their Lordships.'[27] More to the point, it was understood that no first-class ironclad designed in the Admiralty and built in a government dockyard with such a discrepancy would be allowed to go to sea. An inquiry would first be made whether the initial design was off, and if not, how construction was allowed to proceed over months if not years at such obvious variance from the original plans. In any case, fixing the problem would be the order of the day.

Instead, Reed took the opportunity of informing the Controller on 14 March that these reports demonstrated the *Captain* 'cannot possibly prove a satisfactory seagoing ship for Her Majesty's Navy', recommending that the Admiralty immediately suspend further payments to Lairds. The issue was not the ship's inherent *stability* (since this had not be tested in dock much less trialled at sea) as 'whether the guns could be fought in all weathers'. As was well known, he'd already had doubts about Coles trying to improve upon HMS *Monarch* by first reducing her freeboard. This was in the pursuit of a sail-and-turret ironclad which more closely approximated the tactical advantages of (mastless) monitors, which capitalised on their low-freeboard by floating a far greater concentration of armour and heavier guns. Now, 'with the height reduced to the amount already stated,' Reed declared he was 'unable any longer to anticipate a satisfactory result to the trials of the ship in such seas as the *Monarch* has already had to encounter.' Yet by then he had also advocated low-freeboard turret-ships of his own. His large breastwork *Devastation was* expected to fight her guns in a seaway, even without a forecastle as in *Monarch* and *Captain*. The problem here was that not enough was known about the truly revolutionary properties of 'semi-submersion' or 'sub-aquatic' vessels as conceived by John Ericsson. Low-freeboard was a non-starter for a floating gun-platform at sea, but only if the vessel was no more steady than a high-freeboard one pitching and rolling that much more. Would the *Captain* be even steadier as a result of being more submersed like an American monitor, and therefore still prove that her guns could be worked as safely as in a broadside-ironclad at sea?[28]

That Reed was quick to judge only served to further demonstrate to Coles and Lairds the prejudice that animated the Controller's Department. After all, no one had actually tried a low-freeboard sail-and-turret ironclad at sea yet—in terms of its ability to fight, which is what Reed himself had stressed. This is what the Chief Constructor therefore wanted the *Captain* to prove, since 'no conclusion upon this subject will be arrived at until the ship has undergone a lengthened experience at sea'.

27 Ibid., 13. The report by Barnes to Reed was dated 3 March 1870.
28 Ibid., 13-14.

His only expressed concern was that Coles would now try to somehow disassociate himself from the ship as not built upon his own specifications, 'notwithstanding the fact that he has systematically certified his satisfaction with the ship during the various stages of her progress up to the time of the last payment upon her being made.' Even if Coles and Lairds decided to call Reed's challenge and subject the *Captain* to rigorous trials at sea similar to those made by the Channel Squadron (which had indeed exposed many unexpected errors in every British oceangoing ironclad made), Reed was also careful to reiterate that the Admiralty had absolved itself from any responsibility in the ship's design or construction; 'yet my officers were uniformly instructed to mention to Messrs. Laird, as occasion might offer, what they more than once mentioned to me, and what I also saw myself upon my visits to the ships and mentioned to the firm, viz., that throughout the building of the ship iron was put into her in larger quantities than would have been deemed requisite in the building of such a ship in Her Majesty's dockyards, or under my directions'.[29]

* * *

This assertion, however, was not borne out by previous official correspondence. On 15 August 1866, Lairds confirmed their confidence in the design of the *Captain*, nor did they object to any supervision in her construction by Admiralty officers. 'Any suggestions made by the Controller's department as to the details which may differ from those usually adopted in Her Majesty's ships shall receive our careful consideration' they added, 'it being understood that these suggestions are to be confined to modifications of details of construction, and that their adoption, or otherwise, is to be left at our discretion.'[30] At his testimony at the court-martial that September following the disaster, William Laird couldn't point to any specific weights which added to the depth of the *Captain*. He also noted that his team did not expect a relatively low-freeboard ironclad to heel more than ten-degrees steadily, and that even if it did, 'the reserve of stability beyond that was very great and would have admitted of exceeding that angle without any cause for alarm.' This became problematic, however, 'after the inclination immersed the gunwale', affecting the result 'more than in an ordinary ship.' Then again, he thought that the increased submersion of twenty-two-inches, while it decreased the *Captain*'s stability under sail, rather made the ship 'steadier and roll less'—like a monitor. When his brother and business-partner, Henry, testified before the court two days later on 3 October, he was at a loss why the *Captain* heeled more than the *Monarch* during her last cruise but far less during her trial cruise of 29 May when she encountered a gale, offering only

29   Ibid.
30   15 August 1866, Laird Brothers to Secretary of the Admiralty, in *Minute by the First Lord of the Admiralty with Reference to H.M.S. Captain*, 14-15. The letter from Lairds requesting changes to the inner armour was dated 16 July 1867, with Robinson's refusal dated 19 July, as noted in appendices above, 260.

that 100-tons more coal had been added which might have affected her distribution of weight. But he admitted that in building so large a sail-and-turret ironclad they were dealing with a novel design which complicated the issue of added weights, 'and in fact several had to be increased beyond that allowed for them in consequence of experiments made and information obtained after the design was decided upon.' The Admiralty overseers, however, did not enforce 'keeping down the material used…and that while in all ships contracted for since [*Captain*'s] contract, a margin of 5 to 10 per cent is allowed in all iron materials below that specified in her case. We believe that the overseers considered it their duty to see that no materials were employed in her construction that were in any degree below that specified. As a matter of fact, all the materials were provided and worked into her on this understanding.' When Lairds attempted to reduce the scantling in the *Captain* the Admiralty refused, likewise when they later requested to do away with the inner iron backing or skin to the armour, which they felt was ultimately unnecessary and had been subsequently done away with in the *Devastation*-class breastwork monitors currently under construction.[31]

Pakington wrote to Milne on 11 October 1870 expressing his regret that he was not called in by the court martial as a witness, 'having been the responsible Minister by whom the order for the construction of the *Captain* was given.' Indeed, he thought he 'could have prevented some erroneous impressions which appears to have been created by other evidence.' The verdict of the court martial itself he had read 'with great disappointment':

> I suppose the latter part of it is to censure the Admiralty for not having immediately communicated the result of the investigations which were carried on in August after the Ship was at Sea, to yourself and poor Burgoyne. If so, I quite concur in the censure—that communication might have saved the Ship and her precious freight! But one cannot feel sure what is the intended meaning of such a curiously bad composition! I wish you could have been a member of the Committee. You would at least have improved their English. But there is one passage the meaning of which is plain, and which, to best of my recollection, is very incorrect in fact. I refer to the statement that the *Captain* was built 'in opposition to the views and opinions of the Controller of the Navy and his Department' etc. There is a passage of similar import in Reed's letter to *The Times* of 5th instant [5 October]. He says, 'the cause of the *Captain* being designed and constructed was the assumption that the opinions of Sir S. Robinson and myself were not to be trusted.' You and I were together at that time. Do you remember anything to confirm the tenor of these passages? I do not. It is true, no doubt, that Robinson and Reed were free from any responsibility for the design of the *Captain*. But I never felt that their opinions

---

31 Ibid., testimony of 3 October 1870, 170-4.

were not to be trusted, nor do I remember anything on their part to justify the statement about opposition to their views.

As for Pakington's authorisation of the *Captain* being built in the first place, his memory was 'as poor Captain Coles complained of the *Monarch* as not a fair trial of his principle, I though it due to him and to the Public that an invention which had attracted so much attention <u>should</u> be fairly tried, and I therefore sent for Coles, and said "build your own Ship and select your own builder."' In this respect it had nothing to do with the Controller's Department. When the plans later came in, however, the former First Lord of the Admiralty demurred 'to the <u>low free board of eight feet</u>. I eventually gave way upon this point, rather than thwart Coles in his plan, and great was my dismay last winter when the *Captain* made her appearance with <u>six</u> feet instead of <u>eight</u>!' Tormented by these recollections, Pakington asked Milne to confirm or deny his impressions. Milne largely confirmed this account two days later, noting that once the arrangement was made for Coles to design his own seagoing turret-ship, 'the Admiralty would not interfere except to send a person to see that the material and workmanship was good.' Milne clearly remembered 'the model being brought into your Room by Coles', and that when Robinson was called in to examine it he 'at once said that the Model was different from Captain Coles' own views as it was proposed to have a Poop and Forecastle'. As for the eight-foot freeboard he didn't think 'if any special exception was taken…but I do recollect Captain Coles being very strong on that point and as the leading feature of his principles.' Milne's own instinct 'certainly was averse to only 8 feet', but he was also concerned that 'if the Admiralty interfered in any manner with Coles's views it would be considered that he had not his own plans carried out.' Everyone would be back to where they were at the beginning of 1866, reacting to Coles' sharp attack in *The Standard* that the Royal Navy still lacked a powerful first-class turret-ship which could contend with those of other powers. But neither did Milne think a public refutation by Pakington of Reed's letter to *The Times* would do any good. 'The blame at present rests with the Authorities in accepting a Ship drawing 26 inches more than her intended draft', he wrote. 'The Controller's Department ought to have objected to this. Again, if accepted it is clear that her Stability ought to have been tested before she went to sea.' If Reed really thought the *Captain* was unsafe, 'as he appears to have stated to Captain Burgoyne when he went over the Ship with him,' then Milne judged it was 'his duty to have written to the Controller in order that the attention of the Admiralty might have been called to the subject.' In his assessment, a combination of factors had tragically combined to doom the *Captain*: the heeling of the ship to eighteen-degrees while being struck at the same moment 'by a Sea on the weather side forcing her still more over', with a cross swell breaking over her lee deck 'as high as the base of the Turrets', and her unique (and untried) hurricane deck 'acting as a sail' to unnaturally force her over even more. Otherwise, he had 'no recollection of either Robinson or Reed making any special representation of want of safety in the *Captain*.' The truth was that no one really knew what to expect of such a vessel's properties at sea, only that Robinson and Reed generally 'did not approve the "plan" and Coles did not approve of theirs.'[32]

As for Reed's statement to *The Times* that the Board felt himself and Robinson 'were not to be trusted', Pakington omitted the rest of this sentence: 'and that we were showing prejudiced opposition to Captain Coles.' Reed's letter then objected that his testimony was not fully understood when reported by the newspaper; altering the words to his satisfaction but still leaving things somewhat unclear as to whether he was aware of alterations made to the *Captain*'s design during construction '[yes] to specified parts of the design; no, with reference to the many unspecified portions of the design.' At any rate, he didn't dispute the printed transcription of his testimony the previous day at the court martial; that even if Lairds and Coles had been made aware of the test results that the *Captain*'s stability at sea would rapidly vanish after twenty-one-degrees inclination, 'it would have resulted in the strongest possible efforts to prove the Admiralty wrong, and to carry on all sail possible.' This was manifestly an appalling state of affairs, including Reed's own attempt to entirely blame Coles and his supporters for this mutual (and ultimately fatal) lack of trust. It suggested a professional working relationship so malfunctional whereby no one should be surprised if Reed and Robinson themselves quietly chose to bury over any warning signs if they also served to prove their enemies wrong and settle once and for all the great 'turret vs. broadside'-debate in the most comprehensive manner possible. Needless to say, Reed's defensive assertion also publicly insulted the professional integrity of both Lairds and Coles; that their hatred of himself and the Admiralty was so blind and stubborn that they would rather build an unseaworthy ship than take his advice (and would Captain Burgoyne have nonetheless persisted in taking the *Captain* to sea had he been shown the stability tests?) Reed also went further in blaming the loss of Childers' son on the First Lord himself, whom he had entreated not to build any further *Captain*s, and 'when I found that my resistance was useless I retired from duty and undertook to submit the resignation of my office.'[33]

---

32 11 October 1870, Pakington to Milne, and 13 October 1870, Milne to Pakington, Milne Papers, Greenwich, MLN 165/10. Reed had declared that the 'flying deck, which it is proposed to fit over the turrets, from poop to forecastle, and which was ordered some months since for the *Scorpion*, appears to me to be a most valuable addition to the comfort and security of a turret-ship', 20 July 1866, Reed to Robinson, in *Parliamentary Papers, Minute by the First Lord of the Admiralty with Reference to H.M.S.* Captain, 9. See also the discussion on the use of hurricane decks in other British turret-ships, namely HMS *Prince Albert*, in 19 August 1867, Robinson to Board, TNA ADM 1/6019.

33 5 October 1870, *The Times*. Captain Sherard Osborn was indignant with this suggestion by Reed, writing in *The Times* of 11 October that 'had he been brought up as a naval officer he would know that, as a profession, the tendency [to treat due warnings 'with indifference and incredulity'] is quite in a contrary direction. If he meant that Coles or Burgoyne would have attached very little weight to his own opinion, unsupported by data or mathematical demonstration of the seaworthiness of a low-freeboard turret-ship, I think he is right, and he would find hundreds, and I among others, of their way of thinking. Mr.

A *Times* leader the following day, 6 October, noted that whereas the initial question had been 'Why did [the *Captain*] founder?' now it was 'Why was she allowed to go to sea?' It also suggested that 'the theories of Captain Coles' were 'that ocean-cruising frigates could be successfully constructed with low-freeboards on the genuine principles of turret-ships.' In fact, low-freeboard turret-ships were American *monitors*, and all of the previous turret-ships built on Coles' principles were on the pattern of the *Rolf Krake*, the Laird Rams, and the *Huascar*; with superstructures including forecastles, collapsing side bulwarks for ocean journeys, and varying arrays of masts and sails. It was only after the visit of the double-turreted USS *Miantonomoh* to Britain in the summer of 1866 that Coles and his supporters became obsessed with the notion of improving on this design by somehow making the mastless monitor into a turreted-cruiser. Coles advocated a large-hulled sail-and-turret ironclad with lower freeboard than Reed's *Monarch*, and Reed, in finally admitting that artificial ventilation and sole reliance engine power were the way of the future, conceived the mastless breastwork-monitor which at least raised the guns and hatch openings higher out of the water than in the *Miantonomoh* or *Dictator*. Both off-shoots in the conscious evolution of Ericsson's 'Monitor' concept were highly experimental: no other power including the United States had attempted either a low-freeboard sail-and-turret ironclad or a breastwork-monitor. As *The Times* pointed out, there had been a desire 'among naval officers especially' to trial the latest theory of Coles. This was in the sincere belief that somewhere between the successful example of the *Miantonomoh* and the sail-and-turret-ships already built by Lairds and serving abroad the Royal Navy could at last boast a 'response' to not just the broadside-ironclad fleet of France but even to the vaunted flotillas of monitors shielding America and Russia (and who were inexorably extending their reach, and their naval supremacy, with every improved design.) 'The old story, therefore, might have been repeated'—that the *Captain* as a perfect seagoing turret-ship was by definition an impossibility—'and we might have been warned once more against taking the *Captain* for a specimen of what a turret-ship might be.' However, Lairds had written to *The Times* regarding the lower freeboard than expected, 'making light of the miscalculation, and claiming the *Captain* as a success; while as to poor Captain Coles, he was enraptured with the ship as fulfilling his utmost expectation.'[34]

This in itself was perhaps enough to condemn the ship's designers and builders, in answer to the question above. But *The Times* at least was not altogether willing to accept this interpretation of sole responsibility. Clearly the Admiralty had not surrendered 'their rights of inspection, approval, and supervision.' The Controller's Department had been involved with every stage of the *Captain*, including the authorisation for stability tests undertaken at Portsmouth. 'Here, therefore, is the

---

Reed and Sir Spencer Robinson have produced too many melancholy failures in the shape of men-of-war for the service to consider them oracles.'

34 6 October 1870, *The Times*.

opening of a serious controversy.' Both the documented correspondence and the timeline of events suggested that no one even in the Admiralty actually thought the *Captain* critically unstable as a ship, as bound to fail in other respects (like her ability to work her guns in a seaway, next to high-freeboard ironclads including the *Monarch*.) 'Mr. Reed, who certainly thought and spoke as ill of the *Captain* as anybody, says that what he anticipated was that she would first be described as a great success, and then, before she got through her commission, be condemned as utterly unfit for the service.' The unspoken precedent here was the Admiralty's disapproval of the Laird Rams, especially after the trials of the *Wivern* with the Channel Squadron under Yelverton's command in the autumn of 1866.[35]

The next day, 7 October 1870, Robinson submitted his own memo 'relative to the *Captain*' for the President of the Court Martial (Admiral Sir James Hope), 'should he think fit to make use of it.' Here he stressed that once the Board of Admiralty proved determined to let Coles submit his own design for a seagoing turret-ship, the Controller 'made it my business to give no sort of opposition to carrying out exactly and precisely Captain Coles' views.' But not only was his disapproval of these views admittedly 'notorious', so was his belief that '[Coles'] ideas when worked out would prove fallacious'. It was only after the *Captain* had been contracted and was under construction that Reed's team had calculated the inherent risk of cutting down ships-of-the-line into low-freeboard yet fully-masted turret vessels. 'This danger was pointed out in their Reports on these proposals and was made the subject of a Public Lecture by Mr. Reed.' Yet other naval architects (namely Watts and Henwood) had disagreed with Reed's theory, and even then, 'the *Captain* would, if built according to the calculations of her designers, have been very different from the converted Ships because the danger pointed out was owing to an exaggerated lowness of free-board in these ships and the intended height of the *Captain*'s side would have been three times as much as in the former ships.' Hence, Robinson did not think it appropriate to stop Lairds from completing the *Captain*, at least on the assumption she would be floated out as originally planned. If there was any concern of her centre of gravity and stability once it was later found she was too deep, Robinson argued that it was for Lairds 'to have stated it to the Admiralty plainly and without reserve.' In any event, the Controller had asked the Board for permission to accompany both the *Captain* and the *Monarch* to sea for two months, 'hoisting my flag in each ship alternately, and proceeding into the middle of the Atlantic.' Instead he was allowed to accompany them to their rendezvous off Cape Finisterre—and at no time did he have any 'apprehension of imminent danger to the ship' (indeed he was hoping they would be pressed through bad weather, 'under of course proper and seamanlike precaution'). Yet he was also fully prepared to have the *Captain* stripped of her masts and sails, forecastle and poop, thereby destroying her character as a seagoing cruiser, if the reports from her second cruise off the coast of Spain that September had questioned her 'seaworthiness' in

35 Ibid.

any way. That he was willing, perhaps even eager, to then reduce such an expensive and prominent first-rate capital ship down to the status of an ignoble floating battery was shocking enough. After all, there was no mention of trying to alter the vessel positively; to fix her mistakes as much as possible, as had happened with nearly every ironclad launched in Britain since 1860. But Robinson also acknowledged that he saw the *Captain*'s sea-trials as a means 'for further investigations…fully convinced that more light was required on a great many points of great importance than we had yet obtained.' Specifically, the low-freeboard *Captain* might prove useful as a live experiment, while the Controller's Department pressed ahead with Reed's all-important mastless *Devastation* class turret-ships. Thus, in the aftershock of the *Captain*'s sinking and the court martial, Robinson's greatest concern was that the British public would lose confidence in his department and Reed's own designs for turret ironclads currently under construction, assuring the President, finally, 'that catastrophes such as hers will not be repeated.'[36]

36   7 October 1870, Robinson memo, TNA ADM 1/6160.

12

'The Captain is gone, and we who opposed and resisted her have gone too'

When the verdict came in the following week, however, blaming not only 'public opinion' but also the lack of proper professional oversight, *The Times* pointed its finger to a lingering mystery at the Controller's Department, being 'left to bear the responsibility of either neglecting to obtain certain necessary information or withholding it from those entitled to receive it when obtained.' After all, the court had stressed that it was due to the differences between the ship as planned and the ship as delivered which fatally pushed the stability of the *Captain* beyond a safe margin of error; those extra two feet of freeboard might have made all the difference to so many British lives. There was perhaps nothing inherently wrong with Coles' ideas nor the design of the *Captain*, other than Reed and Robinson's sneers that any freeboard lower than the Admiralty designed *Monarch* exposed the *Captain* to less efficiency as a cruising turret-ship, capable of fighting on the open sea (i.e., not her stability). The court martial was frustratingly not going to explore that process in depth; 'that these authorities actually discovered the unseaworthiness of the vessel, and we are left, therefore, in doubt as to the nature of the imputation.'[1]

The First Lord of the Admiralty was also far from satisfied. On 28 October Childers wrote to Milne that he was going to be 'engaged on the minutes about *Captain* and Turret-ship building, which you may have seen that I am preparing', and by 15 November he wrote to Wood that while the Board minute on the court martial was passed that day, he was still working on his own. 'I quite agree with Sir. F. Grey that the order to build a ship not sanctioned by the Controller is unintelligible. From what I hear it was settled off hand by Pakington and Henry Lennox, Milne

---

[1] 11 October 1870, *The Times*. A Letter to the Editor in this same issue by Osborn wanted to know specifically why, if the *Captain* was inclined at Portsmouth on 6 August to test her centre of gravity (and therefore her stability), it took Barnes of the Constructor's Department sixteen days for the calculations to be made, and the results not ready until 22 August? 'To whom was the report on the results…communicated? Did the Board of Admiralty ever receive them; if so, on what date?'

was *non dissentiente*; and Pakington blew a loud trumpet in the House of Commons soon afterwards.' The main culprit was the Chief Constructor; 'doubly committed, positively by his reports on her, and negatively by his reports on other Turret plans where he made want of stability the great objection. His report also on a very similar ship designed by Laird in 1867 is remarkable. There is not one word about stability, though the freeboard was even less than the *Captain*.' A new independent Committee on Ship Designs was, in any case, definitely in the works.[2]

Released to the British public at the end of November 1870, Childers' extremely detailed and comprehensive *Minute* stood as an unparalleled indictment by a First Lord against his own Admiralty and its officers: 42-pages long in print; 115 with appendices (documents); and 276 with the minutes of the court martial including testimonies from the *Captain*'s survivors.[3] As distributed for Parliament it also included the Board's printed minute of 15 November. This had eighty of its own appendices attached, expressing 'surprise' that the court and its witnesses seemed to misuse the expression 'a proper amount of stability' and were unwilling to more distinctly state whether the *Captain* was or was not 'unduly pressed with sail'. Yet the real point of the Board's minute concerned the court martial's conviction of the ship being built 'in deference to public opinion…in opposition to the views and opinions of the Controller and his Department.' How could the court make such a determination when the Controller himself, also a member of the board, had not been called in to testify, nor 'others members or officers of the Board, who, if required, would have been fully prepared to elucidate the circumstances left in doubt and obscurity'? After referring to a history in documents of the *Captain*'s design, contracting, construction and initial cruises, Childers noted that in fact, as late as Vice-Admiral Sir Thomas Symonds's reports on the *Captain*'s second trial at sea (22 May – 6 June 1870) which were forwarded to the Admiralty, there was no reference 'to the question of the ship's stability.' Likewise, until the case of the *Captain*, the calculation for stability at varying degrees of incline was 'not known to have been made as to any actual ship built or building, whether of low or high-freeboard. It was not calculated as to either the *Wyvern* or the *Scorpion*, masted, low-freeboard, turrets ships afloat since 1865, nor as to the *Glatton*, *Thunderer* or *Cyclops* classes of unmasted turret-ships now being built.' Although the *Captain* was found to be seriously overweight, it wasn't until she was undergoing her third cruise that the Controller requested, on 20 July, that a calculation for 'the position of the meta-centre with reference to the centre of gravity' be made. This was done by Barnes nine days later 'in the presence of Captain Coles and Captain Burgoyne',

---

2   28 October 1870, Childers to Milne, Milne Papers, Greenwich, MLN 165/1; 15 November 1870, Childers to Wood, Halifax Papers, Borthwick Institute, A4/90, part 1.
3   Eminent British naval historian Nicholas Rodger excoriates the Childers minute, 'which none of his colleagues saw until it was published in the newspapers "by Command of their Lordships", in which, in the name of the whole Board, he flatly exonerated himself and laid the whole blame on subordinates who could not defend themselves', *The Admiralty*, 111.

but the results were not told (verbally) to Robinson until 9 August—that the centre of gravity was now 2.6 feet below the meta-centre. 'This result, as stated by Messrs. Laird at the Court-martial, almost exactly tallied with their estimate.' Yet by then the *Captain* was already en route to the coast of Spain, and Robinson did not receive the requested curve of stability figures from Barnes until 23 August. That report noted that when the *Captain*'s 'coals, provisions, water, powder, shot and shells have been consumed and her boilers empty', her stability would indeed be 'very small', but this could quickly remedied 'by letting water into the double bottom, for which the necessary means are provided.' If she was damaged in combat, her forecastle and poop shot away or flooded, and her freeboard reduced to six feet (with 500 tons of coals on board), her stability would drop after 21-degrees inclination—but 'the inclination of the deck of the ship to the surface of the wave may reach about 34-degrees (in this case) before the ship would upset. As this angle is large, we do not consider that even with the sides of the poop and forecastle destroyed the *Captain* would be unsafe.' As Childers observed, however, the Controller 'did not call the attention of either the First Sea Lord or myself to Mr. Barnes's imperfect calculation of the *Captain*'s curve of stability (referring to the ship deprived of her poop and forecastle), nor did he recommend that it should be communicated to the Admiral under whose orders the *Captain* at the time was, or to the officers of the ship.'[4]

But what Childers also stressed in the third part of his Minute was that despite the mastless turret-ships agreed to be built, including the four *Cyclops*-class monitors approved that August, 'No proposal to build additional *Captain*s was ever discussed, or even made, since the formation of the present Board, down to the retirement from office of the late Chief Constructor.' The favourable report of Symonds was to be forwarded to Parliament with Robinson's own (negative) comments attached, and a Board minute to the effect that no 'conclusion on the respective merits of the two turret-ships *Captain* and *Monarch*' would be made until their trials were complete. It was clear to the First Lord that Lairds and Coles accepted responsibility for the design and building of the *Captain*, but it was also true that once the experimental sail-and-turret ironclad was completed, the 'Controller of the Navy and his Officers became responsible for the ship's fitness to go to sea; so that if they had reason to apprehend danger from her trials, it was their duty to make representation accordingly.' What the evidence suggested, however, was 'that no such danger was apprehended by the Controller, or by any of his officers.' It was a pity that the Chief Constructor did not follow up Lairds' recommendation on 24 February 1870 for ascertaining the ship's centre of gravity; 'the first intimation received, either by the First Sea Lord or by me,

---

4   'Minute by the First Lord of the Admiralty, with Reference to H.MS. Captain, with the Minutes of the Proceedings of the Court Martial, and the Board Minute Thereon', Parliamentary Papers, 1871 (Minute is dated 30 November 1870), 20, 22, 28, 221 (Appendix S); with the enclosed 15 November 1870 Board of Admiralty 'Minute' on pages 279-81.

of any such proposal, being a submission from the Controller himself, dated the 20th [of July].'[5] Of course, what gave the First Lord's subsequent *Minute* real force was that it was compiled chiefly by a father grieving for his son—seeking justice in the face of an official cover-up whereby no one was to blame except perhaps the dead.

Reed now finally admitted the truth—openly attacking Childers after his *Minute* was not only reproduced in the newspapers up and down the country but discussed at length in Parliament. On 21 December 1870, *The Times* was happy to print another inflammatory letter from the former Chief Constructor. This questioned Childers' assertion 'that he entered office with no prejudice in favour of turret-ships, and that no proposal to build additional *Captain*s was ever made to him':

> I assert, on the contrary, that one of his earliest official acts was to direct me to design a rigged seagoing turret-ship with low-freeboard, and that Sir Spencer Robinson and I opposed it, on the ground that it would capsize in a breeze or gust. We nevertheless had to design a second such ship on larger dimensions, and again declared that she would be unsafe from this cause. Then we persuaded him to let us build such a ship without masts and sails, which caused the danger; hence the *Thunderer, Devastation,* and *Fury.* At a later period he drove me out of office—for a few days only then, as it proved—by the persistence with which he sought to bring the influence of Captain Coles to bear on the designs of ships by appointing him to some office in the Admiralty—which would have resulted in giving the navy nothing but *Captain*s, or else in involving the department in internecine and perpetual controversy. When I resigned my office in July last Mr. Childers actually offered the Chief Constructorship to the designer of the *Captain*, in face of my reports upon her miscalculations and excessive weights.

---

5   Ibid., 39-41. Robinson's lengthy *Reply* to this *Minute* was also printed and distributed to Parliament, 20 February 1871. 'As this Minute contains serious charges of neglect and omissions on the part of myself and others, to which we have had no opportunity to reply, while the accusation against us has been published and sold by your authority,' the Controller wrote to Childers on 10 January 1871, 'I request that you will be so good as to direct that a copy of these remarks (to accompany your Minute and Appendices) may be laid before Parliament.' Among other things, Robinson was emphatic that he had no 'moral' responsibility for the loss of the *Captain*. He also added a 'proximate cause' for the disaster: bad sailing on the part of Burgoyne. 'The sad fact remains…we find her carrying more sail than any other ship in the fleet on a squally night, and with her yards braced up sharper than usual. Every ship in the squadron either shortens sail or has them blown away. The *Captain* does neither.' Robinson also quoted the unpublished letter from the court martial President (Hope) to the Board; that the proper Admiralty Instructions for precautions during dangerous weather had not been followed; 'that the first watch had gone below before they were relieved'; and that 'if her topsails had been lowered in time she would not have foundered'; 21-6. See also the full copy plus materials in TNA ADM 1/6221.

Reed then followed this up in February 1871; that Childers 'always professed the greatest confidence in my professional work, even when he was seeking to force Captain Coles into my department against all my wishes and remonstrances'; and on 22 April *The Times* published another letter from the former Chief Constructor that aside from any 'personal motives' that he was not 'uninfluenced by the acts of the late First Lord of the Admiralty. Mr. Childers considered it his duty to show very great favour to Captain Coles and his ships; I considered it my duty to oppose both; and this conflict of opinion, far more than anything else, led to the breach of that confidence on the part of the late First Lord without which no professional man could possibly have tilled my office with satisfaction and success. Hence arose difficulties, rumours of resignation, offers of other employment, and finally my retirement.' Indeed, Reed was willing to venture that if there had been 'no turret-ship *Captain*, and no turret-ship controversy, I should have been Chief Constructor still, and as wholly devoted as ever to the naval service of my native country.' But history, he felt, had only proven himself and the former Controller (Robinson) right; for 'the *Captain* is gone, and we who opposed and resisted her have gone too, and gone, as I believe, primarily because we did oppose and resist her. This result is, I venture to believe, one of those anomalies of the period which will puzzle historians even more than they puzzle contemporaries.'[6]

The Times, however, was again only acting on the principle that if given enough rope a guilty man will hang himself. On 22 December, its leader noted that Reed's first public reaction to news of the sinking of the *Captain* was to quickly absolve himself of all responsibility—throwing 'the blame of it on the men who, in his oratorical language, had refused to "bring their proud heads down to the altar of science and pay proper homage there."' It likewise found his charges against the First Lord of the Admiralty 'expressed in arrogant terms, and he distinctly accused him of having wanted to build additional *Captain*s before the first was tried, and of having been so infatuated upon the subject as to be incapable of listening to any voice of warning from the scientific advisors of the Admiralty. But the responsibility of building is one thing, and the responsibility of sending on over-masted ship with 500 lives to sea is another; and what is the use of scientific advisors at the Admiralty if they are not, in such a case is this, to say to their superiors— "With those masts and with that freeboard our science shows that the *Captain* will not be safe?"' As with Childers' *Minute*, and the record of correspondence, minutes and reports which came out in the course of the investigation, *The Times* also noted that in fact, Robinson and Reed thought the ship would fail only as a fighting ship, not that it would be unstable. 'Not only is this [the Controller's] view, but he tells us that on the 23rd of August, when the Report of the Department on the *Captain*'s "curve of stability" first reached him, he showed it unofficially to Mr. Reed, "who, after a hasty perusal, considered it satisfactory." That was the very day that on which Mr. Reed wrote the letter to us to which he now

---

6 21 December 1870, 20 February 1871, and 22 April 1871, *The Times*.

refers as having shown that he thought the ship's stability compromised.' Indeed, Reed's own letter of protest finally struck a defensive tone that was as evasive as it was inconsistent: he did not make anything of the stability report because he 'took it for granted she would be tried at sea. She was built for the purpose. It was at sea that she was to prove Captain Coles and Messrs. Laird right, and Sir Spencer Robinson and myself wrong.' He was also rather coldly unsympathetic, bleating that the 'First Lord's theory, that he going to sea depended on my approval, is not tenable…She was built to go to sea; it was at sea that he qualities were to be tested and it was there she fulfilled her object of settling a public controversy—lamentably enough, I admit.' Although he claimed to have had his 'fears for such a ship; they were general and known to all.' He therefore did not feel he needed to bother with any 'exact calculations', and that even if he felt obliged to double-check the stability of a highly experimental—yet rival—sail-and-turret seagoing ship about to go to sea (seeking out bad weather, with 500 men on board), he offered that he 'could not make them without drawings and particulars, which the builders only possessed. I could not, therefore, interpose.'[7]

Likewise, when the court martial announced its verdict in October 1870, the original and overriding *public* question remained unanswered and unspoken. Britain's latest attempt to build an invincible platform for power-projection at sea had miscarried spectacularly, leaving British naval supremacy and national prestige on the world stage even further in doubt. Present on board HMS *Duke of Wellington* when the court martial concluded was American naval observer Commodore Christopher Raymond Perry Rodgers. He had been the commander of the wooden screw-frigate USS *Franklin*, on tour in European waters during the Franco-Prussian War. But he also knew how the best laid plans could come undone, perhaps bitterly recalling his experience as Rear-Admiral Du Pont's fleet captain during the fateful attack of 7 April 1863 against Charleston's defences—crowded into the pilot house of the USS *New Ironsides*, and trying to direct the roaring, smoke-filled battle of Union ironclads against Confederate forts without running aground or being sunk by a mine.[8] 'We are beset on all sides', Childers wrote to the Foreign Secretary on 9 December. 'Our relations with Russia, the U.S., China, even Greece and the Pope, bear on the strength and disposition of the Fleet. You have also been pressing about the Eastern Slave

---

7 22 December 1870, *The Times*.
8 10 October 1870, *The Times*. See for example 15 April 1863, Du Pont to Welles, *ORN*, Series 1, Vol. 14, 5-8; and William H. Roberts, *USS New Ironsides in the Civil War* (Annapolis: Naval Institute Press, 1999), 59-60. 'So dense was the smoke in the channel that I could with difficulty at times see beyond fifty yards from the ship,' reported the Commodore T. Turner of the *New Ironsides*, 'and experienced great embarrassment in training my guns, even when she fell off so that I could use them', 10 April 1863, in *Report of the Secretary of the Navy in Relation to Armored Vessels* (Washington: GPO, 1864), 76-7. According to Confederate testimony the Union flagship did hover above a large electrically-triggered torpedo which nevertheless failed to detonate at the critical moment.

Squadron, the River Plate Squadron, &c.'⁹ It had been far worse with the Imperial Navy of France. On 24 July 1870 a large squadron of seagoing broadside-ironclads set forth from Cherbourg for operations against Prussia. But the strategic island of Heligoland off the German North Sea coast was British, and neutrality dictated that coal could not be sold to either combatant. Soon the deep-draught French ships found themselves in inclement weather, low on fuel, with long lines of supply vessels stretching back to France. The Prussians had quickly taken steps to block the entrances to their major rivers from the sea, augmented by their own ironclads and coastal defences. What's more, there was never any serious plan for landing a French army through the intertidal Wadden Sea, with its shifting shallows and mudflats; no modern navy had a standing flotilla of purpose-built landing craft. Before long it was obvious the best that could be hoped for was blockade, even for the squadron of French ironclads operating in the Baltic. But massed Prussian armies had poured across the French land frontier in early August, and without a coastal assault flotilla which could counter-strike German ports hard and fast, the naval war against Prussia was practically over before it started. By the end of October the French blockading fleet quietly slunk back into Cherbourg. It was perhaps the most execrable failure of sea power in modern history.[10]

* * *

For the British, watching these dramatic events rapidly unfold up close, the question became whether the Royal Navy was any more prepared for real war against a Great Power than the magnificent French ironclad navy—which had found it problematic in the extreme to get at Prussian warships sheltered within the new fortified naval base of Wilhelmshaven, for example. *A Treatise on Coast-Defence* (1868), written by a Prussian mercenary-engineer who had served as a Lieutenant-Colonel and Chief Engineer for the Confederate States Army, stressed that while 'artillery-fire alone will never again prevent a steam-fleet from forcing a passage, the channel of which has not been obstructed…in connection with other obstructions, the torpedo [mine] renders it impossible for any fleet to force a passage under the fire of properly constructed

---

9   9 December 1870, Childers to Granville, Granville Papers, TNA PRO 30-39, 54. Then again, the First Lord was keen to show Gladstone earlier that July that there were more ships in commission and reserve in 1870 (including twenty-three ironclads in service, with eight in reserve) than in 1866 (thirteen and seven, respectively); Return dated 16 July 1870, Gladstone Papers, British Library, Add. Ms., 44,128, Vol. XLIII.

10 And relatively unexplored scholastically; notable examples include Edward Chevalier, *La Marine Française et la Marine Allemande Pendant la Guerre de 1870-71* (Paris: Henri Plon, 1873); chapter XII of H. W. Wilson's popular *Ironclads in Action: A Sketch of Naval Warfare from 1855 to 1895*, 2 vols. (Boston: Little, Brown and Company, 1896), 1: 265-85; Colin Jones, 'The Limits of Naval Power', in John Jordan (ed.), *Warship 2012* (London: Conway, 2012), 162-8; and Ropp, *The Development of a Modern Navy*, 22-5.

shore-batteries.'[11] This was, of course, what had confounded Anglo-French forces during the Crimean War, deployed in the Gulf of Finland before Cronstadt's combined defences in 1855, and which had thwarted the Federal attempt during the American Civil War to make short work of Charleston in 1863. Had the maritime powers learned nothing from these experiences? It was one thing for British contemporaries like Romaine in 1866 (and historians ever since) to pronounce seagoing French ironclads as nothing more than 'a luxury and a vanity'—but was Britain's armoured line-of-battle fleet any different?[12] The sinking of the *Captain* in September 1870 only seemed to confirm the suspicion that valuable time and treasure had been wasted preparing to fight the last great war—against the French Empire under Napoleon Bonaparte, in the age of sail. As Lord Robert Cecil, the Marquess of Salisbury (and future iconic Conservative Prime Minister), complained in the House of Lords on 6 March 1871, British governments always pointed to the fleet to safeguard the country against the threats of increasingly huge and well-equipped nation-state armies. That might have been good enough for the direct defence of the British Isles. But had Belgium actually been threatened, or indeed countries with British guarantees of national sovereignty such as Portugal, Switzerland, Sweden, Greece and Turkey, 'Of what use [was] it, then, to talk of the fleet?'

> Of what value would the fleet be in defending the European or Asiatic frontier of Turkey, or in defending Sweden? Look at the history of the past. Was the fleet of much use in the siege of Sebastopol, or even in the Baltic during the Crimean War?... I do not doubt the courage or vigour of French sailors; but we have seen how perfectly worthless the French fleet has been during the deadly peril of their country. I believe there is no delusion more fatal to this country than to believe that, if we are called upon to sustain our foreign policy with respect to any one

---

11 Victor Ernst Karl Rudolf von Scheliha, *A Treatise on Coast-Defence* (London: E. & F. N. Spon, 1868), 48, 295; also 157. Von Scheliha dedicated his volume to Prince Adalbert of Prussia.

12 The argument that France's naval power was more a 'military one' based on a 'false system' was central to Alfred Thayer Mahan's classic study of *The Influence of Seapower Upon History 1660-1783*, first published in 1890; also Ropp, *The Development of a Modern Navy*, describing the French Navy as having begun life 'as a luxury of the central government that was of no importance in the life of the people at large or in the defense of their interests', yet 'Even in England, the navy in the beginning was partly an instrument of prestige and national glory', 2-3; Jenkins, *History of the French Navy*, 341-4; Robert Gardiner (ed.), *Steam, Steel & Shellfire: The Steam Warship 1815-1905* (London: Conway Maritime Press, 1992), 10-11, 25-6, 57-9; and Hamilton, *Anglo-French Naval Rivalry*, 314-18; see also Norman Friedman's recent analyses in *British Battleships of the Victorian Era* (Barnsley: Seaforth Publishing, 2018), especially 12-14, 174-5. Ballard concluded his assessment of Britain's 'Black Battlefleet' (in which he had served) with the curious assertion that 'It served its purpose…by preventing undeclared enemies from drawing the sword if not by defeating declared enemies in arms', *Black Battlefleet*, 21.

of these guarantees, our fleet is a first line of defence, if so, what have you to oppose to the millions of men of these European Powers?

... It is no use our maintaining a high tone when it is well known how far short our means fall of our great pretensions...My fear is that when the extremity comes we shall look at the obligation, turn it round and round, talk very big, lecture one side or the other, and then when Europe cries shame on us, we shall congratulate ourselves at home upon the moral pinnacle on which we stand. That of late years has generally been our part when we have had inconvenient obligations to encounter, and it will increasingly be our part in the future.

The Earl of Granville in reply commended Salisbury for his lack of party spirit, and that he had 'not shown the inconsistency which some of the critics of Her Majesty's Government have done, who have declared that we are utterly unprepared for war, and yet in the same breath have complained that we did not use language and do things which must inevitably have led to that result.' And just because England was a 'nation of shopkeepers' did not mean that she was not formidable—something which Napoleon himself had learned the hard way. But Salisbury had a point: it was not especially clear recently how British naval power could make its presence felt. As the Earl of Lauderdale remarked, a French admiral had reported that the reason he could do nothing against Prussia in the North Sea was that he had no ships which 'could go near their shores'—and the British fleet was no different. 'We had hardly a single armour vessel afloat for coast and harbour operations; hardly a vessel fit to go in shore and attack forts.' Likewise, of the forty or so ironclads in the Royal Navy, there were scarcely ten 'which were shot-proof against guns of 12 tons or upwards.'[13]

As it turned out, this was a key conclusion of the January 1871 Committee on Ship Designs which Childers established as a direct result of the loss of HMS *Captain*.[14] This had been the most comprehensive review of Britain's past, current and projected ironclad programme ever undertaken. The First Lord invited fellow Cabinet Minister Lord Dufferin to chair a panel of fourteen naval and civilian professionals; shipbuilders, engineers, scientists.[15] Robinson objected to the whole point of such a

13   6 March 1871, 'Motion for Papers', *Hansard*, vol. 204, 1360-80.
14   *Report of the Committee* (1872), referring to the *Devastation*-class of low-freeboard breastwork-monitor as representing 'in its broadest features the first-class fighting ship of the immediate future', and with only the *Hercules*, *Monarch* and *Sultan* to be regarded as 'first-class seagoing ships of war'—thickness of armour and size of gun considered all-important factors, *xiii-iv*. The *Cyclops* class double-turret shallow-draft monitors would be ideal for coast defence, in combination with *Staunch* class gunboats, but also in conjunction with 'vessels whose power, both for attack and defence, is fully equal to that of the most formidable seagoing ships.' The *Glatton*, by contrast, was not a model to be repeated, *xviii*.
15   Frederick Hamilton-Temple-Blackwood, 1st Marquess of Dufferin and Ava, a well-placed aristocratic diplomat, held a sinecure post in Gladstone's Cabinet as Chancellor

'The *Captain* is gone, and we who opposed and resisted her have gone too'   265

review. It would be nothing more than an attack upon himself and Reed. Instead, in early November 1870, he told Childers that he would be willing to resign his post as Controller if he could serve on a Royal Commission of officers to review the history of the *Captain* and all other British ironclads. Here it was obvious that Robinson would largely direct an inquiry into his own policies. When Childers in turn suggested instead a largely civilian committee (in which the Controller would certainly be asked to testify), Robinson protested even more strongly. But he would only agree to resign if the Committee subsequently condemned those designs which his Department had produced, or he was asked to directly by the Government. Presumably such a directive would then see the querulous naval flag officer politely but firmly ask for a detailed explanation, perhaps going public if he disagreed with the reasoning, which was likely. The dogmatic Controller, used to getting his way for a decade, had no intention of making life easy for Childers, Gladstone or anyone else. By now the Board—and the Cabinet—saw him as rather more a public liability than asset. Indeed, after the lengthy public exchange between the First Lord and the Controller over responsibility for the *Captain* disaster it was inconceivable that both men would continue to work harmoniously on the same Board. On 14 December 1870 the two exchanged harsh words about the 'peculiarly hostile relations' between Childers and Reed, which Robinson 'frankly told him' had 'disturbed his judgment'.[16]

    of the Duchy of Lancaster. As Childers had written to Gladstone on 18 October, it was necessary 'to obtain the best scientific opinions on the questions which this calamity has reopened…a commission half professional, half scientific may be desirable', Gladstone Papers, British Library, Add. Ms. 44,128, Vol. XLIII. But five days earlier, the Prime Minister had already written to Wood (a former First Lord of the Admiralty), that 'the time has now come when Childers himself will have to consider the question of an enquiry by Commission respecting iron ships for naval purposes', 13 October 1870, Gladstone to Halifax, Gladstone Papers, British Library, Add. Ms. 44,539, Vol. CCCCLIV. Including the Chair and Secretary (Lieutenant Colonel Charles Pasley, Royal Engineers), there were six Royal Navy senior officers (Admiral George Elliot, Rear-Admiral Geoffrey Hornby, Rear-Admiral Houston Stewart, Rear-Admiral Alfred Ryder, Captain James Goodenough and Captain Arthur Hood), four leading British scientists and engineers (Sir William Thomson, Reverend Dr. Joseph Woolley, Professor William Macquorn Rankine, and William Froude), and three private industrial engineers, naval architects and shipbuilders (George W. Rendel, Peter Denny, George Bidder and Thomas Lloyd.)

16 See Robinson's letter to The *Standard*, 7 March 1871, citing his letter to Gladstone of 4 February 1871. Childers wrote to Gladstone on 19 March 1870 that Robinson was 'a most valuable officer in the management of the Dockyards and construction business; and nothing could be more painful to me than any difference with him.' He acknowledged that he had been appointed in February 1861, with an annual salary of £1,300 (half pay) and that when he became a Lord of the Admiralty in December 1868 this was raised to £1,500 with a £200 house allowance 'besides half pay (now £593)'. Robinson would be entitled to a pension after 10 years' service as Controller, 'and his being retired will not disqualify him from his Lordship of the Admiralty or Controllership', Gladstone Papers, British Library, Add. Ms. 41,128, Vol. XLIII; see also Matthew (ed.) *The Gladstone Diaries*,

Perhaps this also referred to the First Lord's recent decision (in conference with Halifax and Dacres) to slow down completion of 'the great ironclads in hand, e.g., the *Devastation*, *Thunderer* and *Fury*' and devote more resources into building 'as rapidly as we can an additional number of both coast defence and cruising gunboats with the men saved from ironclad building', as well as to construct more 'Anti-*Alabama*s'; something which Gladstone thought was 'decidedly good'.[17] In any case, Childers recalled his unpleasant confrontation with the Controller in a memo before the Cabinet: his authority openly questioned by a junior lord, it was either going to be him or Robinson who had to go. Gladstone then wrote to Robinson on 31 January 1871 that his non-renewal of office had been 'a foregone conclusion'. In the meantime, the First Lord had already informed Gladstone of his own desire to resign. While he felt that 'the great changes made during the last two years' at the Admiralty could 'thoroughly stand the test of critical times', he personally had 'no strength for the work'. He only wished now for the Premier to appoint a successor as soon as possible—and to whom Childers could brief 'in some detail what have been my plans for the future'—before his physical weakness and mental exhaustion increased even more.[18] His eventual replacement, George Goschen, later let slip in the House of Commons on 7 March 1871, 'the relations of Sir Spencer Robinson with some of his colleagues were such, as to interrupt and retard the course of public business, and the Government had to ask themselves whether it was compatible with the interests of the public service that a gallant Admiral, however distinguished might be his ability or high his character, should remain in office under such circumstances.'[19] As powerful

---

    Vol. VII, entries dated 30, 31 January 1870, 440, 441; also 18 April 1871, 481, referring to the lengthy exchange on the subject in Parliament on motion of inquiry by Lennox (18 April 1871; see below).

17 19 December 1870, Childers to Gladstone, Gladstone Papers, British Library, Add. Ms. 44,128, Vol. XLIII; and 20 December 1870, Gladstone to Childers, in Matthew, *Gladstone Diaries*, Vol. VII, 419; also 16 December 1870, Halifax memo to Gladstone, Gladstone Papers, British Library Add. Ms., 44,185, Vol. C.

18 9 and 21 January 1871 (to Gladstone), Gladstone Papers, British Library, Add. Ms. 44,128, Vol. XLIII. He then agreed to take four weeks' rest before committing to any final decision, with both Dacres and Lord Halifax (Sir Charles Wood, to whom Childers often deferred, as Lord Privy Seal in Gladstone's first ministry) agreeing to help manage affairs at the Board in the meantime. See also 30 January 1871, Halifax memo to Gladstone citing the Childers memo of his conversation with Robinson of 14 December, in which the Controller said he would indeed leave office 'when his time was up'—but later refused to go in connection with the publication of Childers' Minute on the *Captain*; by leaving his office, Robinson would not then have access to the papers needed to make a rebuttal. 'Mr. Childers is very anxious that every consideration should be shewn for Sir. Spencer Robinson of whose abilities and services he has the highest opinion, but whose outbursts of temper render him a bad colleague and difficult to act with'; Gladstone Papers, British Library, Add. Ms. 44,185, Vol. C.

19 18 April 1871, 'Motion for a Select Committee', *Hansard*, vol. 205, 1280-1332. Goschen denied the *Captain* disaster had anything to do with Robinson's dismissal—who was not

and forceful as Spencer Robinson had been, he finally overstepped himself against William Gladstone.[20] Captain Robert Hall thus replaced him as both Third Lord and Controller (according to the new Orders in Council of 14 January 1869). Vernon Lushington, the newly designated Permanent Admiralty Secretary—effectively replacing Romaine in June 1869—did not see his rank as an issue since both positions were one in the same 'a Civil Office'.[21]

[20] actually dismissed but not re-appointed after his five year-term expired on 7 February. Robinson, he noted, had also complained to Childers that he could not devote time to the Committee's extensive queries and conduct his normal business at the Department; at that point at least the solution was obvious. The First Lord also added that 'Sir Spencer Robinson has left the service of the Government; but he has not left the Civil Service; he has not ceased to be Admiral. He was superseded in his political appointment on account of differences of opinion between him and his colleagues which rendered it impossible for them to continue to work together in that harmonious way which is absolutely necessary for the well-being of the service.' Gladstone then confirmed where Robinson had finally gone wrong, for 'although it was not the loss of the *Captain* itself, it was the measures which grew out of that loss which led to the rise of most grave practical disagreements between Sir Spencer Robinson and not only the First Lord but other colleagues upon the Board which, in the judgment of Mr. Childers, and in my judgment upon his appeal to me, were incompatible with the advantageous transaction of public business.' When Robinson (unusually) pressed Gladstone's secretary repeatedly for a personal interview with him, Gladstone finally replied (on 7 November 1870) that he would only do so if Robinson would specify 'what you propose should be the subject of our communication that I may consider it with Mr. Childers', Gladstone Papers, British Library, Add. Ms. 44,539, Vol. CCCCLIV.

[20] *The Times* observed on 20 April 1871 that by placing Robinson on the Board (as he had requested), Childers had practically invited him to operate as a colleague rather than a subordinate, while leaving the Controller's Department, also under Robinson's direct control, free to operate separately from the Board ('the papers of which were not in the general course brought under the notice of the permanent Secretary'). The *Army and Navy Gazette* (of 11 February 1871) thought the results could be expected: 'It has been evident for some time past that Sir Spencer has not worked cordially with his present colleagues… The fact is patent that, with a wonderful aptitude for work, with a great amount of zeal for the service of the public, and the possession of no ordinary abilities he was an impracticable man. Although brought up in a profession where obedience to a superior is implicitly exacted, he was impatient of command, and could not brook interference from anyone who did not come up entirely to his standard of excellence.' Worse than this, Robinson was prone to 'a frequent display of an unfortunate temper which was admitted to proceed from habitual ill-health, and a somewhat natural desire to be guided in the transaction of his official work by no other judgment than that of his own. This latter failing could not be tolerated at Whitehall.' In the absence of Childers, Gladstone 'has stepped in and done that which the good nature of the First Lord of the Admiralty would probably have prevented—he has dismissed Sir Spencer—there is no need of being mealy-mouthed—for insubordination'.

[21] 14 February 1871 memo, TNA ADM 1/6210, with enclosed minute by Lushington dated 13 February 1871.

* * *

Reed also condemned the 1871 Committee on Ship Design, from his vantage point as MP for Pembroke: although it was 'powerful', it consisted 'of Gentlemen who knew very little about the subject, and not numbering among them a single shipbuilder.' Then again, he had to admit that while it was 'probably brought together to ban his ships, really blessed them, and he had no fault to find with their Report.' His brother-in-law and former colleague, Nathaniel Barnaby, also thought it valuable in publicly ascertaining that Reed's *Devastation* was going to be much safer than Coles's *Captain*. As he quoted the Committee, 'We believe that our transmarine possessions and other important interests in distant parts of the world, will be more efficiently protected by the establishment, where requisite, of centres of naval power, from which vessels of the *Devastation* class may operate, than by relying upon cruising ships of such limited fighting power as the *Monarch*.'[22] In this assessment, simply 'showing the flag' with the most seaworthy of warships was no longer good enough for the practical projection of Britain's naval standing—and perhaps never had been in the age of the ironclad—in an era of intense rival nationalism combined with rapid industrial and technological advances. Only brute fighting power, as opposed to maritime prowess, mattered. When Sherard Osborn testified before the Committee he recalled how the lower deck of the *Captain* featured 'the most comfortable quarters I had ever seen for a man of war.' Yet while the 'policing of the seas', during peace, was perhaps best left to unarmoured wooden frigates, which also enabled 'the prestige and repute of this country to be maintained all over the world', during war it was obvious that they could 'take no decisive part in great naval actions, either upon the high seas or in breaking into and destroying an enemy's fleet within his own fortresses'.[23]

Robinson's own testimony before the Committee (24 March) rather agreed; 'to defend Jamaica, Bermuda, or Halifax, or attack any hostile port on the other side of the Atlantic' had been the whole *raison d'être* of the new *Devastation*-class of turret-ship. (He did not speculate whether Coles had this in mind with the *Captain* as well.) But he was obliged to acknowledge, before the question posed by civilian engineer George Bidder, that the more range required, and thus the more coal for a mastless vessel, 'you must sacrifice something'—namely a shallower draft for coastal operations or more weight available for guns or armour, versus a monitor. 'If you reduce the dimensions very considerably you might build a ship by sacrificing some of the seagoing qualities of the *Devastation* that would be a better fighting engine than

---

22 13 March 1876, 'British and Foreign Iron-Clad Navies—Observations', *Hansard*, vol. 227, 1891-1918; Barnaby, *Naval Development*, 74-8. David Brown also noted the 1871 Committee 'saw little value in such ships as *Monarch* and *Sultan* as being expensive with little fighting value', yet the 'immediate effect of the committee's report was small, the Board ordering the centre battery ships *Alexandra* and *Temeraire* of the type which they had condemned', in Gardiner (ed.), *Steam, Steel & Shellfire*, 83.
23 Testimony of 25 March 1871, *Report of the Committee* (1872), 86.

the *Devastation*, but only as a fighting machine.' Pressed by Scottish shipbuilder Peter Denny, the former Controller then admitted—in contrast to his previous statements that the best possible ironclad force for Britain would consist of both improved sail-and turret *Monarch*s ('for cruising') and mastless *Devastation*s ('for the day of battle')—that he preferred 'the broadside cruising ship to any cruizing turret design that I have yet seen completed', citing better health and comfort for the crew and the danger of 'accidents' occurring to moving turrets. He still favoured the *Hercules* and could not be convinced of the tactical superiority of either a *Monarch* or *Captain*. When he returned to testify on 3 May he was certain the British navy should be divided 'between ships of the improved *Hercules* or *Sultan* form, and the best type of ships that could be got out of the *Devastation* class.' But he was also now most impressed with the dangers posed by locomotive torpedoes in naval warfare; 'indeed I may say that I had begun considering it, when I was interrupted by other things, in November last, at which time this power became so evident and formidable that I should say instead of turning our attention very much to new *Cyclop*s and new *Sultan*s, as our command of funds is limited, we should do well to turn our attention to the best form of torpedo ship which would be the master even of the *Devastation* and the *Thunderer*.'[24]

However, in Robinson's first interview before the Admiralty committee, on 10 March, he also declared that the shallow-draft breastwork-monitors (ordered up in the autumn of 1870 for coast defence purposes), were likewise 'for those occasions on which the country might think it necessary to send out a great expedition to land an attacking force in shallow water, where vessels of great draught of water could not arrive and take their part in an action.' Here the Chairman, Lord Dufferin, was keen to know more about the actual pre-planned abilities of the British turret-ships, 'if we wished to make an attack upon some forts'. When the ex-Controller of the Navy evasively replied it would be 'merely wasting your time' to speculate, Dufferin interjected:

> But is it not questions of this kind which it is our especial object to anticipate. We have to prepare in time of peace for contingencies which will occur in time of war. It is impossible to foresee what maybe the conditions of any particular attack which may be made, and, therefore, we are bound to furnish ourselves beforehand with the capability of meeting unforeseen contingencies. That was the great mistake which France seems to have made, and many others have made, and perhaps ourselves, in not having provided the necessary means of attack for any contingency which might happen?

Robinson's response was the Admiralty 'had provided such means of attack as the country has thought proper to allow money for…and if we have got too small a navy that is the business of the Government of the day'. In any case, deep water ports

---

24 Testimony of 24 March and 3 May 1871, *Report of the Committee* (1872), 168.

were accessible to the main British ironclad fleet—'if not kept out by torpedoes.' For attacking forts approachable through shallow water, Robinson finally admitted that no armoured vessel currently existed; 'and I do not know that that is a particular want either.'[25] Reed confirmed this in his own testimony to the Committee a month later. The *Cerberus* was built for the unique conditions of Melbourne, Australia only; a fairly sheltered anchorage. For the defence of more exposed ports in the British Isles he thought breastwork-monitors should be seagoing enough to weather the English Channel as well: a significantly modified design which he stated was impossible to speculate upon—even their draft. The former Chief Constructor then added cautiously, 'that the *Cyclops* class was designed under an amount of pressure to accomplish certain objects, which ought not, in my opinion, to have been applied in the designing of harbour defence vessels for the defence of this country.' This included a lighter, weaker hull bottom. He had no idea what the thinking was behind the *Glatton*, and he never 'expressed any opinion in favour of the fitness of the *Glatton* to make ocean voyages.' When invited to comment on whether he considered the USS *Miantonomoh* dangerous at sea, Reed asserted 'Utterly dangerous. Not from capsizing, but from the danger of such a ship getting into a big hollow and being completely overwhelmed, and also from the fact that when you have such a limited freeboard, you have such a small margin for taking water in by accident. That freeboard is the margin of safety.' But when requested specifically if either the British turret vessels could contend with Russian coastal defence ironclads in the Baltic, Reed was bound to reply that 'the Northern Powers will produce vessels superior in fighting powers to those vessels, superior to both the *Glatton* and *Cyclops* classes.'[26]

Thus, it was never very clear to a committee of leading British naval, professional and scientific authorities—nor to the former architects of the Royal Navy's ironclad force between at least 1863 and 1870—how Britain might avoid a humiliation similar to that of Imperial France; not in a lengthy maritime war over 'command of the ocean', but in a short, sharp conflict with nationalised continental powers armed to the teeth. Half a century before the outbreak of the First World War, and doubts had already crept in the Admiralty about laying down a 'close' blockade against a well-defended enemy coast, let alone other forms of classic naval power-projection such as bombardment or amphibious strikes.[27] What was the point of 'naval supremacy', or 'prestige'? How was

25 Ibid., 10 March 1871, 53-7.
26 Ibid., 15 April 1871, 144-54.
27 See for example, Raja Menon, *Maritime Strategy and Continental Wars* (London: Frank Cass, 1998), 56-61, but also page 107, where he notes 'that most of the factors militating against close blockades being undertaken in war today have come from the gradual and relative decline of sea power when pitted against land power…it is conceded that the dynamics attending the closing of an amphibious force to a hostile coast have changed dramatically from what they were 50 years ago, or, for that matter, a century ago'; yet earlier he observes that the American Civil War 'is a grand illustration of a vigorous use of sea skills in every possible way towards the aim of defeating the common continental

it actually applicable—against whom, and with what types of ironclads? Although *The Illustrated London News* in April 1869 depicted the *Royal Sovereign* and *Scorpion*—controversial 'turret-ships of the future'—staging a 'bombardment' of the forts at Dover in an epic two-page spread, this sort of occasional grand review of volunteer British defences by land and sea was designed to thrill tax-paying Victorian spectators rather than as serious wargame exercises in the postmodern sense. Hence the image did not show the twenty-four foot draught of the *Royal Sovereign*, obliging her to keep a greater distance. The sea that day was choppy, meaning the two vessels rolled to the point where any real accuracy would be problematic in the extreme—while the forts apparently were not shown firing back. No mines, obstructions or defending coastal vessels such as fast rams were present; it was a straight fight between ships and shore. What was also missing was the fact that these were two of the only four turret vessels in commission in the Royal Navy at the time, armed with slow-firing, 9-inch 12-ton rifled muzzle-loaded Armstrong guns—intended to penetrate the armour of enemy ironclads, not attempt to silence forts.[28]

Yet as Robinson and others continually maintained during this period and beyond, Britannia had really nothing to be ashamed of. Her navy still commanded the high seas by a considerable margin (especially after the crippling defeat of the Second French Empire by land, not sea in 1870). And other powers, namely America and Russia, were content with their own defences at best—expanding their own interests and empires across their respective continents rather than overseas. Britain was *safe*, and even the Empire was probably able to endure after perhaps some initial shocks from a particularly bold and clever enemy. But neither did these feelings of self-assurance and self-satisfaction entirely overcome the nagging sense of the British public that something important had been somehow lost in the preceding years. Something about Lord Palmerston and 'influence' and 'primacy'. Lost was the dream—the confident expectation—that the globe was becoming a British place in the nineteenth century, thanks in no small part to the long, strong arm of Britain's naval dominance.[29] This was never just about defending the country at home or the empire abroad, but in 'asserting' British 'interests' the world over, Europe included.

---

enemy ... Best of all, [the Union Navy] did not make the excuse that many navies have made in the past; that the force structure designed for an oceanic war precluded any coastal strategy and shallow water operations. Indeed, the evolution of the armoured monitor with revolving turrets was a case of a weapon-platform designed specifically for a land support strategy, and, until the advent of the whole genre of landing ships, represented the best example of naval technology applied specifically to continental warfare,' 52.

28 10 April 1869, 'The Volunteer Review at Dover: View of Dover from the Sea—The Naval Squadron Attacking the Forts', *Illustrated London News*.

29 See for example, Palmerston's declaration in 1848 'that we stand at the head of moral, social and political civilization. Our task is to lead the way and direct the march of other nations', from Martin Lynn, 'British Policy, Trade, and Informal Empire in the Mid-Nineteenth Century', in Porter, *Oxford History*, 102, also 108-9; also Duncan Bell, *The Idea*

Sea power, when maintained properly, had made Britain uniquely invulnerable. The question only remained how far it also made British foreign policies irresistible. That notion was first upset with the French *Gloire* of 1860, and once steps had been taken to meet that serious potential defiance of Palmerstonian primacy in the form of HMS *Warrior* of 1861 (ordered up even a month before Palmerston's second ministry), a far more puzzling challenge appeared on the opposite side of the ocean in the form of the American *Monitor*, in 1862. In the end, Palmerston died before any viable solution to this dilemma was reached, and the American Civil War ended in a way he would not have preferred; not just geo-strategically, but socio-politically the survival of the democratic-republic would reverberate even back to Britain.[30] And while Reed's *Bellerophon* of 1865 and her follow-ons were meant to firmly check the French above all, Italy had been consolidated, and France benefited. Poland had revolted, yet was kept firmly under Russian control as a buffer state. Prussia and Austria had run roughshod over Denmark—and Queen Victoria in the process—and within just a few more years Prussia transformed much of central Europe into a German empire; the Second Reich.[31] It was, meanwhile, was left to Coles and HMS *Captain* of 1869 to comprehensibly answer the monitor riddle: a stealthy, low-freeboard ship-killer boasting the biggest possible guns behind the thickest possible armour, as represented by the USS *Miantonomoh* in the 'Reform Summer' of 1866, yet which could still assert British interests the world over, America included. As Russell, born in 1792, warned the young new First Lord of the Admiralty, Hugh Childers, in February 1869, 'up to a few years ago American statesmen, and generals, and admirals, all thought that at the beginning of a war England would have the best of it; but that opinion had changed, and was then unanimous that the United States would be successful at the commencement of a war between us. Neither Lincoln, nor Johnson, nor Seward wished to try the experiment, but I am by no means confident that Grant may not throw down his glove.' Childers, at 42, was confident, however: while the Americans had 'nothing with which they could think of crossing the Atlantic to attack us…our ironclad fleet is quite equal to offensive operations on their coast.' This was because Britain was 'the only nation who are building seagoing turret-ships'—and 'the crack turret-ship', Childers later wrote to his wife (with a mind where their second son Leonard should serve), was expected to be HMS *Captain*.[32]

---

of Greater Britain: Empire and the Future World Order, 1860-1900 (Princeton: Princeton University Press, 2007).

30 See for example, Bourne, *Britain and the Balance of Power in North America*, especially 203, 252-7, 290.

31 As proclaimed on 18 January 1871 in the Hall of Mirrors, at the (captured) Palace of Versailles.

32 12 February 1869, Russell to Childers, 17 February 1869, Childers to Russell, and 21 September 1869, Childers to Emily Childers, in Childers, *Life and Correspondence*, 1: 171-2, 181-2. Russell replied with relief on 19 February, inasmuch as the '*Alabama* Convention' was to be rejected. 'We may now insist on honourable conditions, or none at all'; 1: 173.

Conclusion

'There was a time when this country was the arbitress of the world'

On King Charles Street, Westminster the new—and first purpose-built—Foreign Office building was finally complete in 1868, after seven years of construction. But the finished structure, like British foreign policy itself by that time, was considered rather a disappointment by the mid-Victorians; not quite Classical, English Baroque or Gothic Revival—which Palmerston had personally opposed as a potential design. Instead, the Italianate style was considered more suitably 'cosmopolitan' when construction began in late 1861—commensurate perhaps with Britain's sense of assertive global identity. By the end of the 1860s, however, much of that self-confidence was gone. Whereas Russell in 1860 hardly cared what the new Foreign Office building might look like on the outside, in one of his last speeches in Parliament, in 1875, the eighty-three year old statesman bemoaned 'that indifference—that carelessness—of foreign policy which I regret we have in recent times allowed to prevail.' By the end of the Napoleonic Wars, great care had been made 'to preserve the position of Great Britain and place her in a situation of considerable power and influence abroad.' But it was clear that by the outbreak of the Franco-Prussian War in 1870, the country had been somehow marginalised in European affairs and was sinking into isolation.[1] 'Neutrality', in the meantime, had become a shameful word.

---

1   Bernard Porter, *The Battle of the Styles: Society, Culture and the Design of the New Foreign Office, 1855-1861* (London: Continuum International Publishing Group, 2011), 111, 132-3; 31 May 1875, *Hansard*, Vol. 224 (Lords), 'Motion for Correspondence', 1091-5. The presiding Foreign Secretary, Lord Stanley, politely objected that 'a policy of non-intervention does not mean a policy of isolation and indifference, and it does not mean that England either is or can be indifferent to the maintenance of European peace', 1099. See also, for example, John Clarke, *British Diplomacy and Foreign Policy 1782-1865: The National Interest* (London: Unwin Hyman, 1989), who refers to the period 1856-1865 as 'The Bluff Exposed', and that if 'there was ever a "British" period in the history of international relations, this must be dated 1815-1864, with a necessary preparatory build up during the Revolutionary and Napoleonic Wars', 258-324.

On 31 October 1870, the Chancellor of the Russian Empire, Prince Gortchakoff, announced that due to various violations by Turkey of the neutrality of the Bosporus Straits in recent years his country no longer felt obliged to honour the Black Sea clauses of the Treaty of 1856, which had ended the Crimean War. Tsar Alexander II and his councillors had calculated, of course, that with France now crippled, and neither Austria nor Italy willing to fight for the sake of neutralisation of the Black Sea, Britain was the only Great Power Russia had left to fear—though at that time of year the Baltic was quite inhospitable for naval operations. The Imperial Russian Navy had also begun construction that July on the *Petr Veliky* (*Peter the Great*), their own version of HMS *Devastation*, with fourteen-inch armour-plating and twelve-inch guns.[2] Gladstone was quick to observe that by unilaterally choosing which parts of a treaty to accept or not the whole essence of such agreements between powers was destroyed. Granville then wrote to Victoria that the Russians' conduct (whether eschewing a conference or by relying upon 'brute force') put them into the wrong, though they clearly already had the backing of Prussia. As for the British people, 'a short time ago [they] would have recoiled from a renewal of a Russian war. It is impossible to say, after the feverishness created by the spectacle of a great war, what would be their feeling now.' The Queen agreed that caution was paramount, 'for a war at the present moment might be very disastrous to us, and do great harm to Turkey instead of good.' She was still bitter that British neutrality in the Franco-Prussian conflict might have only made a future enemy of Germany, now corroborating Russia in her misdeeds. 'However, the great object now must be to do nothing precipitate, so that we may not be driven into a war for so unsatisfactory a cause…by asserting loudly that we are insulted and then cannot recede with honour.' The jingoistic British press is what she feared the most.[3] Childers warned Granville that if there was going to be

---

2   See W. E. Mosse, 'The End of the Crimean System: England, Russia and the Neutrality of the Black Sea, 1870-1', *The Historical Journal*, Vol. 4, No. 2 (1961), 164-90, and W. E. Mosse, *The Rise and Fall of the Crimean System 1855-71: The Story of a Peace Settlement* (London: Macmillan & Co Ltd), 1963, 158-83. Also inspired directly by the visit of the USS *Miantonomoh* (at Cronstadt in July-August 1866), the *Peter the Great* was originally planned to feature limited masts and sails—scrapped after news of the *Captain* disaster; see for example, Stephen McLaughlin, *Russian & Soviet Battleships* (Annapolis: Naval Institute Press, 2003), 1-11., who also suggests not only that the breastwork-monitor concept had been devised originally by Russian Admiral A. A. Popov in 1865—certainly in a memo to the Russian Naval Technical Committee ('MTK') of December 1866—but that 'Reed and Popov were friends, and it is likely they had discussed the idea in their correspondence with one another'; Reed then announcing his ideas at Bourne's paper at the Institution of Civil Engineers in January 1867. As McLaughlin notes, however, Popov's designs still featured masts and sails, until news was received of the sinking of the *Captain*, while Reed cordially advised the Russians in person (during his tour of Russia in 1871) to extend the outer breastwork armour flush with the hull, as had been done on his ships, 3-5.

3   12 November 1870, Granville to Queen Victoria, and 20 November 1870, Victoria to Granville, in Buckle, *Letters of Queen Victoria, Second Series*, 2: 82-3, 85-6; also 10 November 1870, Gladstone memo to Queen, TNA CAB 41/2/46.

a war against Russia then 'every day lost is most injurious'.[4] The navy would have to prepare for such a unique conflict as soon as possible. Yet with Prussian forces stalled in their siege of Paris throughout that autumn and going into winter, the British clamour against Russia was enough to convince Bismarck to pressure St. Petersburg to reconsider; lest France be revitalised by a joint Anglo-French crusade against Imperial Russia, again, and perhaps with Prussia drawn in too. Though Gladstone objected to the notion that Britain was prepared to go to war at all, Granville replied to him candidly enough on 8 December 1870:

> I am afraid that our whole success has been owing to the belief that we would go to war, and to tell the truth, I think war in some shape or other sooner or later, was a possible risk after our note. In any case I would reassure nobody now. Promising peace is as unwise as to threaten war. A sort of sentiment that the bumps of combativeness and destructiveness are to be found somewhere in your head has helped us much during the last five months.[5]

By Christmas both the Tsar and the British Cabinet agreed to an international conference to discuss matters, in London. On 13 March 1871, the Treaty of London confirmed that no power could arbitrarily renounce a treaty or any part of it without reference to the other signing powers, with Turkey retaining her right to 'open the said Straits in time of peace to the vessels of war of friendly and allied Powers'. But the controversial and unpopular clauses in question from the 30 March 1856 Treaty were indeed formally abrogated, and Russia (along with Turkey) was finally allowed to resume her sovereign rights—including the development of her naval power—in the Black Sea again.[6]

Peace had once again been maintained; war averted. And the British public was again both relieved and dissatisfied.[7] After all, the only practical difference between

---

4 Morley, *Life of William Ewart Gladstone*, 2: 351.
5 21 November 1870, Granville to Gladstone, 6 December 1870, Gladstone to Granville, and 8 December 1870, Granville to Gladstone, in Ramm, *Gladstone-Granville Correspondence*, 176-7, 179.
6 As Gladstone observed to Edmund Hammond (1st Baron), the Permanent Under-Secretary of State for Foreign Affairs even before the crisis broke, on 28 October 1870, 'in this country the whole policy of the Crimean War is now almost universally, and very unduly depreciated; and the idea of another armed intervention on behalf of Turkey, whether sole or with allies, is ridiculed', Gladstone Papers, British Library, Add. Ms. 44,539, Vol. CCCCLIV.
7 Gladstone wrote to Granville on 19 November 1870 that 'the tone of the press ... shows me that we have a highly inflammable and suspectable state of the public mind to deal with', exacerbated by the climate of the Franco-Prussian War. Yet 'Russia 'having nothing in the Baltic Sea, an increase of force would mean the thought of attack; I think it would be premature, and I fear might prove mischievous, as with many it would be popular', Gladstone Papers, British Library, Add. Ms. 44,539, Vol. CCCCLIV. 'The shock of the

the spring of 1856 and that of 1871 was in the balance of power. At the close of the Crimean War, the allied fleets of Britain and France reigned supreme, and the Russian army as well as the state was exhausted. By the end of the Franco-Prussian War it was the French who were defeated, their proud navy proven to be more powerful—and more useless—than ever. As one British diplomat confided to Earl Russell on 7 December 1870, '*Then* all the assembled Powers were virtually triumphant, with the exception of one which had been beaten. *Now*, all the Powers have been morally, if not materially worsted, with the exception of one which is so overwhelmingly triumphant as to be virtually the dictatress of any deliberations undertaken with the avowed purpose of *avoiding* a war; for unluckily our complacent parade of that deplorable Anglo-French Alliance places us before Europe in the position of having received a moral defeat by the German victories.'[8] Indeed, the British were by then swimming with doubts. Their model ironclad ship had foundered from either poor design or poor handling, but in any case poor (that is perhaps excessive) administration by the Admiralty seemed to have nurtured its creation. The Royal Navy had struggled with the revolutionary new technology in a way that Palmerston did not expect in 1856, nor respected by 1865. America and Russia, who both seemed susceptible enough to British naval power-politics in 1856, were all-too formidable in their own right by 1871. The *Morning Post* actually pushed for war against Russia 'the sooner the better'; before her strategic system of railways was completed, her troops re-armed with

events of 1864 induced a kind of paralysis of will, an unwillingness to commit British policy in any positive direction for fear of further failures and humiliations', noted Richard Shannon. 'Hence there was a well-defined period of recoil from Europe. But this was an isolation not, as the Cobdenites congratulated themselves it was, of calculation, but of bewilderment, of an inability to understand why policies which had hitherto appeared to answer requirements with complete satisfaction had suddenly ceased to carry conviction and credibility', *The Crisis of Imperialism 1865-1915* (London: Paladin Books 1984 reprint of 1974 original), 41.

8   7 December 1870, Robert Lytton (British attaché at Vienna) to Russell, in G. P. Gooch (ed.), *The Later Correspondence of Lord John Russell 1840-1878*, 2 vols. (London: Longmans, Green and Co., 1925), 2: 373-5. 'In one respect only I fear that you stand quite alone', Lytton later wrote to Russell, after the latter condemned the terms of the Treaty of Washington (resolving the *Alabama* Claims)—in which Gladstone's Government agreed to pay $15.5 million in damages—'and that is the lofty statesmanlike patriotism and old English "pluck"—which rings so true and sound through the whole *tone* of your speech', 25 June 1871, 2: 376. For Russell's speech in the House of Lords see 12 June 1871, 'Motion for Address', *Hansard*, vol. 206, 1823-1901, in which he declared, 'I always looked to Lord Palmerston as the greatest authority on foreign affairs, and when I accepted the seals of the Foreign Office I had great comfort in reflecting that I could always refer to him, who for 14 years had maintained the honour of this country, and had never brought us into the least danger of war.' Granville replied that the Anglo-American negotiations had effectively stalled by the summer of 1870. 'But later in the autumn circumstances occurred which made it desirable to inquire how our relations stood with every country in the world, and when we came to the case of the United States it was impossible to say that our relations were on a perfectly satisfactory footing.'

modern breechloaders, and her navy improved, including completion of the defences of Nikolaev. And this said nothing for far-ranging geo-strategic considerations. 'Not for nought does [Russia] strain her eyes across the Atlantic, to note the first glitter of steel and the first wave of the star-spangled banner', its leader commented on 22 December 1870. 'In 1866, when the *Miantonomoh* was lying at Cronstadt, with hundreds of eager spectators crowding to stare at her double turrets and heavy armament…the compliments showered by the Russians upon their visitors invariably ended in vague menaces against Great Britain, and hints that the two young empires could not do better than make common cause against the old one.'[9]

Peace had not been maintained by British naval supremacy but rather in spite of it. And the 'turret vs. broadside'-debate was not coincidental to this phenomenon. Hence *The Times* was actually critical of Salisbury's speech in March 1871. 'There was a time when this country was the arbitress of the world; she had fleets on every sea, and not only was her brave army ready to go anywhere and do anything in Europe, but there were spirited Statesmen ready to employ it on any enterprise by which glory was to be gained', it parroted. 'Now all that is changed.' Yet the truth was different, and such an outlook was not only at variance with the facts but 'peevish, undignified, and unpatriotic.' It wasn't about gunboat diplomacy so much as 'the relative population, wealth, and military and naval resources of England and other countries of the present and of former days. On these depends the permanent reputation of the country, and we need not fear that the world will be unable to perceive the truth, and to recognise real power, even though we do not display it by plunging into every quarrel.'[10] Then again the 'resources of England' were less perceptible than a powerful ironclad off shore—itself a potent, immediate and incontrovertible demonstration of the latent power of the British Empire. The question then was which symbol of ironclad power would be respected more: turret or broadside. Coles and his followers had been adamant that nothing less than a turret-ship which could also 'go anywhere' *and* 'do anything' would properly defend the interests and uphold the honour of the country. That such interests were indeed 'on every sea', and that any defeat of even a single flagship would be catastrophic to British prestige not just in Europe but around the world, practically dictated the type of armoured vessel required.

---

9   21 November and 22 December 1870, The *Morning Post*. Following the fall of Sevastopol in September 1855 it was reported that the Russians were turning 'Nicolaieff' into a major naval port and arsenal, given its less exposed strategic position up river from the Black Sea, 'and its facility of internal communication with Russia by means of the Dnieper'. Extensive fortifications of the port already underway; 25 September 1855, War Office to Admiralty, TNA ADM 1/5665; also 6 January 1871, Foreign Office to Admiralty, TNA ADM 1/6198. Despite these developments the Allies chose not press the issue given its 'inland' position at the Paris Peace Talks of 1856; see for example, Andrew Lambert, *The Crimean War: British Grand Strategy against Russia, 1853-56* (Farnham: Ashgate, 2011, 2nd ed.), 339-40.
10   7 March 1871, *The Times*.

This turned out to be a tragic illusion. Coles, Reed, and other critics were probably right that the gigantic, stately *Warrior* was nothing more than an albatross—and a sitting duck. But even Ericsson could not deny that such an ironclad vessel indeed represented the overwhelming (and perhaps overbearing) maritime, industrial and economic powers of Britain far better than a compact, more invulnerable version; while the ingenious mechanical powers of the *Monitor*—while she might sink the *Warrior* given the opportunity—at best represented the limits of American resources by comparison. Big as she was, HMS *Warrior* was just the tip of the iceberg. Thus, when U.S. naval officers and engineers toured British facilities during these years they were not just starkly reminded of the disparity of resources in play, but wholly staggered by it.[11] 'It is the old story', Gladstone mused to Cardwell on 23 December 1870, in response to a recent cry for more harbour fortifications; 'the profession wants to make hay when the sun shines':

> At no time for perhaps 30 years, have our harbours been so safe. We are preparing torpedoes & harbour defence vessels in unusual numbers & for one I know of no reason for also setting about forts at such a time. Lord Russell is an historian: but what *are* the innocent & peaceful nations who as he says have been destroyed or assailed by their less happy neighbours out of sheer envy of their prosperity?[12]

* * *

As could be expected, Pakington as President of the Institution of Naval Architects, began their annual meeting of 1871 by addressing the loss of HMS *Captain*. By then Vice-Admiral Sir Robert Spencer Robinson was also listed as a Vice-President, alongside Edward Reed, Hugh Childers, Alexander Milne, Sydney Dacres, John Hay, John Dalrymple Hay (now a rear-admiral), Henry Corry, Frederick Grey, and the new First Lord of the Admiralty, George Goschen. Everyone had come a long way since Pakington's opening address to the Institution in March 1865. He was not only 'personally a sufferer, by the loss of a very near connection…but the share which it was my official duty to take in ordering the construction of that ship'. When he became First Lord in the summer of 1866 the 'public mind had been a long time anxiously attending to the suggestions of the unfortunate and ill-fated Captain Coles', and while the previous Board under Somerset had indeed authorised the construction of HMS *Monarch* to test the concept of a turret-ship as a cruiser it had also allowed Coles to submit his own designs in collaboration with Lairds. Pakington then told

---

11 See for example, *Report of the Chief Engineer, J. W. King, United States Navy, on European Ships of War and Their Armament, Naval Administrations and Economy, Marine Construction, Torpedo-Warfare, Dock-Yards, Etc., Etc.*, Second Edition (Washington: Government Printing Office, 1878).

12 Matthew, *Gladstone Diaries*, Vol. VII, 421.

Coles 'to persevere to build his ship, and I entirely approved of the selection of Messrs. Laird, as being the best persons to whom he could entrust that duty'. When Coles later submitted his design proposal, the former First Lord told him in private that he 'shrunk very much from this freeboard of 8 feet...but I did consent to it on this ground, that the principle on which I was acting was that Captain Coles should solve his own problem, and that as he pressed to have a ship with that freeboard, it would not have been consistent with the principle on which I was acting, to interfere further than to express my doubts and fears with regard to the success of so low a freeboard.' Put in this way, the Admiralty had allowed itself to sacrifice the principle of building the best and safest warships possible in favour of a principle of 'fair play' to Coles. As it had been publicised, he had not received it from the Controller's Department, which clearly preferred seagoing broadside-ironclads over turret ones. Meanwhile that year, foreign powers especially the United States had turret vessels making ocean voyages. One way or another the debate must be resolved, and the *Captain* was meant to do that. Pakington then suggested that his colleagues in 1871 needed to address not just why the Coles turret-ship was built the way it was (at six-feet freeboard), but when that flaw was discovered, 'what steps were taken? Were proper steps taken to test the effect of that deviation on the stability of the ship? If no such steps were taken, why were they not taken, and who was to blame?'[13]

Halifax took an even larger view of the question, writing to Gladstone not just as a respected Cabinet member but trusted confidant on 2 October 1870. The Prime Minister could always summon a Commission of inquiry 'on the construction of these turret-ships', even without consulting Childers. But it was perhaps best to wait until all the evidence had come in. He recalled being First Secretary of the Admiralty—over thirty years before—when the controversy between Captain Sir William Symonds (as surveyor, 1832-1847) and his opponents over his sailing battleship designs was at its height. Even then, after devoting much time and study to the subject of shipbuilding, he thought 'hardly any of those could give a good reason for what they did and that ships sailed equally well built on the most opposite principles.' Thus, while the *Captain* heeled over more than any other ironclad in the squadron that night few had observed that the unarmoured screw-frigate *Inconstant* heeled over still further—and no one in the fleet thought the *Captain* liable to capsize. 'When an accident has happened' he intoned, 'everybody tries to find out some reasons for it; the only one that no answer can be given to is that too much sail was set at the time, and no inquiry by a commission could throw any light on that point.' A letter to *The Times* of 16 March 1871 from old sailing admiral Henry John Rous (then 76 and a veteran of the Napoleonic Wars) also wondered whether the acrimonious feud within the Admiralty over the responsibility for the *Captain*'s sinking was not beside the point: of course the overall design was outlandish, being too deep for narrow seas as a turret-ship

13 30 March 1871, 'Introductory Proceedings', *Transactions of the Institution of Naval Architects*, Volume XII (London, 1871), xxi-xxvi.

and frequently swamped on the high seas. But that just meant she needed 'delicate handling and fine seamanship.' As far as he was concerned the only questions which the court martial needed to address were 1) why were no suitable preparations made to shorten sail with an approaching storm? 2) why were sailors not posted 'by the lee topsail sheets and halyards, according to the custom of every ship of war in respectable discipline'? and 3) 'why were the watch on deck allowed to go below deck before they were relieved, and the deck deserted in the face of the enemy?' The ship had not been killed by Coles, Lairds, Robinson, Reed, or even Burgoyne, but by the 'officer of the watch not knowing how to shorten sail or to keep his men on deck.'[14]

A piercing article in *Fraser's Magazine* of March 1871 by Captain Edmund Robert Fremantle went further. 'The attempt to make sailing ships of our iron-clads we hold to be simply a reactionary blunder, with no redeeming feature to palliate it.' Yet while this referred more to the new trend of economising on coal, 'and the traditions of our officers and men in favour of sailing', the early ironclad navies of both France and Britain had retained sails for the far more serious purpose of retaining the strategic reach of their naval power. 'As to the *Captain* herself, it was clearly shown by Captain Coles' letters published after her loss, that all on board the ill-fated ship were fully bent on proving her capability as a sailing vessel, and this tendency…was undoubtedly one of the principal causes of her loss.' By 1875 Disraeli and the Conservatives were back in power with Gladstone and the Liberal Party's comprehensive defeat at the general election of 1874. Milne was still in post as First Naval Lord, and when contemplating a 'new class of ship to be laid down to add to the Iron clad Fleet' he confirmed the strategic divide which had been at work in British naval power for over a dozen, crucial years—'turret vs. broadside', mastless vs. sailing ironclad: 'For foreign service sail power will have to be retained, but for Home defence and Mediterranean operations as well as special service, the power of the Turret-ship from having the heaviest guns will be the most formidable and efficient type.'[15]

In this wake British foreign policy must continue to follow. Indeed, as Disraeli had sardonically noted on 5 February 1863, 'whatever may have been the disinclination of Her Majesty's Government to interfere in the conflict between the Northern and Southern States, there does not appear to have been any objection to interference in

---

14   2 October 1870, Halifax to Gladstone, Gladstone Papers, British Library, Add. Ms. 44,185, Vol. C; 16 March 1871, *The Times*. Perhaps not surprisingly, Rous couldn't resist adding that 'the boiler has emasculated seamanship. No man can serve two masters—he will hold to the teakettle and despise the canvas.' Halifax later wrote to Gladstone that, given the novelty and controversy surround the *Captain*'s design, 'every possible precaution should have been taken to test her stability before sending her to sea. In point of fact one of the ordinary tests, and in fact the most decisive one[,] was not applied. This appears to me to be the result of the evidence, and it is confirmed by Milne's opinion who is as you know an old Lord of the Admiralty', 12 October 1870, Gladstone Papers, British Library, Add. Ms. 44,185, Vol. C.
15   Milne memo of March 1875, Milne Papers, Greenwich, MLN 144/5.

other States. So far as we can judge of the state of affairs, they have employed the autumn in interfering in almost every part of the world, except America.' A crisis in the Baltic over Poland loomed, another in the North Sea over Denmark. Greece and Italy had been made into trouble spots. China was apparently in a state of 'constant fighting'.[16] A year later, on 5 July 1864, Cobden boldly told the House of Commons 'what one who spoke for the mere sake of popularity would not care to say', for the great fault of Palmerstonian foreign policies, backed by a sense of 'British naval supremacy', was that 'we allow ourselves to be betrayed into something like threats, without duly measuring the power we have to carry out our menaces.' Simply 'Sending a Fleet' would no longer suffice. 'Have those who talk about entering into these continental quarrels, and settling them in a spirit of dictation, ever considered what is our ability to carry out our will in any way on the Continent of Europe? For our own defence at home our powers are, if I may speak it without irreverence, all but omnipotent. All the world could not assail us with success in our island home. But when we talk of our power to coerce military nations on the Continent, we should remember it is very limited indeed.'[17]

Cobden, of course, was right. 'There is, I say, a policy of menace in this country.' It was carried on the sails of every ironclad in Britain's 'Black Battlefleet'. And his exposure of this as both a dangerous bluff and blunder was indeed unpopular. As this study of the great 'turret vs. broadside'-debate has shown, it was not so much that the mid-Victorians were 'misled' by Coles. They were not 'confused' over what they wanted—what they expected to have. They were angry. Angry and afraid. The *Monitor* took something away from them, and the *Captain* promised to give it back. But what the Admiralty could never tell them was, in fact, the truth: there was nothing the Royal Navy could do, at least for now. It would be far easier for the Government to alter its foreign policies than the Controller's Department to bend the laws of physics. Ericsson's Machine had changed the rules by throwing out the game. How could one claim 'supremacy of the sea' when the most powerful ships weren't seaworthy? The British public knew they were being lied to, and this indeed maddened them; they became 'crazed'. But the fear of losing the one thing they held most dear—that gave them a sense of national identity like nothing else—was what led them to commit the lives of 500 of their sons, brothers, fathers and friends to a reckless 'experiment'. The people would right this wrong, which had only led to one national humiliation abroad after another, while the naval professionals pleaded with them not to forget that the sea was a cruel mistress, and that British greatness—even if it was now teetering on the scales of world history—was still good for that generation at least.

The world had changed. The ship would wreck.

One-hundred and fifty years ago.

---

16 5 February 1863, 'Address to Her Majesty on the Lords Commissioners' Speech', *Hansard*, Vol. 169, 66-143.
17 5 July 1864, 'Address to Her Majesty', *Hansard*, Vol. 176, 826-930.

Appendix I

British Ironclads (1860-1870)[1]

NOTE: rounded figures	Builder	Cost	Laid Down	Launched	Completed	Length between perpendiculars; width (feet)	Draught (feet)	Displacement (tons)	Speed (knots)	Special Notes
Warrior	Mare/Thames	£377,000	May 1859	December 1860	October 1861	380; 58	26	9,100	14	Iron-hulled; first British seagoing ironclad
Black Prince	Napier	£377,000	October 1859	February 1861	September 1862	380; 58	26	9,100	14	Iron-hulled
Defence	Palmers	£252,000	December 1859	April 1861	December 1861	280; 54	25	6,100	11	Iron-hulled
Resistance	Westwood & Baillie	£258,000	December 1859	April 1861	July 1862	280; 54	25	6,100	11	Iron-hulled
Hector	Napier	£294,000	March 1861	September 1862	February 1864	280; 56	25	6,700	12	Iron-hulled
Valiant	Westwood & Baillie	£325,000	February 1861	October 1863	September 1868	280; 56	25	6,700	12	Iron-hulled

1. Information mostly taken from George A. Ballard (edited by G. A. Osborn and N. A. M. Rodger), *The Black Battlefleet: A Study of the Capital Ship in Transition* (London: Nautical Publishing Co, Lymington & the Society for Nautical Research, Greenwich, 1980) and Oscar Parkes, *British Battleships, 'Warrior' 1860 to Vanguard' 1950: A History of Design, Construction and Armament* (London: Seeley Service & Co., Ltd., 1970).

Appendix I 283

Achilles	Chatham Dockyard	£469,000	August 1861	December 1863	November 1864	380; 58	27	9,700	14	Iron-hulled; first iron-warship built in a government dockyard
Minotaur	Thames	£478,000	September 1861	December 1863	December 1868	400; 59	28	10,600	14	Iron-hulled
Agincourt	Lairds	£483,000	October 1861	March 1865	June 1867	400; 59	28	10,600	14	Iron-hulled
Northumberland	Mare	£444,000	October 1861	April 1866	October 1868	400; 59	28	10,600	14	Iron-hulled
Royal Oak	Chatham Dockyard	£254,000	May 1860 (wooden line-of-battle ship)	September 1862	April 1863	273; 58	25	6,400	12	Wooden-hulled conversion
Prince Consort	Pembroke Dockyard	£266,000	August 1860 (wooden line-of-battle ship)	June 1862	April 1864	273; 58	27	6,800	12	Wooden-hulled conversion
Caledonia	Woolwich Dockyard	£312,000	October 1860 (wooden line-of-battle ship)	October 1862	July 1865	273; 58	27	6,800	12	Wooden-hulled conversion
Ocean	Devonport Dockyard	£298,000	August 1860 (wooden line-of-battle ship)	March 1863	July 1866	273; 58	27	6,800	12	Wooden-hulled conversion
Royal Sovereign	Portsmouth Dockyard	£180,000	December 1849 (wooden line-of-battle ship)	April 1857	August 1864	240; 62	25	5,100	11	Wooden-hulled conversion; turret-ship

Prince Albert	Samuda	£208,000	April 1862	May 1864	February 1866	240; 48	20	3,900	11	Iron-hulled; turret-ship
Scorpion	Lairds	£111,000	April 1862 (Confederate States Navy)	July 1863	October 1865	224; 42	17	2,700	11	Iron-hulled; turret-ship; ram; incorporated into Royal Navy
Wivern	Lairds	£118,000	April 1862 (Confederate States Navy)	August 1863	October 1865	224; 42	17	2,700	11	Iron-hulled; turret-ship; ram; incorporated into Royal Navy
Research	Pembroke Dockyard	£71,000	September 1861 (wooden sloop)	August 1863	April 1864	195; 39	15	1,900	10	Wooden-hulled conversion; central-battery
Enterprise	Deptford Dockyard	£62,000	May 1862 (wooden sloop)	February 1864	June 1864	180; 36	16	1,300	10	Wooden-hulled conversion; central-battery; composite (upper iron/lower wood) hull
Favorite	Deptford Dockyard	£152,000	August 1860 (wooden corvette)	July 1864	March 1866	225; 47	20	3,200	12	Wooden-hulled conversion; central-battery
Lord Clyde	Pembroke Dockyard	£285,000	September 1863	October 1864	June 1866	280; 59	27	7,800	13	Wooden-hulled; heaviest wooden ships ever built
Lord Warden	Chatham Dockyard	£328,000	December 1863	March 1865	August 1867	280; 59	28	7,800	13	Wooden-hulled; heaviest wooden ships ever built
Pallas	Woolwich Dockyard	£190,000	October 1863	March 1865	March 1866	225; 50	19	3,800	13	Wooden-hulled; central-battery; ram; first compound steam-engines

Appendix I 285

Bellerophon	Chatham Dockyard	£356,000	December 1863	April 1865	April 1866	300; 56	27	7,600	14	Iron-hulled; central-battery; bracket-frame, steel/iron hull; first balanced rudder
Zealous	Pembroke Dockyard	£239,000	October 1859 (wooden line-of-battle ship)	March 1864	October 1866	252; 59	26	6,100	11	Wooden-hulled conversion; central-battery
Royal Alfred	Portsmouth Dockyard	£282,000	December 1859 (wooden line-of-battle ship)	October 1864	March 1867	273; 59	27	6,700	12	Wooden-hulled conversion; central-battery
Viper	Dudgeon	£51,000	March 1864	December 1865	1866	160; 32	11	730	9	Iron-hulled; armoured gunboat
Vixen	Lungley	£54,000	March 1864	November 1865	1866	160; 32	11	750	9	Iron-hulled; armoured gunboat
Waterwitch	Thames	£59,000	October 1864	June 1866	1867	162; 32	11	780	9	Iron-hulled; armoured gunboat; waterjet-propelled
Penelope	Pembroke Dockyard	£397,000	September 1865	June 1867	June 1868	265; 50	17	4,400	13	Iron-hulled; central-battery
Hercules	Chatham Dockyard	£377,000	February 1866	February 1868	November 1868	325; 59	27	8,700	14	Iron-hulled; central-battery
Monarch	Chatham Dockyard	£355,000	June 1866	May 1868	June 1869	330; 57	26	8,300	15	Iron-hulled; sail-and-turret
Captain	Lairds	£336,000	January 1867	March 1869	January 1870	320; 53	25	7,800	14	Iron-hulled; sail-and-turret

Repulse	Woolwich Dockyard	£184,000	April 1858 (wooden line-of-battle ship)	April 1868	January 1870	252; 59	26	6,200	12	Wooden-hulled conversion; central-battery; last wooden British capital ship
Audacious	Napier	£256,000	June 1867	February 1869	September 1870	280; 54	23	6,000	13	Iron-hulled; central-battery
Invincible	Napier	£249,000	June 1867	May 1869	October 1870	280; 54	23	6,000	13	Iron-hulled; central-battery
Cerberus	Palmers	£118,000	September 1867	December 1868	September 1870	225; 45	15	3,300	10	Iron-hulled; breastwork-monitor; for Melbourne; first mastless, low-freeboard ironclad
Vanguard	Lairds	£263,000	October 1867	January 1870	September 1870	280; 54	23	6,000	13	Iron-hulled; central-battery
Sultan	Chatham Dockyard	£375,000	February 1868	May 1870	October 1871	325; 59	28	9,500	14	Iron-hulled; central-battery
Abyssinia	Dudgeon	£117,000	July 1868	February 1870	October 1870	225; 42	14	2,900	9	Iron-hulled; breastwork-monitor; for Bombay
Iron Duke	Pembroke Dockyard	£209,000	August 1868	March 1870	January 1871	280; 54	23	6,000	13	Iron-hulled; central-battery
Swiftsure	Palmers	£257,000	August 1868	June 1870	June 1872	280; 55	26	6,700	14	Iron-hulled; central-battery
Triumph	Palmers	£258,000	August 1868	September 1870	April 1873	280; 55	26	6,700	14	Iron-hulled; central-battery
Glatton	Chatham Dockyard	£223,000	August 1868	March 1871	February 1872	245; 54	19	4,900	12	Iron-hulled; single-turret breastwork-monitor; ram

Magdala	Thames	£132,000	October 1868	March 1870	November 1870	225; 45	15	3,300	10	Iron-hulled; breastwork-monitor; for Bombay
Hotspur	Napier	£176,000	October 1868	March 1870	November 1871	235; 50	20	4,000	12	Iron-hulled; fixed-turret breastwork-monitor; ram
Thunderer	Pembroke Dockyard	£368,000	June 1869	March 1872	May 1877	285; 62	27	9,300	13	Iron-hulled; mastless turret ship
Devastation	Portsmouth Dockyard	£361,000	November 1869	July 1871	April 1873	285; 62	27	9,300	13	Iron-hulled; mastless turret ship
Rupert	Chatham Dockyard	£239,000	June 1870	March 1872	July 1874	250; 53	24	5,400	13	Iron-hulled; single-turret breastwork-monitor; ram
Cyclops	Thames	£157,000	September 1870	July 1871	May 1877	225; 45	16	3,400	11	Iron-hulled; breastwork-monitor
Hecate	Dudgeon	£143,000	September 1870	September 1871	May 1877	225; 45	16	3,400	11	Iron-hulled; breastwork-monitor
Gorgon	Palmers	£141,000	September 1870	October 1871	March 1874	225; 45	16	3,400	11	Iron-hulled; breastwork-monitor
Hydra	Napier	£194,000	September 1870	December 1871	May 1876	225; 45	16	3,400	11	Iron-hulled; breastwork-monitor

Appendix II

British Ironclads (1860-1870) – Armour and Armament[2]

NOTE: SB = Smoothbore RML = Rifled Muzzle-loader BL = Breech-Loader	Side Armour: iron-plating (inches)	Side Armour: wood-backing (inches)	Special Notes	(Original) Armament	Special Notes
Warrior	4½	18 (teak)	Partially-armoured; unprotected ends; armoured bulkheads fore and aft	26—68-pdrs SB 10—110-pdrs BL	8-inch, 95-cwt/4.75-ton (68-pounder shot, 16lb charge; with 1,145 muzzle energy foot-tons) 7-inch, 82-cwt/4.1-ton Armstrong (110-pounder, 14lb charge; with 966 muzzle energy foot-tons)
Black Prince	4½	18 (teak)	Partially-armoured; unprotected ends; armoured bulkheads fore and aft	26—68-pdrs SB 10—110-pdrs BL	

2 Information mostly taken from George A. Ballard (edited by G. A. Osborn and N. A. M. Rodger), *The Black Battlefleet: A Study of the Capital Ship in Transition* (London: Nautical Publishing Co., Lymington & the Society for Nautical Research, Greenwich, 1980) and Oscar Parkes, *British Battleships, 'Warrior' 1860 to 'Vanguard' 1950: A History of Design, Construction and Armament* (London: Seeley Service & Co, Ltd., 1970). See also Captain W. H. Noble, *Report on Various Experiments Carried Out Under the Direction of the Ordnance Select Committee relative to the Penetration of Iron Armour Plates by Steel Shot* (London, 1866). By comparison, the American 11-inch Dahlgren smoothbore gun weighed over 7-tons; with a 30lb charge it fired a 166-pound solid shot with 2,730 muzzle energy foot-tons. The 15-inch Rodman smoothbore weighed over 22-tons; with a 100lb 'battering charge' it fired a 400-pound cored-shot with 7,273 muzzle energy foot-tons, but at 600 yards nearly 30 per cent of its impact-energy was already expended; see Edward W. Very, 'The Development of Armor for Naval Use', *Proceedings of the United States Naval Institute*, Vol. IX, No. 3, 1883.

Defence	4½	18 (teak)	Partially-armoured; unprotected ends; armoured bulkheads fore and aft	10—68-pdrs SB 8—110-pdrs BL	
Resistance	4½	18 (teak)	Partially-armoured; unprotected ends; armoured bulkheads fore and aft	10—68-pdrs SB 6—110-pdrs BL	
Hector	4½	18 (teak)	Partially-armoured; unprotected ends at waterline	20—68-pdrs SB 4—110-pdrs BL	
Valiant	4½	18 (teak)	Partially-armoured; unprotected ends at waterline	20—68-pdrs SB 4—110-pdrs BL	
Achilles	4½	18 (teak)	Partially-armoured; main deck-ends unprotected; armoured bulkheads fore and aft	16—100-pdrs SB 6—68-pdrs SB 4—110-pdrs BL	9-inch, 6¼-ton 'Somerset' (100-pounder; with 25lb charge = 1,540 feet per second initial muzzle-velocity; with 1,580 muzzle energy foot-tons)
Minotaur	5½	10 (teak)	Fully-armoured (stem to stern)	4—12½-ton RMLs 24—6½-ton RMLs 8—24-pdrs SB	9-inch, 12½-ton Armstrong (253-pound shell, 50lb charge = 1,440 feet per second initial muzzle-velocity; with 3,643 muzzle energy foot-tons) 7-inch, 6½-ton Armstrong (112-pound shell, 30lb charge = 1,525 feet per second initial muzzle velocity; with 1,854 muzzle energy foot-tons)
Agincourt	5½	10 (teak)	Fully-armoured (stem to stern)	4—12½-ton RMLs 24—6½-ton RMLs 8—24-pdrs SB	
Northumberland	5½	10 (teak)	Partially-armoured; main deck-ends unprotected; armoured bulkheads fore and aft	4—12½-ton RMLs 22—9-ton RMLs	8-inch, 9-ton Armstrong (174-pound shell, 35lb charge = 1,384 feet per second initial muzzle-velocity; with 2,323 muzzle energy foot-tons)

Ship				
Royal Oak	4½	29½ (wood side)	Fully-armoured (stem to stern); no water-tight subdivisions/bulkheads	24—68-pdrs SB 11—110-pdrs BL	
Prince Consort	4½	29½ (wood side)	Fully-armoured (stem to stern); no water-tight subdivisions/bulkheads	8—100-pdrs SB 16—68-pdrs SB 7—110-pdrs BL	
Caledonia	4½	29½ (wood side)	Fully-armoured (stem to stern); no water-tight subdivisions/bulkheads	8—100-pdrs SB 12—68-pdrs SB 10—110-pdrs BL	
Ocean	4½	29½ (wood side)	Fully-armoured (stem to stern); no water-tight subdivisions/bulkheads	24—6½-ton RMLs	
Royal Sovereign	5½	36 (wood side)	Fully-armoured (stem to stern); no water-tight subdivisions/bulkheads; turret armour 5½-inches/10-inches near ports; 1-inch deck armour	5—150-pdrs SB	10½-inch, 12-ton Armstrong ('300-pounder', never used rifled; round shot 150-pounder; 40lb charge = 1,726 feet per second initial muzzle velocity; with 3,250 muzzle energy foot-tons)
Prince Albert	4½	18 (teak)	Fully-armoured (stem to stern); turret armour 5-inches/10-inches near ports; 1-inch deck armour	4—12½-ton RMLs	
Scorpion	4½	10 (teak)	Fully-armoured (stem to stern); turret armour 5-inches/10-inches near ports	4—12½-ton RMLs	
Wivern	4½	10 (teak)	Fully-armoured (stem to stern); turret armour 5-inches/10-inches near ports	4—12½-ton RMLs	
Research	4½	19½ (wood side)	Partially-armoured; main deck-ends unprotected; armoured bulkheads fore and aft	4—100-pdrs SB	

Appendix II 291

Enterprise	4½	19½ (wood side)	Partially-armoured; main deck-ends unprotected; armoured bulkheads fore and aft	2—100-pdrs SB 2—110-pdrs BL
Favorite	4½	19 (wood side)	Partially-armoured; main deck-ends unprotected; armoured bulkheads fore and aft	8—100-pdrs SB
Lord Clyde	5½ - 4½	31½ (wood side)	Fully-armoured (stem to stern); no water-tight subdivisions/bulkheads; 1½-inch inner iron skin	24—6½-ton RMLs
Lord Warden	5½ - 4½	31½ (wood side)	Fully-armoured (stem to stern); no water-tight subdivisions/bulkheads; 1½-inch inner iron skin	16—9-ton RMLs 4—110-pdrs BL
Pallas	4½	22 (wood side)	Partially-armoured; main deck-ends unprotected; armoured bulkheads fore and aft; no water-tight subdivisions/bulkheads	4—6½-ton RMLs 2—110-pdrs BL
Bellerophon	6 - 5	10 (teak)	Partially-armoured; main deck-ends unprotected; armoured bulkheads fore and aft; 1½-inch inner iron skin; ½-inch deck armour	10—12½-ton RMLs 3—6½-ton RMLs
Zealous	4½	30 (teak)	Partially-armoured; main deck-ends unprotected; armoured bulkheads fore and aft	20—6½-ton RMLs
Royal Alfred	6 - 4	29½ (wood side)	Partially-armoured; main deck-ends unprotected; armoured bulkheads fore and aft; no water-tight subdivisions/bulkheads	10—12½-ton RMLs 8—6½-ton RMLs

Viper	4½	10 (teak)	Partially-armoured; main unprotected; armoured bulkheads fore and aft	2—6½-ton RMLs	
Vixen	4½	10 (teak)	Partially-armoured; main unprotected; armoured bulkheads fore and aft	2—6½-ton RMLs	
Waterwitch	4½	10 (teak)	Partially-armoured; main unprotected; armoured bulkheads fore and aft	2—6½-ton RMLs	
Penelope	6 – 5	11-10 (teak)	Partially-armoured; main deck-ends unprotected; armoured bulkheads fore and aft	8—9-ton RMLs	
Hercules	9 – 8 – 6	12-10 (teak)	Partially-armoured; main deck-ends unprotected; armoured bulkheads fore and aft; 1½-inch inner iron skin	8—18-ton RMLs 2—12½-ton RMLs	10-inch, 18-ton Armstrong (406-pound shell, 70lb charge = 1,379 feet per second initial muzzle-velocity; with 5,356 muzzle energy foot-tons)
Monarch	7 – 4½	12-10 (teak)	Partially-armoured; main deck-ends unprotected; armoured bulkheads fore and aft; turret armour 8-inches/10-inches near ports	4—25-ton RMLs 3—6½-ton RMLs	12-inch, 25-ton Armstrong (608-pound shell, 85lb charge = 1,292 feet per second initial muzzle-velocity; with 7,046 muzzle energy foot-tons)
Captain	8 – 7 – 4	12 (teak)	Partially-armoured; main deck-ends unprotected; 1-inch deck armour; turret armour 9-inches/10-inches near ports	4—25-ton RMLs 2—6½-ton RMLs	
Repulse	6 - 4½	31 (wood side)	Partially-armoured; main deck-ends unprotected; armoured bulkheads fore and aft; no water-tight subdivisions/bulkheads	12—9-ton RMLs	

Audacious	8 – 6	10-8 (teak)	Partially-armoured; main deck-ends unprotected; armoured bulkheads fore and aft; 1¼-inch inner iron skin	10—12½-ton RMLs
Invincible	8 – 6	10-8 (teak)	Partially-armoured; main deck-ends unprotected; armoured bulkheads fore and aft; 1¼-inch inner iron skin	10—12½-ton RMLs
Cerberus	9 – 8 – 6	10-8 (teak)	Fully-armoured (stem to stern); 1¼-inch inner iron skin; 1½-inch deck armour; turret armour 9-inches/10-inches near ports	4—18-ton RMLs
Vanguard	8 – 6	10-8 (teak)	Partially-armoured; main deck-ends unprotected; armoured bulkheads fore and aft; 1¼-inch inner iron skin	10—12½-ton RMLs
Sultan	9 – 8 – 6	12-10 (teak)	Partially-armoured; main deck-ends unprotected; armoured bulkheads fore and aft; 1½-inch inner iron skin	8—18-ton RMLs 4—12½-ton RMLs
Abyssinia	8 – 7 – 6	11-9 (teak)	Fully-armoured (stem to stern); 1¼-inch inner iron skin; 1½-inch deck armour; turret armour 8-inches/10-inches near ports	4—18-ton RMLs
Iron Duke	8 – 6	10-8 (teak)	Partially-armoured; main deck-ends unprotected; armoured bulkheads fore and aft; 1¼-inch inner iron skin	10—12½-ton RMLs
Swiftsure	8 – 6	10-8 (teak)	Partially-armoured; main deck-ends unprotected; armoured bulkheads fore and aft; 1¼-inch inner iron skin	10—12½-ton RMLs

Triumph	8 – 6	10-8 (teak)	Partially-armoured; main deck-ends unprotected; armoured bulkheads fore and aft; 1¼-inch inner iron skin	10—12½-ton RMLs
Glatton	12 – 10	20-18 (teak)	Fully-armoured (stem to stern); 2-inch inner iron skin; 3-inch deck armour; turret armour 12-inches/14-inches near ports	2—25-ton RMLs
Magdala	9 – 8 – 6	11-9 (teak)	Fully-armoured (stem to stern); 1¼-inch inner iron skin; 1½-inch deck armour; turret armour 9-inches/10-inches near ports	4—18-ton RMLs
Hotspur	11 – 8	15-12 (teak)	Fully-armoured (stem to stern); 1¼-inch inner iron skin; 2¾ - 2-inch deck armour; turret armour 8½-inches/10-inches near ports	1—25-ton RML
Thunderer	12 – 10 – 8½	18-16 (teak)	Fully-armoured (stem to stern); 1½-inch inner iron skin; 3 - 2-inch deck armour; turret armour 12-inches/14-inches near ports	4—35-ton RMLs	12-inch, 35-ton Armstrong (706-pound shell, 140lb charge = 1,390 feet per second initial muzzle-velocity; with 9,469 muzzle energy foot-tons)
Devastation	12 – 10 – 8½	18-16 (teak)	Fully-armoured (stem to stern); 1½-inch inner iron skin; 3 - 2-inch deck armour; turret armour 12-inches/14-inches near ports	4—35-ton RMLs	
Rupert	12 –11 – 9	14-12-10 (teak)	Fully-armoured (stem to stern); 1¼-inch inner iron skin; 3 - 2-inch deck armour; turret armour 12-inches/14-inches near ports	2—18-ton RMLs	

Cyclops	9 – 8 – 6	11-9 (teak)	Fully-armoured (stem to stern); 1¼-inch inner iron skin; 1½-inch deck armour; turret armour 9-inches/10-inches near ports	4—18-ton RMLs
Hecate	9 – 8 – 6	11-9 (teak)	Fully-armoured (stem to stern); 1¼-inch inner iron skin; 1½-inch deck armour; turret armour 9-inches/10-inches near ports	4—18-ton RMLs
Gorgon	9 – 8 – 6	11-9 (teak)	Fully-armoured (stem to stern); 1¼-inch inner iron skin; 1½-inch deck armour; turret armour 9-inches/10-inches near ports	4—18-ton RMLs
Hydra	9 – 8 – 6	11-9 (teak)	Fully-armoured (stem to stern); 1¼-inch inner iron skin; 1½-inch deck armour; turret armour 9-inches/10-inches near ports	4—18-ton RMLs

Appendix III

'Penetrating Power of Projectiles Fired from the Service Heavy Muzzle Loading Guns' (Captain C. Orde Browne, 'Firing at Armour-Clads Reduced to a System', *Journal of the Royal United Service Institution*, Vol. 16, 1873, 684-700)

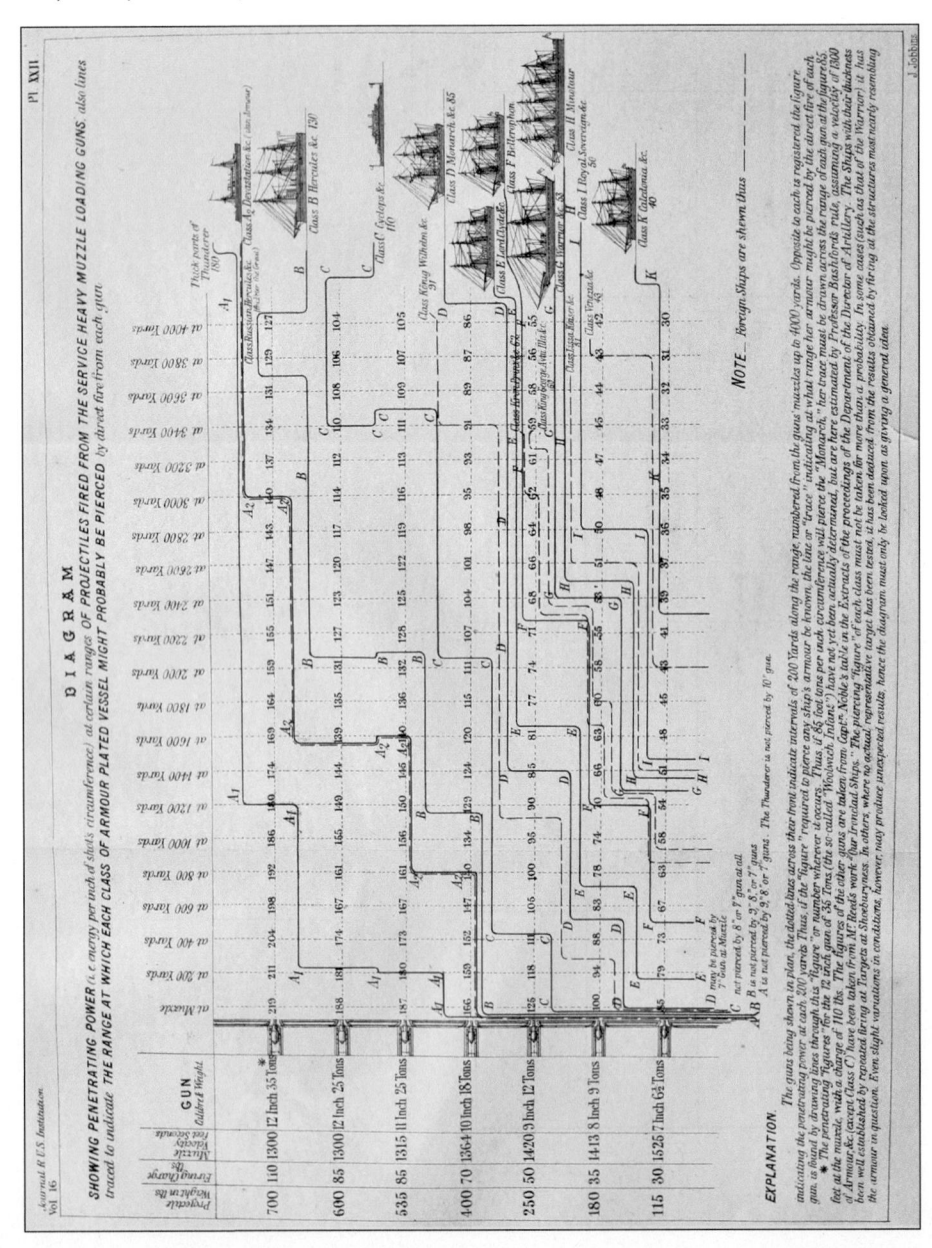

Appendix IV

Captain James Goodenough Reports on the Union Navy (May 1864)

At the U.S. military foundry in Pittsburgh Captain James Goodenough witnessed the successful casting of a truly colossal 20-inch calibre Rodman smoothbore, weighing 51½-tons and capable of firing a 1,000-pound cored shot 4½-miles at 25-degrees. 'The great care and attention paid to the preparation of the cast iron, and the ingenious and exact modes of testing the iron when cast,' he stressed, 'are the principal things which strike one, both at Fort Pitt, and at Mr. Parrott's foundry at Cold Spring; and I am inclined to attribute the great superiority in endurance of American Guns to the attention so bestowed, as it enables them to dispense with the injurious and exaggerated proof strains to which English ordnance are subjected.' The 15-inch Navy Dahlgren guns which armed the monitors were now firing enormous 50-pound service charges safely enough, propelling their large iron spheres at an initial muzzle velocity of 1,200 feet per second—greater than Armstrong's 110-pounder rifled gun capped at 14lb. charges.[1]

By the spring of 1864, Goodenough submitted to Lord Lyons his final report on the Union's ships, guns and personnel (the large-scale officer training at the Newport College formerly at Annapolis being, in his opinion, 'the most important feature of the American Navy'[2]). Before the Civil War, he began, U.S. naval policy tended to emphasise the construction of seagoing warships which were larger and faster than any other navy's, armed 'with a few of the heaviest guns possible having the greatest

---

[1] 13 February 1864, Goodenough to Lyons, TNA FO 115/426; 18 February 1864, Goodenough to Admiralty, TNA ADM 1/5879. See also Marshall J. Bastable, 'From Breechloaders to Monster Guns: Sir William Armstrong and the Invention of Modern Artillery, 1854-1880', *Technology and Culture*, Vol. 33, No. 2 (April 1992), 213-47, and Bastable, *Arms and the State: Sir William Armstrong and the Remaking of British Naval Power, 1854-1914* (Aldershot: Ashgate, 2004), especially 93-4. Even with 10lb. charges the Ordnance Select Committee considered the 110-pounder Armstrong vulnerable to fouling; 6 April 1864, *Abstracts of Proceedings of the Ordnance Select Committee, for the Quarter ending 30th June 1864*, TNA WO 33/14, 208-9.

[2] 13 May 1864, Goodenough to Admiralty, TNA ADM 1/5879.

range'. But the current rapid build-up of the Union fleet was far more purpose-driven, with most of its long-range seagoing warships allocated to coastal squadrons enforcing the blockade of the rebel South. One small squadron cruised the West Indies looking for commerce raiders and blockade runners, and a handful of sloops, corvettes, paddle-steamers and sailing vessels were despatched to mostly European waters hunting for enemy warships like the CSS *Alabama*. New classes of fast wooden screw sloops were currently under construction, however; some 27 of them designed to sacrifice everything 'to the desire of obtaining a continual high speed for 8 to 10 days consecutively under steam', with projected maximum speeds of 15 knots. These were meant to hunt down Confederate wolves but also act as raiders themselves in case of a maritime war with Britain and/or France. 'They will not form a fleet properly so called for their object will be to avoid each other's company but thrown out as a chain across the great lines of commerce, they will be able to destroy an enemy's ships, or if the latter are convoyed will be able to hang about the convoy—cut off stragglers, and evade the pursuit of more heavily armed vessels accompanying it.' Indeed, according to published addresses by the U.S. Secretary of the Navy, the over-arching strategy in such conflicts was to destroy enemy commerce on the high seas while making sure Northern ports and cities were impervious to coastal bombardment or even blockade. This is where the monitors and other Yankee ironclads came in; to make the American littoral a killing zone for enemy warships. Goodenough tallied '1 Ocean ironclad' of 16 guns, six double-turreted monitors, one triple-turreted version, fourteen single turret monitors, and another ten with even lighter draft built or building. In addition to this, he noted five 50-gun screw-frigates mounting 250 heavy guns, six 30-gun frigates mounting 180 guns, seven 16-gun paddlewheel steamers, twenty-two gun sloops of varying armaments, forty converted merchant steamers mounting some '300 guns', twenty-eight powerfully-armed double-ender paddle-steamers, and thirty gunboats mounting 5-guns each.[3] Although the vast majority of this force was built of unseasoned wood which would not last long, many vessels were already in commission and under construction with an aim of being ready within the next year. A major maritime war with Britain would presumably be decided one way or another long before their wooden hulls gave way. As for their actual abilities, he was fairly certain that in an Anglo-American conflict at least the double-turreted monitors would be able 'to make destructive excursions against the blockade and probably, as they are more heavily armoured than any ship yet built to cross the ocean, to relieve the blockade during moderate weather.' The heavy wooden warships ('about equal to French and English frigates of the same nominal force in size and slightly superior in

---

[3] 12 April 1864, ('Confidential') 'Report on Guns and personnel of American Navy' and 'Report on Ships of United States Navy 1864', Captain J. G. Goodenough, TNA ADM 1/5879, 54-62; see also Goodenough's initial draft to Lord Lyons, dated 9 April 1864, in TNA FO 115/426 (From Naval and Colonial, January to June, 1864), and 27 May 1864, Foreign Office to Admiralty, TNA ADM 1/5902.

weight of broadside') would meanwhile patrol off the coast, 'to clear the roads to their own ports on the principal lines of commerce.'[4] This meant that fast U.S. cruisers could proceed to and from their home bases at will. They would not be bottled up as during the second half of the War of 1812. Merchant vessels might also stand a good chance of carrying on trade as need be. Goodenough foresaw the fast paddle-steamers making their way to the Pacific in the early stages of war, where they might 'find sufficient sympathy on the west coast of South America and have sufficient influence in the Sandwich Islands [Hawaii] to enable them to procure supplies of fuel there, as well as in California.' Mississippi squadron gunboats might even be taken apart in Pittsburgh and Cincinnati and moved overland for reassembly on Lake Erie, while those moved up to St. Louis might be similarly reconstructed on Lake Michigan.[5]

The monitors themselves, he detailed, went from quite small to gigantic. The *Kalamazoo*-class of four oceangoing monitors laid down were 345 feet long, nearly twice as long as the original USS *Monitor* or four-fifths the total length of HMS *Warrior*, yet still drawing only 17-feet.[6] Side armour for their upper hull freeboard of three feet was to consist of two rolled 3-inch plates, 6-inches total thickness, with 24-inch wood-backing and three armour stringers 8- by 8-inches placed 8-inches apart. To further support their massive 15-inch thick turrets and armoured decks, 4- by 5-inch wrought iron diagonal braces extended the length and width of the hulls: incredibly strong vessels in the making.[7] The fact that U.S. mills could now forge at least solid 3-inch plates 15-feet long by 3-feet wide was ominous enough. There was every reason to believe that future advances in armour-plate production meant that existing Federal turret ships could be re-armoured with more solid- and less laminated-plating; as the weights were the same, the vessels would not have to be redesigned or replaced altogether.[8] But Goodenough considered the 'semi-

4   12 April 1864, 'Report', 59, 63, 65-6.
5   Ibid., 64-5.
6   Between perpendiculars; *Warrior* is 420 feet long overall.
7   12 April 1864, 'Report'; see also Canney, *The Old Steam Navy*, who also notes deck armour plates 3-inches thick 'over 6-inches of wood, with another 3 inches of planking above'; 'the largest hulls built in a U.S. navy yard to that time,' 124-5.
8   At the 1876 International Exhibition held in Philadelphia, Morgan Iron Works of John Roach & Son (New York City) proudly displayed a solid rolled iron plate measuring 12¾-inches thick, 10-feet long and 3 feet 8 inches wide. As reported by the Centennial Commissioners, up until October 1876 the 14-inch plate also on display by John Brown & Co (Sheffield) was the thickest Britain's leading armour plate manufacturer could forge—until later that month it successfully produced a gargantuan iron plate 24-inches thick and 10 feet wide, *Report of the Board on Behalf of United States Executive Department at the International Exhibition Held at Philadelphia, PA., 1876*, 2 volumes (Washington: GPO, 1884), 1: 606. While Nathan Okun believes the thickest armour plate ever actually *used* was a 33-inch Grüson plate of chilled cast-iron, for coastal fort-turrets (see: http://www.combinedfleet.com/metalprp.htm), by 1877 widely publicized tests at Spezia and elsewhere suggested compound steel armour plating was better at resisting the powerful 80- and 100-ton guns of the day. HMS *Inflexible* (1876) featured a central armoured

submersible' low freeboard concept of the monitors flawed in that 'not one is fit in my opinion to go to sea, except to make a short passage'. Their armament, limited to two very guns in one or two turrets, also indicated a 'want of offensive power', especially in a shore bombardment role, echoing Union Admiral Du Pont's critique that ' "ability to endure is not a sufficient element or wherewith to gain great victories, that endurance must be accompanied with a corresponding power to inflict injury upon the Enemy."' Yet he also doubted the *Atlanta* would have come off so badly against the *Passaic*-class *Weehawken* the previous summer had the Confederate casemate-ram not run aground, and had such a poorly constructed pilot house, which, when damaged by the first shot of the monitor, incapacitated both the *Atlanta*'s pilot and her captain. This then allowed the *Weehawken* to safely take up a position in a blind-spot of the enemy broadside-ironclad at 350 yards. Even then, Goodenough observed, the 15-inch cored shot which soon after struck her side 'failed to penetrate the *Atlanta* and had she possessed an interior lining of iron, would probably have injured but a very few people.' The ability to rotate such heavy iron turrets by steam machinery—controlled by 'the Officer in command of the battery [who] stands in rear of the guns with the lever of a steam valve in each hand'—was, however, a model of 'simplicity, ingenuity and solidity.'[9] In the final analysis, he offered, the Union's large fleet of monitors were most valuable 'in a Maritime war…as a defensive force'. This aspect of their unique character was so acute, and applicable to any navy which invested in them, that he felt obliged to elaborate:

> For the defence of a port the smaller classes would be placed alongside a boom or other temporary defence or might close small channels liable to be attacked by gunboats, and if a port were blockaded, the *Dictator* or *Kalamazoo* might on a fine day do much damage to a blockading force, which would probably be composed of light ships. Indeed, if their speed reaches what it is intended

---

citadel of two layers of 12-inch wrought-iron plates alternated with layers of teak totaling 17-inches; the thickest armour scheme ever floated, even as hardened steel had emerged as the new metal of choice. See also Charles Orde Browne, *Armour, and its Attack by Artillery* (London: Dulau & Co., 1887), 17-34; and David Boursnell, *Forging the Fleet: Naval Armour and the Armour Makers, 1860 to 1916* (Sheffield industrial Museums Trust, 2016), and 'Early British Iron Armour', in John Jordan (ed.), *Warship 2019* (Oxford: Osprey Publishing, 2019), 145-52.

9   12 April 1864, 'Report', 23-31. Goodenough noted that the auxiliary (or 'donkey') steam engine took 1-minute 45-seconds to turn a *Canonicus*-class turret one complete circle, although in the original *Monitor* it took just over thirty-seconds with less than 25-pounds (steam) pressure; see 4 October 1861, Ericsson to Smith, U.S. National Archives, RG 45, Entry 464, Box 49. For elaboration on Goodenough's recommendation for steam machinery to work turrets based on U.S practices see 11 April 1864, Goodenough to Admiralty, TNA ADM 1/5879.

it should, it is very likely that they would capture some of the blockading force unless they were protected by an armour plated vessel.[10]

What he did not venture to speculate on was how a British broadside-ironclad might fare against a Union monitor armed with 15-inch guns. Not surprisingly, before the year was out Ericsson himself wrote to Abraham Lincoln that naval officers 'of all the leading powers…have admitted that Europe has nothing that can cope with the *Dictator*'—at least in terms of 'impregnability and power of armament'. The President could take pride that the Union's ironclad navy had been built on proper principles from the outset, while 'England is now engaged in reconstructing those costly but only partially mailed ships which, but yesterday, she deemed perfect and invincible.'[11]

10   12 April 1864, 'Report', 34.
11   9 December 1864, Ericsson to Lincoln, Ericsson Papers, Philadelphia, Box 2.

Appendix V

The British consider a turret vs. broadside confrontation between the U.S. and Spain at Valparaiso (March 1866)

Since 1859 the latest government of Queen Isabella II had (much like Napoleon III of France) embarked on a series of desperately-needed prestige campaigns, all designed to relieve republican pressures at home with imperial distractions abroad, from Morocco to Indochina to the Caribbean. Spearheading this drive was the new seagoing monster *Numancia*, recently completed by the French at Toulon, and boasting forty 68-pounder smoothbores behind 4½- to 5½-inches of iron armour-plating.[1] In 1865 she arrived off the coast of Peru to enforce a blockade instituted against an 'impudent' former colonial power, in dispute over the nitrate-rich Chincha Islands which Spain had forcibly occupied (14 April 1864). But by 1866, Spanish naval supremacy in the region and diplomatic high-handedness both failed to sufficiently cower the Peruvians or prevent the conflict from drawing in Chile, Bolivia and Ecuador. The new Spanish admiral, Casto Méndez Núñez, unable to come to grips with South American warships sheltering amongst the foreboding reefs and coves of the Chilean coastline, and with his supply lines growing thinner and more precarious with each passing week, now chose to make an example of the undefended port of Valparaiso. European and American merchants were warned that the city was to be subjected to naval bombardment on 31 March, and that there was nothing anyone could do to stop it. British interests in the area were represented by Rear-Admiral Joseph G. Denman,

---

[1] See for example, Lynn M. Case, *French Opinion on War and Diplomacy during the Second Empire* (New York: Octagon Books, 1972), especially, 159-61, 183-6, 209, 272-5. For the *Numancia*, see for example, Christian de Saint Hubert, 'Early Spanish Steam Warships with Special Emphasis on Screw Frigates and Armoured Frigates and Corvettes (1834-70), Part 1', *Warship International*, Vol. 20, No. 4 (1983), 338-67, and Christian de Saint Hubert, 'Early Spanish Steam Warships with Special Emphasis on Screw Frigates and Armoured Frigates and Corvettes (1834-70), Part 2', *Warship International*, Vol. 21, No. 1 (1984), 21-45 (especially 'Section IV').

with two heavily-armed wooden frigates which, however, would be powerless against the *Numancia*.²

Yet even before the Spanish were able to carry out their threat, a small but powerful American squadron centred around the double-turreted U.S.S. *Monadnock* had dropped anchor at Valparaiso, on its way to reinforce the *Passaic*-class monitor *Camanche* at San Francisco via Cape Horn.³ The American commanding officer, Commodore John Rodgers, had commanded the *Camanche*'s sister ship *Weehawken* both in the abortive attempt against Charleston's forts on 7 April 1863, and in her quick defeat of the armoured casemate-ram CSS *Atlanta* later that June. As this seemed a clear case of enforcing the Monroe Doctrine—shielding weaker South American republics from overbearing European monarchies—as well as preventing the wholesale destruction of civilian life and property—Rodgers bluntly assured Denman that the *Monadnock*, if need be, would leave 'only the trucks of the Spanish vessel's masts…above water, thirty minutes after the firing had commenced.' He had seen the same armour plates manufactured by Pétin and Gaudet for the *Numancia* thoroughly smashed by 15-inch smoothbores in target tests conducted during the American Civil War. His heavily-armoured, low-freeboard turreted ironclad had nothing to fear, in turn, from broadside-mounted guns. But when the veiled threat was later made to Núñez directly, the Spanish admiral could only gallantly reply that 'Spain, the Queen, and I prefer honor without ships than ships without honor.'⁴ And since neither the British nor American naval flag officers at the scene were under diplomatic orders to intervene on Chile's behalf, they could only watch helplessly as Valparaiso was duly bombarded after satisfactory time had been given for non-combatants to evacuate the area. Núñez then assured Rodgers that no further attacks would take place—Chile had been sufficiently 'chastised'—and quietly withdrew his forces to the north to operate against Peru. His subsequent attempt on 2 May to bombard Callao,

---

2 See for example, Howard J. Fuller, 'Chilean Standoff: Ironclad-Monitor U.S.S. *Monadnock*, Naval Power-Politics & the Spanish Bombardment of Valparaiso, 1866', *Naval History*, June 2011 (25: 3), 58-65.

3 'No one either at home or abroad feels any special interest for a wooden ship', observed Rodgers, 'but this voyage for an ironclad excites the most lively attention both in our country and in Europe', 2 November 1865, Rodgers to squadron commanders, Rodgers Papers, Library of Congress Manuscript Division. Given the tensions between Imperial Spain and the South American republics in the Pacific, Welles had already conceived that the 'the appearance of the *Monadnock* will…have a good effect there', 6 September 1865, Welles to Fox, Fox Papers, New York, Box 10. Rear-Admiral Francis Gregory had recommended the *Monadnock* for the proposed voyage; see 20 July 1865, Gregory to Welles, U.S. National Archives, RG 19, Entry 1236. See also Robert Royal Miller, 'The *Camanche*: First Monitor of the Pacific', *California Historical Society Quarterly*, Vol. 45, No. 2 (June 1966).

4 Undated Rodgers memo, 'Estimated Guns of the Spanish Fleet', 1866, and 5 and 29 March 1866, John Rodgers to Anne H. Rodgers, Rodgers Family Papers, Library of Congress, Box 23.

which was heavily defended with modern coast defences, was anything but a success. The Spanish admiral was wounded, *Numancia* suffered damage from an Armstrong 300-pounder, and with both ammunition and coal running low, the Spanish fleet withdrew never to return.

Yet it wasn't just the loss of their property which outraged the British merchants at Valparaiso. It was how they were forced to cower before a Spanish ironclad, while the local British rear-admiral had none, and a jaunty American commodore sat there riding the whole affair out in a sort of floating iron fortress. Given his awkward position, Somerset could only attest in the House of Lords in May that Britain's foreign policy of strict neutrality was to blame, and that 'there could have been no use in sending out an iron-clad ship to Denman unless new instructions were sent to him at the same time.' But that still didn't address the question posed to him, what the British flag officer *could* have done with the means at his disposal (i.e., had the Spanish chosen to act in an unhumanitarian manner requiring British honour to forcefully intervene)—or the unspoken question how an American Monitor, on the Pacific coast of South America, might have compelled the Spanish admiral to behave in a more civilised manner in the first place. As Sir Lawrence Palk bitterly remarked in the Commons that same day, 'he had always thought that the object of maintaining fleets at foreign stations was to protect the lives and property of British subjects; but this was evidently a mistake, and when next the Estimates were submitted to the House he hoped some hon. Member would move that they be curtailed, and that for the future English Admirals who were sent to take care of British interests might be sent in a yacht with a broomstick at the masthead.'[5]

There was another question. Even if Somerset had despatched an 'ironclad' to the far side of the world, would it have been able to cope with the *Numancia* with the same certainty Rodgers had with his monitor? 'I have no wish to mix myself up in affairs which are not my business", Rodgers had written to his father-in-law. 'If however the government would like the *Numancia* taken the *Monadnock* can accommodate it.' His whole approach to the Spanish had been to be 'as amiable as invincible, and invincible as amiable', 'exerting here a silent, moral influence, unobtrusive, inoffensive, but not unfelt'.[6] This was precisely what the mid-Victorians had craved with their own naval power—what they felt they had been denied in the final years of Lord Palmerston's ministry—and what Coles promised to restore if he were only given half a chance.

---

5 15 May 1866, *Hansard*, 'War Between Spain and Chile and Peru—Blockade of the Chilean Ports—Bombardment of Valparaiso—Question', Vol. 183, 955-9; 965-86. Sir Lawrence Palk, 1st Baron Haldon, Conservative MP for South Devon.

6 1 March 1866, John Rodgers to his father-in-law, William L. Hodge, and 16 March 1866, to his Anne H. Rodgers, Rodgers Family Papers, Library of Congress, Box 26. See also Robert Erwin Johnson, *Rear Admiral John Rodgers 1812-1882* (Annapolis: United States Naval Institute, 1967), 285-93.

Appendix VI

Admiral Robinson reports on France's ironclad fleet and French naval ordnance (June 1867)

The Paris Exhibition of 1867 left the Controller of the Royal Navy feeling far less satisfied about the comparative strengths of the Anglo-French broadside ironclad fleets, and their respective armaments, than Somerset had assured Russell the year before. Starting with the *Gloire* of 1859, all of the original French armoured frigates were plated with 4.7-inch iron from stem to stern, with ½-inch deck armour. The 6,300-ton *Couronne* was iron-hulled with watertight compartments and was laid down four months before the 9,100-ton *Warrior* (though launched in March 1861, three months after Britain's first seagoing ironclad was). Though wooden-hulled and also relatively short-lived, the *Magenta* and *Solferino* were double-deckers fully-armoured. The ten improved *Gloire*s of the *Provence*-class, laid down in 1861, were likewise wooden-hulled, except for the iron-hulled *Héroïne*, with recorded steam trial speeds that matched the *Warrior*.[1] Stem to stern armour-plating was increased to 6-inches on the waterline and 4.3-inches on the gundeck, armed with ten 7.6-inch smoothbores. By 1867 these were changed to eight 9.4-inch rifled muzzle-loaders. It was reported that the French 5-ton rifled 6.3-inch 100-pounder could safely handle a 28lb. charge, giving it enough power to penetrate 4½-inch iron plate with 18-inches of wood backing and an inner iron skin of 1-inch thickness at 1,089 yards.[2] Rear-Admiral Key's comparative report of 7 June 1867, noted three main types of French

---

1   Early French ironclads were generally barque-rigged, but as they were of considerably less tonnage than British ironclads tended to feature comparable sail areas per displacement. So the 5,600-ton (displacement) *Gloire* hoisted 27,000 square-feet of sail—barque-rigged—whereas *Warrior* ship-rigged 48,400 square-feet on 9100-tons. The 6,000-ton *Provence* was barque-rigged with 21,000 square-feet of sail as opposed to HMS *Achilles* (over 9,800-tons), with an initial spread of 44,000 square-feet of sail (and four main masts) reduced to three main masts and an overall sail area of 30,100 square-feet; from *Conway's All the World's Fighting Ships, 1860-1905* (Greenwich: Conway Maritime Press, 1979), 7-13, 286-88.
2   See Holley, *A Treatise on Ordnance and Armor*, 59.

heavy naval guns: the 6.3-inch, 8-ton 7.48-inch, and 9.45-inch of 14 tons. All of the French guns were breech-loaders, made of cast-iron reinforced by steel bands 'hooped' at the breech. In the absence of any 'authentic record' received on their accuracy or endurance and given the fact that French powder was different (and weaker) from English powder, for example, Key was obliged to extrapolate their performance. Here the older French 6.3-inch gun was calculated as able to 'penetrate a 5.9-inch plate at 328 yards' and at less range would also have 'a serious effect on backing'. The newer 7.48-inch gun fired a 165lb. solid shot would 'seriously damage the side of ships with 5.9-inch plates at 874 yards'; while the big 14-ton gun was expected to seriously damage 5.9-inch plates at '2,187 yards, but it's very efficient action or penetration might be limited to 1,093 yards'. Both of these guns were considered far less powerful than the British 8-inch 9-ton and 9-inch 12-ton rifled muzzle-loaders, which could penetrate the same thickness of plating but at approximately double the range.[3]

But within a week Robinson himself reported to the Board of Admiralty his personal visit to the Paris Exhibition of 1867, in personal company with Whitworth and the Director of Materiel of the Imperial French Navy, Dupuy de Lôme. Here the two models of artillery were more clearly comparable side by side, and the Controller was convinced that 'the French theory gives the constructors and designers of ships a very great advantage over the English':

> They start with a less explosive gunpowder—this enables them to use breech-loaders with security—and to have a longer gun without curtailing the dimensions of hatchways, etc. or running into great width for ships, the security of the sponger and loader[,] the facilities for closing the ports in a sea-way until the gun is run out and fired, the readiness with which the cartridge and projectile are supplied to the breech, the power of taking breechings to the side, and using tackles if preferred to mechanical means for working the gun without any impediment to loading or causing exposure of the loaders[,] the security from the explosion of the muzzle of an adjacent gun damaging the loaders at the breech, and the much longer life of the gun are all advantages for this system, but the less explosive powder requires a longer and therefore heavier gun, and a heavier projectile, to perform exactly what the English gun, with its very strong

---

3   7 June 1867, Key (as Director of Naval Ordnance) to Admiralty, TNA ADM 1/6021. Key thought it obvious that cast-iron guns being weaker than Armstrong's built-up method could not handle higher charges as safely; while the claimed advantages of breech-loaded guns (namely rapidity of fire and safety of gun crews during combat) were 'not so decided' if it also meant greater complexity of guns and possibility of breakdown; see also Ropp, *The Development of a Modern Navy*, 14. By 9 March 1868, Robinson was concerned of a new French 10.63-inch gun firing a 476 lb. shot with a 66lbs. charge which could penetrate the 8-inch plating of the *Ocean* at 1,089 yards—considered the same as the British 12-ton gun, but still inferior to the 18-ton gun. Two of the guns were to be mounted on the *Rochambeau* (*Dunderberg*); 4 March 1868, Robinson to Board, TNA ADM 1/6072.

powder, effects with a shorter gun and lighter projectile. The difference of the two systems is immense. The highly explosive English powder causes the life of the rifled gun to be very short and forbids a breech loader. Muzzle loading involves great exposure of the spongers and loaders, risk from the firing of an adjoining gun, as well as from one overhead, it causes breeching to the side, pivot bars, tackles, etc., to be a very great inconvenience and it is at the foundation of the short projectile which our naval gun adopts, the accuracy of which is undeniably less than that of the longer projectile; the heavier charge requisite for greater precision would destroy too rapidly our naval guns unless we added greatly to the weight.

To sum up, it would appear that the effects produced on Armour Plates by the English 6½-ton and 12½-ton guns are the same as those produced by the French 8- and 14-ton guns…I saw a French 8-inch Armour Plate, with a row of projectiles from a 14 ton gun sticking in it, just as I saw at Shoeburyness an 8-inch Armour Plate for the *Hercules* with a row of projectiles from the 12½-ton gun sticking in it, both plates having ben admirably well backed with timber.

Having visited the same Exhibition, Key later reported, on 20 October 1867, that a French 9.45-inch 14-ton gun was mounted on an iron carriage and slide 'precisely as fitted in *Magnanime*', one of the *Provence*-class ironclads laid down in early 1861 and re-armed in 1866.[4] He thought the sights too weak and noted how four men were needed to elevate the gun 'with difficulty and not smoothly', while the compressor, he felt, must be too small to work effectively therefore 'it is quite useless for controlling the Gun when it is being run-out or-in in a Seaway.' The 12-ton Armstrong was a superior weapon since it weighed two tons less, had a higher initial velocity, and could thus fire further per given angle of elevation. 'This inferiority on the part of the French gun is due to the weakness of the powder, and large windage', he added. But the obvious advantage of a breech-loading gun, which the Controller stressed, was to the Director-General of Naval Ordnance more of a weakness, given the 'simplicity and security from derangement' of muzzle-loaded naval cannon. He also argued that muzzle-loading was just as safe as breech-loading and that the rate of fire was actually higher, again because it was 'simpler'. Robinson's experience in France, however, like his tour of the American *Miantonomoh* the year before, further compelled him to push for even greater armour thicknesses and heavier guns in British ironclads.

---

4   13 June 1867, Robinson to Board, and (enclosed) 20 October 1867, Key to Board, TNA ADM 1/6012; see also 15 July 1867, *Abstracts of Proceedings of the Ordnance Select Committee, for the Quarter ending 30th September, 1867*, comparing English and French powders, TNA WO 33/18; and the printed *Report on the French Artillery 1873*, 5-7, in TNA WO 33/25, giving credit to British excellence in wrought-iron techniques for allowing Armstrong guns to be stronger than the French and cheaper than Krupp's ordnance. The writer, however, thought it 'unnecessary here again to discuss the arguments for or against breech-loading or muzzle-loading'.

Appendix VII

Laminated armour and the 'Law of Resistance'

On July 5 1866 Captain William Henry Noble of the Royal Artillery assured his fellow members of the Ordnance Select Committee that the American 15-inch muzzle-loading smoothbore hardly bore comparison with the Armstrong 9-inch rifled 12-ton gun. Though he had never tested American ordnance himself, his calculations suggested cast-iron projectiles must be 'useless' against ironclads, 'and if the 15-inch gun used a steel shot it would weigh 480 lbs., and the charge would probably have to be reduced to 50 lbs', making the gun relatively harmless. Still, the Director of Ordnance reported that while the Citadel in Quebec was still mounting the ten 7-inch rifled guns sent out the previous October, there was nothing heavier than 32-pounder carronades at Montreal, the works at Toronto and Kingston were incomplete at best, and the main naval base in British North America, Halifax, had twelve 12-ton guns for its defence *on order*, otherwise there were only fifteen of the troublesome 7-inch Armstrong 110-pounder breech-loaders (82 cwt) in place. Bermuda's defences were considered 'in good condition, but inadequate to the requirements of modern defence', with a menagerie of old smoothbores and nothing better than twenty-three of the old Armstrong 110-pounders. Four days later, 11 July, the Admiralty pressed the War Office to finalise its plans for a suitable iron carriage and slides with compressor for the 12-ton gun, 'as the *Bellerophon* is complete for sea with the exception of her armament.'[1]

On 2 May 1866, Noble advanced a theory of 'Law of Resistance', whereby 'the resistance of unbacked wrought-iron plates to absolute penetration by solid steel shot

---

1   5 July 1866, Admiralty memo, TNA ADM 1/5976; 6 July 1866, Minute, 'iron armour plates', *Abstracts of Proceedings of the Ordnance Select Committee, for the Quarter ending 30th September, 1866* (London: George Edward Eyre and William Spottiswoode, 1866), TNA WO 33/17A; *Second Report of the Director of Ordnance Being for the Year 1865-6* (War Office 1866), dated 7 July 1866, TNA WO 33/18, 10-13; 11 July 1866, Minute, "Wrought-iron carriages and platforms for heavy guns', *Abstracts of Proceedings of the Ordnance Select Committee,* (1866), TNA WO 17A, with Admiralty minute dated 28 May 1866.

of similar form and equal diameter ['*vis-viva*'] varies as the square of their thickness only.' Although this was based on experiments going back to at least 1864, it was later discredited; the President of the Ordnance Select Committee noting, 'The fact seems to be established that the resistance of unbacked plates does not in practice follow the simple law of the squares of their thickness, whatever the difference of thicknesses; this is owing perhaps to the difference in quality which exists between thick and thin plates. Thus the resistance of the 10-inch plate is to that of the 5.5-inch, not as 10^2 to 4.5^2, but as $10^{1.68}$ to $5.5^{1.68}$, a very material difference'.[2] As Ericsson wrote to Bureau of Ordnance Chief Henry Wise, recent armour targets conducted at Shoeburyness in 1867 to determine the best possible plating scheme for coastal forts 'were ordered to prove the infallibility of Captain Noble's rule: "that the resisting power of a laminated structure, compared with that of a solid slab, is as the square of the thickness of the thin plates multiplied by their number, is to the square of the thickness of the solid plate", a rule repudiated by the writer, as it would make a 12 inch solid plate 12 times stronger than 12 one inch plates bolted together'. Instead the British discovered that a 15-inch thick target of three 5-inch plates resisted far in excess of this theory. Ericsson then computed that another target 'composed of three thin [2⅓-inch plates] representing the American system, possesses 130/155 part [or 84 per cent] of the strength of the solid plate! This unlooked-for result has greatly perplexed the Ordnance Select Committee and completely upset Captain Noble's theory of the strength of laminated armor. The magnitude of the error of this theory—a theory which we have been told rested on immutable laws, will be seen if we apply the same to the present case...we find by analogy...that a 10-inch solid plate is only equal in strength to a turret 11⅞-inches thick, composed of 2⅓-inch plates.'[3]

2   *Third Report of the Director of Ordnance, Being of the Year 1867-8* (War Office, 1869), TNA WO 33/19, 41; also William Fairbairn, 'On the Law of Resistance of Armour Plates, Composed of One or More Thicknesses', *Transactions of the Institution of Naval Architects*, Volume X (London, 1869), 1-16.
3   11 October 1867, Ericsson Papers, Philadelphia, Box 11. For laminated armour plating on monitors see for example, 18 and 24 October 1861, Ericsson to Smith, U.S. National Archives, RG 45, Entry 464, Box 49, and 23 March 1862, Ericsson to Fox, Fox Papers, New York, Box 3. On 10 June 1862 Ericsson wrote to Fox that solid plating was indeed superior in resisting powers to laminated plates of the same overall thickness; where he expressed that 'one 3 inch plate is fully equal to five 1 inch plates. But for our ability to readily float the greater number, not to mention our inability to obtain thick plates, I never would have employed the thin plates', Fox Papers, New York, Box 3. He had observed to Welles the month before, however, that a convex turret composed of laminated armour plates was 'quite a different structure' than the flat targets as tested in Britain. Lamination, he felt, also helped 'offer just the kind of gradual resistance or yielding which will exhaust the force of impact', 3 May 1862, Ericsson to Welles, Ericsson Papers, Library of Congress. He expanded this idea in his essay on 'Impregnable Armor' to Welles on 18 January 1863; 'of applying laminated protection in order to exhaust the vis viva of the shot by degrees before reaching the solid core intended as the real armor', as in his turret design for the USS *Dictator*. Lamination in a convex (cylindrical) turret structure also

allowed for break-jointing of the plates, removing an inherent weakness with large slabs of (flat) armour plating: their relative dislocation upon impact, as target tests often showed; Ericsson Papers, Library of Congress. For the British tests indicating that 'the resistance to perforation of three 5-inch plates riveted together would equal that of a solid 13-inch plate' see for example 7 October 1867 (Minute 23,289), *Abstracts of Proceedings of the Ordnance Select Committee, for the Quarter ending 31st December, 1867* (London: George Edward Eyre and William Spottiswoode, 1868), 838, TNA WO 33/18.
19 October 1867, 'The "Impregnable" Target Smashed by the Fifteen-Inch Gun', *Army and Navy Journal*. See also 5 November 1867, TNA ADM 1/6021; the Ordnance Select Committee reporting to the Secretary of State for War and the Admiralty that the 25 September 1867 test of the 15-inch Rodman gun with 100lb. charge proved it was 'fully capable of penetrating such a structure as the one referred to ['8 inch Target with *Warrior* backing'], when fired at it direct…at 70 yards.' The Committee further observed, signifiacntly, that 'as the American cast iron shot is almost equal to steel, there is nothing remarkable in the result of the recent trial, further than that the aperture made is of considerable dimensions.' Key commented on 19 October that although current U.S. naval regulations did not stipulate such high battering charges, '80lbs. of [English] powder will probably penetrate any of our ships actually afloat at 70 yards', thus he recommended continued use of such exceptional charges to at least determine the endurance of the American cast-iron smoothbore. By 5 November he was certain that the gun could not penetrate 'the 8" or 9" iron plated portion of *Hercules*' side at any range', as Noble's calculations suggested a necessary force of 200 foot-tons per inch of circumference, requiring a charge of '145lbs.' for the 15-inch gun. On the other hand, none of the British ordnance experts were willing to speculate on the resistance of *Hercules* to the American 20-inch gun, considered wholly experimental. The Americans since 1864 had been casting 20-inch calibre Rodman and Dahlgren smoothbores firing 1,000-pound solid shot with 200lb. charges safely. Despite these titans weighing more than double the Armstrong 600-pounder, Ericsson and Fox had anticipated mounting them on both the single-turreted 4,900-ton *Puritan* and the four 5,600-ton *Kalamazoo*-class double-turreted monitors; see for example, 9 May 1865, Fox to Ericsson, Ericsson Papers, Philadelphia, Box 6. Fox noted to Ericsson that tests with the 20-inch gun confirmed an initial velocity of 1400-feet per second; see 28 March 1867, Ericsson to Fox, Ericsson Papers, Philadelphia, Box 11. As Stimers observed, on 15 March 1867 a 20-inch Rodman at Fort Hamilton, New York (guarding the Narrows) was twice fired with charges of 200 lbs., giving its 1,087 lb. projectiles an initial velocity of 1,370 feet per second, and at 25° elevation, a range of 8,000 yards (4½-miles). When news of this test reached the British naval attaché in Washington he could hardly believe it, adding only that the iron carriage 'was a good deal damaged by the second round'. As slow-firing and unwieldy as the 51½-ton leviathan was, at 500 yards the 20-inch shot fired with a 200lb. charge would strike at a velocity of 1,260 feet, giving a *vis viva* of 12,038 foot tons, or '194 foot tons per inch of circumference of the shot'—perhaps just enough to blast an enormous hole through HMS *Hercules*; 30 July 1867, 'Rodman Guns', The *New York Times*; 26 February 1869 (Minute 26,777), *Abstracts of Proceedings of the Ordnance Select Committee, for the Quarter ending 31st March, 1869* (London: George Edward Eyre and William Spottiswoode, 1869), 50, TNA WO 33/20. The same 20-inch Rodman gun tested at Fort Hamilton remains there today with rows of 20-inch iron shot; a surreal spectacle in John Paul Jones Park, Brooklyn (near the base of the Verrazzano Bridge.) A second one is also preserved at Fort Hancock, Sandy Hook (where it was within range to command the approach to New York Bay).

Appendix VIII

'English and American Iron-Clads Compared' (John Ericsson's critique of Edward Reed's *Our Iron-Clad Ships*, in *Army and Navy Journal*, Vol. 7, No. 26, 12 February 1870, 397-8)

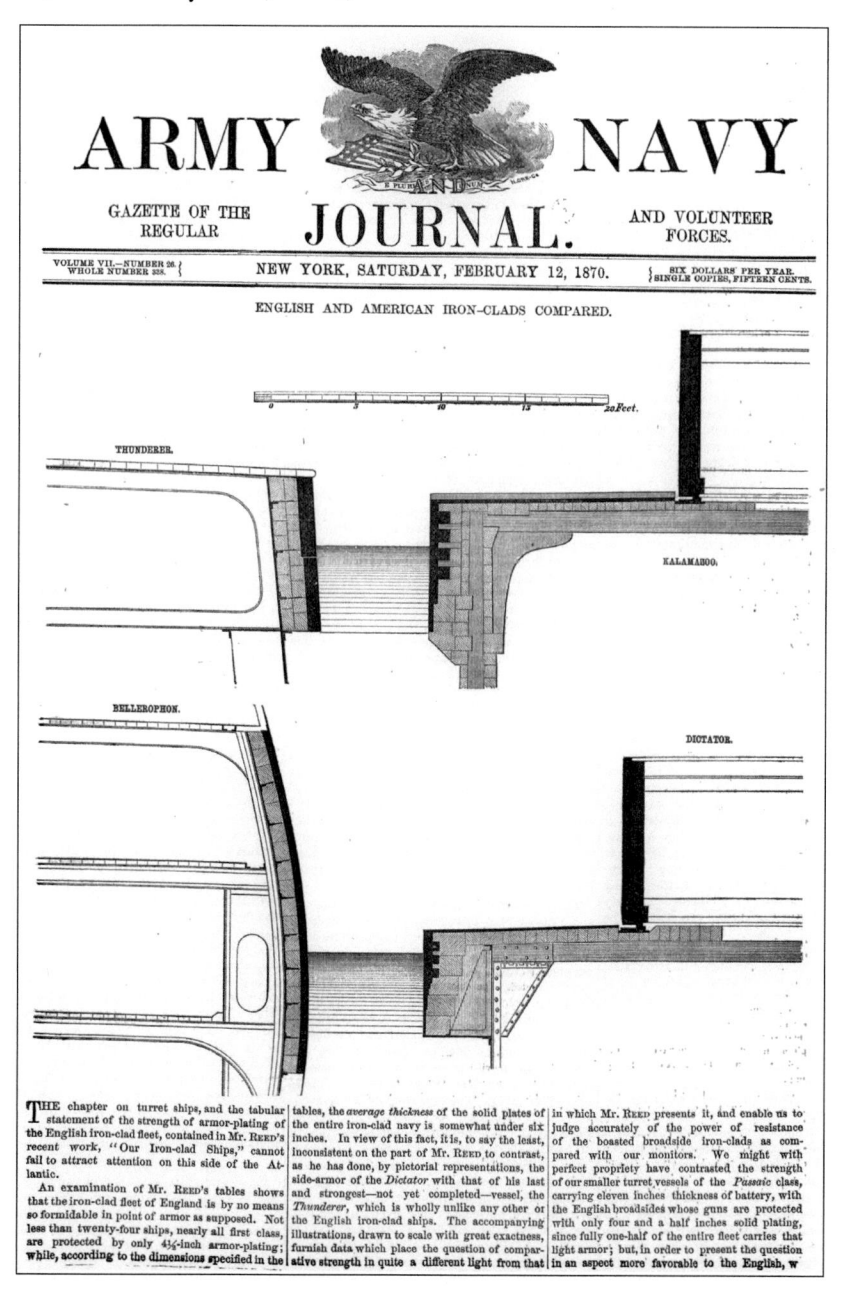

ARMY AND NAVY JOURNAL.

GAZETTE OF THE REGULAR AND VOLUNTEER FORCES.

VOLUME VII.—NUMBER 26. WHOLE NUMBER 338.

NEW YORK, SATURDAY, FEBRUARY 12, 1870.

SIX DOLLARS PER YEAR. SINGLE COPIES, FIFTEEN CENTS.

ENGLISH AND AMERICAN IRON-CLADS COMPARED.

THUNDERER.

KALAMAZOO.

BELLEROPHON.

DICTATOR.

THE chapter on turret ships, and the tabular statement of the strength of armor-plating of the English iron-clad fleet, contained in Mr. REED's recent work, "Our Iron-clad Ships," cannot fail to attract attention on this side of the Atlantic.

An examination of Mr. REED's tables shows that the iron-clad fleet of England is by no means so formidable in point of armor as supposed. Not less than twenty-four ships, nearly all first class, are protected by only 4½-inch armor-plating; while, according to the dimensions specified in the tables, the *average thickness* of the solid plates of the entire iron-clad navy is somewhat under six inches. In view of this fact, it is, to say the least, inconsistent on the part of Mr. REED to contrast, as he has done, by pictorial representations, the side-armor of the *Dictator* with that of his last and strongest—not yet completed—vessel, the *Thunderer*, which is wholly unlike any other or the English iron-clad ships. The accompanying illustrations, drawn to scale with great exactness, furnish data which place the question of comparative strength in quite a different light from that in which Mr. REED presents it, and enable us to judge accurately of the power of resistance of the boasted broadside iron-clads as compared with our monitors. We might with perfect propriety have contrasted the strength of our smaller turret vessels of the *Passaic* class, carrying eleven inches thickness of battery, with the English broadsides whose guns are protected with only four and a half inches solid plating, since fully one-half of the entire fleet carries that light armor; but, in order to present the question in an aspect more favorable to the English, w

398 ARMY AND NAVY JOURNAL. February 12, 1870.

have selected the *Bellerophon* for comparison, her solid armor-plating representing the average thickness of the whole English armored fleet. We have, however, not followed Mr. Reed's example, of contrasting our thickest side-armor with that of the English average strength. Accordingly, we have placed the section of the *Dictator* against that of the *Bellerophon*, and the section of the *Kalamazoo* against that of the *Thunderer*.

We cannot pass unnoticed Mr. Reed's deceptive method of keeping the strength of the battery out of view in comparing the resisting power of iron-clads. No one understands better than the constructor of the "breastwork monitor" *Thunderer* the leading feature of the monitor system, the submerging the hull so nearly as to render the *side-armor* of but secondary importance. Besides, the side-armor of a monitor is not intended to protect the guns. We need scarcely urge that, under such circumstances, it is highly improper to exclude the battery from an illustration put forth for the purpose of imparting information as to the relative offensive and defensive power of broadside ships and monitors.

The sections of the *Bellerophon* and the *Dictator*, represented by our engravings, furnish conclusive evidence that the former could not successfully oppose the latter. The 6-inch plating, 10-inch wood backing, and 1½-inch skin of the *Bellerophon*, offer protection so utterly inadequate to contend against turret guns of adequate power, worked behind fifteen inches thickness of iron, that no question can be raised as to the result of a conflict between these vessels, especially at such ranges as would prevail during harbor defence. It should be borne in mind, with reference to the side-armor, that, during defensive operations, a monitor can almost invariably point the bow towards the assailant, in which case, apart from the protection which results from deep immersion, the angle of the armor of the bow is so acute that every kind of projectile will be deflected.

Respecting the inferior resisting power of a series of thin plates, as compared with an equal thickness of solid armor-plating, we repeat what we have so frequently urged, that the superiority of the monitor over the broadside vessel is not affected by the difference of strength of laminated and solid armor. It is all-sufficient that monitors do carry turrets from eleven inches to fifteen inches in thickness, and that turrets of such enormous thickness are readily handled. The number of plates composing that thickness has obviously nothing to do with the principle. The weight being alike in both cases, all we have to do is to substitute solid for laminated plating.

Much has been said by English writers about the weakness of the wrought-iron armor-stringers placed behind the plates for the protection of the upper part of the submerged hulls of monitors. We readily admit that broad, solid plates are better; but our iron works during the war could only supply the stringers and the thin plates. It should be observed, however, that they fully answered the purpose, not a single life being lost within a monitor hull or turret during the protracted contest with fixed forts, notwithstanding that our adversaries had the advantage of steady aim and an accurate knowledge of ranges. The armor of the hull of the *Kalamazoo* consists, as shown by the engraving, of four wrought stringers of eight inches square, together with two plates, each three inches thick. The aggregate weight of these stringers and plates being the same as a solid plate ten inches thick, we have only to substitute such a plate to render the vessel's hull practically impregnable.

As our engraving furnishes precise data for comparing the armor of English and American iron-clads, and also points out very clearly the unsatisfactory character of the pictorial representations in Mr. Reed's work, we dismiss the subject of armor-plating and pass on to the chapter headed "Turret Ships." We do not propose to criticise Mr. Reed's views with reference to the turrets applied to full-rigged ships, or his disparaging comparisons between Coles's turret ship the *Captain* and the broadside ship *Hercules;* but we cannot refrain from observing that while his demonstration about the importance of an all-round fire is unanswerable and fatal to Coles's ship, he overestimates the advantage of the "simultaneous fire of the *Hercules* in six separate directions," and commits a serious mistake in assuming that four guns in two turrets can only fire in *two* directions. If loading, aiming, and firing could all be effected in an instant, the argument would no doubt be sound; but such not being the case, the firing may alternate, viz., one gun may fire while the other is being loaded. By this method objects separated thirty degrees may be kept under fire as effectually as if two guns in broadside were applied. Evidently, the turret may be as well moved from a given position and returned to it, during loading, as to remain stationary. Indeed, reasons are not wanting why it is better to keep moving than remaining still. We have alluded to this subject to correct the general impression that both guns in a monitor turret must necessarily fire in the same direction. Mr. Reed deems the assumed necessity of firing both guns in the same direction to be a great disadvantage, and thinks that it "assuredly deserves the most serious attention of naval men."

No one who is thoroughly acquainted with the monitor system can peruse the chapter under consideration without arriving at the conclusion that the author of "Our Iron-clad Ships" possesses no accurate knowledge of the American monitor. He comprehends the general features of the system; he finds that by dispensing with freeboard and sails he can apply side-armor of such thickness as to insure impregnability and secure the advantage of an all-round fire; but he evidently is not acquainted with the mechanical detail of an American monitor, nor has he given due reflection to the subject, as will be seen from the following brief examination of his views and quotations. The chief constructor of the English navy thinks that our turrets "are especially liable to be driven out of their proper position by the spindle becoming bent when struck by heavy shot." The proposition that a weight of 200 tons, kept in place by a vertical wrought-iron shaft of twelve inches diameter, should be driven out of position by a shot, is too absurd to demand refutation. In disparagement of the monitor turret, he quotes an erroneous account written by a civil engineer at St. Louis concerning the *base ring*, although it is well known through Bourne's work and other publications, that a base ring forms no part of a monitor turret, such a ring having been applied simply as an expedient to strengthen turrets made of very thin plates. Several other disparaging statements are quoted from the account published by the civil engineer mentioned, who has no personal experience on the subject other than building, to plans furnished, some small turrets for certain river boats, misnamed monitors. The readers of "Our Iron-clad Ships" also learn from the same source that the rotation of the turret is liable to be stopped "by the downward swelling caused by the impact of heavy shot." We have pointed out, on former occasions, that this assumption is a gross mistake; that stoppage from such a cause is impossible, since the outer plating—comprising more than three-quarters of the entire thickness—does not reach the deck.

The central shaft of the monitor is also criticised, and Coles's plan of revolving the turret recommended. The chief constructor apparently does not comprehend that the settling of the deck does not affect a turret which, like a mill-stone on its spindle, is supported on a central shaft; while on Coles's plan such settling causes the rollers to recede from the base which they are intended to support. The views expressed relative to turning the ports away during conflict ignore the fact that the American monitors are provided with massive port-stoppers, which are always shut except at the moment of firing. The important circumstance is also wholly overlooked that the turret, during an engagement with a single opponent, is always kept in position by the officer in charge, the gunner having in fact nothing to do with lateral aim; he fires whenever the roll or elevation suits. Again, a *single*-turreted monitor, in nearly all cases, fires over the bow, obviously uninfluenced by the rolling, and but little affected by the state of the weather, as it happens but seldom that the ports are flooded when pointed towards the bow.

The assumed "bending" of the turret shaft is purely imaginary, as the following explanation will show. The deck ring which supports the base of the turret rests upon four bulkheads, all as deep as the vessel, two being placed transversely and two longitudinally. The tops of these bulkheads cannot be, and never have been, out of a true plane in our monitors with iron hulls. *Wooden* monitors, be it observed, are makeshifts, incompatible with the turret system. As no constructor understands this better than Mr. Reed, why does he put before his readers, as a serious objection against the monitor turret, the statement of an inexperienced civil engineer concerning the settling of the deck of the wooden turret vessel *Miantonomoh?* And why does he advance as a point against the *system* the fact that the base of our wooden vessels had "coats round the turrets to keep them water-tight" while crossing the ocean? He knows that the turrets of the monitor fleet, exposed to the waves of the Atlantic during the war, were at all times ready for action. Those who saw the monitors during the gale off Fort Fisher, with their turrets half submerged, can estimate exactly the strength of the objection urged. In fine, the assumption that the joint between the base of the turret and the deck is liable to leak so as to endanger the safety of the vessel, is mere conjecture based on inferences drawn by those who are not correctly informed of the true cause of the foundering of the original *Monitor*—an accident wholly unconnected with any defects of construction.

Referring to the "breastwork monitors" *Thunderer* and *Devastation*, without masts and sails, we are of opinion that they will prove the most powerful ships in existence; but they are costly, first-class iron ships, protected with solid armor, such as only England can produce at the present time, and they draw twenty-five feet of water. Our experienced naval officers well know that such vessels are not calculated for the defence of the several harbors, dock-yards, and maritime cities of this country; they know that the points to be defended are too numerous to admit of our employing such costly structures as the *Thunderer* and *Devastation;* and that the American monitor, with its impregnable turret, submerged hull, and light draught of water, is better adapted for our shallow waters.

The writer of the chapter on turret ships, apart from his erroneous views of the American monitor, appears to have forgotten what took place subsequently to Admiral Du Pont being relieved from his command at Charleston. The report of Du Pont that the monitors "are totally unfit for blockading duties" being quoted, it will be asked, why is the report of his successor, Admiral Dahlgren, omitted? The former was detached before he had time to become at all acquainted with the new system; while the latter, during two years, blockaded Charleston with the monitors so effectually that the Confederate stronghold was completely sealed. The report of the several commanders of the monitors during the first demonstration against Charleston, under Du Pont's command, is quoted as decisive against the monitor turret; but no reference whatever is made to the important fact that these officers were wholly inexperienced with them, and that the vessels were brought directly from the engine establishments to the enemy's batteries. Had the fleet not been brought into action again, the reference to the reports from the commanders during this their first essay would have been unavoidable; but what are the facts? Admiral Dahlgren afterward engaged the Confederate batteries, with these same monitors, nineteen times between July 18th and September 8th. The report of this experienced commander and accomplished naval artillerist concludes thus: "The battering received was without precedent. The *Montauk* had been struck two hundred and fourteen times, the *Weehawken* one hundred and eighty-seven times, and almost entirely with 10-inch shot."

Captain J. MacDougall, of the Danish Royal Navy, is now on a mission to the United States to study the improvements that have been made in armor-plated ships of war since the return of General Von Rasloff from America, where he was formerly accredited as the Danish Envoy at Washington.

Bibliography

Primary Sources

The National Archives (Kew, London)
Admiralty, War Office, Colonial Office, Foreign Office, and Cabinet—as noted

U.S. National Archives (Washington, D.C., and College Park, Maryland)
Record Groups—as noted

Russian National Archives (St. Petersburg)
Russian State Archive of the Navy—as noted
Russian State Historical Archive—as noted

Personal paper collections (UK)
Major General Sir John Charles Ardagh Papers, The National Archives (Kew)
Henry Herbert, 4th Earl of Carnarvon Papers, The National Archives (Kew)
Richard Cobden Papers, Chichester, West Sussex Record Office
Cochrane Family Papers, Royal Naval Museum Archives, Portsmouth
Cowper Phipps Coles Folios (CCC), National Maritime Museum, Greenwich
Lord Cowley Papers, The National Archives (Kew)
Earl of Ellenborough Papers, The National Archives (Kew)
Gladstone Papers, British Library
2nd Earl Granville Papers, The National Archives (Kew)
General Charles Grey Papers, Durham University Library (Archives & Special Collections) Durham, Palace Green
Rear Admiral Sir Frederick W. Grey, Private Letterbook, 1861-66, National Archives of Scotland, Edinburgh, General Register House
Hickleton (Halifax) Papers, Borthwick Institute (University of York)
Halifax Papers, British Library
Sir George Cornewall Lewis Papers, Harpton Court Estate Records, National Library of Wales, Aberystwyth
Sir Alexander Milne Papers, National Maritime Museum, Greenwich
Sir Charles Napier Papers, The National Archives (Kew)

Napier Papers, Add. Ms. 40027, British Library
Palmerston Papers (Henry John Temple, 3rd Viscount), MS 62 ('Broadlands'), University of Southampton, Southampton
Palmerston Papers, Private Letterbook, British Library
Russell Papers, The National Archives (Kew)
Somerset Papers (Edward Adolphus Seymour, 12th Duke of Somerset), Buckinghamshire Record Office, Aylesbury
Somerset Papers (Ref 3799M), Devon Archives Record Office, Exeter
Sir William Stuart Papers, The National Archives (Kew)

Personal paper collections (US)
John Dahlgren Papers, Library of Congress, Manuscript Division, Washington, D.C.
John Ericsson Papers, American-Swedish Historical Foundation, Philadelphia, PA
John Ericsson Papers, Library of Congress, Manuscript Division, Washington, D.C.
Gustavus Vasa Fox Papers, New York Historical Society Library Manuscripts, New York, NY
Abraham Lincoln Papers, Library of Congress, Manuscript Division, Washington, D.C.
David Dixon Porter Family Papers, Library of Congress, Manuscript Division, Washington, D.C.
Rodgers Family Papers, Naval Historical Foundation Collection, Library of Congress, Manuscript Division, Washington, D.C.
Gideon Welles Papers, Library of Congress, Manuscript Division, Washington, D.C.

Personal paper collections (Russia)
Papers of Alexander Sergeyevich Menshikov, St. Petersburg National Archives
Letters of Konstantin Nikolaevich, St. Petersburg National Archives
Russian National Library, Department of Manuscripts

Parliamentary Papers
Session 1861, Paper number 150; 591, "Return of Number of Steam Battle-Ships, Iron-cased Ships, Frigates, Corvettes, Sloops, and Gun-Boats, March 1859 and 1861"
Session 1861, Paper number 207; 597, "Correspondence between the Admiralty and the Contractors who built the Warrior *in reference to the Non-fulfilment of their Contract within the stipulated Time"*
Session 1861, Paper number 347: 637, "Return of the Makers' Names, and Mode of Manufacturing the Armour Plates of the Warrior, *the Quantities of Iron or Armour Plates Condemned, and the Date and Reason of their Condemnation"*
Session 1861, Paper number 361; 389, "Return of Iron-cased Ships as to Date of Contract, Time for Completion and Penalties"
Session 1862, Paper number 392; 891, "Return of Number of Proposals or Plans for Shot-Proof Ships received at Admiralty, May 1859-62"

Session 1862, Paper number 68; 895, "Return of Total Cost of the Warrior *before being Ready for Sea"*
Session 1862, Paper number 432; 887, "Return of Iron-cased Ships and Floating Batteries building or afloat"
Session 1862, Paper number 507; 125, "Return of Number and Area of Basins and Dockyards of Chatham, Deptford, Woolwich, Sheerness, Portsmouth, Devonport, Keyham and Pembroke; Number of Docks capable of admitting Iron-cased Ships"
Session 1862, Paper number 3063; 887, "Correspondence relating to Civil War in U.S.A."
Session 1863, Paper number 83; 301, "Statement relating to the Advantages of Iron and Wood, and the relative Cost of these Materials in the Construction of Ships for Her Majesty's Navy"
Session 1863, Paper number 86; 293, "Return of Iron-cased Floating Batteries, from Date of Launching to March 1862"
Session 1863, Paper number 190; 295, "Return of Cost of Iron-plated Ships fitted for Sea since Warrior"
Session 1864, Paper number 145; 25, "Admiral Kuper's Official Report of Performance of Armstrong Guns in Action at Kagosima"
Session 1864, Paper number 176; 555, "Account of Guns and Munitions of War shipped from port of Liverpool to America, 1861 and 1862"
Session 1864, Paper number 408; 605, "Correspondence from Commander-in-Chief at Devonport, on Inspection of H.M.S. Research*"*
Session 1865, [Bill] Paper number 51; 189, "Bill to make better provision for Naval Defence of Colonies"
Session 1865, Paper number 156; 553, "Return of Alterations and Repairs on Royal Sovereign *and* Prince Consort; *Estimated Cost of altering* Royal Alfred*"*
Session 1865, Paper number 279; 309, "Report of Admiral Kuper in reference to Armstrong Guns in Action of Simonosaki"
Session 1865, Paper number 307; 321, "Return of Expenses of Armstrong Guns; Number of Armstrong Guns exchanged from Ships of Channel Squadron at Plymouth, May 1864"
Session 1865, Paper number 367; 519, "Return of Iron-plated Ships and Batteries built, building or ordered to be built"
Session 1865, Paper number 3511; 125, "Correspondence arising out of Conflict between Kearsage *and* Alabama"
Session 1866, Paper number 87; 367, "Report of Admiralty Committee on Turret Ships; Correspondence between Admiralty and Captain Cowper Coles"
Session 1866, Paper number 121; 591, "Return of iron-clads built of Wood, adapted or converted from Wooden Ships in course of Construction built in Royal and Private Yards"
Session 1866, Paper number 416; 217, "Supplementary Estimate of Navy: 1866-67 (Completion of H.M.S. Northumberland*)"*
Session 1867, Paper number 537; 279, "Return of Armour-clad Ships and Batteries built by Contract for H.M. Service, 1855-67"

Session 1867-68, Paper number 166; 641, "Papers on Progress of Shipbuilding in H.M. Dockyards, 1868-69"

Session 1867-68, Paper number 167; 637, "Return of Number of H.M. Ships on Station, 1847-67"

Session 1867-68, Paper number 283; 773, "Controller's Report on Trials of Warrior, Minotaur *and* Bellerophon"

Session 1868-69, Paper Number 415; 569, "Return of the Number of Serviceable Rifled Guns and Carriages; Number of Guns required for Fortifications and Iron-clad Ships; Number of Guns under Manufacture at Royal Arsenal at Woolwich"

Session 1877, Paper number 369; 717, "Official Despatches from Rear-Admiral de Horsey reporting Encounter between H.M.S. Shah *and* Amethyst, *and Peruvian Iron-clad Ram* Huascar"

War Have Recently Been Constructed (London: Harrison and Sons, 1872)

1871 Report of the Committee…to Examine the Designs Upon Which Ships of War Have Recently Been Constructed—Dissenting Report by Admiral George Elliot and Rear-Admiral A. P. Ryder (London: Harrison and Sons, 1872)

Hansard—Parliamentary Debates

Congressional Reports:
Miscellaneous Documents of the House of Representatives, 37th Congress, 2nd Session, 1861-62 (Washington: GPO, 1862):
- Misc. Doc. 70, Letter of the Secretary of the Navy to the Chairman of the Committee on Naval Affairs of the Senate of the United States, in relation to the construction of iron-clad steamers, &c., 25 March, 1862
- Misc. Doc. No. 82, Iron-Clad Ships, Ordnance, &c., &c., Letter from the Secretary of the Navy, March 25, 1862

Executive Documents, 37th Congress, 2nd Session, 1861-62 (Washington: GPO, 1862):
- Ex. Doc. No. 6, Estimates for Fortifications, Letter from the Secretary of War, December 10, 1861
- Ex. Doc. No. 8 (Senate), Message of the President of the United States Transmitting A Correspondence between the Secretary of State and the authorities of Great and France, in relation to the recent removal of certain citizens of the United States from the British mail-steamer Trent, December 30, 1861
- Ex. Doc. No. 14, Fortification of the Sea-Coast and Lakes, Message from the President of the United States, December 17, 1861
- Ex. Doc. No. 23, Iron Steam Battery, Letter from the Secretary of the Navy, January 6, 1862
- Ex. Doc. No. 41 (Senate), Letter of the Secretary of War Communicating the Report of Edwin F. Johnson, upon the Defences of Maine, April 5, 1862
- Ex. Doc. No. 103, Forts and Other Means of Defence, Letter from the Secretary of War, April 18, 1862

Ex. Doc. No. 115, *Change of Materials and Construction of Forts, Letter from the Secretary of War, May 12, 1862*
Ex. Doc. No. 128, *Enlargement of the Locks of the Erie and Oswego Canals, Message from the President of the United States, June 13, 1862*
Ex. Doc. No. 148, *Relations Between the United States and Foreign Powers, Message from the President of the United States, July 12, 1862*

Reports of Committees of the House of Representatives and Courts of Claims, 37th Congress, 2nd Session, 1861-62 (Washington: GPO, 1862):
Report No. 22, *Reciprocity Treaty with Great Britain, February 5, 1862*
Report No. 23, *Harbor Defences on Great Lakes and Rivers, February 12, 1862*
Report No. 86, *Permanent Fortifications and Sea-Coast Defences, April 23, 1862*
Report No. 114, *Enlargement of the Locks of the Erie and Oswego Canals, June 3, 1862*

Reports of Committees of the House of Representatives and Courts of Claims, 37th Congress, 3rd Session, 1862-63 (Washington: GPO, 1863):
Report No. 4, *The Naval Defences of the Great Lakes, January 8, 1863*
Report No. 53, *Niagara Ship Canal, March 3, 1863*

Executive Documents, 38th Congress, 1st Session, 1863-64 (Washington: GPO, 1864):
Ex. Doc. No. 69, *Armored Vessels in the Attack on Charleston, Letter from the Secretary of the Navy, April 11, 1864*

Executive Documents, 55th Congress, 2nd Session, 1888-89 (Washington: GPO, 1889):
Ex. Doc. No. 197 (Senate), "Moses Stuyvesant, Monitors v. Battle Ships", March 21, 1898

Report of the Secretary of the Navy in Relation to Armored Vessels (Washington: GPO, 1864)

Congressional Globe
Official Records of the Union and Confederate Navies in the War of the Rebellion, 30 vols. (Washington, D.C.: GPO, 1894-1922)
Official Records of the War of the Rebellion, Union, and Confederate Armies, 120 vols. (Washington, D.C.: GPO, 1880-1901)

Periodicals

Army and Navy Journal
Blackwood's Edinburgh Magazine
The Broad Arrow
Colburn's United Service Journal
Cornhill Magazine
The Daily News
The Daily Telegraph
Edinburgh Review
English Nautical Magazine
The Evening Standard

Fraser's Magazine
Gentleman's Magazine
The Graphic
Hampshire Chronicle
Harper's Weekly
Harper's Monthly
The Illustrated London News
Journal of the Royal United Service Institution
Liverpool Daily Post
London Engineer
The Times (London)
Macmillan's Magazine
Morning Post
Nautical Magazine
Naval Science
New York Herald
The New York Times
Philadelphia Inquirer
Punch, or the London Charivari
Quarterly Review
Saturday Review
Scientific American
The Standard
Sydney Morning Herald
Transactions of the Institute of Naval Architects
The United Service Gazette

Published collections

Evelyn Ashley, *The Life and Correspondence of Henry John Temple, Viscount Palmerston*, 2 vols. (London: Richard Bentley & Son, 1879)
George Douglas Eight of Duke of Argyll—*Autobiography and Memoirs*, 2 vols. (London: John Murray, 1906)
Roy P. Basler (ed.), *The Collected Works of Abraham Lincoln*, 9 vols. (New Brunswick: Rutgers University Press, 1953-55)
Winfried Baumgart (ed.), *Akten zur Geschichte des Krimkriegs*, Series III, *Englische Akten zur Geschichte des Krimkriegs*, Band 4, (Vienna: R. Oldenbourg, 1988)
Howard K. Beale (ed.), *Diary of Gideon Welles: Secretary of the Navy under Lincoln and Johnson*, 3 vols. (New York: W. W. Norton & Company, Inc., 1960)
John Beeler (ed.), *The Milne Papers: The Papers of Admiral of the Fleet Sir Alexander Milne, Bt., K.C.B. (1806-1896)—Vol. I, 1820-1859*, (Aldershot: Ashgate, for the Navy Records Society, 2004)

_____, *The Milne Papers: The Papers of Admiral of the Fleet Sir Alexander Milne, Bt., K.C.B. (1806-1896)—Vol. II, The Royal Navy, and the Outbreak of the American Civil War, 1860-1862*, (Farnham: Ashgate, for the Navy Records Society, 2015)

Arthur Benson and Viscount Esher (eds.), *The Letters of Queen Victoria: 1837-1861*, vol. 3 (London: John Murray, 1907)

D. Bonner-Smith (ed.), *Russian War, 1855—Baltic—Official Correspondence* (Navy Records Society, 1954)

A. J. Butler (ed.), *Bismarck: The Man and the Statesman, being the Reflections and Reminiscences of Otto Prince von Bismarck* (London: Smith, Elder, & Co., 1898)

Hector Bolitho (ed.), *Further Letters of Queen Victoria, From the Archives of the House of Brandenburg-Prussia* (London: Thornton Butterworth, Ltd., 1938)

Kenneth Bourne (ed.), *The Letters of the Third Viscount Palmerston to Laurence and Elizabeth Sulivan 1804-1863* (London: Royal Historical Society, 1979)

_____, *British Documents on Foreign Affairs: Reports and Papers from the Foreign Office Confidential Print, Part I, Series C, North America, 1837-1914, Vol. 5, The Civil War Years, 1859-1861* (University Publication of America, 1986)

_____, *British Documents on Foreign Affairs: Reports and Papers from the Foreign Office Confidential Print, Part I, Series C, North America, 1837-1914, Vol. 6, The Civil War Years, 1862-1865* (University Publication of America, 1986)

_____, *British Documents on Foreign Affairs: Reports and Papers from the Foreign Office Confidential Print, Part I, Series C, North America, 1837-1914, Vol. 7, The Aftermath of the Civil War, 1866-1871* (University Publication of America, 1986)

John Bright and James E. Thorold Rogers (eds.), *Speeches on Questions of Public Policy by Richard Cobden, M.P.*, 2 vols. (London: Macmillan and Co., 1870)

John Bright, *The Diaries of John Bright, with a Foreword by Philip Bright* (London: Cassell & Company Ltd, 1930)

George M. Brook, Jr., (ed.), *Ironclads and Big Guns of the Confederacy: The Journal and Letters of John M. Brooke* (Columbia: University of South Carolina Press, 2002)

John Brooke and Mary Sorensen (eds.), *The Prime Ministers Paper Series, W. E. Gladstone III: Autobiographical Memoranda 1845-1866* (London: HMSO, 1981)

_____, *The Prime Ministers Paper Series, W. E. Gladstone IV: Autobiographical Memoranda 1868-1894* (London: HMSO, 1978)

George Earle Buckle (ed.), *The Letters of Queen Victoria, 1862-1878, Second Series*, 2 vols. (London: John Murray, 1926)

Montagu Burrows, *Memoir of Admiral Sir Henry Ducie Chads* (Portsea: Griffin and Co., 1869)

Spencer Childers (ed.), *The Life and Correspondence of the Right Hon. Hugh C. E. Childers 1827-1896*, 2 vols. (London: John Murray, 1901)

P. H. Colomb (ed.), *Memoirs of Admiral the Right Honble. Sir Astley Cooper Key* (London: Methuen & Co., 1898)

Brian Connell, *Regina vs. Palmerston: The Private Correspondence between Queen Victoria and Her Foreign Minister* (New York: Doubleday & Co., 1961)

Madeleine V. Dahlgren, *Memoir of John A. Dahlgren, Rear Admiral United States Navy, by His Widow* (New York: C. L. Webster, 1891)

Arthur Irwin Dasent (ed.), *John Thadeus Delane, Editor of the 'Times', His Life and Correspondence*, 2 vols. (London: John Murray, 1908)

William Gerard Don, *Reminiscences of the Baltic Fleet of 1855* (D. H. Edwards, 1894)

David Duncan (ed.), *The Life and Letters of Herbert Spencer* (London: Willaims & Norgate, 1911)

Official Dispatches and Letters of Rear Admiral Du Pont, U.S. Navy, 1846-48, 1861-63 (Wilmington: Ferris Bros., 1883)

Sydney Eardley-Wilmot, *An Admiral's Memories: Sixty-Five Years Afloat and Ashore* (London: Sampson Low, Marston & Co., Ltd., ca. late 1920s)

_____, (ed.), *Life of Vice-Admiral Edmund, Lord Lyons* (London: Sampson Low, Marston and Company, 1898)

Fred Egerton, *Admiral of the Fleet Sir Geoffrey Phipps Hornby: A Biography* (William Blackwood and Sons, Edinburgh, 1896)

Don E. Fehrenbacher (ed.), *Abraham Lincoln: Speeches and Writings 1859-1865* (New York: Literary Classics, Inc., 1989)

Tytus Filipowicz (ed.), *Confidential Correspondence of the British Government Respecting the Insurrection in Poland 1863* (Paris: Librairie H. Le Soldier, 1914)

Worthington Chauncey Ford (ed.), *A Cycle of Adams Letters, 1861-1865*, 2 vols. (Boston: Houghton Mifflin Company, 1920)

Sie Edmud E. Fremantle, *The Navy as I Have Known It 1849-1899* (London: Cassell and Company, Limited, 1904)

G. P. Gooch (ed.), *The Later Correspondence of Lord John Russell 1840-1878*, 2 vols. (London: Longmans, Green and Co., 1925)

Victoria Goodenough, *Memoir of Commodore Goodenough, with Extracts from His Letters and Journals*, 3rd edition (London: C. Kegan Paul & Co., 1878)

Charles Greville and Henry Reeve, *The Greville Memoirs: A Journal of the Reign of Queen Victoria, From 1852-1860*, 2 vols., (London: Elibron reprint, 2004)

Philip Guedalla (ed.), *The Palmerston Papers: Gladstone and Palmerston, being the Correspondence of Lord Palmerston with Mr. Gladstone 1851-1865* (London: Victor Gollancz, Ltd., 1928)

C. I. Hamilton (ed.), *Portsmouth Record Series, Portsmouth Dockyard Papers 1852-1869: From Wood to Iron* (Winchester: Hampshire County Council, 2005)

James Howard Harris Malmesbury, *Memoirs of an Ex-Minister: An Autobiography*, 2 vols. (London: Longmans, Green, and Co., 1884)

Angus Hawkins and John Powell (eds.), *The Journal of John Wodehouse—First Earl of Kimberley for 1862-1902, Vol. 9* (London: Royal Historical Society), 1997

John D. Hayes (ed.), *Samuel Francis Du Pont: A Selection From His Civil War Letters*, 3 vols. (Ithaca: Cornell Univ. Press, 1969)

W. H. Hallock and Lady Gwendolen Ramsden (eds.), *Letters, Remains, and Memoirs of Edward Adolphus Seymour Twelfth Duke of Somerset* (London: Richard Bentley and Son, 1893)

Anthony Howe and Simon Morgan (eds.), *The Letters of Richard Cobden Volume Three 1854-1859* (Oxford: University Press, 2012)

Kurt Jagow (ed.), *Letters of the Prince Consort 1831-1861* (London: John Murray, 1938)

T. A. Jenkins (ed.), *The Parliamentary Diaries of Sir John Trelawny, 1858-1865, Camden Fourth Series, Volume 40* (London: Royal Historical Society, 1990)

Robert Underwood Johnson and Clarence Clough Buel (eds.), *Battles and Leaders of the Civil War*, 4 vols. (Edison: Castle Books, 1956, reprint of 1884-88 original series)

John F. V. Keiger (ed.), *British Documents on Foreign Affairs: Reports and Papers from the Foreign Office Confidential Print, Part I, Series F, Europe, 1848-1914, Vol. 9 France, 1847-1878* (University Publication of America, 1989)

Andrew Lang (ed.), *Life, Letters, and Diaries of Sir Stafford Northcote First Earl of Iddesleigh*, 2 vols. (Edinburgh: William Blackwood and Sons, 1890)

John Laughton (ed.), *Memoirs of the Life and Correspondence of Henry Reeve, C.B., D.C.L.*, 2 vols. (London: Longmans Green & Co., 1898)

H. J. Leech (ed.), *The Public Letters of the Right Hon. John Bright* (London: Sampson, Low, Marston, Searle, and Rivington, 1885)

Tresham Lever (ed.), *The Letters of Lady Palmerston* (London: John Murray, 1957)

Dominic Lieven (ed.), *British Documents on Foreign Affairs: Reports and Papers from the Foreign Office Confidential Print, Part I, Series A, Russia, 1859-1914, Vol. 1 Russia, 1859-1880* (University Publication of America, 1983)

Gilbert Frankland Lewis (ed.), *Letters of the Right Hon. Sir George Cornewall Lewis, Bart. to Various Friends* (London: Longmans, Green, and Co., 1870)

Theodore Martin (ed.), *The Life of His Royal Highness The Prince Consort*, 5 vols., (London: Smith, Elder, & Co., 1879)

H. C. G. Matthew (ed.), *The Gladstone Diaries*, Volume VI: 1861-1868, 9 vols (Oxford: Oxford University Press, 1978)

_____, *The Gladstone Diaries*, Volume VII: January 1869 – June 1871, 9 vols (Oxford: Clarendon Press, 1982)

Herbert Maxwell (ed.), *The Life and Letters of Earl of George William Frederick, Fourth Earl of Clarendon*, 2 vols., (London: Edward Arnold: 1913)

Bowen Stilon Mends, *Life of Admiral Sir William Robert Mends, G. C. B.: Late Director of Transports* (London: John Murray, 1899)

Peter von Meyendorff and Otto Hoetzch (eds.), *Peter von Meyendorff, Ein russicher Diplomat an den Höfen von Berlin und Wien*, vol. 3. (Berlin: Walter de Gruyter, 1923)

Nancy Mitford (ed.), *The Stanleys of Alderley: Their Letters Between the Years 1851-1865* (London: Chapman & Hall Ltd., 1939)

Markus Mosslang, Chris Manias and Torston Riotte (eds.), *British Envoys to Germany 1816-1866, Volume IV: 1851-1866* (Cambridge: Cambridge University Press, 2010)

Major-General Elers Napier, *The Life and Correspondence of Admiral Sir Charles Napier*, 2 vols. (London: Hurst and Blackett, 1862)

Arthur Otway (ed.), *Autobiography and Journals of Admiral Lord Clarence E. Paget* (London: Chapman & Hall, Ltd., 1896)
Beverly Wilson Palmer (ed.), *The Selected Letters of Charles Sumner*, 2 vols. (Boston: Northeastern University Press, 1990)
Charles Stuart Parker (ed.), *Life and Letters of Sir James Graham*, 2 vols. (London: John Murray, 1907)
Edward L. Pierce (ed.), *Memoir and Letters of Charles Sumner*, 2 vols. (London: Sampson Low, Marston and Company, 1893)
Agatha Ramm (ed.), *The Political Correspondence of Mr. Gladstone and Lord Granville 1868-1876, vols. 81-82* (London: Royal Historical Society, 1952)
Henry Reeve (ed.), *St. Petersburg and London in the Years 1852-1864, Reminiscences of Charles Frederick Vitzthum von Eckstaedt*, 2 vols. (London: Longmans, Green, and Co., 1887)
Ernest Rhys (ed.), *Selected Speeches of the Rt. Honble John Bright, M.P., on Public Questions* (London: J. M. Dent & Co., 1907)
Warren Ripley (ed.), *Siege Train: The Journal of a Confederate Artilleryman in the Defense of Charleston* (Columbia: University of South Carolina Press, 1986)
John Earl Russell, *Recollections and Suggestions, 1813-1873* (Boston: Roberts Brothers, 1875, reprint of London, Longmans, Green, 1873)
Elizabeth D. Samet (ed.), *Annotated Memoirs of Ulysses S. Grant* (New York: Liveright Publishing Corporation, 2019)
T. H. Sanderson and E. S. Roscoe (eds.), *Speeches and Addresses of Edward Henry XVth Earl of Derby K.G.*, 2 vols. (London: Longmans, Green, and Co., 1894)
David Stevenson (ed.), *British Documents on Foreign Affairs: Reports and Papers from the Foreign Office Confidential Print, Part I, Series F, Europe, 1848-1914, Vol. 17 Denmark, 1848-1914* (University Publication of America, 1990)
_____, *British Documents on Foreign Affairs: Reports and Papers from the Foreign Office Confidential Print, Part I, Series F, Europe, 1848-1914, Vol. 18 Germany, 1848-1897* (University Publication of America, 1990)
Lord Sudley (ed.), *The Lieven-Palmerston Correspondence 1828-1856* (London: John Murray, 1943)
Henry Norton Sulivan and Sir George Henry Richards, *Life and Letters of the Late Admiral Sir Bartholomew James Sulivan, K.C.B., 1810-1890* (London: J. Murray, 1896)
Robert M. Thompson and Richard Wainwright (eds.), *Confidential Correspondence of Gustavus V. Fox, Assistant Secretary of the Navy, 1861-1865*, 2 vols. (New York: New World Book Manufacturing: 1918-19)
John Vincent (ed.), *A Selection from the Diaries of Edward Henry Stanley, 15th Earl of Derby (1826-93), Between September 1869 and March 1878, Vol. 4* (London: Royal Historical Society, 1994)
_____(ed.), *Disraeli, Derby and the Conservative Party: Journals and Memoirs of Edward Henry, Lord Stanley 1849-1869* (Hassocks: The Harvester Press, 1978)

Sarah Agnes Wallace and Frances Elma Gillespie (eds.), *The Journal of Benjamin Moran 1857-1865*, 2 vols. (Chicago: The University of Chicago Press, 1949)
Henry Richard Charles Wellesley (ed.), *The Paris Embassy during the Second Empire: Selections from the Papers of Henry Richard Charles Wellesley 1st Earl Cowley, Ambassador at Paris 1852-1867* (London: Thornton Butterworth, Limited, 1928)
Rosslyn Wemyss (ed.), *Memoirs and Letters of the Right Hon. Sir Robert Morier*, 2 vols. (London: Edward Arnold, 1911)
William White, *The Inner Life of the House of Commons* (Richmond: The Richmond Publishing Co. Ltd., 1973)
M. G. Wiebe, Mary S. Millar, and Ann P. Robson (eds.), *Benjamin Disraeli Letters, Volume Six 1852-1856* (Toronto: University of Toronto Press, 1997)
_____, *Benjamin Disraeli Letters, Volume Eight 1860-1864* (Toronto: University of Toronto Press, 2009)
Michel W. Pharand, Ellen L. Hawman, Mary S. Millar, Sandra Den Otter and M.G. Wiebe (eds.), *Benjamin Disraeli Letters Volume Nine 1865-1867* (Toronto: University of Toronto Press, 2013)
_____, *Benjamin Disraeli Letters Volume Ten 1868* (Toronto: University of Toronto Press, 2014)
H. Noel Williams, *The Life and Letters of Admiral Sir Charles Napier* (London: Hutchinson & Co., 1917)
Lucien Wolf (ed.), *Life of the First Marquess of Ripon*, 2 vols. (London: John Murray, 1921)
George Wrottesley, *Life and Correspondence of Field Marshall Sir John Burgoyne*, 2 vols. (London: Richard Bentley & Son, 1873)
_____, *The Military Opinions of General Sir John Fox Burgoyne* (London: Richard Bentley, 1859)
The History of the Times, 2 vols., (London: 1939)

Secondary Works

Henry L. Abbot, *Course of Lectures upon the Defence of the Sea-Coast of the United States, Delivered Before the U.S. Naval War College* (New York: D. Van Nostrand, 1888)
Charles Francis Adams, Jr., *Charles Francis Adams* (Boston: Houghton-Mifflin, 1900)
Ephraim Douglas Adams, *Great Britain and the American Civil War*, 2 vols. (New York: Russell and Russell, 1925)
A. R. Allinson (ed.), *Intimate Memoirs of Napoleon III, by the Late Baron D'Ambes* (Boston: Little Brown, and Company, 1912)
Daniel Ammen, *The Navy in the Civil War: The Atlantic Coast* (New York: The Blue & The Gray Press, 1905, reprint of Charles Scribner's Sons, 1898)
_____, *The Old Navy and the New* (Philadelphia: J. B. Lippincott, 1891)
Philip Appleman, William A. Madden and Michael Wolff (eds.), *1859: Entering an Age of Crisis* (Bloomington: Indiana University Press, 1959)

Thomas Archer and Alfred Thomas Story, *William Ewart Gladstone and His Contemporaries: Seventy Years of Social and Political Progress*, 4 vols. (London: The Gresham Publishing Co., 1899)
Stephen Badsey, *The Franco-Prussian War 1870-1871* (Oxford: Osprey, 2003)
Philip S. Bagwell and G. E. Mingay, *Britain and America: A Study of Economic Change, 1850-1939* (London: Routledge & Kegan Paul, 1970)
George A. Ballard (edited by G. A. Osborn and N. A. M. Rodger), *The Black Battlefleet: A Study of the Capital Ship in Transition* (London: Nautical Publishing Co., Lymington & the Society for Nautical Research, Greenwich, 1980)
K. C. Barnaby, *The Institution of Naval Architects, 1860-1960: An Historical Survey of the Institution's Transactions and Activities over 100 Years* (London: George Allen and Unwin, 1960)
Nathaniel Barnaby, *Naval Development in the Century* (London: W. & R. Chambers, Limited, 1904)
J. G. Barnard, *The Dangers and Defences of New York* (New York: D. Van Nostrand, 1859)
_____, *Notes on Sea-Coast Defence* (New York: D. Van Nostrand, 1861)
_____, *A Report on the Defenses of Washington* (Washington: GPO, 1871)
James J. Barnes and Patience P. Barnes (eds.), *The American Civil War through British Eyes: Dispatches from British Diplomats*, 2 vols. (London: Caliban Books, 2005)
Correlli Barnett, *The Pride and the Fall: The Dream and Illusion of Britain as a Great Nation* (New York: The Free Press, 1987)
_____, *The Collapse of British Power* (Gloucester: Alan Sutton, 1972)
Patrick Barry, *Dockyard Economy and Naval Power* (London: Sampson Low, Son, and Co., 1863)
_____, *The Dockyards, Shipyards and Marine of France* (London: Simpkin, Marshall, and Co., 1864)
_____, *Shoeburyness and the Guns: A Philosophical Discourse* (London: Sampson Low, Son, and Marston, 1865)
C. J. Bartlett, *Great Britain and Sea Power, 1815-1853* (Oxford: Clarendon Press, 1963)
_____, *Defence and Diplomacy: Great Britain and the Great Powers 1815-1914* (Manchester: Manchester University Press, 1993)
_____, (ed.), *Britain Pre-Eminent: Studies in British World Influence in the Nineteenth Century* (London: Macmillan and Co., Ltd, 1969)
K. C. Barnaby, *Some Ship Disasters and their Causes* (London: Hutchinson & Co., Ltd., 1968)
Marshall J. Bastable, *Arms and the State: Sir William Armstrong and the Remaking of British Naval Power, 1854-1914* (Burlington: Ashgate, 2004)
Darrell Bates, *The Abyssinian Difficulty: The Emperor Theodorus and the Magdala Campaign 1867-68* (Oxford: Oxford University Press, 1979)
Winfried Baumgart, translated by Ann Pottinger Saab, *The Peace of Paris 1865: Studies in War, Diplomacy, and Peacemaking* (Santa Barbara: ABC-Clio, 1981)

James Phinney Baxter 3rd, *The Introduction of the Ironclad Warship* (Cambridge: Harvard University Press, 1933)
Edward Beasley, *Mid-Victorian Imperialists: British Gentlemen and the Empire of the Mind* (London: Routledge, 2005)
John F. Beeler, *British Naval Policy in the Gladstone-Disraeli Era 1866-1880* (Stanford: Stanford University Press, 1997)
_____, *Birth of the Battleship: British Capital Ship Design 1870-1881* (London: Caxton Publishing 2003, reprint of Chatham Publishing, 2001)
Duncan Bell, *The Idea of Greater Britain: Empire and the Future World Order, 1860-1900* (Princeton: Princeton University Press, 2007)
Herbert C. F. Bell, *Lord Palmerston*, 2 vols. (Hamden: Archon Books, 1966, reprint of London, Longmans Green & Co., 1936)
Frank M. Bennett, *The Steam Navy of the United States* (Westport: Greenwood Press, 1896)
_____, *The Monitor and the Navy Under Steam* (Boston: Houghton, Mifflin and Company, 1900)
George Bennett (ed.), *The Concept of Empire: Burke to Attlee, 1774-1947* (London: Adam and Charles Black, 1967)
Michael Bentley, *Politics Without Democracy 1815-1914: Perception and Preoccupation in British Government*, 2nd ed. (Oxford: Blackwell Publishers, 1996)
Eugene H. Berwanger, *The British Foreign Service and the American Civil War* (Lexington: The University Press of Kentucky Press, 1994)
Geoffrey Best, *Mid-Victorian Britain 1851-75* (London: Fontana Press, 1971)
George J. Billy, *Palmerston's Foreign Policy: 1848* (New York: Peter Lang, 1993)
Robert C. Binkley, *Realism and Nationalism 1852-1871* (New York: Harper & Brothers Publishers, 1935)
Saxon T. Bisbee, *Engines of Rebellion: Confederate Ironclads and Steam Engineering in the American Civil War* (Tuscaloosa, University of Alabama Press, 2018)
Jeremy Black, *A History of Diplomacy* (London: Reaktion Books, Ltd., 2010)
_____, *Fighting for North America: The Struggle for Mastery in North America, 1519-1871* (Bloomington: Indiana University Press, 2011)
R. J. M. Blackett, *Divided Hearts: Britain and the American Civil War* (Baton Rouge: Louisiana State University 2001)
William Blackwell, *The Beginnings of Russian Industrialization 1800-1860* (Princeton: Princeton University Press, 1968)
C. A. Bodelsen, *Studies in Mid-Victorian Imperialism* (London: Heinemann, 1960)
Kenneth Bourne (ed.), *The Foreign Policy of Victorian England 1830-1902* (Oxford: Clarendon Press, 1970)
_____, *Britain and the Balance of Power in North America 1815-1908* (London: Longmans, Green and Co. Ltd., 1967)
Charles B. Boynton, *The Navies of England, France, America and Russia, Being an Extract from a Work on English and French Neutrality, and The Anglo-French Alliance*

(New York: John F. Trow, 1865, reprinted in 1866 by C. F. Vent & Co. as *The Four Great Powers*)

_____, *The History of the Navy During the Rebellion*, 2 vols. (New York: D. Appleton & Co., 1867-68)

Kenneth Bourne and D. C. Watt (eds.), *Studies in International History* (Hamden: Archon Books, 1967)

J. D. Brandt, *Gunnery Catechism, as Applied to the Service of Naval Ordnance* (New York: D. Van Nostrand, 1865)

Thomas Brassey, *The British Navy: Its Strength, Resources, and Administration*, 6 vols. (London: Longmans, Green, and Co., 1882-83)

Fenton Bresler, *Napoleon III: A Life* (London: Harper Collins, 1999)

Asa Briggs, *Victorian Cities* (Harmondsworth: Penguin Books Ltd., 1982 reprint of Odhams Press 1963 original)

_____, *Victorian People* (Chicago: The University of Chicago Press, 1970)

John Henry Briggs (edited by Lady Briggs), *Naval Administrations 1827 to 1892: The Experience of 65 Years* (London: Sampson Low, Marston & Company, 1897)

Bernard Brodie, *Sea Power in the Machine Age* (Princeton: Princeton University Press, 1941)

George M. Brook, Jr., (ed.), *Ironclads and Big Guns of the Confederacy: The Journal and Letters of John M. Brooke* (Columbia: University of South Carolina Press, 2002)

David Brown, *Palmerston and the Politics of Foreign Policy 1846-55* (Manchester: Manchester University press, 2002)

David Brown and Miles Taylor (eds.), *Palmerston Studies II* (Southampton: University of Southampton, 2007)

David K. Brown, *Before the Ironclad: Development of Ship Design, Propulsion and Armament in the Royal Navy, 1815-1860* (London: Conway Maritime Press, 1990)

_____, *Warrior to Dreadnought: Warship Development 1860-1905* (London: Chatham Publishing, 1997)

Charles Orde Browne, *Armour, and Its Attack by Artillery* (London: Dulau & Co., 1887)

Samuel T. Browne, *First Cruise of the Montauk—Soldiers and Sailors Historical Society of Rhode Island—Personal Narratives of Events in the War of the Rebellion* (Providence: N. Bangs Williams Co., 1880)

Robert S. Browning, III, *Two If By Sea: The Development of American Coastal Defence Policy* (Westport: Greenwood Publishing, 1983)

Robert M. Browning, Jr., *From Cape Charles to Cape Fear: the North Atlantic Blockading Squadron During the Civil War* (Tuscaloosa: University of Alabama Press, 1993)

_____, *Success Is All That Was Expected: The South Atlantic Blockading Squadron During the Civil War* (Washington, D.C.: Brassey's Inc., 2002)

Robert V. Bruce, *Lincoln and the Tools of War* (Chicago: University of Illinois Press, 1989)

James D. Bulloch, *The Secret Service of the Confederate States of in Europe, or How the Confederate Cruisers Were Equipped*, 2 vols. (London: Richard Bentley & Son, 1883, reprint New York: Sagamore /Thomas Yoseloff, 1959)
W. L. Burn, *The Age of Equipoise; A Study of the Mid-Victorian Generation* (New York: W. W. Norton & Company, Inc., 1964)
E. Milby Burton, *The Siege of Charleston, 1861-1865* (Columbia: University of South Carolina Press, 1970)
J. P. T. Bury, *Napoleon III and the Second Empire* (London: The English Universities Press, Ltd., 1970)
Hans Busk, *The Navies of the World; Their Present State and Future Capabilities* (London: Routledge, Warnes, and Routledge, 1859)
James Cable, *Gunboat Diplomacy 1919-1979: Political Applications of Limited Naval Force* (London: The Macmillan Press Ltd., 1981
_____, *The Political Influence of Naval Force in Naval History* (London: Macmillan Press, Ltd., 1998)
Charles S. Campbell, *From Revolution to Rapprochement: The United States and Great Britain, 1783-1900* (New York: John Wiley & Sons, Inc., 1974)
Duncan Andrew Campbell, *English Public Opinion and the American Civil War* (Woodbridge, The Boydell Press, 2003)
_____, *Unlikely Allies: Britain, America and the Victorian Origins of the Special Relationship* (London: Hambledon Continuum, 2007)
Eugene B. Canfield, *Civil War Naval Ordnance* (Washington: Navy Department, Naval History Division, 1969)
Donald L. Canney, *The Old Steam Navy, Volume Two: The Ironclads, 1842-1885* (Annapolis: Naval Institute Press, 1993)
, *Lincoln's Navy: The Ships, Men and Organization, 1861-65* (Annapolis: Naval Institute Press, 1998)
Stephen P. Carlson, *Charlestown Navy Yard Historic Resource Study*, Volume 3 of 3 (Boston: National Park Service, 2010)
Lynn M. Case, *French Opinion on War and Diplomacy During the Second Empire* (New York: Octagon Books, 1972)
Lynn M. Case, and Warren F. Spencer, *The United States and France: Civil War Diplomacy* (Philadelphia: University of Pennsylvania Press, 1970)
Algernon Cecil, *British Foreign Secretaries, 1807-1916, Studies in Personality and Policy* (London: G. Bell and Sons, Ltd., 1927)
Muriel E. Chamberlain, *British Foreign Policy in the Age of Palmerston* (London: Longman Group Limited, 1980)
_____, *Lord Palmerston* (Washington, D.C.: Catholic University Press, 1988)
_____,*Lord Aberdeen: A Political Biography* (London: Longman, 1983)
_____, *'Pax Britannica'? British Foreign Policy 1789-1914* (Harlow: Longman Group UK Limited, 1988)

John D. Champlin, Jr. (ed.), *Narrative of the Mission to Russia, in 1866, of the Hon. Gustavus Vasa Fox, Assistant-Secretary of the Navy, from the journal and Notes of J. F. Loubat* (New York: D. Appleton and Company, 1873)

John Charmley, *Splendid Isolation? Britain, the Balance of Power and the Origins of the First World War* (London: Hodder & Stoughton, 1999)

Edward Chevalier, *La Marine Française et la Marine Allemande Pendant la Guerre de 1870-71* (Paris: Henri Plon, 1873)

Gregory Claeys, *Imperial Sceptics: British Critics of Empire 1850-1920* (Cambridge: University Press, 2010)

George Sydenham Clarke, *Imperial Defence* (London: The Imperial Press Limited, 1897)

John Clarke, *British Diplomacy and Foreign Policy 1782-1865: The National Interest* (London: Unwin Hyman, 1989)

Michael Clodfelter, *Warfare and Armed Conflicts: A Statistical Encyclopedia of Casualty and Other Figures, 1492-2015* (Jefferson: McFarland & Company, Inc., 2017, 4th ed.)

William Laird Clowes, *The Royal Navy: A History from the Earliest Times to 1900*, Volume VII (London: Chatham Publishing, 1997, first published by Sampson Low, Marston and Company, 1903)

J. B. Conacher, *Britain and the Crimea, 1855-56: Problems of War and Peace* (London: The Macmillan Press, Ltd., 1987)

_____, *The Aberdeen Coalition 1852-1855: A Study in Mid-Nineteenth-century Party Politics* (Cambridge: University press, 1968)

William Conant Church, *The Life of John Ericsson*, 2 vols. (New York: Charles Scribner's Sons, 1890)

Adrian Cook, *The Alabama Claims: American Politics and Anglo-American Relations, 1865-1872* (Ithaca: Cornell University Press, 1975)

John M. Coski, *Capital Navy: The Men, Ships and Operations of the James River Squadron* (Campbell: Savas Publishing Company, 1996)

Regis A. Courtemanche, *No Need of Glory: The British Navy in American Waters 1860-64* (Annapolis: Naval Institute Press, 1977)

Maurice Cowling, *1867—Disraeli, Gladstone and Revolution: The Passing of the Second Reform Bill* (Cambridge: Cambridge University Press, 1967)

Martin Crawford, *The Anglo-American Crisis of the Mid-Nineteenth Century: The Times and America* (Athens: The University of Georgia Press, 1987)

Donald Creighton, *The Road to Confederation: The Emergence of Canada: 1863-1867* (Toronto: Macmillan of Canada, 1964)

Timothy Crick, *Ramparts of Empire: The Fortifications of Sir William Jervois, Royal Engineer, 1821-1897* (Exeter: The Exeter Press, Ltd., 2012)

David Paul Crook, *The North, the South, and the Powers 1861-65* (New York: John Wiley & Sons, Inc., 1974)

_____, *Diplomacy During the American Civil War* (New York: John Wiley & Sons, Inc., 1975)

Michele Cunningham, *Mexico and the Foreign Policy of Napoleon III* (New York: Palgrave, 2001)
Jack A. Dabbs, *The French Army in Mexico 1861-1867* (Hague: Walter De Gruyter Inc., 1963)
John A. Dahlgren, *Shells and Shell-Guns* (Philadelphia: King & Baird, 1857)
John Darwin, *Unfinished Empire: The Global Expansion of Britain* (London: Penguin Group, 2012)
Lance E. Davis and Robert A. Huttenback, *Mammon and the Pursuit of Empire: The Political Economy of British Imperialism 1860-1912* (Cambridge: Cambridge University Press, 1988)
James Tertius DeKay, *Monitor: The Story of the Legendary Civil War Ironclad and the Man Whose Invention Changed the Course of History* (Pimlico: Random House, 1999)
Simon Dentith, *Epic and Empire in Nineteenth-Century Britain* (Cambridge: University Press, 2006)
Conrad Dixon, *Ships of the Victorian Navy* (Southampton: Society for Nautical Research/Ashford Press, 1987)
Jeffrey M. Dorwart, Fort Mifflin of Philadelphia: An Illustrated History (Philadelphia: University of Pennsylvania Press, 1998)
David Dougan, *The Great Gun-Maker: The Story of Lord Armstrong* (Newcastle: Frank Graham, 1971)
Howard Douglas, *On Naval Warfare with Steam* (London: John Murray, Albemarle Street, 1858)
_____, *A Treatise on Naval Gunnery*, 5th edition (London: John Murray, 1860)
Alan Dowty, *The Limits of American Isolation: The United States and the Crimean War* (New York: New York University Press, 1971)
Peter Duckers, *The Crimean War at Sea: The Naval Campaigns Against Russia 1854-56* (Barnsley: Pen & Sword, 2011)
James B. Eads, *System of Naval Defences* (New York: D. Van Nostrand, 1868)
G. Butler Earp (ed.), *The History of the Baltic Campaign of 1854, From the Documents and Other Materials Furnished by Vice-Admiral Sir C. Napier* (London: Richard Bentley, 1857)
Nicholas C. Edsall, *Richard Cobden—Independent Radical* (Cambridge: Harvard University Press, 1986)
C. C. Eldridge (ed.), *British Imperialism in the Nineteenth Century* (London: Macmillan Publishers, Ltd., 1984)
Bruce A. Elleman and S. C. M. Paine (eds.), *Naval Blockades and Seapower: Strategies and Counter-Strategies, 1805-2005* (London: Routledge, 2006)
_____, *Naval Coalition Warfare: From the Napoleonic War to Operation Iraqi Freedom* (London: Routledge, 2008)
Arthur Elliot (ed.), *The Life of George Joachim Goschen, First Viscount Goschen 1831-1907*, 2 vols. (London: Longmans, Green, and Co.), 1911

George S. Emmerson, *John Scott Russell: A Great Victorian Engineer and Naval Architect* (London: John Murray, 1977)
John Ericsson, *Contributions to the Centennial Exhibition* (New York: Nation Press, 1876)
Arvel B. Erickson, *The Public Career of Sir James Graham* (Oxford: Basil Blackwell, 1952)
David Evans, *Building the Steam Navy: Dockyards, Technology and the Creation of the Victorian Battle Fleet, 1830-1906* (London: Conway Maritime Press, 2004)
William Fairburn, *Treatise on Iron Shipbuilding: Its History and Progress* (London, 1865)
R.W.D. Fenn, *The Life and Times of Sir George Cornewall Lewis, Bart—A Radnorshire Gentlemen* (Woonton: Logaston Press, 2005)
Laurence Fenton, *Palmerston and* The Times: *Foreign Policy, the Press and Public Opinion in Mid-Victorian Britain* (London: I. B. Taurus, 2013)
Norman. B. Ferris, *Desperate Diplomacy: William H. Seward's Foreign Policy* (Knoxville: University of Tennessee Press, 1976)
_____, *The Trent Affair* (Knoxville: University of Tennessee Press, 1977)
E. Gardiner Fishbourne, *Our Ironclads and Merchant Ships* (London: E. & F. N., 1874)
John Fisher and Antony Best (eds.), *On the Fringes of Diplomacy: Influences on British Foreign Policy, 1800-1945* (London: Ashgate, 2011)
J. S. Fishman, *Diplomacy and Revolution: The London Conference of 1830 and the Belgian Revolt* (Amsterdam: Charles E. Vos, 1988)
Edmond Fitzmaurice, *The Life of Granville George Leveson Gower, Second Earl Granville K. G. 1815-1891*, 2 vols. (London: Longmans, Green, and Co., 1905)
R. A. Fletcher, *Warships and Their Story* (London: Cassell and Company, Ltd., 1911)
Charles Stuart Forbes, *A Standing Navy: Its Necessity and Organisation* (London: John Murray, 1861)
Stig Forster and Jorg Nagler (eds.), *On the Road to Total War: The American Civil War and the German Wars of Unification, 1861-1871* (Washington, D.C.: German Historical Institute, 1997)
William M. Fowler, *Under Two Flags: The American Navy in the Civil War* (New York: Norton, 1990)
George Henry Francis (ed.), *Opinions and Policy of the Right Honourable Viscount Palmerston* (London: Elibron Classics, 2006 reprint from 1852 original)
Norman Friedman, *British Battleships of the Victorian Era* (Barnsley: Seaforth Publishing, 2018)
Howard J. Fuller, *Clad in Iron: The American Civil War and the Challenge of British Naval Power* (Annapolis: Naval Institute Press, 2008)
_____, *Empire, Technology and Seapower: Royal Navy Crisis in the Age of Palmerston* (London: Routledge, 2013)
William C. Fuller, Jr., *Strategy and Power in Russia 1600-1914* (New York: The Free Press, 1992)

W. Craig Gaines, *Enclyclopedia of Civil War Shipwrecks* (Baton Rouge: Louisiana State Press, 2008)
John Gallagher, *The Decline, Revival and Fall of the British Empire* (Cambridge: University Press, 1982)
A. G. Gardiner, *The Life of Sir William Harcourt*, 2 vols. (London: Constable & Company Ltd., 1923)
Robert Gardiner (ed.), *Conway's History of the Ship Series—The Advent of Steam: The Merchant Steamship Before 1900* (London: Conway Maritime Press, 1993)
_____(ed.), Conway's History of the Ship Series—Steam, Steel & Shellfire: The Steam Warship 1815-1905 (London: Conway Maritime Press, 1992)
David Gillard, *The Struggle for Asia 1828-1914: A Study in British and Russian Imperialism* (London: Methuen & Co. Ltd., 1977)
Quincy A, Gillmore, *Engineer and Artillery Operations against the Defences of Charleston Harbour in 1863* (New York: D. Van Nostrand, 1865)
_____, *Supplementary Report on Operations Against Charleston* (New York: D. Van Nostrand, 1868)
John Howes Gleason, *The Genesis of Russophobia in Great Britain: A Study of the Interaction of Policy and Opinion* (Cambridge: Harvard University Press, 1950)
Jan Glete, *Navies and Nations: Warships, Navies and State Building in Europe and America 1500-1860*, 2 vols. (Stockholm: Coronet Books, Inc., 1993)
David M. Goldfrank, *The Origins of the Crimean War* (London: Longman, 1994)
Erik Goldstein and B. J. C. McKercher (eds.), *Power and Stability: British Foreign Policy, 1865-1965* (London: Frank Cass, 2003)
W. P. Gossett, *The Lost Ships of the Royal Navy 1793-1900* (London: Mansell Publishing Limited, 1986)
Barry M. Gough, *The Royal Navy and the Northwest Coast of North America, 1810-1914: A Study of British Maritime Ascendancy* (Vancouver: University of British Columbia Press, 1971)
_____, *Pax Britannica: Ruling the Waves and Keeping the Peace before Armageddon* (Basingstoke: Palgrave Macmillan, 2014)
G. S. Graham, *The Politics of Naval Supremacy: Studies in British Maritime Ascendancy* (London: Cambridge University Press, 1965)
John D. Grainger, *The First Pacific War—Britain and Russia, 1854-1856* (Woodbridge: The Boydell Press, 2008)
Alfred Grant, *The American Civil War and the British Press* (Jefferson: McFarland & Co., Inc., 2000)
Jack Greene and Alessandro Massignani, *Ironclads at War: The Origin and Development of the Armored Warship, 1854-1891* (Conshohocken: Combined Publishing, 1998)
Basil Greenhill and Ann Giffard, *The British Assault on Finland 1854-1855: A Forgotten Naval War* (London: Conway Maritime Press, 1988)
_____, *Steam, Politics & Patronage: The Transformation of the Royal Navy 1815-54* (London: Conway Maritime Press, 1994)

Edwyn Gray, *Nineteenth-Century Torpedoes and Their Inventors* (Annapolis: Naval Institute Press, 2004)

Edward Grierson, *The Imperial Dream: British Commonwealth and Empire 1775-1969* (Newton Abbot, Readers Union Limited, 1972)

Baron Louis Antoine Richild Grivel, *De la guerre maritime. Attaque et défense avant et depuis les nouvelles inventions* (Paris: Bertrand-Dumaine, 1869)

Philip Guedalla, *Palmerston* (London: Hodder and Stoughton, 1926)

J. M. Haas, *A Management Odyssey: The Royal Dockyards, 1714-1914* (Lanham: University Press of America, 1994)

H. J. Habakkuk, *American and British Technology in the Nineteenth Century: The Search for Labour-Saving Inventions* (Cambridge: University Press, 1962)

Kurt Hackemer, *The U.S. Navy and the Origins of the Military-Industrial Complex 1847-1883* (Annapolis: Naval Institute Press, 2001)

Barton Hacker (ed.), *Astride Two Worlds: Technology and the American Civil War* (Washington, D.C.: Smithsonian Institution Scholarly Press, 2016)

J. A. Hall, *The Law of Naval Warfare* (London: Chapman & Hall, Ltd.), 1921

H. W. Halleck, *Elements of Military Art and Science: Course of Instruction in Strategy, Fortification, Tactics of Battles, Etc.* (New York: D. Appleton & Company, 1861)

C. I. Hamilton, *Anglo-French Naval Rivalry 1840-1870* (Oxford: Clarendon Press, 1993)

_____, *The Making of the Modern Admiralty: British Naval Policy-Making, 1805-1927* (Cambridge: Cambridge University Press: 2011)

George Hamilton, *Parliamentary Reminiscences and Reflections 1868-1885* (London: John Murray, 1916)

Charles Hamley, *Fleets and Navies* (London: William Blackwood and Sons, 1860)

Alfred Jackson Hanna and Kathryn Abbey Hanna, *Napoleon III and Mexico: American Triumph over Monarchy* (Chapel Hill: University of North Carolina Press, 1971)

Frank Hardie, *The Political Influence of Queen Victoria: 1861-1901* (London: Frank Cass & Co. Ltd., 1963)

Richard Harding, *Modern Naval History: Debates and Prospects* (London: Bloomsbury, 2016)

Jerry Harlowe, *Monitors: The Men, Machines and Mystique* (Gettysburg: Thomas Publications, 2001)

William Snow Harris, *Our Dockyards: Past and Present State of Naval Construction in the Government Service* (Plymouth: 1863)

John B. Hattendorf, R.J.B. Knight, A.W.H. Pearsall, N. A. M. Rodger, and Geoffrey Till (eds.), *British Naval Documents, 1204-1960* (Aldershot: Scolar Press for the Navy Records Society, 1993)

Arthur Hawkey, *Black Night Off Finisterre: The Tragic Tale of an Early British Ironclad* (Annapolis: Naval Institute Press, 1999)

Angus Hawkins, *Parliament, Party and the Art of Politics in Britain, 1855-59* (Stanford: Stanford University Press, 1987)

_____, *The Forgotten Prime Minister: The 14th Earl of Derby, Volume II Achievement: 1851-1869* (Oxford University Press, 2008)

James Headlam-Morley, *Studies in Diplomatic History* (London: Methuen & Co. Ltd., 1930).

P. C. Headley, *The Miner Boy and His Monitor, or The Career and Achievements of John Ericsson* (New York: William H. Appleton, 1865)

Daniel R. Headrick, *The Tools of Empire: Technology and European Imperialism in the Nineteenth Century* (Oxford: Oxford University Press, 1981)

F. J. C. Hearnshaw (ed.), *The Political Principles of Some Notable Prime Ministers of the Nineteenth Century* (London: Macmillan and Co., 1926)

Gavin Burns Henderson, *Crimean War Diplomacy and Other Historical Essays* (Glasgow: Jackson, Son & Company, 1947)

Emanuel Hertz (ed.), *Lincoln Talks: A Biography in Anecdote* (New York: Viking Press, 1939)

Martin Hewitt (ed.), *Age of Equipoise? Reassessing Mid-Victorian Britain* (Aldershot: Ashgate Publishing Group, 2000)

Christopher Hibbert, *The Illustrated London News: Social History of Victorian Britain* (London: Book Club Associates, 1976)

Richard Hill, *War at Sea in the Ironclad Age* (London: Cassell, 2000)

Gertrude Himmelfarb, *Victorian Minds: A Study of Intellectuals in Crisis and Ideologies in Transition* (Chicago: Ivan R. Dee, 1968)

Wendy Hinde, *Richard Cobden: A Victorian Outsider* (New Haven: Yale University Press, 1987)

Wilfred Hindle, *The Morning Post 1772-1937: Portrait of a Newspaper* (Westport: Greenwood Press, 1974)

J. A. Hobson, *Richard Cobden: The International Man* (New York: Henry Holt and Company, 1919)

Rolf Hobson and Tom Kristiansen (eds.), *Navies in Northern Waters 1721-2000* (London: Frank Cass, 2004)

Ian V. Hogg, *Coast Defences of England and Wales, 1856-1956* (Newton Abbot: David & Charles Publishers, 1974)

Ian Hogg and John Batchelor, *Naval Gun* (Poole: Blanford Press, 1978)

Alexander L. Holley, *A Treatise on Ordnance and Armor* (New York: D. Van Nostrand, 1865)

Anna Gibson Holloway and Jonathan W. White, *'Our Little Monitor': The Greatest Invention of the Civil War* (Kent: The Kent State University Press, 2018)

Harold Holzer and Tim Mulligan (eds.), *The Battle of Hampton Roads: New Perspectives on the USS* Monitor *and CSS* Virginia (New York: Fordham University Press, 2006)

Peter Hore (ed.), *Seapower Ashore: 200 Years of Royal Navy Operations on Land* (London: Chatham Publishing, 2001)

Michael Howard, *The Franco-Prussian War* (London: William Clowes and Sons, Limited, 1961)

Christopher Howard, *Britain and the Casus Belli 1822-1902: A Study of Britain's International Position from Canning to Salisbury* (London: The Athlone Press, 1974)
Richard Humble, *Before the Dreadnought: The Royal Navy from Nelson to Fisher* (London: Macdonald & Jane's Publishers, Ltd., 1976)
_____, *The Rise and Fall of the British Navy* (London: Queen Anne Press, 1986)
Alvah F. Hunter (edited by Craig L. Symonds), *A Year on a Monitor and the Destruction of Fort Sumter* (Columbia: University of South Carolina Press, 1987)
Ronald Hyam, *Britain's Imperial Century, 1815-1914: A Study of Empire and Expansion*, 2nd ed. (Basingstoke: Palgrave, 1993)
_____, *Understanding the British Empire* (Cambridge: University Press, 2010)
Edward Ingram, *The British Empire as a World Power* (London: Frank Cass, 2001)
Peter J. Jagger (ed.), *Gladstone* (London: The Hambledon Press, 1998)
Fred T. Jane, *The British Battle-Fleet: Its Inception and Growth throughout the Centuries*, Introduction by Anthony Preston (London: Conway Maritime Press: 1997, reprint from London; S.W. Partridge & Co., Ltd., 1912)
Brian Jenkins, *Britain and the War for the Union*, 2 vols. (Montreal: McGill-Queen's University Press, 1974)
E. H. Jenkins, *A History of the French Navy: From its Beginnings to the Present Day* (London: Macdonald and Jane's, 1973)
Mark Jenkins, *Lord Lyons: A Diplomat in an Age of Nationalism and War* (Montreal: McGill-Queen's University Press, 2014)
Roy Jenkins, *Gladstone* (London: Macmillan Publishing, 1995)
T. A. Jenkins, *The Liberal Ascendancy, 1830-1886* (London: Macmillan Press, Ltd., 1994)
John Johnson, *The Defense of Charleston Harbor, Including Fort Sumter and Adjacent Islands, 1863-1865* (Charleston: Walker, Evans and Cogswell, 1890)
Robert Erwin Johnson, *Rear Admiral John Rodgers 1812-1882* (Annapolis: United States Naval Institute, 1967)
Howard Jones, *Union in Peril: The Crisis over British Intervention in the Civil War* (Chapel Hill: University of North Carolina Press, 1992)
Raymond A. Jones, *The British Diplomatic Service 1815-1914* (Gerrards Cross: Colin Smythe, 1983)
Wilbur Devereux Jones, *The Confederate Rams at Birkenhead: A Chapter in Anglo-American Relations* (Tuscaloosa: Confederate Publishing Co., 1961)
Donaldson Jordan and Edwin J. Pratt, *Europe and the American Civil War* (Boston: Houghton Mifflin Company, 1931)
Gerald B. Kauvar and Gerald C. Sorensen (eds.), *The Victorian Mind* (London: Cassell & Company, 1969)
Greg Kennedy (ed.), *Imperial Defence: The Old World Order 1856-1956* (London: Routledge, 2008)
Paul Kennedy, *The Rise and Fall of British Naval Mastery* (Malabar: Robert E. Krieger Publishing Company, 1982, reprint of Harold Ober, 1976)

_____, *The Realities Behind Diplomacy: Background Influences on British External Policy, 1865-1980* (London: George Allen & Unwin, 1981)

_____, *Strategy and Diplomacy 1870-1945, Eight Studies* (London: George Allen & Unwin, 1983)

_____, *The Rise and Fall of the Great Powers: Economic Change and Military Conflict from 1500 to 2000* (London: Fontana Press, 1988)

David Killingray, Margarette Lincoln and Nigel Rigby (eds.), *Maritime Empires: British Imperial Maritime Trade in the Nineteenth Century* (Woodbridge: The Boydell Press and National Maritime Museum, 2004)

J. W. King, *The Warships of Europe* (London: Griffin and Co., 1878)

Paul Knaplund, *Gladstone and Britain's Imperial Policy* (London: Frank Cass & Co., Ltd., 1966)

David F. Krein, *The Last Palmerston Government* (Ames: Iowa State University Press, 1978)

C. Douglas Kroll, *'Friends in Peace and War': The Russian Navy's Landmark Visit to Civil War San Francisco* (Washington DC: Potomac Books, Inc., 2007)

Roy C. Laible (ed.), *Ballistic Materials and Penetration Mechanics* (New York: Elsevier Scientific Publishing Company, 1980)

Andrew Lambert, *Battleships in Transition: The Creation of the Steam Battlefleet 1815-1860* (London: Conway Maritime Press, 1984)

_____, *Warrior: The World's First Ironclad Then and Now* (London: Conway Maritime Press, Ltd., 1987)

_____, *The Crimean War: British Grand Strategy against Russia, 1853-56* (Farnham: Ashgate, 2011, second edition)

_____, *The Last Sailing Battlefleet: Maintaining Naval Mastery 1815-1860* (London: Conway Maritime Press, 1991)

Nelson H. Lawry, Glen M. Williford, and Leo K. Polaski, *Portsmouth Harbor's Military and Naval Heritage* (Charleston: Arcadia Publishing, 2004)

John P. LeDonne, *The Russian Empire and the World 1700-1917: The Geopolitics of Expansion and Containment* (Oxford: Oxford University Press, 1997)

Don Leggett, *Shaping the Royal Navy: Technology, Authority and Naval Architecture, c1830-1906* (Manchester: Manchester University Press, 2015)

Don Leggett and Richard Dunn (eds.), *Re-inventing the Ship: Science, Technology and the Maritime World, 1800-1918* (Farnham: Ashgate publishing Limited, 2012)

Susanna Michele Lee, *Claiming the Union: Citizenship in the Post-Civil War South* (New York: Cambridge University Press, 2014)

Emanuel Raymond Lewis, *Sea Coast Fortifications of the United States: An Introductory History* (Annapolis: Naval Institute Press, 1979, reprint of Smithsonian, 1970)

Michael Lindberg and Daniel Todd, *Brown, Green and Blue-Water Fleets: The Influence of Geography on Naval Warfare, 1861 to the Present* (Westport: Greenwood Press, 2002)

Jay Luvaas, *The Military Legacy of the Civil War: The European Inheritance* (Lawrence: University Press of Kansas, 1988, reprint of University of Chicago Press, 1959)

Raimondo Luraghi, *A History of the Confederate Navy* (London: Chatham Publishing, 1996)
David Lyon and Rif Winfield, *The Sail and Steam Navy List: All the Ships of the Royal Navy 1815-1889* (London: Chatham Publishing, 2004)
Robert MacBride, *Civil War Ironclads: The Dawn of Naval Armor* (Philadelphia: Chilton, 1962)
Philip Macdougall (ed.), *Chatham Dockyard, 1815-1865: The Industrial Transformation* (Farnham: Ashgate, Navy Records Society, 2009)
_____, *Royal Dockyards* (Newton Abbot: David & Charles, 1982)
John M. MacKenzie (ed.), *Popular Imperialism and the Military 1850-1950* (Manchester: Manchester University Press, 1992)
Philip Magnus, *Gladstone: A Biography* (London: John Murray, 1970, reprint of 1954 original)
Alfred Thayer Mahan, *The Influence of Seapower Upon History 1660-1783* (New York: Hill and Wang, American Century Series, 1957, reprint of 1890 original)
_____, *Naval Strategy Compared and Contrasted with the Principles and Practice of Military Operations on Land* (Boston: Little, Brown, 1911)
Dean B. Mahin, *One War at a Time: The International Dimensions of the American Civil War* (Washington D.C.: Brassey's, 1999)
Curt von Maltzahn, *Naval Warfare: Its Historical Development from the Age of the Great Geographical Discoveries to the Present Time* (London: Longmans, Green, and Co., 1908)
Greg Marquis, *In Armageddon's Shadow: The Civil War and Canada's Maritime Provinces* (Montreal: McGill-Queen's University Press, 1998)
Ian Marshall, *Armored Ships: The Ships, Their Settings, and the Ascendancy That They Sustained for 80 Years* (Charlottesville: Howell Press, Inc., 1993)
_____, *Ironclads and Paddlers* (Charlottesville: Howell Press, Inc., 1993)
B. Kingsley Martin, *The Triumph of Lord Palmerston: A Study of Public Opinion in England Before the Crimean War* (London: George Allen & Unwin Ltd., 1924)
Percy F. Martin, *Maximilian in Mexico: The Story of the French Intervention (1861-1867)* (New York: Charles Scribner's Sons, 1914)
Rebecca Berens Matzke, *Deterrence through Strength: British Naval Power and Foreign Policy Under Pax Britannica* (Lincoln: University of Nebraska Press, 2011)
Robert E. May (ed.), *The Union, the Confederacy, and the Atlantic Rim* (West Lafayette: Purdue University Press, 1995)
R. B. McDowell, *British Conservatism 1832-1914* (London: Faber and Faber, 1959)
Peter McKenzie, *W. G. Armstrong: The Life and Times of Sir William George Armstrong, Baron Armstrong of Cragside* (Newcastle: Longhirst Press, 1983)
Stephen McLaughlin, *Russian & Soviet Battleships* (Annapolis: Naval Institute Press, 2003)
James M. McPherson, *Ordeal by Fire: The Civil War and Reconstruction* (New York: McGraw-Hill, 2009)

W. N. Medlicott, *Bismarck, Gladstone, and the Concert of Europe* (London: The Athlone Press, 1956)
R.M. Melnikov, V.Yu. Gribovsky, I.I. Chernikov (eds.), *The First Russian Ironclads, Articles and Documents* (St. Petersburg, 1999)
Maurice Melton, *The Confederate Ironclads* (New York: Thomas Yoseloff, 1968)
Raja Menon, *Maritime Strategy and Continental Wars* (London: Frank Cass Publishers, 1998)
Frank J. Merli, *Great Britain and the Confederate Navy, 1861-1865* (Bloomington: Indiana University Press, 1970)
_____, David M. Fahey (ed.), *The Alabama, British Neutrality, and the American Civil War* (Bloomington: Indiana University Press, 2004)
Bowen Stilon Mends, *Life of Admiral Sir William Robert Mends, G. C. B.: Late Director of Transports* (London: John Murray, 1899)
Edward M. Miller, *U.S.S. Monitor: The Ship That Launched A Modern Navy* (Annapolis: Leeward Publications, Inc., 1978)
Richard Millman, *British Foreign Policy and the Coming of the Franco-Prussian War* (Oxford: Clarendon Press, 1965)
David A. Mindell, *War, Technology, and Experience aboard the U.S.S. Monitor* (Baltimore: John Hopkins University Press, 2000)
Mairin Mitchell, *The Maritime History of Russia 848-1948* (London: Sidgwick and Jackson Limited, 1949)
Jay Monaghan, *Diplomat in Carpet Slippers: Abraham Lincoln Deals with Foreign Affairs* (New York: Bobbs-Merrill, 1945)
N. Monasterev and L'Serge Terestchenko, *Historie de la Marine Russe*, translated by Jean Perceau (Paris: Payot, 1932)
John Morley, *The Life of Richard Cobden*, 2 vols. (London: Chapman and Hall, 1881)
W. P. Morrell, *British Colonial Policy in the Mid-Victorian Age: South Africa, New Zealand, The West Indies* (Oxford: Clarendon Press, 1969)
Roger Morriss, *Naval Power and British Culture, 1760-1850: Public Trust and Government Ideology* (London: Ashgate, 2004)
W. E. Mosse, *The Rise and Fall of the Crimean System 1855-71: The Story of a Peace Settlement* (London: Macmillan & Co., Ltd., 1963)
_____, *The European Powers and the German Question 1848-71, with Special Reference to England and Russia* (Cambridge: Cambridge University Press, 1958)
R. B. Mowat, *The Diplomatic Relations of Great Britain and the United States* (London: Edward Arnold & Co., 1925)
F. Darrell Munsell, *The Unfortunate Duke: Henry Pelham, Fifth Duke of Newcastle, 1811-1864* (Columbia: University of Missouri Press, 1985)
Ivan Musicant, *Divided Waters: The Naval History of the Civil War* (Edison: Castle Books, 2000, reprint of 1995 original)
Mark E. Neely and Harold Holzer (eds.), *The Union Image: Popular Prints of the Civil War North* (Chapel Hill: The University of North Carolina Press, 2000)

Keith Neilson and Greg Kenendy (eds.), *Far-Flung Lines: Studies in Imperial Defence in Honour of Donald Mackenzie Schurman* (Abingdon: Routledge, 1997)

David Newsome, *The Victorian World Picture: Perceptions and Introspections in an Age of Change* (New Brunswick: Rutgers University Press, 1997)

Lord Newton, *Lord Lyons: A Record of British Diplomacy*, 2 vols. (London: Edward Arnold, 1913)

John Niven, *Gideon Welles: Lincoln's Secretary of the Navy* (Baton Rouge: Louisiana State Press, 1973)

David H. Olivier, *German Naval Strategy 1856-1888: Forerunners of Tirpitz* (London: Frank Cass, 2004)

Frank Lawrence Owsley, *King Cotton Diplomacy: Foreign Relations of the Confederate States of America* (Chicago: 1959)

John C. Paget, *Naval Powers and Their Policies* (London: Longmans and Co., 1876)

Oscar Parkes, *British Battleships, 'Warrior' 1860 to 'Vanguard' 1950: A History of Design, Construction and Armament* (London: Seeley Service & Co., Ltd., 1970)

Roger Parkinson, *The Late Victorian Navy: The Pre-Dreadnought Era and the Origins of the First World War* (Woodbridge: The Boydell Press, 2008)

Bah Parritt, *The Intelligencers: The History of British Military Intelligence up to 1914*, 2nd ed. (Ashford: Intelligence Corps Association, 1983)

Jonathan Parry, *The Rise and Fall of Liberal Government in Victorian Britain* (New Haven: Yale University Press, 1993)

Michael Stephen Partridge, *Military Planning for the Defence of the United Kingdom, 1814-1870* (New York: Greenwood Press, 1989)

Michael S. Partridge and Karen E. Partridge (eds.), *Lord Palmerston 1784-1865: A Bibliography* (Westport: Greenwood Press, 1994)

A. W. H. Pearsall, C. I. Hamilton, and Andrew Lambert (eds.), *Publications of the Navy Record Society, Vol. 131, British Naval Documents 1204-1960* (Aldershot: Scolar Press, 1993)

Hugh B. Peebles, *Warshipbuilding on the Clyde: Naval Orders and the Prosperity of the Clyde Shipbuilding Industry, 1889-1939* (Edinburgh: John Donald Publishers, Ltd., 1987)

Geoffrey Penn, *Up Funnel, Down Screw: The Story of the Naval Engineer* (London: Hollis & Carter, 1955)

David Perry, *Bluff, Bluster, Lies and Spies: The Lincoln Foreign Policy, 1861-1865* (Philadelphia: Casemate, 2016)

(Victor Fialin) de Persigny, *Memoires du Duc de Persigny* (Paris: 1896)

Harold L. Peterson, *Notes on Ordnance of the American Civil War, 1861-1865* (Washington: American Ordnance Assn., 1959)

Harry Piers, *The Evolution of the Halifax Fortress 1749-1928* (Halifax: Public Archives of Nova Scotia, 1947)

Albert D. Pionke, *The Ritual Culture of Victorian Professionals: Competing for Ceremonial Status, 1838-1877* (Abingdon: Routledge, 2016 reprint of 2013 original)

D. C. M. Platt, *Finance, Trade, and Politics in British Foreign Policy 1815-1914* (Oxford: Clarendon Press, 1968)
Leo Polaski and Glen Williford, *New York City's Harbor Defenses* (Charleston: Arcadia Publishing, 2003)
Andrew Porter (ed.), *The Oxford History of the British Empire: The Nineteenth Century* (Oxford: Oxford University Press, 1999)
Bernard Porter, *Critics of Empire: British Radicals and the Imperial Challenge* (London: I. B. Tauris, 1968)
———, *The Absent-Minded Imperialists: Empire, Society, and Culture in Britain* (Oxford: University Press, 2004)
———, *The Battle of the Styles: Society, Culture and the Design of the New Foreign Office, 1855-1861* (London: Continuum International Publishing Group, 2011)
David D. Porter, *Naval History of the Civil War* (Secaucus: Castle, 1984, reprint of Sherman, 1886)
Raymond Postgate and Aylmer Vallance, *England Goes to Press: The English People's Opinion on Foreign Affairs as Reflected in Their Newspapers Since Waterloo (1815-1937)* (Indianapolis: The Bobbs-Merrill Company, 1937)
John Prest, *Lord John Russell* (London: The Macmillan Press Ltd., 1972)
Anthony Preston, and John Major, *'Send a Gunboat': A Study of the Gunboat and Its Role in British Policy, 1854-1904* (London: Longmans, Green and Co. Ltd., 1967)
Philip Pugh, *The Cost of Seapower: The Influence of Money on Naval Affairs from 1815 to the Present Day* (London: Conway Maritime Press, 1986)
R. K. I. Quested, *The Expansion of Russia in East Asia 1857-1860* (Singapore: University of Malaya Press, 1968)
Hugh Ragsdale (ed.), *Imperial Russian Foreign Policy* (Cambridge: Woodrow Wilson Center Press, 1993)
A. A. Ramsay, *Idealism and Foreign Policy: A Study of the Relations of Great Britain with Germany and France, 1860-1878* (London: John Murray, 1925)
Bryan Ranft (ed.), *Technical Change and British Naval Policy, 1860-1939* (London: Morrison & Gibb, Ltd., 1977)
A. A. Rasdolgin and Y. A. Skorikov, Кронштадтская крепость, *The Fortress of Cronstadt* (Leningrad: Stroyizdat, 1988)
Andrew C. Rath, *The Crimean War in Imperial Context, 1854-1856* (New York: Palgrave Macmillan, 2015)
Dora Neill Raymond, *British Policy and Opinion During the Franco-Prussian War* (New York: AMS Press, Inc., 1967)
E. J. Reed, *Our Iron-Clad Ships: Their Qualities, Performances, and Cost* (London: John Murray, 1869)
———, *Shipbuilding in Iron and Steel* (London: John Murray, 1869)
———, *Our Naval Coast Defences* (London: John Murray, 1871)
———, *Letters from Russia in 1875* (London: John Murray, 1876)
Rowena Reed, *Combined Operations in the Civil War* (Annapolis: Naval Institute Press, 1978)

Clark G. Reynolds, *Command of the Sea: The History and Strategy of Maritime Empires*, 2 vols. (Malabar: Robert E. Krieger Publishing Company, 1983, reprint of William Morrow & Company, 1974)
_____, *History and the Sea: Essays on Maritime Strategies* (Columbia: University of South Carolina Press, 1989)
David S. Reynolds (ed.), *Lincoln's Selected Writings* (New York: W.W. Norton & Company, 2015)
Norman Rich, *Why the Crimea? A Cautionary Tale* (New York: McGraw-Hill, Inc., 1991 reprint)
Thomas Richards, *The Imperial Archive: Knowledge and the Fantasy of Empire* (London: Verso, 1993)
Herbert W. Richmond, *The Invasion of Britain: An Account of Plans, Attempts & Counter-Measures from 1586-1918* (London: Methuen & Co Ltd., 1941)
Jasper Ridley, *Lord Palmerston* (London: Constable & Co. Ltd, 1970)
_____, *Maximilian and Juárez* (London: Phoenix Press, 1992)
Warren Ripley, *Artillery and Ammunition of the Civil War* (New York: Van Nostrand Reinhold Co., 1970)
James Ewing Ritchie, *The Life and Times of Viscount Palmerston*, 2 vols., (London: The London Printing and Publishing Company, Limited, 1866)
Keith Robbins, *Politicians, Diplomacy and War in Modern British History* (London: The Hambledon Press, 1994)
William H. Roberts, *USS New Ironsides in the Civil War* (Annapolis: Naval Institute Press, 1999)
_____, *Civil War Ironclads: The U.S. Navy and Industrial Mobilization* (Baltimore: The John Hopkins University Press, 2002)
_____, *Now for the Contest: Coastal and Oceanic Naval Operations in the Civil War* (Lincoln: University of Nebraska Press, 2004)
Charles M. Robinson III, *Hurricane of Fire: The Union Assault on Fort Fisher* (Annapolis: Naval Institute Press, 1998)
Charles N. Robinson, *The British Fleet: The Growth, Achievements and Duties of the Navy of the Empire* (London: George Bell & Sons, 1894)
N. A. M. Rodger, *The Admiralty* (Lavenham: Terence Dalton Ltd., 1979)
H. C. B. Rogers, *A History of Artillery* (Secaucus: The Citadel Press, 1975)
Theodore Ropp (edited by Stephen S. Roberts), *The Development of a Modern Navy: French Naval Policy 1871-1904* (Annapolis: Naval Institute Press, 1987)
John Scott Russell, *The Fleet of the Future: Iron or Wood?* (London: Longman, Green, Longman and Roberts, 1861)
Imbert de Saint-Amand, *Napoleon III at the Height of His Power* (New York: Charles Scribner's Sons, 1912)
Raphael Samuel (ed.), *Patriotism: The Making and Unmaking of British National Identity, Volume I: History and Politics* (London: Routledge, 1989)
_____, *Patriotism: The Making and Unmaking of British National Identity, Volume III: National Fictions* (London: Routledge, 1989)

Carl Sandburg, *Abraham Lincoln: The War Years*, 4 vols. (New York: Harcourt, Brace & Company, 1939)

Keith A. P. Sandiford, *Great Britain and the Schleswig-Holstein Question 1848-64* (Toronto: University of Toronto Press, 1975)

Stanley Sandler, *The Emergence of the Modern Capital Ship* (Newark: University of Delaware Press, 1979)

_____, *Battleships: An Illustrated History of Their Impact* (Santa Barbara: ABC-CLIO, 2004)

Norman E. Saul, *Distant Friends: The United States and Russia, 1763-1867* (Lawrence: University Press of Kansas, 1991)

Andrew Saunders, *English Heritage Book of Channel Defences* (London: B. T. Batsford, 1997)

Robert J. Schneller, Jr., *A Quest for Glory: A Biography of Rear Admiral John A. Dahlgren* (Annapolis: Naval Institute Press, 1996)

Paul W. Schroeder, *Austria, Great Britain, and the Crimean War: The Destruction of the European Concert* (Ithaca: Cornell University Press, 1972)

Donald Mackenzie Schurman, *The Education of a Navy: The Development of British Naval Strategic Thought, 1867-1914* (London: Cassell, 1965)

_____(edited by John F. Beeler), *Imperial Defence 1868-1887* (London: Frank Cass & Co., 2000)

Albert Seaton, *The Crimean War: A Russian Chronicle* (London: B. T. Batsford Ltd., 1977)

Bernard Semmel, *Liberalism and Naval Strategy: Ideology, Interest, and Sea Power During the Pax Britannica* (London: Allen & Unwin, Inc., 1986)

Jay Sexton, *Debtor Diplomacy: Finance and American Foreign Relations in the Civil War Era 1837-1873* (Oxford: Clarendon Press, 2005)

Richard Shannon, *Gladstone, Volume 1: 1809-1865* (London: Hamish Hamilton, 1982)

_____, *The Crisis of Imperialism 1865-1915* (London: Paladin Books, 1979, reprint of 1974 original)

A. G. L. Shaw (ed.), *Great Britain and the Colonies 1815-1865* (London: Methuen & Co., Ltd., 1970)

Belle Becker Sideman and Lillian Friedman (eds.), *Europe Looks at the Civil War* (New York: Orion Press, 1962, reprint of 1960 original)

Jennifer Siegel, *Endgame: Britain, Russia and the Final Struggle for Central Asia* (London: I. B. Tauris Publishers, 2002)

Paul H. Silverstone, *Warships of the Civil War Navies* (Annapolis: Naval Institute Press: 1989)

Edward Simpson, *A Treatise on Ordnance and Naval Gunnery: Compiled and arranged as a Text-Book for the U.S. Naval Academy* (New York: D. Van Nostrand, 1863)

Edward William Sloan III, *Benjamin Franklin Isherwood, Naval Engineer* (Annapolis: Naval Institute Press, 1965)

Goldwyn Smith, *The Empire: A Series of Letters Published in the 'Daily News,' 1862, 1863* (Cambridge: University Press, 2010)

Mark A. Smith, *Engineering Security: The Corps of Engineers and the Third System Defense Policy, 1815-1861* (Tuscaloosa: The University of Alabama Press, 2009)
The Duke of Somerset, *Monarchy and Democracy: Phases of Modern Politics* (London: James Bain, 1880)
Michael Somerville, *Bull Run to Boer War: How the American Civil War Changed the British Army* (Warwick: Helion & Company Limited, 2019)
Lawrence Sondhaus, *Naval Warfare 1815-1914* (London: Routledge, 2001)
_____, *Preparing for Weltpolitik: German Sea Power before the Tirpitz Era* (Annapolis: Naval Institute Press, 1997)
Raymond James Sontag, *Germany and England: Background of Conflict 1848-1894* (New York: W. W. Norton & Company Inc., 1969)
Donald Southgate, *'The Most English Minister...' The Policies and Politics of Palmerston* (New York: St. Martin's Press, 1966)
Warren F. Spencer, *The Confederate Navy the Europe* (Tuscaloosa: The University of Alabama Press, 1983)
Thomas J. Spinner, Jr., *George Joachim Goschen: The Transformation of a Victorian Liberal* (Cambridge: University Press, 1973)
C. P. Stacey, *Canada and the British Army 1846-1871* (Toronto: University of Toronto Press, 1963)
E. D. Steele, *Palmerston and Liberalism, 1855-1865* (Cambridge: Cambridge University Press, 1991)
William N. Still, Jr., *Confederate Shipbuilding* (Athens: University of Georgia Pres, 1969)
_____, *Iron Afloat*: The Story of the Confederate Armorclads (Nashville: Vanderbilt University Press, 1971)
William N. Still, Jr., John M. Taylor, and Norman C. Delaney, *Raiders and Blockaders: The American Civil War Afloat* (Washington, D.C.: Brassey's Inc., 1998)
David G. Surdam, *Northern Naval Superiority and the Economics of the American Civil War* (Columbia: University of South Carolina Press, 2001)
Marvin Swartz, *The Politics of British Foreign Policy in the Era of Disraeli and Gladstone* (Basingstoke: The Macmillan Press Ltd., 1985)
Craig Symonds (ed.), *Union Combined Operations in the Civil War* (New York: Fordham University Press, 2010)
A. J. P. Taylor, *The Struggle for Mastery in Europe: 1848-1918* (Oxford: Oxford University Press, 1954)
_____, *The Trouble Makers: Dissent Over Foreign Policy 1792-1939* (London: Pimlico, 1957)
Harold Temperley and Lillian M. Penson (eds.), *Foundations of British Foreign Policy from Pitt (1792) to Salisbury (1902) or Documents, Old and New* (Cambridge: The University Press, 1938)
William H. Thiesen, *Industrializing American Shipbuilding: The Transformation of Ship Design and Construction, 1820-1920* (Gainesville: University Press of Florida, 2006)

A. Wyatt Tilby, *Lord John Russell: A Study in Civil and Religious Liberty* (London: Cassell & Company, Ltd., 1930)
Geoffrey Till (ed.), *Seapower: Theory and Practice* (Ilford: Frank Cass & Co. Ltd, 1994)
_____, *The Development of British Naval Thinking: Essays in Memory of Bryan McLaren Ranft* (London: Routledge, 2006)
Herbert Henry Todd, *The Building of the Confederate States Navy in Europe* (Nashville: Tennessee Joint Universities Libraries, 1941)
Daniel Todd, and Michael Lindberg, *Navies and Shipbuilding Industries: The Strained Symbiosis* (Westport: Greenwood Publishing Group, 1996)
John Tredrea and Eduard Sozaev, *Russian Warships in the Age of Sail 1696-1860: Design, Construction, Careers and Fates* (Barnsley: Seaforth Publishing, 2010)
George Macaulay Trevelyan, *The Life of John Bright* (Boston: Houghton Mifflin Company, 1914)
Spencer Tucker, *Arming the Fleet: U.S. Navy Ordnance in the Muzzle-Loading Era* (Annapolis: Naval Institute Press, 1989)
Brian Tunstall, *The Realities of Naval History* (London: George Allen & Unwin Ltd., 1936)
Glyndon G. Van Deusen, *William Henry Seward* (New York: Oxford University Press, 1967)
Sheldon Vanauken, *The Glittering Illusion: English Sympathy for the Southern Confederacy* (Washington, D.C.: Regnery Gateway, 1989)
J. Don Vann and Rosemary T. Van Arsdel (eds.), *Victorian Periodicals and Victorian Society* (Toronto" University of Toronto Press, 1994)
George Villiers, *A Vanished Victorian: Being the Life of George Villiers, Fourth Earl of Clarendon 1800-1870* (London: Eyre & Spottiswoode, 1938)
Brougham Villiers and W. H. Chesson, *Anglo-American Relations 1861-1865* (London: T. Fisher Unwin: 1919)
John Vincent, *The Formation of the British Liberal Party 1857-1868* (London: Penguin Books, 1972, reprint of Constable 1966)
Spencer Walpole, *The Life of Lord John Russell*, 2 vols. (London: Longmans, Green, and Co., 1891)
Adolphus William Ward and George Peabody Gooch (eds.), *The Cambridge History of British Foreign Policy, 1783-1919, Volume II: 1815-1866* (Cambridge: University Press, 2012)
D. R. Ward, *Foreign Affairs 1815-1865* (London: Collins, 1972)
Gordon H. Warren, *Fountain of Discontent: The* Trent *Affair and Freedom of the Seas* (Boston: Northeastern University Press, 1981)
Kenneth Warren, *Steel, Ships and Men: Cammell Laird, 1824-1993* (Liverpool: Liverpool University Press, 1998)
Geoffrey Wawro, *The Franco-Prussian War: The German Conquest of France in 1870-1871* (Cambridge: Cambridge University Press, 2003)

John R. Weaver II, *A Legacy in Brick and Stone: American Coastal Defense Forts of the Third System, 1816-1867* (Missoula: Pictorial Histoires Publishing Company, 2001)

Richard H. Webber, *Monitors of the U.S. Navy 1861-1937* (Washington, D.C.: Naval History Division, Navy Department, 1969)

Charles Webster, *The Foreign Policy of Palmerston 1830-1841: Britain, The Liberal Movement and the Eastern Question*, 2 vols. (London: G. Bell & Sons, Ltd., 1951)

Kevin J. Weddle, *Lincoln's Tragic Admiral: The Life of Samuel Francis Du Pont* (Charlottesville: University of Virginia Press, 2005)

Stanley Weintraub, *Disraeli: A Biography* (London: Hamish Hamilton, 1993)

J. J. Welch, *A Text Book of Naval Architecture for the Use of Officers of the Royal Navy* (London: Darling & Son, Ltd., 1891)

John Wells, *The Immortal Warrior: Britain's First and Last Battleship* (Emsworth: Kenneth Mason, 1987)

Richard S. West, Jr., *Gideon Welles, Lincoln's Navy Department* (New York: Bobbs-Merrill Co., 1943)

_____, *The Second Admiral: A Life of David Dixon Porter, 1813-1891* (New York: Coward-McCann, 1937)

Francis Brown Wheeler, *John F. Winslow, L.L.D. and the* Monitor (New York: Poughkeepsie, 1893)

Ruth White, *Yankee From Sweden: The Dream and the Reality in the Days of John Ericsson* (New York: Henry Holt and Company, 1960)

Roger Willcock, *Bulwark of Empire: Bermuda's Fortified Naval Base 1860-1920* (Princeton: Roger Willcock, 1962)

Harry Williams, *The Steam Navy of England: Past, Present and Future* (London: W. H. Allen & Co., Limited, 1895)

Sydney Eardley-Wilmot, *The British Navy: Past & Present* (London: The Navy League, 1904)

H. W. Wilson, *Ironclads in Action: A Sketch of Naval Warfare from 1855 to 1895 With Some Account of the Development of the Battleship in England*, 2 vols., 5th edition (London: Sampson Low, Marston & Co., 1897)

_____, *Battleships in Action*, 2 vols. (London: Conway Maritime Press, 1995, reprint from Sampson Low, Marston & Co., 1926)

Stephen R. Wise, *Lifeline of the Confederacy: Blockade Running During the Civil War* (Columbia: University of South Carolina Press, 1988)

_____, *Gate of Hell: Campaign for Charleston Harbor, 1863* (Columbia: University of South Carolina Press, 1994)

Anthony Wood, *Nineteenth Century Britain 1815-1914* (Harlow: Longman Group, Ltd., 1982, reprint of 1960 original)

Cecil Woodham-Smith, *Queen Victoria: Her Life and Times, Volume 1 1818-1861* (London: Book Club Associates, 1972)

Llewellyn Woodward, *The Oxford History of England: The Age of Reform 1815-1870* (Oxford: Clarendon Press, 1962, reprint of 1938 original)

C. D. Yonge, *The History of the British Navy from the Earliest Period to the Present Time*, 3 vols. (London: Richard Bentley, 1866)

(Anon.) *Imperial Strategy: By the Military Correspondent of the Times, with Maps* (London: John Murray, 1906)

Articles

Dean C. Allard, 'Naval Technology During the American Civil War', *The American Neptune*, Vol. 49, No. 2 (Spring 1989)

Francis J. Allen, '*Roanoke*: A Civil War Battleship', *Warship*, No. 35 (July 1985)

Bern Anderson, 'The Naval Strategy of the Civil War', *Military Affairs*, Vol. 26, No.1 (Spring 1962)

Neil Ashcroft, 'British Trade with the Confederacy and the Effectiveness of Union Maritime Strategy During the Civil War', *International Journal of Maritime History*, Vol. 10, No. 2 (December, 1998)

John Bach, 'The Imperial Defense of the Pacific Ocean in the Mid-Nineteenth Century: Ships and Bases', *The American Neptune*, Vol. 32, No. 4 (October 1972)

G. A. Ballard, 'British Battleships of 1870: The *Captain*', *The Mariner's Mirror*, Vol. 17, No. 3 (1931)

C. J. Bartlett, 'The Mid-Victorian Reappraisal of Naval Policy', in Kenneth Bourne, and D. C. Watts (eds.), *Studies in International History: Essays Presented to W. Norton Medlicott* (Hamden: Archon Books, 1967)

Richard M. Basoco, William E. Geoghegan, and Frank J. Merli (eds.), 'A British View of the Union Navy, 1864: A Report Addressed to Her Majesty's Minister at Washington', *The American Neptune*, Vol. 27, No. 1 (January 1967),

K. Jack Bauer, 'Naval Shipbuilding Programs 1794-1860', *Military Affairs*, Vol. 29, No. 1 (Spring 1965)

Colin F. Baxter, 'The Duke of Somerset and the Creation of the British Ironclad Navy, 1859-1866', *The Mariner's Mirror*, Vol. 66, No. 3 (August 1977)

James P. Baxter III, 'The British Government and Neutral Rights, 1861-1865', *The American Historical Review*, Vol. 34, No. 1 (October 1928)

John F. Beeler, 'A One Power Standard? Great Britain and the Balance of Naval Power, 1860-1880', *Journal of Strategic Studies*, Vol. 15, No. 4 (December 1992)

George E. Belknap, 'Reminiscent of the 'New Ironsides' off Charleston', *The United Service*, Vol. 1 (January 1879)

George L. Bernstein 'Special Relationship and Appeasement: Liberal Policy Towards America in the Age of Palmerston', *The Historical Journal*, Vol. 41, No. 3 (1998)

Stellan Bojerud, 'Monitors and Armored Gunboats of the Royal Swedish Navy: Part 1', *Warship International*, Vol. 23, No. 2 (1986)

John Bourne, 'Ships of War', *Proceedings of the Institution of Civil Engineers* 26 (1866-67)

Kenneth Bourne, 'British Preparations for War with the North, 1861-1862', *English Historical Review*, Vol. 76 (October 1961)

Kenneth Bourne, 'Lord Palmerston's "Ginger-beer" Triumph, 1 July 1856', in Kenneth Bourne and D. C. Watt (eds.), *Studies in International History* (Hamden: Archon Books, 1967)
Edgar M. Branch, *American Literature*, 'Major Perry and the Monitor *Camanche*: An Early Mark Twain Speech, Vol. 39, Issue 2 (May 1967)
Jan S. Breemer, 'The Great Race: Innovation and Counter-Innovation at Sea, 1840-1890', *Corbett Paper No. 2, Corbett Centre for Maritime Policy Studies*, King's College, London (January 2011)
Bernard Brodie, 'Military Demonstration and Disclosure of New Weapons', *World Politics*, Vol. 5, No. 3 (April 1953)
Peter Brook, 'Warships Built By Armstrong: H.M.S. *Glatton* (ex-*Bjoergvin*) and *Gorgon* (ex-*Nidaros*)', *Warship International*, Vol. 22, No. 2 (1985)
David K. Brown, 'Introduction of the Screw Propeller into the Royal Navy', *Warship*, No. 1, January 1977
_____, 'Technical Topics: Roughness and Fouling', *Warship*, No. 12, October 1979
_____, 'Shells at Sevastopol', *Warship* 3 (1979)
_____, 'Technical Topics: Where the Power Goes', *Warship*, No. 16, October 1980
_____, 'Attack and Defence', Parts 1-2, *Warship*, Nos. 18 and 21, 1981-1982
_____, 'Developing the Armour of HMS *Warrior*', *Warship*, No. 40, October 1986
_____, 'H.M.S. *Warrior*—The Design Aspects', Royal Institution of Naval Architects, 129, (Spring 1986)
_____, 'Seaworthy by Design', *Warship International*, Vol. 24, No. 4 (1988)
_____, 'British Warship Design Methods 1860-1905', *Warship International*, Vol. 32, No. 1 (1995)
_____, 'Wood, Sail, and Cannonballs to Steel, Steam, and Shells, 1815-1895', in J. R. Hill (ed.), *The Oxford Illustrated History of the Royal Navy* (London: BCA, 1995)
Lance C. Buhl, 'Mariners and Machines: Resistance to Technological Change in the American Navy, 1865-1869', *The Journal of American History*, Vol. 61, No. 3 (December 1974)
James Morton Callahan, 'Russo-American Relations During the American Civil War', *Diplomatic History*, Series 1, No. 1 (January 1908)
Donald L. Canney, 'The Union Navy During the Civil War, 1861-65', in John Roberts (ed.), *Warship* 1995 (London: Conway Maritime Press, 1995)
Christina Carroll, 'Imperial Ideologies in the Second Empire: The Mexican Expedition and the Royaume Arabe', *French Historical Studies*, Vol. 21, No. 1 (February 2019)
Francis M. Carroll, 'The American Civil War and British Intervention: The Threat of Anglo-American Conflict', *Canadian Journal of History*, Vol. XVVII (Spring 2012)
Lynn M. Case, 'French Opinion and Napoleon III's Decision After Sadowa', *The Public Opinion Quarterly*, Vol. 13, No. 3 (Autumn, 1949)
Martin P. Claussen, 'Peace Factors in Anglo-American Relations, 1861-1865', *Mississippi Valley Historical Review*, Vol. 26, No. 4 (March, 1940)

W. F. Durand, 'John Ericsson: Navies of Commerce', in John Lord (ed.), *Beacon Lights of History*, vol. 14 (New York: James Clarke and Co., 1902)
Niels Eichhorn, 'The Intervention Crisis of 1862: A British Diplomatic Dilemma?', *American Nineteenth Century History*, Vol. 15, No. 3 (2014)
R. B. Ely, 'This Filthy Ironpot', *American Heritage*, Vol. 19, No. 2 (1968)
William C. Emerson, 'U.S.S. *New Ironsides*: America's First Broadside Ironclad', *Warship*, 1993
John Ericsson, 'The Monitors', *The Century Magazine*, Vol. 31, No. 2 (December 1885)
D. Evans, 'The Royal Navy and the Development of Mobile Logistics 1851-1894', *The Mariner's Mirror*, Vol. 83, No. 3 (August 1997)
Howard J. Fuller, ' "The fiery focus": An Analysis of the Union Ironclad Repulse at Charleston, 7 April, 1863', *The International Journal of Naval History*, Vol. 1, No. 1. (April 2002)
_____, ' "The Whole Character of Maritime Life": British Reactions to the U.S.S. *Monitor* and the American Ironclad Experience', *The Mariner's Mirror*, Vol. 88, No. 3 (August 2002)
_____,'"This Country Now Occupies the Vantage Ground": Understanding John Ericsson's Monitors and the American Union's War Against British Naval Supremacy', *The American Neptune*, Vol. 62, No. 1 (Winter 2002)
_____, '"Seagoing purposes indispensable to the defence of this country": Policy-Pitfalls of Great Britain's Early Ironclads', *The Northern Mariner/Le Marin du nord*, Vol. 13, No. 1 (January 2003)
_____, " 'The absence of decisive results': British Assessments of Union Combined Operations", in Craig Symonds (ed.), *Union Combined Operations in the Civil War* (New York: Fordham University Press, 2010)
_____, 'Chilean Standoff: Ironclad-Monitor U.S.S. *Monadnock*, Naval Power-Politics & the Spanish Bombardment of Valparaiso, 1866', *Naval History*, June 2011 (25: 3)
_____, 'The *Warrior's* Influence Abroad: The American Civil War', *International Journal of Naval History*, Vol. 10., No. 1 (October 2013)
Frank A. Golder, 'The American Civil War Through the Eyes of a Russian Diplomat', *American Historical Review*, Vol. 26, No. 3 (April 1921)
Norman A. Graebner, "Northern Diplomacy and European Neutrality", in David Donald (ed.), *Why the North Won the Civil War* (New York: Collier, 1962)
Jack Greene, 'The *Re d'Italia*', *Warship International*, Vol. 13, No. 4 (1976)
C. I. Hamilton, 'Sir James Graham, the Baltic Campaign and War Planning at the Admiralty in 1854', *The Historical Journal*, Vol. 19 (1976)
_____, 'The Victorian Navy', *The Historical Journal*, Vol. 25, No. 2 (1982)
_____, (ed.), 'Selections from the Phinn Committee of Inquiry of October-November 1855 into the State of the Office of Secretary to the Admiralty', in N.A.M. Rodger (ed.), *The Naval Miscellany Volume V* (London: George Allen & Unwin, 1984)

Freda Harcourt, 'Disraeli's Imperialism, 1866-1868: A Question of Timing', *The Historical Journal*, Vol. 23, No. 1 (1980)
Daniel G. Harris, 'The Swedish Monitors', *Warship*, Vol. 18 (1994)
Daniel R. Headrick, 'The Tools of Imperialism: Technology and the Expansion of European Colonial Empires in the Nineteenth Century', *The Journal of Modern History*, Vol. 51, No. 2 (June 1979)
William Ray Heitzmann, 'The Ironclad *Weehawken* in the Civil War', *The American Neptune*, Vol. 42, No. 3 (July 1982)
Robin D. S. Higham, 'The Russian Fleet on the Eastern Seaboard, 1863-1864: A Maritime Chronology', *The American Neptune*, 20, No. 1 (January 1960)
Lothar W. Hilbert, 'The Early Years of the Military Attaché Service in British Diplomacy', *Journal of the Society for Army Historical Research*, Vol. 37, No. 152 (December 1959)
Peter J. Hugill, 'The American Challenge to British Hegemony, 1861-1947', *The Geographical Review*, vol. 99, no. 3 (July 2009)
Barbara Jelavich, 'British Means of Offense against Russia in the Nineteenth Century', *Russian History*, Vol. 1, No. 2 (1974)
Mark F. Jenkins, 'The Technology of the Ironclads', *Naval Gazette*, Vol. 2, No. 6, and Vol. 3, No. 1 (1998)
Robert Erwin Johnson, 'Investment by Sea: The Civil War Blockade', *The American Neptune*, Vol. 32, No. 1 (January 1972)
_____'Ships Against Forts: Charleston, 7 April 1863', *The American Neptune*, Vol. 57, No. 2 (Spring 1997)
Colin Jones, '*Monarch* and *Captain*', in Antony Preston, John Jordan and Stephen Dent (eds.), *Warship* 2009 (London: Conway: 2009)
_____, Colin Jones, 'The Limits of Naval Power', in John Jordan (ed.), *Warship 2012* (London: Conway, 2012)
Howard Jones, 'History and Mythology: The Crisis over British Intervention in the Civil War', in Robert E. May (ed.), *The Union, the Confederacy, and the Atlantic Rim* (West Lafayette: Purdue University Press, 1995)
Frank Joseph, 'A Strategic Reassessment: Ironclads at Hampton Roads', *Command Magazine*, 45 (October 1977)
Klari Kingston, 'Gunboat Liberalism? Palmerston, Europe and 1848', *History Today*, Vol. 47, No. 2 (February 1997)
Jacob W. Kipp, 'Consequences of Defeat: Modernizing the Russian Navy, 1856-1863', *Jahrbücher für Geschichte Osteuropas, Neue Folge*, Vol. 20, No. 2 (June 1972)
S. Kirby, 'USS *Keokuk*' in John Roberts (ed.), *Warship Volume VII* (London: Conway Maritime Press, 1983)
Howard I. Kushner, 'The Russian Fleet and the American Civil War: Another View', *The Historian*, 34: 4 (August 1972)
Andrew Lambert, 'The Royal Navy, 1856-1914: Deterrence and The Strategy of World Power', in Keith Neilson and Elizabeth Jane Errington (eds.), *Navies and Global Defense: Theories and Strategy* (Westport: Praeger Publishers, 1995)

_____, 'The Shield of Empire, 1815-1895', in J. R. Hill (ed.), *The Oxford Illustrated History of the Royal Navy* (London: BCA, 1995)

_____, ' "Part of a Long Line of Circumvallation to Confine the Future Expansion of Russia": Great Britain and the Baltic 1809 – 1895', in Rystad Goran, Klaus Bohme and Wilhelm Carlgren (eds.), *In Quest of Trade and Security: The Baltic in Power Politics, 1500- 1990*, vol. 1 of 2 (Lund: Lund University Press, 1994)

_____, 'Politics, Technology and Policy-Making, 1859-1865: Palmerston, Gladstone and the Management of the Ironclad Naval Race', *The Northern Mariner*, Vol. 3, No. 3 (July 1998)

_____, 'Australia, the *Trent* Crisis of 1861, and the Strategy of Imperial Defence', in David Stevens and John Reeve (eds.), *Southern Trident: Strategy, History and the Rise of Australian Naval Power* (Crows Nest: Allen & Unwin, 2001)

_____, 'Economic Power, Technological Advantage, and Imperial Strength: Britain as a Unique Global Power, 1860-1890', *International Journal of Naval History* (www.ijnhonline.org), Vol. 5, No. 2 (August 2006)

_____, (ed.), 'Sir Henry Keppel's Account, Capture of Bomarsund, August 1854', in N.A.M. Rodger (ed.), *The Naval Miscellany Volume V* (London: George Allen & Unwin, 1984)

Paul D. Lockhart, 'The Confederate Naval Squadron at Charleston and the Failure of Naval Harbor Defense', The American Neptune, Vol. 44, No. 4 (Fall 1984)

Charles W. Maccord, 'Ericsson and His 'Monitor', *The North American Review*, Vol. 149, No. 395 (October 1889)

Seymour H. Mauskopf, 'Pellets, Pebbles and Prisms: British Munitions for Larger Guns, 1860-1885', in Brenda J. Buchanan (ed.), *Gunpowder, Explosives and the State: A Technological History* (Aldershot: Ashgate Publishing Limited, 2006)

Douglas H. Maynard, 'Plotting the Escape of the *Alabama*', *The Journal of Southern History*, Vol. 20, No. 2 (May 1954)

Philip Melvin, 'Stephen Russell Mallory, Southern Naval Statesman', *The Journal of Southern History*, Vol. 10, Issue 2 (May 1944)

John D. Milligan, 'From Theory to Application: The Emergence of the American Ironclad War Vessel', *Military Affairs*, Vol. 48, No. 3 (July 1984)

Walter Millis, 'The Iron Sea Elephants', *The American Neptune*, Vol. 10, No. 1 (January 1950)

Iwan Rhys Morus, '"The nervous system of Britain": Space, Time and the Electric Telegraph in the Victorian Age', *The British Journal for the History of Science*, Vol. 33, No. 4 (December 2000)

W. E. Mosse, 'The Crown and Foreign Policy: Queen Victoria and the Austro-Prussian Conflict, March-May, 1866', *Cambridge Historical Journal*, Vol. 10, No. 2 (1951)

Nathan Okun, 'Armor and its Application to Warships', *Warship International*, Vol. 15, No. 4 (1978)

_____, 'Face Hardened Armor', *Warship International*, Vol. 26, No. 3 (1989)

G. A. Osborn, 'The First of the Ironclads—The Armoured Batteries of the 1850s', *The Mariner's Mirror*, Vol. 50, No. 3 (1964)
_____, 'The Crimean Gunboats', Parts 1 and 2, *The Mariner's Mirror*, Vol. 51, Nos. 2-3 (1965)
Philip Ransom Osborn, 'The American Monitors', *U.S. Naval Institute Proceedings*, Vol. 63, No. 408 (1937)
Marc-William Palen, 'The Civil War's Forgotten Transatlantic Tariff Debate and the Confederacy's Free Trade Diplomacy, *Journal of the Civil War Era*, Vol. 3, No. 1 (March 2013)
Erika Pani, 'Law, Allegiance, and Sovereignty in Civil War Mexico, 1857-1867', *Journal of the Civil War Era*, Vol. 7, No. 4 (December 2017)
J. P. Parry, 'The Impact of Napoleon III on British Politics, 1851-1880', in *Transactions of the Royal Historical Society*, Sixth Series, Vol. XI (Cambridge: University Press, 2001)
Charles Oscar Paullin, 'President Lincoln and the Navy', *The American Historical Review*, Vol. 14, No. 2 (January 1909)
Arnold A. Putnam, 'The Introduction of the Revolving Turret', *The American Neptune*, No. 56, No. 2 (Spring 1996)
_____, '*Rolf Krake*: Europe's First turreted Ironclad', *The Mariner's Mirror*, Vol. 84, No. 1 (February 1998)
Bryan Ranft, 'Parliamentary Debate, Economic Vulnerability and British Naval Expansion, 1860-1905', in Lawrence Freedman, Paul Hayes, and Robert O'Neill (eds.), *War, Strategy, and International Politic(s: Essays in Honour of Sir Michael Howard* (Oxford: Clarendon Press, 1992)
E. J. Reed, 'State of the British Navy'; 'The Ironclad Reconstruction of the Navy', *Quarterly Review*, Vol. 134 (1873)
Rowena Reed, 'The Siege of Charleston', in William C. Davis (ed.), *The Image of War 1861-1865*, 6 vols. (New York: Doubleday & Company, Inc., 1983), 4
Stephen S. Roberts, 'The French Coast Defense Ship *Rochambeau*', *Warship International*, Vol. 30, No. 4 (1993)
William H. Roberts, 'The Neglected Ironclad: A Design and Constructural Analysis of the U.S.S. *New Ironsides*', *Warship International*, Vol. 26, No. 2 (1989)
_____' "Thunder Mountain"—The Ironclad Ram *Dunderberg*', *Warship International*, Vol. 30, No. 4 (1993)
_____, '"The Name of Ericsson": Political Engineering in the Union Ironclad Program, 1861-1863', *Journal of Military History*, Vol. 63, No. 4 (1999)
_____, '"The Sudden Destruction of Bright Hopes": Union Shipbuilding Management, 1862-1865', in Randy Carol Balano and Craig L. Symonds (eds.), *New Interpretations in Naval History* (Annapolis: Naval Institute Press, 2001)
Robert Spencer Robinson, 'England as a Naval Power', *The Nineteenth Century*, No. 37 (March 1880)

N. A. M. Rodger, 'British Naval Thought and Naval Policy, 1820-1890: Strategic Thought in an Era of Technological Change', in Craig L. Symonds (ed.), *New Aspects of Naval History* (Annapolis: U.S. Naval Institute, 1981)
_____, 'The Dark Ages of the Admiralty, 1869-85 Part I: 'Business Methods', 1869-74', *The Mariner's Mirror*, Vol. 61, No. 4 (1975)
_____, 'The Design of the *Inconstant*', *The Mariner's Mirror*, Vol. 61, No. 1 (1975)
Nini Rogers, 'The Abyssinian Expedition of 1867-1868: Disraeli's Imperialism or James Murray's War?', *The Historical Journal*, Vol. 27, No. 1 (1984)
Christian de Saint Hubert, 'Early Spanish Steam Warships with Special Emphasis on Screw Frigates and Armoured-frigates and Corvettes (1834-70), Part 1', *Warship International*, Vol. 20, No. 4 (1983)
_____, 'Early Spanish Steam Warships with Special Emphasis on Screw Frigates and Armoured-frigates and Corvettes (1834-70), Part 2', *Warship International*, Vol. 21, No. 1 (1984)
_____, 'Main Shipyards, Engine-builders and Manufacturers of Guns and Armour Plate in the Saint Petersburg Area Up to 1917', *Warship International*, Vol. 22, No. 4 (1985)
Stanley Sandler, 'A Navy in Decay: Some Strategic Technological Results of Disarmament, 1865-69 in the U.S. Navy', *Military Affairs*, Vol. 35, No. 4 (December 1971)
_____, 'The Day of the Ram', *Military Affairs*, Vol. 40, No. 4 (December 1976)
_____, 'The Royal Navy's Coastal Craze: Technological Results of Strategic Confusion in the Early Ironclad Era', *The American Neptune*, Vol. 51, No. 3 (Summer 1991)
_____, Stanley Sandler, '"In Deference to Public Opinion": The Loss of HMS *Captain*', *The Mariner's Mirror*, Vol. 59, No. 1 (1973)
David Saunders, 'Charles Mitchell, Tyneside and Russia's First Ironclads', *Northern History*, Vol. XLVIII (March 2011)
Paul W. Schroeder, 'The Nineteenth Century System: Balance of Power or Political Equilibrium?' *Review of International Studies*, 15 (1989)
G. N. Shumkin, '"The continuous experimentation of our artillery scientists have yielded magnificent results": The Creation of Armor-Piercing Coastal Artillery in the Mid-Nineteenth Century', Voenno-istoricheskii zhurnal (*Military History Journal*), 2020, No. 4
Edward Simpson, 'The Monitor *Passaic*', *The United Service*, Vol. 2 (April 1880)
_____, 'Ironclads', in *Hammersly's Naval Encyclopedia* (Philadelphia: L. R. Hamersly & Co., 1881)
Ernest F. Slaymarker, 'The Armament of HMS *Warrior*', parts 1-3, *Warship*, No. 37, (January 1986); No. 38 (April 1986); No. 39 (July 1986)
Valerii L. Stepanov, 'The Crimean War and the Russian Economy', *Russian Studies in History*, Vol. 51, No. 1 (Summer 2012)
Jon Stephenson, 'Deterrence in Stone: Seacoast Fortresses of the 19th Century', *Journal of America's Military Past*, Vol. XX, No. 2 (Summer 1993)

William N. Still, Jr., 'Confederate Naval Strategy: The Ironclad', *The Journal of Southern History*, Vol. 27, No. 3 (August 1961)

_____, '*Monitor* Companies: A Study of the Major Firms That Built the U.S.S. *Monitor*', *The American Neptune*, Vol. 48, No. 2 (Spring 1988)

David G. Surdam, 'The Union Navy's Blockade of the Confederacy: Tradition-Bound or a Betrayal of America's Birthright', in Peter N. Stearns (ed.), *The American Civil War in a Global Context* (Richmond: Virginia Sesquicentennial of the American Civil War Commission, 2015)

Richard H. Thompson, 'The Rise and Fall of the Monitor 1862-1973', *The Mariner's Mirror*, Vol. 60, No. 3 (August 1974)

Stephen C. Thompson, 'The Design and Construction of "USS Monitor"', *Warship International*, Vol. 27, No. 3 (1990)

W. C. B. Tunstall, 'Imperial Defence, 1815-1870', in J. Holland Rose, A. P. Newton, and E. A. Benians (eds.), *The Cambridge History of the British Empire* (Cambridge: Cambridge University Press, 1940)

Edward W. Very, 'The Development of Armor for Naval Use', *Proceedings of the United States Naval Institute*, Vol. IX, No. 3, 1883

Samuel J. Watson, 'Knowledge, Interest and the Limits of Military Professionalism: The Discourse on American Coastal Defence, 1815-60', *War in History*, Vol. 5, No. 3 (1998)

Donald B. Webster, Jr., 'Rodman's Great Guns', *Ordnance* (July-August 1962)

Kevin J. Weddle, ' "There Should Be No Bungling About this Blockade": The Blockade Board of 1861 and the Making of Union Naval Strategy', *The International Journal of Naval History*, Vol. 1, No. 1, (April 2002)

Gideon Welles, 'The Capture and Release of Mason and Slidell', *The Galaxy*, Vol. 7 (May 1873)

Charles S. Williams and Frank J. Merli (eds.), 'The *Normandie* shows the way: report of a voyage from Cherbourg to Vera Cruz, 4 September 1862', *The Mariner's Mirror*, Vol. 54 (1968), 153-162

Christopher C. Wright, 'The New London Naval Station: The First Years 1862-1885', *Warship International*, Vol. 30, No. 2 (1993)

Theses

Colin F. Baxter, 'Admiralty Problems During the Second Palmerston Administration, 1859-1865', University of Georgia Ph.D. Thesis (1965)

Martin Paul Claussen, 'The United States and Great Britain, 1861-1865; Peace Factors in International Relations', University of Illinois Ph.D. thesis (1938)

Martin S. Crawford, '*The Times* and America 1850-1865: A Study in the Anglo-American Relationship', Oxford University Ph.D. thesis (1979)

Arthur Thomas Frame, 'The U.S. Military Commission to the Crimean War and its Influence on the U.S. Army Before the American Civil War', University of Kansas Ph.D. thesis (1993)

T. S. Good, 'The British Parliament & the American Civil War', Durham University M.A. thesis (1993)
T. Keiser, 'The English Press and the American Civil War', Reading University Ph.D. thesis (1971)
John S. Kinross, 'The Palmerston Forts in the South West: Why Were They Built?' Exeter University M.A. thesis (1995)
David B. McGee, 'Floating Bodies, Naval Science: Science, Design and the *Captain* Controversy, 1860-1870', University of Toronto Ph.D. thesis (1994)
Russell Reed Price, 'American Coastal Defense: The Third System of Fortification, 1816-1864', Mississippi State University Ph.D. thesis (1999)
W. Wilson West, Jr., 'Monitor Madness: Union Ironclad Construction at New York City, 1862-1864', University of Alabama Ph.D. thesis (2003)

Index

Aberdeen, George Hamilton-Gordon (4th Earl of), 39-40
Aboukoff, General, 130
Abyssinian Expedition (1866-7), 221
Act of Union (1707), 36n2
Adalbert, Prince (Prussia), 263n11
Adams, Charles Francis, Sr., 77, 141n23
    co-hosts tour of *Miantonomoh* at Sheerness, 186
Adams, Charles Francis, Jr., 77
Adlersparre, Captain Axel, 159n12
Adriatic Sea, 112-13, 115, 189
Afghanistan (invasion of 1839), 37
Alabama Claims, 141, 218n6, 272n32, 276n8, 218, 272n32, 276n8
Aland Islands, 50
Alaska Purchase, 217
Albert, Prince Consort, 46, 48, 51n50, 61, 67, 139
Alderson, Major-General Henry James, 117, 118n17
Alexander, Brigadier-General Barton Stone, 120
Alexander II, Nikolaevich, Tsar, 36n1, 42-3, 49-50, 89, 90n48
    assassination attempt, 180
    risks abrogating Black Sea Clauses (1870), 274-5
Alexandroffski, 130
Alma, Battle of, 38
American Civil War, *xxxiii*, *xxxv*, 64-73, 81-9, 105, 115, 118-23, 127-9, 139-41, 143-4, 158-9, 173, 181, 229, 270n27, 272, 280-1, 297, 303
American Revolutionary War, *xxiii*, 139, 144, 273n1

Ammen, Rear-Admiral Daniel, 181-2
Anglo-French naval fête, (1865), 158-9, 180-1
Antietam, Battle of, 81, 140n22
Antigua, 103
Antwerp, 131n48
Appomattox, 135n7, 158
Apponyi, Rudolf (Count), 112, 115
Ardagh, Major General John Charles, 220n12
Argyll, George John Douglas Campbell (8th Duke of), 101
Armour-plating, 40-4, 55, 57-60, 62-4, 69-72, 74-5, 77-81, 83, 86-8, 94, 99, 103-5, 116, 119, 122-5, 130-1, 133, 136-8, 142, 145-6, 156-7, 272, 274, 299-310
Armstrong, William George (1st Baron), 56n12, 94, 107, 156, 232, 306n3
Army and Navy Gazette, 218, 246, 267n20
Army & Navy Journal, 122, 146n32, 158, 212-14, 311-12
Army of Châlons, 246
Army of Northern Virginia, 81, 118, 127, 135n7
Army of the Potomac, 75, 81, 118
Atlas Works (see John Brown & Company)
Australia, 193
Austria, 45-7, 49-50, 53, 82, 91, 100-2, 112-14, 123, 174, 178, 183, 239-40, 272, 274
Austrian Navy, 98, 100-1, 112-13, 189
Austro-Prussian War, 174, 178, 183, 186, 239

Bahamas, 66, 68
Balaclava, Battle of, 38

'Balance of Power' considerations, *xxxiv*, 37, 53-4, 58-60, 80, 82-4, 89-91, 100, 102n30, 113-14, 119, 121, 136, 158-9, 178, 180-1, 240, 242, 272-7
Ballard, Admiral George A., *xx*n3, *xxviii-xxix*, 200n10, 263n12
Baltic Sea, 63, 98n15, 112, 115, 121, 143, 201n11, 231, 241, 262, 270, 274, 275n7, 281
　open to Russian naval expansion, 165
Baltic Campaigns (1854, 1855), 38-49, 51, 53, 58-9, 62, 115, 263
Barbados, 103, 132
Baring, Arthur Napier Thomas, *xxiii*
Baring, Thomas George (1st Earl of Northbrook), *xxiii*, 177n5
Barnaby, Nathaniel, *xxxi*, 124, 142, 199n6, 200n9
　1871 Committee on Ship Design, 268
　assesses *Captain*'s construction, 247
　central-battery design innovations, 222n15
　opposes Bourne on need for monitor turret-ship navy, 207
Barnard, Major John G., 70n54
Barnes, Frederick Kynaston, 205n16, 248, 256n1, 257-8
Barry, Patrick, 138n15, 142-3, 145
Bartlett, C. J., *xxxv*n27
Baxter, James Phinney (*The Introduction of the Ironclad Warship*), *xxix*, 73n1
Beaufort (North Carolina), 85
Beaumont, Commander John C., 181, 185n25, 186n28
Beeler, John (*British Policy in the Gladstone-Disraeli Era*), 126n38
Belcher, Admiral Edward, 125
Belgium, 95, 178n7, 240-2
Benbow, John, *xxiv*
Berlin, 99n21, 100
Bermuda (imperial naval base), 66, 69, 80, 97, 103, 107, 110, 116, 128, 177, 183n20, 232n37, 268, 308
Bidder, George Parker, 264n15, 268-9
Birkenhead, *xxii*, 168, 203
Bismarck, Otto Eduard Leopold, von, 91, 239-41
　contempt of British power, 179
　urges Russia to consider negotiations (1870), 275
Blackwood's Edinburgh Magazine, 73, 200

Black Sea, *xxxii*, 38, 39n8, 40, 47, 62, 274-275, 277n9
Black Sea Clauses, 46, 274-5
Black Sea Fleet (British), 41
Black Sea Fleet (Russian), 37
Blockships, 58
Board of Admiralty, *xix*, *xxix-xxx*, *xxxii*, 43, 68, 73, 77, 79, 88, 93-4, 104-5, 107, 117n14, 118n18, 134n4, 147-8, 169n32, 171, 180, 184n22, 189-90, 238, 243, 256n1, 298n3
　allows Coles to submit *Captain* design, 176-7, 278-9
　and early seagoing ironclads, 57-63, 173, 213-14
　and Reed's claim for extra pay, 225, 228, 230, 233-4
　Anglo-French naval balance of power, 53-6, 59, 63, 69, 110-11, 119-20, 126, 130-1, 180, 188, 193-4, 207, 210, 218, 221, 228, 231-2, 242-3, 253, 263, 271-2, 280, 305-7
　approve *Audacious*-class ventral-battery ironclads, 218-20, 234
　approves *Monarch* design, 160, 176-7, 229, 278
　cautious against more turret-ships until *Monarch*, *Captain* trials, 201-2, 219-20, 228-9, 234, 242, 258
　Childers' Board restructure (1868), 230n32, 242, 244
　coastal assault-defence breastwork-monitors authorised, 242, 243n15, 264n14
　considers 1867 proposal for seagoing mastless turret-ship, 218-20
　Crimean War, 39, 43, 45, 47, 54, 58, 69, 98, 114, 177, 193, 263
　dismisses Coles, 164-8
　establishes turret-ship committee (1865), 151-3
　formulation of naval strategies, 206n19, 232, 263, 269-70
　influenced by Robinson and Reed, 163-4, 166, 176, 193, 197-202, 208-11, 218-27, 229-34, 236-8, 243-6, 257, 265-7, 279
　ironclad shipbuilding policies, 99-100, 108-9, 124-6, 128-9, 145-51, 156, 158, 160, 163-4, 168, 173, 176-7, 188-9, 191, 193, 197-202, 205-11,

213-14, 218-19, 222-35, 237-8, 242-6, 253, 264-6, 268-72, 276, 278-80
lays responsibility for *Captain* design upon Lairds, 203-5, 247-52, 256-62, 265, 279
orders conversion of *Royal Sovereign*, 80, 99
outraged by Coles letter to *The Standard* (1866), 164-5
relationship with Coles, 146, 156, 164-8, 176-7, 186, 188, 190-1, 226, 228-9, 243n17, 252-4, 258-61, 278-9
sanctions HMS *Monarch*, 156, 168, 229
split between turret-ships and central-battery ironclads, 81, 107, 154-5, 176-7, 189, 197-202, 208-11, 227-9, 268-72, 278-80
tenders for 2nd-class ironclads (1867), 208, 219-20, 234
tours *Miantonomoh* at Spithead, 185, 235
urges ordnance production, 103, 120, 131-2, 157, 308
Bolivia, 302
Bolt, Peter, 42n21
Bonaparte, Napoleon, 100, 264
Bonaparte, Napoleon III, Charles-Louis (Emperor), 49n44, 53, 55, 81-2, 118-19, 143
and Franco-Prussian War, 239-41, 246
imperial ambitions of, 178, 217, 240-1, 272, 302
surrenders at Sedan, 246
Bosporus Straits, 274-5
Boston, 69, 94, 116
Boston Navy Yard, 83, 94
Bourne, John, 165n24, 170-4, 200, 202n13, 229
lecture on 'Ships of War' (1867), 205-6
writes to Pakington urging monitor-ironclads, 189
Bourne, Kenneth (*Britain and the Balance of Power in North America*), 66n41
Boxer, Edward Mounier, *xxiii*
Boxer, Edward William Frederick, *xxiii*
Brand, Henry Bouverie William (1st Viscount Hampden), 179-80
Brazil, 130
Brassey, Thomas (1st Earl), 201n11
Breastwork-monitor (ironclad design), *xxx*, 199-200, 201n11, 206-8, 218-20, 225, 231-4, 242, 244, 248, 250, 253, 264n14, 269-70, 274n2, 269-70
Cyclops-class authorised, 242, 264n14
Reed proposal of 1869, 231-3, 253
Robinson' strategy for, 231-4, 264n14, 268-70
Russian *Peter the Great* design, 274n2
Bright, John, *xxxiii*, 64, 70, 134n6, 135, 218
Brighton, 48
British Association, 190
British foreign policy, *xxxiv-xxxv*, 39n8, 53, 81-2, 100-2, 105, 110, 112-15, 121-3, 129, 139, 158-60, 179, 261-4, 273-7, 280-1
during Austro-Prussian War, 178-9
during Franco-Prussian War, 240-2, 262, 271, 273-4
loss of national prestige during Palmerston's Second Ministry, 160, 173, 178-9, 188, 240, 271-3
perception of British naval power affecting, 200-1, 210, 221, 240, 261-4, 270-2, 278, 280-1, 304
response to Russian abrogation of Black Sea Clauses, 274-7
British isolation, *xxxii-xxxiii*, *xxxv*, 89, 101-2, 114-15, 121-3, 139-40, 263-4, 271-3, 275-8, 280-1, 304
Broager, 99
Brooke, Commander John Mercer, 136n11
Brooklyn, 117
Brooklyn Navy Yard, 74, 83, 172
Brown, David K., 38n5, 47n41, 268n22
misquotes Bythesea testimony, 183n20
objects to Victorian public sensationalising *Miantonomoh*, 200n9
on Isaac Watts, 164n22
on seaworthiness, 175n1
Bruce, Frederick William Adolphus, 119n21, 142n25, 158, 159n11
notes criticisms of U.S. ironclads, 211-13
Brunel, Isambard Kingdom, 55
Buffalo, 83
Bull Run (1st Battle of), 71
Bureau of (Ship) Construction and Repair (U.S.), 74, 76, 238
Bureau of Steam Engineering (U.S.), 239
Burgoyne, Captain Hugh Talbot, *xix-xxiii*, 236, 250-2, 257, 259n5, 280
Burgoyne, General John, *xxiii*
Burgoyne, Field-Marshal John Fox (1st Baronet), *xxiii*, *xxvii*, 53, 58, 70n54, 107, 236

Burnley, J. Hume, 141
Burroughs, Peter (*The Oxford History of the British Empire*), xxxiv
Bythesea, Rear-Admiral John, 83-4, 120n25
   co-hosts Admiralty visit aboard *Miantonomoh*, 185
   joins *Miantonomoh* to Britain, 181-3
   notes tonnage of American monitors, 168n31

Cadogan, Major General George, 192n41
Caldwell, Captain Henry, 151, 154
Callao, bombardment of, 184, 303-4
California, 299
Canada (British North America), 73, 82, 121, 159, 181, 186n28, 242
   imperial defence of, 83, 115-17, 122, 128-9, 131-2, 138-9, 232n37, 308
Cape Fear River, 127
Cape Finisterre, 236, 254
Cape of Good Hope and West Coast of Africa Station, 62, 201n11, 222
Cape Hatteras, 85
Cape Horn, 303
Captain Coles and the Admiralty, By the Son of An Old Naval Officer (1866), 170
Captain Court Martial (1870), xxvi, 246-7, 249-50, 254-6, 261, 268, 280
Cardwell Edward (1st Viscount), 241-2, 278
Caribbean Sea, 172, 302, 302
Central America, 51
Central-battery (ironclad design), xxx, 80-1, 93, 103, 105-6, 108-10, 124, 142, 145-7, 149-52, 154-5
   as prevailing design in Controller's Department, 166, 178, 197-8, 205-7, 218-25, 227-8, 233-4, 236, 243n17, 244-5
   as safer experiment than turreted vessels, 161-2, 175, 198, 207, 218-21, 233
   French versions, 232n36
   gradually eclipsed by turret-based armaments, 224-5, 236, 244-5, 264n14, 268n22
   recessed gunports, 222
   to handle 12-ton guns, 160, 177
Chads, Admiral Henry Ducie, 37n4
Channel Squadron, xix, 53, 58, 97, 113, 115, 126, 148, 169, 193, 220
   combined cruise of (1870), 240-2, 246

   initial cruise of 1870, 236-7
   trial cruise of (1866), 195-7, 209, 222-3, 249, 254
Charleston (South Carolina), 84-8, 96, 137, 303
   naval assault on, 86-8, 95-6, 261, 263, 303
Chatham Dockyard, 59, 103, 157, 222, 283, 284, 285, 286, 287
Cherbourg, 54, 82n26, 185-6, 262
Chevalier, Michael, xxxv, 240, 242n14
Chicago, 83
Childers, Hugh, xxiii, xxvii, xxix-xxx, 232-3, 242, 264, 278
   advises Milne to not spare coal for sea trials, 241n10
   appointed First Lord of the Admiralty (1868), 227n27, 230
   assures Russell seagoing turret-ships will command American coasts, 272
   combined squadron-cruise (1870) to 'shew strength', 241
   commends Controller's Department in Commons, 228
   defends new ironclad programme, reforms, 234
   greater resources for coast defence, gunboats and cruisers, 266
   Minute questioning *Captain* court martial findings, 256-61, 266n18
   navy will need time to prepare for war against Russia (1870), 274-5
   notes foreign relations issues (1870), 261-2
   on Reed's threat to resign ('over pay'), 225, 245n20
   on Robinson's status within Admiralty, 245n20, 265-6
   prefers additional *Captain* over *Monarch*, 244, 252, 258-60
   presses for seagoing turret-ship, 230, 259-60
   writes Wood that building a ship not sanctioned by Controller 'unintelligible', 256-7
Childers, Leonard, xxiii, 252, 259, 272
Chile, 302-3
China, 53, 261, 281
China Station, 114
Chincha Islands, 302
Cincinnati, 299

Circassia, 46n37
Civil Rights Act (1866), 216
Clarendon, George William Frederick Villiers (4th Earl), 45-6, 119n21, 183n20
   death of, 241
   naval demonstration against United States (1856), 52
   negotiations at Paris (1856), 49-51
   objects to Palmerston's threat to Apponyi, 113
   Queen anxious over Austro-Prussian War, 178-9
   warns against un-backed naval demonstrations, 178-9
Cleveland, 83
Close blockade, 270
Clowes, William Laird, *xxviii*, 38n5
Coastal assault, bombardment, 37-42, 47-51, 53-4, 56, 58, 62-3, 98, 102-4, 112-120, 126-30, 143, 155, 242, 263, 268
   defending Halifax, 232n37
   during American Civil War, 69-70, 73, 84-9, 95-6, 127-8, 136, 261, 298, 300
   Franco-Prussian War, 261-4, 269-70
   monitors for coast defence, 158, 185, 197, 210-13, 218-19, 225, 242-3, 269-71, 298
Cobden, Richard, 65n35, 103, 128, 134n6, 135, 242n14, 275n7
   and dangers of gunboat diplomacy, 281
   argues with Reed, 105
   laments shipbuilding policies, 107-8
   speech at Rochdale, 123
Cobden-Chevalier Treaty, *xxxv*, 240, 242n14
Colburn's United Service Magazine, 70
Cold Spring Foundry (New York), 297
College of Naval Architecture, 95
Coles, Captain Cowper Phipps, *xix-xxiv, xv, xxvii, xxix, xxxi-xxxii*, 63n29, 80, 95, 99, 105-8, 124, 131n48, 143, 146, 156, 188, 200, 212-13, 239n6, 243, 257, 278, 280
   1860 cupola ship submission, 60-1
   accused of building turret-ships for foreign powers, 226
   apologises for letter to *The Standard*, 165-7
   asks for copies of Scott's carriage and slide designs for *Monarch*, 226
   attacks Reed in *The Standard* (1866), 162, 164-5
   complains of Admiralty favouritism of Reed's ironclads, 103, 146-7, 161-2, 199, 208-11
   conversion of *Royal Sovereign*, 169
   criticises naval estimates, 145
   design of HMS *Captain*, 202-5, 243, 248-9, 252, 258, 272, 277
   disclaims himself a 'shipbuilder', 190, 203-5, 249
   dismissed by Admiralty (January 1866), 164-6
   endorses Reed's *Devastation*, 234n40
   invited by Admiralty to submit design seagoing turret-ship (*Captain*), 176-7
   intrigued by low-freeboard, 190, 202, 209-10, 248-9, 253
   joins *Captain* for final cruise, 242-3
   notes *Monadnock* deployed to the Pacific, 161, 175
   objects to live-fire test against *Royal Sovereign*, 177-8
   objects to *Monarch* design, 156-7, 160, 162, 164, 168, 175-7, 243, 248
   patent issues, 167
   pay from Admiralty appointment, 166n27, 167
   pleads with Somerset to consider seagoing turret-ship, 107-8, 277, 304
   presentations at RUSI, Institution of Naval Architects (1863), 92-3
   presentation at RUSI, with extended debate (1867), 208-11
   questions new heavy guns on large vs. small ironclads, 160
   reacts to Battle of Hampton Roads, 78, 80
   reacts to Fort Fisher campaign, 128
   requests Admiralty draughtsman (1866), 199n7
   restores association with Admiralty, 168
   tours *Miantonomoh* at Spithead, 185, 253
   submits single-turret *Pallas*-type, 149-55, 157, 169
Colonial Naval Defence Act, 139
Colonial Office, 129
Committee on Board of Admiralty (1871), 206n19
Committee on Coles Turret-Ship (1865), 149-55, 157, 169, 177, 183n20, 199
Committee on Royal Dockyards, 223

Committee on Ship Design (1871), 168n31, 182, 200n9, 257, 264n14, 264-5, 268-70
Conacher, J. B., 36n1
'Concert of Europe', 53-4, 178
Confederate commerce raiders, 90, 100-1, 298
Confederate Constitution, 65
Confederate States of America, 65, 71, 82, 84, 102, 115, 118, 138, 297
Confederate States Army, 262
Confederate States Navy, 71, 88, 97, 101, 172, 211
Congress (U.S.), 51, 65, 71, 73, 75-6, 87, 121, 141, 238
 appoints 'Mission to Russia', 180-1
Congress of Vienna (1815), 36, 178
Conservative (Tory) Party, *xxix*, 39, 55n6, 102, 123, 139, 168n31, 179n11, 218, 230, 263, 280
Copenhagen, 100
Cork (Ireland), 185n26, 231
Cornhill Magazine, 169
Corry, Harriet Anne (Ashley-Cooper) Lowry-, 226n24
Corry, Henry Thomas Lowry-, 278
 against naval cutbacks, 221
 annoyed with Reed's pushiness, 225-6
 approves Reed's claims for extra pay, 228
 becomes First Lord of the Admiralty (1867), 218, 225
 believes sail-and-turret ironclads will be failures, 228n28
 difficulties with Controller's Department, 226
 doubts Reed's objectivity judging ironclad proposals, 219
 opposes mastless *Devastation* concept, 234
 questions Paget over *Monarch* design, 168
 replaced as First Lord by Childers, 230
Court of St. James's, 186
Cowley, Henry Richard Charles Wellesley (1st Earl), 49n44, 51, 178
Crater, Battle of the, 118
Crimean War, 36-51, 53-6, 58-60, 62, 89, 92, 114-15, 117, 143, 193, 236, 246n24, 274, 276
Cronstadt, 38, 40-5, 47-51, 89-90, 122, 130, 143, 210, 263, 275n6, 277
Cuba, 66

Cuxhaven, 98

Dacres, Admiral Sydney Colpoys, 97n15, 148, 226n26, 232, 242, 278
 cautions against more turret-ships until *Monarch, Captain* trials, 201-2, 220, 242
 made First Naval Lord (1868), 230n32
 mastless turret-ships to convince pubic of Admiralty's impartiality, 243n15
 stresses need for cruisers to protect commerce, 189, 207, 266
Dahlgren, Rear-Admiral John Adolphus Bernard, 83, 88
 opinion of monitors, 96, 108
 relative efficiency of rifled ordnance, 143
Daily News, *xxii*, 210-11
Daily Post (Liverpool), *xxii*
Daily Telegraph, *xxii*, *xxiv*
Dalrymple-Hay, John (3rd Baronet), 192, 212, 278
 suggests private firms build *Audacious*-class, 220
Dartmouth, 197n4
Dasent, George Webbe, 242n13
Davis, C.S. President Jefferson, 118, 158
Delafield, Major-General Richard, 51, 117, 120
Delane, John Thadeus, 91
 opinion of Gladstone's government (1870), 242
Denman, Rear-Admiral Joseph George, 302-4
Denmark, 91, 97-8, 100, 102, 108, 112-15, 123, 172n42, 174, 240, 272, 280
Denny, Peter, 264n15, 269
Deptford Dockyard, 284
Derby, Edward George Geoffrey Smith-Stanley (14th Earl), *xxix*, 39, 48n42, 139, 168n31
 Conservative ministry (1866), 179, 218, 226n26
Detroit, 83
Devonport, *xxii*
Devonport Dockyard, 37n2, 195n1, 199n7, 283
Disraeli, Benjamin (1st Earl of Beaconsfield), 48n42, 102n30, 179
 endorses Abyssinian Expedition, 221
 fall of first Ministry, 227n27
 rejects call for supplemental naval

estimate, 218
scrutinises Palmerstonian interventions, 280-1
second Ministry (1875), 280
Dnieper River, 277n9
Dockyards and Naval Economy, 142
Douglas, General Howard (3rd Baronet), 58n17, 107
Dover, 271
Downing Street, 73
Dowson, Captain C. S., 93
Duckers, Peter (*The Crimean War at Sea*), 47n41
Dufferin, Frederick Temple Hamilton-Temple-Blackwood, 1st Marquess of Dufferin and Ava), 264
　presses Robinson on need for coastal ironclads, 269-70
Dundas, Vice-Admiral Richard Saunders, 40-1, 43, 44n27, 44n29, 45, 47-9, 62, 64n32
Du Pont, Rear-Admiral Samuel Francis, 85n32, 86-8, 261, 300

Eads, James Buchanan, 144n29
East India Company, 37, 60n22
East Indies Station, 261-2
Ecuador, 302
Edinburgh, Duke of (Prince Alfred Ernest Albert)
　tours *Miantonomoh* at Sheerness, 186
Edinburgh Review
　on monitors for the Royal Navy, 188, 189n34
Edward VII, Albert, King (as Prince of Wales)
　tours *Miantonomoh* at Sheerness, 186
Eider River, 98
Elbe River, 98
Ellenborough, Edward Law (1st Earl), 123
Elliot, Admiral George Augustus, 264n15
Elliot, Henry George, 192n41
Elms Despatch, 240
Emancipation Proclamation, 81, 90n48, 140n22
Engineering, 165, 213
English Channel, 53-4, 58, 106, 220, 231, 270
Ericsson, John, *xxix, xxxi*, 76, 79, 83, 85, 156, 159n12, 175, 189, 205-6, 216, 232, 239, 248, 278, 300n9

　advocates *Monitor* to Lincoln, 71, 76, 301
　and British trials of 15-inch Rodman gun (1867), 213-15
　answers criticisms of monitors in *Army and Navy Journal* (1866), 212-13
　claims invention of turreted warships, 143, 145, 211-13
　correspondence with John Bourne, 165n24, 170-4
　design of *Dictator*, 171-3
　disgusted with Reed's breastwork 'mutilation', 199-200
　doubts success of monitors against forts, 87
　explains *Monitor* concept to Ironclad Board, 72
　monitors for the Royal Navy, 172-3
　monitor vs. broadside-ironclads, 158, 212-13
　names *Monitor*, 73
　notes post-war construction limits, 217
　offers improved monitors, 74-7
　patent vibrating engines, 183n20
　power of 15-inch gun, 87-8, 212-13
　predicts Reed will appropriate monitor concept for Royal Navy, 202n13, 229
　seaworthiness of monitors, 153, 158, 212, 248
　'surprised' by Laird's report of *Captain*'s seaworthiness, 239, 272
　theory of laminated armour-resistance, 309-10
　war-machines negating seapower, 108, 171n35, 172-4, 184, 206, 239, 281
Erie and Hudson Canal, 83
Eslington, Liddell, Henry George 2nd Earl of Ravensworth), 179n11

Fanshawe, Vice-Admiral Arthur, 70n54
Faraday, Michael, 44n31
Farragut, Admiral David Glasgow, 84, 144n29
Fayetteville (North Carolina), 135n7
Fenians, 128, 178, 181
Finland, 46n37, 48
First World War, 270
Fishbourne, Captain Edmund Gardiner, 58n18, 209
Floating batteries, 71, 116, 171, 185, 239n6, 255

British Crimean War ironclad batteries, 36, 39-41, 44-5, 48, 50, 54, 58, 69, 98
French Crimean War ironclad batteries, 40-2, 58, 62
Foreign Office, 42-3, 45n32, 89n46, 99n21, 118n18, 127, 184n22, 212, 222, 238, 241, 273, 298n3
Forts (coastal fortifications), 54, 58, 73, 84, 220
    Alexander (Russian), 37, 45n33
    Battery Bee (Confederate), 87n38
    Battery Weed/Fort Wadsworth (U.S.), 117
    Constantine (Russian), 37, 41
    Darling (Confederate), 85
    Dover, 271
    Fisher (Confederate), 127-8, 136
    Gorges (U.S.), 84
    Hamilton (U.S.), 117, 309n3
    Hancock (U.S.), 309n3
    Lafayette (U.S.), 117
    Malakoff (Russian), 45, 127
    Monroe (U.S.), 74-5, 215n35, 239n6
    Moultrie (Confederate), 86, 87n38, 96n11
    Pitt (U.S.), 297
    Preble (U.S.), 84
    Redan (Russian), 45
    Richmond (U.S.), 117
    Scammel (U.S.), 84
    Solent, 54, 78, 104, 220
    Sumter (U.S., Confederate), 84, 86, 87n38
    Tompkins (U.S.), 117
Fox, Charles, 48
Fox, Gustavus Vasa, 84, 87, 170n34, 309n3
    and Reconstruction issues, 216
    design of *Dictator*, 171, 173
    diplomatic mission to Russia, 181-6, 210
    monitors for the Royal Navy, 172-3
    offers exchange of fire between *Miantonomoh* and British ironclads, 185
    post-war naval construction, 216-17
    recounts opposition to Ericsson from Lenthall and Isherwood, 239
    reminds Russia of lack of seagoing turret-ships, 210
    report on *Miantonomoh* voyage, 182
    willing to challenge combined Anglo-French ironclad fleets, 159

France, *xix*, *xxxv*, 36, 45-7, 50, 53, 59, 63, 65, 75-6, 89-91, 98, 100, 102n30, 110, 112-14, 118n18, 124, 141, 145, 159, 169, 172n42, 188, 193, 198, 298
    and Austro-Prussian War, 178-9, 239
    and Franco-Prussian War, 206n19, 239-42, 246, 262, 269-71, 274-6
    intervention in Mexico, 66, 82, 118-19, 141, 181, 217, 240
    potential threat to Belgium, 240-1
    proposes co-mediation in American Civil War, 81-2
Franco-Austrian War, 60
Franco-Prussian War, *xix*, 111, 206n19, 239-42, 246, 261, 273-6
Fraser's Magazine, 280
Frederick VIII, King (Denmark), 91
Frederick, Admiral Charles, 183
Fremantle, Admiral Charles Howe, 195n1
Fremantle, Admiral Edmund Robert, *xxiii*8, 280
French Ministry of Marine, 36
French naval power, 36n2, 53-5, 59-61, 63, 69, 79, 110-11, 119, 126, 127, 130-1, 135, 158-9, 173, 180, 187-8, 218
    Anglo-French naval balance-of-power, 53-6, 59, 63, 69, 110-11, 119-20, 126, 130-1, 142, 180, 187-8, 193-4, 207, 210, 218, 221, 228, 242-3, 253, 263, 271-2, 276, 280, 305-7
    considered a 'luxury', 193, 263
    during Franco-Prussian War, 241, 262-4, 269-70, 276
    Fox doubts ability to overcome British naval supremacy, 210
    local strategic advantage of, 231-2
Froude, William, 264n15

Galicia, 47, 49n45
Gallwey, Lieutenant-General Thomas Lionel, 117, 118n17, 118n18, 136-7
Genoa, *xxxiii*
George III, William Frederick, King, 134
Georgia (Caucasus), 46n37
Germany, *xxxv*, 91, 102n30, 111-12, 114-15, 206n19, 240-1, 246, 272, 274
German Second Reich, *xxxv*, 272
German Wars of Unification, *xxxv*, 239-41, 246, 272
Gettysburg Address, 135n7, 144
Gettysburg, Battle of, 144

Gibraltar, 69, 97, 113, 127, 241
Gladstone, William Ewart, *xxiii, xxvii*n7, 59, 107, 218, 242, 262n9, 279-80
  and *Alabama* Claims, 276n8
  approves decision to invest in cruisers, 266
  contemplates despatching British troops to Antwerp, 242
  Crimean War budget, 39
  downplays strategic threats to British security, 278
  failure of Reform Bill (1866), 179
  favours mediation in American Civil War, 81
  government of (1868), 226, 230, 241
  on Robinson's status within Admiralty, 245n20, 265-7
  opposes fortifying Canada, 138
  popularity of, 179, 226
  questions increased defence budgets, 111, 122-3, 128, 160
  response to Russian abrogation of Black Sea Clauses, 274-5
  tours *Royal Sovereign*, 108
Glasgow, 56n11, 89
Globe,
  and Reed's influence over the Board of Admiralty, 228
Gloucester (Massachusetts), 116
Godon, Rear-Admiral Sylvanus W., 172n41
Goldsborough, Rear-Admiral Louis Malesherbes, 96
Goodenough, Commodore James Graham, 94, 120n25, 264n15, 298n3
  report on U.S. Navy (1864), 297-301
Gordon, Charles (10th Marquess of Huntly), *xxiii*
Gordon, Lewis, *xxiii*
Gortchakoff, Alexander Mikhailovich, Prince, 274
Goschen, George Joachim (1st Viscount), 266, 278
Graham, James Robert George (2nd Baronet), 38n5, 39
Gramont, Antoine Alfred Agénor (10th Duke of), 240
Grant, General Ulysses S., 118, 119n21, 135n7, 272
  opposes sending *Miantonomoh* to Britain, 182
Granville, George Leveson-Gower (2nd Earl), 46, 50n46, 82n27, 112, 241, 262n9, 276n8
  on British policy of non-intervention (1871), 264
  response to Russian abrogation of Black Sea Clauses, 274-5
Great Britain, *xxv-xxvii, xxxi, xxxiii-xxxv*, 36, 47, 50, 53, 74-6, 88, 90-1, 172n42, 271-2, 278, 304
  and American Civil War, 65-71, 73, 81-2, 91, 94, 97, 100, 115-23, 126-9, 131-42, 145, 158-9, 169, 280-1, 298-301
  and Austro-Prussian War, 178-9
  and Denmark (1864), 91, 97-8, 100-2, 112-15, 272, 281
  and Franco-Prussian War, 239-42, 246, 262, 271, 273-4
  and technological developments, 54, 78, 123-7, 143-5, 173, 188, 200n9, 205-7, 230-2, 245, 268, 276, 278, 299n8
  coastal fortifications, 58, 78, 104, 107, 128, 148, 169, 271, 278
  considers co-mediation with France, 81-2
  intervention in Mexico, 66
  liberalism, *xxix, xxxiii*, 39, 53, 89, 102, 121-3, 179
  Reform movements, 134n6, 179, 186, 189, 218, 272
  Russian abrogation of Black Sea Clauses (1870), 274-7
Great Exhibition (1851), 54
'Great Game', 37
Greece, 37, 261, 263, 281
Greek revolts, 36-7
Green & Company (Poplar), 131n48
Greenwich, 162
Gregory, Rear-Admiral Francis Hoyt, 77n10
Grey, Admiral Frederick William, 40, 68-9, 92, 109, 116, 120, 148-9, 278
  denies Coles a clerk, 160
  feels Coles sufficiently humbled to re-appoint, 167
  resigns 1866, 186
  suggests Coles submit his own design for seagoing turret-ship, 176, 256
Grey, George (2nd Baronet), 101n29
Grey, Henry George (3rd Earl), 98n16
Greytown (Nicaragua), 52
Grimes, James Wilson, 181

Gulf of Finland, 38, 130, 165, 173, 263
Gulf of Mexico, 76, 83
Guns
   24-pounder SB (British), 69
   32-pounder SB (British), 44n29, 60, 69, 94
   60-pounder SB (Russian), 43n24, 44n29, 90
   68-pounder SB, 95-cwt (British), 44, 56-7, 69, 80, 102, 104-6, 120, 134, 214, 288
     on *Numancia*, 302
   110-pounder Armstrong RBL (British), 56-7, 69, 80, 93, 102, 103n32, 106, 120, 149, 288, 297, 308
   6.3-inch, 5-ton BL, 100-pounder (French), 304-5
   6.4-inch Brooke RML (Confederate), 136n11
   7-inch Brooke RML (Confederate), 87n38, 136, 138
   7-inch, 6½-ton Armstrong RML (British), 103n33, 120n24, 131-2, 149, 187, 289, 307-8
     on *Lord Clyde*, 197n3
   7.48-inch, 8-ton BL, 165-pounder (French), 306
   7.6-inch shell-gun SB (French), 305
   8-inch shell-gun SB, 65-cwt (British), 94
   8-inch, 7-ton Armstrong RML (British), 94, 219
     on *Monarch*'s bow
   8-inch, 9-ton Armstrong RML (British), 119, 131-2, 147, 289, 306
     on *Lord Clyde*, 197n3
   8.2-inch, 9½-ton Krupp RML (German), 99n18
   9-inch Dahlgren SB (U.S.), 69
   9-inch, 6¼-ton SB (British, 'Somerset'), 103, 106, 119-20, 289
     on *Research*
   9-inch, 12½-ton Armstrong RML (British, 1865), 103-4, 119, 124, 131-3, 150n40, 153, 155, 177n5, 188, 234, 264, 271, 289, 306-8
     carriage problems, 106, 157, 308
     fired against *Royal Sovereign*, 177-8
     on *Bellerophon*, 177-8
     on *Hercules*, 157, 222
     on *Minotaur*, 160-1, 187
     on *Scorpion, Wivern*, 160-1, 236, 271
   9-inch Krupp, 18-ton BL (German), 122, 130
   9.4-inch, 14-ton RML (French), 305-6
   10-inch Rodman SB (U.S., 'Columbiad'), 84n29, 87n38, 96
   10-inch, 18-ton Armstrong RML (British, 1868), 208, 234, 292, 306n3
     for *Cyclops*-class breastwork-monitors, 242
     on *Ant*-gunboat, 242
     on *Cerberus*, 200n9
     on *Hercules*, 187, 222
   10½-inch, 12-ton Armstrong RML (British, '300-pounder', pre-1865), 77, 80, 93-4, 100n22, 103-4, 106, 109, 119, 131-3, 184n22, 234, 290, 304
     on *Royal Sovereign*, 100n22, 177n5, 187
     on *Wivern* 187
   10.63-inch BL, 476-pounder (French), 306n3
   11-inch, 7-ton Dahlgren SB (U.S.), 72, 75, 79-80, 86, 119, 127, 133, 135, 144n29
   11-inch, 14-ton Blakely RML (British), 130
   12-inch, 25-ton Armstrong RML (British), *xix, xxi*, 103, 234, 292
     on *Captain*, *xix*n1, 189n35, 203, 225, 237
     on *Glatton*, 232
     on *Hotspur*, 232
     on *Monarch*, 187, 225
   12-inch, 35-ton Armstrong RML (British), 224-5, 294
   13.3-inch, 22½-ton RML (British, '600-pounder'), 103, 116, 132, 149, 150n40, 153, 168, 198, 208, 219
     Unable to penetrate *Hercules* Target, 215
   15-inch, 20-ton Dahlgren SB (U.S), 75-6, 77, 79, 86-8, 103, 117, 124, 127, 133, 134n4, 136-8, 158n9, 213-14, 217, 297, 300
     on *Dictator*, 171
     on *Miantonomoh*, 180, 184-5, 200n9, 213
     on *Monadnock*, 161, 172n41, 303
     on *Roanoke*, 239n6
     on *Weehawken*, 300

15-inch, 22½-ton Rodman SB (U.S.), 70n54, 77, 94, 117, 124, 134n4, 136-8, 158n9, 215n35, 217, 308
British tests of (1867), 213-15, 309n3
20-inch 44½-ton Dahlgren SB (U.S.), 75-6, 83, 184, 217, 309n3
20-inch 51½-ton Rodman SB (U.S.), 217, 297, 309n3
Parrott rifle RML (U.S.), 69, 136
'Guns vs. Armour' race, 54, 94, 104-5, 119-20, 122, 126, 130-8, 142-3, 147-50, 153, 157, 296, 308-10
   Anglo-French developments, 180, 187, 305-7
   coastal ironclads' heavier guns, thicker armour-plating, 158, 173, 199-201, 205-6, 211-12, 299
   gradually favouring turret- over broadside-mounts, 224-5, 231-2
   Hercules Target, 215
   monitors best suited for, 170-1, 173-5, 180, 183-6, 189, 191-2, 197-201, 205-12, 231-2, 264n14, 299, 303
   Reed promises impenetrable ironclads (1866), 197-8
   Rodman 15-inch gun vs. 8-inch *Warrior* Target, 213-15

Hale, John P., 76n8
Halifax (imperial naval base), 69, 103, 110, 119, 230-1, 232n37, 268, 308
Hall, Vice-Admiral Robert, 267
Halstead, Vice-Admiral Edward Pellew
   delays in adopting Coles seagoing turret-ship, 161
   proposes cutting down ships-of-the-line into low-freeboard turret-ships, 225, 238
   wants independent committee to review ironclad proposals, 223-4
Hamburg, 98-9
Hamelin, Admiral Ferdinand, 55n7
Hamilton, C. I., *xxx*
Hammond, Edmund (1st Baron), 275n6
Hammond, James Henry, 65
Hampshire Chronicle, *xxiii*
Hampshire Telegraph and Naval Chronicle, *xxi*n3
Hampton Roads (Virginia), 69, 74, 77, 88, 144, 239n6
Hampton Roads, Battle of, *xxviii*, 74-8, 144,

147, 158n8, 169, 171, 191, 217
Harper's Weekly, 66n40, 141
Harris, William Snow, 95
Harrison, Captain Arthur, 148
Hart, Edward, 76n9
Havana, 172
Hawkey, Arthur (*Black Night off Finisterre*), *xxix*
Hay, Admiral Lord John, 188, 230n32, 278
Heligoland, 262
Helsinki (Helsingfors), 44, 48
Henwood, Charles Frederic, 60n23, 238, 254
Herbert, Sidney (1st Baron Herbert of Lea), *xxiii*
Herbert, Sidney (14th Earl of Pembroke), *xxiii*
Herbert, William Reginald, *xxiii*
Himmelfarb, Gertrude, *Victorian Minds: A Study of Intellectuals in Crisis and Ideologies in Transition*, 180n13
History of the Navy During the Rebellion, 144, 145n30
Hodge, William L., 304n6
Holley, Alexander Lyman (*Treatise on Ordnance and Armor*), 137
Hood, Admiral Arthur William Acland (1st Baron Hood of Avalon), 264n15
Hope, Admiral James, 97, 103, 120-1, 132, 177, 254-5, 259n5
Hore, Captain Edward George, 130
Hornby, Admiral Geoffrey Thomas Phipps, 126, 222, 264n15
House of Commons, *xxxii*, 52, 54, 59, 63, 66, 78, 92, 95, 102, 105, 109, 113, 129, 131, 139-40, 145, 148, 170n34, 187, 227, 238, 242, 246, 281, 304
   and Channel Squadron reports, 222-3
   deliberates Austro-Prussian War, 178
   on *Captain* sinking, 257
   pressures Admiralty to build more turret-ships, 200, 243n15
   rallies around Coles, 167-8
   Reform Bill (1866) defeated, 179
   Return of Correspondence relative to Navy (Turret-ships), 177
   Robinson's place in the Admiralty, 266
   votes emergency military and naval supplement (1870), 242
House of Lords, 41, 66, 139-40, 276n8, 304
   debates Admiralty relationship with

Coles, 168-9
Hyde Park (demonstrations), 189

Illinois River, 83
India, 193
Indian ('Sepoy') Mutiny, 53, 60n22, 81, 91
Indochina, 302
Inkerman, Battle of, 38
Institution of Civil Engineers
    Bourne lecture on 'Ships of War', 205-6
Institution of Naval Architects, 62, 92-3, 123, 142, 169-71, 215, 225, 229n31, 278
International Exhibition (1876), 299n8
Ireland, 178, 183
Irish Channel, 145
Ironclad Board (1861), 71-2
Ironclad Oath of Allegiance, 158
Ironclad 'revolution', *xxix, xxxi, xxxiv*, 43, 55-6, 59, 62, 76, 78, 107, 111, 169-71, 224
Iron Plate Committee, 104, 142, 148, 151
Iron targets, 142-3, 149n38, 308-10
    Gloire, 104
    Hercules (8-inch *Warrior*), 213-15, 309n3
    Hercules (Admiralty), 215
    list of British, 138n15
    Lord Warden, 104
    U.S., 136-8
    Warrior, 147
Isabella II, Queen (Spain), 240, 302-3
Isherwood, Rear-Admiral Benjamin Franklin, 76, 183n20, 239
Isle of Wight, 184
Italian Navy, 189
Italian unification, *xxxv*, 53, 89, 272
Italy, *xxxv*, 100, 130, 178, 198, 274, 281
    declares war on Austria, 183

J & W Dudgeon (Millwall), 285, 286, 287
Jamaica (colony), 268
James River, 75, 85
Jane, John Frederick Thomas, *xxviii*
Japan, 102, 123
    desires American monitors, 172n43
Jane's Fighting Ships (mentioned), *xxviii*
Jervois, Lieutenant-General William Francis Drummond, 103, 115-16, 139, 220n12, 232n37
John Brown & Company (Sheffield), 79, 131n48, 138, 299n8
John Bull, *xxxv*, 90n48, 139, 170n34, 217
John Roach & Son (New York City), 299n8

Johnson, U.S. President Andrew, 134, 272
    dubious of 'Mission to Russia', 181-2
    impeachment of, 216
Jones, Colin, *xxviin*5

Kagosima, 102, 103n32
Kars, Siege of, 36n1, 46, 50
Kattegat (Danish Straits), 98
Kennedy, Captain John James, 151
Key, Admiral Astley Cooper, 94, 131, 133-4, 136, 138, 155-6, 309n3
    appointed Acting Director General of Naval Ordnance, 187n32
    argues against 'defensive fleet', 192
    endorses Reed's *Devastation*, 234n40
    report on French naval ordnance (1867), 305-6
    tours *Miantonomoh* at Spithead, 185
Kiel, 98, 130
Kinburn, Battle of, 40-1, 44n29, 62
Kingston, 116, 131, 308
Kolpino, 130n47
Königgrätz, Battle of, 186
Konstaninov (Colonel), 45n33
Kotlin Island, 38, 40, 42, 43n24
Krupp guns, 95, 99n18, 122, 130
Kudryavtsev, S. G., 43
Kuper, Admiral Augustus Leopold, 102

Laird Brothers (Birkenhead), *xxii*, 64, 97, 101-2, 147, 177, 190, 238, 280, 283, 284, 285, 286
    construction of *Captain*, 247-50, 253-4, 258
    design of HMS *Captain*, 202-5, 249-50, 278-9
    requests Admiralty to incline-test *Captain*, 247-9, 252-3, 256n1, 258
    seagoing turret-ships built for foreign navies, 186, 226
    proposes improved 2nd-class *Captain* (1867), 219-20, 257
Laird, Henry, 249-50
Laird, John, 139, 168, 188, 222, 227-8
    writes to Ericsson of *Captain*'s success, 239
Laird, William, 249, 258
Laird Rams, 97, 101-2, 125n36, 155n2, 160, 169, 177, 180, 187, 211, 221, 253
    armament of, 160-1, 187, 236, 271
    seakeeping abilities, 190, 195-6, 201,

209, 236, 254, 257
Lake Erie, 299
Lake Michigan, 83, 299
Lake Ontario, 83, 116
Laminated armour plating, 74, 183n20, 308-10
   American monitor turrets', 212, 299, 309-10
   Reed's opinion of American monitor armour, 189n35
Lamport, Charles, 126, 229n31
Lee, General Robert E., 81, 118, 127, 135n7, 158
Lennox, Henry George Charles Gordon-, 226n26, 228, 256, 265n16
Lenthall, John, 76, 238-9
Leopold I, King of the Belgians, 65, 118
Leopold, Prince of Hohenzollern, 240
Lewis, George Cornewall (2nd Baronet), 82-3
Liberal Party, *xxvii*n7, *xxix*, 167, 179-80, 230, 280
Lichtenburg (St. Petersburg), 45
Lincoln, 223
Lincoln, U.S. President Abraham, 65, 67, 71n58, 72, 76, 81, 90n48, 108, 119, 133, 135n7, 140, 144, 272, 301
   assassination of, 158, 180
Lisbon, 100
Lissa, Battle of, 189, 196
   tactics of, 192
Liverpool, *xxii*, 97
Lloyd, Thomas, 265n15
Lôme, Dupuy de, 55, 306
London, *xxxiv*, 66, 117, 135, 185, 207, 212, 226, 235, 275
London Conference (1830), 241
London Straits Convention, 37
Low-freeboard, *xxxi*n19, 72, 76-7, 85, 87-8, 107, 143, 152-3, 228n28, 234
   Bourne against high-freeboard turret-ships, 170, 205-6
   Coles notes on U.S. monitors, 161, 175, 253, 272
   comparative freeboard of *Monarch*, 163, 175-6, 229, 237-8, 243-4, 248, 254, 256, 264n14, 268-9
   Ericsson stresses only applicable to mastless monitors, 239, 253
   Goodenough condemns on U.S. monitors, 299-300

   of *Captain*, *xx*, *xxiv*, *xxvi*, *xxvii*, 190, 202-3, 205n16, 209, 237-9, 243, 247-9, 251, 253-4, 256-8, 272, 279
   of *Cerberus*, 200n9, 207-8, 270
   of *Miantonomoh*, 182-6, 201n11, 235
   Reed's assessment of low-freeboard monitors' stability under canvas, 225, 229, 233, 257
   Robinson argues against, 210, 232, 237-8, 243-4, 248, 254, 256
Lungley, Charles, 62, 285
Lushington, Vernon, 267
Lyons, Admiral Edmund (1st Baron), 41, 48, 70n54
Lyons, Richard Bickerton Pemell (1st Viscount), 94, 97, 100, 102-3, 117n15, 118, 122, 141, 239-40, 297, 298n3
Lyveden, Robert Vernon (1st Baron), 139
Lytton, Robert Bulwer- (1st Earl), 276n8

Macmillan's Magazine, 140
Madrid Gazette, 184n22
Mahan, Alfred Thayer (*The Influence of Seapower Upon History*), 263n12
Maine, 84, 181
Maitland, Admiral Thomas (11th Earl of Lauderdale), 151
   endorses Reed's *Devastation*, 234n40
   lack of coastal assault vessels in Royal Navy, 264
Mallory, Stephen, 71
'Manifest Destiny', 59
Marblehead (Massachusetts), 116
Mare & Company (Millwall), 64, 282, 283
Martin, Daniel. B., 74n4
Marx, Karl, 140n22
Mason, James, 66-7
Mason-Dixon Line, 65
Maximilian I, Ferdinand (Archduke), 118-19, 217
McClellan, General George B., 75, 81
Mechanics' Magazine, 180
Mediterranean Sea, 37, 57, 59, 63, 97, 121, 172, 201n11, 220, 231, 280
Mediterranean Squadron, *xix*, 100, 163, 193, 241
Melbourne, 207, 225, 270, 286
Meingard (St. Petersburg), 43
Mends, Admiral William Robert, 41
Meuse River, 246
Meyendorff, Peter, 49n45

Mexico, 66, 82, 118-19
  1861 allied intervention, 66
  French occupation, 82, 118-19, 141, 159, 181, 217, 240
Millwall Ironworks, 64n33, 131n48, 145, 177, 219
Milne, Vice-Admiral Sir Alexander, *xix-xx*, 45n32, 66, 88, 97, 110, 197-8, 221, 223, 230n32, 250, 256, 278
  as First Naval Lord (1866), 187
  against sail-and-turret ironclad proposal (1867), 220
  averse to wooden ships-of-the-line, 68, 80
  blames Controller's Department for overlooking *Captain*, 251
  cautions against more turret-ships until *Monarch*, *Captain* trials, 201-2
  contemplates operations against U.S. during *Trent* Affair, 68-9
  favours conversion of *Repulse* to central-battery ironclad, 197
  implores Reed not to resign, 225-6
  opposes monitors for Royal Navy, 193, 201-2
  recalls approval of *Captain* design, 251
  recommends sailing ironclads for foreign service, but turret-ships stronger, 280
  reports loss of HMS *Captain*, 246-7
  thicker armour necessary for new ironclads, 189
  to command combined Channel-Mediterranean fleet (1870), 240-1
  tours Northern States, 90
  warns of drastic naval budget cuts (1867), 207, 218
  worries Robinson will dominate the Admiralty (1868), 227
Mines ('torpedoes')
  American Civil War, 86, 117, 120n25, 261-3
  for harbour defence, 269-71, 278
  French use of, 130
  proposals to sweep, 44n30, 47-9
  Russian sea-mines (or 'squibs') during Crimean War, 43n26, 44-5, 263
  to help defend Halifax, 232n37
Mississippi River, 83
Mobile (Alabama), 96
Mobile Bay, Battle of, 144n29
Moir, Captain James, 67

Monitors (ironclad design), *xxx-xxxi*, 72, 74-80, 82-9, 94-6, 107-8, 110, 116-18, 128-9, 131, 137, 140, 152-3, 155
  adopted by foreign powers, 165-6, 172-4, 186, 210-11, 226, 231-2
  armour-weight ratios of, 79, 216-17, 268, 231-2, 264n14, 268-9, 280, 299, 303
  as 'machines', *xxxv*, 72, 77, 87, 170-2, 184, 206-7, 235, 239, 281
  Dictator design, 171-3, 309n3
  ideal for coast defence, 189, 197-8, 202, 210-11, 268-70, 280, 298-301
  habitability of, 170-1, 182, 184, 235, 269
  popularity of in America, 157-8, 170, 191-2, 205-6, 211, 216-18
  Reed's assessment of their stability under canvas, 225, 229, 231, 233, 248
  Robinson denies usefulness of comparing with seagoing broadside-ironclads, 166, 210, 269-70
  seagoing qualities of, 168, 171-2, 182-3, 201-2, 207, 210, 212, 229, 231-3, 248, 268-9, 299-301
  spreading around the world, 161, 165-6, 169, 172-4, 303
  voyage of *Miantonomoh* to Russia, 180-6, 189, 200, 201n11, 210, 272, 277
Monroe Doctrine, 64, 118-19, 141, 217, 303
Montreal, 116, 129, 308
Morgan Iron Works, 299n8
Morning Post, 134, 246, 276-7
Morocco, 302
Morrill Tariff, *xxxv*
Mortars, 40n13, 41-2, 45, 70, 84

Napier, Admiral Charles John, 38-40, 44, 68
Napier, Francis (1st Baron Ettrick), 89
Napier & Sons (Glasgow), 56n11, 99, 177, 226, 282, 286, 287
Napoleonic Wars, 36, 169, 263, 273, 279
Nautical Magazine, 165, 211
Navarino, Battle of, 37
Navy Board, 163
Nelson, Vice-Admiral Horatio (1st Viscount), *xxiii*, *xxviii*, *xxxii*
Neva River, 45n31
Newburyport (Massachusetts), 116
New Orleans, 96
New Orleans, Battle of, 84
Newport (Rhode Island), 83

Newport College, 297
Newport News (Virginia), 74, 183n20
New York, 83, 181
New York City, 69-71, 76, 84, 90, 116-17, 120, 141n24, 309n3
New Zealand, 123
Nice, 60
Nicholas I, Pavlovich, Tsar, 36, 42
Nickolayevich, Konstantin (Grand Duke), 43, 49n45
Nikolaev, *xxxii*, 277
Nobel Alfred, 45n32
Noble, Major-General William Henry, 308-9
Nordin (General), 45n32
Nore, the, 186
Norfolk (U.S. naval base), 71, 74-5, 172
North America and West Indies Station, *xxxiii*, 66, 94, 97, 110, 120, 122, 151n44, 193
North Sea, 97-8, 112-13, 115, 262, 264, 281
Núñez, Admiral, Casto Méndez, 302-4

Obstructions, 40, 42, 47-8, 85-7, 117, 120, 130, 262, 271, 300
Okun, Nathan, 299n8
Ordnance Select Committee, 104, 133-8, 142, 187n32, 215n36, 297n1, 308-9
  opposed by Robinson, 224
  tests Rodman 15-inch smoothbore, 213-14
Orlov, Prince Alexey Fyodorovich, 50
Osborn, Rear-Admiral Sherard, *xxiv*, 62, 106-7, 151, 177
  denounces for Reed suggesting Coles and Burgoyne blind to *Captain*'s faults, 252n33
  questions incline test of *Captain*, 256n1
  turret-ships needed for naval battles, coastal assault, 268
  replaces Key on Ordnance Select Committee, 187n32
Ottoman Empire (Turkey), 36-7, 46, 130, 226n26, 263, 274-5
Overland Campaign, 118

Pacific Station, 222
Paget, Admiral Clarence Edward, 61, 80, 83n28, 95, 101, 145-6, 165n23, 187
  attacked in Parliament over Admiralty ironclad policy, 168, 170n34

Coles treated like a 'spoilt child', 164
control of ship designs by Controller's Department, 163-4
resigns, 177
Walker also sensitive to criticism, 164n22
Pakenham, General William Lygon (4th Earl of Longford), 187n32
Pakington, John Somerset (1st Baron), *xxix*, 55n6, 93n2, 105, 123, 193, 207, 218, 225
  becomes of Secretary of State for War (1867), 218, 242
  complains of inability to purchase *Konig Wilhelm/Fatikh*, 226n26
  criticises Reed, 145-6, 250-1
  denies 'distrust' of Robinson and Reed, 250-2
  First Lord of the Admiralty again (1866), 186
  invites Milne to be First naval Lord, 186-7
  need for unified decision-making, 197
  recollection of *Captain* approval, 251, 256-7, 278-9
  reflects on loss of *Captain*, 278-9
  suggests Coles treated unfairly, 167, 251, 279
  wishes for seagoing turret-ship, 160
Palk, Lawrence (1st Baron Haldon), 304
Palmer Brothers & Company, 177, 219, 282, 286, 287
Palmerston, Henry John Temple (3rd Viscount), *xxn2*, *xxviin7*, *xxxii*, 55, 79, 81n23, 107, 120, 122, 141, 142n25, 179-80, 187, 218, 271, 276n8
  and democracy, 134n6, 135, 179-80, 272
  and Denmark crisis (1864), 98, 100, 112-15
  and the *Trent* Affair, *xxxiii*, 66-8
  Anglo-American relations, 51, 64, 82, 90-1, 115, 119, 128, 159, 272, 276, 280-1
  anti-French sentiments, 159
  British neutrality and CSS *Alabama*, 101
  death of, 158-60
  desires test of Crimean War submarine, 45n32, 48
  disapproves of new Foreign Office design, 273
  dissatisfied with *Warrior*, 60, 276
  doubts ability of Dundas, 48

increased armaments for Britain, 59, 128, 130
Laird Rams, 101-2
negotiations at Paris (1856), 50-1
on monarchical government for Mexico, 118-19
opinion of *Royal Sovereign*, 106
opposes naval reductions, 123, 128
Polish insurrection, 89-91
Prime Minister, 1855, 40, 45-6
Second Ministry, 61, 138, 272
speech at Tiverton, 114-15
urgent need for heavier naval ordnance against U.S., 119-20
warns of French power, ambition, 54, 82, 90-1, 159
Panama Canal, 52, 240
'Pax Britannica', *xxxiii*n23, *xxxiv-xxxv*, 271-3
Paris, 48, 49n44, 135, 178, 234
  Siege of, 275
Paris Exhibition (1867), 305-7
Parkes, Oscar (*British Battleships*), 109n46, 197n4, 199n6, 222n15
Parrott, Captain Robert Parker, 297
Paskevich (Field-Marshall), 49n45
Pasley, Major-General Charles, 264n15
Pasley, Admiral Thomas Sabine (2nd Baronet), 184-5, 192
Pearl Harbor, Battle of, 74
Peel, Jonathan, 218
Peel, Robert (2nd Baronet), 168n31
Peelites, 40
Pembroke, 162, 228, 268
Pembroke Dockyard, 147, 283, 284, 285, 286, 287
Peninsula Campaign, 75
Penn trunk engines, 56, 197
Pennefather, Lieutenant-General John, 70n54
Persigny, Jean Gilbert Victor Fialin (Duke of), 46n37
Peru, 184, 302-3, 304n5
Petersburg, Siege of, 118, 127
Pétin and Gaudet, 138, 303
Peto, Samuel Morton (1st Baronet), 168
Philadelphia, 116, 2998
Philadelphia Navy Yard, 83
Phillimore, Admiral Henry Bouchier, 151
Phipps, Colonel Charles Beaumont, 113n4
Pittsburgh, 297, 299

Pius IX, Pope, 261
Plymouth, *xxii*, 97
Plymouth (Massachusetts), 116
Pola (Austrian naval base), 98, 112
Polish intervention crisis, *xxxv*n27, 89-91, 102, 111, 114-15, 122, 272, 280
Popov, Admiral Andrei Alexandrovich, *xxxii*, 274n2
Porter, Admiral David Dixon, 127-8, 238, 239n6
Portland, *xxvii*
Portland (Maine), 84, 116
Port Royal (South Carolina), 85
Portsmouth, *xxii*, 97, 104, 137, 157, 159, 183, 248
Portsmouth Dockyard, *xxviii*, 37n4, 57, 81, 95, 99, 108, 184, 232, 246, 256n1, 283, 285, 287
Portsmouth Navy Yard (Maine), 83, 116
Portugal, *xix*, 263
Potomac River, 120
Press (British), agitation of, *xxviii-xxix*, *xxxii*, 45, 66, 78, 105-9, 113-14, 142, 150-1, 156-61, 176, 271
  Admiralty condemns Coles for public attacks, 164-8
  Admiralty stalling on introduction of turret-ships, 211, 225, 236, 243n17, 279
  as a result of *Miantonomoh* visit (1866), 182-6, 188-91, 200
  blamed for *Captain* disaster, *xxvi*, *xxix-xxxii*, 92, 160, 164-5, 168, 177, 184, 188, 190-1, 222-3, 256-7, 261, 278, 281
  calls for naval economy, modernisation of ships, 222, 226
  loss of national prestige during Palmerston's Second Ministry, 160, 211, 273, 275-7
  naval review and (1869), 271
  Paget notes having to defend broadside and central-battery ironclads, 164
  questions Reed's integrity, 236, 244-5
  Rodman gun trials (1867) and, 213-15
  '*Royal Sovereign* vs. *Bellerophon*'-test, 177-8, 184-5, 212-13
  war with Russia (1870), 274-7
Prestige (notions of), *xxvi*, *xxvii-xxviii*, *xxxii-xxxv*, 45-6, 56, 61, 87, 92, 100, 104, 112-15, 121-2, 125, 134-5, 138-43, 145-6,

150-1, 210, 234, 245, 302
  American naval, 143-5, 157-8, 181, 188, 191, 211-14, 216-18
  based on British Navy, Napoleonic Wars, 159, 169, 263, 273
  challenged by regional monitor-ironclads, 161, 173-4, 188, 200-1, 211-14, 270-1, 281
  loss of national prestige during Palmerston's Second Ministry, 160, 169, 178-9, 191, 200-1, 211, 271-3, 276
  naval economy and, 122-3, 160, 207, 218, 221, 226, 234, 264, 269-70
  neutralised by American coastal defence, 158, 173-4, 211-15, 270-1, 276, 281
  perception of British naval power affecting, 200-1, 210, 221, 240, 261, 263-4, 270-1, 276-7, 280-1
  shaken by domestic turmoil, 218, 224, 263-4
Price, Arthur, 151
Proceedings of the Royal Artillery Institution, 149
Prussia, *xix*, 54, 91, 97-8, 100-2, 112-14, 123, 130, 174, 178, 239-41, 246, 262, 272, 274-5
Prussian Army, 113, 186, 206n19, 246, 275
Prussian Navy, 98-101, 130, 173, 207, 226, 241
Punch, or The London Charivari, xxxiin21, xxxv, 39, 90n48, 102, 114, 118, 133-4, 159
  'Captain Coles and His Turret-Ship' (1866), 188
  ' "The Critic" (Slightly Altered)' (1866), 190-1

Quebec, 116, 129, 308
Queenstown (Ireland), 182-3

Rankine, William John Macquorn, 264n15
Reciprocity Treaty, 121
Reed, Edward James, *xxiv*, *xv*, *xxvii*, *xxviii*-*xxxii*, 62, 95, 103, 105-6, 116, 123, 126, 145-8, 156, 161, 166-7, 171, 186, 192, 202n13, 211n28, 265, 278, 280
  absolves himself from *Captain* design responsibility, 202-4, 243, 247-54, 256-7, 260-1
  advises converting *Repulse* as central-battery ironclad, 197
  advocates *Hercules* design, 157, 197-8, 210, 215
  argues with Cobden in *The Times*, 105
  attacks Childers *Minute* in *Times*, 259-60
  Bellerophon steam trials, 211n28
  branded as anti-turret, 168, 199, 209-11, 229, 243n17, 244-5, 252, 257, 279
  claims for gratuities, 225, 228, 230, 233-4
  condemns Coles single-turret *Pallas* proposal, 149-55, 169
  critiques *Captain* design, 198, 243-4, 248, 256
  debates Coles at Institution of Naval Architects (1863), 93
  debates Coles at RUSI (1867), 208-11
  defends 12-ton guns on broadside mounts, 161n16
  denies writing anti-turret letter to *The Times* (1866), 165
  Devastation design proposal, 232, 248
  disagrees with Bourne on necessity for turret-ships, 189, 206-7
  dispute with Coles over *Pallas* plans, 108-9, 169
  depicted in *Illustrated London News*, 162
  endorsed by Robinson, 80-1, 95
  essay on *Seagoing Turret-ships and Lowness of Freeboard* (1868), 229
  introduces breastwork-monitor concept, 199-201, 206-8
  liberal resources allocated to, 197, 243n17
  objects to 1871 Committee on Ship Design, 268
  offers new ironclad schemes (1866), 197-8, 200-1
  Our Iron-Clad Ships (1869), 233, 236, 311-12
  paper 'On the Stability of Monitors Under Canvas', 225
  persuasiveness of, 229n31, 230n31, 236, 244-6
  plans for Great Lakes monitors, 128, 131
  plans for imperial defence monitors, 207
  political ambitions, 162, 228, 244, 268
  promises sustained prestige during ironclad revolution, 169-70, 210, 215,

272
  proposes mastless turret-ship, 197-202, 206-8, 218-19
  questions low-freeboard monitors, 170, 199, 206-10, 225, 229, 248, 270
  quits Admiralty, 233, 244-6, 252259-60
  recommends Admiralty suspend payment to Lairds for *Captain* faults, 248
  regards Parliamentary inquiry as personal attack (1868), 224
  resents Coles, 239, 243, 245, 252
  salary of, 201
  seakeeping not compromised by greater armour protection, 125, 142, 215
  skewed comparison of *Monarch* with *Captain*, 189n35, 198, 229, 233, 236, 243-4, 254, 256
  special breastwork-monitors required for separate locales, 270
  submits *Monarch* design, 160, 163, 175-7
  suggests only the largest mastless turret-ships can be seagoing, 230-1, 244
  threatens to resign (1868), 225-6, 228
  urges wooden ironclads' deployment abroad before rotting, 197n3
Refo, Carter Beaumont, 185n25
Reform movements, 179, 189, 218, 224
Rendel, George Wightwick, 264n15
Retrenchment issues, 39, 53, 121-3, 141-2, 207, 218, 221-4, 226, 269-70
Reval, 49n44
Rhine Provinces, 178n7
Rice, Admiral Ernest, 236-7
Richmond (Virginia), 75, 85, 118, 127, 135n7
Ripon, George Frederick Samuel Robinson, Earl de Grey and (1st Marquess of Ripon), 100, 120n23, 138, 149
Robinson, Admiral Robert Spencer, *xxv, xxvii, xxix-xxx*, 64, 93-4, 105, 126, 134n4, 160, 169n32, 186, 198, 249n30, 278, 280
  admires many French naval practices, 238n4, 305-7
  admits nothing in Royal Navy for tackling coastal defences, 269-70
  advocates central-battery designs of Reed, 80-1, 109-11, 154-5, 197-8, 210, 218-21, 224, 229, 242-3, 269, 279
  and 1871 Committee on Ship Design, 264-5, 268-70
  and Iron Plate Committee, 104, 148-9
  appointed Controller (1861), 62, 265n16
  appointment as Controller renewed (February 1866), 166, 244
  argues for fast ironclads to match foreign powers, 192
  assesses HMS *Captain* after initial cruise, 236-8, 252, 254-5
  believes U.S. coast 'unassailable', 88, 128-9
  British firms building ironclads for foreign powers, 130, 131n48, 226
  complains of Parliamentary scrutiny, 222-5
  condemns Coles single-turret *Pallas* proposal, 149-55, 169
  considers sail-and-turret ironclads dead-ends, 201n11, 210, 220, 229, 231-2, 237-8, 243, 252-5, 269
  converting ships-of-the-line into broadside-ironclads, 63, 124
  defends 12-ton guns on broadside mounts, 161n16
  desires to be made full Board member, 226-7
  discredits Coles, 147-8, 164-6, 210, 226, 238, 243n17, 252, 254
  disparages claims of Laird, 190, 238
  dominates Admiralty shipbuilding policy, 148-51, 163, 176-7, 193, 196-8, 206n19, 208-11, 218-26, 229, 238, 242-7, 250-8, 264-6, 267n20, 269-70, 279
  forced out of office (1871), 233, 244, 265-7
  improved naval ordnance, 131-2
  limits of seagoing turret-ships, 107, 149-52, 154-5, 210-11, 218-20, 229, 231-2, 236-8, 254-6, 259, 269
  made full Board member (1868), 230, 265n16
  memo on 'New ships required to be built' (1867), 221
  monitors for defence of Canada, 116-17, 128-9, 131
  objectivity of questioned by Board, 219
  objects to supplying Coles correspondence to Parliament, 169n32, 177

objects to Coles (1863) pamphlet, 92n1
opinion of *Monarch*, 176, 229, 236-7, 242-3, 256, 269
outlines 'Wants of the Navy' (1866), 193, 207
placed on 'Retired List', 244-6
proponent of *Devastation*-class breastwork-monitor, 201n11, 210, 218-19, 231-2, 237-8, 255, 268-9
publicly debates Coles at RUSI (1867, 208-11
pushes for more scientific training, 175
questions Channel Squadron reports (1866), 196-7, 209, 211n28, 222-3
recommends double-turreted monitors for coastal defence, 193, 210, 218-19, 269-70
replies to published Childers *Minute*, 259n5
reports on French naval ordnance at Paris Exhibition (1867), 305-7
responsibility for *Captain* design, 203-5, 237-8, 247-56, 259-61, 265
salary of, 265n16
stalls on *Monarch*, 156, 162-3
stresses need for newer, heavier naval armaments, 187, 218-19
testifies naval strategy never discussed at Board of Admiralty, 206n19
tours *Miantonomoh* at Spithead, 185, 270, 307
views on turret-mounted guns, 95, 162-3, 177-8, 218-19, 229, 237, 268-9
Rochdale, 123
Rockets (Russian), 45
Rodger, Nicholas, *xxix*, 230n31, 257n3
Rodgers, Anne H., 85n34, 303n4, 304n6
Rodgers, Rear-Admiral Christopher Raymond Perry, 86n38, 261
Rodgers, Rear-Admiral John, 85n34
  confronts Spanish over Valparaiso bombardment, 303-4
Rodman, Brigadier-General Thomas Jackson, 94, 137n13, 142
Romaine, William Govett, 81n21, 95, 151n45, 160n15, 162, 167, 168n30, 190, 197, 199n7, 263, 267
  believes Robinson power-mad, 227
  Coles designing turret-ships for foreign powers, 226n26
  recommends vast ironclad shipbuilding programme, 193
Rous, Admiral Henry John, 279
Royal Artillery Institution, 148
Royal Commission on Dockyards, 110
Royal Gun Factory (Woolwich), 56n12
Royal School of Naval Architecture and Marine Engineering (London), 124
Royal United Service Institution, 92, 146
Rush-Bagot Treaty (1817), 121
Russell, John (1st Earl), *xxvii*n7, *xxix*, 40, 61, 64, 67, 81n23, 89n46, 90, 103, 119, 180, 276, 278, 305
  and *Trent* Affair, 139
  concerns of American aggression, 97, 118, 122, 141, 158-9, 272
  condemns Treaty of Washington (*Alabama* Claims), 276n8
  considers naval reductions, 160
  Denmark crisis, 97-8, 100, 102, 112-14
  downplays Anglo-American tensions, 139
  Laird Rams, 101-2
  loss of British prestige, 272-3
  premiership of, 167, 179, 211-12
  reaction to Battle of Hampton Roads, 79
  resigns as Prime Minister, 179
Russell, John Scott, 124-5
  The Modern System of Naval Architecture for Commerce and War, 175
  plans for submarine, 45n32, 48
Russia, *xxxii*, *xxxv*, 36, 42, 45-7, 49-51, 58-9, 82, 89-91, 100, 102, 111-12, 121-2, 185n25, 217, 261, 272
  abrogation of Black Sea Clauses, 274-6
  and Franco-Prussian War, 240, 274
  as a continental power, 159, 231, 270-1
  emancipation of serfs, 59, 90n48, 180
  expansion of, 276-7
  relations with U.S., 180-2, 217
Russian Baltic Fleet, 38, 89n46, 90, 122, 165, 173, 210, 231
Russian circular ironclads, *xxxii*
Russian ironclads of the Crimean War, 42-4
  armoured pontoon-rafts, 43-4
Russian monitors, 165-6, 173, 210, 231, 253, 270, 276
Russian Naval Technical Committee, 274n2
Ryder, Admiral Alfred Phillipps, 264n15

Sackets Harbor, 83
Saint Albans (Vermont), 121

Saint Johns (Newfoundland), 182
Saint Lawrence River, 116, 119-20, 129, 170
Saint Louis (Missouri), 299
Saint Petersburg, 38, 43, 45-6, 89, 130n30, 275
Saint Thomas (Virgin Islands), 172n42
Salem (Massachusetts), 116
Salisbury, Robert Arthur Talbot Gascoyne-Cecil (3rd Marquess), 263-4, 277
Samuda Brothers (Isle of Dogs), 99, 131n48, 177, 207, 219, 238, 284
Samuda, Joseph d'Aguilar, 234
Sandler, Stanley, *xxx*
Sandwich Islands (Hawaii), 299
Sandy Hook, 117, 309n3
San Francisco, 303
San Juan Islands, 100, 123
Saratoga, Battle of, *xxiii*
Savannah, 87
Savoy, 60
Scientific American, 71
    worried *Miantonomoh* 'counselling enemies', 189
Scott, Rear-Admiral Robert Anthony Edwards, 136n11
    carriage and slide designs of, 226
Scullard, Joseph, 149n39, 199n7
Seaton, Albert (*The Crimean War: A Russian Chronicle*), 38n5
Second Reform Act of 1867, 218, 230, 272
Second Schleswig (Danish) War, *xxxv*n27, 91, 97-102, 108, 111-15, 123, 174, 272, 281
Second World War, 127n40
Sedan, 246
Sedan, Battle of, 246
Sedgwick, Charles B., 76n8
Seely, Charles, 223, 227
Senate Committee on Naval Affairs, 74-5, 181
Sevastopol, 36n1, 112, 143
    Siege of, 37-8, 42, 45, 49-50, 121, 127, 263, 277n9
Seward, William Henry, 68, 77, 141, 272
    plan to buy Danish West Indies, 172n42
    urges Fox to showcase American naval prestige to Europe, 181
Seymour, Vice-Admiral George Henry, 189
Seymour, Admiral Michael, 45
Shankland, Lieutenant William F., 144n29
Sheerness, 184n22, 186, 245n20

Sherman, General William Tecumseh, 135n7
Ships
    Abyssinia, HMS, 207, 286, 293
    Achilles, HMS, 60, 63, 107, 124, 142, 147n34, 183, 185n26, 189, 283, 289
        sail-rig, 305n1
        seakeeping abilities, 195-6, 211n28, 223n17
    Aetna, HMS, 42n21
    Agamemnon, HMS (1852), 38n5, 41, 69
    Agamemnon, HMS (1879), *xxxi*n19
    Agincourt, HMS, 64, 126, 132, 203, 283, 289
        1870 cruise, 241
    Ajax, HMS, *xxxi*n19
    Alabama, CSS, 100-1, 119, 135, 141, 266, 298
    Albion, HMS, 38n5
    Alexandra, HMS, 268n22
    Amazon, HMS, 120, 193
    Ammonoosuc, USS, 94n4
    Ant, HMS, 242
    Arethusa, HMS, 38n5
    Arminius (Prussian), 99, 207
    Ashuelot, USS, 185n26
    Atlanta, CSS, 87-8, 138, 300, 303
    Audacious, HMS, *xxxi*, 218-21, 286, 293
    Augusta, USS, 182, 185n26
    Bahia (Brazil), 186
    Bellerophon, HMS, *xxx*, *xxxiv*, 103-4, 107, 110, 124, 132, 147, 151-2, 158, 161, 165, 184, 195, 206, 223n17, 272, 285, 291
        1870 cruise, 241
        armament of, 187, 308
        critiqued by Coles, 209
        design changes, 162
        speed-trials, 190, 211n28
        test-fires against *Royal Sovereign*, 177-8, 184
        tonnage of, 168n31
    Belliqueuse (French), 232n36
    Bellona, later *Lima Barros* (Brazil), 186
    Black Prince, HMS, 55, 56n11, 63, 66-7, 70n55, 100, 113, 183, 282, 288
    Britannia, HMS (former *Prince of Wales*), 197n4
    Bulldog, HMS, 39n8
    Caledonia, HMS, 63, 283, 290
        1870 cruise, 241

seakeeping abilities, 195
Camanche, USS, 303
Canonicus, USS, 77, 85n33, 127, 172, 300n9
Captain, HMS (1787), *xxiii*
Captain, HMS (1869), *xxxiv–xxxv*, 93n2, 219, 230, 285, 292
  armament of, *xix*n1, 189n35, 203, 226, 237
  compliment of, 205, 247
  construction of, 203-5, 222, 243, 247-9
  court martial, *xxvi*, 246-7, 249-50, 254-6, 258, 261, 268, 280
  design of, *xxvii*, *xxix–xxx*, 180, 189n35, 190, 198, 202, 208-9, 237-8, 243-4, 247-8, 250-1, 254-7, 268
  expected to fail, 203-5, 229, 236-8, 243-4, 247-9, 251-7
  habitability of, 208, 238n3, 268
  launch of, *xxx*
  low-freeboard of, *xx*, *xxiv*, *xxvi*, *xxvii*, 190, 202-3, 205n16, 208-9, 236-8, 243-4, 247-9, 251, 254, 256-8, 279-80
  rationale of, *xxxi*, 158, 160, 176-7, 236, 248, 253, 265, 272, 277, 279-81
  sinking of, *xix–xxiv*, *xxvi*, *xxix*, *xxxiv*, 36, 182, 233, 242n14, 246-7, 253, 255-7, 259n5, 260, 263-4, 266n19, 274n2, 276, 278-80
  speed of, 190, 202-3
  stability of, *xxi*n5, 236, 248-54, 256-8, 260-1, 268, 279-80
  survivors of, *xxi*n6, *xxiii*n8
  tonnage, *xx*, 168n31
  trials of, 201-2, 228, 236-7, 241-4, 247, 249-50, 254-5, 257-8
Casco, USS, 94n4
Catskill, USS, 87n38
Cerberus, HMVS, 225, 243n15, 270, 286, 293
  compared with *Miantonomoh*, 200n9
  initial designs for, 199-200, 207
Challenger, HMS, 151n44
Colossus, HMS, *xxxi*n19
Congress, USS, 74
Conqueror, HMS, 68
Contoocook, USS, 94n4

Couronne (French), 55, 305
Cumberland, USS, 74, 78
Cyclops, HMS, 242, 257-8, 264n14, 269-70, 287, 295
Defence, HMS, 57, 63, 70n55, 93, 97n15, 100, 114, 155, 187, 282, 289
Devastation, HMS, *xxviii*, *xxviii*n9, *xxxi*n19, *xxxiv*, 36, 237-8, 243-4, 255, 259, 266, 274, 287, 294
  as the 'first modern battleship', *xxx–xxxi*, 200, 233, 264n14
  critiques of, 234-5
  design of, 232, 244, 248, 250, 268-9
Dictator, USS, 103-4, 170-3, 199, 217n4, 253, 301
  armour of, 309n3
  seaworthiness of, 206, 229, 236, 300-1
  tonnage of, 171n38
Don Juan D'Austria (Austrian), 98
Drache (Austrian), 98
Dreadnought, HMS (1875), *xxxi*n19
Duke of Wellington, HMS, 40, 236, 261
Duncan, HMS, 94
Dunderberg, USS (French *Rochambeau*), 306n3
Edinburgh, HMS, *xxxi*n19
Enterprise, HMS (*Circassian*), 81, 103, 114, 146, 150, 221, 225, 284, 291
  sailing qualities, 162
Erebus, HMS, 42n21
Erzherzog Ferdinand Max (Austrian), 192
Excellent, HMS (gunnery school), 37n4, 94, 131, 133, 185
Favorite, HMS, 93, 110, 146, 284, 291
  armament of, 187
Franklin, USS, 261
Fury, HMS, 39n8, 243, 259, 266
Galena, USS, 72, 85
Georgia, CSS, 90
Glatton, HMS (1855), 42n21
Glatton, HMS (1871), 232, 234n40, 257, 264n14, 270, 286, 294
Gloire (French), *xxxiv*, 53, 55-6, 60, 63, 88, 272, 305
  sail-rig, 305n1
Gorgon, HMS, 242, 287, 295
Great Eastern, 55
Hecate, HMS, 242, 287, 295
Hector, HMS, 62-3, 97n15, 100, 113,

184, 187, 282, 289
  seakeeping abilities, 195-6
Hercules, HMS, *xxx*, 126, 150, 157, 216-17, 226, 243n15, 264n14, 285, 292, 307, 309n3
  1870 cruise, 241
  armament of, 187, 222
  design of, 189n35, 269
  launch of, 222
  trials, 236
Héroïne (French), 305
Hotspur, HMS, 232, 287, 294
Huascar (Peru), 186, 190, 253
Hydra, HMS, 242, 287, 295
Inconstant, HMS, 193, 241, 279
Inflexible, HMS, *xxx*in19, 299n8
Invincible (French), 55
Invincible, HMS, 218-21, 286, 293
Iron Duke, HMS, 221, 286, 293
Kaiser (Austrian), 98
Kaiser Max (Austrian), 98
Kalamazoo, USS, 159n12, 300-1, 309n3
  armour qualities of, 159n12, 212, 299
Kearsage, USS, 119
Keokuk, USS, 86
Keystone State, USS, 69
Konig Wilhelm, formerly *Fatikh* (Prussian), 226
Lord Clyde, HMS, 104, 125n36, 284, 291
  armament of, 187, 197n3
  need to deploy abroad soon, 197n3
  trials of, 195-6, 211n28
  vulnerability against turret-ship, 196
Lord Warden, HMS, *xx*, 104, 196, 223n17, 241, 246, 291
Louisiana, CSS, 84
Magdala, HMS, 207, 287, 294
Magenta (French), 59, 63, 305
Magnanime (French), 307
Mahopac, USS, 127
Meteor, HMS, 42n21
Miantonomoh, USS, *xxxi*, *xxxiv*, 188n33, 201n11, 234n40, 270, 277
  armour of, 183n20
  coal bunkerage of, 182, 183n20
  engines of, 183n20
  tonnage of, 169n31
  visit to Britain, 180-6, 189, 200, 235, 253, 272, 279
Milwaukee, USS, 144n29

Minnesota, USS, 74
Minotaur, HMS (*Elephant*), 64, 107, 145, 150, 155, 158, 283, 289
  1870 cruise, 241
  sea trials of, 211n28
  with 12-ton guns, 160
Mississippi, CSS, 84
Monadnock, USS, 94n4, 116, 127, 141, 158, 199, 234n40
  armament of, 303
  confronts broadside-ironclad *Numancia*, 181n18, 303-4
  engines of, 183n20
  going to the Pacific, 161, 168, 175, 182, 279
  relative power of armament, 169, 212-13
  sent to intercept *Stonewall*, 172
  tonnage of, 169n31
Monarch, HMS, *xxviin5, xxviii*, 93n2, 170, 236, 243, 264n14, 285, 292
  armament of, 187, 215, 226
  decision to build, *xxx*, 156-7, 160, 169, 278
  design of, 160, 162, 164, 168, 175-7, 189n35, 190, 202-3, 215, 237, 243-4, 248
  launch of, 222
  stability of, *xxin5*, 176, 249
  to be side-lined, 166, 203, 268-9
  tonnage of, 168n31, 169
  trials of, 201-2, 228, 236-7, 241, 249-50
  turret-rotation of, 300n9
Monitor, USS, *xxviii, xxxi, xxxiv-xxxv*, 44, 78-80, 108, 144, 157, 169, 191, 200, 232, 235, 272, 278, 281, 299
  confrontation with CSS *Virginia*, 74-5
  decision to build, 72, 191
  defects of, 74
  popularity in America, 157-8, 170, 191-2
  sinking of, 85, 229
  stability of, 72
Montauk, USS, 85, 87n38, 96
Nahant, USS, 87n38
Nantucket, USS, 87n38
'Naughty Child', 93, 146
Nausett, USS, 94n4
New Ironsides, USS, 72, 83, 85, 88, 96,

127, 261
Nile, HMS, 80
Normandie (French), 55, 82
Northumberland, HMS, 64, 145, 241, 283, 289
Numancia (Spain), 130-1, 181n18, 184n22, 232n36
  confronted by USS *Monadnock* (1866), 302-4
Océan (French), 306n3
Ocean, HMS, 63, 195, 283, 290
Osborne, HMY, 185
Palestro (Italian)
  set on fire at Lissa, 196
Pallas, HMS, 108-9, 120, 147n34, 149, 151-2, 157, 162, 184, 236, 284, 291
  armament of, 187
  design changes, 162
  seakeeping abilities, 195
Passaic, USS, 77, 85-6, 89n46, 96, 182n19, 300, 303
  armour of, 212n29
  Russian versions, 165-6, 231, 253
  seaworthiness questioned by Reed, 229, 236
Patapsco, USS, 86n38, 182n19
Penelope, HMS, 147, 187, 198, 285, 292
  launch of, 222
Petr Veliky/Peter the Great (Russia)
  Reed's influence, 274
Pompanoosuc, USS, 94n4, 193
Prince Albert, HMS, 80, 93, 125n36, 132, 146, 148, 209, 284, 290
  armament of, 187
Prince Consort, HMS (*Triumph*), 63, 97n15, 100, 113, 145, 146n32, 283, 290
  1870 cruise, 241
Prince of Wales, HMS (1860)
  engines removed for *Repulse* conversion, 197
Princess Royal, HMS, 102
Prinz Eugene (Austrian), 98
Provence (French), 63, 305, 307
  sail-rig, 305n1
Puritan, USS,
  20-inch guns for, 184, 309n3
  completion of, 216-17
Re d'Italia (Italian)
  sunk at Lissa by ramming, 192
Repulse, HMS, 286, 292

  converted as central-battery ironclad, 197
Research, HMS, 103, 105, 114, 146, 157, 195, 221, 284, 290
  as value for money, 161n16
  sailing qualities, 162
Resistance, HMS, 57, 63, 70n55, 100, 126, 187, 282, 289
Roanoke, USS, 74, 239n6
Rolf Krake (Prussian), 99, 105, 108, 253
Royal Albert, HMS, 41
Royal Alfred, HMS, 63, 145, 187, 285, 291
Royal George, HMS, *xxiii*
Royal Oak, HMS, 63, 88, 97, 100, 124, 155, 187, 283, 290
  1870 cruise, 241
  rolling of, 196
Royal Sovereign, HMS, *xxxii*, *xxxiv*, 77, 80, 93, 95, 99, 100n22, 103, 106-7, 125n26, 146-8, 151, 155-6, 184, 212, 283, 290
  armament of, 100n22, 177n5, 187, 271
  design of, 176
  high-freeboard of, 207
  more habitable than *Miantonomoh*, 184
  neglection of, 162
  opposed by Reed, 169
  tested under live-fire (June 1866), 177-8, 184, 212-13
Rupert, HMS, 287, 294
St. Lawrence, USS, 74
Salamander (Austrian), 98
San Jacinto, USS, 66
Saugus, USS, 127
Scorpion, HMS ('Laird Ram'), 97, 101-2, 125n36, 155n2, 160-1, 169, 177, 180, 211, 221, 252-3, 257, 284, 290
  armament of, 160-1, 236
  seakeeping abilities, 190, 196, 201, 209, 236
Solferino (French), 59, 63, 130, 305
Squando, USS, 94n4
Staunch, HMS, 264n14
Stonewall, CSS, 172
Sultan, HMS, 126, 236, 242-3, 264n14, 268n22, 269, 286, 293
Swiftsure, HMS, 286, 293
Tallapoosa, USS, 120n25

Taureau (French), 130
Temeraire, HMS (1876), 268n22
Tennessee, CSS, 144n29
Terrible, HMS, 39n8
Terror, HMS, 42n21, 177
Thunder, HMS, 42n21
Thunderbolt, HMS, 42n21
Thunderer, HMS, *xxxi*n19, 234n40, 237-8, 243n15, 257, 259, 266, 269, 287, 294
Trent, RMS, 66
Triumph, HMS, 126, 286, 294
Trusty, HMS, 42n21, 63n29, 80, 108
Valiant, HMS, 62-3, 187, 282, 289
Vanguard, HMS, *xxxi*, 221, 286, 293
Vengeance, HMS, 39n8
Victoria, HMS, 56
Viper, HMS, 285, 292
Virginia, CSS (formerly USS *Merrimack*), *xxviii*, 44, 71, 74-5, 78-80, 144, 169, 235
Vixen, HMS, 285, 292
Wampanoag, USS, 193, 238
Warrior, HMS, *xx*n3, *xxxi*, *xxxiv-xxxv*, 36, 53, 61, 64, 66-7, 70, 71n59, 77, 93n2, 97n15, 100, 113, 150, 155, 157, 186, 196, 272, 282, 288, 299, 305
  1870 cruise, 241
  design rationale of, 55-8, 124-5, 127
  draught of, 171
  improved armament for, 186
  sail-rig, 305n1
  weaknesses, 57, 60, 63, 78-80, 88, 126-7, 161, 232, 278
Waterwitch, HMS, 285, 292
Weehawken, USS, 85, 86n38, 87-8, 96, 300, 303
Winnebago, USS, 144n29
Wivern, HMS ('Laird Ram'), 97, 101-2, 125n36, 132, 155n2, 160-1, 180, 211, 221, 253, 257, 284, 290
  armament of, 160-1, 187, 236
  seakeeping abilities, 190, 195-6, 201, 209, 236, 254
Zealous, HMS, 187, 285, 291
  inadequate armour, 197n4
  unarmoured wooden ends vulnerable to fire, 196
Ships vs. Forts, 37, 53-4, 56, 58-60, 62-3, 68-70, 73, 84-5, 95-6, 103-4, 130, 143, 220

Allied naval attack on Sevastopol, 17 October 1854, 38
American Civil War, 69-70, 73, 84-9, 95-6, 127-8, 136, 261-3
  British monitors and, 218-19, 264n14, 268-71
  Cronstadt's defences, 1854-1856, 38-45, 47-51, 62, 89, 122, 130, 143, 210, 263
  defences of Bermuda, Halifax, 232n37
  Fort Fisher, 127-8
  Kagosima, 102
  Second Schleswig (Danish) War, 97-9, 115
  Spanish attack on Callao, 184n22
  Union naval assault on Charleston, 86-8, 95-6
  U.S. shore defences, 83-4, 115-20, 128-9
Shoeburyness, 37n4, 103-4, 137, 187n32, 213-14, 220n12, 309
Shoeburyness and the Guns, 142, 145n31
Sinclair, Charles, *xxiii*
Sinclair, George (2nd Baronet), 102n30
Sinope, Battle of, 37
Slidell, John, 66-7
Smith, A. B., 74n6
Smith, Goldwin, 140
Smith, Lieutenant-General John Mark Frederick, 78
Smith, Rear-Admiral Joseph, 74n4, 300n9, 309n3
Société Nouvelle des Forges et Chantiers de la Méditerranée, 130-1
Somerset, Edward Adolphus Seymour (12th Duke of), *xx*n2, *xxix*, 57-8, 97, 104n34, 107, 111, 120-1, 128, 130-2, 148, 159, 160n2, 161
  advises against defence cuts, 122-3, 160
  advocates Colonial Naval Defence Act, 139
  and extension of the franchise, 134n6, 135
  approves central-battery proposals, 81
  armour-plate manufacturing, 78-9
  concern over mediation proposal, 82
  critiqued by *The Times*, 167
  defends *Monarch* design, 169, 176
  disapproves of *Devastation* concept, 235
  doubts over ironclad flotilla for Canada, 129
  dubious of Laird Rams, 101

French naval power, 60, 63, 180
House of Lords inquiry on Coles, 169
intervention in Denmark, 97-8, 100, 113-14
invites Coles to produce *Captain* design, 176-7, 278
Monarchy and Democracy (1880), *xxxiii*, 135
need for naval attaché to U.S., 103
neutrality of Britain in the Pacific (1866), 304
notes high powder-charges of U.S. guns, 185
opinion of Coles, *xxviii*
orders turret-ship committee to assess Coles design (1865), 151
parting acknowledgment of Robinson and Reed, 186, 226, 235
pre-eminence of the United States, *xxxiii*
reassures Russell of new naval ordnance, 119, 180, 305
shortage of wooden ships in the Navy, 187
South Atlantic Blockading Squadron, 86-8, 96
South East Coast of America Station, 261-2
Southsea (Portsmouth), 178, 203
Spain, 66, 131, 172n42, 181, 240-1, 246, 254, 258, 303
war against Chile, Peru (1866), 302-4
Spezia, 299n8
Spithead, *xxvii*, 50, 78, 180, 189n34
Spratt, Vice-Admiral Thomas Abel Brimage, 70n54
Stanley, Edward Henry (15th Earl of Derby), 112, 179, 211-13, 222
disagrees that non-intervention means indifference, 273n1
Stanton, Edwin McMasters, 134
Staten Island, 117
Stevens, Rear-Admiral Thomas Holdup, Jr., 144n29
Stewart, Rear-Admiral Houston, 70n54, 264n15
Stimers, Chief Engineer Alban Crocker, 215n35
Stockmar, Christian Friedrich Freiherr von, 51n50
Stokes Bay, 247-8
Sulivan, Admiral Bartholomew James, 47-8, 70n54, 155
Sulivan, George, 47
Sulivan, Laurence, 68n47
Sweaborg, 38n5, 41, 44, 48, 49n44
Sweden, 46n37, 91, 173, 263
Switzerland, 263
Symonds, Admiral Thomas Matthew Charles, 236, 244, 257
Symonds, Rear-Admiral William, 279

Tarleton, Admiral John Walter, 126n38
Tenniel, John, 114, 190-1
Thames Ironworks & Shipbuilding (Blackwall), 57, 64, 131n48, 177, 219, 238, 282, 283, 287
launch *Konig Wilhelm* for Prussian Navy, 226
Thames River, 131n48, 172
The Broad Arrow, *xxiii*
The Critic, 189-90
The Engineer, 161, 165
condemns American monitors, 161-2
mocks 15-inch Rodman gun, 213
The Evening Standard, 236
The Illustrated London News, *xxiii*, 60, 78-9, 104, 122, 130
features Reed, *Pallas*, 162
HMS *Minotaur* completion
Miantonomoh and '*Royal Sovereign*' vs. *Bellerophon*'-test, 185
mock bombardment of Dover forts, 271
Prussian ironclad fleet (1870), 241
The Modern System of Naval Architecture for Commerce and War (1865), 175
The Standard,
Coles letter (10 January 1866), 162, 164-5, 251
on Reed's resignation, 244-7
Robinson's letter to (1871), 265n16
The Sydney Morning Herald, 44n27
The Times (London), *xxii*, *xxiv*, *xxvi*, *xxvii-xxviii*, *xxxii*, 78, 92, 105, 146, 155, 161n16, 165, 182, 187
and American Civil War, 134
and British foreign policy, 101-2, 121-2
and Fort Fisher, 127
and Reed's influence over the Board of Admiralty, 228, 245-6
and Rodman 15-inch gun trials, 213-15
approves of *Our Iron-Clad Ships* (1869), 233-4

blames Controller's Department for lack of *Captain* construction oversight, 253-6, 259-61
calls for naval economy, modernisation of ships, 222, 234
Coles and, 160, 169, 178, 243n17, 244, 252-3
concern of French threat to Belgium, 241
critiques Somerset, 167, 169
defends non-intervention policies, 277
impressed by *Miantonomoh*, 183-6
on American acquisition of Alaska, 2175
on Palmerston's death, 160
opinion of Federal monitors, 95-6, 156, 158, 183-6, 188, 191-2
Polish insurrection, 89
reaction to Battle of Hampton Roads, 79
Robinson's power over the Board of Admiralty, 267n20
Spithead Naval Review (1856), 50
threat of commerce raiders, 101
unconvinced by Reed's defence against Childers *Minute*, 259-61
urges turret-ship construction, 99, 106-8, 145-6, 150-1, 157, 169, 184-6, 188, 191-2, 243-4
used by Russians as intelligence, 42
The Times (New York), 103, 218
The United Service Gazette, xxiv
Thirteenth Amendment (U.S. Constitution), 141
Thomson, William (1st Baron Kelvin), 264n15
Thornton, Edward (2nd Count of Cacilhas), 238
Tilburina, 191
Tiverton, 114-15
Todleben, General Franz Edward Graf von, 38, 42
Toledo, 83
Toronto, 116, 308
Torpedoes (locomotive), 172, 269
Toulon naval base, 130, 302
Trafalgar, Battle of, 192
Trafalgar Square, 186
Treasury, 39, 101, 216, 226, 228n29, 230
Treatise on Coast-Defence, 262
Treaty of London (1871), 275
Treaty of Paris (1856), 36n1, 43, 45-6, 50-1, 274-5, 277n9
Treaty of Washington (1871), 276n8
Trevelyan, George Otto (2nd Baronet), 230n32
Trent Affair, xxxi, xxxiii, 66-71, 73, 76-7, 82, 84, 111, 116, 139, 242
'Turret Craze', xxviii-xxix, xxxi, 96, 143-5, 157-8, 169, 184-6, 218, 224-5, 229, 233-6, 243n15, 244-5, 271, 277, 280-1, 300
Turret ships, high-freeboard (ironclad design), xix-xxi, xxiv, xxvi-xxxii, 60-1, 73n1, 74, 76-78, 80, 92-3, 95, 106-8, 123-4, 128, 143-5
Admiralty cautious of building more until *Monarch*, *Captain* trials, 201-2, 228, 234, 242
built by Lairds for smaller powers, 186, 253
Captain an example of, according to Reed, 243-4, 248
Coles *Pallas*-type proposal (1865), 149-55, 157, 169
design of *Dictator*, 170-3, 206, 253
habitability of, 184, 208, 235
high-freeboard vulnerability of, 207, 213, 234, 237, 243, 268-9
lack of suitable designs for, 145, 147-9, 157, 175-7, 196, 206-7, 212, 228-32, 233-5, 248, 272, 280
HMS *Monarch*, 156, 160, 162-3, 168-9, 175-7, 229, 236-7, 243-4, 253-4, 264n14, 268-9
Laird Rams, 97, 101-2, 125n36, 155n2, 160, 169, 177, 180, 187, 190, 195-6, 253-4, 271
Prussian, 99
RUSI debate over (1867), 208-11
USS *Roanoke* failure, 239n6
Yelverton, Warden favour in Channel Squadron reports, 195-6, 209
Twisleton, Edward Turner Boyd, 82n25

Uncle Sam, 139, 217
Union naval blockade of Southern Confederacy, 65, 67, 97, 122-3, 298
U.S. Army, 75, 81, 116, 118, 127
U.S. Constitution, 135
U.S. Navy (Union Navy), xxxi, xxxiv, 71, 74-5, 79, 81, 83, 86-90, 96, 101, 108, 111, 119-20, 128-9, 144-5, 153, 157-8, 239n6,

297-8
  oceangoing monitors for, 170-2, 185, 212, 253, 299-301, 303-4
  post-war demobilisation of, 216-18, 238
  war-time ship construction for, 173, 216n1, 238, 270n27, 298-9
United States of America, *xxvi, xxxiii, xxxv*, 46, 51-3, 58, 94, 101, 103, 105
  as a continental power, 159, 170-1, 270-1
  nationalism, 144-5, 158, 216-17, 272
  outbreak of American Civil War, 64
  possible war with Britain and France, 82-3, 88-9, 94, 101, 111, 115-23, 126-9, 131-42, 145, 158, 169, 172, 178, 181-2, 193, 211-12, 218, 232n37, 240, 261, 272, 276, 280-1, 298-301
  Reconstruction issues, 216-18, 238
  relations with Russia, 180-2, 217, 277
  response to *Trent* Affair, 71, 83
  tensions with Imperial Spain, 181, 303-4

Valparaiso, 181, 302-4
Venetia, 178n7
Venetian Quadrilateral, 178
Venice, *xxxiii*
Vera Cruz, 66, 82n26
Verrazzano Bridge, 309n3
Versailles, 272n31
Victoria, Alexandrina, Queen, *xxviii*, 46, 50, 65, 68n48, 139, 186n28, 242n14
  anxious over Austro-Prussian War, 178
  concern of popular clamour of war with Russia (1870), 274
  opposes intervention in Denmark, 112-14, 123, 272
  protests Russell's resignation, 179
Victoria (colony), 139
Vienna, 100, 276n8
Vigo, 246
Virginia, 74-5, 81, 96, 118
Virilio, Paul, *xxv*

Walker, Admiral Baldwin Wake (1st Baronet), *xxiii*, 54-5, 57-9, 61-2, 233
  salary of, 201
  sensitive to criticism, 164n22
  tours *Miantonomoh* at Sheerness, 186
War of 1812, 299
Ward, Admiral William John, 238
Warden, Rear-Admiral Frederick, 195-7, 209, 211n28, 223n17
War Office, 56n12, 56n13, 94, 98, 100n22, 103, 104n34, 120, 148, 149n38, 157, 187, 277n9, 308
  dubious of Canadian defence, 232n37
  tests Rodman 15-inch smoothbore, 213-15
Washington, D.C., 52, 66, 82, 87, 94, 97, 100, 103, 116, 118, 120, 135, 158, 238, 309n3
Washington, George, *xxiii*, 134
Washington, Rear-Admiral John, 69
Washington Navy Yard, 76, 83, 137, 138m15
Watertight compartments, 55, 57, 124-5
  on *Cerberus*, 200n9
  on *Miantonomoh*, 183n20
Watts, Isaac, 64, 79-81, 127, 146, 233, 254
  as an autocrat, 164n22
Welles, Gideon, 71, 74, 77n10, 85n32, 87, 96, 127n40, 143n28, 144n29, 217, 239, 298, 309n3
  monitors in the Pacific will have a 'good effect', 303n3
  opinion of mission to Russia (1866), 181
  opposes plan to buy Danish West Indies, 172n42
  potential Anglo-American conflict, 84
  Report of (1864), 216n1
  Report of (1867), 216
  requests ironclad build-up from Congress, 75
  sends monitors to intercept *Stonewall*, 172
  warns Dahlgren not to lose monitors in harbour assault role, 88
West Indies, 201n11, 298
Westminster, 273
Westwood & Baillie (shipbuilders), 282
Whigs, 40, 179n11
Whitehall, *xxxii*, 60, 107-8, 130, 222, 234, 267n20
White House, 71, 121
Whitworth, Joseph (1st Baronet), 244n19, 306
Whitworths, 244-5
Wigram & Sons (Blackwall), 177
Wilhelm I, William Frederick Louis, King (Prussia), 240-1
Wilhelmshaven, 262
Wilkes, Rear-Admiral Charles, 66-7
Williams, Richard, 67

Wilmington, 85, 96, 127
Wise, Captain Henry Augustus, 134n4, 135-6, 309
Wood, Charles (1st Viscount Halifax), 40-1, 42n21, 44n29, 45n32, 46, 60, 91, 98n16, 187, 256, 264n15, 266
   Captain disaster an exercise in scapegoating, 279, 280n14
   naval demonstration against United States (1856), 52
   notes public scrutiny during Crimean War, 4
   prospects of 1856 Baltic campaign, 47-9
Woolley, Joseph, 264n15
Woolwich (Arsenal), 108
Woolwich Dockyard, 283, 284, 286
Worden, Rear-Admiral John Lorimer, 158n8

Yelverton, Admiral Hastings Reginald, 151
   1870 Channel Squadron cruise, 241, 247
   reports on Channel Squadron cruise (1866), 195-7, 209, 254
   sympathy with Milne on loss of *Captain*, 247

Wolverhampton Military Studies
www.helion.co.uk/wolverhamptonmilitarystudies

Editorial board

Professor Stephen Badsey
Wolverhampton University

Professor Michael Bechthold
Wilfred Laurier University

Professor John Buckley
Wolverhampton University

Major General (Retired) John Drewienkiewicz
Ashley Ekins
Australian War Memorial

Dr Howard Fuller
Wolverhampton University

Dr Spencer Jones
Wolverhampton University

Nigel de Lee
Norwegian War Academy

Major General (Retired) Mungo Melvin President of the British Commission for Military History

Dr Michael Neiberg
US Army War College

Dr Eamonn O'Kane
Wolverhampton University

Professor Fransjohan Pretorius
University of Pretoria

Dr Simon Robbins
Imperial War Museum

Professor Gary Sheffield
Wolverhampton University

Commander Steve Tatham PhD
Royal Navy
The Influence Advisory Panel

Professor Malcolm Wanklyn
Wolverhampton University

Professor Andrew Wiest University of Southern Mississippi

Submissions

The publishers would be pleased to receive submissions for this series. Please contact us via email (info@helion.co.uk), or in writing to Helion & Company Limited, 26 Willow Road, Solihull, West Midlands, B91 1UE.

Titles

No.1 *Stemming the Tide. Officers and Leadership in the British Expeditionary Force 1914* Edited by Spencer Jones (ISBN 978-1-909384-45-3)

No.2 *'Theirs Not To Reason Why': Horsing the British Army 1875–1925* Graham Winton (ISBN 978-1-909384-48-4)

No.3 *A Military Transformed? Adaptation and Innovation in the British Military, 1792–1945* Edited by Michael LoCicero, Ross Mahoney and Stuart Mitchell (ISBN 978-1-909384-46-0)

No.4 *Get Tough Stay Tough. Shaping the Canadian Corps, 1914–1918* Kenneth Radley (ISBN 978-1-909982-86-4)

No.5 *A Moonlight Massacre: The Night Operation on the Passchendaele Ridge, 2 December 1917. The Forgotten Last Act of the Third Battle of Ypres* Michael LoCicero
  (ISBN 978-1-909982-92-5)

No.6 *Shellshocked Prophets. Former Anglican Army Chaplains in Interwar Britain* Linda Parker (ISBN 978-1-909982-25-3)

No.7 *Flight Plan Africa: Portuguese Airpower in Counterinsurgency, 1961–1974* John P. Cann (ISBN 978-1-909982-06-2)

No.8 *Mud, Blood and Determination. The History of the 46th (North Midland) Division in the Great War* Simon Peaple (ISBN 978 1 910294 66 6)

No.9 *Commanding Far Eastern Skies. A Critical Analysis of the Royal Air Force Superiority Campaign in India, Burma and Malaya 1941–1945* Peter Preston-Hough (ISBN 978 1 910294 44 4)

No.10 *Courage Without Glory. The British Army on the Western Front 1915* Edited by Spencer Jones (ISBN 978 1 910777 18 3)

No.11 *The Airborne Forces Experimental Establishment: The Development of British Airborne Technology 1940–1950* Tim Jenkins (ISBN 978-1-910777-06-0)

No.12 *'Allies are a Tiresome Lot' – The British Army in Italy in the First World War* John Dillon (ISBN 978 1 910777 32 9)

No.13 *Monty's Functional Doctrine: Combined Arms Doctrine in British 21st Army Group in Northwest Europe, 1944–45* Charles Forrester (ISBN 978-1-910777-26-8)

No.14 *Early Modern Systems of Command: Queen Anne's Generals, Staff Officers and the Direction of Allied Warfare in the Low Countries and Germany, 1702–11* Stewart Stansfield (ISBN 978 1 910294 47 5)

No.15 *They Didn't Want To Die Virgins: Sex and Morale in the British Army on the Western Front 1914–1918* Bruce Cherry (ISBN 978-1-910777-70-1)

No.16 *From Tobruk to Tunis: The Impact of Terrain on British Operations and Doctrine in North Africa, 1940–1943* Neal Dando (ISBN 978-1-910294-00-0)

No.17 *Crossing No Man's Land: Experience and Learning with the Northumberland Fusiliers in the Great War* Tony Ball (ISBN 978-1-910777-73-2)

No.18 *"Everything worked like clockwork": The Mechanization of the British Cavalry between the Two World Wars* Roger E Salmon (ISBN 978-1-910777-96-1)

No.19 *Attack on the Somme: 1st Anzac Corps and the Battle of Pozi.res Ridge, 1916* Meleah Hampton (ISBN 978-1-910777-65-7)

No.20 *Operation Market Garden: The Campaign for the Low Countries, Autumn 1944: Seventy Years On* Edited by John Buckley & Peter Preston Hough (ISBN 978 1 910777 15 2)

No.21 *Enduring the Whirlwind: The German Army and the Russo-German War 1941-1943* Gregory Liedtke (ISBN 978-1-910777-75-6)

No.22 *'Glum Heroes': Hardship, fear and death – Resilience and Coping in the British Army on the Western Front 1914–1918* Peter E. Hodgkinson (ISBN 978-1-910777-78-7)

No.23 *Much Embarrassed: Civil War Intelligence and the Gettysburg Campaign* George Donne (ISBN 978-1-910777-86-2)

No.24 *They Called It Shell Shock: Combat Stress in the First World War* Stefanie Linden (ISBN 978-1-911096-35-1)

No. 25 *New Approaches to the Military History of the English Civil War. Proceedings of the First Helion & Company 'Century of the Soldier' Conference* Ismini Pells (editor) (ISBN 978-1-911096-44-3)

No.26 *Reconographers: Intelligence and Reconnaissance in British Tank Operations on the Western Front 1916-18* Colin Hardy (ISBN: 978-1-911096-28-3)

No.27 *Britain's Quest for Oil: The First World War and the Peace Conferences* Martin Gibson (ISBN: 978-1-911512-07-3)

No.28 *Unfailing Gallantry: 8th (Regular) Division in the Great War 1914–1919* Alun Thomas (ISBN: 978-1-910777-61-9)

No.29 *An Army of Brigadiers: British Brigade Commanders at the Battle of Arras 1917* Trevor Harvey (ISBN: 978-1-911512-00-4)

No.30 *At All Costs: The British Army on the Western Front 1916* Edited by Spencer Jones (ISBN 978-1-912174-88-1)

No.31 *The German Corpse Factory: A Study in First World War Propaganda* Stephen Badsey (ISBN 978-1-911628-27-9)

No.32 *Bull Run to Boer War: How the American Civil War Changed the Victorian British Army* Michael Somerville (ISBN 978-1-912866-25-0)

No.33 *Turret versus Broadside: An Anatomy of British Naval Prestige, Revolution and Disaster, 1860-1870* Howard J. Fuller (ISBN 978-1-913336-22-6)